The Lamp for Integrating the Practices

(*Caryāmelāpakapradīpa*)

Treasury of the Buddhist Sciences Series

Editor-in-Chief: Robert A.F. Thurman, Jey Tsong Khapa Professor of Indo-Tibetan Buddhist Studies, Columbia University

Executive Editor: Thomas F. Yarnall, Columbia University

Series Committee: Daniel Aitken, David Kittelstrom, Tim McNeill, Robert A.F. Thurman, Christian K. Wedemeyer, Thomas F. Yarnall

Editorial Board: Ryuichi Abé, Jay Garfield, David Gray, Laura Harrington, Thupten Jinpa, Joseph Loizzo, Gary Tubb, Vesna Wallace, Christian Wedemeyer, Chun-fang Yu

The *Treasury of the Buddhist Sciences* series is copublished by the American Institute of Buddhist Studies and Wisdom Publications in association with the Columbia University Center for Buddhist Studies and Tibet House US.

The American Institute of Buddhist Studies (AIBS) established the *Treasury of the Buddhist Sciences* series to provide authoritative translations, studies, and editions of the texts of the Tibetan Tengyur (*bstan 'gyur*) and its associated literature. The Tibetan Tengyur is a vast collection of over 4,000 classical Indian Buddhist scientific treatises (*śāstra*) written in Sanskrit by over 700 authors from the first millennium CE, now preserved mainly in systematic 7th–12th century Tibetan translation. Its topics span all of India's "outer" arts and sciences, including linguistics, medicine, astronomy, socio-political theory, ethics, art, and so on, as well as all of her "inner" arts and sciences such as philosophy, psychology ("mind science"), meditation, and yoga.

Volumes in this series are numbered with catalogue numbers corresponding to both the "Comparative" (*dpe bsdur ma*) Kangyur and Tengyur ("CK" and "CT," respectively) and Derge (Tōhoku number) recensions of the Tibetan Tripiṭaka.

THE DALAI LAMA

Message

The foremost scholars of the holy land of India were based for many centuries at Nālandā Monastic University. Their deep and vast study and practice explored the creative potential of the human mind with the aim of eliminating suffering and making life truly joyful and worthwhile. They composed numerous excellent and meaningful texts. I regularly recollect the kindness of these immaculate scholars and aspire to follow them with unflinching faith. At the present time, when there is great emphasis on scientific and technological progress, it is extremely important that those of us who follow the Buddha should rely on a sound understanding of his teaching, for which the great works of the renowned Nālandā scholars provide an indispensable basis.

In their outward conduct the great scholars of Nālandā observed ethical discipline that followed the Pāli tradition, in their internal practice they emphasized the awakening mind of *bodhichitta*, enlightened altruism, and in secret they practised tantra. The Buddhist culture that flourished in Tibet can rightly be seen to derive from the pure tradition of Nālandā, which comprises the most complete presentation of the Buddhist teachings. As for me personally, I consider myself a practitioner of the Nālandā tradition of wisdom. Masters of Nālandā such as Nāgārjuna, Āryadeva, Āryāsaṅga, Dharmakīrti, Chandrakīrti, and Śāntideva wrote the scriptures that we Tibetan Buddhists study and practice. They are all my gurus. When I read their books and reflect upon their names, I feel a connection with them.

The works of these Nālandā masters are presently preserved in the collection of their writings that in Tibetan translation we call the Tengyur (*bstan 'gyur*). It took teams of Indian masters and great Tibetan translators over four centuries to accomplish the historic task of translating them into

Tibetan. Most of these books were later lost in their Sanskrit originals, and relatively few were translated into Chinese. Therefore, the Tengyur is truly one of Tibet's most precious treasures, a mine of understanding that we have preserved in Tibet for the benefit of the whole world.

Keeping all this in mind I am very happy to encourage a long-term project of the American Institute of Buddhist Studies, originally established by the late Venerable Mongolian Geshe Wangyal and now at the Columbia University Center for Buddhist Studies, and Tibet House US, to translate the Tengyur into English and other modern languages, and to publish the many works in a collection called *The Treasury of the Buddhist Sciences.* When I recently visited Columbia University, I joked that it would take those currently working at the Institute at least three "reincarnations" to complete the task; it surely will require the intelligent and creative efforts of generations of translators from every tradition of Tibetan Buddhism, in the spirit of the scholars of Nālandā, although we may hope that using computers may help complete the work more quickly. As it grows, the *Treasury* series will serve as an invaluable reference library of the Buddhist Sciences and Arts. This collection of literature has been of immeasurable benefit to us Tibetans over the centuries, so we are very happy to share it with all the people of the world. As someone who has been personally inspired by the works it contains, I firmly believe that the methods for cultivating wisdom and compassion originally developed in India and described in these books preserved in Tibetan translation will be of great benefit to many scholars, philosophers, and scientists, as well as ordinary people.

I wish the American Institute of Buddhist Studies at the Columbia Center for Buddhist Studies and Tibet House US every success and pray that this ambitious and far-reaching project to create *The Treasury of the Buddhist Sciences* will be accomplished according to plan. I also request others, who may be interested, to extend whatever assistance they can, financial or otherwise, to help ensure the success of this historic project.

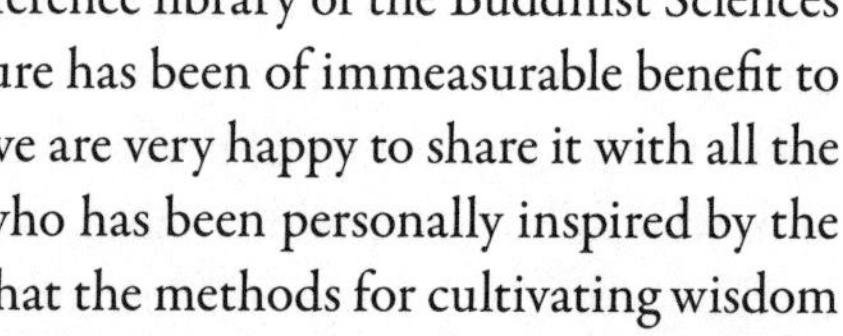

May 15, 2007

• TREASURY OF THE BUDDHIST SCIENCES •

The Lamp for Integrating the Practices

(*Caryāmelāpakapradīpa*)

by Āryadeva

The Gradual Path of Vajrayāna Buddhism

Translated with an introduction by
Christian K. Wedemeyer

TREASURY OF THE BUDDHIST SCIENCES SERIES
TENGYUR TRANSLATION INITIATIVE
CT 708 (TŌH. 1803)

COPUBLISHED BY
THE AMERICAN INSTITUTE OF BUDDHIST STUDIES AND WISDOM PUBLICATIONS
IN ASSOCIATION WITH THE COLUMBIA UNIVERSITY CENTER
FOR BUDDHIST STUDIES AND TIBET HOUSE US

Wisdom

Treasury of the Buddhist Sciences series
Tengyur Translation Initiative
A refereed series published by:

American Institute of Buddhist Studies
Columbia University
80 Claremont Avenue, Room 303
New York, NY 10027
www.aibs.columbia.edu

Wisdom Publications
199 Elm Street
Somerville, MA 02144 USA
www.wisdomexperience.org

In association with Columbia University's Center for Buddhist Studies
and Tibet House US.
Distributed by Wisdom Publications.

Library of Congress Cataloging-in-Publication Data
Names: Wedemeyer, Christian K., translator, writer of introduction.
Title: The lamp for integrating the practices (Caryāmelāpakapradīpa) by Āryadeva: the gradual path of Vajrayāna Buddhism / translated with an introduction by Christian K. Wedemeyer.
Other titles: Āryadeva's Lamp that integrates the practices (Caryāmelāpakapradīpa)
Description: Second edition. | New York, NY: The American Institute of Buddhist Studies; Somerville, MA: Wisdom Publications, [2021] | Series: The treasury of the Buddhist sciences series | "In association with Columbia University's Center for Buddhist Studies and Tibet House US." | Includes bibliographical references and index. | English, Sanskrit and Tibetan.
Identifiers: LCCN 2020044305 (print) | LCCN 2020044306 (ebook) | ISBN 9781949163186 (hardcover) | ISBN 9781949163193 (ebook)
Subjects: LCSH: Tripiṭaka. Sūtrapiṭaka. Tantra. Guhyasamājatantra—Commentaries—Early works to 1800.
Classification: LCC BQ2155 .A82 2021 (print) | LCC BQ2155 (ebook) | DDC 294.3/85—dc23
LC record available at https://lccn.loc.gov/2020044305
LC ebook record available at https://lccn.loc.gov/2020044306

ISBN 978-1-949163-18-6 (hardcover) ebook ISBN 978-1-949163-19-3
25 24 23 22 21 1 2 3 4 5

Cover and interior design by Gopa&Ted2. Set in Diacritical Garamond Pro 11/14.

Printed on acid-free paper and meets the guidelines for permanence and durability of the Production Guidelines for Book Longevity of the Council on Library Resources.

Printed in the United States of America.

For
My Parents
and
My Children,
With Love and Profound Gratitude

Contents

Series Editor's Preface to the First and Second Editions ... xiii
Author's Prefaces to the First Edition ... xix
Author's Preface to the Second Edition ... xxvii
Abbreviations and Sigla ... xxxi

Part One: Introduction

Prologue ... 3
History of the Noble Tradition ... 7
  Through the Glass of Modern Scholarship, Darkly ... 9
  Traditional History: Treasures and Visions ... 14
  Concluding Reflections ... 33
Canon of the Noble Tradition: Scriptural Authorities and Commentarial Literature ... 41
  Root and Explanatory Tantras ... 41
  Commentarial Literature ... 46
    The Works of Nāgārjuna ... 46
    The Works of Āryadeva ... 49
    The Works of Nāgabodhi, Śākyamitra, and Candrakīrti ... 55
The Lamp for Integrating the Practices and its Subject Matter ... 60
  Nature and Purpose of the Work ... 60
  Structure of the Work ... 65
  Analytical Summaries of Individual Chapters ... 72
Conventions in the Translation ... 116

Part Two: Translation

[Title page and homages] ... 119

1. Resolution of Doubts {about the Integration of Enlightenment} ... 121
2. Resolution of Doubts about the Integration of Body Isolation ... 133
3. Resolution of Doubts about the Integration of Speech Isolation ... 157
4. Resolution of Doubts about the Integration of Mind Isolation ... 187
5. Resolution of Doubts about the Integration of the Discernment of the Consequences of Action (*karma*) ... 209
6. Resolution of Doubts about the Integration of Superficial Reality ... 219
7. Resolution of Doubts about the Integration of Ultimate Reality ... 229
8. Resolution of Doubts about the Integration of the Realm of Unlocated Nirvāṇa ... 239
9. Resolution of Doubts about the Integration of the Bodhisattva Practice with Elaboration, the Enlightenment of the Reality-Source, According to the Method of the *Union of All Buddhas: Magical Supreme Bliss of the Ḍākiṇīs* ... 253
10. Resolution of Doubts about the Integration of the Practice without Elaboration ... 281
11. Resolution of Doubts about the Integration of the Practice Completely without Elaboration ... 291

Appendixes, Bibliography, Indexes

Appendix I: English–Sanskrit–Tibetan Glossary ... 309

Appendix II: Index of Scriptural Authorities Cited in the CMP ... 339

Appendix III: Charts of the One Hundred Buddha Families ... 345

Appendix IV: Charts of the Eighty Prototypes of the Subtle Mind ... 351

Appendix V: Schema of Questions Posed in the CMP ... 355

Appendix VI: Notes on the Textual Editions of the CMP ... 359

Bibliography ... 371

Indexes

Index of Canonical Authors Cited 393

Index of Canonical Texts Cited 395

General Index 397

Series Editor's Preface to the First and Second Editions

THIS *Treasury* series is dedicated to making available in English and other languages the entire Tengyur (*bsTan 'gyur*), the collection of Sanskrit works preserved in Tibetan translations. Āryadeva's *Lamp for Integrating the Practices* is a key work in Indo-Tibetan Buddhism. Along with Nāgārjuna's *Five Stages*, the *Lamp* is considered by the living representatives of the spiritual and intellectual tradition it illuminates to be one of two foundational instruction manuals covering the theory and practice of that type of Mahāyāna Buddhism that is interwoven with the contemplative technology of the vehicle of Mantra or Tantra. It is with great pride and delight that we present a second edition of Christian Wedemeyer's brilliant, comprehensive, and thorough study, translation, and critical editions of Āryadeva's *Lamp*.[1]

The *Lamp* has a charming structure, its information given in the form of a dialogue between a Vajraguru and a Vajrashiṣya, a Diamond Mentor and Diamond Student. It closely parallels Nāgārjuna's *Five Stages* in its structure, proceeding up through the five stages of perfection stage practices: (1) body isolation, (2) speech isolation, (3) mind isolation / self consecration / magic body, (4) clearlight transparency, and (5) communion (according to one of several ways of counting the five), though it is more detailed and discursive (mostly in prose). Before this work of Wedemeyer's, there have been many things about the unexcelled yoga tantras that have been obscure to the community of scholars that study them. Making

1. The Sanskrit and Tibetan critical editions published in the first edition of this book can now be found in the online reading room at wisdomexperience.org. A slightly corrected version of the Sanskrit critical edition is also available at sarit.indology.info/caryamelapakapradipa.xml.

Āryadeva's masterpiece available in English translation, together with its Sanskrit and Tibetan foundations, sheds much light on them.

Of course, the full understanding of this recondite and subtle subject will continue to remain somewhat difficult. It may well be that the whole complex literature of the *Esoteric Community Tantra*—its five explanatory tantras, Nāgārjuna's *Five Stages,* Nāgabodhi's *Stages of Arrangement,* the Esoteric Community works of Nāropa, the many Tibetan commentaries, especially those of Tsongkhapa, and finally the instructions of the living Tibetan mentors of the practice of these traditions—all must be translated, studied, and made accessible for any scholar without knowledge of Tibetan to gain a real grip on what it is all about. Whatever the fate of the field, the present work represents a major step in the right direction.

A continuing issue that persistently confronts us all, always resisting any easy solution, is that of the authorship of the original work. The "Vajra" Nāgārjuna is said to be the author of the *Five Stages*; the "Vajra" Chandrakīrti, in his *Illuminating Lamp*, refers to his mentor as Nāgārjuna; and the "Vajra" Āryadeva, in the prefatory remarks of this work, also refers to his mentor as Nāgārjuna, at least in some recensions of the texts. Thus, the "Noble" (*ārya*) lineage of instruction in the *Esoteric Community Tantra* cult and literature is inseparable from *a* Noble Nāgārjuna, who is claimed in the works themselves to be the mentor of *an* Āryadeva and *a* Chandrakīrti.

Christian Wedemeyer takes great care to consider the evidence of references to datable texts in order to establish a firm dating for the author of this work as an Āryadeva who lived in the 9th century or so, many centuries later than the famous Āryadeva of Mādhyamika fame, also reputed to be the direct disciple of the Mādhyamika founder Nāgārjuna. The Mādhyamika Nāgārjuna and Āryadeva are loosely dated in modern historiography in the 2nd–3rd century CE, and the Mādhyamika philosopher Chandrakīrti is placed in the 7th century CE; but all three of the tantric writers are dated in the 8th through 9th centuries. Therefore we have (at least) two sets of the three famous persons: the philosophical set dated in the 2nd and maybe 3rd centuries, and likely the 7th century, respectively, and the tantric set dated in the 8th through 9th centuries.

The Indo-Tibetan Buddhist scholarly tradition almost unanimously considers the two sets to be one set, not bothered by what for modern scholars is the major dating problem—namely that this postulates a six hundred year lifespan for Nāgārjuna, considers Āryadeva to be a miraculously born and nearly immortal saint, and considers the very same famous Chandrakīrti to have been both a Mādhyamika philosopher and a tantric adept. It seems strange that such sophisticated thinkers and scholars as the Indian masters of the last half of the first millennium and the equally distinguished Tibetan masters who followed them in the first half of the second millennium would so easily accept the traditional attribution of authorship of the tantric works to the same individuals, which means accepting their personal relationships across centuries of time. As Wedemeyer indicates, they often critically reject attributions that contradict internal evidence in the texts attributed, and it is not true that they have no sense of "history," which plays as strong an authenticating role for them as it does for modernist scholars. It thus appears that here we have a clash of cosmologies and therefore a clash of "histories"—what seems plausible and realistic to the Indian and Tibetan Buddhist seems fantastic to the modern scholars; what seems plausible and realistic to the modern scholars, seems spiritually blind and dogmatically materialistic to the Buddhists. Neither side can be expected to capitulate to the other. But should they simply condemn each other? Or is there something each can understand from this?

Perhaps what the Buddhists can learn from the moderns is the instability of texts, their transformability as they are transmitted, and the mixing of originals with commentarial notes from the hands of new generations; Wedemeyer's careful comparisons of the various Sanskrit texts and the Tibetan translations is useful for this. What the moderns can learn from the Buddhists is the imprecision of "history," how nothing relative can ever be asserted as absolute objective fact, how in a universe we do not fully understand we live tolerably only by cultivating a tolerance of cognitive dissonance. And eventually they might also learn that it is a form of cognitive imperialism to insist on inscribing the events in the Indic and Tibetan past into the materialist history of the modern West, dismissing as childish, deluded, primitive, superstitious, and unrealistic those who do not accept the hegemony of the Eurocentric and modernist presumptions regarding the nature of reality. After all, a glance at any number of recent writings on string theory, dark matter, dark energy, the wave-particle paradox, nonlocality, and so on, immediately reveals that we do not understand what "matter" is; so how can we be so certain about our "laws of scientific materialism" or the concrete factuality of our presumed "history"?

The traditional tantric scholars, still in modern times, recount a history wherein the founders of the tantric traditions worked at the very founding of the Mahāyāna itself; however, with the Vajrayāna being the esoteric aspect of the Mahāyāna, they kept the tantric teachings secret with no circulation of any kind of written text for up to seven hundred years. They observed serious vows of secrecy for good social reasons, and they had prodigious memories that could keep oral texts in relatively stable form without committing things to writing. This would allow the main Nāgārjuna and the main Āryadeva to have established the teachings in the *Five Stages* and the *Lamp* during their lifetimes in probably much shorter memory-preserved texts than those we have today after fifteen hundred years of handwritten and variously printed textual transmission. And as for the claims of meetings, these may have occurred on the visionary level. So with a touch of open-mindedness, it might be possible for modern scholars to bracket their sense of the really real and retain respect for the traditional tantric scholars.

Once we bracket as presently unknowable the historical facts of when and how long different persons lived, we must base our sense of which Nāgārjuna, which Āryadeva, and so on, on the internal evidence in the texts ascribed to them by responsible scholars. Thus, for example, the Tibetan scholar-adept Tsongkhapa (1357–1419) studied the Centrist philosophies and the Esoteric Community meditational practices during years of advanced study and practice in the 1390s, as did many other Tibetan monastic scholar-adepts, over centuries before and after him. All these master scholars eventually thought they did achieve remarkable results, and all recognized in the teachings they received and implemented the hands of the same teachers. Thus, after comprehensive study and sustained practice, they all reported that the two types of teachings complement each other and are best pursued in some form of coordination. It therefore seemed logical to them that the original teachers taught them in a coordinated way.

Either to verify or to reject these claims is beyond our present powers and understandings. Therefore, while staying skeptical, we can at least be open-minded and respect those who make such claims as being possibly more correct than us. We can go beyond our dogmatic self-enclosure in a smug sense of intellectual and scientific "modernist" superiority and reach a level field where we can engage in the healthy "contestation of truth-claims" (Peter Berger's felicitous phrase) with our counterparts from another civilization, without fixed prejudice as to the outcome.

It is in this spirit that we offer for your exploration and contemplation this *Lamp for Integrating the Practices.* Whether its original is eleven hundred years old or eighteen hundred years old, it is accessible for study in the present. Whether it is a sophisticated investigation of how the body and mind of a human being fit together and come apart in life and death, and ultimately evolve into an extraordinary state called "full enlightenment," or an elaborate fantasy about such matters from an era before the development of modern neuroscience, it is fascinating in its intricacy of detail, its grandeur of conceptual scheme, and its clarity in explaining how a community of tantric practitioners thought and lived in India and Tibet over many centuries.

I congratulate Christian Wedemeyer for his great scholarly and intellectual achievement in producing this book, maintaining his focus through many years of strenuous labor and unrelenting critical insight. I also add my sincere thanks to the international group of fine scholars he remembers and thanks for their skilled assistance, and a special acknowledgment of the labor of love and skill given by Thomas Yarnall, our designer, meticulous scholarly colleague, and executive editor.

Finally, it is a pleasure to present this second edition of Wedemeyer's wonderful work twelve years after the first edition, this time in collaboration with our new copublishing partners, the publishers and staff of Wisdom Publications. The work has stood the test of time, sold out some time ago, and as we evaluated it in the light of the intervening years of scholarship in the field, we found very little that needed changing. We have changed our way of handling the Sanskrit and Tibetan language critical editions, providing them to the scholarly readership online rather than printing them on paper, though we retain herein in Appendix VI the detailed explanation of the critical edition of the originals, Sanskrit and Tibetan, that introduces the online editions. I would like to thank Daniel Aitken, Ben Gleason, and the whole Wisdom Publications design and production team for their diligent and skilled work on this beautiful second edition.

Robert A.F. Thurman
Columbia University
August 3, 2007 CE
Tibetan Royal Year 2134, Fire Pig

Amended:
March 8, 2020 CE
Tibetan Royal Year 2147, Iron Mouse

Author's Preface to the First Edition

THE TEXT BEFORE YOU is the product of a sustained encounter between the author and a literary work over the course of about twelve years (1993–2005). Or, more precisely—since a literary work is rarely, if ever, properly instantiated in concrete, textual form—the text before you is the product of a sustained encounter between the author (myself by no means self-identical over the same period) and two primary, four secondary, and numerous tertiary texts over the course of about twelve years. During this period, I have attempted to reconstruct two literary works in two distinct languages and to present another afresh in yet a third. The two works whose reconstruction has been attempted are: a) a late first-millennium guide, composed in Sanskrit, detailing the gradual path of esoteric Buddhist yoga, and b) its eleventh-century translation into Tibetan. That which is to be presented afresh is an annotated English translation that attempts, within the typical limitations of the genre,[2] to communicate the ideas contained in the first two works.

The work to which I allude, you may well surmise, is the *Caryāmelāpakapradīpa* (CMP) of Āryadeva. When first pointed in the direction of this book by my doctoral advisor in 1993, I had little idea of the journey upon which I was about to embark. At the time, the work was only available in Tibetan translation; and it was in this form that I worked on it from 1993 until 1999, when a translation of it appeared as an appendix to my doctoral dissertation.[3] In early 1999, however, as work on the dissertation neared completion, I discovered that scholars at the Central Institute for Higher

2. As Edmond Jaloux has written (with apologies for the less-than-politically-correct phraseology), "les traductions sont comme les femmes: quand elles sont belles, elles ne sont pas fidèles, et quand elles sont fidèles, elles ne sont pas belles."

3. Christian K. Wedemeyer, "Vajrayāna and its Doubles," 232–356.

Tibetan Studies (Sarnath, Varanasi, India) had recently identified two manuscripts (or, more exactly, two halves of one manuscript) of this work in India and Nepal. Having long since been requested to publish a translation of the CMP in the Treasury of the Buddhist Sciences series, I realized that my old work was now obsolete and, begging the indulgence and patience of the publishers, set about obtaining the necessary manuscripts so as to update the translation with reference to the newly-available Sanskrit materials. By mid-2000, I had the MSS in hand, along with an advance copy of Dr. Janardan Pandey's edition, published later that year,[4] and set about what I assumed would be the brief work of revising the translation in light of the Sanskrit texts.

The next few years, however, witnessed the "goal posts" of this project progressively receding further and further from where I had at first imagined them to be. As I was setting about reworking my translation in light of these initial materials, I simultaneously (May 2000) discovered the existence of yet another manuscript that had previously escaped notice—in the Rahul Sāṅkṛtyāyan collection in Patna.[5] The results of my initial work at revision (which had very quickly revealed rather significant problems with Pandey's *editio princeps*) and the revelation of the new manuscript—combined with a little prodding by my senior colleague at the time, Prof. Kenneth Zysk—led me, by early 2001, to undertake a new edition of the Sanskrit to accompany the revised translation. Further work in this direction—coupled with my personal sense of unease at working on a *Sanskrit* edition while anticipating review for a promotion in my position directing the University of Copenhagen's *Tibetan* Studies program—led me in 2002 further to undertake an edition of the canonical Tibetan translation of Śraddhākaravarman and Rinchen Zangpo. These expansions of the scope of the project, along with no less than four international moves (from New York to India, India to Florida and back to New York, New York to Copenhagen, Copenhagen to Chicago), a seemingly interminable academic job search, and a heavy teaching load for three years, conspired to demand three more years to complete the work, completely revise long-obsolete introduc-

4. Janardan Shastri Pandey, *Caryāmelāpakapradīpam of Ācārya Āryadeva.*

5. Having identified this MS by the chapter titles listed in Sāṅkṛtyāyan's second article, I later discovered that it had previously been identified by German and Japanese scholars: see Tsukamoto et al., *Descriptive Bibliography* (237) and Bandurski, "Übersicht" (66).

tory material, and bring this volume at last to press. Though numerous flaws no doubt remain, I offer it here in the hope that it represents at least a small improvement over previous works and that it will make some helpful (if minor) contribution to knowledge and study of this important document of Indian esoteric Buddhist literature, the traditions of which it speaks, and to the study of religion as a whole.

Contributing over the years to this encounter of man and text(s) have been numerous others who have given generously of their time, energy, love, and consideration. It is my privilege here to acknowledge them and to thank them for their invaluable contribution to the work here presented. First and foremost, I should mention Robert A.F. Thurman, who was first responsible for setting me on the trail of Āryadeva and his *Lamp*. His patience, insight, and encouragement throughout my doctoral program at Columbia were invaluable. "Second readers" Ryuichi Abé and Gary Tubb were also of inestimable aid in helping me through the historical, linguistic, and interpretative issues posed by the work. Prof. Tubb contributed yet further to the very end of the process, generously agreeing to help me (in January 2005) to work through a last few editorial difficulties that had proven intractable.

Colleagues at the various academic institutions with which I have been affiliated during these last years have contributed in countless ways: some clearly apparent, many in less apparent, but all in important ways. At Columbia, deserving of special mention are Rachel McDermott, Frances Pritchett, Tom Yarnall, and David Mellins. At Antioch University: Robert Pryor, Pema Tenzin, Karma Lekshe Tsomo, Rebecca Manring, Peter Friedlander, and Abraham Zablocki. Among colleagues and staff at the University of Copenhagen's (erstwhile) Department of Asian Studies, I should mention Kenneth Zysk, Don Wagner, Viggo Brun, Pankaj Mohan, Stefan Baums, Cynthia Chou, Margaret Mehl, Anne Burchardi, Hartmut Buescher, Ole Lillelund, Leif Littrup, and the librarians of the institute library, Jens Østergaard Petersen and Merete Pedersen; my M.A. students in Copenhagen—Trine Brox, Heidi Köppl, Thomas Doctor, and Tina Rasmussen—have also been a source of inspiration. More recently, the faculty and staff of the University of Chicago Divinity School have distinguished themselves as absolutely outstanding colleagues, among whom Richard Rosengarten, Wendy Doniger, Matthew Kapstein, Bruce Lincoln, Martin Riesebrodt, Winifred Sullivan, Clark Gilpin, Steven Collins, and

Daniel Arnold figure prominently. Colleagues at other institutions have also been very generous, among whom especially should be mentioned Ashok Aklujkar, José Cabezón, Jacob Dalton, Georges Dreyfus, Stephen Hodge, Anne MacDonald, Patrick Olivelle, Isabel Onians, Kurtis Schaeffer, and Tōru Tomabechi.

Though not contributing directly to this project, I would like to thank my many teachers over the years: J. H. Stone II, Janet Gyatso, Janice Willis, Lou Nordstrom, Andrew Szegedy-Maszak, G. Thomas Tanselle, Peter Awn, John Sutula, Angela Irvine, Jack Thorpe, Tim Vincent, Betty Highlands, Bob Kaelin, and Mike O'Neill, as well as others too numerous to mention. None of this could have been accomplished without my many language teachers: Tibetan teachers Geshe Lhundup Sopa and Khamlung Tulku, Tsetan Chonjore, Tinley Dhondup, Tsering Wangyal, and Robert Thurman; and Sanskrit teachers Ted Riccardi, Nadine Berardi, Timothy Lubin, and Gary Tubb. Also deserving of gratitude are the many Tibetan scholar-practitioners who have taught, debated, and conversed with me over the years, including Geshe Pema Wangchen, Geshe Jigme Dawa, Kirti Tsenshab Rinpoche, Khensur Lobsang Nyima Rinpoche, Khensur Wangdag, Chokyi Nima Rinpoche, Geshe Lama Lhundup, Bokar Rinpoche, and His Holiness the Dalai Lama XIV. Nor can I omit to mention the significant contributions of my dear friends of many years: Greg Anderson, Dan Capper, Grady Clouse, Jerry Garcia, David Gimbel, Jessica Glass, Dominique Jones, Andy Kaufman, Joe Kennedy, Christian Svanes Kolding and Adriana Estrada, Ben Lund, Chase McClister, Dan Nothmann, Aaron Pomerantz, Larry Rosansky, Josefina og David Rosenkvist (og selvfølgelig også lille Andrea), Andy Ruskin, Sanjay Talwani, Ganden Thurman, Chris Trimble, Michael Unger, and Rick Weinstein. All these and many others who have shared beauty and knowledge with me, I thank most appreciatively.

Many persons gave assistance in obtaining the manuscript and other materials needed. Among these I would like to thank: the Asiatic Society of Bengal and their General Secretaries, Manabendu Banerjee and Ramakanta Chakrabarty, for their generous help with MS A and for generously granting permission to publish; Hena Basu, who did the actual legwork of procuring a copy of this manuscript; the very helpful staff of the Nepal-German Manuscript Preservation Project, through whose offices I obtained MS B—in particular Anne MacDonald, Johannes Vagt, and Klaus-Dieter Mathes; Mrs. Sarala Manandhar, Chief of the National Archives of Nepal, for assistance in consulting MS B and for generous permission to publish my results; Reinhold Grünendahl, Helmut Rohlfing, and the staff of the manuscript section of the library of Göttingens Universität for help in procuring microfilms of MSS from the Rāhul Sāṅkṛtyāyan Collection in Patna, including a film and print of MS C; Tōru Tomabechi, who confirmed for me the identity of MS C and initially directed me to the library at Göttingen; Janardan Pandey for sharing an advance copy of his edition of the CMP; the staff of Columbia University's Lehman Library, particularly David Magier and Peter Banos; the staff of New College's Cook Library, for extremely efficient ILL services; the staff of the Danish Royal Library (Det Kongelige Bibliotek), København, Denmark, for their kindness and assistance with accessing their excellent collection of Tibetan texts; and the staff of the University of Chicago's Regenstein Library, who, when their own outstanding collection fell short, went the extra mile to extract essential ILL materials from recalcitrant Ivy League libraries that shall go unmentioned.

Financial support, for its part, was not forthcoming for much of this work—textual scholarship of this ilk not being much in favor these days. One notable exception, to whom especial thanks are due, is Robert Schiffman, for his invaluable support of my work and for his faith in standing up against an array of obstacles in order to secure my research stay at New College, Sarasota, Florida. The semester I spent there as a Research Scholar allowed me both to produce my first published article and to begin the work on the Sanskrit manuscripts of this project—the indispensable foundation to bringing this book, ultimately, to completion. In this regard, thanks also are due to New College Trustee Darilyn Avery, Dean of the Humanities Stephen Miles, and Humanities secretary Nedra Hartley. On the other end of the process, the University of Chicago Divinity School and Committee on South Asian Studies (COSAS) have provided crucial support, both financial and moral, toward the completion of this project. I would also like to express appreciation to the University Seminars at Columbia University for their help in publication. Material in this work was presented to the University Seminar on Buddhist Studies. The late Aaron Warner and Robert Belknap, Directors of the Seminars, were most helpful and encouraging.

My research assistant of the last two years, Brad Aaron, provided crucial assistance in the final stages of the project, translating the computer files into a Unicode-friendly word processor in 2003 and then back again to the original (updated) program in 2004, producing the architecture for the glossary, formatting the marginal page numbers, and re-collating the Cone CMP, among other inestimable services. While preparing the typescript for publication, in Brad's absence, Amanda Huffer was also a great help in time of need. Many, many thanks are also due to Ngawang Jorden for his close reading of my Tibetan edition, which caught several careless typos and inadvertent errors. Wendy Doniger, Matthew Kapstein, Yigal Bronner, Losang Jamspal, and Stefan Baums all gave much needed and valued critical feedback on textual problems. Dan Arnold gave helpful feedback on part of the introduction. And especially, I must express my sincere, deep, and lasting gratitude to Harunaga Isaacson for his reading and correction of the Introduction and all three texts, generously offered even as he faced the challenges of new parenthood. Even though I have had the benefit of so much support, learned criticism, and guidance of all sorts, numerous errors and oversights no doubt remain—for which I own complete responsibility.

I could not have accomplished any of this without the support of my family. Endless thanks are due to my wife, Gitanjali Kapila who, as usual, gave invaluable help with both my thinking and my prose. Her patience and her love have kept me going all these years, without which I could never have persevered. Given the burdens she has had to shoulder in the course of it, she is no doubt as glad as I to see this project reach completion. Homage and gratitude are due as well as to the rest of my family: Phillips Wedemeyer, Anne Wedemeyer, Josephine Wedemeyer, Hope, Larry and Henry Wedemeyer-Salzer, Bill Wedemeyer and Jennifer Ekstrom, Margarete Wiener, Bina Kapila, Rajender Kapila, Vik, Kanan, Lola, and Kairavi Kapila, Jennifer, Alison and Sue Stanton and their families, and all the rest of the Wedemeyer and Kapila clans.

Finally, I need to mention a word about the two beautiful people whose names grace the dedication page of this work. As a young graduate student at Columbia, I was blessed to be classmates with Acarya Pema Losang Chögyen, an absolutely first-rate human being and very promising scholar of Buddhism, whom I am honored to have called my friend. Though I and the world were robbed of Pema's warm and generous presence as this work was commencing, in completing the project I have happily been blessed with a new friend, the other dedicatee of this work: my precious daughter

Maitreya, who daily gives me confidence that there really could be buddhas in the future. Along with them, this work is gratefully dedicated to you, my dear reader.

Christian K. Wedemeyer
Chicago, Illinois
19 August 2005

Addendum

THOUGH THIS WORK was "completed" over two years ago, it has by no means lain fallow in the interval. While a tremendous amount of time and effort went into writing it, no less remarkable an amount of care and attention has since been lavished in bringing these "chips from an American workshop" at last to press. The editors of this series, Robert A.F. Thurman and Thomas F. Yarnall, have been exemplary in their consistent concern for quality and in their no-less-appreciated patience with a highly opinionated and occasionally rather stubborn author. Dr. Yarnall, in particular, has been an outstandingly helpful and accommodating midwife: humoring my many persnickety demands for niceties such as marginal cross-pagination and a gargantuan glossary, incorporating much new material shamelessly smuggled into the margins of galleys long into the production process, enduring my at times "phantasmicly" idiosyncratic translation choices—even bearing up under my last-minute demand to include an addendum to the Preface! In the face of all these (and more) challenges, with a consummate skill Dr. Yarnall has crafted this handsome *nirmāṇa*—a public face—for the *dharma* (lowercase-d) produced in my private researches. The labor has been long and exhausting; the birth at last a joy and relief. As with all midwives, whatever thanks I can here offer will be inadequate, though they be nonetheless earnest and heartfelt.

Christian K. Wedemeyer
Chicago, Illinois
21 September 2007

Author's Preface to the Second Edition

As I observed at the beginning of the Preface to the first edition of this book, Aryadeva's *Lamp for Integrating the Practices* was my intellectual sparring partner for nearly twelve years—challenging me, frustrating me, and thrilling me, as I labored to develop the skills necessary to conduct advanced research into Buddhist literature and pursue a career as a professor of the History of Religions. Some further years have passed since I sent what understanding of it I was able to acquire in those years out into the world at large. At present, just over another dozen years has passed since its first birth as a published book.

I recall the early days, soon after I first agreed (against my better judgment) to follow Bob Thurman's advice to work on the *Lamp* for my dissertation project. Walking on a sunny New York day, I bumped into Alex Wayman on the street in front of Ollie's Noodle Shop at 113th Street and Broadway. As Wayman was at that time the only person to have published a monograph on the traditions of the Guhyasamāja Tantra, I asked him if I might come by to see him sometime to discuss sources I should consult. I was taken aback by his reply: "Oh! The Guhyasamāja! I wrote a book about that. You should just read the book. Everything I know is in the book." At the age of twenty-four, I could only surmise that this rejoinder reflected advanced senility on the part of this emeritus professor, for how could it be that he had nothing more to offer a student new to the field than the contents of his book, published only seventeen years previously? Yet, time is an unsparing teacher; and well before seventeen years had passed since the publication of what was to become my own book on the subject (whose second edition you hold in your hands), I found myself empathizing with Prof. Wayman, having moved on to other sparring partners, to other projects and ideas—with their thrills, challenges, and frustrations—and realized that I, too, retained only a rapidly fading recollection of the topics I had written about. Reviewing it recently in preparing it again for publication, I am happy to say that I find the author of this book seems to have done a pretty decent job under the circumstances, and seems not to have been nearly the fool as is his elder successor, the author of this Preface.

It has long been my hope that a more compact and affordable, English-only edition of the CMP may become available; and, now, the remarkable collaboration of Wisdom Publications and the American Institute of Buddhist Studies has made it a reality. The original edition was very much a scholar's tome: comprehensive in its scope and analysis of texts in three languages, but designed primarily for the use of researchers conversant in Sanskrit and Tibetan. Weighing in at 826 pages, it was a prime offender of the Greek dictum attributed to Callimachus, μέγα βιβλίον μέγα κακόν: "a big book is a big evil." Yet it was not an unmixed evil; and I hope those who aspire to such things may still be able to benefit from the (now out-of-print) first edition, lovingly produced by the magisterial efforts of Tom Yarnall and the AIBS team. Speaking another ancient-yet-modern tongue, H.H. the Dalai Lama XIV has stressed the crucial importance of Āryadeva's work for understanding the Tantric traditions of India and Tibet; and, referring to the fact that I had translated the book into English, he commented དཔེ་ཡག་པོ་འདུག ("outstanding!"). So, the book has that going for it, which is nice.

The current edition consists of all of the English-language contents of the first, excluding only the critical editions I had made of the Sanskrit of Āryadeva and the Tibetan translation of Śraddhākaravarman and Rinchen Zangpo. With the exception of only minor corrections and emendations, the introduction and translation remain essentially unaltered, although completely re-typeset. The appendixes from the original have been included, allowing further insight into the terminology of the treatise, its dialogical structure, and the sources it cites as authorities for its claims. There are no doubt improvements I could make, were I to revisit the work in a sustained manner; but for now, it remains what it is.

I hope soon to supplement this work with a companion volume of translations of the most essential Noble Tradition[6] works of liturgy (*sādhana*)

6. Like the Four "Noble Truths" of Buddhism, which are best rendered as the Four Truths of the [Spiritually] Noble (who understand them)—there being nothing particularly "noble" about facts such as universal suffering—what is herein rendered the "Noble Tradition" is also best understood as the Tradition of the Noble Ones (Nāgārjuna, Āryadeva, Nāgabuddhi/ Nāgabodhi, Candrakīrti, etc.).

and theory of liturgy, including those by Nāgārjuna, Candrakīrti, Nāgabuddhi/Nāgabodhi, Abhayākaragupta, and others. Taken in conjunction with the forthcoming AIBS translation of the *Guhyasamāja Tantra* itself—and the many other important works being produced on the classics of Indian Tantric Buddhism (by AIBS, Wisdom, and others)—a significant body of English-language sources are now available for the research, study, and/or practice of modern readers. (Indeed, the Dalai Lama himself commented that a large proportion of Tibetans today must themselves rely upon English translations for understanding their own traditions.)

The most significant development related to the contents of this volume and my own research—one that could not neatly be incorporated into a new edition—is the "discovery" of the parameters and larger significance of the "practices" (*caryā*) referred to in the title of Āryadeva's work. It was reflecting on the distinctive schematization found in the *Lamp* that led me subsequently to interrogate the broader Tantric literature to determine how these "practices" appeared outside of Āryadeva's system. What I learned was that the term "practice" (*caryā*) that appears in the title and last three chapters of Āryadeva's work, with its frequent synonym "observance" (*vrata*), which had hitherto been construed by readers (scholars and practitioners alike) as "practice" in the generic, is correctly to be understood as "(1) a highly specific term of art [already] in the literature of the Buddhist Mahāyoga and Yoginī Tantras, signifying a very precise undertaking, (2) that close attention to the semiology of the rite reveals a very clear ritual intent that is evident throughout the Buddhist literature, and (3) that the sources explicitly (if at times somewhat obliquely) stress that this rite is appropriate only in quite specific and elite ritual contexts with very specific prerequisites."[7] That is, while Āryadeva's systematic analysis of (what I think is thus best called) The Practice (*caryā*) or The Practice Observance (*caryāvrata*) is innovative and constitutes one of his distinctive interventions in the theory of the Buddhist Tantric traditions, it is important to understand that systematic transgression of moral and ritual purity norms was never understood as "Tantric practice" in general, but was always a special time-delimited undertaking for advanced practitioners. Since I first presented these ideas in 2007, I have been gratified to find that—aside

7. See Wedemeyer, *Making Sense of Tantric Buddhism*, 136, where further discussion of this issue may be found.

from exciting one scholar's *ressentiment* (allegedly based on some concern about my explicit use of synchronic historical method)—most have found my interpretation compelling. That this insight has since enabled others to uncover new and fascinating features of the Buddhist Tantric traditions, both in India and Tibet, is the stuff of which scholarly dreams are made.

The new edition carries a new dedication: to my parents, of whom I cannot begin to express my love, devotion, and gratitude for their many blessings over half a century now; and to my two daughters, Maitreya, to whom the first edition was dedicated, and now Isolde, born as the first edition was in press. It is my firm hope that, in the end, our time together may likewise have the good fortune of unfolding over at least half a century. I am daily grateful for their presence in my life, bringing some sorrows as well as joys, but mainly delight and pride, meaning and purpose.

Christian K. Wedemeyer
Chicago, Illinois
Day of Miracles (ཆོ་འཕྲུལ་དུས་ཆེན) 9 March 2020

Abbreviations & Sigla

Primary Textual Sources

Skt Edited Sanskrit text of the *Caryāmelāpakapradīpa* of Āryadeva, based on sources as follows:

A Microfilm copy of Sanskrit manuscript held by the Asiatic Society of Bengal: manuscript no. 4837; catalogued as *Vajrayānasādhanāṅgānī*; palm leaf, 36 leaves, Old Newari/Proto-Bengali script, 28.5 3 5 cm. (The first half of ms B.)

B Microfilm copy of Sanskrit manuscript held by the National Archives, Kathmandu, Nepal: manuscript no. 3-363/vi, bauddhatantra 8; catalogued as *Saṃśaya-pariccheda*; palm leaf, 36 leaves, Old Newari/Proto-Bengali script, 28.5 3 5 cm; NGMPP reel no. A48/6, filmed on 19 October 1970. (The second half of ms A, minus the last folio.)

C Microfilm copy of photograph of Sanskrit manuscript made by Rāhul Sāṅkṛtyāyan in Tibet (Ngor Monastery); paper, 69 leaves (final 27 containing CMP), Old Bengali script, 12.33 3 2.17 in., 9 lines per side, Bandurski no. Xc 14/30.

Pn *editio princeps* of Janardan Pandey (See Pandey 2000).

Tib Edited text of *Spyod pa bsdus pa'i sgron ma*—the Tibetan translation of the *Caryāmelāpakapradīpa* by Śraddhākaravarman and Rin-chen bZang-po.

Co Co-ne edition; microform copy by IASWR held in library of American Institute of Buddhist Studies/ Columbia Center for Buddhist Studies, Columbia University, New York.

D sDe-dge edition; facsimile reprint of xylographic edition in *poṭhi* format, published as part of the dGongs-rdzogs of H.E. the Karmapa XVI (Delhi: Delhi Karmapae Choedhey, 1984) held in Columbia University Libraries.

N	sNar-thang edition; xylographic copy held by the Danish Royal Library (Det Kongelige Bibliotek), Copenhagen, Denmark.
P	Peking edition; facsimile edition of the copy of Otani University (as *Chibetto Daijōkyō—Tibetan Tripitaka*, ed. D. T. Suzuki) held at the Danish Royal Library.
Tib[Chag]	Readings from Chag Lo-tsā-ba's translation of CMP found in RṄSG.

Other Textual Citations

AKṬ	*Amṛtakaṇikā-ṭippaṇī* of Raviśrījñāna (See Lal 1994)
AKU	*Abhibodhikramopadeśa* attributed to Āryadeva (Tōh. 1806)
AKUN	*Amṛtakaṇikodyota-nibandha* of Vibhūticandra (See Lal 1994)
ĀM	Kambala's *Ālokamālā* (See Lindtner 2003)
ASPP	*Aṣṭasāhasrikā-prajñāpāramitā Sūtra* (See Vaidya 1960)
AVS	*Advayavajra-saṃgraha* (See Shāstrī 1927)
BHSD	Buddhist Hybrid Sanskrit Dictionary (See Edgerton 1957)
CGKV	*Caryāgītikoṣavṛtti* of Munidatta (See Kværne 1977)
Chandra Das	*A Tibetan-English Dictionary*, ed. Sarat Chandra Das (see Das 1899)
CMP	*Caryāmelāpakapradīpa* of Āryadeva
CS(Tucci)	*Catuḥstava* of Nāgārjuna (See Tucci 1932)
CS(Patel)	*Catuḥstava* of Nāgārjuna (See Patel 1932)
CVP	*Cittaviśuddhiprakaraṇa* attributed to Āryadeva (See Shāstrī 1898 and Patel 1949)
DK	sDe-dge bKa'-'gyur
DN	*Dīgha-nikāya* (See Davids and Carpenter 1903)
GS	*Guhyasiddhi* of Padmavajra (See Rinpoche and Dwivedi 1987)
GST	*Guhyasamāja Tantra* (See Matsunaga 1978)
GSUT	*Guhyasamāja Uttaratantra* (See Bhattacharyya 1931)

HJ	*Hobson-Jobson* (See Yule and Burnell 1886)
Jäschke	*A Tibetan-English Dictionary* of H.A. Jäschke (See Jäschke 1881)
KP	*Kāśyapa-parivarta* (See von Staël-Holstein 1977)
KRP	*Kinnara-rāja-paripṛcchā* (See Harrison 1992)
LAS	*Laṅkāvatārasūtra* (See Nanjio 1923)
MNS	*Mañjuśrī-nāma-saṃgīti* (See Davidson 1981)
MV	*Mahāyāna-viṃśikā* of Nāgārjuna (See Tucci 1982)
M-W	*A Sanskrit-English Dictionary*, ed. M. Monier-Williams (See Monier-Williams 1899)
NTED	*The New Tibetan-English Dictionary of Modern Tibetan* (See Goldstein 2001)
PED	Pali-English Dictionary (See Davids and Stede [1921–25] 1999)
PK	*Pañcakrama* of Nāgārjuna (See Mimaki and Tomabechi 1994)
PK-Poussin	*Pañcakrama* of Nāgārjuna (See La Vallée Poussin 1894)
PKṬ	*Pañcakramaṭippaṇī* of Parahitarakṣita (See La Vallée Poussin 1894)
PKṬYM	*Pañcakramaṭippaṇī Yogīmanoharā* of Muniśrībhadra (See Jiang and Tomabechi 1996)
PSED	*A Practical Sanskrit-English Dictionary* by V.S Apte (See Apte 1890)
PU	*Pradīpoddyotana-nāma-ṭīkā-ṣaṭkoṭi-vyākhyā* of Candrakīrti (See Chakravarti 1984)
RD	*Rahasyadīpikā* commentary of Vanaratna on *Vasantatilakā Tantra* (See Rinpoche and Dwivedi 1990)
RṄGC	*Rim lnga 'grel chen* (or *sLob dpon klu sgrub mdzad pa'i rim lnga'i 'grel chen rdo rje 'chang chen po'i dgongs pa zhes bya ba*) of Jo-nang Tāranātha (See Tāranātha 1976)

RṄSG	*Rim lnga gsal sgron* (or *Rgyud kyi rgyal po dpal gsang ba 'dus pa'i man ngag rim pa lnga rab tu gsal ba'i sgron me*) of rJe Rinpoche bLo-bzang Grags-pa (See Tsong-kha-pa, *The Collected Works*, 1975–, vol. 11
SBS	*Sarvabuddhasamāyoga Tantra*
S[K]P	*Svādhiṣṭhāna-[krama-]prabheda* of Āryadeva (See Pāṇḍey 1990)
SRS	*Samādhirājasūtra* (See Vaidya 1961)
SS	*Subhāṣitasaṃgraha* (See Bendall 1905)
STTS	*Sarvatathāgata-tattva-saṃgraha* (See Horiyuchi 1968)
SUṬ	*Sekoddeśaṭīkā* of Nadapāda (See Carelli 1941)
SUT	*Saṃvarodaya Tantra* (See Tsuda 1974)
YST	*Yoginīsaṃcāra Tantra* (See Pāṇḍey 1998)

Typographical Conventions and Miscellaneous Abbreviations

[...]	Material added by translator
{...}	Material found only in the Sanskrit
(...)	Material found only in the Tibetan translation
**saṃskṛta*	Sanskrit terms reconstructed from Tibetan testimony
**bod skad*	Tibetan terms reconstructed from Sanskrit testimony
†	Page break in MS A and B
‡	Page break in MS C
MS(S)	Manuscript(s)
SKT.	Edited Sanskrit text of the *Caryāmelāpakapradīpa* of Āryadeva (See Wedemeyer 2007), based on sources as follows:
TIB.	Edited text of *Spyod pa bsdus pa'i sgron ma* (See Wedemeyer 2007)—the Tibetan translation of the *Caryāmelāpakapradīpa* by Śraddhākaravarman and Rin-chen bZang-po

Part One

INTRODUCTION

Introduction

Prologue

Āryadeva's *Lamp for Integrating the Practices* (*Caryā-melāpaka-pradīpa*, hereafter CMP or the *Lamp*) is among the most important and influential works in the history of esoteric Buddhist thought. One may infer as much from the fact that it is cited in numerous Indian commentaries of the late first and early second millennia, including the *Sekoddeśaṭīkā* of Naḍapāda (Nāropā) and the *Pañcakrama-ṭippaṇī Yogi-manoharā* of Muniśrībhadra. In Tibet, it has been considered of the highest authority by authors from all of the various traditional lineages over many centuries. In Gö Kugpa Lhaytsay's eleventh-century *Survey of the Esoteric Community* (*gSang 'dus stong thun*)—the earliest extant Tibetan treatise on the Noble Tradition's practice of the *Esoteric Community* (*Guhyasamāja*) *Tantra*—it is the first and arguably the most prominent textual authority cited; and it was closely studied and cited by a wide range of Tibetan scholar-monks from this time until at least the seventeenth century. Perhaps most notably, the *Lamp* served as a definitive template for the early fifteenth-century systematization of esoteric practice by the founder of the Ganden (later Geluk) Tradition, Je Rinpoche Lozang Drakpa (1357–1419; a.k.a. Tsongkhapa), through which it continues to exercise a decisive (if second-hand) influence on much of contemporary Tibetan practice of the esoteric traditions to this very day.

It may be considered remarkable, then, that the *Lamp* has not generated much comment by modern scholars of Buddhism, who have tended (insofar as they have taken notice of the esoteric traditions at all) to focus their attention on the few Vajrayāna works edited and published in the early twentieth century—a number among which the CMP does not figure. A work that *was* so edited and published, however, and that accordingly has been noticed and commented on since the very inception of the modern study of the Buddhist traditions, is the *Pañcakrama*, or *Five Stages*, of Nāgārjuna (hereafter PK). This latter is intimately related to the CMP, for it is the central idea of the PK that the CMP seeks to elaborate and legitimate.

The existence, and to a limited extent the importance, of the PK was noted as early as 1844 in what has come to be considered the foundational document of the modern academic study of Buddhism: Eugène Burnouf's *Introduction à l'Histoire du Buddhisme Indien*. Burnouf was not, however, much impressed by Nāgārjuna's work—indeed, he was rather volubly put off by its antinomian rhetoric—and, aside from a few elementary observations about its use of maṇḍalas and the mantra *oṃ śūnyatā-jñāna-svabhāvātmako 'ham*, he did not have much to contribute to its study or analysis.[8] Further research in this area was left to his self-appointed successor, Louis de La Vallée Poussin, who took up work on the PK and one of its commentaries in the 1890s. In 1894, La Vallée Poussin published an initial notice of this work, entitled "Note sur le Pañcakrama," which was subsequently republished as the introduction to his critical edition in 1896.[9] Since the publication of that work, the PK has been a touchstone of the published works of esoteric Buddhism, referred to and cited in a variety of contexts.

There has not, however, been equal attention paid to works in the same tradition preserved unpublished in manuscript form or solely in Tibetan translation, as was the CMP until quite recently. The earliest mention of the CMP in modern scholarship seems to have been in Ferdinand Lessing and Alex Wayman's 1967 translation of the *Fundamentals of the Buddhist Tantras* (*rGyud sde spyi rnam*) of Kaydrup Je Gelek Palzang (1385–1438), a major disciple of Tsongkhapa.[10] Further brief reference was subsequently made by Wayman in an article entitled "Early Literary History of the Buddhist Tantras, especially the Guhyasamāja Tantra."[11] Much of this discussion was taken over verbatim into Wayman's 1977 *Yoga of the Guhyasamāja Tantra*, which seems to represent what is to date the most extensive discussion of this work and its related traditions in a European language.

8. For a translation of Burnouf's entire comment on PK, see Christian K. Wedemeyer, "Vajrayāna and its Doubles," 40–41; original French in Burnouf, *Introduction* (1844), 557–58.

9. See Louis de La Vallée Poussin, "Note sur le Pañcakrama," 137–46 and *Études et Textes Tantriques: Pañcakrama*.

10. Ferdinand D. Lessing and Alex Wayman, eds. and trans., *Mkhas-grub-rje's Fundamentals of the Buddhist Tantras* (The Hague: Mouton, 1967), see esp. p. 35.

11. Reprinted in Alex Wayman, *The Buddhist Tantras,* 12–23.

Wayman emphasized the importance of the *Lamp*, writing that "in this tradition the greatest work on important phases of tantric praxis is Āryadeva's *Caryāmelāpakapradīpa*."[12]

The "tradition" he speaks of is one that Tibetan intellectuals refer to as the Noble Tradition of the Esoteric Community (*gsang 'dus 'phags lugs*). Since the work of Wayman and others, this moniker[13] has been taken up into scholarly usage. While we have no evidence that Indian tradition likewise had a special name for this school of thought and practice, the literature of the tradition itself is sufficiently coherent and self-referential that it may confidently be said to form a consistent school of thought. Thus, though the name may not be of Indian origin, its application in this case seems apposite. Nonetheless, it should always be borne in mind that the "canon" of commentarial literature this name implies does not appear to have been explicitly so-called in the Indian context.

That said, what is "the Noble Tradition of the Esoteric Community?" In brief, the Noble Tradition comprises a group of authors (and their spiritual descendents) who commented in distinctive ways upon the literature and praxis of the *Guhyasamāja Tantra*, or *Esoteric Community Tantra* (hereafter GST or *Esoteric Community*)—one of the most important scriptures of Indian esoteric Buddhism.[14] Perhaps the idea most central to the Noble Tradition (though by no means exclusive to it) is that the goal of Buddhist enlightenment is to be reached through a gradual yogic process, rather than through a "sudden" or immediate experience. There is, of course, more to it than this, which will be explored in greater detail below. In the meantime, as a working definition, we may postulate that the Noble Tradition asserts

12. Alex Wayman, *Yoga of the Guhyasamāja Tantra*, 93. It could legitimately be debated whether or not Wayman's use of a superlative here is warranted; but there can be no doubt whatsoever that, in such a contest, the CMP would be a serious contender.

13. Or, rather, other variations on this moniker. Most scholars have tended to "back-translate" the name into Sanskrit, yielding the "Ārya Tradition (or "School") of the Guhyasamāja Tantra." Others refer to it as the "Saint School," which term is the one most frequently used in Japanese scholarship, owing to the influence of Yūkei Matsunaga.

14. Most scholars, I think it is fair to say, do not translate the name of this scripture (or other esoteric scriptures) in their writings (unlike, say, the *Diamond* or *Lotus* scriptures). While I am not entirely satisfied with the term Esoteric Community, I have not yet devised another that is to my liking. Note, too, that I will occasionally distinguish the Esoteric Community understood as either the deity or its associated traditions, from the *Esoteric Community* qua scripture.

that full and complete realization as an enlightened world teacher (*samyaksaṃbuddha*) is a) only possible through the practice of yogic techniques revealed in the *Esoteric Community Tantra*, b) that further essential components of these techniques are only taught in a set of auxiliary "explanatory tantras" (*vyākhyā-tantra*), and c) that these techniques effect a gradual process of transformation whose main features may be reduced to a schema of discrete stages.

In what follows, I will attempt both to unpack the richness condensed into these three propositions and to provide the background necessary to appreciate and to understand the significance and the thought of the *Lamp* and the school of which it is an authoritative statement. To date, modern scholarship on these traditions has (it seems to me) made little effort to communicate the fundamental concerns of these Buddhist thinkers—either to other specialists or to a more general public. While there have been some few articles discussing the Noble Tradition, nowhere have its constitution and its main contributions to Buddhist thought and practice been clearly and succinctly outlined. Wayman's remains the only book-length contribution in this area. As valuable as Wayman's work may have been in its time and place (and I will leave that for the enterprising reader to determine), *Yoga* does not succeed in communicating clearly and systematically the thought of the Noble Tradition, although it is devoted precisely to elucidating the same. Unfortunately, as in the case of much scholarship on the esoteric Buddhist traditions, Wayman seems not fully to believe that the tradition even *has* a coherent, explicable system of thought to elucidate, referring as he does to its doctrines as "arcane lore."

In attempting to rectify this lacuna, I proceed on the understanding that the teachings of this tradition are not at all "arcane," except in the limited sense that it may at one time have been restricted to initiated practitioners (and even this proposition is open to serious question).[15] The thought of the tradition is herein communicated through the vehicle of a translation and explanation of the CMP, a work ideally suited to this task insofar as it constitutes an unusually lucid and direct presentation of the yogic system and doctrinal underpinnings of the Esoteric Community as mediated through

15. It is not inconceivable that this "esoteric" literature may have been meant in part for a larger, non-initiate audience. As I will argue below (see p. 75), there are qualities of the CMP that suggest that its target audience may have included those outside the tradition.

the interpretative lens of Nāgārjuna's school. This introduction seeks to give an overall sense of the parameters of the tradition—its history, literature, and major figures—as well as to explain its yogic platform in terms accessible to both specialist scholars of Indic religions and the educated public. I begin by addressing the historical context of the tradition and its authors; I then give an overview of the major monuments of the literature of the school; this is followed by an analysis and close reading of the CMP. The introduction concludes with some observations concerning the materials and methods used in editing and translating the work.

History of the Noble Tradition

The Noble Tradition is a school of Buddhist esoteric thought and practice centering on the *Esoteric Community Tantra* (though making frequent and wide reference to other esoteric scriptures). It is styled "Noble" by Tibetan exegetes in deference to its central thinker, the Noble (i.e., Ārya) Nāgārjuna (Tib. [*dpal mgon*] *'phags pa klu sgrub*), whose PK is the most authoritative statement of the school's yogic technologies—as contrasted with the other major tradition so identified, which bears the name of its chief thinker, Jñānapāda.[16] In addition to Nāgārjuna and Āryadeva, its most significant authors bear the names Nāgabodhi and Candrakīrti. To anyone with even a passing acquaintance with Mahāyāna Buddhist thought, these names will not be unfamiliar, and their conjunction as members of a common "school" will come as no surprise: for these are none other than the names of the more famous thinkers of the exoteric Mahāyāna Centrist Tradition (*madhyamaka, dbu ma*). Thus, the attributions of these esoteric works to these authors suggests a link between the exoteric school of the Centrists and the esoteric school of the Noble Tradition.

The exact nature of this link, however, has been a matter of some dispute; and there are, accordingly, divergent views concerning the history of the

16. Modern scholarship tends to hold the view that the Jñānapāda Tradition (*ye shes zhabs lugs*) is older than the Noble Tradition; traditional sources are generally silent on this issue, though the attribution of the Noble works to Nāgārjuna et al., would tend to suggest that they consider the Nobles to be prior (though, on this, see my analysis of the indigenous historiography, below, esp. p. 40). The lineages differ in their central deities (Mañjuvajra for Jñānapāda, Akṣobhyavajra for the Nobles) and the number of deities in the maṇḍala (nineteen versus thirty-two, respectively).

Noble Tradition and its authors, and their relationship (if any) with the famous authors of the Centrist Tradition. Though in what follows I will problematize this formulation, the contrast may most succinctly be stated as follows. The Tibetan tradition has accepted—from its earliest encounter with these texts until the present—that the authorship of the esoteric works may be attributed to those authors bearing the same names who composed the exoteric philosophical works of the Centrist (Madhyamaka) School. That is, they maintain that the famous Nāgārjuna who penned the *Fundamental Verses of Centrism*[17] was also a tantric yogin who wrote the *Five Stages* and other important works of Buddhist esoterism.[18] Modern scholars of Buddhism, in contrast, have tended to find this position untenable if not utterly inconceivable. Based on the conviction that esoteric Buddhism constitutes a much later phase in the development of Indian Buddhist literature, they have concluded that the esoteric writings could not possibly have been written by the Centrist authors.

In part, this difference of opinion reflects the fact that these two groups approach this literature with rather different concerns—though there is perhaps more consonance between the two camps than the "ideal types" here presented might imply. For while the Tibetan tradition is, to be sure, rather deeply invested in Nāgārjuna's role as an authoritative source for the esoteric practices, it is not entirely uninterested in (nor entirely unaffected by) the results of critical, historical scholarship. Modern scholarship, too—if it seeks not merely to "know better" than the tradition itself, but also to understand its internal ideo-historical dynamics—needs be alert to the indigenous construction of the tradition's own self-imagining if it is properly to evaluate its claims.

A suitably-nuanced scholarly understanding of the history and historiography of this literature, then, requires that each of these ideal positions be somewhat rethought. On the one hand, there are clear problems with

17. *Mūla-madhyamaka-kārikā*; this work has attracted an enormous amount of interest in modern scholarship. For a recent translation see, e.g., Jay Garfield, trans., *Fundamental Wisdom of the Middle Way*.

18. Interestingly, though the Noble Tradition of the Esoteric Community was not transmitted there, other esoteric schools in Japan (and China) nonetheless maintain that Nāgārjuna played a significant role in the transmission of their traditions. An influential and formative narrative maintains that he was the recipient of esoteric lineages and transmitted them from the Iron Tower in southern India. On this, see, e.g., Ryuichi Abé, *The Weaving of Mantra*, 221.

the "traditional view" as so constructed. Taken in the aggregate, the extant evidence suggests that the authors of the esoteric writings lived rather later than the homonymous authors of the exoteric texts. On the other hand, modern scholarship has in general taken a rather myopic approach to the issue. A tendency simply to rest satisfied in the smug assertion of difference has prevented scholars from probing more deeply into the complex of issues involved. In particular, having overlooked features of the construction of authorship culturally-specific to first-millennium Indian Buddhist communities, they have failed to engage the issue in such a way as would illuminate the important dynamics of religious history and ideology that lie behind the attribution. In what follows, we shall accordingly endeavor to reconsider these positions, taking into account heretofore-overlooked evidence from the Indo-Tibetan historiographical tradition that suggests a more subtle (and more accurate) way of understanding the indigenous views concerning the emergence of these texts and their noteworthy attributions.

Through the Glass of Modern Scholarship, Darkly

Although the Library of Congress catalogs the esoteric writings attributed to Āryadeva under the rubric "Āryadeva, 3rd cent."—seemingly assenting to the traditional attribution—on the whole, modern scholarship has not considered this credible. It was an early axiom of scholarship on Buddhism that the esoteric traditions were morally degenerate and, precisely to that extent, of correspondingly late date.[19] Though poorly argued and predicated on only the weakest evidentiary footing, a consensus was quickly reached that led inexorably to the conclusion that the works of the Esoteric Community Noble Tradition *could not possibly* have been composed by the homonymous authors of the Centrist Tradition.

The incredulity of the modern scholarly community early found its most unambiguous voice in the scornful comment of Louis de La Vallée Poussin who, in his *Bouddhisme: Opinions sur l'Histoire de la Dogmatique*, wrote that:

19. Implicit here is an historiographical axiom to the effect that all phenomena follow the same historical laws and conform to the same pattern—that of the organic life-cycle of birth-maturity-decay-and-death. Also implicit is the notion that this "decay" generally reflects moral failings. A full discussion of this may be found in Christian K. Wedemeyer, "Tropes, Typologies, and Turnarounds," 227–34.

> There are, no doubt, some tantric writings whose promulgation is attributed to Nāgārjuna, Saraha, [and] Āryadeva—illustrious doctors of the Great Vehicle. But this literary fraud cannot fool anyone, and the authors of our books are very probably the sorcerers subsequent to the sixth century that are described by Tāranātha—by profession "evokers" of divinities of the second rank, with a smattering of Buddhist philosophy, but totally foreign to the spirit of the Good Law.[20]

Much the same has been repeatedly asserted by the most prominent scholars of esoteric Buddhism, such as Benoytosh Bhattacharyya,[21] S. B. Dasgupta,[22] David Seyfort Ruegg,[23] and David Snellgrove.[24] That is to say, modern scholars have tended to give one of two explanations for the Tibetan assertion of the identity of the exoteric and esoteric authors: either they were "confused" or they were the victims of a crude (but effective) "literary fraud." There has been no effort to engage the traditional attribution in more detail or to attempt to understand the logic internal to it. Scholarly consensus in this case has not resulted in any uniformity of opinion concerning their respective *floruit*,[25] nor in any greater insight as to the ideological import of this noteworthy attribution than La Vallée Poussin's view that it was noth-

20. Louis de La Vallée-Poussin, *Bouddhisme: Opinions sur l'Histoire de la Dogmatique*, 382–83. [my translation]

21. "The Tibetan sources have hopelessly mixed up together the accounts of Nāgārjuna—the disciple of Aśvaghoṣa, with Nāgārjuna—the disciple of Saraha.... [A]s these two persons are taken erroneously to be the same, a serious confusion has arisen." B. Bhattacharyya, *Introduction to Buddhist Esoterism*, 67.

22. "The Tibetan account perhaps makes a confusion between Nāgārjuna, the Tāntric, and Nāgārjuna, the great philosopher." S. B. Dasgupta, *Introduction to Tāntric Buddhism*, 54.

23. "The Indo-Tibetan records frequently identify these Vajrayānist masters with the illustrious teachers of the early Madhyamaka school whose names they bore, and to whom these records accordingly ascribe extraordinarily long life-spans." D. Seyfort Ruegg, *Literature of the Madhyamaka School*, 106.

24. "*Pañcakrama* (Fivefold Series) [was] written by a certain Nāgārjuna, whom Tibetan tradition identifies with the renowned Madhyamaka teacher." D. Snellgrove, *Indo-Tibetan Buddhism*, 285.

25. The consensus concerning the date of the Centrist Nāgārjuna still floats somewhere between the first and the early fourth centuries of the Common Era (though most tend to stick to a first/second century date); whereas the Noble Nāgārjuna has been placed anywhere from the fifth to the tenth centuries.

ing more than a simpleminded attempt to commandeer the authority of the "illustrious doctors of the Great Vehicle."

Before interrogating the traditional attribution further, it will perhaps be instructive to digress a moment on the evidence available for dating the Noble Tradition literature. For despite the ineptitude with which the modern scholarly view has generally been presented,[26] it is in fact possible to argue fairly persuasively that the Āryadeva who authored the CMP was not contemporaneous with the person who authored the *Catuḥśataka*.[27] This is possible based upon the wide range of sources cited in the CMP—sources the nature of which allow us to begin to make some claims about a *terminus post quem* for its author—and sources that themselves cite the CMP, which allow us to fix a *terminus ante quem*.[28] Given the notorious difficulty of assigning dates to the scriptural corpus of revealed sūtras and tantras, it is the śāstric literature that will concern us here.[29] Of śāstras, the CMP cites the following two known works: Kambala's *Ālokamālā* (ĀM) and Padmavajra's *Guhyasiddhi* (GS).

The citation of ĀM alone would allow us fairly confidently to conclude that the Āryadeva who authored the CMP is not the Āryadeva who authored the *Catuḥśataka*. Christian Lindtner has argued that the ĀM demonstrates "acquaintance with Bhartṛhari (ca. 450–510) and Dignāga (ca. 480–540, or a few decades earlier)."[30] If we accept this, then we must accordingly date the author of the CMP as at least one century posterior

26. For a detailed discussion of scholarly arguments concerning the dating of esoteric schools such as the Noble Tradition, see Wedemeyer, "Tropes, Typologies, and Turnarounds," 235–56.

27. Which work we may take as definitive of the identity of the Centrist Āryadeva in much the same way in which the *Mūlamadhyamakakārikā* is taken as definitive of the Centrist Nāgārjuna. On the *Catuḥśataka*, see Karen Lang, *Āryadeva's Catuḥśataka*, and P. L. Vaidya, *Études sur Āryadeva et son Catuḥśataka*.

28. In arguing in this way for the dating of the CMP, I am following the method I advocated in my doctoral dissertation. Therein, I suggested that a more fruitful approach to dating the esoteric literature would be to construct a relative chronology of works, based on their frequent citations one of another, which could then be connected to an absolute chronology via the dating of one or more known figures. This, I suggest, is a more sound method than the previous one of relying for the relative chronology on traditional lineage lists (*saṃpradāya*).

29. Sūtras and tantras are revealed scriptures whose authorship is attributed to transcendent authors, such as buddhas; śāstras are commentarial or systematic treatises whose authorship is attributed to named, human individuals.

30. Christian Lindtner, *A Garland of Light*, 7.

to that of the *Catuḥśataka*. However, it is not at all certain how much later the citation of the ĀM allows us to place the CMP. If we follow Lindtner, it would be no later than this same period, that is, the late fifth/early sixth centuries (ca. 450–525).

However, Lindtner's placing the date of the ĀM so early is based in part on the ascription of the *Madhyamakaratnapradīpa* to Bhavya/ Bhāvaviveka (ca. 490–570), which ascription (I think it is fair to say) is highly controversial.[31] Lindtner bases further argument for this early date upon the existence of a commentary on the ĀM by *Asvabhāva, of whom a commentary on the *Mahāyānasaṃgraha* was translated into Chinese in 648–49. While this may turn out to be sound reasoning, I feel it is premature to rely too heavily on this argument, as so little is known of this author and his range of authentic works. Thus, the evidence of the ĀM citation allows us to rather confidently place the CMP posterior to the fifth century, though further work on the date of Kambala may require us to push this date back somewhat.

The citation of GS suggests that we ought to situate the authorship of the CMP rather later in the second half of the first millennium. Wayman (on rather dubious premises) puts its author, Padmavajra, in the latter half of the eighth century,[32] while Ronald Davidson (more reliably) locates him in the second quarter of the ninth century.[33] Given the relative security of these dates (which views are also supported by Yukei Matsunaga),[34] it seems

31. See, for instance, the reasons to the contrary adduced by Yasunori Ejima cited in Christian Lindtner, "Adversaria Buddhica," 182–84. van der Kuijp ("Earliest Indian Reference," 187) comments that Lindtner's article "contains much about Bhāvaviveka/ Bhavya and his/ their oeuvre with which one cannot but disagree."

32. Alex Wayman, *Yoga of the Guhyasamājatantra*, 96.

33. Ronald M. Davidson, personal email communication 28 April 2005: "Padmavajra looks to me to be active in the second quarter of the ninth century, particularly based on the vocabulary that he uses in that text and his other works. He certainly is later than Buddhaguhya, whose *Tantrārthāvatāra* he comments on, and he is earlier than the *Hevajra-tantra*, which I believe to be a late ninth or early tenth century work. Padmavajra also uses vocabulary slightly more advanced than Buddhajñānapāda, but only slightly more so, and I would put Buddhajñānapāda in the early ninth century, since he studied with Haribhadra and Vilāsavajra, both of whom wrote at the very end of the eighth or early ninth centuries. These figures are actually part of our solid points of reference in the history of the tradition."

34. See Yukei Matsunaga, ed., *The Guhyasamāja Tantra*, xxv–xxvi.

we must move the CMP yet further back into at least the mid-to-late ninth century.

Having thus established on the basis of the works it cites a tentative *terminus post quem* for the CMP, we may now turn to evidence that allows us to determine with rather more certainty a *terminus ante quem* —that is, the evidence provided by sources that themselves cite the CMP. The CMP is cited in several extant works both in Sanskrit and Tibetan. It is, for example, cited in the anonymous *Subhāṣitasaṃgraha* (SS)[35] and the *Pañcakramaṭippaṇī Yogimanoharā* (PKṬYM) of Muniśrībhadra.[36] These two works, however, are of little help in the task at hand—the former because it is of rather uncertain date (and I suspect later than the earliest Tibetan references), the latter because it, too, likely postdates the earliest Tibetan reference to our text.[37] Much the same is true of the *Caryāgītikośavṛtti* (CGKV) of Munidatta, which was likely composed in the thirteenth century.[38]

We are on firmer ground, however, when we consider the citation of the CMP at the end of the *Sekoddeśaṭīkā* (SUṬ) of Naḍapāda (Nāropā).[39] Adopting the date 1040 for the death of Naḍapāda,[40] we may presume that the SUṬ was written in the early eleventh century. The *terminus ante quem* this establishes (early eleventh century) is supported by the earliest Tibetan reference to the CMP. As noted above, the *Survey of the Esoteric Community* (*gSang 'dus stong thun*) of Gö Kugpa Lhaytsay frequently cites the CMP.[41] While the date of Gö is somewhat vague, it seems certain that he flourished in the mid-eleventh century. He does not cite Āryadeva as one of his many

35. Cecil Bendall, ed., *Subhāṣita-saṃgraha.*

36. Zhongxin Jiang and Tōru Tomabechi, eds., *The Pañcakramaṭippaṇī of Muniśrībhadra.*

37. This latter is by no means as clear as it could be. In the introduction to their work (*Pañcakramaṭippaṇī*, xiv–xv) Jiang and Tomabechi propose Muniśrībhadra's date to be ca. 1200; however, this is based on rather little evidence and rather a lot of speculation. Without evidence to the contrary, the PKṬYM has little to offer us at present.

38. See Per Kværne, *An Anthology of Buddhist Tantric Songs*, 2.

39. Mario E. Carelli, *Sekoddeśaṭīkā of Naḍapāda (Nāropā)*, see esp. pp. 70–71.

40. See Turrell Wylie, "Dating the Death of Nāropa," 691.

41. 'Gos Khug-pa Lhas-btsas, *Gsaṅ 'dus stoṅ thun*. I am currently preparing an article for publication that treats of this author and his works, entitled "Sex and Death in Eleventh-century Tibetan gSar-ma Esoterism: 'Gos Khug-pa Lhas-btsas, *spyod pa* (*caryā*), and *mngon par spyod pa* (*abhicāra*)."

Indian gurus, so we may presume that there was at least one generation of teachers, and probably two, between Gö and Āryadeva.

Thus, the evidence here cited suggests that the CMP (and, by extension, its author) is the product of the period between ca. 850 CE and 1000 CE. This is, no doubt, rather a large window, capacious enough to encompass the lives of three or more persons. By Indological standards, however, it is relatively precise; and, for now, it will have to do.[42] It is certainly enough, at the least, for our present purposes, in that it provides relatively reliable grounds on which to maintain that the Noble author of the CMP is not the same person as the Centrist author of the *Catuḥśataka*.

Traditional History: Treasures and Visions

What, then, is one to make of the traditional attribution? Is it in fact the case that the Tibetan tradition has "hopelessly mixed up" two or more historical figures? Or were they, on the contrary, either the victims or the later propagators of a literary fraud: a nefarious scriptural "bait-and-switch?" I do not believe either hypothesis fits the case. A closer look at the materials available reveals a much more complex picture of the "traditional view" on the authorship of the Noble Tradition literature than has hitherto been recognized by modern scholarship. For while it is certainly the case that Tibetan tradition accepts that (in some sense at least) the author of the *Catuḥśataka* and the *Caryāmelāpakapradīpa* are the "same person," it is by no means entirely clear what precisely is meant by this claim. I contend that this assertion should be taken not as a strictly historical claim about concrete figures (though some may have come to this conclusion), but as an "auctorative" assertion about the validity and prestige of the literature concerned.[43]

The first of the modern contentions—that Tibetan tradition has merely "confused" two distinct authors—is untenable at best, condescending at worst. There is, on the one hand, abundant evidence of a critical stance with

42. If we credit Tāranātha's claim (on which more below, p. 21) that these works were spread during the reign of King Devapāla and son, this would suggest a narrower range of ca. 875–925.

43. I regret the neologism, but there does not seem to be an English term with precisely this meaning, to wit "conferring or establishing authorial identity or prestige" (qv. auctorizate, auctorial).

regard to authorial attribution among Tibetan religious thinkers. Traditional scholars frequently demonstrate an awareness of the phenomenon of multiple authors bearing the same name, not to mention the inverse phenomenon of a unitary author writing under several names.[44] Furthermore, it is quite evident that the Tibetans were not the initiators, but the inheritors of a well-established Indian tradition to the effect that the Noble and the Centrist authors were identical. Though it may be argued that we have little or no direct textual evidence that the esoteric authors "Nāgārjuna," "Āryadeva," and "Candrakīrti" themselves claimed identity with the exoteric authors,[45] I think there is a good *prima facie* case to be made that such is implicit in their writings. These names are not common, so the hypothesis that the correspondence is a mere coincidence is rather a weak one from the start. Their conjunction in a *group* of authors who form an inter-referential school of thought, however, is so remarkable as to speak overwhelmingly for the position that these texts were deliberately claiming derivation from authors of renown. There are, in addition, several ways in which an affiliation with Centrist doctrines is implicit in the Noble literature: most notably in their technical nomenclature.[46] Thus, I think it is safe to say that the notion of the identity of the Nobles and the Centrists is an Indian one, presumably intrinsic to the composition of the Noble works themselves, and transmitted as such by Indian teachers of the tradition in Tibet. It was by no means the result of carelessness or confusion on the part of the Tibetans.

The other hypothesis typical of modern scholarship to date—that the Tibetans were the dupes of a literary fraud perpetrated by their Indian masters—is less easy to dismiss but, as I will argue below, nonetheless equally

44. Nearly all Tibetan scholia on esoteric literature begin with a critical survey of the authoritative corpus; these frequently involve notices of such phenomena as these. To give a few examples, see the writings of Bu-ston, Tsongkhapa, mKhas-grub-rje, Amyes-zhabs, etc.

45. Tib (DCo) does have Āryadeva describing Nāgārjuna as "my teacher" (*bdag gi slob dpon*), but this is not found in the original Sanskrit, nor in Tib (NP). Likewise, in the PU, Candrakīrti merely notes that he "obtained [the instructions] from Nāgārjuna" (*śrīnāgārjunāptaṃ*). This does not necessarily entail personal transmission and, indeed, his later reference to Nāgārjuna as the first in a series of teachers (*śrī-nāgārjuna-bhaṭṭāraka-pādād ārabhya nidhanam iva guru-parva-krameṇa guru-vaktrāt samājikānām asmin janmani buddhatva-bhājanānāṃ santāne saṃkrāmati*) suggests that (as one would expect) he was not a direct disciple of Nāgārjuna. See PU, 1 and 229.

46. This is suggested, for instance, by the central role the notion of "two truths" (*satya-dvaya*) plays in the doctrinal formulations of both systems. See below, pp. 38–40.

problematic. There is no end of evidence to the effect that Tibetans were highly critical of putative Indic authorities and were not wont to accept the attribution of works uncritically[47]—there being an extensive literature dealing with issues of "literary fraud" and the issue of how to determine genuine religious authority. Thus, even if one insists on describing the attribution of the Noble Tradition works as a "fraud," the Tibetans—if credulous—were by no means the simpleminded dupes they are implied to be, but went into it with their eyes open. However, there are further, fatal difficulties with this hypothesis, such that the Tibetan votaries of this tradition are perhaps better described as conscious participants in a widespread (and arguably salutary) Buddhist tendency to ratify religious innovation through a distinctive kind of "soft history."

Tibetan historical literature—presumably the source for modern scholars' construction of the "traditional Tibetan view"—reveals rather a different understanding of the historical issues surrounding the Noble Literature than has hitherto been recognized. I believe this evidence compels us to construct an alternative understanding of the indigenous historiography. First and foremost, there should be no doubt that traditional historians were well aware of the historiographical difficulties they confronted—not only with regard to the attribution of the literature of the Noble Tradition, but also to the attribution of its source scriptures to the "historical" Buddha (a similar example wherein modern scholars have uncritically maintained that the tradition is guilty of a simpleminded literary fraud). On the contrary, the traditional sources can be read as reflecting a clear, if

47. The problem of apocryphal scriptures and commentaries was well known in Indian and Tibetan intellectual circles. There is considerable discussion in later works of the validity of authorial attributions—not infrequently resulting in the rejection of certain works as fraudulent. For instance (to take one example pretty much at random), mKhas-grub dGe-legs dPal-bzang in his major work on the creation stage of the Guhyasamāja, the *Guhyasamāja Creation Stage Ocean of Accomplishment*, is quite forthright in asserting that:

> Since the commentary on the Root Tantra and the maṇḍala rite ascribed to the Noble [Nāgārjuna], the *Rosary of Jewels*, *Clear Import*, and *Summarized Stages* ascribed to Nāgabodhi, the *Ornament of Realizations* root and autocommentary ascribed to Candra[kīrti], and so on, are nothing but mis-ascribed counterfeits, one should not rely on them. (*gSang 'dus bskyed rim dngos grub rgya mtsho*, f. 18a$^{4-5}$).

Though the criteria they employ diverge in important ways from modern critical practice, this and many similar critical observations throughout the scholastic literature bear witness to the existence of a vigorous critical practice in the Tibetan tradition.

largely implicit, awareness of this problem. That, on the whole, they do not explicitly so address it reflects the fact that, to them, the problem was not a *problem*. I mean this not in the sense that they did not recognize that the attributions posed significant historical difficulties (which they did), but in the sense that for the tradition this "problem" was in fact the *solution* to a prior—and presumably more pressing—difficulty: that of the legitimacy of ongoing scriptural revelation.

For while it *is* uniformly accepted that the exoteric and esoteric authors are in some important sense "identical," traditional sources nonetheless reflect the "cognitive dissonance" that such a claim creates with respect to historical plausibility. This is perhaps most clearly seen in an analysis of the nature of this authorial "identity" by the early seventeenth-century Tibetan historian Jo-nang Tāranātha (1575–1634) who expresses this dissonance in an unusually explicit manner. His treatment of this issue represents a thoughtful and creative attempt to harmonize a critical approach to historical fact with the theologically exigent concern for the auctorization of the traditional sources of his lineage. While it may legitimately be objected that Tāranātha's confrontation of this issue demonstrates nothing more than his own distinctively critical stance, other parallel historical narratives concerning the revelation of several earlier Buddhist traditions (both exo- and esoteric) suggest that Tāranātha's view might plausibly be considered not the novel hypothesis of a creative, critical mind (which his undoubtedly was), but simply the straightforward expression of what I argue is the *de facto* (if implicit) position of most traditional authorities on the historical question.

In his *Great Commentary on the Five Stages* (*Rim lnga 'grel chen*, hereafter RṄGC), Tāranātha stresses the point that the esoteric works of the Noble Tradition are "uncontestably the work of the Father [Nāgārjuna] and Sons."[48] However, this assertion—noteworthy in its direct advocacy of a view most authors treat as part of the axiomatic background of the tradition—comes at the end of a discussion in which he confronts directly the historical problem of attributing the Noble literature to the early period of the Centrist authors. In fact, he no less stringently maintains that these works were *not* in fact propagated during the lifetime of the Centrist Nāgārjuna. He writes:

48. Tāranātha, RṄGC, f. 5a$^{2-3}$.

> These teachings of the Esoteric Community Noble literature were not openly [and] widely spread to common and uncommon students during the time when the Noble Father [Nāgārjuna] and Sons were actually residing in this world. At that time, as appropriate, they greatly clarified the tradition of the [exoteric] scriptures and clarified the [esoteric] secret mantra practices [of] the Ritual and Practice Tantras. Hence, [the Esoteric Community Noble literature] was not spread at that time as were Nāgārjuna's collections of advice, reasoning, and praises. Likewise, the *Illumination of the Lamp* [Commentary on the *Esoteric Community* (PU)] was not composed and spread while Candrakīrti was actually active in the human realm.[49]

On one level, Tāranātha here unambiguously asserts precisely the position maintained by modern scholarship: that the Esoteric Community Noble Tradition literature was not the product of the early first millennium, nor even of so late a period as that of the seventh-century Centrist Candrakīrti. And, it may be worth noting, Tāranātha makes this point some two hundred and fifty years prior to the moment when European scholarship would arrogate to itself the responsibility to propagate these same views in ostensibly overturning the native ignorance that allegedly held the opposite. However, for all their agreement about the chronological question, there remains a significant divergence between Tāranātha's position and that of most modern scholars: that is, he maintains that these works are nonetheless properly attributable to those authors. How is this possible? How could a thinker of his caliber maintain two such seemingly contradictory propositions?

He does so by recourse to the notion that the active agency of these authors is not restricted to conventional, historical time and place—a presumption, I think it is fair to say, that would have been shared by most of his Mahāyāna co-religionists. He goes on to assert that their works were

49. RṄGC, f. 4b$^{4-6}$: *gsang 'dus 'phags skor gyi chos 'di rnams | 'phags pa yab sras 'dzam bu gling du dngos su bzhugs pa'i dus su thun mongs dang thun mongs ma yin pa'i slob ma rnams la mngon mtshan du rgya cher dar ba ni ma yin te | de'i tshe ni mdo lugs nyid shin tu gsal bar mdzad pa dang | gsang sngags spyod pa yang bya ba dang spyod pa'i rgyud nyid ci rigs par gsal bar mdzad do | | des na | klu sgrub kyi gtam tshogs dang rigs tshogs dang bstod tshogs bzhin du | de'i skabs dar bar gyur pa ma yin no | | de bzhin du sgron gsal yang | zla grags dngos su mi yul du spyod pa'i tshe mdzad cing dar ba ma yin te |.*

propagated in a later period by one Nāgabodhi, alleged to be an actual disciple of Nāgārjuna who had attained a "rainbow body" (*'ja' lus*, i.e., a kind of immortality), who preserved the teachings in some form until the late first millennium.[50] Tāranātha is less definitive when it comes to the question of the form in which these works were so preserved, and he advances two hypotheses for his learned readers to consider:

> The Father [Nāgārjuna] and Sons may have composed these treatises in an earlier time and commanded [Nāgabodhi] to propagate [them] when [the proper] disciples of these teachings would emerge in the future; or it is also possible that, when the disciples' time had come, [they] composed those treatises in the body of a *vidyādhara* and taught them to fortunate ones.[51]

That is, Tāranātha does not come down firmly here on the question of whether or not the works as we have them were even composed during the early first millennium. He is willing to entertain the notion that they were, and were then subsequently preserved and propagated by Nāgabodhi; or, alternatively, that they were not, and that Nāgārjuna et al. themselves composed these works at a later point while embodied in a kind of mystical, immortal *vidyādhara*-form (*rig pa 'dzin pa'i lus*). Given his commitment to the authenticity of the tradition, however, Tāranātha does come down firmly on one point, concluding (as we have already observed) that "however that may be, [they are] uncontestably the work of the Father and Sons."[52]

In his rather more famous *History of Buddhism in India* (*rGya gar chos 'byung*, a work widely consulted and regularly cited by modern scholars since the nineteenth century), Tāranātha makes similar claims—claims

50. RṄGC, ff. $4b^{6}$–$5a^{1}$: *chos 'di dag ni | klu sgrub kyi dngos slob slob dpon klu'i byang chub kyis 'ja' lus rdo rje'i sku brnyes nas 'gro ba'i don du dpal gyi ri bor bzhugs shing | de las rgyud de phyis sngags kyi theg pa mngon mtshan du spyod cing dar ba'i tshe | chos skor 'di rnams kyang mi yul du dar bar gyur to |.*

51. RṄGC, f. $5a^{1-2}$: *des na yab sras de rnams kyis sngon gyi dus nyid du | bstan bcos 'di dag mdzad nas ma 'ongs pa na chos 'di'i gdul bya dag byung ba na spel shig par gdams te bzhag pa'am | yang gdul bya dus la bab pa nyid na | rig pa 'dzin pa'i lus nyid kyis bstan bcos de dag mdzad de | skal ldan rnams la bstan pa yang yin srid de |.*

52. RṄGC, f. $5a^{2-3}$: *gang ltar yang yab sras de rnams kyi mdzad par rtsod pa med la |.*

strangely overlooked by modern scholarship.[53] While discussing the esoteric saint Mātaṅgīpā, who is traditionally held to be a disciple of Nāgārjuna and Āryadeva and an important link in the transmission of the Noble Tradition, he states quite unambiguously that "though it is said that Mātaṅgī was a disciple of *ācārya* Nāgārjuna and his disciple [Āryadeva], he could not have lived at that time."[54] Yet he does not reject the traditional ascription of authority implicit in this history. How is it possible that Mātaṅgīpā could nonetheless be considered the disciple of these saints? Simply stated, "he could have had their vision later (*phyis zhal mthong ba'o*)," that is, he qualifies due to having received their teachings in a miraculous vision.

In his *History*, then, as in his *Great Commentary*, Tāranātha makes much the same assertion concerning the provenance of the Noble Tradition's literature—they are theologically authentic, though historically anachronistic works. Elsewhere in his *History*, he further adds a rather provocative analogy in which he compares this phenomenon with two others presumably more familiar to his readers, drawn from specifically Tibetan religious experience of which the above cases of Nāgārjuna and Mātaṅgīpā may serve as illustrative examples. What Tāranātha suggests is that the writings of the Nobles were either sequestered revelations along the lines of the Treasure Teachings (*gter ma*) famous in the rNying-ma School of Tibetan Buddhism,[55] or they

53. Indeed, given the heavy reliance on this source by modern scholars, it is truly astounding that these passages have not been commented on by *any* of those who have explored this issue. One must, I think, conclude from this that there has been far too much reliance on the available, not-particularly-reliable translations that do not capture the true significance of these passages. (One may profitably compare these translations with those I provide in what follows; see notes 57 and 59, below.) The result of this failure to consult original sources has been a rather marked misconstrual of the nature and contents of the Tibetan historiographical tradition.

54. Tāranātha, *rGya gar chos 'byung*, f. $43a^{6}$–$43b^{1}$: grub thob ma tang gi yang klu sgrub yab sras kyi slob mar grags pa ni dus 'di skabs byung ba ni min |.

55. Though by no means exclusive to that school—there have been numerous treasure revealers (*gter ston*) who belonged to other lineages, such as the dGe-lugs. According to what became the dominant understanding, these traditions are believed to derive from the teachings of the eighth-century saint Padmasambhava, intended for revelation at a suitable time in the future (recall Tāranātha's earlier comment about the Noble Tradition works being reserved until suitable disciples were to be found), and concealed in the meantime by various strategems (some quite ordinarily hidden in caves, others implanted in the minds of saints, or communicated through angels) until the time was ripe for them to have the maximum salvific effect. On Treasures in general, see Janet Gyatso, "Drawn from the Tibetan Treasury." For a provocative piece on the diversity of early Treasure traditions, before the

were revealed as mystical visions. Speaking of such literary monuments of the Noble Tradition as the *Pañcakrama* (PK) and *Caryāmelāpakapradīpa* (CMP), he writes,

> Those treatises did not become widely known like works such as the [Six] Logical Treatises of the Middle Way.[56] Since they were entrusted solely to Nāgabodhi, who attained the [immortal] state of *vidyādhara*-hood, they were spread later in the time of King Devapāla 'father and son.' That is the reason that the lineage of the Noble literature and the Buddhakapāla literature is short. For example, it is like the Tibetan Vision Teachings (*bod gyi yang dag snang gi chos*) and those Treasure Teachings that are not counterfeit (*gter chos rdzun gso ba med pa*).[57]

---

imposition of the hegemonic, Padmasambhava-centric model, see Ronald M. Davidson, "Imperial Agency in the gSar ma Treasure Texts."

56. *Rigs tshogs drug*: a standard Tibetan list of Nāgārjuna's major exoteric works comprising the *Mūlamadhyamakakārikā, Vigrahavyāvartanī, Yuktiṣaṣṭikā, Śūnyatāsaptati, Ratnāvalī*, and *Vaidalyaprakaraṇa*. See Christian Lindtner, *Nagarjuniana* for a detailed discussion of the authenticity of the various writings attributed to this author.

57. Tāranātha, *Chos 'byung*, f. 52a³⁻⁵: *bstan bcos de dag kyang dbu ma rigs tshogs drug la sogs pa'i gzhung bzhin du yongs khyab tu grags pa ni ma yin te | klu'i byang chub rig pa 'dzin pa'i gnas brnyed pa de kho na la gtad pas | phyis rgyal po de wa pā la yab sras kyi dus su dar bar gyur pa yin te | de'i phyir 'phags skor dang sangs rgyas thod pa'i skor sogs la brgyud thag nye mor 'byung ba'i rgyu mtshan yang de yin no | | dper na bod kyi yang dag snang gi chos dang | gter chos rdzun gso ba med pa rnams dang 'dra'o |*.

The previous translations do not adequately communicate the meaning of this passage. Here, and in note 59, I provide the full text of these versions, as an object lesson in the necessity of consulting original sources. The Schiefner translation (available to scholars from 1869) reads:

> Diese Çâstra's die Madhjamikavidjâgaṇa's u. s. w. waren ihrem Text nach nicht allgemein bekannt, sondern wurden erst dem Nâgabodhi, als er die Stufe eines Vidjâdhara erreichte, übergeben und verbreiteten sich in der Folge zur Zeit der Königs Devapâla und seines Sohnes. Das ist auch die Ursache davon, dass in der nächsten Zeit die ehrwürdige Abtheilung, die Buddhakapâla-Abtheilung und die übringen entstanden, ähnlich wie in Tibet das gänzlich helle Gesetz und das ungefälschte Gesetz des Schatzes. (Schiefner, *Geschichte*, 105–6).

The Chimpa/Chattopadhyaya translation runs:

> Besides, even these treatises are not as well-known as the collection of the Mādhyamika *śāstra*-s. These were entrusted only to Nāgabodhi, who attained the vidyādhara-sthāna and these were made extensively available later on during the period of king Devapāla and his son. Hence the absence of any remote succession accounts for the purity of the *Ārya* and *Buddhakapāla* [*Tantras*], as in Tibet there

It is hard to overestimate how remarkable this passage is. Again, Tāranātha clearly denies that the works of the Nobles can be properly ascribed to the early first millennium era of the "real" Nāgārjuna, *et al.* Instead, he here explicitly states his view that they were propagated during the reign of the Pāla Dynasty's King Devapāla (ca. 810–850) and his son.[58] His analogy to the Treasures or Visions is meant to communicate that these are books that, while allegedly composed (or, at least inspired) in an earlier period by a distinguished buddhalogian-saint, were not actually transmitted until a later period. While it could be argued that this is a distinctively Tibetan understanding applied *ex post facto* to the Noble Tradition, I would suggest that his invocation here of the concept of Treasure is only meant to be clarificatory—that he is not thereby doing anything new historiographically, but merely providing an example of an analogous, more highly and explicitly theorized phenomenon for the benefit of his Tibetan readers. This case will be made in more detail below. For now, let us return for a moment to one remaining, important passage from Tāranātha's *History*.

Subsequent to his previous declaration, in the chapter specifically devoted to the era of King Devapāla, Tāranātha finishes the story, describing the manner in which these "Treasures" were revealed.

> At this time, the son of a Mātaṅga [outcaste] met Āryadeva and, through his blessing, came to a thorough knowledge of the Dharma. Meditating, he achieved accomplishment (*siddhi*). He obtained the esoteric works of Ārya Nāgārjuna, father and son. He appropriately explained them. [He was] Mātaṅgīpā.
>
> In addition, in Koṅkana, Ācārya *Rakṣitapāda actually studied under Candrakīrti; the text of the *Illumination of the Lamp* appeared also. Likewise, Paṇḍita Rāhula [śrībhadra] is said to have met Nāgabodhi. The Noble Tradition teaching began to spread a bit. Later, at the time of the four latter-day Pālas, it spread extensively.[59]

---

is no corruption of the works in circulation [because these are copies from] sealed texts. (*History*, 152–53)

58. Which, as we have seen, is on the earlier end of, but consonant with, our postulated range of 850–1000 CE.

59. Tāranātha, *Chos 'byung*, f. 101b^{4}–101b^{6}: | *'di'i dus gdol pa'i bu zhig ā rya de wa dang*

Here we find three separate mystical revelations as the sources of the Noble Tradition teachings. Āryadeva appeared in a vision to Mātaṅgīpā—presumably transmitting the text of the CMP, if nothing else; Candrakīrti appeared to one *Rakṣitapāda,[60] transmitting the PU; and Rāhulaśrībhadra

---

mjal byin gyis brlabs pas chos tol shes su byung | bsgoms pas grub pa thob ste | 'phags pa klu sgrub yab sras kyi sngags gzhung mtha' dag rnyed | ci rigs par bshad de ma tang gi pa'o | | yang kong ka na ru slob dpon srung ba'i zhabs zhes bya ba des zla grags la dngos su mnyan nas | sgron gsal gyi glegs bam yang byung | de bzhin du paṇḍi ta sgra gcan 'dzin zer bas kyang klu byang dang mjal zer te | chos 'phags skor mgo dar ba tsam byung | phyis pā la phyi ma bzhi'i dus su lhag par dar ro | | mkha' la nyi zla rnam gnyis dang | sa la gsal ba rnam gnyis zer ba byung skad |.

Again, neither available translation has captured the reference to the Noble Tradition. Schiefner reads:

> Zu dieser Zeit wurde der Sohn eines Tschaṇḍâla, der mit Ârjadeva zusammengetroffen und von ihm gesegnet war, ein Kenner des Kerns der Lehre, nachdem er sich der Beschauung hingegeben und die Siddhi erlangt hatte, fand er alle Mantra-Texte des Nâgârdschuna und seines (geistlichen) Sohnes auf, nach der Behauptung mehrerer ist er Mâtanga. Nachdem ferner der Âtschârja Rakschitapâda von Koṅkana Tschandrakîrti in Wirklichkeit gehörte hatte, kam das Werk Pradîpoddjotana zum Vorschein. Ebenso soll auch der Paṇḍita Râhula mit Nâgabodhi zusammengetroffen sein und der Anfang der ehrwürdigen Kreises der Lehre sich verbreitet haben; späte, zur Zeit der letzten vier Pâla's verbreitete er sich überaus. (215–16)

Chimpa and Chattopadhyaya (*Tāranātha's History*, 272–73) reads as follows:

> During this time, a son of a Caṇḍāla had the vision of (lit., met) Āryadeva and under his blessings received the knowledge of the Doctrine without much effort. He meditated and attained *siddhi*. He received all the Tantra-śāstras of Nāgārjuna 'the father and son.' He also expounded some of these. This one was Mātaṅgī-pā.
>
> *Ācārya* Rakṣita-pāda of Koṅkana composed the *Pradīpodyotana* under the direct instruction of Candrakīrti.
>
> Similarly, *paṇḍita* Rāhula also met Nāgabodhi. This was only the beginning of the Dharma-viśiṣta-maṇḍala. Afterwards during the four later Pālas, this was widely spread.

60. This *Rakṣitapāda (Srung ba'i zhabs) may perhaps be the paṇḍit-translator known from the bsTan-'gyur as Tathāgatarakṣita (or perhaps one of the teachers of the latter). Tathāgatarakṣita was the paṇḍit on the team that translated the *Vajrasattvasādhana* of Candrakīrti (Pek. 2679). The colophon to this work states that the translation was done at the temple of Śrī Vikramaśīla by Tathāgatarakṣita and Lo tsā ba glog [read: klog] kya gzhon nu 'bar (Peking bsTan-'gyur, rGyud-'grel, vol. gi, ff. $177b^7$–$178a^2$). The former, as a contemporary of Rin-chen bZang-po, is dated by Tucci between 950 and 1075 (*Rin-chen-bzaṅ-po*, 49). If this is so, and we credit the tradition reported by Tāranātha, this would allow us tentatively to date the revelation of the *Pradīpoddyotana* to the late tenth or early eleventh centuries. On the other hand, the *Blue Annals* reports a tradition whereby a *Rakṣitapāda (bSrung

is said to have also received an unspecified revelation—perhaps of the PK, since this saint appears in the lineage lists as a recipient of Nāgārjuna's teaching. The import, however, is the same: the historical origin of the Noble literature is located by a "traditional" author in the late ninth century.

At least according to the testimony of Tāranātha, then, the Tibetan tradition was well aware of the historical problems posed by the attribution of the Noble Tradition literature to the authors of the Centrist School. Nonetheless, one may legitimately entertain the possibility that Tāranātha was unique in this regard, and that, far from reflecting the mainstream of traditional understanding, his account merely represents his own (or, perhaps, one of his teachers') attempt to assuage a personal sense of unease with the putative "traditional history." It is, after all, (as far as I am aware) the only explicit appearance in the early literature of this notion regarding the origin of the Noble Tradition corpus.[61] We have no evidence of a Treasure tradition *per se* in India; so, one must wonder if Tāranātha is merely anachronistically (and anatopistically) imputing second-millennium Tibetan practices to first-millennium India. As Tāranātha drew from Indian sources whose dates of composition and authors are not known to us, as well as drawing on oral information from his Indian teachers, one may plausibly entertain the hypothesis that this story emerged sometime between the eleventh and seventeenth centuries.

On the other hand, Tāranātha's formulation might also (indeed, might better) be understood as a seventeenth-century Tibetan articulation of a widespread pattern of historical understanding evident in a broad range of Indian (and Tibetan) Buddhist contexts since the early first millennium. His presentation encapsulates a set of distinctive motifs that are pandemic in the historiography of Buddhist scriptural production. The theoretical models underpinning his discussion are neither restricted to esoteric nor to Tibetan historiography, but have functioned throughout the Buddhist world as devices for those traditions discursively to digest the conspicu-

ba'i zhabs) was a student, not of Candrakīrti, but of Nāgārjuna, and an elder contemporary of Buddhajñānapāda (*Blue Annals*, vol. I, 368). Thanks to Paul Hackett for this latter reference.

61. Though it does not (to my knowledge) appear in earlier sources, by the time of the most recent bDud-'joms Rinpoche 'Jigs-bral Ye-shes rDo-rje (1904–1987), Tāranātha's presentation seems to be taken for granted. The last passage we treated (about Mātaṅgīpā's vision) appears verbatim in Dudjom Rinpoche's *The Nying-ma School of Tibetan Buddhism* (see Dorje and Kapstein, trans., 464). See also pp. 502 and 596 for concurring claims.

ous fact of near constant scriptural revelation over the course of (at least) a millennium, while simultaneously validating these revelations by referring their origins to beings of unimpeachable authority: generally buddhas, bodhisattvas, or major saints.

To begin with an example near to our own, one may consider the traditional narrative concerning the initial preaching of the *Esoteric Community Tantra* (GST). Here, too, scholars have decried the fraud and/or confusion they see as implicit in the traditional depiction of these teachings as having been taught by Buddha Śākyamuni. A more careful reading, however, again reveals a more complex picture. For in this narrative, although care is taken to emphasize that the initial preaching of the Tantra may be attributed to Śākyamuni (thus validating the revelation as being equally as authoritative as other examples of the Buddha's gospel [*buddha-vacana*]), the narrative also contains (though it does not elaborate upon) a similar tale of revelation "lost and regained" as found in Tāranātha's account of the Noble Tradition. In this influential story, the Esoteric Community is said to have been taught on behalf of a King Indrabhūti, who wanted to follow the Buddha's path but could not bring himself to "go forth from home into homelessness" as had the Buddha and his community of monks. The following account appears in the seventeenth-century *History of the Esoteric Community* (*gSang 'dus chos 'byung*) written by the Sakya lay scholar Jamgön Amey Zhab:

> Previously, when the Lord [Buddha Śākyamuni] was present [in this world], in the western land of Udyāna, a king called Indrabhūti saw a community of renunciants (*śrāvaka*) who, using their religious robes as wings, flew in the morning from east to west, and in the evening flew in the sky from west to east. Inquiring of his domestic minister, and so forth—who could not explain [it]—he asked the people of the city what it was. The citizens said, "to the east of here in the city called Śrāvastī, King Śuddhodana's son, Sarvārthasiddha, called the Buddha Śākyamuni, is residing turning the wheel of Dharma for his disciples. They are his renunciants."
>
> Upon [hearing] their reply, the religious instincts of the King were awakened. Immediately upon hearing the name "Buddha," the hair on his body stood on end and an unexcelled faith in the Teacher was born. On account of that, he had a direct vision of

the Teacher and retinue staying in Śrāvastī. Having asked them, "please won't you come and visit me tomorrow," the next morning the Lord and his retinue miraculously appeared. Having pleased them through worship and service, he requested, "please establish us on the stage of omniscience."

The Lord said, "Go forth from home into homelessness and practice the three educations."

The King replied, "since we cannot abandon the objects of desire, please teach a method of enlightenment involving the enjoyment of the objects of desire."

The Teacher . . . emanated the maṇḍala of the Esoteric Community and gave initiation to those with the good fortune to hear, such as the Great King Indrabhūti, and so forth. The King attained great success (*mahāsiddhi*) at the very time of initiation. . . .

Then the Teacher proclaimed the Root and Explanatory Tantras of the Esoteric Community to the King. He entrusted them to Vajrapāṇi. There, the King wrote the tantras on gold paper with melted sapphire [ink], and he also made a building to house them. Then, everyone living in that land ruled by the King, even down to the crows who ate their scraps of food, attained success.

Gradually, as that land became empty, it became a great lake. Many snake-spirits (*nāgas*) lived in that lake, and gradually a town was built on its shores. Then, Vajrapāṇi, having again given initiation to the snake-spirits who lived in the lake, explained the Tantra, and taught the path. Many snake-spirits became heroes and *yoginīs*. Then, when the lake dried up [and] the house that the king had earlier built for the texts emerged without having been damaged by the water, it was given the name "chapel of the self-emergent Heruka." It is said that even today that very [chapel] stands in the sky and one or two fortunate ones see it.[62]

62. A-myes-zhabs, *gSang 'dus chos 'byung*, ff. 7a^4–8a^4: *sngon bcom ldan 'das bzhugs pa'i dus su*

As this passage demonstrates, the narrative of Śākyamuni's preaching of the GST preserved by Tibetan tradition contains embedded within itself the notion that, although it was originally taught by the Buddha (and thus derives its spiritual authority from a valid source), all trace of this original teaching was subsequently obliterated from the face of the Earth and, therefore, the immediate source of the spread of these teachings was a text or texts recovered from a miraculously-appearing shrine. In fact, the narrative suggests that a significant lapse of time must have occurred after the time of the Buddha (enough to allow for a large lake to form, another town to develop on its shores, and the lake to dry up again) before the chapel, its contents, and spiritual message were (re)revealed in the world. This account is also related in no less than three separate works of Butön (1290–1364).[63] Substantially the same narrative may be found (for which the same analysis

---

nub phyogs o rgyan gyi yul na rgyal po indra bhū ti zhes bya bas | nyan thos kyi dge 'dun rnams chos gos kyis gshog pa byas snga dro shar na nub phyogs la 'phur 'gro | dgongs mo nub phyogs nas shar la nam mkhar 'phur nas 'gro ba gzigs nas | nang blon sogs kha dris pas | ma shes par | grong khyer gyi mi rnams la ci yin dris pas | grong khyer ba dag na re | 'di nas shar phyogs na grong khyer mnyan yod ces bya bar rgyal po zas gtsang ma'i sras don thams cad grub pa | sangs rgyas pa'i mtshan shākya thub pa zhes bya ba gdul bya rnams la chos kyi 'khor lo bskor bzhin par bzhugs pa de'i nyan thos yin zhus pas | rgyal po chos kyi bag chags sad de sangs rgyas zhes pa'i mtshan thos ma thag lus kyi ba spu gyo zhing ston pa la dad pa bla na med pa 'khrungs | de'i rkyen gyis ston pa 'khor bcas mnyan yod na bzhugs pa mngon sum du mthong ste | sang gi nyin bdag gi 'dir gdugs tshod la gshegs su gsol zhes zhus pas | nang par bcom ldan 'das 'khor bcas rdzu 'phrul gyis byon pa la mchod pa dang bsnyen bkur gyis mnyes par byas nas | bdag cag kyang thams cad mkhyen pa'i go 'phang la 'god par zhu zhus pas | bcom ldan 'das kyis khyim nas khyim med par rab tu byung la bslab pa gsum la slobs shig ces bka' stsal | rgyal pos bdag cag gi 'dod yon spong mi nus pas 'dod yon la longs spyod bzhin du 'tshang rgya ba'i thabs zhu 'tshal zhes zhus pas | ston pa 'dis . . . dpal gsang ba 'dus pa'i dkyil 'khor sprul nas rgyal chen indra bhū ti la sogs te | nyan pa'i skal pa dang ldan pa rnams la 'dis dbang bskur pas | rgyal pos dbang dus nyid du grub pa chen po thob bo | |. . . | | de nas ston pas rgyal po la gsang ba 'dus pa'i rtsa ba dang bshad pa'i rgyud rnams gsungs | phyag na rdo rje la gtad | der rgyal pos rgyud rnams gser gyi shog bu la bai dū rya zhun mas bris te | de dag bzhugs pa'i khang bu yang byas so | de nas rgyal po'i 'khor yul khams de na gnas pa'i mi thams cad dang | bya rog tshun chad kyang gtor zan zos pas grub pa thob ste | rim gyis yul khams de stongs nas mtsho chen po gcig tu gyur | mtsho de la klu mang po gnas shing mtsho 'gram du rim pas grong yang chags | de nas slar yang phyag na rdo rjes mtshor gnas pa'i klu rnams la dbang bskur | rgyud bshad | lam bstan pas klu las byung ba'i dpa' bo dang rnal 'byor ma mang du byung ngo | | de nas mtsho de skam pas sngar rgyal pos bzhengs pa'i dpe khang de chus ma nyams par byung bas | he ru ka rang byung gi gandho la zhes ming du btags | de nyid deng sang yang bar snang la bzhugs shing skal ldan 'ga' res mthong ba yin par bshad do |.

63. The *rGyud sde'i zab don sgo 'byed rin chen gces pa'i sde mig*, the *dPal gsang ba 'dus pa'i rgyud 'grel gyi bshad thabs kyi yan lag gsang ba'i sgo 'byed*, and the *bDe mchog rtsa rgyud kyi 'grel pa*. On this narrative, see also Giuseppe Tucci, *Tibetan Painted Scrolls*, 212–13.

holds) in the *Blue Annals*, which interposes the emptying of the land and the mediation of a snake-spirit *yoginī* between the Buddha's immediate disciple Indrabhūti and the later Noble Tradition.[64]

It is worth stressing that, although this is the most common history related in Tibetan sources, it does not appear to be of Tibetan origin. Ronald M. Davidson has drawn attention to a very early version of this narrative found in an Indic work, a commentary on the *Prajñāpāramitā-nayaśata-pañcāśatikā*.[65] Another variant, though structurally similar, tale of the revelation of the esoteric scriptures—one that uses the Vision, rather than the Treasure model—may be found in one of the earliest Tibetan histories, Nyang Ral Nyima Özer's eleventh-century *Essence of Flower, Nectar of Honey: A History of Buddhism*.[66] This latter, in the chapter entitled "The Manner in which the Adamantine Vehicle of Secret Mantra Spread in the World," specifies that twenty-eight years had passed since the Buddha's death before the revelation of the Vajrayāna took place.[67] That is, although

64. 'Gos Lotsāwa gZhon-nu-dpal's *Blue Annals*, gives the following account:

> According to the Community-ists (*'dus pa ba*), by the power of a request by the Great King of Oḍiyaṇa, called Indrabhūti, the Lord of Sages (Buddha Śākyamuni) went there, gave initiation into this Community Tantra and taught the Tantra. The king and his retinue, by practicing diligently the practice with elaboration, became vidyādharas; and Oḍiyaṇa became emptied. A yoginī who was a snake-spirit (nāga) learned the Tantra from the king and explained it to the southern king Visukalpa.
>
> | *de la 'dus pa ba rnams zhal 'thun par 'dus pa'i rgyud 'di o ḍi ya ṇa'i rgyal po chen po indra bhūti zhes bya bas gsol ba btab pa'i mthus | thub pa'i dbang pos der byon nas dbang bskur zhing rgyud bstan te | rgyal po 'khor bcas kyis kyang spros bcas kyi spyod pas legs par bsgrubs pas rig pa 'dzin par gyur nas | o ḍi ya ṇa'i gnas stongs pa lta bur gyur | de yang klu las gyur pa'i rnal 'byor ma zhig gis rgyal po las mnyan nas | des lho phyogs kyi sa bdag bi su kalpa la bshad* | (*Deb gter sngon po*, vol. ja, f. $4b^{2-4}$).

The reference here to the "practice with elaboration" is interesting. On this practice, see below, p. 107ff.

65. See Ronald M. Davidson, *Indian Esoteric Buddhism*, 242–43.

66. Nyang-ral Nyi-ma 'Od-zer, *Chos 'byung me tog snying po sbrang rtsi'i bcud*.

67. "When twenty-eight years had passed since the nirvāṇa of the Great Sage, incited by the compassion of the Blissful Ones, the Lord of Secrets, Vajradhara himself came manifestly to Mount Malaya and . . . taught the Adamantine Vehicle" (Nyang-ral, *Chos 'byung*, 88: *thub pa chen po mya ngan las 'das nas lo nyi shu rtsa brgyad lon pa'i dus der | bde bar gshegs pa rnams kyi thugs rjes bskul nas | gsang ba'i bdag po rdo rje 'chang nyid | ri ma la yar mngon sum du byon te | . . . rdo rje theg pa gsungs so |*).

they may properly be attributed to the Buddha ("auctoritatively"), these teachings were propagated ("historically") via mystical revelation.

It is not too great a reach, I think, to postulate that these narratives were originally crafted to account for the fact of the manifestly anachronistic revelation of esoteric traditions such as the GST. Its authors and propagators were presumably aware of the difficulties in maintaining that there had been a continual, worldly transmission of the textual tradition of the GST since the time of the Buddha. Thus, the notion of the texts being hidden in an underwater chapel (or revealed in mystical glory on Mt. Malaya) allowed these revelations to have the authority of buddhic authorship, while simultaneously explaining their posterior historical derivation. That we see here precisely the same pattern presented in the historiography of the Noble Tradition—an auctorative assertion of derivation from ancient authority coupled with a narrative trope of revelation, disappearance/latency, and re-revelation—is, I argue, not a matter of coincidence or confusion,[68] but reflective of broader patterns in Buddhist historiography of scripture. Thus, the historiographical paradigm of an early revelation by an authoritative (*prāmāṇika*) source, only revealed in later historical time, occurs

68. It is worth noting that one of the more perceptive commentators on these narratives, Giuseppe Tucci, recognized the coincidence of these themes across multiple narratives, but did not take the further step of understanding that the "cognitive dissonance" they imply is integral to the cultural logic of the historiography so constructed. For him, the accounts are merely "confused." He writes:

> As the reader may have seen, these legends are complex, a mixture of different themes: the theme of a revelation *ab antiquo*, of a written version of the texts, hidden and then found again; of the nāgas who are the depositories of these texts, as in another narrative alluded to above; of the *mk'a' ạgro ma*, who in their turn become the keepers of the texts; of Indrabhūti, implicitly considered present when the first revelation of the Tantras took place, so that his word has the weight of an eyewitness's evidence. There is no doubt that these traditions are confused, independent of any chronology; they consider Indrabhūti a contemporary of the Buddha and state that he was present when the *gSaṅ ạdus* was revealed. There is only one point on which the traditions agree: namely that the *Guhyasamāja* was revealed to King Indrabhūti in Uḍḍiyāna; the meaning of this, for us, is that the *Guhyasamāja* was elaborated in the Swat valley, in or about the epoch of this personage, which seems to be, more or less, the end of the VIIth and the beginning of the VIIIth century AD. (*Tibetan Painted Scrolls*, 213)

The conclusion is typical of scholarship to date: resting content with the assessment of the "correct" historical date, without investigating how it is that such learned traditions could maintain such "confused" accounts over centuries.

throughout the extant indigenous historiography of Buddhism—both as it relates to its revealed scriptures and to problematic commentarial literature such as that of the Noble Tradition. This pattern is an ancient and pervasive Buddhist strategy for dealing with scriptural innovation.

Perhaps the earliest example of this strategy may be found among the schools that developed the Abhidharma literature. When it was first introduced, the Abhidharma corpus was by no means universally accepted by the Buddhist faithful.[69] Like the later Mahāyāna and Vajrayāna scriptures, the fact of their novelty was palpable. Thus, some accommodation was necessary in order to ensure that this inconvenient historical fact did not impugn the authority of the new scriptures. Hence, at least by the early first millennium, the mainstream Buddhist schools developed the notion that although the Abhidharma was understood (*adhigata*) by the Buddha in his enlightenment experience, and reflected on (*vicita*) during his weeks of subsequent meditation, it was not taught by him until his legendary visit to teach his mother in the Trayastriṃśas Heaven.[70] Though this tradition maintains that he also taught the texts to Śāriputra at that time (who would thus be considered responsible for propagating them), I believe that—given the documented controversy over the attribution of these works to the Buddha—the structural similarity of the narrative to our other examples suggests a similar desire to resolve the tension between contested historical origins and the desire for authoritative scriptural status. The clear implication is that Queen Mahāmāyā acted as an intermediary, like the nāgas in the

69. Thus, for instance, the Sautrāntika (or "Scripturalist") School was in part defined by their refusal to accept the Abhidharma-piṭaka as the word of the Buddha. The same is reported of the Mahāsaṃgītikas in *Dīpavaṃsa*, v. 37. See Etienne Lamotte, *History of Indian Buddhism*, 181.

70. Lamotte, *History of Indian Buddhism*, 182–83. It should be noted that the Theravāda is the only Abhidharma tradition to claim such supernatural origins (as asserted in the *Abhidhammāttakathā*). Other Abhidharmas have more terrestrial (if equally problematic) myths of origins, being attributed to human authors such as Śāriputra. However, the Pāli Abhidhamma is by no means the only work of the late first millennium BC/early first millennium CE to claim mystical transmission via Trayastriṃśas. In a recent address given at the XIVth Conference of the International Association of Buddhist Studies, Peter Skilling has noted that, for example, several Avadānas, *Majjhima Nikāya* 134, the "Āryatrayastriṃśaparivarta" (found in the "Sanghabhedavastu" of the *Mūlasarvāstivāda Vinaya*), and the *Sarvadurgatipariśodhana Tantra*—as well as several Thai "apocrypha"—either take place in or claim to have been revealed in the Trayastriṃśas Heaven. See Skilling, "Trayastriṃśas Heaven and the Production of Scriptures."

GST narrative: the teachings were given to her by an authoritative source, she acted as repository until a later historical moment, and they were then propagated in the world.[71]

In its turn, Mahāyāna Buddhism devised similar ways by which the creative expansion of its scriptural resources could be authenticated, while acknowledging their later historical provenance. For instance, the remarkable scripture *Samādhi of Direct Encounter with the Buddhas of the Present* studied by Paul Harrison—which figures among the earliest Mahāyāna scriptures—presents the outlines of a mode of mystical revelation by which practitioners may meditatively cultivate the perception of enlightened beings from whom they may learn new scriptures to reveal and propagate in the world.[72] In fact, this scripture is especially notable in that it also represents an example of the very phenomenon it describes. That is, this work contains a narrative of its own revelation and re-revelation not dissimilar to those we have been discussing. For the Buddha states therein that some years after his death the scripture will disappear, going "into a hole in the ground." Five hundred disciples present among the congregation thereupon vow to re-reveal it at a later point during the prophesied decline of Buddhism.[73] Thus, this text gives scriptural warrant to both of the modes of subsequent revelation suggested by Tāranātha: mystical revelation through direct contact with enlightened beings ("Vision Teachings," *dag snang gi chos*) and concealed, re-revealed teachings ("Treasures," *gter ma*).

Both of these models thus have Indian prototypes and scriptural sanction as early as the second century.[74] Both of them also appear in narratives

71. Indeed, it might be argued that the inclusion of Śāriputra in the tale is extraneous and may represent a later attempt to preserve a patriarchal lineage for these teachings.

72. Paul M. Harrison, *The Samādhi of Direct Encounter with the Buddhas of the Present*. As Harrison writes (xx): "one of the main aims of the *samādhi* that gives our *sūtra* its title is to provide practitioners with the means to translate themselves into the presence of this or that particular manifestation of the Buddha-principle for the purpose of hearing the Dharma, which they subsequently remember and propagate to others. This can be seen not only as a legitimation device justifying the continuing production of Mahāyāna *sūtras* (or 'dharmas hitherto unheard,' in the words of the text)—and a bold one at that, insofar as it removes the necessity for strictly historical claims to authenticity—but also as an indication of the means by which at least some Mahāyāna *sūtras* were composed, i.e., as a result of meditational inspiration."

73. See Harrison, *Samādhi*, 96–108.

74. It is worth noting that examples like the ones I cite here have also been referenced by

of specific scriptural revelations. For instance, the traditional tale of Asaṅga's cultivation of a direct, visionary encounter with Maitreya, resulting in Asaṅga's revelation of Maitreya's *Five Books* (*Byams chos lnga*), reflects the self-same historiographical move intended to lend authority to these new scriptures through claiming direct, mystical revelation of a scriptural corpus.[75] The "Treasure" pattern, on the other hand, may be observed in the well-known tale of Nāgārjuna's receiving the scriptures on the Transcendent Virtue of Wisdom (*Prajñāpāramitāsūtra*) from the undersea world of the nāgas, where they had allegedly been preserved since the time of the Buddha.

Once one begins to attend to it, this pattern—involving an awareness of the difficulties of chronology coupled with a desire for auctorization—is evident throughout Buddhist historiography. Aside from the Vision and Treasure models, there also exist other strategies that reveal the same auctorizing/historicizing tension. One is to attribute an extraordinary lifespan to certain authors. This can be seen in Tāranātha's tale of Nāgabodhi's attainment of the rainbow body, rendering him immortal.[76] To consider merely one further example, one might consider the famous tradition of Nāgārjuna's having lived six hundred years (as related, for instance, in Butön's *History of Buddhism*[77]). This may be understood as another strategy to deal with chronological difficulties, bringing Nāgārjuna's active life up to the period in which he was understood to have composed and taught the PK. One may also detect another strategy in some sources, including some related to Nāgārjuna's life: a narrative of rebirth. According to one account,

---

indigenous Tibetan apologists for the Treasure tradition, such as the thirteenth-century author Guru Chos-dbang. I hope it is clear that my intention is somewhat different: not to establish the "truth" of these Buddhist ideas, but to establish them as operative discursive models within the Buddhist world of which we speak. Indeed, Guru Chos-dbang's citation of them precisely proves my point. On this issue, see Janet Gyatso, "Drawn from the Tibetan Treasury," 153.

75. Interestingly, the chronological dynamic is here reversed: the auctorizing gesture is to a figure in the future (Maitreya), rather than the past (Śākyamuni, Nāgārjuna, etc.).

76. This tradition would seem to have Indic sanction, insofar as the colophon to one of the works attributed to Nāgabodhi in the Tibetan canon notes that it "was composed by the great teacher Nāgabuddhi who still resides on Śrīparvata, having discovered the magical power (*siddhi*) of the *vidyādharas*" (*slob dpon chen po klu'i blo rig pa 'dzin pa'i dngos grub brnyes nas da dung dpal gyi ri la bzhugs pa'i zhal snga nas mdzad pa*); see *Rim pa khongs su bsdu ba'i man ngag ces bya ba'i rab tu byed ba*, sDe-dge bsTan-'gyur, rGyud, vol. ngi, f. 148b³.

77. See E. Obermiller, trans., *History of Buddhism*, 127.

the jealous son of a king whose life force was linked to that of the immortal Nāgārjuna, being desirous of ascending to royal power, killed the sage, thus ending the life of the king. However, from the neck of the deceased Nāgārjuna issued the following stanza: "I, having gone to the realm of Sukhāvatī, will again enter this body." And we are told, "neither the head nor the body decaying, each year they came nearer to each other and, having ultimately united, he is said to have performed deeds for the teaching and the benefit of beings."[78] This narrative, too, could be mobilized to account for literary activity several centuries after the early first millennium *floruit* of the Centrist Nāgārjuna. However, on the whole, the Vision and Treasure models seem to have been predominant.

Given this multitude of examples, I think it is safe to conclude that these several narrative modes of legitimation were widespread—indeed something of a cliché—among Indian Buddhist communities of the first millennium struggling to come to terms with an ever-expanding scriptural tradition. Thus, Tāranātha's use of them to resolve the chronological problem of the Noble Tradition literature invokes a longstanding Buddhist strategy for accommodating such growth in sacred literature, and may reflect traditions handed down to him from earlier sources. From this perspective, his invoking of such distinctively Tibetan notions as Treasures and Visions may be considered simply an attempt to illustrate these patterns in terms intelligible to his contemporaries—a novel nomenclature applied to a longstanding Indic discourse about scriptural revelation, not an innovative approach to the historiography of these traditions.

Concluding Reflections

What, then, are we left to conclude about the history of the Noble Tradition and its authors? For one, it seems certain that the development of this school took place in the ninth and early tenth centuries. Furthermore, it seems certain that the traditional authorities were aware of this fact, such that the early seventeenth-century Tibetan author Tāranātha could locate its origins in the ninth-century reign of King Devapāla and his son.

78. *Bu-ston Chos-'byung*, 148: *ske'i rtsa ba nas | nga ni bde ba can gyi 'jig rten du | phyin nas lus 'di la yang 'jug par 'gyur | zhes tshig bcad byung ngo | |... | | dbu dang sku lus gnyis ka ma nyams par lo re zhing nyer song nas mthar 'byar nas bstan pa dang 'gro don mdzad ces grag go* |.

Nonetheless, it is important to note that these authorities simultaneously maintained that the central works of the school are attributable to early first-millennium Centrist authors such as Nāgārjuna and Āryadeva. We have seen that this reflects a larger, well attested, and accepted pattern of Buddhist historiography relative to ongoing developments in scriptural and commentarial production. That is, by the ninth century, Buddhist communities were quite accustomed to the ongoing efflorescence of its sacred literature being attributed to either direct divine revelation or the emergence of previously-concealed revelations. The Noble Tradition, in this sense, was merely one more example of a centuries-old process of scriptural production and auctorization.

Thus, the modern scholarly consensus that the attribution was somehow based upon either confusion or fraud has significantly misconstrued the "traditional view," having failed to read the relevant materials with the sensitivity necessary to properly grasp the historiographical dynamic they contain.[79] It is remarkable how similar the scholarly discourse on this literature has been to the discourses that have characterized the discussion of the Tibetan Treasure traditions, based as they are on a parallel historiographical conceit. One sees the same dynamic of quick dismissal on the grounds of apparent conflict with "historical fact," without further interrogating the meaning of the attribution within its proper cultural context.[80] The treatment has been consistent: to identify the corpus (on historical grounds) as spurious and to treat the attribution as a case of contemporary authorial

79. Indeed, the materials were not even reliably read, much less interpreted.

80. It may be said, however, that this dismissal is more characteristic of older scholarship on Tibetan Buddhism. Thus, for instance, Austine Waddell writes of the "fictitious 'revelations' or *Terma* books" that "pretend to be the composition of St. Padma, the founder of Lāmaism." Of the *gter ston*, he writes: "these so-called 'revealers' [are] really the composers of these *Terma* treatises." He treats them as cheap and juvenile frauds, meant only "to legitimize many of their unorthodox practices . . . and to admit of further laxity." See Waddell, *Buddhism of Tibet*, 165 and 57.

More recently, some have begun to complain that the general tenor of scholarship on the Treasure traditions has been overly credulous. For instance, Donald Lopez has lamented that "the pious fiction of authenticity has been tacitly maintained . . . by scholars of Tibet" (Lopez, *Prisoners of Shangri-La*, 243n32). In making this claim, he bases himself on the more detailed comments of Michael Aris who, while critiquing the kid-glove treatment of scholars such as Snellgrove and Richardson, replicates (in 1989) the older pattern of importing alien cultural assumptions, writing that "the whole cult depended on conscious pretense and fraud." See Aris, *Hidden Treasures, Secret Lives*, 96–98.

fraud, like the "Hitler diaries" or (less recently) William Henry Ireland's "lost plays of Shakespeare." This approach, however, is fundamentally misguided. Scholars have been captivated by the false dilemma of "authenticity" versus "fraud"—a set of alternatives "natural" within the commodity culture in which modern Buddhist Studies takes place, yet inappropriate (as so constructed) to the classical South Asian context. Consequently, scholars have been able to appreciate neither that which the tradition speaks of itself nor what that presentation reveals of its ideology. A more promising approach to these South Asian materials has been indicated by scholars such as Matthew Kapstein, who has suggested that "the question that we must ask . . . is not so much whether [such works] were real or fake, but rather why it was that . . . creativity so often masked itself as the retrieval of the past."[81]

For to construct these phenomena as examples of "rogues" seeking to "pass off" their own work for personal gain[82] is rather remarkably, anachronistically, and anatopistically to misconstrue the nature of the phenomenon by situating it against the cultural and legal presuppositions of the contemporary capitalist West, rather than those of late first-millennium India. The cultural constructions of authorship regnant in these Indian Buddhist circles were rather different than we are accustomed to today. The notion of authorship has varied over time and in different social contexts. As Raymond Williams (among others) has noted, "authorial identification . . . [is] subject to historically variable conventions":

> In its root and some of its surviving associations[, the word "author"] carries a sense of decisive origination. . . . Its most general early uses included a regular reference to God or Christ, as the authors of man's condition, and its continuing association with "authority" is significant. Its literary use, in medieval and Renaissance thought, was closely connected with a sense of "authors" as "authorities": the "classical" writers and their texts. In the modern period there is an observable relation between the

81. Matthew Kapstein, *Tibetan Assimilation of Buddhism*, 136. The article cited here and below, "The Purificatory Gem and its Cleansing," is very insightful and provocative with regard to the problem of authenticity and "apocrypha" in Buddhist literature and should be read by anyone interested in these issues.

82. This is how the treasure revealer Pemalingpa is characterized by Aris. See *Hidden Treasures, Secret Lives*, 97.

> idea of an author and the idea of "literary property": notably in the organization of authors to protect their work, by copyright and similar means, within a bourgeois market.[83]

With regard to first millennium Indian Buddhist circles, I think we are safe in asserting that the prevailing conception of authorship was not one designed to function to restrict reproduction and exchange of textual materials in a market economy. Rather, it was closer to the Renaissance notion of author as "authority" which, while clearly a terrain of ideological struggle, was nonetheless flexible in culturally distinctive ways, and diverged in important respects from the cultural assumptions subtending the description of such attributions as a type of "fraud."

It is important to understand, then, that the Buddhist tradition was quite comfortable in maintaining a rather loose conception of authorship, such that it may legitimately be claimed on hermeneutical grounds, even when strict historical contiguity is manifestly absent.[84] Though in certain circumstances the ongoing attribution of new literature to ancient authorities was evidently resisted by conservative elements, and at times such resistance certainly did appeal to notions of historical reality, the category of authorship as it related to Buddhist sacred literature was rarely, if ever, beholden to such considerations."[85] The Buddhist concept of authorship was situated in larger networks of Buddhist axioms about the nature of the individual, and thus not bound to a criterion of strict historical realism as we (and, indeed, they) understand it. Commonly held Buddhist beliefs such as the possibility of interaction with timeless divine beings, rebirth, communication in dreams and visions, and the possibility of personal immortality all allow for a more flexible and expansive range of possible modes of authorship than fall under the terms of the Berne Convention.[86] Although the perspective adopted by the tradition may seem incoherent or fantastic to us, this is due

83. Raymond Williams, *Marxism and Literature*, 174 and 192.

84. For an excellent treatment of such issues, see Ronald M. Davidson, "An Introduction to the Standards of Scriptural Authority in Indian Buddhism."

85. As Kapstein has noted "there is no evidence to suggest . . . that anyone within the Buddhist tradition ever actually held" the rigid position that the revealed word of the Buddha included only those dispensations taught between "the first turning of the wheel at Ṛṣipatana and . . . the *parinirvāṇa* at Kuśinagara"; see his *Tibetan Assimilation of Buddhism*, 124.

86. That is, the 1886 Berne Convention for the Protection of Literary and Artistic Works

merely to the fact that we do not share their cultural presuppositions. We have internalized the construction of authorship contemporary in our society such that it seems "natural" to us, and it is only with some difficulty that we can attempt to think outside this box. Our notion of authorship, however, is predicated on a set of contingent social choices—choices not shared by the societies of classical India, wherein its range of possible forms was evidently more extensive. Writing of critical, historical scholarship in the Tibetan Buddhist world, Kapstein comments that:

> If a critical tradition similar to that of the post-Renaissance West never blossomed, one reason can perhaps be seen in the ancient rejection of the historical realism that is methodologically required for historical philology (even if in the end it is to be overturned), and the concomitant failure to determine suitable criteria for the historical authenticity of the Buddha's word.[87]

While I agree with the general tenor of Kapstein's discussion, I would further suggest that what one sees is not the wholesale rejection of historical realism, but merely a restriction of its appropriate scope of application. The Tibetan historical tradition seems to have been quite capable of understanding and appreciating historical argument, and deployed it in certain circumstances (including the debunking of others' claims to authenticity). However, faced with the widely accepted and frequent occurrence of mystical revelations of literary works, historical considerations were not infrequently trumped by the exigencies of auctorization.

There still remains, however, the question of why the PK, CMP, and so on, were attributed to human saints, rather than celestial buddhas or bodhisattvas, who would seem to be more authoritative still. After all, the explanatory tantras that the Nobles draw on (and that were likely composed either by them or their immediate predecessors) were attributed the full status of scripture, revealed by the Buddha. It would seem a small thing to encapsulate the teachings of the PK and CMP in the literary form of a tantra, thus lending it even more traditional authority. Why go the route of attributing

(established in part at the instigation of Victor Hugo), the first in a series of protocols whose aim is to protect the fiduciary interests of the producers of literary and other works.

87. Kapstein, *Tibetan Assimilation of Buddhism*, 135.

them to human agents, of less-than-absolute enlightened status? That is, one might object that, simply because we have identified the narrative trope operative in this context—and have identified it as a common Buddhist move—we have not thereby ascertained exactly the "cultural logic" behind the specific attribution in this case.[88]

It seems likely that an ascription to Nāgārjuna and his tradition may already have been suggested by earlier currents in Buddhist esoterism. For instance, though it does not seem to appear in the surviving Indic materials, the Sino-Japanese esoteric schools trace their lineages back through Nāgārjuna, relating a history that puts the sage as the first human link after Vajrasattva.[89] Though these tales may be limited to East Asia, there is corroborating evidence in the scriptural corpus of the Esoteric Community that hints at an affiliation with the Centrists. Of interest in this regard is the striking correspondence, noted by Harunaga Isaacson, between what is likely the earliest description of the two stages (*krama-dvaya*) of esoteric practice and a (presumably earlier) verse of the Centrist Nāgārjuna describing the two realities (*satya-dvaya*) of the Madhyamaka system.[90] The parallelism is evidently deliberate, leading Isaacson to comment that "this echo is in fact an indication of a basic point that I suggest underlies the original conception of the division into two kramas and remained an important factor in the thought of most teachers"[91]—that is, that the two stages of the

88. In this regard, it may be instructive to consider a parallel example from the non-Buddhist Indian tradition. The *Law Code of Manu* is a work on duties (*dharma-śāstra*) composed roughly around the beginning of the Common Era. As Patrick Olivelle has noted, "the clear intent [of attributing the work to Manu] was to make the work more authoritative" by attributing its authorship to an ancient sage. However, Olivelle also notes the cultural logic behind the specific attribution. As Manu is the name both of "the sage responsible for the famous proverbial sayings and [of] the first king of humankind," this attribution fit with the ideology of the work in countering Buddhist influence by re-establishing "the old alliance between priesthood and royalty" (Olivelle, *Law Code of Manu*, xxi and xliii).

89. See note 18, above.

90. The original verse (*Mūlamadhyamakakārikā* XXIV.8) reads: *dve satye samupāśritya buddhānāṃ dharma-deśanā | lokasaṃvṛtisatyaṃ ca satyaṃ ca paramārthataḥ* |. The *Esoteric Community Appendix Tantra* (*Guhyasamājottaratantra*, XVIII.84), as edited by Isaacson, reads: *krama-dvayaṃ upāśritya vajriṇāṃ dharma-deśanā | kramaṃ autpattikaṃ caiva kramaṃ autpannakaṃ tathā* |. See Harunaga Isaacson, "Ratnākaraśānti's *Hevajrasahajasadyoga*," 469.

91. Harunaga Isaacson, "Ratnākaraśānti's *Hevajrasahajasadyoga*," 469. Note 92 on this page

esoteric practice are analogous to the two realities. I would suggest that this verse also functions to affiliate the Esoteric Community with the Centrists.

This affiliation further enabled the Nobles to align their doctrinal formulations with those of their philosophical forebears, manipulating the familiar discourses of the Centrists such that the later developments of the Nobles had a familiar ring to them, making intuitive "sense" to readers steeped in Centrist thought. Thus, one finds in the central yogic terminology of the Noble system the notion of the two realities or truths (*satya-dvaya*: perhaps *the* fulcrum concept in the Centrist lingo) serving as two stages of esoteric practice that are mastered and integrated in the final realization of the Noble system. The immediately antecedent stages, called the "three isolations," draw further on the familiar Transcendent Virtue of Wisdom (*Prajñāpāramitā*) terminology of isolation (often found in this literature in conjunction with the notion of voidness/*śūnyatā*)—again playing on discursive themes common among the Mahāyāna wisdom traditions of which Nāgārjuna was considered the principal master. In these several ways, then, the Nobles were able to manipulate the well-established terminology of the Centrists in communicating the details of their yogic model in a way striking, familiar, and memorable to their fellow Buddhists—and in which a derivation from the sage Nāgārjuna would be readily comprehensible.

In a similar way, Āryadeva can be seen to be manipulating the established terminology of the "Vast" and "Profound" Traditions of the Mahāyāna to argue his case for the primacy and indispensability of the esoteric traditions. These terms had emerged in Indian Buddhist discourse to describe the traditions of the Yogācāra and Madhyamaka, respectively. The latter was the "profound" tradition, that allowed the attainment of buddhahood through its penetration of the nature of reality. The former taught the effective expression of this attainment through the "vast" path of the bodhisattva's deeds. In a very interesting move, the Noble Āryadeva aligns the (exoteric) Mahāyāna as a whole (including, presumably, Centrism) with the "vast" tradition and the Vajrayāna with the profound.[92] The implication seems to be much the same: that the "profound" tradition of the Esoteric Community was the essential mode of understanding reality and thus attaining

further speculates that this parallelism may have been intended to "protect" the gradualist approach to these practices against subitist encroachments.

92. See CMP, f. 55a.

enlightenment, which was expressed through the normative perspective of the exoteric Mahāyāna.

Appeal to this sort of intellectual consonance is not to suggest that other, less subtle, considerations may not also have been involved. Taken from another perspective, the attribution may be understood as one strategy in an attempt to resolve auctorative difficulties with regard to the Noble Tradition's explanatory tantras and their relationship to the (chronologically prior) Esoteric Community Jñānapāda Tradition. As we have alluded above (and will discuss further below), the primary yogic and hermeneutical innovations of the Noble Tradition were encapsulated in a set of auxiliary "explanatory tantras" that claim the status of revealed truth. However, the current state of research on this topic suggests that these explanatory tantras were still in a formative state at the time the Noble Tradition works were redacted.[93] Thus, the auctorization of their authorizing scriptures themselves was as yet unsettled as they sought to validate their tradition alongside that of Jñānapāda. That is, it was incumbent upon the Nobles to demonstrate the credentials of their novel doctrines relative to the prior prestige of the other tradition—for which they needed to be able to deflect the charge that their explanatory tantras were of lesser authority as they postdated the works of the Jñānapādists. One way to accomplish this would be to produce allegedly anterior commentarial works that cite these explanatory tantras, which is exactly what the PK and the other Noble works do. As the Centrist Nāgārjuna, Āryadeva, et al. were well known to have lived prior to Jñānapāda, this would lend the explanatory tantras a long and distinguished pedigree. Not only were they then established as attested from the early part of the millennium, but their authority was greatly reinforced: after all, if they were considered authoritative by Nāgārjuna, who would argue with that?

Though further insight into this issue must await a more comprehensive analysis than is possible here, I hope nonetheless to have succeeded in suggesting a preferable mode of appreciating the indigenous historiography of the Noble Tradition. It is important for modern scholarship to recognize that the Indian and Tibetan Buddhist traditions were not so deluded about the chronology of their own scriptures as has generally been maintained. At least in the case of Tāranātha—and, as I have argued, quite plausibly universally—the Noble Tradition has been well aware of the historical

93. See Matsunaga, "A Doubt to Authority of the Guhyasamāja-Ākhyāna-tantras."

difficulties the attribution of its chief literature raises. Nonetheless, from the perspective of late first-millennium India—given the importance of validation from antiquity in this cultural context, the prevalence of such modes of revelation throughout the Indian Buddhist world, and the seeming discursive consonance of the yoga of the Nobles with the dialectics of the Centrists—the attribution "works." Grasping this allows us to begin to transcend the ersatz scholarly debate about "fraud" and "authenticity," and to begin to interrogate the tradition in a manner that highlights its distinctive ideology, through situating its "preposterous" attributions in larger—even typical—patterns of Buddhist discourse and practice. With this in the background, let us now turn to the corpus of the Noble literature itself to try to understand something of what it contributed to the intellectual and religious life of late first-millennium Buddhist India.

Canon of the Noble Tradition: Scriptural Authorities and Commentarial Literature

Root and Explanatory Tantras

The central and most important scripture of the Noble Tradition is the *Esoteric Community* (or *Guhyasamāja*) *Tantra* (GST)—perhaps the esoteric scripture best known to modern scholars since it was first published by Benoytosh Bhattacharyya in 1931.[94] In general, the GST is understood to consist of seventeen chapters.[95] What is sometimes included as its "eighteenth chapter" is the scripture's *uttaratantra*, or "appendix tantra," which comments on the previous seventeen chapters.[96] The contents of the scripture are difficult to give a clear and succinct account of, especially since (as

94. Though it might be said that David Snellgrove's 1959 publication of the *Hevajra Tantra* somewhat displaced it, as he included not only an edition, but an English translation and Sanskrit commentary. Nonetheless, the GST (or, at least, Bhattacharyya's comments on it) has been among the most cited sources on Buddhist esoterism. For a recent translation of the first twelve chapters of the GST together with its commentary by Candrakīrti, see Campbell et al., trans. and ed., *The Esoteric Community Tantra (Guhyasamāja Tantra)*, 2021.

95. Many scholars believe that this scripture consists of two parts: an older version consisting of the first twelve chapters, later supplemented by chapters thirteen to seventeen. For discussion of this thesis, see, e.g., Alex Wayman, *Yoga of the Guhyasamāja Tantra*, 142.

96. It is quite common, in general, for esoteric Buddhist scriptures to have companion works supplementing them, for which "appendix tantra" (*uttara-tantra*) is the generic

is true of most esoteric works) the hermeneutical issues surrounding the proper mode(s) of interpreting it are still much in dispute. At the risk of doing a great injustice, it may be encapsulated as follows. The work begins by elaborating a maṇḍala (or divine assembly/world) of the deity Esoteric Community (here called Sarvatathāgata-bodhicitta-vajra or Mahāvairocana). This assembly consists of thirteen deities: the five central transcendent lords (Akṣobhya, Vairocana, Ratnaketu,[97] Lokeśvara,[98] and Amoghasiddhi), four goddesses (Dveṣarati, Moharati, Rāgarati, and Vajrarati),[99] and four wrathful protectors (Yamāntakṛt, Prajñāntakṛt, Padmāntakṛt, and Vighnāntakṛt).[100] There are discussions in the early chapters (one to twelve, considered by many modern scholars to have originally circulated as a complete, independent text) concerning the nature of the spirit of enlightenment (*bodhicitta*), yogic visualizations, instructions for constructing a ritual maṇḍala, the antinomian practices of the esoteric adept (including eating of and worshipping with polluting substances, ritual sexual union, and the like), invoking deities through their seed-syllables, visionary and alchemical procedures for the attainment of magical powers, and similar practices of the esoteric bodhisattva. In the later chapters (thirteen to seventeen) most of these same topics are addressed, though in greater ritual detail.

A distinctive claim of the Noble Tradition is that this fundamental, or "root" (*mūla, rtsa ba*), scripture is supplemented and clarified by auxiliary scriptures, called "explanatory tantras" (*vyākhyātantra, bshad rgyud*). The question of explanatory tantras is of especial significance for a discussion of the Noble Tradition, for this school is distinctive in its reliance on such scriptures in the construction of their yogic system.[101] One of the major

name. Generally, these are considered separate works; the ambiguous classification of the GSUT as either a separate scripture or as the final chapter is unusual.

97. In the commentarial materials of the Noble Tradition, as in most later sources, this transcendent lord's name is given as Ratnasambhava.

98. Again, among the Nobles and most others, this transcendent lord is known as Amitābha.

99. These four goddesses of the GST maṇḍala are typically known (as in the CMP) as: Locanā, Māmakī, Pāṇḍaravāsinī, and Tārā.

100. Though ten protectors (*daśa-krodha*) are featured in this maṇḍala in both the Jñānapāda and Noble Traditions, they are not enumerated as such in the opening chapter of the GST.

101. Indeed, it has been argued that these scriptures are unique to the Noble Tradition, which used them to legitimate their innovative approach to interpretation and praxis. See, e.g., Yūkei Matsunaga, "A Doubt to Authority of the Guhyasamāja-Ākhyāna-tantras," 16–25.

emphases of this school is the manner in which the root and explanatory tantras may be connected so as to yield a proper understanding of the Tantra. In the *Pañcakrama*, for instance, Nāgārjuna states that, "This reality (*tattva*) [is] fixed, well-sealed in the *Glorious* [*Esoteric*] *Community Tantra*; [it is] to be understood from the mouth of the guru in accordance with the explanatory tantra[s]."[102] Āryadeva similarly indicates the importance of these scriptures, when he observes that the so-called "air reality"—that is, the quintessential yogic practice of manipulating the vital airs—is not to be obtained without recourse to the explanatory tantras. He writes, "the air reality is not stated clearly in the root tantras ... and the appendix tantras. [This is] because it is spoken of intentionally. But in the explanatory tantra, it is spoken of literally."[103] In a similar vein, a later Tibetan votary of the Noble Tradition, Je Tsongkhapa, ascribes the motivation behind the composition of the Noble Tradition works to just such a concern with establishing an interpretation based on the explanatory tantras:

> Having seen that those who could explain [the teachings] through the guru's connecting of root and explanatory tantras (as explained above) would be hard to come by in latter days, and that if the instructions obtained from connecting root and explanatory tantras by that sort of guru were written down they would remain for a long period, the Noble Father and Sons composed many texts of instructions on the two stages, such as the *Five Stages* and the *Lamp for Integrating the Practices*.[104]

On its face, this comment offers an explanation of why these (allegedly oral) instructions of the lineage of gurus were put into writing. This is, of course, difficult (if not impossible) to corroborate, and the testimony of a

102. PK I.9: *etat tattvaṃ sthitaṃ tantre śrīsamāje sumudritam* | *vyākhyā-tantrānusāreṇa boddhavyaṃ guruvaktrataḥ* ||. The Tibetan reads: *dpal ldan 'dus pa'i rgyud du ni* | *de nyid 'di dag rgyas btab gnas* | *bshad pa'i rgyud kyi rjes 'brangs nas* | *bla ma'i kha las rtogs par bya* ||.

103. CMP, f. 18b.

104. Tsongkhapa, *Rim lnga gsal sgron* (RṄSG), f. 76a[4–5]: *sngar bshad pa ltar gyi bla mas rtsa bshad sbyar nas 'chad shes pa phyi dus su rnyed dka' zhing* | *de 'dra'i bla mas rtsa bshad kyi rgyud sbyar ba las rnyed pa'i man ngag yi ger bris pa na [text reads: ni] dus ring po'i bar du yang gnas par gzigs nas* | *'phags pa yab sras rnams kyis rim lnga dang spyod bsdus la sogs pa'i rim gnyis kyi man ngag gi gzhung mang du mdzad de* |.

fifteenth-century Tibetan may or may not be reliable in this regard. What it does demonstrate quite clearly, however, is that the subsequent representatives of the tradition continued to be quite conscious of the fact that the authority of the Noble Tradition's teachings is predicated largely on that of its explanatory tantras. There is considerable discussion among Tibetan commentators as to the nature of the category itself, which scriptures are appropriately considered "explanatory tantras" of the GST, the issue of whether scriptures may be "common" or "uncommon" explanatory tantras (i.e., whether certain scriptures function in this capacity for more than one esoteric tradition), and the like. Though important in the intellectual history of Tibetan Buddhism, the niceties of these debates need not concern us here. It is enough for our purposes to note the existence of the category—attested in the usage of Āryadeva in the CMP (as Nāgārjuna in the PK), wherein he refers to certain texts specifically as "explanatory tantras."[105]

What special teachings do these explanatory Tantras provide that are not found in the Root Tantra itself? From the perspective of the tradition's hermeneutical apologetics, of course, nothing—since all the required ideas have been "sealed" into the Root Tantra by its authorial buddha. Given the central importance of ancient and timeless authority in these traditions, there is little scope for an acknowledgement of innovation. Instead, they claim that the explanatory tantras merely indicate explicitly that which is already present in the fundamental scripture. By following the explanatory tantras, they claim, one is enabled to "break the seals" on these implicit teachings and demystify the elliptical instructions found in the GST. On the other hand, as Āryadeva comments more than once in the CMP, it is only through the medium of the explanatory tantras that one may learn key elements of the Noble Tradition system, such as the essential instructions on the yoga of the vital airs.

According to many later interpreters, in addition to the *Esoteric Community Appendix Tantra* (GSUT), there are four explanatory tantras that form the key sources of the Noble Tradition, as established by their citation as such in the PK and CMP. These are: the *Enquiry of the Four Goddesses*

105. For instance, he refers specifically to the *Explanation of the Intention* (*Saṃdhyāvyākaraṇa*: CMP, f. 16b), *Vajra Rosary* (*Vajramālā*: CMP, f. 18b), the *Gnosis Vajra Compendium* (*Jñānavajrasamuccaya*: CMP, f. 27a), and perhaps the *Vajra Maṇḍala Ornament* (*Vajramaṇḍalālaṃkāra*: CMP, f. 72a) as explanatory tantras.

(*Caturdevīparipṛcchā*), the *Gnosis Vajra Compendium* (*Jñānavajrasamuccaya*), the *Vajra Rosary* (*Vajramālā*), and the *Explanation of the Intention* (*Saṃdhyāvyākaraṇa*).[106] These works can be classified as either exegetical/hermeneutical or yogic in import. The *Explanation of the Intention* and the *Gnosis Vajra Compendium* belong in the former category—detailing techniques of scriptural exegesis and the Tradition's hermeneutical model.[107] The former (by far the more extensive of the two) takes the form of a verbal commentary on the text—setting out what it takes to be the proper interpretation—while the latter describes in more brief and general terms the distinctive interpretative techniques used to arrive at such an interpretation: the so-called six parameters and four procedures (*ṣaṭkoṭi, caturnyāya; mtha' drug, tshul bzhi*) that constitute the primary hermeneutical approaches advocated by the Noble Tradition.[108] The division into exegetical and yogic texts should not be taken as exclusive, however, as, for example, the *Explanation of the Intention* also outlines the yogic process of the vajra recitation (*vajra-jāpa-krama*—the topic of CMP chapter 3), as evidenced by its citation in this context by the PK and the CMP.

The latter two explanatory tantras of the Esoteric Community—the *Vajra Rosary* and the *Enquiry of the Four Goddesses*—explain chiefly the yogic techniques of the tradition, preeminent among which figures the practice of the yogas of the vital airs (*prāṇāyāma*). The *Enquiry of the Four Goddesses* is a quite brief work in verse, cast in the form of a dialogue between Vajrasattva and the four goddesses of the Esoteric Community maṇḍala, that addresses some questions concerning the yoga of vital airs and drops of the subtle body. The *Vajra Rosary*, by contrast, is a wide-ranging and voluminous work, consisting of a series of eighty-two questions posed by Vajrapāṇi and their answers, comprising sixty-nine folio pages in its Tibetan translation.

106. See, e.g., A-myes-zhabs, *gSang 'dus chos 'byung*, f. 8b; and Tsongkhapa, RṄSG, f. 17a$^{1-2}$.

107. According to the Tibetan commentator A-myes-zhabs Ngag-dbang Kun-dga' bsod-nams (1597–1662), the *Explanation of the Intention* principally treats of the words of the Tantra, while the *Gnosis Vajra Compendium* illuminates its meaning (*ye shes rdo rje kun las btus kyis mtha' drug dang tshul bzhi sogs rtsa rgyud kyi don gyi cha ston | dgongs pa lung ston kyis tshig gi don gtso bor ston |*); see A-myes-zhabs, *gSang 'dus chos 'byung*, f. 8b$^{3-4}$.

108. These techniques are further discussed and applied to the interpretation of the words of the GST in Candrakīrti's PU commentary. For discussion of these hermeneutical strategies, see Robert A.F. Thurman, "Vajra Hermeneutics," and Ernst Steinkellner, "Remarks on Tantristic Hermeneutics."

Most significantly, perhaps, the final chapter of the *Vajra Rosary* serves as the main scriptural authority for the doctrine of the five stages that Nāgārjuna and Āryadeva elaborate. As Matsunaga has suggested, its date of redaction may have overlapped somewhat with the PK itself, such that the two works may have mutually influenced each other.[109]

It is on the basis of these works that the authors of Nāgārjuna's school composed their commentarial and explanatory treatises. They form the central wellspring of ideas that are developed and refined in the commentarial works. They are frequently cited in the CMP, the PK, and related works in the tradition.

Commentarial Literature

The Works of Nāgārjuna

The writings of Noble Nāgārjuna serve as the primary and principal touchstone for interpretation and practice—the ultimate authority—of the Noble Tradition. There are numerous works on esoteric subjects attributed to Nāgārjuna, including several on topics affiliated with the Esoteric Community. Here, we will only be concerned with three works that are generally accepted as authoritative by the tradition and that form part of the essential corpus of Noble Tradition thought. The first two works concern the creation stage of esoteric practice and the third addresses the perfection stage.[110] The former are the *Condensed Sādhana*[111] (*Piṇḍīkṛta-sādhana*, also called the *Piṇḍīkrama-sādhana* or "*Globule Stage Sādhana*") and the [*Sādhana that*] *Integrates Scriptural Citations* (*Sūtramelāpaka*). The former work is an abbreviated map of the rites and visualizations involved in the

109. Matsunaga, "A Doubt to Authority," 24.

110. This is a crucial distinction in Buddhist esoterism. In brief, the creation stage (*utpattikrama, bskyed rim*) involves the cultivation of a clear self-identification as a deity and culminates (in part) in the ability to visualize the entire maṇḍala in a drop the size of a sesame seed on the tip of one's nose. The perfection stage (*niṣpannakrama, rdzogs rim*) involves the actualization of this divine identity and realm through the yogic manipulation of the vital airs. This latter is the primary subject matter of the PK and CMP.

111. The *sādhana* is the most central ritual form in later Buddhist esoterism, serving as the fundamental template for all other rituals (such as fire-offering, consecration, initiation, etc.). It involves the dissolution of the conventional sense of self and the emergence in and consecration of a new, enlightened identity as a Buddhist divinity.

creation stage yoga of the Esoteric Community, including the invocation of wrathful protector deities to secure the site of practice, the evolution of a maṇḍala-cosmos out of the subtle elements of the world, establishing a divine mansion in this world, emanation of the thirty-two deities of the maṇḍala, merging this world with one's own body (in a "body maṇḍala"), consecrating this body by arraying seed-syllables in its key places, blessing the "three vajras" of body, speech, and mind, preparing and uniting with a consort, re-creating the thirty-two-deity maṇḍala and meditating on it the size of a mustard seed at one's nose tip through the subtle yoga. It does not cite any scriptural authority, but simply teaches these points in a straightforward, didactic manner.

The latter text, the [*Sādhana that*] *Integrates Scriptural Citations*, is also a creation stage sādhana of the Esoteric Community, but its approach is different. Its primary aim is to legitimate the Noble Tradition's ritual template (its sādhana) by identifying its validating sources in the root scripture, the GST. It "integrates citations" in the sense that the text enumerates each of the phases of the practice in prose and, at each point, quotes an applicable verse from the Root Tantra. The implication is that one way in which the Esoteric Community tradition was mystified—so as to make its secrets unavailable to the uninitiated—was to take its various teachings, such as that of the sādhana, chop them up, and scatter the pieces in different chapters of the text. Nāgārjuna's work, then, reassembles this teaching, indicating where the parts had been hidden. Thus, this work is of particular importance, insofar as it constitutes—not a theoretical discussion of—but a concrete instantiation of textual exegesis in this tradition.

Nāgārjuna's main contribution to the explanation of the perfection stage yogas is the *Pañcakrama* (PK), or *Five Stages*, which stands at the forefront of his esoteric *œuvre*. It is here that the perfection stage is analyzed into sequential phases and elucidated. Although all authorities agree on there being five stages, there is some variation, both in the names applied to these stages and to the actual identity of the five. In the titles of the chapters of the PK, the names of the successive stages appear as follows: vajra recitation stage (*vajrajāpakrama*), universally pure stage (*sarvaśuddhiviśuddhi-krama*), self-consecration stage (*svādhiṣṭhāna-krama*), supremely-secret-bliss enlightenment stage (*parama-rahasya-sukhābhisambodhi-krama*), and communion stage (*yuganaddha-krama*).

This sequence is accepted by a number of commentators.[112] Another mode of classifying the stages includes the propædeutic "globule stage" (*piṇḍīkrama*, detailed in the eponymous sādhana text) as the first stage and omits the universally pure stage, on the argument that the chapter describing this stage is not the work of Nāgārjuna.[113]

The former interpretation would seem to be suggested by the following passage from the PK that presents the stages in brief as a sequential array:

> The yogī standing in vajra recitation
> Should attain the mind-objective [stage].
> Standing in the phantasmic samādhi,
> [He] should be purified by the reality limit (*bhūtakoṭi*).
>
> Arising from the reality limit,
> [He] should attain the nondual gnosis.
> The one who stands in the communion samādhi
> Learns nothing further.
>
> He is called "one of perfected yoga"—
> He is also Mahāvajradhara;
> Endowed with the supreme of all forms,
> The omniscient one is born from that [process].[114]

112. These include the *Pañcakramaṭīkā Maṇimālā* and *Pañcakramārthabhāskaraṇa* attributed to Nāgabodhi (Tōh. 1840 and 1833), the *Pañcakramapañjikā Arthaprabhāsa-nāma* of Vīrabhadra (Tōh. 1830), and the *Pañcakramaṭīkā Kramārthaprakāśikā* attributed to Lakṣmī (Tōh. 1842). See Katsumi Mimaki and Tōru Tomabechi, *Pañcakrama*, ix, n. 10.

113. In fact, it is generally accepted that this chapter was not written by Nāgārjuna, though this is not universally taken as a reason to exclude it from the five stage system. In short, the colophon of the second chapter—on the "universally pure stage"—unmistakably indicates that the author was someone named "Śākyamitra." Furthermore, there is special mention of the fact that this chapter bears its own unique title (*aparanāma*), the *Unexcelled Intention* (*Anuttarasaṃdhi*). Similarly, when this part of the PK is quoted in the CMP, it is in fact cited as the *Unexcelled Intention*, not as the *Five Stages*—strong evidence for its status as a discrete text (though it is not, of course, unusual for a work or part of a work to have more than one name).

The works that maintain this alternative system include: Muniśrībhadra's *Pañcakramaṭippaṇī Yogimanoharā* (PKṬYM, Tōh. 1813), Samayavajra's *Pañcakramapañjikā* (Tōh. 1841), Abhayākaragupta's *Pañcakramamataṭīkā* (Tōh. 1831), and Līlāvajra's *Pañcakramavivaraṇa* (Tōh. 1839). See Mimaki and Tomabechi, *Pañcakrama*, x, n. 14.

114. PK, I.5–7: *vajrajāpa-sthito mantrī citta-nidhyaptim āpnuyāt | māyopama-samādhi-stho*

Here we see Nāgārjuna using alternative names for these five stages. The second stage after the vajra recitation, the "universally pure" stage, is here called the "mind-objective" (*citta-nidhyapti*)—a term also used in the *Pradīpoddyotana* of Candrakīrti.[115] The process continues with the attainment of the phantasmic samādhi (*māyopama-samādhi*), which is a synonym for the self-consecration stage. Then follows the reality limit (*bhūta-koṭi*), an equivalent for the supremely-secret-bliss enlightenment stage, which leads to the communion stage. These stages, their various names, and their precise nature will be discussed at greater length below in the context of our discussion of Āryadeva's CMP, so for now we shall be content with this brief overview of the work and its schema of five stages.

The Works of Āryadeva

There are twelve works attributed to Āryadeva in the Tantric Commentary section (*rgyud 'grel*) of the Peking edition of the Tibetan canon —fourteen in the Derge. Of these, six deal with some aspect of the Guhyasamāja system.[116] Of this number, two works—the CMP and the *Svādhiṣṭhānaprabheda* (SP)—seem to me to merit the most serious consideration as authentic works of the esoteric author Āryadeva, though further research is necessary before any final determination can be made.[117] Two others—the famous *Cittaviśuddhiprakaraṇa* and the (rather less well-known)

---

bhūtakoṭyā viśodhayet || *bhūtakoṭeḥ samuttiṣṭhann advaya-jñānam āpnuyāt* | *yuganaddha-samādhi-stho na kiṃcic chikṣate punaḥ* || *ayaṃ niṣpanna-yogākhyo mahāvajradharaś ca saḥ* | *sarvākāravaropetaḥ sarvajño jāyate tataḥ* ||.

115. See PU, 1. For a translation of this passage, see Thurman, "Vajra Hermeneutics."

116. The eight that deal with other esoteric systems are: 1. *Śrī-caturpīṭha-yogatantra-sādhana* (Tōh. 1610: *rNal 'byor gyi rgyud dpal ldan bzhi pa'i sgrub thabs*); 2. *Jñāneśvarī-sādhana-nāma* (Tōh. 1612: *Ye shes dbang phyug ma'i sgrub thabs*); 3. *Śrī-caturpīṭha-tantrarāja-maṇḍalavidhi-sārasamuccaya-nāma* (Tōh. 1613: *rGyud gyi rgyal po dpal ldan bzhi pa zhes bya ba'i dkyil 'khor gyi cho ga snying po mdor bsags pa zhes bya ba*); 4. *Śrī-catuḥpīṭha-gūḍhārthanirdeśa-ekadruma-pañjikā* (Tōh. 1614: *dPal ldan bzhi pa'i zab don ston pa shing gcig gi dka' 'grel*); 5. *Vajraghaṇṭa-pūjasādhana-krama* (Tōh. 1615: *rDo rje dril thabs kyi mchod pa'i thabs kyi rim pa*); 6. *Nirvikalpa-prakaraṇa* (Tōh. 2279: *rNam par mi rtog pa'i rab tu byed pa*); 7. *Pratipattisāra-śataka* (Tōh. 2334: *Go bar byed pa snying po brgya pa*); and 8. *Dug lnga sbas pa'i lam mchog tu gsang ba bsam gyis mi khyab pa zhes bya ba* (Tōh. 2457).

117. In making this determination, I take the CMP as the definitive work of the Noble Āryadeva, much as the *Mūlamadhyamaka-kārikā* have been taken as the starting point for determining the works of the Centrist Nāgārjuna.

Abhibodhikramopadeśa—are considered authoritative by a significant number of authors in the tradition, but I believe these do not hold up under analysis, for reasons I will detail below. There are also several other works attributed to this author in the Tibetan canons, but these are not accepted as authoritative by most traditional authorities, so I will not discuss them here.[118]

By universal acclaim, Āryadeva's *magnum opus* on esoteric yoga is the *Caryāmelāpakapradīpa* (CMP), the focus of the present study. This work expands on the details of the various stages of the path of Vajrayāna Buddhism as set forth in the *Pañcakrama*, elaborating on many of the same issues and also clarifying the broader context within which the five stages are to be understood. For ease of comprehension, the following chart demonstrates the correlation of the eleven chapters of the CMP to the five chapters of the *Pañcakrama*.

CMP chapter	PK chapter
1. Awakening (sudden or gradual)	
2. Body Isolation	(Globule Stage)
3. Speech Isolation	1. Vajra Recitation Stage
4. Mind Isolation	2. Universally Pure Stage
5. Consequences of Action (karma)	
6. Superficial Reality	3. Self-consecration Stage
7. Ultimate Reality	4. Enlightenment Stage
8. Communion	5. Communion Stage
9. Practice with Elaboration	
10. Practice without Elaboration	
11. Practice completely w/o Elaboration	

The relationship of these two works is thus extremely close, though the

118. These include the *Śmaśāna-vidhi* (Tōh. 1807: *Ro sreg pa'i cho ga*) and the *Pradīpoddyotana-nāma-ṭīkā* (Tōh. 1794: *sGron ma gsal ba zhes bya ba'i 'grel bshad*).

CMP is more comprehensive in its scope. The central theme of both works is the same, and the CMP cites many of the same authoritative scriptures of the Esoteric Community literature as PK in the same pedagogical contexts. This is especially evident in the correspondence between the first chapter (*vajrajāpakrama*) of PK and the third chapter (*vāgviveka-saṃśaya-paricchedа*) of the CMP. It is important to note, however, that although the correspondences are great in terms of subject matter and structure, the CMP does not bill itself as a commentary on the PK.[119]

The title is interesting in this regard and bears some reflection. The final element is, I think, unproblematic. To call a śāstric text a lamp (*pradīpa*) is rather a cliché—such a work is a "lamp" in that it sheds needed light in areas of exegetical obscurity. The rest of the title is more difficult to unpack. What kind of a lamp is it? It is a lamp that is a *melāpaka*—a causative agentive form derived from the root √*mil*, "to meet." Thus, a *melāpaka* is one that causes things to meet or blend—that "integrates" disparate elements. The object of this verbal agent is *caryā*—usually a general term for religious practice, such as the "practices of a bodhisattva" (*bodhisattva-caryā*).

Taken in this generic sense, the CMP is a work that "sheds light" (*pradīpa*) on its subject by integrating all the various practices of the tradition it describes. This interpretation is fairly plausible, as the CMP does indeed take a comprehensive perspective on the practice of the Esoteric Community, presenting all the elements in their proper order with respect to one another and integrating them into one cohesive program. Thus, the CMP would be that work which synthesizes the entire span of religious praxis in this tradition.

However, there is another reading that I think is worth considering, and which better captures the distinctive contribution of the CMP to the system set forth in PK. For in the context of this tradition, *caryā* has a distinctive, restricted sense. The final three chapters of the CMP (chapters nine to eleven) are devoted to explaining and justifying a set of three types of practices in which the esoteric yogin sets out to experience an array of sensual pleasures in order to "destroy the vestiges of beginningless defilement"

119. Many detailed commentaries on the PK were written and are preserved in both Sanskrit and Tibetan translation (see notes 112 and 113, above). The thirteenth-century Tibetan commentator Bu-ston refers to the CMP as a "meaning commentary" (*don 'grel*) on the PK, and this is echoed in the writings of Tsongkhapa.

(CMP, f. 54a). Such practices—though generally taken as definitive of the "tantric" traditions—are not mentioned at all in PK. Thus, the *Lamp* may also be understood as a work that sheds light on the subject of the five stages (*pañca-krama*) by demonstrating the manner in which the three *caryā* (not mentioned in the PK) form an integral part of the overall approach to esoteric practice advocated by Nāgārjuna.

Though nowhere does the author reflect directly on the implication of this title, we can derive some information in this regard from the CMP itself. The term *melāpaka* appears in three contexts within the CMP: in chapters 1, 4, and 7. In the first instance, the word is used in the conventional declaration of intent to compose found at the beginning of most śāstras. Āryadeva writes that, in order to clarify the five stages, he will set forth a *sūtra-melāpaka*—a work that integrates scriptural citations.[120] The word is used again in chapter 4 (f. 29b) where, after giving a scriptural citation, Āryadeva writes that the "summary teaching" (*uddeśa*) contained in that passage will be followed by a *nirdeśa-melāpaka*—that is, by a teaching that includes the full instruction (*nirdeśa*). The final instance in which the term is employed comes at the end of chapter 7 (f. 48b), where its usage seems to be something like "introducing" something or "adding more"—in this context, adding more names to an extensive list of synonyms for the absolute.[121] Thus, all the occurrences seem to involve supplementing something with another thing: supplementing the explanations with scriptural citations, adding detail to a summary teaching, and extending a list of synonyms. If this analysis of Āryadeva's use of *melāpaka* is correct, it would seem to lend further warrant to interpreting the *caryā* of the title in the restricted sense.

One other possible source for guidance in grasping the meaning of the title is the commentary on the CMP attributed to Śākyamitra, which offers this interpretation: "'integrates the practices' [means it] abbreviates the practices, for fear of prolixity."[122] On this reading, the CMP would be

120. This use echoes the title of Nāgārjuna's sādhana cited above (p. 47). While the reading *sūtramelāpaka* is found in MS B, MS C reads *sūtaka-melāpaka*, which may correspond to TIB "<u>sū</u>tras, <u>ta</u>ntras, and ritual texts (<u>ka</u>lpa)." Indeed, the CMP is generally cited in Sanskrit works as the *Sūtaka*—the title *Caryāmelāpakapradīpa* is, to my knowledge, unattested.

121. The root √*mil* occurs one other time in the work: in the form *mīlanaṃ kṛtvā*, "having brought together" (CMP, f. 70b). This would seem to lend further support to this reading.

122. *spyod pa bsdus pa ni spyod pa nyung du byas pa ste | gzhung rgyas pas 'jigs pa'o |*; see Śākyamitra, *Spyod pa bsdus pa'i sgron ma zhes bya ba'i rgya cher bshad pa* (sDe-dge bsTan-'gyur, rGyud-'grel, vol. ci, 245a^2).

a work that condenses or abbreviates the teaching of the practices (presumably to be taken in the generic sense—the commentator does not elaborate on this). There are numerous difficulties with this reading. For one, the CMP is longer than the PK, not shorter—there is little ground on which to claim that it is at all meant to be a concise work; in fact, it appears quite the opposite. Furthermore, as I argue in more detail below in considering the Noble Tradition works of Śākyamitra,[123] this very gloss is one example of several indications in this work that lead me to the conclusion that this commentary is not what it claims to be: it is not of Indic origin. I doubt very much that *melāpaka* would or could be interpreted in this way in an Indic context. Its interpretation of the meaning of the title, thus, is rather suspect.

The CMP is accompanied in the Tibetan canons by three smaller works that appear as companion pieces, each dealing with one of the three median stages of the five: the *Citta-viśuddhi-prakaraṇa* (CVP: on the mental purification [*citta-viśuddhi*] or mind isolation [*citta-viveka*] stage), the *Svādhiṣṭhāna-prabheda* (S[K]P: on the self-consecration [*svādhiṣṭhana*] or phantasm body [*māyā-deha*] stage), and the *Abhisambodhi-kramopadeśa* (AKU: on the enlightenment [*abhisambodhi*] or brilliance [*prabhāsvara*] stage). There are many questionable features of these works that call into doubt the interrelationship of the comprehensive CMP and these three ancillary works. On the one hand, it appears highly likely that the author of the CMP was also the author of the S[K]P. The S[K]P is a systematic work in sixty verses dealing with issues concerning the phantasm body and the dissolution of the subtle mind into the brilliance.[124] The terminology used, the topics covered, and the deliberate argumentative style strike me as consonant with those found in the CMP.[125] The same may not be said, however, of the AKU and the CVP.

123. See below, pp. 57ff.

124. A detailed discussion of these yogas appears in the next section on the subject matter of the CMP. A provisional translation (based on the text published in *Dhīḥ*, vol. 10) may be found in Wedemeyer, "Vajrayāna and its Doubles," 383–91.

125. It is noteworthy that the S[K]P refers to the CMP. The S[K]P refers the reader to the *Sūtaka* as a source for the teaching of the hundred buddha clans. The CMP is frequently referred to in Sanskrit commentarial literature by this name; and this is reflected in the fact that the Tibetan translators of the S[K]P rendered the term *Sūtaka* by *sPyod bsdus*—the typical Tibetan abbreviation of the *Caryāmelāpaka[pradīpa]*. It is not unlikely that the author of such interrelated treatises would have revised them together and added suitable

The CVP is an interesting case, as this work—the first published esoteric work attributed to Āryadeva—has accordingly since been taken as definitive of "Tantric Āryadeva." This work is cited again and again in works on Buddhist Tantrism—A. L. Basham having gone so far as to have it stand as an exemplar not merely of Āryadeva, but of Buddhist Tantrism as a whole.[126] The CVP is, however, a highly idiosyncratic text, more in the nature of a compendium than a deliberate work on esoteric practice.[127] It does not treat of the mind isolation stage as presented in the CMP, but a wide range of general esoteric themes, chiefly the nature of the mind and the general tantric theme of forbidden acts as vehicles for liberation.[128] Its polyvocality was noted early on by Louis de La Vallée Poussin, who commented on his surprise in finding sloppy and unprofessional verses rubbing elbows with some that are quite elegant.[129] This inchoate and inconsistent quality contrasts sharply with the composition of the CMP and the S[K]P. These latter are coherent, well written, and deliberately argued. Hence, though it is attributed to Āryadeva by several traditional authorities,[130] I do not think it can be rightly taken as sharing the same author as the CMP.

The AKU is even more dubious than the CVP.[131] For one, it is not widely accepted by traditional authorities as an authentic work of Āryadeva. Tsongkhapa, for instance, writes that:

> Concerning the claim that this teacher [Āryadeva] composed the *Abhibodhi-kramopadeśa*, the [earlier] Tibetan scholars say

cross-references so as to make them easier to use in concert. One may compare, in this regard, the inter-referentiality of Abhayākaragupta's *Vajrāvalī* and *Niṣpannayogāvalī*.

126. See W. T. deBary, ed., *The Buddhist Tradition*, 118–20.

127. Indeed, its manuscript was catalogued under the title "Collection of Buddhist Verses" (*Bauddhaśloka-saṃgraha*). Evidently, the cataloguer also felt it to be a diffuse work.

128. A provisional translation of the CVP may be found in Wedemeyer, "Vajrayāna and its Doubles," 357–82.

129. See L. de La Vallée Poussin, "À propos du Cittaviśuddhiprakaraṇa d'Āryadeva," 414.

130. Tsongkhapa, for instance, notes that the authenticity of the CVP is seemingly vouched for by the fact that it is cited as such by the famous Indian Buddhist author Abhayākaragupta, though he evidently has lingering doubts on the issue. See RṄSG. f. 29a[1–2].

131. A provisional translation of the AKU may be found in Wedemeyer, "Vajrayāna and its Doubles," 392–98.

> that it seems to be rather dubious; [and] as it seems to disagree greatly with the *Caryā-melāpaka-pradīpa*, it is a fake.[132]

It is not entirely clear to me how he believes that the *Abhibodhi-kramopadeśa* contradicts the CMP (there are a number of possibilities, but Tsongkhapa does not spell them out here), yet it is undeniably a rather suspicious text. For one, it too lacks the clarity and cohesion of the CMP and the S[K]P. Furthermore, there is the curious fact that the CMP cites two verses also found in the AKU, though it does not mention this work by name. These verses are cited at the beginning of the seventh chapter of the CMP (which itself concerns the *abhibodhi-krama*). Āryadeva does not specifically note the source of the verses, introducing them as found in "scriptural discourse" (*deśanā-pāṭha*). As he uses this term elsewhere,[133] it seems to apply exclusively to revealed scriptures, not to śāstric treatises. Hence, it seems likely that these verses are not Āryadeva's own composition (in the AKU) later cited by him in the CMP, or he would not attribute them to scripture. The AKU also features eight unmarked verses that are drawn from the GST. As in general Āryadeva (both in the prose CMP and the verse S[K]P) is quite consistent in marking verses that are not his own,[134] the presence of unmarked citations in the AKU speaks against the notion that the Noble Āryadeva was its author. It seems more likely that the AKU—like the CVP—is a composite work, though (unlike the CVP) it does seem fairly consistently to treat of themes associated with the Noble Tradition presentation of the enlightenment stage.[135]

The Works of Nāgabodhi, Śākyamitra, and Candrakīrti

Supplementing these seminal works of Nāgārjuna and Āryadeva are the writings of three other putative disciples of Nāgārjuna: Nāgabodhi,

132. Tsongkhapa, f. 29a$^{2-3}$: *mngon par byang chub pa'i rim pa slob dpon 'dis mdzad zer ba la | bod kyi mkhas pa dag the tshom gyi gzhir snang gsung ba ltar spyod bsdus dang mi mthun pa chen po snang bas kha g.yar ro.*

133. See CMP, ff. 2a, 26b, 35b, 40b, and 54a.

134. The same may be said of Nāgārjuna, who is careful in the PK to mark verses cited from other sources.

135. Though some of the systematic statements seem to suggest a later commentarial hand than the early Nobles such as Nāgārjuna and Āryadeva.

Śākyamitra, and Candrakīrti. Of these, the first and last are of particular importance given the authority in which their works are held by subsequent commentators. The major works of Nāgabodhi and Candrakīrti stand alongside the PK and CMP as essential reference points for the tradition. The two works attributed to Śākyamitra, on the other hand, exert a mixed influence—one being authoritative (though not universally attributed to him) and the other (quite rightly) generally considered spurious by indigenous critics.

Nāgabodhi is a writer of great importance in the Noble Tradition. If Āryadeva's contribution to an understanding of the *Esoteric Community Tantra* may be said to focus on the perfection stage, Nāgabodhi has made a similar contribution with regard to the creation stage. His most influential works on the Esoteric Community are the *Maṇḍala Rite Twenty* (*Śrī-guhyasamāja-maṇḍalopāyikā-viṃśati-vidhi-nāma*)—which describes the initiation ritual—and a work on creation stage meditation entitled *Arranged Stages of the Community Sādhana* (*Samājasādhana-vyavastholi-krama*). This latter work, in particular, has had tremendous influence in the tradition. It describes the processes of birth, death, and the between state, and the way in which the sādhana transforms the ordinary forms of these processes into the emanation of a divine form. In so doing, it provides an alternative perspective on the yogic processes also described in the CMP, spelling out in greater detail much of the background knowledge Āryadeva assumes in his readers.[136]

In addition to these works, there are two commentaries on the *Pañca-krama* attributed to Nāgabodhi, both of which, however, are considered apocryphal by most later commentators. These are the *Five Stages Commentary called "Jewel Rosary"*[137] and the *Clarification of the Meaning of the Five Stages*.[138] The Tibetan canons also preserve a curious work entitled *Instruc-*

136. See below, "Nature and Purpose of the Work," for my own attempt to spell out some of these presuppositions (minus Nāgabodhi's discussion of embryology). Yael Bentor has been working on later Tibetan interpretations of the *Arranged Stages*, which work should be forthcoming shortly.

137. *Nor bu'i 'phreng-ba*; a commentary on PK, called *Pañcakrama-ṭīkā-maṇimālā-nāma* (Pek. 2697, Tōh. 1840). Bu-ston, however, seems to accept this work at least as authentic in his *History of Buddhism*. Cf. Obermiller, trans., 132.

138. *Don gsal*; another work on PK: the *Pañcakramārtha-bhāskaraṇa-nāma* (Pek. 2702, Tōh. 1833)

tion on Nesting the Stages that is also attributed to Nāgabodhi.[139] This brief discourse attempts to demonstrate that each of the five stages of Nāgārjuna's system contains each of the others, thus subdividing each by five, yielding twenty-five stages. There is some dispute about the authorship of this text also, and some Tibetans suggest it may have been composed by another author by the name of Nāgabodhi.[140]

Candrakīrti's primary contribution to the literature of the Esoteric Community is his extremely influential commentary on the GST, the *Six-parameter Commentary on the Esoteric Community, called "Illumination of the Lamp"* (*Guhyasamājatantra-pradīpoddyotana-nāma-ṭīkā-ṣatkoṭivyākhyā*: PU).[141] This work is held in high esteem by the later tradition, as it is the highest authority that elaborates on the interpretative procedures of the Esoteric traditions. It is also of great significance for modern scholarship, as it is the only commentary on the GST to have survived in its original Sanskrit. In the prologue to this commentary, Candrakīrti further develops the hermeneutical model of "six parameters" and "four methods" for interpreting the esoteric scriptures that was first set out in the explanatory tantra, the *Gnosis Vajra Compendium*.[142] After detailing the various categories of statements made in the esoteric texts, Candrakīrti then parses the text of the *Esoteric Community Tantra*, indicating which statements are to be taken in which sense(s). He then comments at length on the Tantra, unpacking its meaning through gloss and paraphrase, while also providing a wealth of information on the ritual forms alluded to in the work.

It is not quite clear where to place Śākyamitra in regard to the Noble Tradition. Aside from the works attributed to him in the Tibetan canons, the tradition has little to offer in the way of information about his personality,

139. *Rim pa khongs su bsdu ba*; the *Kramāntarbhāvopadeśa-nāma-prakaraṇa* (Pek. 2677, Tōh. 1812).

140. Tsongkhapa (RṄSG, f. 30a[1–2]) attributes this theory to Chag Lotsāwa.

141. There are two other works on the Esoteric Community attributed to Candrakīrti which, however, are not in general accepted as authentic by later Tibetan tradition: a *Vajrasattva Sādhana* (*rDo rje sems dpa'i sgrub thabs*, Tōh. 1814) and an *Esoteric Community Ornament of Realizations Commentary* (*gSang ba 'dus pa'i mngon par rtogs pa'i rgyan gyi 'grel pa*, Tōh. 1817). The former is quite an interesting piece, though traditional authors (Tsongkhapa and A-myes-zhabs among others) believe it contradicts the sādhana as set out by Nāgārjuna. According to A-myes-zhabs (*gSang 'dus chos 'byung*, f. 18b), Sa-skya Paṇḍita (1182–1251) suggested that it might have been composed by a "Candrakīrti II."

142. See above, p. 44.

such that he seems rather a shadowy character whom even traditional sources consider somewhat marginal. As noted above, the colophon of the second chapter of the PK, the *Unexcelled Intention*, ascribes its authorship to him. This issue sparked quite a bit of controversy in later periods. Butön, for example, tried to argue for Nāgārjuna's authorship of this chapter by suggesting that "Śākyamitra" was perhaps Nāgārjuna's ordination name.[143] Tsongkhapa, seemingly dissatisfied with this approach, suggests that the *Unexcelled Intention* was written partially by Nāgārjuna and partially by his disciple Śākyamitra.[144] He further mentions a number of discussions regarding this by a range of commentators—all of whom, it seems, felt this issue demanded resolution.[145]

Other than the chapter of the PK attributed to him, there is only one work of his on the Esoteric Community—a partial commentary on the CMP (chapters one to eight). This work, called the *Extensive Explanation of the "Lamp for Integrating the Practices"* (*Spyod pa bsdus pa'i sgron ma zhes bya ba'i rgya cher bshad pa*), is (to my knowledge) not accepted as authentic by any classical authority. Tsongkhapa is quite straightforward: "the commentary on the CMP attributed to Śākyamitra might possibly be by some author of a similar name, but if it is supposed to be the Śākyamitra [who was a] disciple of the Noble [Nāgārjuna], it is definitely not his work."[146] Jamgön Amey Zhab is equally terse in his assessment. He says:

> Of the four Heart Sons [of Nāgārjuna], the one called "Śākya

143. See Obermiller, trans., *History of Buddhism*, 129–30.

144. In this, he may be following a tradition mentioned by A-myes-zhabs, who cites a passage from 'Gos, author of the *Survey of the Esoteric Community* (*gSang dus stong thun*), that "Up to 'you will certainly be liberated from the prison of existence' was composed by the Master Nāgārjuna, after 'this nature of wisdom' is Śākyamitra's supplement and he put his name at the end of the second stage of the Five Stages." (Cf. A-myes, *gSang 'dus chos 'bung*, f. 17b) If we credit this tradition, this would make verses 1–44 of PK II the work of Nāgārjuna and verses 45–87 that of Śākyamitra. It is interesting in light of this that Āryadeva's work does not cite any verses from PK II after verse 44.

145. According to Tsongkhapa (RṄSG, ff. 27b¹–28b³), Rin-chen bzang-po felt that all five texts were composed by Nāgārjuna. Chag Lotsāwa avoided the issue (of which five were the "five stages") by translating all five as separate texts. Abhaya and Samayavajra hold that the *Unexcelled Intention* is by Śākyamitra, and that the *Condensed Sādhana* is the first of the five stages. It is worth noting that the multi-work Sanskrit MS C, from which the CMP was herein edited, contains the *Unexcelled Intention* as a separate work.

146. Tsongkhapa, RṄSG, f. 30a⁶–30b¹.

> bShes-gnyen," or "Śākyamitra," is the author of the second stage of the *Five Stages*, as demonstrated above. . . . The "Śākyamitra" who composed a commentary on the *Lamp for Integrating the Practices* is not the same.[147]

My own reading of this text suggests that the situation is rather more dramatic than these traditional authors maintain. I believe that this commentary, though included in the Tibetan canon as a translation of an allegedly authentic Indian work, was in fact composed by a Tibetan and passed off as an Indic translation. In brief, as we have noted above, the explanation of the title of the CMP given in this commentary suggests that the author was working in an exclusively Tibetan medium. It states, "'integrates the practices' [means it] abbreviates the practices, for fear of prolixity."[148] I believe what we see here is not a Sanskritophone author commenting on the term *melāpaka*, but rather a Tibetophone author explaining the meaning of its Tibetan counterpart, the term *bsdus*, which serves to render more than one Sanskrit term. In one of its meanings (the one explicitly referenced by the author of the commentary), *bsdus* means "the opposite of vast."[149] This is not a viable meaning of *melāpaka*, however, which corresponds to another of the meanings of *bsdus*, to wit "to come or approach together, to meet, to interlace."[150] That this is the case is further confirmed by the erroneous Sanskrit title given in the Tibetan "translation." It reads *Carya-samucchaya-pradīpaṃ-ṭīkā* (*sic*). Of course, *samuccaya* does not mean "abbreviated" either, but it is one of the most common Sanskrit equivalencies for Tibetan *bsdus*, suggesting that the title was concocted by a Tibetan without (or without much) knowledge of Sanskrit. Consequently, the commentary on the CMP attributed to Śākyamitra may be fairly confidently classified as a

147. A-myes-zhabs, *gSang 'dus chos 'byung*. f. 41b$^{1-4}$: *yang thugs sras bzhi'i shā kya bshes gnyen nam shā kya mi tra ni gong du bstan pa ltar rim lnga'i rim pa gnyis pa mdzad mkhan de yin* | . . . | *yang spyod bsdus la 'grel pa mdzad mkhan gyi shā kya bshes gnyen bya ba gcig byung ba de yang 'di dang mi gcig cing* |.

148. *spyod pa bsdus pa ni spyod pa nyung du byas ba ste* | *gzhung rgyas pas 'jigs pa'o* |: see sDe-dge bsTan-'gyur, rGyud-'grel, vol. ci, 245a^{2}.

149. rgyas pa'i ldog phyogs: Yisun Zhang, *Tshig-mdzod chen-mo*, 1489.

150. 'dzoms par byed pa: Zhang, *Tshig mdzod chen mo*, 1470; English definition of *'dzom pa* cited from Candra Das, 1056.

Tibetan work to which has been attributed Indic origins and authorship.[151] Hence, excepting the possibility of his authorship (or partial authorship) of the second chapter of the *Pañcakrama*, no other works of the relevant Śākyamitra on the Noble Tradition have come down to us.

The *Lamp for Integrating the Practices* and its Subject Matter

With this broad overview of the major authors of the tradition and their most important writings in mind, let us turn now to a detailed examination of the contents of the CMP. At first, I aim to give a brief résumé of the main presuppositions and doctrines of the work—the necessary background to understanding the discussions found therein. Then, I give a thumbnail sketch of the work, briefly summarizing the purport of each chapter. Finally, I explore each chapter in depth, restating their arguments in a current English idiom and identifying some of the "hot button" issues of the text, both in its original context and with respect to the modern study of Buddhism. It is to be hoped that this will allow readers unfamiliar with the terms and rhetorical style of esoteric Buddhist treatises to understand and appreciate the translation that follows.

Nature and Purpose of the Work

At its most general level, the CMP seeks to elucidate the stages of Esoteric Community practice through an unpacking in prose of the details presented in brief, versified form in the *Pañcakrama*, while simultaneously drawing attention to passages from authoritative scriptural sources that (ostensibly) teach (and thus validate) these various points. In addition to the added detail, the CMP also analyzes the structure of the Noble Tradition path in a way slightly divergent from that found in the PK. As previously noted, the Noble Tradition as a whole makes three major claims: a) that enlightenment is only possible through the practice of the Esoteric Community; b) that essential teachings of this tradition are only to be found in the explanatory tantras; and c) that these practices entail a gradual process of enlightenment. The CMP makes all of these claims and more. The major

151. I have argued this point at greater length in "On the Authenticity of the *Caryāmelapakapradīpa Commentary* Attributed to Śākyamitra."

arguments of the CMP (many of which overlap with the PK) are: a) the fivefold process (*pañca-krama*) can only be interpreted as a gradual path, not a sudden attainment; b) that the five stages can be further analyzed into a sixfold schema (of "three isolations," "two realities," and communion); and c) that essential to the path of enlightenment are three types of practice involving the ritual enjoyment of sense pleasures.[152] Before exploring these points in detail, let us first consider some of the presuppositions shared by the Noble Tradition authors.

The Noble Tradition, as a school of Buddhist teaching, advocates its yogas as a method for attaining enlightenment (*bodhi, nirvāṇa*). Thus, it is predicated on the basic Buddhist teaching that the life-cycle (*saṃsāra*) is unsatisfactory, and that one should seek liberation (*mokṣa*) from this cycle of suffering and rebirth. As a tradition that follows the Universal Way (Mahāyāna), the Nobles advocate as the ideal mode of this enlightenment, not a pursuit of individual freedom, but the messianic goal of acting as a savior for all beings. As a school of the esoteric Adamantine Way (Vajrayāna), the Nobles further accept its critique of the exoteric Universal Way: that, although it may not be deficient in the accumulation of gnosis (*jñāna-sambhāra*) that leads to the attainment of the (self)liberated reality body of a buddha (*dharma-kāya*), it does not provide a suitable technique for the perfection of the accumulation of merit (*puṇya-sambhāra*) that yields an other-oriented, palpable form body (*rūpa-kāya*) through which to act for the benefit of others. It is precisely a technique of this latter sort that is advocated by the Noble Tradition.

The method for doing this is predicated on the notion that the production of a buddha's form body comes about through the selfsame processes by which an unenlightened being takes rebirth in a new, ordinary body after death. Thus, in advocating their esoteric yogas, the Nobles advance a comprehensive understanding of the ordinary death and rebirth process that, they assert, may be redirected to the production of a divine form. Central to this understanding is the notion that all beings emerge from, and periodically return to, a fundamental, enlightenment-like state of nonduality called the "brilliance" (*prabhāsvara*).[153] Due to their karma,

152. On this last point, the reader is encouraged to consult Wedemeyer, *Making Sense of Tantric Buddhism*, chapter 5.

153. In most modern works on Buddhist esoterism, this is called the "clear light" (a

however, unenlightened beings do not rest in this state, but are driven to evolve into coarse forms. This evolution is said to follow the pattern of the evolution of the external universe: from the fundamental brilliance evolve in series three levels of the subtle mind, which subsequently coarsen further through re-involvement with the subtle elements. That is, consciousness, having evolved through the levels of the subtle mind—called brilliance, imminence, radiance, and luminance—thereupon, as in the process of the formation of the cosmos, gradually reintegrates with coarser and coarser levels of the material world beginning with the "subtle element" air, and proceeding through fire, water, and earth.[154] Thereupon, the being is fully reintegrated with the coarse world in a new rebirth.

Upon death, this process is reversed. The elements of the dying person's body gradually "dissolve" their connection to its subtle consciousness: earth into water, water into fire, fire into air. The subtle consciousnesses then dawn and evolve in reverse order: luminance into radiance, radiance into imminence, imminence into brilliance. At this point, due to karmic imprints, the consciousness re-evolves through the same process into a subtle body of the between state (*antarābhava*)[155] that reflects the karmic instincts of the person. This body is composed only of subtle material, thus approximating a kind of "spirit" form that can pass through ordinary matter. Such a being is also believed to have supernatural powers of sense perception and travel. After a brief period in this state, while awaiting the necessary conditions to take concrete rebirth, the being again experiences the death process—that is, the between-being dies—and again experiences the evolution process, culminating in concrete rebirth.[156]

---

translation of the Tibetan term *'od gsal*). This is a nondual state in that there is said to be no distinction between subject and object or between mind and matter at this most subtle level of reality.

154. These four elements add motility, warmth, cohesion, and solidity (respectively) to the newly created organism.

155. This doctrine, though of long Indian Buddhist pedigree, is also better known today by its Tibetan moniker, the "Bardo."

156. A description of this process is found the CMP (chapter 4: f. 35a): "Having further abandoned their body by the process of entering the ultimate reality maṇḍala, one is taken up by the air-element, bound to feeling, trailing along behind craving, fallen from the realm of reality, seized by recollection, bound to attend to virtue and non-virtue, like a child of five or six years seeing all, nourished by scents, undaunted by vajras, and so on, endowed with all the marks, and moving with the speed of action and miracle (*ṛddhi*). After seven days,

The Noble Tradition's system of yoga involves the conscious redirection of this process (normally under the unconscious direction of karmic imprints) toward rebirth in the form body of an enlightened being. First, however, the aspiring yogin must develop familiarity with what the process should ideally look like, by means of visualization exercises. This is called the creation stage (*utpatti-krama, bskyed rim*), in which the practitioner follows the ritual form meant to create the divine body, but does not actually intervene in the subtle processes of death and rebirth.[157] In so doing, they simulate dying as a coarse person and resting in the state of brilliance (thus approximating the experience of attainment of a buddha's reality body [*dharma-kāya*]). They then visualize their emergence into a between-state form (simulating a buddha's attainment of a beatific body [*sambhoga-kāya*]), later dissolving this and re-emerging as an emanated body (*nirmāṇa-kāya*) through which they may interact with beings, guiding them toward enlightenment.

This ideal template is meant to be actualized in what is called the perfection stage (*niṣpanna-krama, rdzogs rim*), the main topic of the PK and CMP, wherein the subtle fabric of the universe is reconfigured to effect in actuality what had previously been imagined. The mastery of this process is said to develop through several stages. Here, we will follow the schema advanced by Āryadeva in the CMP, which is more elaborate than that presented in the PK. His presentation involves six processes: three isolations, two realities, and the final stage of communion.[158]

The three isolations are: body isolation, speech isolation, and mind isolation (*kāya-*, *vāg-*, and *citta-viveka*). The first is considered by Āryadeva to be a part of the creation stage, not the perfection stage. In brief, this practice involves the cultivation of the insight that the entire world is not the unenlightened place we think it is, but the unfolding of a cosmic play entirely

---

standing in the interval between rebirths, when impelled by the good and evil actions born from their own conceptuality and having met with the proper causes and conditions, that one takes rebirth in the five realms again and again."

157. As such, the creation stage is sometimes referred to as the "imaginative yoga" (*kalpita-yoga*).

158. It is worth noting the compression implicit in this structure (not, however, commented upon by any traditional authors) that seems to mimic similar themes in the literature (i.e., the assimilation of the hundred clans into five, three, and one). Here, the three isolations (body, speech, and mind) are assimilated into two realities (body and mind) that are finally unified in the attainment of communion.

composed of enlightened beings. Thus, it is integral to the esoteric practice of the creation stage, that seeks to develop the "divine pride" of oneself as an "always already" enlightened being. The speech and mind isolations involve primarily the mastery of two interrelated sets of skills necessary for the perfection stage practices. Speech isolation is largely devoted to recognizing and controlling the subtle vital airs—five airs that regulate bodily functions, and five others that are the physical counterpart to sensory processes. The control of these airs is a vital key to activating the processes of death and rebirth and thus form part of the basic skill set of an esoteric Buddhist yogin. Mind isolation focuses on the subjective aspect of the vital airs: what are called the prototypes and radiances. The three radiances (*ābhāsa-traya*, also called the three consciousnesses, *vijñāna-traya*) are the levels of the subtle mind mentioned above—luminance, radiance, and imminence—that prefigure the dawning of the subtlest mind of brilliance. The prototypes (*prakṛti*) are basic behavioral and psychological patternings encoded in these levels of the subtle mind. By developing the ability to identify when these prototypes are active, the yogin is enabled to identify with accuracy what level of the subtle mind is operative, thus maintaining awareness throughout the dissolution (and re-evolution) process.[159]

Having attained skill in manipulating the vital airs of the subtle body and gaining familiarity with the architecture of the subtle mind, the yogin then puts these skills to use in mastering two attainments, called the two realities (*satya-dvaya*). In essence, this involves the creation of enlightened body and mind. The first reality, superficial reality (*saṃvṛti-satya*), is sometimes asserted to be the central teaching of the *Esoteric Community Tantra*: how to produce "a deity body from mere gnosis" (CMP, f. 41a). This process is also called the self-consecration (*svādhiṣṭhāna*), the phantasmic samādhi (*māyopama-samādhi*), or the phantasm body (*māyā-deha*). The second reality, ultimate reality (*paramārtha-satya*), also called the "reality limit" (*bhūta-koṭi*), involves guiding one's vital airs and mind through the stages of dissolution, such that one may experience the fundamental brilliance mind without actually dying. This is considered to be tantamount to a personal liberation—the accomplishment of the actual mind of a buddha. A passive enlightened being, however, is of no soteric use to beings and thus

159. It is maintained that the radiances are not perceptible directly, thus they must be identified by inference from the functioning of their corresponding prototypes. On this, see CMP chapter 4 (f. 32b).

anathema to Buddhists of the Universal Way. Hence, the final process of communion (*yuganaddha*) involves uniting the two realities (as object and subject, body and mind) into a comprehensive enlightened embodiment—arising out of the brilliance through the self-consecration process into the fully enlightened form of a world-teaching buddha.

In addition to this yogic process, the CMP is distinctive in that it devotes considerable space to analyzing and describing what it calls the "practices" (*caryā*), the "practices of spiritual discipline" (*vrata-caryā*), or the "consort discipline" (*vidyā-vrata*).[160] Āryadeva categorizes the practices into three sorts: those with elaboration (*prapañcatā*), without elaboration (*niṣprapañcatā*), and completely without elaboration (*atyanta-niṣprapañcatā*). In brief, these three involve the systematic experience of sensual pleasures in order to consummate the enlightenment experience by eradicating the vestigial instincts (*vāsanā*) of the defiled, unenlightened state.

Structure of the Work

The text is composed in eleven chapters, each of which is called a *saṃśaya-pariccheda*, or removal of doubts, concerning the integration of a given stage or aspect of esoteric practice within the overall schema of the Nāgārjunian system. The first chapter is devoted to a general removal of doubts about the nature of enlightenment—whether it is to be understood as a "sudden" or a "gradual" attainment. The next three chapters deal with problematic points relating to the stages of body isolation, speech isolation, and mind isolation. There then follows a chapter concerning the "Consequences of Action (*karmānta*)," in which the processes of death—the central focus of yogic intervention in the Buddhist esoteric traditions—are explained and clarified. The sequence of stages is then resumed with two chapters detailing the nature of the two realities, the superficial and the ultimate—or the phantasm body and brilliance. The eighth chapter describes the coalescence of these into a divine body of communion. There then follow three concluding chapters that explain the details of and legitimation for each of the three "practices."

The work is cast in the form of a dialogue: a series of questions being

160. For detailed discussion of the theorization of these practices in the wider Tantric traditions, see Wedemeyer, *Making Sense of Tantric Buddhism*, chapter 5.

posed by a Vajra Student (*vajra-śiṣya*) to his Vajra Mentor (*vajra-guru*).[161] In this regard, the CMP is rather typical of Indic treatises (*śāstras*) that are often structured in this way. However, in this case, the Vajra Mentor in the CMP may be intended as more than just a stock character. It may in fact be intended to represent—not a generic guru—but Nāgārjuna himself, with the Vajra Student presumably representing Āryadeva. I advance this as a possible interpretation as, at the beginning of chapter 6, the Vajra Student refers to his teacher as Venerable Master (*bhaṭṭāraka-pāda*; CMP, f. 40a)—a term that elsewhere in the CMP is used only to refer to Nāgārjuna.[162]

The work begins with some prefatory discussion, setting the composition of the work within the development of esoteric literature as seen by the author. The basic claim being made (which, as with all the following discussion in this section, will be more elaborately treated in the subsequent section) is that Āryadeva's work is unusual in presenting its topics in explicit, clear terms (*uttāna-śabda*). He claims that previous teachers did not need to present the subject so, as they could rely on their students to be of such high quality that they could learn the tradition based on cryptic expressions (*nigūḍha-śabda*). Āryadeva observes that they could do so, since they lived in earlier, purer times. Writing in the final, degenerate Age of Contention (*kali-yuga*), Āryadeva must be more direct in his presentation, as he cannot rely on the virtue and intelligence of his readers.

Thereafter, the first chapter is devoted to arguing for gradualism in esoteric practice. After an initial excursus on the nature of "Reality" (*tattva*) that adumbrates the later discussion of the communion of the two realities, the Vajra Student inquires whether the esoteric path of the Adamantine Way is "sudden" or "gradual." In addressing this question, Āryadeva takes his stand firmly in the camp of gradualists; though, as is perhaps typical of the Buddhist tradition of this era, the "sudden/gradual" problem is here resolved by reference to an "instantaneous" purification at the end of the "gradual" process. In so doing, he enumerates the sequential stages of the gradual path of the Nobles. Chapter 1 concludes with a claim of the unique efficacy of this tradition as a means to enlightenment.

The second chapter elucidates the teaching of body isolation. The intent here is to erode the instinctual sense of the reality of the ordinary body and

161. All the questions posed by the Vajra Student are abstracted and listed in Appendix V.
162. CMP, ff. 39b and 51b.

to establish instead that all the inner and outer elements are in fact constituted (*adhiṣṭhita*) of the Five Transcendent Lords (*pañca-tathāgata*). To this end, the Vajra Mentor reminds his Student of the Buddha's teaching that the body has no real existence—that it is merely a "heap" or "accumulation" of various substances. He asserts that the reason they perdure in such a manner is through "ordinary pride"—that type of ego-function by which a practitioner identifies with her ordinary, limited form, thereby alienating her from what the esoteric schools consider her fundamental, divine, enlightened nature (and the responsibilities associated therewith).

The task for the Student at this stage is to learn to recognize the world, him/herself, and all beings as composed of buddhas (*buddha-maya*)—that the very stuff of reality is holy and pure, in line with the esoteric doctrine that, as a central mantra puts it, "all things are intrinsically pure, I am intrinsically pure."[163] To this end, the Master teaches what becomes known as the doctrine of the hundred clans. In short, the elements of reality (as analyzed by the Buddhist *abhidharma*)—the five aggregates, the four elements (both as interior and exterior), the six sense media, the five sensory airs, and the gnoses—are all subdivided into five and correlated with the Five Transcendent Lords: Akṣobhya, Vairocana, Amitābha, Ratnasambhava, and Amoghasiddhi.[164] In this way, the Student learns to view him/herself as inhabiting a divine body "composed of the fine atoms of all transcendent lords" (CMP, ff. 7b, 14a). The Mentor then teaches the manner in which these hundred are assimilated to five clans, three clans, and one clan, and clarifies the nature of the creation of a vajra body.

The third and fourth chapters detail the speech and mind isolations in which these, too, are isolated from the ordinary appearances privileged by ordinary pride. The former consists primarily of the advanced esoteric practice of vitality control (*prāṇāyāma*), the yoga of the vital airs, by which a practitioner is able to access the subtle levels of the body/mind complex. The latter chapter describes the fundamental nature of mind, free of its modifications, and, most importantly, constitutes an extremely influential discussion of the architecture of the subtle mind: the doctrine of the three radiances (*ābhāsa*) and the eighty prototypes (*prakṛti*). In this context,

163. *Oṃ svabhāva-śuddhāḥ sarvadharmāḥ svabhāva-śuddho 'ham.*

164. A complete chart of these correspondences, based on chapter 2 of the CMP, can be found in Appendix III.

Āryadeva describes in some detail the processes of death, the between, and rebirth.

The Mentor notes that speech isolation is "not the sphere of those who practice the creation stage," signaling that it is this point in the process that marks the boundary between the creation and perfection stages. He notes that the techniques he is about to describe—"air reality," the practice of *prāṇāyāma*—must be mastered in order to attain speech isolation, or "mantra reality." He explains the yoga of the subtle airs and enumerates the names and functions of the five vital and the five sensory airs. The chapter concludes with a discussion of the power of mantras and the qualities of the yogin who abides in this speech-vajra samādhi.

Chapter 4 addresses the nature of and progress through the next stage, that of mind isolation. Here, the Mentor urges the Student to seek the nature of his own mind. To begin with, he teaches him about the nature of the mind according to general Buddhist notions, drawing on scriptures such as the *Journey to Laṅka* and the *Enquiry of Bhadrapāli*. This is basically an evolution of the teaching found in Buddhist literature from its earliest strata—that the mind is fundamentally brilliance (*prabhāsvara*), merely obscured by adventitious defilements.[165] As the Mentor says, "the scriptures of the Universal Vehicle teach that consciousness has no color, no characteristics, and no shape, being mere self-aware gnosis." That is the ultimate nature of mind. To know its superficial nature, however, one needs to consult esoteric tantras such as the *Esoteric Community*. The Mentor then presents the crucial conception of the creation of beings from the fundamental brilliance mind through the stages of imminence, radiance, luminance, air, fire, water, and earth—and their subsequent dissolution in reverse order during the death process. The Mentor gives the important characteristics of these states of mind—in particular the "three radiances" (luminance, radiance, and imminence)—and completely enumerates the eighty prototypes (*prakṛti*) that are correlated with these states. As the Mentor assures his Student, "the yogin who understands the categories of the appearance of the prototypes and their air-mounts will know the fluctuation of the mental activities of all sentient beings of the past, present, and future" (CMP, f. 33b–34a). That is, if one understands the "science" of the subtle mind, one has penetrated the functioning of the life-cycle and will gain the omni-

165. See, e.g., *Aṅguttara Nikāya* I.10.

science of enlightenment. The chapter ends with a discussion of how these airs and minds function to create the processes of death, the between, and rebirth.

This discussion leads quite naturally into the topic of chapter 5, which is a short digression on the issue of the "Consequences of Action"—that is, on the question of how a purified mental body (as advocated in the Tantras) can be produced by the very same processes that result in an ordinary body bound by karma. The Mentor begins by explaining the ten paths of non-virtuous action in a quite conventional manner. He then explains that the one who has realized mind isolation does not become involved in the creation of either virtuous or non-virtuous action. A number of scriptural sources are cited in support of this perspective.

Chapters 6 and 7 go on to discuss the two realities: the superficial and the ultimate. The Vajra Student observes that the processes described up to this point do not result in the creation of an actual divine body, only facsimiles thereof. He seeks to learn the special procedure through which one can create an actual deity body from mere gnosis—the teaching known as "divinity reality"—which even tenth-stage bodhisattvas of the exoteric tradition do not know. An operative question here is how, given the common Buddhist idea that mind and body are interdependent, can a "divine body endowed with all marks such as hands and feet, and so on" (CMP, f. 40b) be created from mind alone. In response, the Mentor describes how a phantasmic divine body "with five-colored light rays and endowed with various qualities" emerges. He demonstrates the structural similarity of this process with that of ordinary transmigration. He also discusses the similarity of these with states of sleep and dream. He concludes by illustrating how the transcendent lords manipulate these processes in their divine activity, "[residing] for as long as the life-cycle lasts by means of the phantasmic samādhi" (CMP, f. 44a).

The subsequent chapter, which clarifies doubts about the "ultimate reality," describes the fundamental brilliance awareness (the "reality limit," *bhūta-koṭi*) in which the practitioner is said to immerse and purify the divine body created by the process of self-consecration. The focus here is on the mind so, at this point, having developed the ability to create an actual divine body, the practitioner again enacts becoming insubstantial and bodiless, via a process analogous with the dissolution process of death/apocalypse. There is an excellent description of a ritual procedure in which the

Student offers a "well-educated consort" and other offerings to the Mentor, praises him, and is then given a series of initiations and instructions that enable him to manifest the brilliance mind. After a brief comment on the "outer" and "inner" enlightenments—a recapitulation of the treatment of the radiances from previous chapters—the Mentor gives a long list of names used to refer to ultimate reality in general Buddhist discourse—in effect, identifying the achievement of this school with the common goals of the Buddhist traditions *in toto*. It is here, at the end of chapter 7, that Āryadeva gives an important description of the enlightenment of Buddha Śākyamuni. This enlightenment—which is reached also by the Vajra Student at this point in the text—is known as communion, which stage is described in the succeeding chapter.

Chapter 8, then, deals with the characteristics of the perfected state of communion, in which the phantasm body and the brilliance awareness are brought to final consummation. This attainment is also called the adamantine samādhi (*vajropama-samādhi*). The Mentor describes the final yogic emergence of the enlightened being in an:

> adamantine body—imperishable, free of impurity (*anāsrava*), free of the vestiges of all defilements, [with] mastery [of others] at will. Like a fish [leaping] out of water [or one] awakened [from] sleep, the proper form of the body of supreme joy is created. Because [it] is the nature of mind and body [it is called] 'Mahāvajradhara.' (CMP, f. 50b)

He cites numerous scriptural verses that characterize this perfected state —ultimately, of course, ineffable—and again enumerates a list of common Buddhist epithets applicable to this state.

Finally, chapters 9, 10, and 11 discuss the three types of esoteric practices commonly known as *caryā*: those with, without, or completely without elaborations—here taken to mean, not the ordinary mental fabrications found in exoteric Buddhist works, but the ritual accoutrements used in the rites. Āryadeva devotes one chapter to each of these types of practice. Though it is not explicit here, given the overall gradualist message, the placement of this discussion after the chapter on the enlightenment phase may suggest that Āryadeva considered the practices to be advanced techniques to be reserved for this virtuoso context. There are other strands in the Noble literature that also suggest that this might be the case;[166] however, there are some additional indications that suggest the opposite. Further research on this topic is clearly a desideratum.

Chapter 9 begins by noting that, for one who has attained this level of perfection, there is no distinction between meditation and non-meditation, or between an accomplisher, an accomplishment, and the accomplishing; that is, there is nothing to be done. However, even at this stage there still remain the vestiges of defilement. This notion is typical of Buddhist soteriology: although one may have eliminated the coarse manifestation of various defiled behaviors and thoughts, their subtle impress continues to afflict the practitioner until they, too, are eliminated. These impressions are called "vestiges," or "vestigial instincts" (*vāsanā*), and are sometimes analogized to the subtle lingering of scent in a perfume bottle after the perfume itself has been removed. The aim of engaging in "practices," then, seems to be the exhaustion of these subtle vestiges that are the final obstacle to the attainment of complete enlightenment.[167] The Mentor says:

> clearing up the stains of the vestiges of beginningless defilement by means of equipoise in the signless samādhi, doing away with thoughts of 'I will or will not perform the practices,' and conquering the eight worldly concerns, the one who seeks to secure the effortless result should practice. (CMP, f. 54b)

Also called the "practices of spiritual discipline" (*vrata-caryā*: a usage, I believe, with some palpable irony), these constitute the esoteric dharma of passion *par excellence*, for as Āryadeva indicates, "from the distinctive cause, the distinctive effect arises" and "one-pointedness of mind will not be won by ascetic practices, for they annihilate the five senses" (CMP, f. 55b). The Mentor briefly addresses the Student's concern that this seems to contradict the Buddha's teaching regarding passion, hatred, and delusion as three poisons. In response, the Mentor offers a résumé of the Mahāyāna position

166. I advance this argument in greater detail in "Antinomianism and Gradualism."

167. It is important to note that I here differ from later Tibetan traditional understanding that maintains that the practices may be employed in a variety of contexts over the course of the esoteric path, not merely at the end. See my "Antinomianism and Gradualism," 190–95.

on the relativity of poison and medicine: poisons becoming medicines and medicines becoming poisons, depending on circumstance. He concludes:

> there is no other practice (*sādhana*) to reach the result of unexcelled, great bliss—which [itself] becomes the cause for perfecting the distinctive result—than the distinctive transference (*samāropa*) and the distinctive transformation (*pariṇāma*). Therefore, the perfection of the omniscient [state], such as the eight superhuman powers, is realized by means of pleasurable food, residence, and so on. (CMP, ff. 56b–57a)

The rest of the chapter describes how to arrange the yogin's residence, the manner of arraying the female attendants as goddesses around the maṇḍala, a fire-offering of foodstuffs, various erotic techniques to be employed with the companion-goddesses, the secret esoteric verbal and somatic signs, and so forth.

Chapter 10 continues with a treatment of the practices without elaboration. This also describes setting up a residence, but involves a merely visualized maṇḍala and does without the ritual gestures, fire-pit, and so forth. There is an alternative array of goddesses and further detail concerning erotic techniques. Chapter 11 details the practices thoroughly without elaboration. Another alternative yogic procedure is presented, in which the yogin unites with a "gnosis consort." Yogic dissolution of the airs and the deities of the body maṇḍala is described again and the practitioner is told to "perform the practices of a *bhusuku*" (CMP, f. 71b). Such a *bhusuku* is devoted solely to eating (*bhu*), sleeping (*su*), and defecation (*ku*).[168] The result is said to be the accomplishment of the Great Seal (*mahāmudrā*)—an enlightened body with the eight lordly qualities.

Analytical Summaries of Individual Chapters

Chapter 1: Enlightenment

The first chapter takes as its declared focus the topic of "enlightenment" or "awakening" (*prabodhana*). Herein, Āryadeva presents a scripturally-

168. This etymology is unpacked at CMP, f. 71b.

based argument for a gradual approach to enlightenment. Subitism is rejected in no uncertain terms; and the gradual path of this particular tradition is detailed, with the entire sequence of stages listed in abbreviated form. This discussion is noteworthy since, although a gradualist message is implicit in the *Pañcakrama*, the message tends to remain under the surface. Nāgārjuna never belabors the point; he describes the process as "like a staircase," presents the stages in order, and leaves it at that. This is not true of Āryadeva's work. The issue is of such import in his eyes, that he devotes the greater part of the opening chapter to tackling this point head-on. We may with some justification, then, deduce that this was a vital issue for the audience he was seeking to address.[169] Clearly, a major aim of these authors is to establish not only the details, but the very legitimation of a graduated path to enlightenment in the esoteric tradition.[170]

Before commencing this argument, however, Āryadeva discusses the motivation behind his decision to compose the work, "situating" himself in the larger context of the production of esoteric Buddhist literature. Previously, he claims, the "supremely erudite" teachers of the Adamantine Way produced treatises that were composed of what he calls "cryptic expressions" (*nigūḍha-śabda*). These works, we are told, extracted the inchoate words of the esoteric scriptures and organized them into systematic patterns for ritual meditative praxis (*sādhana*). That is to say, he claims that

169. It may be noted that similar debates raged over a broad spectrum of Buddhist communities in the mid-to-late first millennium, as can be seen from works such as the *Laṅkāvatāra Sūtra* and Kamalaśīla's *Bhāvanākrama*-s, as well as the reports of a subitist/ gradualist conflict in imperial Tibet. See, e.g., Luis O. Gomez, "Indian Materials on the Doctrine of Sudden Enlightenment" and David Seyfort Ruegg, *Buddha-nature, Mind, and the Problem of Gradualism*.

170. It has been suggested (Snellgrove, *Indo-Tibetan Buddhism*, 152–53) that this view contradicts that of Indrabhūti, who claims in his *Jñānasiddhi* (chapter 15: see Bhattacharyya, *Two Vajrayāna Works*, 81) that enlightenment is not gradual but sudden. However, it is by no means apparent that the *Jñānasiddhi* is so clear about this. Rather, what seems most interesting is that there exist two variant manuscript traditions of the JS—one that reads "gradual" (*krameṇa*) and another that reads "sudden" (*yugapat*). What this suggests to me is that someone at some time (or times) was tinkering with the JS and altered this passage to fit their ideology. The question then becomes: which reading was original? It may be hard to argue one way or the other with certainty; yet, given the following reading "they are established by this very process" (*anenaîva nyāyena saṃsthitā*), I am inclined to believe that the original reading is "gradual"—especially since the passage in the GST it refers to describes a sequential unfolding of goddesses of the maṇḍala.

the scriptures themselves are full of "cryptic expressions" (albeit "meaningful," "elegant," and "lovely") which the "naïve" cannot properly understand. Thus, teachers prior to Āryadeva restricted themselves to extracting the most relevant passages and reordering them into manuals of religious practice. In contrast, Āryadeva claims that his own work will use "straightforward expressions" (*uttāna-śabda*) that can be understood by all. The earlier masters, he tells us, were writing for a more sophisticated audience: the hardy, ethical, and insightful folk of the three early, pure eras. These could be expected to understand the cryptic expressions of the scriptures, requiring merely that they be arranged in their proper order. Āryadeva's audience, however, consists of the sickly, immoral, and dense folk of the final, degenerate era of this world-cycle. They are confused by allusive expressions, needing the teaching to be spelled out in explicit detail. It is this clientele that the CMP seeks to address.

The key question here, of course, is to whom Āryadeva is alluding. What literature could he be speaking of that presents the sādhana in the form of cryptic expressions extracted from the Tantras, arranged in order? While there are perhaps several possibilities, the most obvious referent to my mind is the author's predecessor in the Noble Tradition, Nāgārjuna, who composed a sādhana exactly on this order. His **Sūtramelāpaka* is structured in precisely the fashion described by Āryadeva in this passage.[171] In Nāgārjuna's work, each stage of the sādhana is described in prose, with a verse from the relevant chapter of the *Esoteric Community Tantra* appended in legitimation of it. These citations are drawn from disparate chapters of the Tantra, rearranged to create and legitimate the ritual form advocated by Nāgārjuna. Āryadeva may also have been alluding to the PK (a kind of extended, perfection stage sādhana)—the better part of the first chapter of which also consists chiefly of citations from "authentic tantras." Āryadeva refers, however, not merely to one teacher, but to "teachers" in the plural. Presumably, then, he means to indicate a variety of authors, not solely Nāgārjuna, though I suspect that the latter is his primary referent.

This is not, however, the position taken by another scholar who has studied this literature closely. Tōru Tomabechi argues that this opening depiction is intended as a reference to—indeed a critique of—the elabo-

171. Furthermore, the title of the *Caryā-melāpaka-pradīpa* may be thought to allude to the title of this sādhana, especially since the CMP (f. 2a) refers to itself as a *sūtra-melāpaka*.

rate literary style of Jñānapāda (at least, and perhaps also of his school as a whole).[172] According to Tomabechi, Vitapāda (a disciple of Jñānapāda) describes his master's style in similar terms; and, Tomabechi further argues, the surviving fragments of Jñānapāda's writings bear this out. While I have great respect for the close study Tomabechi has made of the literature of the Esoteric Community and of the CMP in particular, I do not believe this argument can be sustained. First and foremost, the description found in this first paragraph cannot, I believe, accurately be called a "critique" of an elaborate literary style used by commentators. The "cryptic expressions" that he finds obsolete in esoteric pedagogy—glossed as "elegant and lovely words spoken in verses and songs, prose and verse"—are derived, not from commentarial works by his competitors, but from the scriptures themselves, authored (in Āryadeva's view) by enlightened beings, who are presumably exempted from such criticism. What he is criticizing is the attempt to clarify the practices by "the compositional arrangement of cryptic expressions," rather than doing so explicitly and independently. He thus validates his own approach as a necessary restatement, for a degenerate age.

I would also suggest that that this passage implies (contrary to the opinion currently popular that esoteric works are only meant for a restricted audience of initiates) that this work is meant for a relatively open public, as it is written "using straightforward expressions common to both students who are ritually prepared and those who are not" (CMP, f. 2a). This is borne out by the fact that the CMP devotes so much energy to legitimating its practices from the perspective of the broader Buddhist tradition. For instance, there would be little point in raising the objection found in chapter 9 (concerning the conflict of esoteric practices of sensual enjoyment with mainstream Buddhist teachings) among a sympathetic crowd of committed esoteric Buddhists. Similarly, the final question posed by the Vajra Student—that is, can ordinary working stiffs, who don't have the resources or time to run off and frolic in ritual celebration for six months, still achieve enlightenment through this tradition?—seems to be addressed

172. Tōru Tomabechi (personal email communication, 17 November 2000). This argument has since been advanced in his doctoral dissertation, *Étude du Pañcakrama* (Université de Lausanne, 2006), which deals with the *Pañcakrama* and its literary history. Apparently, the position that this opening passage of the CMP refers to Jñānapāda is a central premise in an historical argument to the effect that the Noble Tradition postdates the Jñānapāda Tradition.

to an interested laity, not the "choir" of professional esoterists. Indeed, the discussion of gradualism, it might be speculated, could represent an attempt to reassure concerned mainstream Mahāyāna Buddhists that this esoteric tradition, unlike some others, is committed to the same gradualist perspective advocated in exoteric circles. It may, of course, be objected that these questions may be meant merely to provide "sound bites" for debate with outsiders, rather than anticipating them as an actual, direct audience.[173] There is no clear way to determine this with any degree of certainty. I merely suggest it here as one way of thinking about the intended audience of the work.

However that may be, Āryadeva proceeds to claim that having "grasped this pivotal point" (that a more explicit treatment is needed), he "attained the samādhi of the perfection process, following in order [from/ after] the creation process from the tradition of Glorious Nāgārjunapāda." It is noteworthy that some Tibetan redactions (DCo) here specify that Nāgārjuna was Āryadeva's own teacher (*bdag gi slob dpon*). This is not found in the Sanskrit text, nor in other Tibetan versions (NP), which refer only to the "tradition" (*āmnāya*) of Nāgārjuna.[174] This latter term is ambiguous: *āmnāya* can refer both to distant traditions (i.e., the Vedas, Upaniṣads, etc.) or to more personal teachings/instructions. One does not gain from this text a clear sense of whether this author wanted to claim to be a direct disciple of Nāgārjuna or not.

Āryadeva then expresses his "commitment to compose" the text, as is traditional in Indic śāstras. The reader is told that the author proposes to "clarify the fivefold process"—the five stages or *pañcakrama*—by setting forth a new work. Here is the first mention of the schema of the five stages. He lists four topics of especial interest that he calls "mantra reality, seal reality, self reality, [and] divinity reality." The first and the last are fairly clear: mantra reality consists of the teachings of vitality control (*prāṇāyāma*, the topic of

173. Works of this sort—crib notes for those preparing debates or the like—do exist: for example, the fascinating Dun-huang text Pélliot Tibétain 116. However, the style of the CMP does not support its inclusion in such a genre.

174. The confusion in Tib (DCo) seems to have arisen from the Tibetans translators' decision to render Skt "Glorious Nāgārjunapāda" (*śrīnāgārjunapāda*) with "teacher/mentor Nāgārjuna" (*slob dpon klu sgrub*). From this, it was an easy error to move from "I . . . teacher" (*bdag gis slob dpon*) to "my teacher" (*bdag gi slob dpon*). Thanks to Dr. Losang Jamspal for drawing my attention to this variant.

the latter half of chapter 3), whereas divinity reality is the production of a divine body from mere gnosis (the topic of chapter 6). The two others are not mentioned elsewhere in the work, so it is difficult to assert with confidence what referent Āryadeva had in mind. The Tibetan translation lists five realities here, rather than four. It adds "dharma reality" (*chos kyi de kho na nyid*, **dharma-tattva*) between self reality and divinity reality. As such, it seems as if the intent of the Tibetan is to align these five with the five stages.[175] Although this is true of the "standard," canonical Tibetan translation, a citation of this passage in Tāranātha's RṄGC does not so include this "extra" reality.

One should also note that this introductory passage describes the CMP not as "integrating the practices" (*caryā-melāpaka*), but as "integrating scriptural [quotations]" (*sūtra-melāpaka*). This is rather strange —the more so, as Nāgārjuna's sādhana bears exactly this title. However, the fact is that if there is one thing that is strikingly characteristic of the CMP, it is the sheer quantity of scriptural citations it contains. Thus, it is not unreasonable for the author to stress this point in introducing his work.

With the conclusion of this prefatory statement, the real substance of the CMP begins. The Student begins by asking about the nature of Reality: what is it that those of the pure ages understood directly from the Tantras, but which beings of this age can no longer grasp? There then follows a quick exchange in which the Mentor equates Reality (*tattva*) with the real (*bhūta*), the non-deceptive (*avisaṃvādaka*), and the samādhi whose nature conduces to the real (*bhūta-nayātmaka-samādhi*). This latter is said to be that which is the nondual form of the two realities (*satya*), the superficial (*saṃvṛti*) and the ultimate (*paramārtha*). He then cites the *Vajra Crown-Protrusion* (*Vajroṣṇīṣa*) *Tantra*, which describes the ultimate reality as existing everywhere and in all things, though in an inexpressible, inconceivable way. The superficial reality is the dream-like manifestation of the ultimate reality. The

175. A similar correlation is, in fact, explicitly made by the apocryphal Tibetan commentary attributed to Śākyamitra; see sDe-dge bsTan-'gyur, Rgyud-'grel, vol. ci, f. 239b^{7}–240a^{1}, which reads: "mantra reality [refers to] the vajra recitation [stage]. Seal reality [refers to] the creation stage and the phantasmic [samādhi]. Subjective reality [refers to] the mind-objective [stage]. Objective reality [refers to] the brilliance. Divinity reality [refers to] the body of communion." (*sngags kyi de kho na nyid ni dor rje bzlas pa'o | phyag rgya'i de kho na nyid ni bskyed pa'i rim pa dang | sgyu ma lta bu'o | bdag gi de kho na nyid ni sems la dmigs pa'o | chos kyi de kho na nyid ni 'od gsal ba'o | lha'i de kho na nyid zung du 'jug pa'i sku'o |*). On the authorship of this commentary, see above, pp. 57ff.

citation equates this explicitly with the "phantasmic samādhi" (*māyopama-samādhi*), which elsewhere in this work is understood as a synonym for the phantasm body (*māyādeha*). We can thus understand that (in this context at least) the ultimate reality refers to the brilliance that is integrated with the phantasm body in the final stage of communion (*yuganaddha*): what is here and elsewhere (CMP, ff. 39b and 60b) called the "samādhi whose nature conduces to the real" (*bhūta-nayātmaka-samādhi*) where it clearly denotes the unification of the phantasm body with the brilliance. Thus, the upshot of this exchange is this: Reality is found through the yogic process wherein one unites a divine phantasm body with the realization of the fundamental brilliance of mind—the "communion" that is the goal of the Noble Tradition.

The Student then asks the central question of this chapter: is this enlightenment learned "according to a [gradual] process" (*krama-vṛttyā*) or does it take place instantaneously (*jhaṭiti*)? This seems to have been a major point of dispute among various Buddhist schools of the mid-to-late first millennium, both in an exoteric and an esoteric context. In formulating his response, the Vajra Mentor comes down clearly on the side of gradualists, though his final formulation is telling and, perhaps, typical: he claims that the experience of enlightenment is an instantaneous experience *capping* a long and gradual process. In making this argument, the Vajra Mentor cites first the *Journey to Laṅka* (*Laṅkāvatāra*) *Scripture* (a sūtra, incidentally, much beloved of East Asian subitists)—a passage that asserts that "one's own continuum of mental experience" (*svacittadṛśyadhārā*) is purified gradually, not instantaneously. A series of analogies is used: fruits ripening, potters making vessels, vegetation growing, and learning artistic skills are all gradual processes. Likewise, it is said, mental purification is also a gradual process. A citation from the *Hero's Progress Samādhi Scripture* (*Śūraṃgama-samādhi Sūtra*) makes a similar point. Here there is one analogy: an archery student learns to gradually improve his aim, training on successively smaller targets until he can hit unerringly. A bodhisattva's practice and attainment of the hero's march (*śūraṃgama*) samādhi is said to occur in a similar manner.

The Vajra Mentor then unpacks this latter analogy with particular reference to his own (i.e., Āryadeva's) tradition. This is quite interesting as, in so doing, he sets out in an ordered list the complete set of sequential stages of the esoteric Vajrayāna path, not merely the "five stages" of the perfection stage which form the focus of this work. He says (CMP, ff. 5a–5b), first one learns the inclination (*āśaya*) toward the Buddha Way, then the samādhi of single-mindedness on this way, then the imaginative yoga, then the beginners' samādhi, then (the sequence that is subsequently described in detail in this book): body isolation, speech isolation, mind isolation, superficial reality, ultimate reality, and the perfection (communion) samādhi. At this point, the Vajra Mentor explains, one is a complete buddha; there is nothing further to learn or do. This latter sequence, from body isolation on, is the central topic of the CMP, and we will learn more about this below. The

Āryadeva's Terminology	**Method/Means**	**Corresponding Samādhi**
Body isolation	Hundred buddha clans	Body-vajra samādhi
Speech isolation	Vowels and consonants OR Vitality control OR Vajra recitation	Speech-vajra samādhi
Mind isolation	Radiances and prototypes	Mind-vajra samādhi
Superficial reality	Twelve similes of phantasm	Phantasmic samādhi OR Universal buddha initiation
Ultimate reality	Eighteen great voidnesses	Purification of all defilements
Communion	Process of gnosis	Perfection samādhi OR All transcendent and worldly accomplishments (*siddhi*)

former sequence, then, corresponds to Āryadeva's schematization of the creation stage, which does not figure as a topic of discussion here.

This formulation yields a series of equivalencies, which are important to grasp if one is to follow discussions in the Noble Tradition literature. We have already commented on the variety of names of the stages within this tradition. To this we may now add the following set of equivalencies:

This sequence is again asserted to be a gradual process, in which each stage is necessary to the next. This discussion is capped by the statement that "when one has learned the perfection stage by a gradual process, one's own continuum of mental experience is purified instantaneously" (f. 6a). This may be taken to be a somewhat typical resolution of the sudden/gradual controversy—privileging gradualism, but recognizing and accommodating the subitist strands in some Buddhist scriptural sources. This synthetic gradual/sudden perspective is then justified by another citation from the *Journey to Laṅka Scripture* (*Laṅkāvatāra Sūtra*: previously cited in a gradualist vein)—this time in defense of a sudden illumination, like images in a mirror, or objects illuminated by the sun.

Āryadeva ends the chapter with a verse seemingly taken from Kambala's *Ālokamālā* (ĀM) that states that the Buddha, from pedagogical concerns, arranged the path to enlightenment in stages like a staircase. He further adds a special comment to the effect that "without the sequence of the five stages, one cannot realize the perfection stage samādhi." In essence, according to Āryadeva, the Noble Tradition—arranged as it is around a sequence of five stages—is the only method for achieving full buddhahood.

Chapter 2: Body Isolation

With the sequence of stages thus set out as a set of three "isolations," two "realities," and the final stage of "communion," chapter 2 begins with the Vajra Student asking how one is to learn the first of these: body isolation. The answer leads us into an interesting region: a kind of Vajrayāna Abhidharma, in which the ordinary body and world are reenvisioned as constituted of the Five Transcendent Lords. Twenty sets of phenomena are subdivided by five, yielding one hundred "buddha clans," which are meant to comprise the totality of observable reality.[176] In essence, what is taught is a pantheistic vision of a universe that is thoroughly divine in its essence, yet misperceived by the unenlightened as an ordinary, troubled world.[177]

176. See Appendix III for a chart detailing these correspondences.

177. A similar perspective, it might be argued, is communicated in the opening chapter of the

The Vajra Mentor begins his teaching by explaining that the body is merely a "heap" (*rāśi*) of various constituents (flesh, organs, connective tissue, hair, etc.) and that this heap has the same status as a heap of grains or pulses—i.e., it does not possess an intrinsic identity or self nature. The same is true of mental phenomena. He then proceeds to the special teaching that the perception of the ordinary body, as composed of (the Abhidharmic categories) of aggregates, elements, and media (*skandha-dhātv-āyatana*), is "predicated on the beginningless ordinary pride" (*prākṛtāhaṃkāra*). The Vajra Mentor then sets about teaching that the body is by nature composed of fine atoms (another Abhidharmism) that are in reality the Five Transcendent Lords. He quotes a passage from the *Esoteric Community Tantra* that equates the five aggregates with the five buddhas, the media with the six bodhisattvas, and the elements with the four goddesses, concluding with the injunction that "the mantrin always meditates on forms, sounds, and so on [i.e., the manifest world] as divine."

There then follows a discussion of the hundred buddha clans in some detail, for which the *Secret Moon Drop* (*Guhyendutilaka*) is taken as the authoritative source. A chart of these correspondences in full can be found in Appendix III. What one finds is, again, a quasi-Abhidharmic discussion, in which aggregates, elements, and media are defined, subdivided, and associated with corresponding divinities. These subdivisions are said to be the "constitution" of their associated divinity. The term I translate "constitution" (*adhiṣṭhāna*) is an important and wide-ranging term in Buddhist esoterism. Elsewhere in this work, in the context of the superficial reality stage (also called the *svādhiṣṭhāna-krama*), it is translated as "consecration."[178] In this context, however, the import is that the constituent elements of the outer and inner worlds are constituted of, or are the residence of—in the final analysis *are*—the five buddhas, four goddesses, and six bodhisattvas.

The description of the mental sense, the constitution of Samantabhadra, is noteworthy. Having described the sense media (*āyatana*) associated with the five basic senses and shown the correlation of their subdivision with the five buddha clans, Āryadeva describes the (Buddhist) "sixth sense" of mind in a

---

Vimalakīrti-nirdeśa-sūtra, in which the Buddha reveals the true nature of his buddha-field to be that of a pure, bejeweled universe, misperceived by narrow-minded disciples like Śāriputra to be "full of ordure." See Robert A.F. Thurman, trans., *The Holy Teaching of Vimalakīrti*, 18–19.

178. See note 277 to chapter 2 of the translation for more on this choice of terminology.

unitary and soteriological mode. The mental sense is defined here, not in a traditional Abhidharmic mode, but as "the consciousness of the three radiances in the interior of the body." It is this mental sense that is of supreme soteric importance, as it is this faculty that, focused on the unreality of all things (the "Realm of Reality" or *dharmadhātu*) and reconstructed through esoteric techniques (the "enlightenment process of the phantasmic web" or *māyājālābhisambodhikrama*—presumably the process described in chapter 7, below), becomes endowed with all buddha-qualities and traverses the buddha-fields.

Particular attention is then paid to the element "air" in the form of the ten vital airs of the body, an understanding of which is crucial to the subsequent discussion in chapter 3 of "vitality control" (*prāṇāyāma*), in which these vital airs are manipulated for yogic ends. Ten vital airs are detailed: five primary and five auxiliary. The first five—vitality (*prāṇa*), evacuating (*apāna*), ascending (*udāna*), metabolic (*samāna*) and pervading (*vyāna*)—are understood to be the chief "neural" energies that govern bodily functions: the preservation of life, evacuation of waste and emission of sexual fluids, evacuation through nose and mouth (sneezing, vomiting, etc.), digestion of food, and movement of the limbs, respectively. The latter five—up-moving (*udvāha*), re-moving (*vivāha*), co-moving (*saṃvāha*), out-moving (*nirvāha*), and well-moving (*pravāha*)—are understood to be the "neural" energies associated with sensory perception. They govern sight, sound, scent, taste, and touch, respectively.

With the analysis of the five auxiliary airs as the constitution of the Five Transcendent Lords, the delineation of the hundred clans is finished. The discussion is capped by a verse that suggests the significance of this teaching: "aggregates, elements, and . . . media, divided five by five, are each the constitution of the Five Transcendent Lords: how could life-cycle-action (*saṃsāra-karma*) occur?" That is, one is presented with a kind of theodicy: if the very fabric of the world is constituted of enlightened being (i.e., it is *buddha-maya*), how is it possible that "evil" (in the specifically Buddhist sense of bondage to the cycle of birth and death) could occur? The implication is that it could not—it only appears to be so, due to misperception of the world as not a pure play of enlightened consciousness, due to the influence of the ordinary pride (*prākṛtāhaṃkāra*), which conceives of the world as base or mundane. The practice of the "hundred buddha clans," we are to understand, counteracts this false, empirical pride and suggests a reenvisioning of the world as "always already" divine.

The Vajra Student then asks about the teaching that the perception of the hundred clans is to be yogically refined into a vision of five clans. In short, this involves reidentifying the world as divine, based on a division into five elements—the four common elements (earth, air, fire, water) and the consciousness element. The earth element corresponds to the transcendent lord clan (*tathāgata-kula*), constituted of/by Vairocana; the water element is the jewel clan (*ratna-kula*), constituted of/by Ratnasambhava; the fire element is the lotus clan (*abja-kula*), constituted of/by Amitābha; the air element is the action clan (*karma-kula*), constituted of/by Amoghasiddhi; and the consciousness element corresponds to the adamant clan (*vajra-kula*), constituted of/by Akṣobhya.

The Student then inquires of the teaching of three clans. The Mentor teaches that this involves reducing the perception of the world to enlightened (vajra) body, speech, and mind. These correspond to the three transcendent lords Vairocana, Amitābha, and Akṣobhya.[179] Those things corresponding to Ratnasambhava are collapsed into the Vairocana/body vajra rubric; and those belonging to Amoghasiddhi are subsumed under Amitābha/speech vajra. Akṣobhya and Vajrasattva (the "sixth transcendent lord") constitute the arena of the mind vajra. The yogic process here, we are told, involves collecting the highly-ramified hundred clans into one's own body, speech, and mind. There follow citations from the GST and the *Union of All Buddhas* (*Sarvabuddhasamāyoga* or SBS) that describe a process of the practitioner envisioning his/her body, speech, and mind as divine. The discussion concludes with the Student inquiring of the terminal point of the body-isolation yoga, wherein the three clans are reduced to one: "the body vajra with the nature of the indivisible three vajras," also called the "body-vajra samādhi—the final consummation of this stage of practice.

Chapter 3: Speech Isolation

Chapter 3 commences with the Vajra Student asking the Vajra Mentor for instruction concerning the next stage of practice: speech isolation (*vāgviveka*), also called the vajra recitation stage (*vajrajāpa-krama*). The Mentor

179. These, it may be noted, correspond in their colors to these arenas. Thus Vairocana and body vajra (oṃ) are white; Amitābha and speech vajra (āḥ) are red; and Akṣobhya and mind vajra (hūṃ) are blue/black.

begins with an important statement on the distinction of the creation stage and perfection stage. He comments that the body isolation just described is a coarse yoga, "common to all." Speech isolation, on the other hand, is the "extremely subtle gnosis of the yogins," which is not shared by those who practice the (exoteric) Mahāyāna nor yet by those engaged in merely the creation stage of the Vajrayāna. This is an important assertion as to the relative division of yogas between the two stages, a topic of some debate within the commentarial traditions. The Mentor then goes on to distinguish two sub-stages to this practice: a propædeutic stage of "air reality" (*vāyu-tattva*) and the actual practice of speech isolation, or "mantra reality" (*mantra-tattva*).[180] The former entails a more detailed teaching of the vital airs of the subtle body, whose manipulation is central to (or even definitive of) the practices of the perfection stage.

"Air reality," then, is synonymous with the classical yogic term "vitality control" (*prāṇāyāma*). The Mentor cites a famous verse from the GST, which describes meditating on a five-colored jewel the size of a mustard seed on the tip of one's nose. He asserts that this verse may be interpreted in two ways: either as referring to a creation stage or to a perfection stage yoga. The former involves meditating on the symbol of one's own deity (i.e., either a wheel, a jewel, a lotus, a sword, or a vajra for, respectively, Vairocana, Ratnasambhava, Amitābha, Amoghasiddhi, or Akṣobhya) on the tip of one's nose for the purpose of attaining stability of mind (presumably a kind of esoteric calming, or *śamatha*, meditation). The latter yoga is to be described herein: the "harnessing" of the "three-syllabled" (*tryakṣara*, in this context, the syllables *oṃ āḥ hūṃ*) to the breath—and, thus, to the three cosmogenic processes of entering, abiding, and emerging—according to a sequence of four elemental maṇḍalas. This is the process of vajra recitation: the preeminent process of vitality control according to this tradition.

The Vajra Student then inquires about the various vital airs manipulated in the practice of vitality control. The Mentor cites the *Explanation of the Intention*, which gives ten names for the airs. In this passage, the five primary airs are given their standard names: vitality, evacuative, metabolic, ascending, and pervasive. The five auxiliary airs, however, are given special names: snake (*nāga*), tortoise (*kūrma*), partridge (*kṛkala*), gift of the gods (*devadatta*), and champion (*dhanaṃjaya*). He then states that they are

180. This distinction is found at PK I.4ab: *vāyu-tattvānupūrveṇa mantra-tattvaṃ samāviśet* |.

also known by an esoteric jargon as: koṭākhyaḥ, koṭavaḥ, koṭaḥ, koṭābhaḥ, kaṭīrakaḥ, kolākhyaḥ, kolavaḥ, kolaḥ, kolābhaḥ, and kaliḥ. He cites the *Vajra Door {Goddess}* (*Vajramukhī*) *Tantra* as the source of the terms he prefers (vitality, etc., and up-moving, etc.).

The Student thereupon asks for further information about these ten airs, beyond merely their names. The Mentor specifies that the five principal airs reside in the body and perform its functions, while the five auxiliary airs reside in the sense media and perform sensory functions. He comments on the importance of the airs, given their (yogic) correspondence with the four elemental maṇḍalas, the goddesses, the elements, the gnoses, the light rays, and the transcendent lords. They are, he states, the medium for the vajra recitation when connected with the syllables *oṃ āḥ hūṃ;* and, further, are the basis of all speech, since this air/breath is the foundation of the primal vocalic sound: ə (represented by the Sanskritic letter *a*). At a yet more refined yogic level, they reach (or dissolve into) the "unstruck sound" (the *anāhata*, known in Tibetan sources as the "indestructible [drop]" [*mi shigs pa'i thig le*]), wherein they become "insubstantial."

The Student then asks about the processes by which these airs day and night emerge from and recollect in the body. The Mentor makes an interesting comment that "the air reality is not stated clearly in the root tantras and appendix tantras" such as the *Compendium of Realities* (*Tattvasaṃgraha*). Assuming his reference to root tantras and appendix tantras refers equally to Mahāyoga Tantras such as the GST, and not merely to Yoga Tantras (such as the one mentioned), we can take this to mean that it is only in the explanatory tantras that the details of *prāṇāyāma* are elaborated in this tradition. One way of reading this would be that the practice of yogic manipulation of the vital airs was not developed until a later stage of Buddhist esoterism, whereupon explanatory tantras were composed to account for, legitimate, and explain them. The explanation given here by Āryadeva is that such a teaching *is* found in the primary scriptures, though it is expressed in allusive terms (*saṃdhyābhāṣā*), rather than literally described. This issue is important for reconstructing the intellectual history of these traditions, and merits further study.

In this regard, the Vajra Mentor cites the *Vajra Rosary Tantra*, which describes the motion of five airs in the body, how they are issued from the nostrils, and their correspondence with the maṇḍalas of the Five Transcendent Lords. This passage does not identify the airs by name but, based on what we have learned in the previous chapter, we can summarize the teaching thus: The ascending air (*udāna*) issues from the right nostril, corresponds to the red fire maṇḍala, and is governed by Amitābha. The metabolic air (*samāna*) issues from the left nostril, corresponds to the green air maṇḍala, and is governed by Amoghasiddhi. The evacuative air (*apāna*) issues from both nostrils, corresponds to the yellow earth maṇḍala, and is governed by Ratnasambhava. The vital air (*prāṇa*) issues in a languid, slow manner, corresponds to the (white) water maṇḍala, and is governed by Akṣobhya. And the pervasive air (*vyāna*), which is the ultimate material fundament of beings and outer world, issues forth only at death, does not correspond to an elemental maṇḍala (or only to the "consciousness element"), and is governed by Vairocana. These four maṇḍalas, and presumably the fifth, maṇḍala-less air, are the focus of recitative practice (*japa*) by the yogin. The explanation of these airs and their yogic use concludes with the caution that these "individual" airs/maṇḍalas are not in fact independent but, like the elements themselves, are inextricably linked: "for all four elements are pervaded by each single elemental maṇḍala." Thus, it seems, the entire yogic/cosmogenic process of entering, abiding, and emerging, correlated with the three-syllabled mantra (*oṃ āḥ hūṃ*) is nested within the yogic manipulation of each elemental air.

This concludes the discussion of the practice of "air reality," or vitality control, which is preparatory to the actual cultivation of speech isolation, or "mantra reality"; and the Vajra Student now inquires about the practice of the latter process. Here again, the Mentor comments that this teaching is not found in the root and appendix tantras, of which the *Compendium of Realities* is again referenced—reflecting its important place in the background of these traditions.[181] According to the Mentor, only the mantras themselves are described in these primary scriptures. The extraction (*uddhāra*), signification (*saṃketa*), and meaning (*artha*) of the mantras, and the key teaching of mantra reality, are only described in the explanatory tantras. So the Mentor promises to teach these topics as they are presented in these scriptures. In this chapter, the explanatory tantras cited are the

181. Āryadeva's citation of the *Compendium of Realities* as a "root" text was notable enough to invite comment by later Tibetans. Tsongkhapa writes: "It appears to be the intention of the *Lamp for Integrating the Practices* also to consider the *Compendium of Realities* to be a root tantra with respect to the *Community*" (*'dus pa la bltos nas de nyid bsdus pa rtsa rgyud yin pa 'di spyod bsdus kyi'ang dgongs par snang ngo*); see RṄSG, f. 16a[4].

Explanation of the Intention and, perhaps also, the *Vajra Maṇḍala Ornament* (*Vajramaṇḍalālaṃkāra*).

This teaching constitutes a kind of esoteric linguistics, and Indic linguistic science is the assumed common point of reference. All mantras, we are told, "are born from the vowels and consonants." That is, the vowels and consonants of the Sanskritic syllabary[182] are considered to constitute all possible sounds. It is from these elements that mantras are assembled. The essence of all mantras is said to be the three-syllabled mantra (*oṃ āḥ hūṃ*), which is arisen from the unstruck sound (*anāhata*). That is to say, this fundamental, primordial sound of the universe—which is the aural counterpart to the subtlest level of reality, wherein mind [of brilliance] and matter [the indestructible drop] become nondual—is the source of the three-syllabled mantra. On this analogy, the three-syllabled, the "overlord of all mantras," may be taken to be the *sambhogakāya* emanation of the fundamental *dharmakāya* sound, the unstruck. This, then, becomes further manifest as all other mantras, the *nirmāṇakāya* sound. These mantras are further ramified as feminine, masculine, or neuter, depending on their composition.

The Mentor then describes a variety of ways in which the three-syllabled mantra functions and may be manipulated for ritual and yogic ends. First, the "union of the three" produces a divine body (i.e., presumably, from the union of vajra body, speech, and mind, a divine body is produced). Its elements are correlated with the three cosmogenic/yogic processes of entering, abiding, and emerging—which mimic the processes of embryonic conception; and, thus, it "causes embodiment." It is related to the seminal drop, and so, when the semen is emitted, it "produces masses of beings." Manipulated yogically, it is drawn upward, "opens the doors of the sense organs," is engaged in the vajra recitation, and "purifies the obscurations of previous action (*karma*)." It also functions in the ritual actions such as pacification of obstacles, increase of prosperity, domination, and destruction. It is employed in the purification of edibles for ritual consumption. It manifests and functions in all these ways, yet it never loses its foundational connection to the primal state, the "unstruck" [sound/center], wherein it may return before again taking embodiment in the conventional world.

182. This consists of sixteen vowels (a, ā, i, ī, u, ū, ṛ, ṝ, ḷ, ḹ, e, ai, o, au, aṃ, and aḥ) and thirty-three consonants (ka, kha, ga, gha, ṅa, ca, cha, ja, jha, ña, ṭa, ṭha, ḍa, ḍha, ṇa, ta, tha, da, dha, na, pa, pha, ba, bha, ma, ya, ra, la, va, śa, ṣa, sa, and ha).

This discursus is followed by a lengthy citation from the *Explanation of the Intention*, which describes in a more elliptical way the extraction (*uddhāra*) of the syllables *oṃ āḥ hūṃ* and the manner in which, via the practice of the vajra recitation, the breath may be utilized as a vehicle for the recitation of this three-syllabled mantra, and thus the practice of enlightenment "24/7." This, the Vajra Mentor concludes, is the so-called "mantra reality," the first of the "five stages" of Nāgārjuna's system.

The Vajra Student then inquires further about the nature of the primary sound of all language, the syllable ə (a). The Mentor begins with a critique of prosaic grammatical knowledge, claiming that the "hidebound" (*prāvacanikāḥ*) who, although they may have mastered the technicalities of Pāṇinian grammar, do not understand the real manifestation of sound, as this is only evident to enlightened consciousness. He begins by explaining the Sanskritic syllabary of sixteen vowels (*āli*) and thirty-three consonants (*kāli*),[183] and he gives a kind of laundry list of central topics of Sanskritic grammar: types of words, phonology, declension and conjugation, and a range of suffixes. Based on these conventions, he says, more complex significations are created, including various forms of sacred and secular literature. By relying on these forms of literature, the Mentor declares, all accomplishments (*siddhi*) are attained. That is to say, significant language, in reliance on phonemes and graphemes,[184] is the source of all goodness and spiritual success. An illustrative verse is cited from the *Laṅkāvatāra Sūtra* to illustrate this point: conceptual speech is like a lamp that illuminates the "wealth" of spiritual attainment.

However, all those ramified forms known through grammar and literary study are likened to (inert) bodies, which are enlivened by the syllable ə (*a*), which is their "very consciousness" (*vijñāna-bhūta*). This is predicated on the grammatical truism that consonant stops do not make a sound without a vowel informing them. "K" is not a sound; only when conjoined with a vowel, as in "ka," for example, is it perceptible as a vocal sound. This is supported by a citation from the *Song of the Names* [*of Mañjuśrī*] ([*Mañjuśrī*] *nāmasaṃgīti*), which extols the greatness of this primal, primary sound

183. On these, see note 182, above.

184. It is noteworthy that Āryadeva does not speak in an exclusively phonetic mode, as is typical of orthodox Indian grammar. He makes specific reference to *lipika* (graphemes), which are the elements of significant expression.

ə (*a*), the "chief phoneme." This is further illuminated by a citation from the *Vajra Maṇḍala Ornament*, which seems to suggest that it is ə (*a*) itself that is the "unstruck [sound]" (*anāhata*), which resides in the heart center. The Vajra Mentor's commentary also describes this sound as uncreated and connate (*sahaja*), which latter term has important connotations in esoteric Buddhism.[185]

The Mentor then declares that, based on this fundamental understanding of the primal, unstruck sound which is the source of all significant speech, the buddhas teach beings liberation based on the specific conditions of their bondage, "without regard for the niceties of grammar." There then follow two citations to illustrate this point. The first is a standard passage from the *Journey to Laṅka Scripture* (alluded to earlier, though not cited as such, in chapter 1), which cautions against mistaking the letter for the spirit or meaning. Using a classical Buddhist analogy, those who cling to the letter, the signifier, are likened to those ignorant ones who, when the moon is indicated to them by a pointing finger, stare at the finger, not the moon.[186] So one is cautioned to rely on the meaning, not the letter, and, even more, to rely on those spiritual friends who are learned in the spirit/meaning, rather than those who are pedantic followers of the mere letter.

The second citation is a less commonly cited passage from the same scripture, which distinguishes four types of speech (*vāc*). The relevance of this passage is not at all clear to me. The distinction it lays out is not further developed in this work, nor in other esoteric works of which I am aware. Perhaps further knowledge of the implications of this distinction in Yogācāra literature would help in the interpretation of this citation. The conclusion drawn from this passage (which is nowhere mentioned in it) is that sound, which is born from ə/a is undestroyed (*akṣara*—a standard term for syllables insofar as they are unanalyzable) and, thus, "that which has the space-like [infinite] nature," the perfection stage of esoteric practice, is reached "through the door of [i.e., by means of] sound." This makes sense in this context, as Āryadeva is claiming that the practice of vajra recitation—

185. See, for instance, Ronald M. Davidson, "Reframing Sahaja"; an earlier, more diffuse, discussion may be found in Per Kværne, "On the Concept of Sahaja."

186. Note that Candrakīrti uses the same, classical metaphor at the end of his PU (230), where he writes, "the one who sees only the letter does not see Reality; it is like one who wishes to see the moon gazing at the finger [that points at it]" (*tattvaṃ na paśyati hi so 'kṣaramātradarśī candraṃ didṛkṣur iva câṅgulim īkṣamāṇaḥ*).

focused on the vocalic and consonantal sounds in conjunction with the vital airs—is the gateway to mastery of the first of the five stages of the perfection stage.

With this observation, the technical discussion of this chapter is over. What remains is devoted to more general assertions about the power of mantra and the nature of the purification of speech. Overall, the intent seems to be to "domesticate" the advanced, technical approach of the Noble Tradition (as enunciated in the explanatory tantra) into the vocabulary and discourses of more "mainstream" exoteric and "lower" esoteric traditions. It does so through extensive citation of works of those sorts.

The first citation is from the *Teaching of One Method Scripture* (*Ekanayanirdeśa Sūtra*) to the effect that, though words and languages are used to teach things/realities (*dharma*), these words and languages are ultimately without a fundamental reality (they are "unfindable"), and thus are not a secure basis in and of themselves. There then follows a lengthy passage from the *Enlightenment of Vairocana* (*Vairocanābhisambodhi*) *Tantra*, that treats of the nature of mantric power. It asserts that mantric power is not something created by the buddhas or other enlightened beings. They are a "given" (*sthita*) part of reality, and can be accessed whether or not enlightened beings arise in the world to teach them. Various worldly deities are said to have magical spells (*vidyā*) that create various effects; and ordinary magicians can create illusions by means of mantric power. They may also use them in worship, so as to gain happiness or boons from the divine powers. Concluding, the passage maintains that "the potency of mantra should be firmly believed in," though its power cannot be traced to either its own nature, any material substance, or the power of its reciter. Yet, it is claimed, mantra "works," due to the "inconceivable dependent origination."

The above citations are given, the reader is told, to "demonstrate the inconceivable power of . . . mantras." At this point, further citations are marshalled to establish the credentials of the notion of "speech purification"—in this context, another term for speech isolation, but one with an exoteric pedigree. This is first demonstrated by a citation from the *Enquiry of the Kinnara King* (*Kinnara-rāja-paripṛcchā*). Addressing the question of the source of the vocal sounds of all beings, it is asserted that such sound could come neither from the body nor the mind, as the former is inanimate and the latter is imperceptible. Thus, vocal sound must emerge from the expanse of space itself. Like all things, it is both inconceivable and limitless like space, yet also "mere vocalization . . . delimited by conventions." From this insight, the chapter concludes with a claim about the nature of the one who has completed the stage of speech isolation, asserting that "the great yogin who abides in the speech-vajra samādhi" does not conceive thoughts of attachment or aversion based on conventional speech. S/he "has understood all sounds" and so sees through the fantastic worlds they signify. Such a one, we are told, is not afflicted by the eight worldly concerns. S/he has, moreover, attained the eighth bodhisattva stage and, firmly established in the perfection stage yogas, proceeds to focus on mind isolation, under the guidance of a spiritual friend (*kalyāṇa-mitra*).

Chapter 4: Mind Isolation

The central topic of chapter four, devoted to the practice of mind isolation (*citta-viveka*) is the teaching of the nature of mind. In particular, in this context, this means the teaching of the structure of the subtle mind, its levels of "radiance" (*ābhāsa*) and their corresponding behavioral "prototypes" (*prakṛti*). Through the manipulation of the subtle airs, which are the motile vehicles or "mounts" of various consciousnesses, the yogin is said to be enabled to be aware of the various levels of the subtle mind.[187] Later, this skill is used to guide the consciousness through the dissolution process (homologous with the death process), whereupon the subtlest consciousness—the "brilliance" (*prabhāsvara*), wherein mind and matter, subject and object, are nondual—may be understood, inhabited, and employed to manifest the enlightened state of buddhahood. This dissolution leads through the three subtle levels of consciousness, "luminance" (*āloka*), "radiance" (*ābhāsa*), and "imminence" (*upalabdhaka*). As these "three radiances" (*ābhāsa-traya*), and the fundamental nature of mind they presage, are difficult to discern directly (i.e., with *pratyakṣa*), eighty behavioral prototypes encoded in these subtle minds are taught, so that the practitioner may be able to discern them by means of inference (*anumāna*).[188] Thus recognizing

187. Note that, in the yogas of the subtle levels of reality, the vital airs are the material correlate of the subtle mind. That is, they form the "bodies" with which the subtle mind is interrelated.

188. In general, Buddhist philosophical schools accept two modes of epistemic authority (*pramāṇa*): direct perception (*pratyakṣa*) and inference (*anumāna*).

and taking charge of the "reins" of the subtle mental mechanism of the death and rebirth process, one is freed from habitual, compelled rebirth, and gains control over the life-cycle (*saṃsāra*).

The discourse begins in very general terms. The Vajra Student inquires as to the nature of mind isolation. The Vajra Mentor commends his question and begins a general discourse about the nature of mind, the thorough knowledge of which is said in many Mahāyāna and Vajrayāna Buddhist sources to be tantamount to enlightenment. As the Mentor notes:

> As the Lord said in all the scriptural discourses, "the nature of mind is rootless, unlocated, without foundation, signless, colorless, shapeless, beyond the senses, not the sphere of the logicians." Hence, the nature of one's own mind is to be sought by the one who, desiring buddhahood, relies on the Adamantine Way [having] honored a spiritual guide.

There follow three brief citations (from the *Compendium of Realities*, the *Enlightenment of Vairocana*, and the *Method of the Three Baskets*) to the effect that meditative discernment of the nature of mind leads to enlightenment. Here, in brief, we see again a conscious situating of the advanced yogic practices of the Noble Tradition in mainstream Mahāyāna and established esoteric discourses.

The Mentor teaches that the one who desires the "phantasmic samādhi"—i.e., one who seeks to manifest a phantasm body, the next major stage of this yogic process—should seek to understand the radiances and the prototypes. This is so, in part, because the entire perceptible world is a derivation of the three radiances, or three consciousnesses—the levels of the subtle mind. This claim is supported by a citation from the *Enquiry of Bhadrapāli* (*Bhadrapāli-paripṛcchā*), a work particularly devoted to the rebirth process, which describes the consciousness-element (*vijñāna-dhātu*) as the creator of the body. It also analogizes this consciousness-element with sunbeams that remain pure, even though they contact the impure. Similarly, the scripture maintains, the consciousness-element remains pure even though it takes rebirth in impure states. It further describes consciousness as being like a seed, which carries imprints from one place to another. This consciousness-seed, carrying the imprint of its previous karma, gives rise to ("sprouts") a new body, having passed through the death and between states. Thus, the

Mentor concludes, the esoteric teaching that follows is continuous with these mainstream Mahāyāna teachings.

However, although it is "indicated in the scriptures of the Universal Way [that] consciousness [is] colorless, signless, shapeless, selfless, [and] mere self-awareness," the esoteric teachings add something that is not found in the exoteric presentations. Thus, we are led to the important claim that "without having entered the Great Adamantine Way [via] the Great Yoga Tantra, the *Glorious Esoteric Community*, one is not able" to recognize the fundamental nature of mind and, thus, cannot attain full enlightenment. This is so, because it is only in this tradition (actually, only in the explanatory tantras of this tradition) that the three radiances/consciousnesses, which constitute the true nature of the mind, are taught. The Mentor then turns to these explanatory tantras to elucidate this essential teaching. First, he cites a *locus classicus* for this doctrine in the explanatory tantra, the *Gnosis Vajra Compendium* (*Jñānavajrasamuccaya*). Then he gives a more extensive explanation of this model of mental functioning. He gives a series of synonymous terms used in the literature for the three radiances: luminance, radiance, and imminence, respectively. Some are technical terms taken over from the exoteric treatises: critical wisdom, liberative art, and imminence; mind, mentation, and consciousness; other-dependent, imagined, and accomplished; passion, hatred, and ignorance, etc. Some are distinctive of the esoteric literature: void, extremely void, and great void; mind, mental functions, and delusion; and passion, dispassion, and moderate passion.

The natures of the three radiances of the subtle mind are then described. All three are said to be formless, without body or speech. Luminance is said to appear like the "radiance of stainless moonbeams in an autumn sky." The yogically adept can conceive it by means of the syllable *aṃ*, though lesser beings engage it by means of conventional symbols such as a moon-disk, a lotus, or other forms. Radiance is said to appear like sunbeams pervading an autumn sky. The yogically adept, again, can conceive it by means of the syllable *aḥ*, though lesser beings engage it by means of conventional symbols such as a sun-disk, a vajra, jewel, or other forms. Imminence is said to appear like the darkness of twilight. It is unconscious, without perceptible content, and has no seed-syllable nor conventional forms by which it may be engaged.

Having given such an overview of the three levels of the subtle mind, the Mentor then gives a list of the eighty prototypes (*prakṛti*), which are encoded at each level. There are thirty-three related to luminance, forty related to radiance, and seven related to imminence. These eighty constitute a kind of esoteric mental Abhidharma. That is, one finds here a list of mental states rather similar, but not corresponding to the lists of mental events (*manāsika-dharma*) found in the mainstream Abhidharmic analysis of mind. These are called "prototypes" (*prakṛti*), presumably because they function as the basic instincts that manifest themselves as their corresponding mental event and behavior (which would be their *vikṛti* or *ākṛti*). Thus, onc finds hunger, fear, shame, doubt, delight, laughter, sucking, spite, forgetfulness, and sloth. The Vajra Mentor comments that they "function day and night" and thus should not be divided by male and female.[189] The division into day and night yields one hundred and sixty, which number is sometimes used for the prototypes.

The Vajra Student then asks rather a bold question. He is satisfied with the teaching of the eighty prototypes, but he is not satisfied that this teaching has the sanction of authoritative scripture (*āgama*). So he asks the Mentor for such, whereupon the Mentor performs what can only be considered a bit of commentarial "sleight of hand." He claims it is authenticated by a famous verse in the *Esoteric Community Appendix Tantra* (GSUT), which gives a [hermeneutical] etymology of the term "mantra." However, the verse as it appears in this source does not say what the Mentor claims. The etymology given in the source text is: *man-* refers to mentation (*manas*) and *-tra* refers to protection (*trāṇana*). The verse given by the Mentor, on the other hand, reads: "that mind is called 'eighty' (*aśīti*). The syllable 'tra' is derived from 'protection.'"

Thus the syllable *man-* is not referred to *manas*, but instead called *aśīti* ("eighty"), a term with no etymological connection (hermeneutical or no) to *man*. Thus, it may not appear to be an etymology at all. However, in classical commentary, such an etymology (*nirukti*) need only comment on one element of the term—it need not give the derivation of all elements.[190] Thus, it does qualify as an etymological verse; but one wonders how such a non-standard verse would have been accepted in this context. That is, the Vajra Student is asking precisely for an authoritative scriptural pronounce-

189. The specification of day/night or male/female seems to be related to a dispute within the prior commentarial tradition that I have not been able to locate.

190. This was indicated to me by Professor Ashok Aklujkar in personal conversation, 26 July 2002.

ment to clear away his concerns about the legitimacy of the teaching. To then cite a doctored verse—not referred to some untraceable source, but attributed to a scripture wherein the verse is well-known in its standard form—strikes me as rather missing the point, if not counter-productive.

However it may have struck its readers, the virtual interlocutor, the Vajra Student, is predictably compliant. Accepting the authority of this verse and its source, he proceeds to ask a further question regarding the functioning and manifestation of the three radiances in the body and, most importantly, how they can be perceived. The Mentor replies that, yes, the radiances are mind conjoined with vital air; thus they are imperceptible in principle. However, just as the external air element may be perceived inferentially on the basis of the motion of tree limbs and the like, one may perceive the three consciousnesses inferentially on the basis of the changes they induce—that is, the functioning of the prototypes. This analogy is supported by a citation from the *Enquiry of Bhadrapāli*.

The Mentor then cites a passage from the *Unexcelled Intention* (=PK II) that describes the dependence of consciousness on air for its functioning, and states that the prototypes become active through the functioning of the vital airs. In explaining this, the Mentor notes that radiances only appear for an instant during the dissolution process. They are thus difficult to discern. However, they may be discerned on the basis of their corresponding prototypes. And the one who understands the prototypes and radiances (and how they function in conjunction with the vital airs) "knows the pulsating thought-deeds of all beings—past, present, and future." That is, they know the minds of others—a characteristic accomplishment of a buddha, as described in the subsequent citation from the *Enquiry of the Kinnara King*.

The import of this chapter is then summarized. Those who do not understand the nature of mind and its functioning—i.e., those who do not know the radiances and prototypes of the subtle mind—are "[trapped] in the beginningless life-cycle due to the bonds of action and defilement (*karma-kleśa*) born from their own conceptuality—like a cocoon-weaving [silk] worm." Life after life they suffer and die, whereupon they "enter the ultimate reality maṇḍala"—i.e., their coarse minds dissolve into the fundamental brilliance of mind. Not controlling this process, they are pushed along in the rebirth process at the mercy of their karmic momentum. Arising as an immaterial between-state being ("like a child of five or six . . . moving with the speed of action and miracle"), they experience the between for "seven days" before taking birth in one of the realms of existence "impelled by the good and evil actions born from their own conceptuality." In this way, "one takes rebirth in the five realms again and again in the manner of an irrigation machine and experiences the suffering of the life-cycle" (f. 35a).

Chapter 5: The Consequences of Action (Karma)

This analysis of the mechanics of death and rebirth from the esoteric perspective leads to a digression of sorts—the only such (chapter-length) one in the book. That is, rather than go on immediately to the discussion of the next yogic stage, the conventional reality or phantasm body, Āryadeva turns to a discussion of action and its consequences (*karmānta-vibhāga*). The Vajra Student gives voice to doubts about the reality and mechanics of karmic effects. The basic question is: if everything involved in karmic functioning—including the radiances and prototypes, the vital airs, and karma itself—is formless and void, how does it work? Why should one be "bound to the beginningless wheel of existence by good and evil action" if that is somehow unreal? Further, he asks the fundamental question of karmic theory: how does karma function in a future time? That is, how does one have a cause here and now, and an effect there and then? And, is karma derived from another source, or from one's own mind?

The Vajra Mentor again congratulates his Student on asking such probing and fundamental questions about what he terms "the purification of action" (*karma-viśuddhi*). He begins his answer with a review of the basic model of the "ten paths of unvirtuous action," as related (with an esoteric spin) in the *Vajra Crown-Protrusion Tantra*. This scripture, beginning with the standard division of unvirtuous actions into three of body, four of speech, and three of mind, further specifies two categories of body and speech misdeeds: the "common" (*sāmānya*), which corresponds to the standard lists, and the "grave" (*guru*), which relate to mother, father, and "respectable persons" (*gurujana*).

The misdeeds of mind are subjected to a separate treatment. These are categorized, not according to grave and common, but according to their "prototype" (*prakṛti*)—those that have mind, mental factors, or delusion as their prototype. The implied equivalency between these categories and the three levels of the subtle mind (also called mind, mental factors, and delusion—see chapter 4, f. 30a) is clear. The actual extent of the correspondence is less clear. The dispassion (*virakta*), passion (*rāga*), and forgetting (*vismṛti*) of the three categories in the *Vajra Crown-Protrusion Tantra* seem to correspond to the *virāga*, *rāga*, and *vismṛti* of the three categories of prototypes, but the other correspondences do not seem to be overwhelmingly precise. Unfortunately, this scripture has not survived either in Sanskrit or Tibetan translation. So further research into the extant fragments of this text is necessary to determine if this is indeed a formative source for this tradition, or if Āryadeva is again engaging in commentarial acrobatics.

On this basis, the Mentor distinguishes the ignorant (*ajñānin*) from the wise (*jñānin*). The ignorant do not recognize that good and evil deeds are the effects (*vikṛti*) of the prototypes encoded into the subtle mind. Hence, they perform good and evil deeds conceiving of "I and mine," which course leads to "good and bad rebirths." The wise, however, understanding the mechanics of the subtle mind with its radiances, prototypes, and vital airs, do not cling to conceptual thought regarding good and evil deeds. Their prototypes—both good and evil—merely arise and decay moment by moment into the fundamental brilliance of mind. They are, thus, free of the compelling effects of karmic action. This position is legitimated by a citation from the *Unexcelled Intention* that says much the same, ending with a typical esoteric verse to the effect that "that by which the ignorant are bound [here, the radiances and prototypes], the wise are liberated."[191] A further scriptural warrant is drawn from the *Enquiry of the Kinnara King*, which also asserts that, "knowing the prototypes of mind . . . there will be no . . . defilement at all."

There then follow two citations (from the *Diamond Cutter Scripture* [*Vajracchedika Sūtra*] and the GST) that express the bodhisattva's transcendence of conventions of good and evil. A further passage is drawn from the *Eight-Thousand-Line Transcendent Virtue of Wisdom Scripture* (*Aṣṭasāhasrikā Prajñāpāramitā Sūtra*) that addresses the fundamental question first raised by the Vajra Student: how, if all is void (*śūnya*) and isolated (*vivikta*) does (karmic) purity and defilement occur? The answer is plain: they work

191. Similar verses are found, e.g., in the *Hevajra Tantra* (v. II.ii.50) and the *Cittaviśuddhiprakaraṇa* attributed to Āryadeva (v. 6)—but the stock verse form is widespread in Buddhist esoteric literature.

even though they are void. Indeed, as Nāgārjuna insists in his exoteric writings, they would not work if they were not.[192]

A slightly different spin is given by the *Purification of All Karmic Obscurations Scripture* (*Sarvakarmāvaraṇaviśodhana Sūtra*) that asserts that, since all beings are ultimately unproduced, they do not really exist, and so cannot take rebirth in bad states. It claims, notably—like many Buddhist scriptures, exoteric and esoteric, mainstream and Mahāyāna—that "all things are brilliance (*prabhāsvara*)." Therefore, it is only through misconception (and, thus, misperception) of reality that naïve beings (*bāla*), alienated from their true nature (*pṛthagjana*), experience themselves as being in hell or an animal realm or the like. A similar sentiment is cited from the *Secret Treasury of the Transcendent Lords Scripture* (*Tathāgataguhyakoṣa Sūtra*): since all things are primordially pure (*ādiśuddha*), there is ultimately no real existence of suffering in lower rebirths, and the like. Three verses attributed to Nāgārjuna are cited to much the same effect.

With this, the chapter ends. It is only left to conclude that scripture and reasoning both concur in describing the functioning of karma in this way, and that the compassionate buddhas, seeing naïve, deluded beings whose nature is pure brilliance suffering unnecessarily due to misperception of reality, act in the world in order to establish them in the "samādhi whose nature conduces to the real." That is, buddhas do not remain in a quiescent state; they see the delusion of beings and emanate in the world in order to interact with these deluded ones, so that they may be conducted to the blissful state of enlightenment themselves. The means by which they emanate is the creation of a phantasm body, the technique for creating which is the topic of the next chapter.

Chapter 6: Superficial Reality/Phantasm body

This chapter addresses what is perhaps the most important element of the esoteric process in this tradition. For, the contribution of the esoteric traditions of the Mahāyoga Tantras is not to the ultimate side, the realization of emptiness, but to the techniques of engaging the world via a com-

192. Cf. Nāgārjuna, *Mūlamadhyamakakārikā* XXIV.20: "if all this were not empty, there would be neither creation nor destruction" (*yadi aśūnyam idaṃ sarvam udayo nāsti na vyayaḥ*)

passionate, omnipotent, divine emanation body (*nirmāṇa-kāya*).[193] This method of constructing a divine body from subtle vital airs and subtle mind patterns is known in this tradition as the self-consecration (*svādhiṣṭhāna*) or superficial reality (*saṃvṛti-satya*). It is of this process that the Vajra Student now inquires.

His questioning begins by noting that such a divine emanation body is not taught at the previous stages of the three isolations of body, speech, and mind. He concludes, "without a foundation in the superficial reality, one does not obtain establishment as a deity." The term here rendered "establishment" (*pratiṣṭhā*) is most often used in reference to the consecration of statues and images. Hence, an analogy is implied: in just the same way as a statue is consecrated—that is, transformed from an insentient mass of material into a living body inhabited by the sentience of the deity it represents—just so is the practitioner's enlightened mind to be installed in a suitable receptacle through which devotees and other needy beings may interact with an enlightened buddha. In order for this to happen, a suitable "body/image" needs to be created. This is done by means of the self-consecration, which involves the "production of a deity [body] by means of mere gnosis." The Mentor promises to teach this method, also called "divine reality" (*devatā-tattva*), which is "the assuming of a divine form, endowed with all the marks [of a great being], by merely the prototypes and radiances." This body is described by twelve similes (detailed below) and is said to be the "mind-made body" (*manomaya-kāya*) of the buddhas.[194]

Before this teaching is given, the Vajra Student again intervenes. He reiterates that mind and body are interdependent; therefore, the creation of a body by mind alone is problematic according to commonly held Buddhist assumptions. He notes that "those who hold objectifying views"—that is, presumably, the skeptical—"will not accept [this teaching] without [proofs based on] scripture and reasoning." He therefore asks the Mentor to teach this technique with an eye to scriptural legitimation, so that those with doubts will have their reservations addressed.

The Mentor is pleased and alludes to the irony of those attached to the exoteric path, or even those of the creation stage, who recite standard

193. This position is asserted by a number of Tibetan interpreters, including but not limited to Tsongkhapa. It seems a reasonable claim, based on my reading of the Indian materials.

194. A term with a prior exoteric pedigree; see, e.g., the *Laṅkāvatāra Sūtra*.

Buddhist similes like phantasm, dream, reflection, etc. (which are here used to refer to the phantasmic divine body), without understanding them to refer to this higher teaching, "the production of a divine [form], made of mind, by mere gnosis." This teaching, in short, is that the formless mind, mere radiance, is linked with the air element, both being subtle, quick, and nimble. From the union of subtle mind and subtle air, a divine body is produced. Air provides the substance and motility needed by the quiescent and insubstantial mind so as to engage the world. This teaching is authenticated by reference to the *Enquiry of Bhadrapāli*, here called the *Transmigration of Consciousness Scripture* (*Vijñānasaṃkrānti Sūtra*), which speaks of consciousness, after death, taking on a new form of its own, like a reflection in water. The Mentor draws a further analogy between the body a consciousness evolves during the between state (*antarābhava, bar do*) and the divine body created through the self-consecration process. The former is the fate of "naïve, ordinary beings," while the latter is achieved by those "who have obtained the personal precept of all the buddhas through the successive generations of mentors." This "phantasm body" is likened to a rainbow in a verse cited from the *Enlightenment of Vairocana Tantra*.

The Vajra Student then begins a new line of questioning—this time concerning sleep, rather than death. How is it that one's consciousness passes out of the body during sleep and experiences visions elsewhere, yet returns subsequently to the body? How is it that one accumulates karma from deeds done in a dream? The dream state was of great interest to Buddhist yogins, and the question of whether or not one is accountable for karma produced while asleep was one continually debated within Buddhist circles from an early time. Here, Āryadeva is using the Vajra Student to set up a discussion of the esoteric Buddhist Mahāyoga answer to these recurrent questions about dream and karma.

The Vajra Mentor is pleased with these questions for two reasons. For one, he says, they will serve as a point of departure for further clarifying the self-consecration stage. Also, by focusing on dreams and, in particular, the reality of dream experience, the question implicitly criticizes the "beginningless ordinary pride of those suffering from the disease of clinging to physicality." That is, unenlightened people believe that their conception of themselves as ordinary, physical beings (which characterizes the waking state of most people) is their true self; they are thus alienated from their miraculous divine identity. Emphasizing the reality of dream—and its analogy to the miraculous divine body—will help to "heal" this "disease." He then announces his intention to teach the method by which this divine body may be attained by yogic manipulation of the dream state.

He cites an unidentified scriptural source that states that from the great voidness of sleep, beings experience various dream visions "by the force of vital air"—that is, the vital airs continue to function during sleep, not engaging (putatively) external objects, but creating dream experiences. While this happens, the body "remains like a mere [lump of] earth." Due to the residual karmic force of the being, the vital airs do not depart from the body, even though it is unconscious. They return and reanimate it, like a new birth: "the air again proceeds to birth here." That is—and this is crucial in the esoteric yogic context—falling asleep is like death, the dream body is like the between-state body, and waking up is like a rebirth. The dream body is like the beatific body (*sambhoga-kāya*) of the buddhas. Just as these "victorious lords," who have no solid physical bodies, may enter into "emanated bodies" (*nirmāṇa-kāya*) made of coarse physical elements, just so does the dreaming mind waken into its own physical "emanation."

As "all things are like a dream" there is no essential difference between waking and dreaming experiences: neither is given ontological or epistemological priority. Much the same is stated in two further citations from the *Purification of All Karmic Obscurations* and the GST. A third citation, from the *Gnosis Vajra Compendium*, gives the "twelve similes of phantasm" (*dvādaśa-māyā-dṛṣṭānta*), which describe the bodies emanated by the enlightened beings. They are said to be like: a phantasm, a moon in water, a phantom double, a mirage, a dream, an echo, a city of the gandharvas, Indra's net (an optical illusion), Śakra's bow (a rainbow), lightning, water bubbles, and a mirror-image. It is in such a "phantasm body" (*māyā-deha*, here called the "phantasmic samādhi) that all the buddhas "reside for as long as the life-cycle lasts." With such an unlimited body, "endowed with all the qualities (of an omniscient one)," they are able to pass "from buddha-field to buddha-field"—unimpeded in intellect and motility—for the benefit of unenlightened beings.

Chapter 7: Ultimate Reality/Brilliance

The next chapter is devoted to explaining the stage in which the yogin experiences and controls the fundamental state of brilliance, the subtlest level of the mind/body. This is the "ultimate reality" to the "superficial reality" of the phantasm body; and is also the subjective pole of the final enlightenment process, "the state of purified perception," which will subsequently be unified with its objective correlate—the phantasm body—in the ultimate stage of communion (*yuganaddha*). The Vajra Mentor confesses to difficulty in describing such a thing: while the divine body may be hinted at using the twelve similes of phantasm, the subjective mind of brilliance is "incomparable" and only to be known though introspective discernment, guided by the instructions of the Mentor. He gives an interesting simile to describe this brilliance, a simile that is very similar to yogic ideas about the true self (*ātman*) as described in early Vedāntic literature. The simile is this: just as one cannot see the radiance of a lamp while it sits under a clay pot, yet the light shines out if the pot is broken; just so, the light of buddhagnosis is concealed by the ordinary body—when the latter is shattered via the Mentor's instruction, the former "bursts into view." It is interesting that this verse seems to equate ("objective") "Reality" (*tattva*) with (subjective) buddha-gnosis (*buddha-jñāna*) or, at the very least, suggests that buddhagnosis is the flame of the lamp of Reality. The Mentor emphasizes again the inexpressible nature of the ultimate reality/brilliance, again citing the same verse from the *Teaching of One Method Scripture* that was cited before in chapter 3.

There then follows a description of a rite of initiation that would seem to correspond to the secret initiation (*guhyābhiṣeka*), the second of the four higher initiations. Therein, the Student offers a consort to the Mentor and, regarding him as a real, manifest enlightened being, offers praises and requests initiation. Thus requested by the Student, the Mentor—presumably after ritual intercourse with the offered consort—emits his spirit of enlightenment (here, referring to semen) into a conch shell and offers it, mixed with that of the consort, to the student-initiate as a pledge (*samaya*). The text specifies a sequence of nine (previous) initiations to be given: garland, water, buddha, vajra, bell, mirror, name, teacher, and permission. Initiating the Student in that way, the Mentor is to transmit to the Student "the sacred tradition that comes from the successive generations of mentors."

The process of realizing the brilliance of mind, here called "ultimate reality," is also known in this tradition as the "enlightenment process/stage" (*abhisambodhi-krama*) and is believed to correspond to the enlightenment process experienced by each buddha at the foot of their respective tree of enlightenment (*bodhi-vṛkṣa*). Typically, this process is said to proceed by stages according to the successive periods of the night. The Mentor then goes on to describe these stages as they are experienced externally and internally. Externally, the "outer enlightenment" is experienced as such: dawn is the luminance-imminence "of delusion-darkness"; between dawn and sunrise is the brilliance; sunrise is luminance-radiance; sunset again is luminance-imminence; and moonrise is luminance. This corresponds to the inner experience of the yogin. The process of dissolution of the subtle airs is perceived internally as follows: before the experience of the first subtle mind, the meditator experiences a vision "like a mirage, a mass of five-colored light rays" (f. 47a). Then, one sees luminance, white like the moon. Then one sees radiance, red like the sun. Then utter darkness—the blackness of imminence. Emerging from the experience of darkness, the yogin sees "brilliance, extremely bright, the nature of perpetual luminance, the ultimate reality, the particular."

Having had such a direct perception of the universal void (*sarva-śūnya*) of brilliance, the yogin is instructed to practice the "twofold meditation" (*dvividhaṃ dhyānaṃ*), which—though referred to elsewhere—is here described in brief for the only time in this work. These two meditations are the "dissolving" (*anubheda, rjes su gzhig pa*) and the "holistic" (*piṇḍa-grāha, ril bur 'dzin pa*). Both are processes used to dissolve the airs and thus incite the experience of the fundamental brilliance. The "dissolving" process is said to resemble a globule melting in stainless water. The "holistic" process simulates the gradual disappearance of the vapor of breath from a mirror. I believe that this is a type of visualization-guided meditation, which involves the dissolution of the practitioner's divine form into voidness, envisioned as resembling either of the two natural processes described.

The Vajra Mentor then proceeds to an extensive digression enumerating the various names for the ultimate reality/brilliance/ enlightenment-process. These consist of a laundry list of major terms for the absolute or other elevated persons/states from throughout the Buddhist heritage. Many of them are old, mainstream epithets of nirvāṇa—unarisen, unceasing, inconceivable, uncompounded, peaceful, etc. Others are more esoteric: vajra gnosis, secret accomplishment. Still others are redolent of the Mahāyāna vocabulary of the Transcendent Virtue of Wisdom scriptures (mother of all buddhas, transcendent virtue of wisdom). The Mentor then notes that this enlightenment process is also described by the "six stanzas on the spirit of enlightenment" (*ṣaḍ bodhicitta-gāthāḥ*), which are the famous verses spoken in the second chapter of the *Guhyasamāja Tantra* by the Six Transcendent Lords.

He further cites verses that describe the "supreme maṇḍala" that is "beyond the head and the drop" (*mātrā-bindu-samātīta*). Given the context in which this is spoken, I believe we are meant to interpret this comment in light of the previous discussion of the two processes of dissolution. In these visualizations, the practitioner's divine body is dissolved into its seed syllable (often *hūṃ*: ཧཱུྃ), which then dissolves from the bottom up. The final stage of the dissolution of this graphic syllable involves the body of the letter entering the top line ("head": ྃ) and, subsequently, the dot above ("drop": ྂ). This, then, dissolves either into voidness directly (as seemingly advocated here) or, often in contemporary practice, first into the *nāḍa* (traditionally, a subtle sound-energy, but understood in contemporary Tibet to refer to another graphical element looking like a squiggle on top of the drop: ʿ), and then into voidness. Thus, the "supreme maṇḍala" described here is what is elsewhere in the CMP called the "ultimate reality maṇḍala"—the fundamental brilliance mind experienced upon the dissolution of the airs. "It is to be entered by all living things"—i.e., it is experienced upon death by all beings; it is also "to be entered" in the process of liberation from the lifecycle via these yogas. It is "stainless" and "formless." It is beyond dualities such as pure and impure. The Mentor concludes that there is no use multiplying words to describe this reality, which is the ultimate reference of all the teachings of the buddhas.

The Vajra Student is then described as having understood the foregoing (the description of the outer and inner enlightenment processes, the two dissolution methods, and the names of ultimate reality) and, "casting off adherence to conceptual thought," he praises the Mentor as the expression of enlightened reality. The Mentor, for his part, regards the Student as a veritable buddha and, uttering a praise of the primordially-unarisen voidness of mind, actually bestows the wisdom-gnosis initiation. According to the tradition taught here, the initiation process is not a ritual form created in first-millennium India, but rather reflects the experience of all previous buddhas up to, including, and beyond the Buddha Śākyamuni—whose enlightenment story concludes this chapter. The author, Āryadeva himself, comments in his own voice that it was by this process that the Buddha became enlightened. Deep in the "unshakeable samādhi," he was "roused by all the transcendent lords," whereupon he seated himself under the Bodhi Tree, realized brilliance at midnight, and emerged in a phantasm body to "turn the wheel of Dharma for beings."

This is considered the *locus classicus* of this esoteric Mahāyoga tale of enlightenment by the fifteenth-century Tibetan commentator Kaydrup Je Gelek Palzang, who states that the "method by which the Lord and Teacher became a buddha according to the tradition of the Unexcelled [Tantra]" according to the Noble Tradition is described in Āryadeva's *Lamp for Integrating the Practices*.[195] He then goes on to relate a more elaborate story than that given in the CMP, in which the buddhas summon a divine girl as consort and bestow upon him the wisdom-gnosis initiation, the third of the four higher initiations, whereupon he engaged in the dissolution process, was given the fourth and final initiation, and emerged at dawn as a complete buddha. A similar account is given in Ratnākaraśānti's *"Jewel Rosary" Commentary on [Nāgārjuna's] Abbreviated Sādhana*.[196] In this version, the buddhas tell Śākyamuni that the "unshakeable samādhi" will not cause him to attain the ultimate state and they counsel him to abandon it. He sees them with his divine eye, prostrates four times, and inquires of the authentic samādhi. Hearing this, the buddhas emanate "gnosis" (i.e., immaterial) forms of the four goddesses from their hearts. He receives the initiations; attains buddhahood at midnight; defeats Māra at dawn; and proceeds up to Tuṣita Heaven. One can see in all of these accounts, a desire to legitimate the yogic processes of the esoteric traditions by making them instrumental in the enlightenment process of Śākyamuni—a narrative incorporation typical of innovative Buddhist traditions.

Chapter 8: Unlocated Nirvāṇa/Communion

In some sense, this chapter marks the culmination point of Āryadeva's exegesis. Its topic is the stage of Communion (*yuganaddha*), which is the

195. mKhas-grub-rje, *Rgyud sde spyi rnam*: see Lessing and Wayman, ed., *Mkhas-grub-rje's Fundamentals of the Buddhist Tantras*, 34: *bla med kyi lugs la ston pa bcom ldan 'das sangs rgyas tshul ni | . . . 'phags lugs kyi a rya de ba'i spyod bsdus nas gsungs |*.

196. Ratnākaraśānti, *mDor bsdus pa'i sgrub thabs kyi 'grel pa rin chen phreng ba*: sDe-dge bsTan-'gyur, rGyud-'grel, vol. ci, f. 1b^4–2b^4.

fifth and final stage in the Nāgārjunian system, equivalent to buddha- or vajradhara-hood itself. In fact, he titles this chapter, not the "Stage of Communion," but the "Realm of Unlocated Nirvāṇa," drawing an equivalency between this highest achievement of esoteric yoga and the old Mahāyānist notion of an enlightenment (*nirvāṇa*) that is not localizable (*apratiṣṭhita*). The questions posed at the outset by the Vajra Student are somewhat unclear. That is, the chief question is very clear, but the set of subsidiary queries seems unsystematic. The first and chief question concerns the manner in which the yogin, having mastered the process of creating a divine body "from mere gnosis" and the technique by which one thoroughly purifies the substratum of one's mind by means of dissolution into the "ultimate reality maṇḍala," arises in a completely enlightened divine body-mind.

The auxiliary questions are these: Who experiences true bliss? What is the irreversible? What is the meaning of liberation? And from what is one liberated? The first question is the most problematic. For one, the text is not entirely certain. My reading of "true bliss" (*sat-sukhaṃ*) is based upon the testimony of Tsongkhapa concerning an "alternative translation" of the CMP by Chag Lotsāwa. The sole manuscript evidence, however, reads *sva-sukhaṃ* ("self-bliss"); and the "standard Tibetan translation" reads something like "confrontation" (*mngon par phyogs pa*), suggesting something like *abhimukhīṃ*. Nowhere in the subsequent discussion is any of these terms mentioned. Indeed, the text seems to skip directly from the answer to the first question (which concludes with a citation from the LAS) to the answer to the third. Thus, one is uncertain how to interpret the very existence of this second question, much less settle on a definitive reading.

The answer to the question about irreversibility is more straightforward. The notion of irreversibility has been an important one in Buddhist thought from quite early on. In essence, there arose the idea that a practitioner, at a certain point in their development, reached a point at which buddhahood was certain. There was nothing they could do to backslide on the path—it was all downhill until buddhahood. Although this (and the related idea of "prophecy" [*vyākaraṇa*]) was the subject of some vigorous debate, it was a widely accepted idea. Thus, the Vajra Student is asking, "at what point does the practitioner of the Noble Tradition become 'irreversible'?" The answer is that they become so after they have achieved mastery over the fourth stage of brilliance. Until this point, the Vajra Student is told, "the three radiances [are] not purified" (CMP, f. 50a). Until this is so (i.e., until the mastery of brilliance), there is the "linked continuity of defilement" and, thus, rebirth. After the consummation of brilliance, one may be said to be destined for liberation. After all, the practitioner has only to arise from the ultimate brilliance using the (previously mastered) process of self-consecration to effect enlightenment.

The Vajra Master then goes on to describe the emergence from brilliance, traversing the four voids in reverse order, which culminates in the practitioner emerging in the "body of supreme joy" that emerges "like a fish [leaping] out of water" (CMP, f. 50b). This, we are told, is Vajradhara; it is liberation. This is validated by a series of citations from scriptures that describe the enlightened body created by esoteric practices: the *Secret Accomplishment* (*Guhyasiddhi*), the GST, PK/*Niraupamyastava*, *Compendium of All Rituals* (*Sarvakalpasamuccaya*), *King of Samādhi Scripture* (*Samādhirājasūtra*), and *Transcendent Virtue of Wisdom Scripture*. The remainder of the chapter is devoted to giving a detailed listing of the synonyms of enlightenment in the Buddhist tradition. This may be understood as answering the question (only found in Tib) "who is liberated?" It may also (like the similar list in chapter 7) be thought to serve the function of validating this attainment from a general Buddhist perspective. That is, in marshalling an array of terms for enlightenment from across the spectrum of Buddhist discourse, the author is, in effect, incorporating and superceding them.

Chapter 9: Practice with Elaboration

With the description of the communion stage in chapter 8, the CMP has concluded its chief subject matter. Nonetheless, a topic of central importance remains to be addressed. Indeed, over a quarter of the work remains, and is entirely devoted to this topic: that is, the "practices" (*caryā*). In brief, these practices consist principally in the enjoyment of the five objects of sensory desire (*pañca-kāma-guṇāḥ*) and, in particular, the enjoyment of tactile objects, preeminent among which figures the enjoyment of *dvayendriya-samāpatti* (or *-prayoga*), the "union of the two (sexual) organs." In brief, Āryadeva characterizes the practices as follows: "The practices of enlightenment, born from passion, are of three kinds: with elaboration (*prapañcatā*), without elaboration (*niṣprapañcatā*), and thoroughly without elaboration (*atyantaniṣprapañcatā*). . . . By the three types of practice, [they] will attain the level of Mahāvajradhara."[197] These three types of practices are the subject matter, respectively, of chapters 9, 10, and 11 of the CMP.

The Vajra Student initiates the discussion by inquiring of the conduct of the yogin "exerting himself . . . in the causal condition" who desires to manifest "the perfection of omniscience." The Vajra Mentor replies with his usual enthusiasm, implying in the process that the practices are for those who want to obtain the eight superhuman powers in this very life. This suggests that one of the purposes of the practices is the effecting of such powers (*siddhis*), rather than merely the purification of the vestiges (*vasanā*) of defilement.[198] He divides the topic into two subtopics: the purification of [meditative] cultivation and the purification of practice.

He begins his discussion by referring to the principle that, seen from the highest perspective, there is no intrinsic difference between the enlightened and the unenlightened states. Nonetheless, in keeping with his gradualist standpoint, the Mentor insists that "in the context of exerting oneself [in practice]" there *is* a critical distinction between cause and effect, the unenlightened practitioner and the enlightened result. Thus, he addresses these practices in conventional terms, for "without the practices of [spiritual] discipline (*vrata-caryā*), [one] cannot destroy the vestiges of beginningless defilement" (CMP, f. 54a).

He begins by again invoking the example of Buddha Śākyamuni. He describes three careers of the Buddha by which he undertook three types of realization (of the Four Noble Truths, objective selflessness, and nonduality) and addressed three different types of disciples (corresponding to the three ways: Hīnayāna, Mahāyāna, and Vajrayāna). The first two—which he calls the ways of the Śrāvakas and the Scripturalists[199]—the Mentor asserts, are "not suitable" for attaining the highest goal. This is established by

197. CMP, f. 57a–b: *rāgaja-bodhicaryā trividhā* | *yad uta prapañcatā niṣprapañcatā atyantaniṣprapañcatā ceti* | . . . *trividhacaryābhir mahāvajra[dhara]padaṃ niṣpādayanti* |.

198. This is, indeed, what Tsongkhapa claims in his RṄSG: that the "practices" effect the mundane powers on the creation stage, and the transcendental power of enlightenment on the perfection stage. However, this position seems somewhat problematic with regard to the Indian sources. See my "Antinomianism and Gradualism."

199. Here, he seems to be using the term Scripturalist (*sautrāntika*) for all the practitioners of the Mahāyāna, rather than in its more restricted sense of a school of Buddhist thought. Jacob Dalton (personal email communication, 21 December 2005) has indicated that this usage is typical of the (roughly contemporaneous) Tibetan materials from Dun-huang.

citations from the *Enlightenment of Vairocana* and the GST and two unidentified scriptures. The chief distinction he seeks to draw is that the two lower ways depend on mortification of the body, whereas the highest way does not, involving rather the yogic use of sense pleasure. This is supported by citations from the *Supreme Prime* (*Paramādya*) *Tantra* and the GST.

The Vajra Student then asks the "million-dollar question" with respect to esoteric Buddhist practice: since the Buddha taught that sense indulgence leads to lower rebirth *not* buddhahood, how is it that this does not contradict the esoteric teaching of using sense pleasure for enlightenment? Adding to the piquancy of his question is the fact that the verse he cites in support of the Buddha's stance against sense pleasure[200] is drawn, not from a major mainstream Buddhist scripture, but from an esoteric text (the *Mahāmāyūrī-vidyārājñī*).[201] Such a seemingly manifest contradiction cannot be so easily dismissed by the Mentor.

Delighted (of course) by the Student's question, which will obviate the doubts of those who engage in the practices of passion, the Vajra Mentor gives this answer:

> The Lord [Buddha] himself taught in the scriptures that the defilements such as passion are the cause of lower rebirth for those with objectifying views such as Śrāvakas, as [they] do not thoroughly understand the intrinsic nature of defilement; while, through thorough understanding of the intrinsic nature [of defilement], they become the cause for enlightenment.

This is supported by citations to this effect, from the *Supreme Prime*, the *Kāśyapa Chapter* (*Kāśyapaparivarta*: an important scripture in the Jewel Heap [Ratnakūṭa] class), and the (otherwise unknown) *Unfailing Success in Discipline* (*Vinayāmoghasiddhi*) *Tantra*. This is, of course, fairly standard esoteric theory (with roots in the Mahāyāna scriptures, as evident in the *Kāśyapa Chapter* citation; one might also cite the "Family of the Buddhas"

200. "Passion, hatred, and ignorance are the three poisons in the world" (*rāgo dveṣaś ca mohaś ca ete loke trayo viṣāḥ*).

201. At least the verse is found there; it may also have a more mainstream pedigree.

chapter of the *Vimalakīrti Sūtra*,[202] among others). The same view is also put forth in other works of the Noble Tradition—for instance, Nāgabodhi in his *Arranged Stages* (*Vyavastholikrama*) claims that "in the initial context when the ordinary body is saturated by lust, hatred, and delusion, [such practices] are the cause of *saṃsāra*; later, when their nature has been thoroughly understood and purified, [they] become the cause of the accomplishment of omniscience."[203] The Mentor concludes that there is no other practice for effecting great bliss—which is the *sine qua non* for enlightenment—than these practices, which he here calls the "distinctive transference (*samāropa*) and the distinctive transformation (*pariṇāma*)." Thus, the state of omniscience (i.e., buddhahood)—of which the eight superhuman powers are a metonym—"is realized by means of pleasurable food, residence, and so on" (CMP, f. 57a).

The Mentor then introduces the three categories of practice—with, without, and completely without elaboration—and defines them. The first is the extensive play (*āralli*—a key term, likely related to the term *oralli* as found in orthodox "Hindu" esoterism)[204] of the transcendent lords as taught in the *Union of All Buddhas Tantra*. The second is a more condensed form, for those whose time is short due to the necessity of business commitments (*kārya*). The last is even more truncated—involving only the practitioner. The categories of practice are aligned with different scriptural authorities. There are two categories of practice with elaboration, which follow the dictates of either the *Compendium of Realities* or the *Supreme Prime*. The GST, however, only teaches the practices without and completely without elaboration. With this overview of the varieties of practice complete, the discussion then turns to the central topic of this chapter: the practice with elaboration. It is, presumably given the extent of its "elaboration," the longest of the three discussions—dealing in detail with the various arrangements that may be made for yogic enjoyment by esoteric Buddhist communities.

The first topic is the construction of a building in which the practices may be performed. The ideal structure is three-storied, with a kitchen on

202. See Thurman, trans., *Holy Teaching of Vimalakīrti*, 64–72.

203. *tha mal pa'i lus la 'dod chags dang zhe sdang dang gti mug la sogs pas brlan pa'i sngon gyi gnas skabs su 'khor ba'i rgyu yin la phyis rang bzhin yongs su shes shing yongs su dag pas thams cad mkhyen pa grub pa'i rgyur 'gyur ba*: Nāgabodhi, *Samāja-sādhanaṃ Vyavastholi-krama* (*'Dus pa'i sgrub pa'i thabs rnam par gzhag pa'i rim pa*), sDe-dge bsTan-'gyur, vol. 48, 29a$^{5-6}$.

204. See s.v. *Tāntrikābhidhānakośa* II.

the first, a chapel on the second with provision for musical worship, and a room on the top floor for the practitioners to enact the maṇḍala of gods and goddesses. However, allowance may also be made for a single-story structure, imagined as such an elaborate celestial palace (*kūṭāgāra*). It is to be adorned (and/or envisioned) as the maṇḍala palace of the central deity: four-doored, eight-pillared, strung with garlands, yak tails, etc. Here, the practitioner "should engage the practice of the Great Seal (Mahāmudrā)" in the company of two sets of female consorts: the companions (*sahacarī*) and attendants (*anucarī*).

The Mentor then describes a yogic enactment of the maṇḍala, in which the practitioner focuses on "ultimate reality" (i.e., dissolves him/herself into the brilliance/voidness) and emerges (by the self-consecration process) in the form of the lord of the maṇḍala, Vajrasattva, in order to enjoy pleasure with the goddesses. These latter are then described in detail with their names, appearances, and locations in the maṇḍala. Note that the maṇḍala so described would seem to be that of the SBS, not the GST. There are four companions (*sahacarī*) in the four cardinal directions; there are four more in the intermediate directions; four performing-arts goddesses in the outer intermediate directions; four offering goddesses in the intermediate directions outside the curtain; and four door-guardians at the four cardinal gateways; for a total of twenty-one deities (Vajrasattva and twenty goddesses).

A rite is then described in which the practitioner begins by consecrating food and the objects of sight, sound, and smell, consumes them, and transforms the bliss into the elixir of immortality (*rasāyana*). Then the practitioner gratifies the "body vajra" by means of the fifth sense: touch. This involves selecting one of the twenty goddesses as a consort, setting her in his lap, and engaging in a variety of sexual activities, described in some detail (CMP, ff. 60b–62a). This sexual stimulation precipitates the dissolution of "the transcendent lords who have the nature of the aggregates, and so on," causing them to descend through the subtle psychic veins in a process that seems equivalent to that of dissolving the subtle mind into brilliance through the levels of luminance, radiance, and imminence. Having mastered this process, the yogin may "mature" beings through the application of what are here called "inducements and deterrents" (*nigraha-anugraha*). These are effected by means of the four yogic powers: pacification, prosperity, control, and destruction. Each power corresponds to a different central deity and a different type of disciple-being.

The discussion then turns to the secret tokens (*cchomā*), verbal and bodily, of the esoteric community of practitioners. Much has been written on this subject; and there has been much confusion—most notably conflating these tokens with the practice of intentional speech (*saṃdhyā-vacana*). It is not the place here to address the many issues surrounding the proper interpretation of these facets of esoteric Buddhist culture. Suffice it to say that we are here presented with one important list of the secret verbal and bodily signs—material that bears further analysis in light of the other, similar lists. The yogin who undertakes this practice is compared to the mythical king (and esoteric practitioner) Indrabhūti who "having transformed his body . . . [and] become a vajra body, disappearing together with his harem, goes from buddha-field to buddha-field endowed with the eight masteries" (CMP, f. 63b).[205] The discussion concludes with another statement to the effect that, if one cannot afford the cost (in time and money) of such elaborate erotic play (*krīḍā*), the SBS also authorizes practice without and completely without elaboration. Citations from this scripture are given to validate this claim.

Chapter 10: Practice without Elaboration

This chapter is devoted to the more sparse practices without elaboration. As will be seen, this practice does not differ greatly from those with elaboration—there is only one consort, but much of the associated ritual remains the same. Hence, our discussion here will be more cursory than the rest, so as not to go over old ground. The Mentor begins by specifying that the location be a remote one. The previous practices were said to be performed in "an agreeable place free of unfortunate ones such as Śrāvakas and the like." Here, the Mentor cites the GST's authority that one should practice in a great wilderness, an isolated location. There, in a single-story cottage or on a ritual platform, the practitioner again visualizes a celestial palace and, together with one consort and the host of disciples (*śiṣya-gaṇa*), practices the Great Seal (*mahāmudrā*). There, again preceded by dissolution (into brilliance) and emergence (through the self-consecration), the practitioner visualizes the entire maṇḍala in his/her own body. Then the practitioner

205. The attentive reader will recall that the character of Indrabhūti plays a central role in the myth of origins of the Esoteric Community. See p. 25, above.

and consort again dissolve into brilliance/voidness and emerge (again via self-consecration) and "frolic . . . in order to enjoy the savor of supreme joy." Again, the four senses (sight, sound, smell, and taste) are first gratified. Then, to gratify the sense of touch, the yogin unites with his consort in sexual union. Here, there is greater stress on antinomian behavior. The consort is specified to belong to unclean or inauspicious communities. Subsequent to their union, the yogin consecrates the pledge [substances] (*samaya*)—here presumably at least the sexual fluid of yogin and yoginī, if not also the entire array of "five meats and five ambrosias"[206]—and consumes them. Noteworthy here is the specification that such consumption is to be done "in a private place" (*pracchanne pradeśe*). Further stress is laid on the notion that the yogin involved in such practices is completely absorbed in internal yogic processes, and does not engage in the external practices, such as the rituals, astrology, etc. advocated in the "lower" esoteric traditions.

Then a truncated maṇḍala is taught for the erotic practices, for one who cannot afford the entire array as described in chapter 9. This retinue consists of merely five goddesses—corresponding to the five sense objects—in the four intermediate directions and in one's lap. Again a process is described (CMP, ff. 67a–b) in which a variety of sexual techniques result in the dissolution of the transcendent lords (of the "body maṇḍala") into the psychic veins and a corresponding great bliss. If five consorts are not available, we are told, one may perform it with one goddess alone (Sparśavajrā, Touch Adamant, in one's lap), visualizing all of the transcendent lords in the bodies of the two practitioners. This discussion is capped by a citation of the *locus classicus* of the "consort discipline" (*vidyāvrata*) from GST chapter 16.

Chapter 11: Practice completely without Elaboration

The final chapter begins in a distinctive way: it is the only chapter (after the first) that does not begin with a question posed by the Vajra Student. The Vajra Mentor simply continues, describing the nature of the practices completely without elaboration. Its beginning is strongly reminiscent of that of chapter 10, citing a similar verse describing the site to be used for practice (*sādhana-*

206. Two sets of conventionally defiling substances (cow, dog, horse, elephant, and human meat; and blood, semen, urine, feces, and marrow). On the interpretation of these substances in esoteric ritual, see my "Beef, Dog, and Other Mythologies."

sthāna)—again, a lovely yet remote place. Here, however, as the practitioner is engaged in the practices alone, provision must be made for food. This can be done by means of supernatural help (invoking dryads [*yakṣinī*] or other spirits for assistance), or by arranging help from a ritual assistant (*uttara-sādhaka*).

The practice itself is more ascetic (relatively speaking, of course): one is reminded to recall the suffering of the life-cycle, to abandon all social interaction, to abandon the desire to possess objects, and to have no regard for body or life. Nor, indeed, should this practitioner desire either minor powers or the eight great powers cited in the last two chapters as one goal of the practices. These, the Mentor says, are "distracting and mutable"—the practice completely free of elaboration is devoted solely to the "non-conceptual power," Mahāvajradharahood itself. This is to be attained through union with a gnosis consort (*jñāna-mudrā*), rather than a physical consort (*karma-mudrā*).

After a brief résumé of the prototypes, radiances, and air, the Mentor describes a yogic process of using the sleep/dream dissolution process (rather than that of sexual union) as a means of perceiving ultimate reality/brilliance. This is called the "inner enlightenment" (f. 71a), said to result in the transformation of the ordinary body into a vajra body "more quickly." This process, which eschews "all play (*āralli*) and attachment to sense objects," is also called the "practice of a *bhusuku*"—i.e., of one who is devoted solely to eating (*bhu*), sleeping (*su*), and defecating (*ku*). This is subsequently called the "mad spiritual discipline" (*unmatta-vrata*) and is said to derive from the teachings of the explanatory tantra[s].

The accomplishment of this practice—said to take either a fortnight, a month, or six months—results in the attainment of a vajra body:

> Subtle in form, light to the touch,
> Having obtained omnipresence,
> Brightness and firmness,
> [Self-]mastery, [and] having come to the end of desire.

Dream portents, which indicate success in the practice, are cited from the *Esoteric Community Tantra*.

At this point, the Vajra Student finally asks what will be his final question: how essential are these practices? If a practitioner is too overwhelmed with day-to-day concerns such as farming, trade, etc., and can't do all this erotic play or mad wandering—if they have seen reality, can they nonetheless attain enlightenment upon death? Or will they return to ordinary *saṃsāra*? The Vajra Mentor is unequivocal at first: if one has seen reality, one has by definition accomplished the perfection stage and, thus, will be enlightened. Some qualification is needed, however.

First of all, he gives a brief discourse on the apparent paradox of rebirth without a self, using traditional analogies from the mainstream Buddhist tradition, such as the continuity of a flame from flame, seal-impressions, etc. He then stresses the phantasmic nature of all this, including the birth and death of the Buddha. He cites the well-known *Golden Radiance Scripture* (*Suvarṇābhāsa-sūtra*) verse about the docetic nature of the Buddha's career. The perfection stage yogin is likewise said to be an enlightened being, making a show of birth, death, and enlightenment for the sake of others. Such scriptural niceties aside, he then comes to the heart of the matter. One may attain enlightenment without the practices, through using the actual death experience as a vehicle for the yoga of the perfection stage. The practitioner "generates the firm resolution that 'having cast off the ordinary aggregates, I will arise by the process of self-consecration.'" That is, having died and entered the brilliance upon the dissolution of his vital airs, the yogin arises in the between state as a fully perfected buddha. This teaching becomes especially important in Tibetan monastic esoterism, insofar as it provides the rationale for foregoing the radical, unmonkish "practices" in favor of reaching enlightenment in the between state after death.[207]

At the outset of the work, Āryadeva described the earlier masters as composing works in order to clarify the "meaningful words" of the scriptures. He concludes his work by returning to this notion. He states that beings cannot grasp these words, as they are as hard to obtain as a drop of oil floating on stormy seas. Working the analogy somewhat, he concludes that he has taken up a little of this oil in the foregoing—as fuel for his *Lamp*, to light the "minds of fortunate beings." With this, the CMP concludes. Little remains now but to stand aside and present my own English translation. First, though, a word or two is in order concerning the constitution of, and typographical conventions found in, this translation.

207. The dGe-lugs Tradition asserts this of its founder, Tsongkhapa, to account for how he could attain enlightenment via esoteric means without taking a consort and thus violating his monastic vows.

Conventions in the Translation

Though the translation is meant to reflect in the main the edited Sanskrit text provided in the first edition (and now available in the online reading room at wisdomexperience.org), when possible I have tried to indicate divergences between the Tibetan and Sanskrit in the main text. Following the practice of some translations of multi-language works (e.g., Descartes' Latin and French *Meditations on First Philosophy*), I have used brackets to indicate which materials are exclusive to different versions. Thus, all readings found in the Sanskrit for which there is no equivalent in the Tibetan translation are set off by curly brackets: {...}. Likewise, elements found in the Tibetan but not the Sanskrit, insofar as they are not inappropriate, have been incorporated yet set off by parentheses: (...).[208] Tibetan readings that are contradictory or incompatible with the Sanskrit text have been relegated to the footnotes. Clarificatory elements added by myself have, according to long-standing practice, been set off in square brackets: [...].

An asterisk before a Sanskrit or Tibetan word signifies a form reconstructed on the basis of a form in the other language not actually attested in that context. The names of cited works are set in italic type. Paragraph breaks are my own, and I have endeavored to keep them consistent across the texts.

The issue of gendered language has presented some difficulties in the execution of the translation. Like traditional English usage, the masculine pronoun of classical Sanskrit is frequently inclusive of both genders. However, given the changes that have taken place in contemporary English due to principled considerations of gender, translating the masculine pronoun by gender-inclusive equivalents would seem to be preferable in many contexts. However, given the strongly gendered language of some (particularly the later) chapters of the CMP, I have decided to render the Sanskrit pronouns throughout with their strict, gendered equivalents. In reading the translation, then, the reader should keep in mind that masculine pronouns and forms (he, his, yogin, etc.) *may* be appropriately taken in a gender-inclusive manner (i.e., as s/he, her/his, yogin/ī, etc.).

208. Glosses are also set off by parentheses, but these should be self-evident enough as not to cause any confusion between the two.

Part Two

Translation

(In Sanskrit: *Caryāmelāpakapradīpa*
In Tibetan: *Spyod pa bsdus pa'i sgron ma*)

††{Homage to Glorious Vajrasattva!} A:1b
(Homage to the bodhisattva, the great one, Mañjuśrī, the gnosis-being!)[209] C:42a

{Pay} homage to the space-like, essenceless and pure!
{Pay} homage to the wholly unspoken and inexpressible![210]
{Pay} homage to the omnipresent in past and future![211]
{Pay} homage to the ubiquitous, total universal void![212]

209. Presumably the Tibetan translator's homage (*'gyur phyag*).

210. *aśeṣam anakṣaram avācyam*; Tib reads *ma lus tshig med yi ge bral*, "wholly wordless and syllable-less," which is another way of interpreting the expression.

211. Following ms C and Tib: *namatātītānāgatasarvagataṃ*, *'das dang ma byon kun du son la phyag 'tshal lo*. ms A reads, "Pay homage to the Blissful One, omnipresent in future!" (*namatānāgatasarvagaṃ sugataṃ*).

212. *samastāśeṣasarvaśūnyam*; Tib suggests "perpetual, ubiquitous universal void" (*kun du ma lus thams cad stong*).

I. Resolution of Doubts {About the Integration of Enlightenment}

Here in the Adamantine Way, the teachers of the two types of practice by means of mantra—[that is,] those devoted to mantra and those devoted to interior [transformation][213]—supremely erudite and aiming to care for all beings, in order to clarify the meaningful words[214] proclaimed in the scriptures[215] through the compositional arrangement of the cryptic expressions [found therein]—such as the many elegant and lovely[216] words spoken in verses and songs, prose and verse—extracted [these words] from the authentic tantras and established the divisions of the art of accomplishment (*sādhana*) [to act] (like) lamps in order that the naïve should understand.[217]

213. These precise terms are not used elsewhere in the CMP, though at f. 20a those "who devote themselves to outer mantras" (*bāhya-mantra-parāyaṇāḥ*) are equated with those who do not understand the explanatory tantras. These terms do appear in PU (e.g., p. 180), where they are correlated with the bodhisattvas and the buddhas, whose practices are "sign-ful" and "signless," respectively (*sanimittānimitta*). According to dbYangs-can dGa'-ba'i bLo-gros's (eighteenth/nineteenth-century) work, *Stages and Paths of Mantra According to the Noble Tradition of the Glorious Esoteric Community*, "yoga devoted to mantra" (*sngags la gzhol ba'i rnal 'byor*) is a synonym for coarse creation stage yoga and "yoga devoted to interior [transformation]" (*nang la gzhol ba'i rnal 'byor*) is a synonym for subtle creation stage yoga. He continues, "Tantric commentaries repeatedly apply the term 'one devoted to mantra' to the yogin who has completed the coarse creation stage, and the term 'one devoted to interior [transformation]' to the yogin who has completed the subtle creation stage" (*bskyed rim rangs pa mthar phyin pa'i rnal 'byor pa la sngags la mchog tu gzhol ba zhes pa dang | bskyed rim phra mo mthar phyin pa'i rnal 'byor pa la nang la mchog tu gzhol ba zhes pa'i tha snyad rgyud 'grel las yang yang gsungs so* |); see dbYangs-can dGa'-ba'i bLo-gros, *Sa lam rnam gzhag*, f. $3b^{2-5}$.

214. *artha-vacana*; Tib reads "words of scripture" (*lung gi tshig*; **āgama-vacana*?).

215. Reading *sūtra* with ms A; ms C reads *sūtaka*, which may correspond to Tib "sūtras, tantras, and kalpas" (*mdo sde dang rgyud dang rtog pa dag*).

216. *lalita*; Tib reads "elaborate" (*rgya che ba*).

217. Tib has taken some liberties with the grammar of this opening statement, presumably in order to make it more clear. It reads: "Undertaking practices through the portal of mantra

That was appropriate[218] [previously] in the Perfect, Threefold, and Twofold Eras.[219] (Why?) [In those eras,] folk were blessed with vitality and health, and were endowed with the blessed qualities of the practices of generosity, ethics, and so forth. Through deep investigation of the foundations of the sciences (*śāstra*), [they] became endowed with the gnosis of Reality (*tattva-jñāna*). [Hence,] when Reality was demonstrated [to them] by means of cryptic expressions—such as lovely words, and so forth—they understood.

But now, in this Contentious Era, folk lack the blessings of vitality and
A:2a health, are crafty, deceitful, haughty, {envious}, †and jealous; they lack
C:42b critical wisdom and [hold] false views; they take pleasure in bad actions.‡ Insofar as [they are] incapable of[220] ascertaining the meaning of the cryptic expressions—such as lovely words, and so on—[they] do not investigate Reality. Hence, not understanding Reality due to neglecting deep investigation of the exoteric sciences,[221] [their] time comes [to die, and they] become devoted to virtuous and unvirtuous action (*karma*). Hence, it is pointless for those who desire liberation to resort to literary conceits such as lovely words, elegance, and so on, since [verbal] expressions are like a raft.[222] Just

---

in this Adamantine Way is twofold—devotion to secret mantra and devotion to interior [transformation]—the mentors [who teach these two], the erudite who care for all sentient beings—in order to clarify the words of scripture proclaimed in the sūtras, tantras, and ritual texts . . ." (*rdo rje theg pa 'di la sngags kyi sgor spyod pa ni rnam pa gnyis te | slob dpon gsang sngags la mchog tu gzhol ba dang | nang la mchog tu gzhol ba ste | thos pa'i pha rol tu son pa rnams kyis sems can thams cad rjes su gzung bar bya ba'i don du | mdo sde dang rgyud dang rtog pa dang las yang dag par gsungs pa'i lung gi tshig rnam par gsal bar bya ba'i phyir*).

218. Following Skt's reading of *yuktaṃ*; Tib reads "inappropriate" (*mi rigs*, **ayuktaṃ*).

219. These are the first three (of four) eras of the Indian cosmic cycle of decline: *kṛta-yuga*, *tretā-yuga*, and *dvāpara-yuga*. The final (and current) era is the "Contentious Era" (*kali-yuga*). The principle of this classification is that an initial set of four qualities declines over the eras, one disappearing in each. Stefan Baums has suggested to me that the first era may also be rendered the "Fourfold era," as it has been argued (cf. Mayrhofer, *Etymologisches Wörterbuch*, s.v.) that *kṛta* is an old numerical term related to *catur*.

220. *aśaktatvāt*; Tib reads, "As they do not rejoice in . . ." (*mi dga' bas*, **asaktatvāt*).

221. Skt *bāhya-śāstra*; Tibetan reads *dang po'i bstan bcos*, "primary sciences/texts."

222. Skt *kola*; Tib reads "ship" (*gzings*). I take this metaphor to mean the words are like a raft in that they conduct one to the meaning, not the typical use of this analogy in the sense of a raft that helps one cross the ocean of *saṃsāra*. This use of the raft metaphor is found in Asaṅga's *Mahāyānasūtrālaṃkāra* XIII.2 where its intention is declared to be the "elimina-

as the Lord said, "[one] should rely on the meaning; as for the word[s], let them be any old way."[223]

Having grasped this crucial point, through the tradition[224] of {Glorious} Nāgārjuna{pāda}, I[225] attained the samādhi of the perfection process following in order [after] the creation process. In order to clarify the mantra reality, seal reality, self reality, divinity reality, [and] the fivefold process (*pañca-krama*),[226] I will set forth [this *Lamp*] that integrates scriptural [citations][227] using straightforward expressions common to both students who are ritually prepared and those who are not.[228]

---

tion of satisfaction with (mere) learning" (*śrutatuṣṭiprahāṇāya*). This usage would appear to be consonant with that found here.

223. This is a reference to the injunction that the bodhisattva should follow the meaning, not the 'letter' (cf. CMP chapter 3, below, which cites the same sentiment from the *Laṅkāvatārasūtra*). Tib reads, "one should follow the meaning, not the words" (*don gyi rjes su 'brang bar bya'i sgra ji bzhin par ma yin no*).

224. *āmnāya*; Tib reads "personal instructions" (*man ngag*). Note that Tib also refers to Nāgārjuna as the author's "own teacher" (*bdag gi slob dpon*), whereas Skt does not.

225. Tib (PN) seems to conform to Skt, reading *bdag gis*. Tib (DCo), however, reads "of my mentor Nāgārjuna" (*bdag gi slob dpon klu sgrub*). Presumably, these editors altered the instrumental to genitive in relation to the following "mentor" (*slob dpon*), which stands in for Skt "Glorious" (*śrī*). Thanks to Dr. Losang Jamspal here.

226. Tib adds an extra "reality" between "self reality" and "divinity reality," a so-called "dharma reality" (*chos kyi de kho na nyid*, **dharma-tattva*), which is not found in either Skt or RṄGC. It is not clear whether this is integral to Tib, or is the result of subsequent textual corruption. One suspects that it was added in order to make the realities come up to a list of five, to correspond to the fivefold process. Its absence from RṄGC leads me to suspect that it was not originally to be found in Tib, though I have retained it in my edition. Since it occurs in the apocryphal commentary of "Śākyamitra," it is of early provenance.

227. Note the use here of the term *melāpaka*, as found in the title of the work. The author signals here the character of this composition, in that it marshalls scriptural authority to legitimate the practices of his tradition. I read *sūtra-melāpaka* (following ms A), though the reading of ms C (*sūtaka-melāpaka*) may be preferable insofar as Tōru Tomabechi suggests that it may correspond to Tib "sūtras, tantras, and ritual texts (kalpa)" (*mdo sde dang rgyud dang rtog pa rnams*). This is less than perfectly clear, however. For, just below, ms A reads *sūtraka* (and ms C *sūtaka*), which is rendered in Tib merely by "sutras and so on" (*mdo sde la sogs pa*).

228. *saṃskṛtāsaṃskṛta-śiṣya*, *'dus byas pa dang 'dus ma byas pa'i slob ma*. Traditionally in Indian religion this refers to individuals who have been ritually purified for study or practice. The relevance of this distinction here is not clear, as one would presume all the students engaged in Tantric Buddhist study would have been ritually prepared or initiated in some way.

It was said by the Lord in all the scriptural discourses [such as] the sūtras, and so on: "those who lack [understanding of] Reality will not succeed
A:2b even in billions[229] of æons." †As the Lord said in the Great Yoga Tantra *Enquiry of the Four Goddesses*:[230]

> Those who do not know Reality
> In the eighty-four thousand Dharma teachings
> Of the Great Sage,
> They [are] all barren of results.[231]

The Vajra Student inquired,[232] "Since the Lord has said, 'without the gnosis of Reality, there could be no buddhahood,' I wish to learn the so-called 'characteristic of Reality' according to scriptural tradition (*pravacana*). As the practitioners of the Universal Way, the logicians (*tārkika*), and so forth, taking their stand on the interpretable meaning,[233] conceptualize Reality in manifold ways—in order to communicate with them, speak, Lord! What is 'Reality?'"

The Vajra Mentor replied, "That which is real (*bhūtaṃ*), that is 'Reality' (*tattvaṃ*)."

The Vajra Student inquired: "Lord, what is 'real?'"

"That which is non-deceptive[234] is real."

229. *koṭi-śata*, "one hundred ten millions"; Tib reads merely *bye ba*, "ten million."

230. *Caturdevīparipṛcchā*, *Lha mo bzhis zhus pa*; A Sanskrit text of this important explanatory tantra of the GST has not come to light. A Tibetan translation (by Smṛtijñāna-kīrti) may be found at: DK, rGyud, vol. ca, ff. $277b^3$–$281b^7$.

231. This citation may be found at DK, rGyud, vol. ca, f. $279a^{5-6}$. The bKa'-'gyur reading diverges, omitting 'Great Sage'; see also PKṬYM and CGKV.

232. The rest of Āryadeva's work is presented as a dialogue between a Vajra Mentor (*vajra-guru*) and his Vajra Student (*vajra-śiṣya*), who interrogates him about the nature and sequence of the various practices on the Vajrayāna path. A complete list of the questions posed, somewhat abstracted, is found in Appendix V. See the Introduction above regarding the possible identity of this Vajra Mentor.

233. Tib reads "this very idea."

234. *avisaṃvādaka*: a term with strong epistemological overtones, suitable to the discussion at hand. The real/existent (*bhūtaṃ*) is accessed through an authoritative source (*pramāṇa*—

"What is 'non-deceptive?'"

"The samādhi whose nature conduces to the real[235] is non-deceptive."

"What is that 'samādhi whose nature conduces to the real?'"

"That whose character is to make the two realities nondual is the samādhi whose nature conduces to the real."

"What are those two realities, Lord?"

"The first is superficial reality; the second† is ultimate reality." A:3a

"What [are] the distinguishing characteristic[s] of the two realities, Lord?"

The Vajra Mentor answered: "It was described by the Lord in the *Vajra Crown-Protrusion Tantra*:[236]

> Vajrapāṇi asked, 'Lord, what is the ultimate reality, the foundation (*ālaya*) of all things?'
>
> The Lord said, 'Overlord of Secret Ones, all things—{those having the nature of} aggregates, elements, media, (and) all beings, animate and inanimate—are the dwelling places (*āśraya*) of the ultimate reality [and], since [it stands] in a non-static manner, the ultimate reality† is selfless, undominated, universally void. [It C:43a is] without increase, without decrease, thoroughly pure, space-like, stainless in nature, unspoken, inexpressible,[237] free of body, speech, and mind. It does not exist, nor is it nonexistent; [it is]

---

in Buddhist terms, generally an authoritative/valid direct perception or authoritative/valid inference), one of the primary characteristics of which is its non-deceptiveness.

235. *bhūta-nayātmakaḥ samādhiḥ, yang dag pa'i tshul gyi bdag nyid can gyi ting nge 'dzin.*

236. *Vajroṣṇīṣa-tantra, rDo rje gtsug tor gyi rgyud.* This scripture does not seem to have been translated into Tibetan, nor has it been found in Sanskrit. It is not infrequently cited in Tibetan commentarial literature, drawing from passages cited in works such as this one.

237. *anakṣaram avācyam*; see note 210 on the title page of the translation, above.

> not animate, nor inanimate, not far, not near, not void, not non-void, nor yet a middle [thing] is this ultimate reality. Therefore, that supremely profound, difficult to fathom, birthless, ceaseless [ultimate reality] is the [fundamental pre-]condition of the superficial reality.[238] This superficial reality, insofar as it is like a dream, an optical illusion, (and) a reflection {in a mirror}, is the phantasmic samādhi. By its intrinsic character it is the cause of the four pure abodes (*brahma-vihāra*). The process leading to the communion of those two is this samādhi whose nature conduces to the real.† [It is] the eradication of all objectification. All that is 'Reality.'"

The Vajra Student inquired: "Ordinary beings like ourselves who, due to beginningless obsession with various external objects, are obsessed with concepts whose cause is the vestigial instinct [to conceive] natures (such as) existent and nonexistent, unity, non-unity, both, [or] neither, non-existence, non-nonexistence, permanence, impermanence, (and so on)—when learning the (successive) samādhis of the perfection stage, do they learn according to a [sequential] process or will they be illuminated instantaneously by the personal instructions of the guru?"

The Vajra Mentor replied: "They learn by a gradual method, not immediately. The Lord himself stated in the *Journey to Laṅka Scripture*:[239]

> Then {indeed} the bodhisattva, the great one, Mahāmati asked the Lord again in order to purify the continuum of his own mental experience, 'Lord, how is the continuum of one's own mental experience purified: immediately or by a gradual method?'

238. Literally, "has the superficial reality condition." N and P follow SKT here. D and Co omit this last phrase. All Tibetan versions add "the superficial reality is born from causes and conditions" (*rgyu rkyen gyis 'byung ba ni kun rdzob kyi bden pa ste)*.

239. *Laṅkāvatārasūtra, Lang kar gshegs pa'i mdo*. An extremely influential scripture of Mahāyāna Buddhism, the LAS has been edited in its original Sanskrit by Bunyiu Nanjio (see Nanjio, ed., *Laṅkāvatāra Sūtra*) and P. L. Vaidya (see Vaidya, ed., *Saddharmalaṅkāvatārasūtra*). A Tibetan translation (by 'Gos Chos-grub) can be found in DK, mDo, vol. ca, ff. 56a[1]–191b[7] (Tōh. 107). An English translation (D. T. Suzuki, *The Laṅkāvatāra Sūtra*) is also available, though it is not very reliable.

> The Lord replied, 'Mahāmati, the continuum of one's own mental experience is purified by a gradual method, not immediately. Thus, for instance, Mahāmati, mango fruits ripen gradually, not immediately. Likewise, Mahāmati, the continua of beings' own mental experience are purified {by the Transcendent Lord} gradually, not immediately.
>
> 'Thus, for instance, Mahāmati, a potter makes vessels gradually, not immediately. Likewise, Mahāmati, the Transcendent Lord † purifies the continua of all beings' own mental experience gradually, not immediately. A:4a
>
> 'For instance, Mahāmati, on the Earth, grasses, thickets, vegetation, and large trees[240] shoot forth in a gradual manner, not immediately. Likewise, Mahāmati, the Transcendent Lord purifies the continua of all beings' own mental experience gradually, not immediately.
>
> 'For instance, Mahāmati, those skilled in [arts such as] comedy, dance, singing, cymbals, guitar, and painting[241] become so gradually, not immediately. Likewise,‡ Mahāmati, the Transcendent Lord purifies the continua of all beings' own mental experience gradually, not immediately.'[242] C:43b

"This very sequentiality is also demonstrated clearly in the *Hero's March (Samādhi) Scripture*,[243] which says:

240. *tṛṇa-gulmauṣadhi-vanaspati*; TIB reads "grasses, large trees, medicinal herbs and groves" (*rtsva dang | shing gel ba dang | sman dang | nags tshal rnams*).

241. TIB reads "comedy, music, songs, guitar, cymbals, and music" (*bzhad gad dang rol mo dang glu dang pi wang dang sil snyan dang rol mo dag*). Perhaps the second *rol mo* should be emended to read *ris mo*. I have translated the term *citra* as "cymbals," based on its seeming correspondence to the term *sil snyan* in the Tibetan.

242. The Sanskrit text of this citation is essentially identical to that found in the edition of Nanjio, p. 55, lines 2–17. The Tibetan can be found at DK, mDo, vol. ca, $76a^7$–$76b^5$.

243. *Śūraṅgama-samādhi-sūtra, dPa' bar 'gro ba'i ting nge 'dzin gyi mdo*. This scripture has apparently not come down to us in its original Sanskrit. For a Tibetan translation (by Śākyaprabha and Ratnarakṣita), see DK, mDo, vol. da, $253b^5$–$316b^6$ (Tōh. 132). For an English translation, see Lamotte (Boin-Webb, trans.) *Śūraṃgamasamādhisūtra*.

Then, {indeed,} the bodhisattva, the great one, Dṛḍhamati said this {to the Lord}: 'Lord, how is the bodhisattva, the great one, educated who here learns the hero's march samādhi without conceit for [all] his learning?'

{Thus addressed,} the Lord then said this to Dṛḍhamati, the bodhisattva, (the great one): 'Dṛḍhamati, in all likelihood the student of an archery teacher[244] first hits a [wooden] post.[245]
A:4b When one becomes skilled with a post,† one hits a plank. When one becomes skilled with a plank, one hits a target. When one becomes skilled with a target, one hits a stick. When one becomes skilled with a stick, one hits one hundred hairs. When one becomes skilled with one hundred hairs, one hits ten hairs. When one becomes skilled with ten hairs, one hits a single hair. When one becomes skilled with a single hair, one hits even by the sound [alone]. When one becomes skilled in hitting by sound [alone], one hits unerringly. When one becomes skilled in hitting unerringly, one has completely mastered the study of archery. [If] he wishes, [even] in the blinding darkness of night, the arrow will go effortlessly and unerringly to the vicinity of whatever sounds he hears, whether human or non-human.

'The one who can hit by sound [alone], learns nothing (further). Why? Because it has been well learned previously. All {the aforementioned} targets are manifest to that one. Likewise,†
A:5a Dṛḍhamati, the bodhisattva established here in this hero's march samādhi has nothing to learn (subsequently). Why? Since that

244. Reading *iṣvastrācāryāntevāsī*. Tib text seems to read "an archery teacher *or* an archery student" (*'phong gi slob dpon nam | 'phong gi slob ma*).

245. Concerning the term "[wooden] post": Tib is most clear, but seemingly at variance with Skt; it reads *ba lang gi ko ba*, "a cow hide." Ms C reads *gokiliṅgaṃ*. Pandey reads *gokilaṃ*, which (as he notes) the *Medinī Dictionary* glosses as *muśale hale*: a "club" or, perhaps, a "plough" (though that would seem to be a strange target) or, perhaps, a post to which cows were tied (?). The reading "post" would seem to be supported by M-W *kiliñca*, "thin plank, board." PED *kilañja* could suport Tib, as "mat, screen," but it also has "faggot." Dr. Losang Jamspal reports that in Ladakh wet goat skin stretched on a willow twig bent in an oval shape is used as a target, and that in India a cow hide was used.

very samādhi has been well learned previously, all the qualities of a bodhisattva are manifest (in that one).'[246]

"(Also,) by this reasoning, the one who desires to learn the hero's march samādhi in reliance on the Adamantine Way should learn according to these (very) stages. The stages are these: first of all, one learns the inclination (*āśaya*) toward the Buddha Way. When one has learned the inclination toward the Buddha Way, one learns the new way, the samādhi of single-mindedness.[247] When one has learned (single-mindedness on) the new way, one learns the imaginative yoga.[248] (When one has learned the imaginative yoga, one becomes established in the beginner's samādhi.)[249] When one has become established in the beginner's samādhi, one enters the divisions‡ of the hundred clans.[250] When, through (skill in) the process of the hundred clans, one knows body isolation, one becomes established in the body-vajra samādhi. C:44a

"Stationed in body isolation, one enters speech isolation through the door of the vowels and consonants. When one has realized vitality control (*prāṇāyāma*) through the process of vajra recitation, †one becomes A:5b

246. This citation integrates two passages found at: DK, vol. da, fol. 271b²–271b⁷, 272b⁷–273a². Cf. Lamotte (trans. Boin-Webb), 138–39, 149.

247. *ekasmṛti, dran pa gcig pa*. This term does not appear elsewhere in the CMP. According to dbYangs-can dGa'-blo, "the coarse yoga of the creation stage . . . is called the coarse yoga of single-mindedness" (*bskyed rim rags pa'i rnal 'byor . . . rags pa dran pa gcig pa'i rnal 'byor zhes brjod pa . . .*); see *Sa-lam rnam gzhag*, f. 3b⁶.

248. *kalpita-yoga, rtog pa'i rnal 'byor*. This term does not appear elsewhere in the CMP, though it does appear frequently in PU where it seems to be a synonym for the creation stage: e.g., p. 60 where "those who stand in the samādhi of the yoga of the perfection stage" (*niṣpannakramayogasamādhisthāḥ*) are said to be superior to the imaginative yogins (*kalpitayoginaḥ*). This is borne out in dbYangs-can dGa'-blo, who writes, "the subtle yoga of the creation stage . . . is called the subtle imaginative yoga" (*bskyed rim phra mo'i rnal 'byor . . . phra ba rtog pa'i rnal 'byor zhes brjod pa . . .*); see *Sa-lam* f. 4a¹⁻².

249. *ādikarmika-samādhi, las dang po pa'i ting nge 'dzin*. This sentence is not found in the SKT MSS, but as it is found in TIB and seems to follow the pattern established, I assume it belongs. One could theorize that the imaginative yoga is synonymous with the beginner's samādhi and the Tibetans have erroneously divided them, but it is doubtful. I am confident that further study will be able to decide this.

250. These will also be treated in chapter 2 below. They are arrived at by taking the five transcendent lords (qua five aggregates), the four goddesses (qua four elements), the five bodhisattvas (qua sense media), the five auxiliary airs, and gnosis, and subdividing each and correlating these with the five buddha clans.

established in the speech-vajra samādhi. Stationed in speech isolation, one enters mind isolation through the process of the radiances and the prototypes.[251] When one has learned the radiances and the prototypes classified according to their air-mounts just as they are, one becomes equipoised in the mind-{vajra} samādhi. Stationed in the thorough knowledge of the mind just as it is, one enters superficial reality[252] via the twelve similes of phantasm. When one becomes equipoised in the phantasmic samādhi, one obtains the {universal} buddha initiation.[253] (When one obtains initiation, then,) stationed in the phantasmic samādhi, one enters ultimate reality[254] via the sequence of the eighteen great void{nesse}s. When one enters the reality limit[255] by the holistic [samādhi] and the dissolving samādhi,[256] one becomes purified of all defilements. When, having arisen through the process of gnosis, the self that is the prototypical brilliance is perfectly enlightened by making the two realities nondual, one has learned the perfection samādhi.[257]

251. *prakṛtyābhāsa-krameṇa*. I am (obviously) taking the Sanskrit compound *prakṛtyābhāsa* as a *dvandva*, which is typically marked with a genitive in Tibetan translation. However, all the Tibetan texts I collated read an instrumental: *rang bzhin gyis snang ba*. While the compound could be resolved this way (presumably as an instrumental *tatpuruṣa*), a genitive marking a *dvandva* would seem to make more sense. This, in fact, is the reading of such early Tibetan works on the Noble Tradition as the (eleventh-century) *gSang-'dus stong-thun* of 'Gos Khug-pa Lhas-btsas. It seems likely, then, that later Tibetan tradition may have "corrected," or misconstrued, an originally genitive marker (*gyi*) of a *dvandva* as a Tibetan-style instrumental adverbial form (i.e., "naturally luminous"), on the pattern of such common exoteric (Madhyamaka) expressions as "intrinsically void" (*rang bzhin gyis stong pa*).

252. In this context, a synonym for the phantasm body (*māyā-deha, sgyu lus*) or self-consecration (*svādhiṣṭhāna, bdag byin brlab*). See chapter 6, below.

253. *sarvabuddhābhiṣeka*; Tib reads merely *sangs rgyas kyi dbang bskur* (**buddhābhiṣeka*).

254. Here, as synonym for brilliance (*prabhāsvara, 'od gsal*). See chapter 7, below.

255. *bhūta-koṭi, yang dag pa'i mtha'*; also (and throughout this work) a synonym for the brilliance. This term was very important in earlier Indian Mahāyāna Buddhism. It is found as a synonym for nirvāṇa in the *Aṣṭasāhasrikāprajñāpāramitā Sūtra*, and its commentator Haribhadra gives the following synonyms: reality body (*bhūtakāya*), perfection of the dharma body (*dharmakāyaparinispatti*), and Realm of Reality (*dharmadhātu*). These latter are most telling with regard to Āryadeva's usage, for the mind of brilliance is considered an analogue to the pure, formless existence of a buddha in dharmakāya. See Lewis R. Lancaster, "The Oldest Mahāyāna Sūtra," 38–39.

256. *piṇḍagrāha-, ril bur 'dzin pa*; *anubheda-, rjes su gzhig pa*. These yogic processes (techniques for entering the most subtle state) are briefly described below in chapter 7 (CMP, f. 47a).

257. Following the reading in Skt (*yadā jñānakrameṇa vyutthāya prakṛtiprabhāsvaraṃ*

"A {great} yogin equipoised in the perfection samādhi learns nothing (further). (Why so?) For it was well learned previously; just as the archery master who can [find his mark] by sound alone learns nothing (further).† Why? A:6a
Because it has been well learned previously—it becomes manifest through the force of that one's prior impetus. Likewise, one who is established in the perfection samādhi has nothing (further) to learn, for it was (extremely) well learned previously. The transcendent and worldly accomplishments (*siddhi*) of that one manifest effortlessly.

"Thus, one learning the perfection stage samādhi learns by a gradual method, not immediately. Hence, without body isolation, speech isolation cannot be known. One who lacks speech isolation cannot realize mind isolation. Without {realizing} (the samādhi of) the radiance[s] and the prototypes (of the mind), one cannot make manifest the superficial reality. Without realizing superficial reality, one cannot make manifest the ultimate reality. Without realizing ultimate reality, one cannot manifest the process {that leads to} communion.[258]

"Having perceived this crucial point, the Lord said that one learns by a gradual process, not immediately. [The fact that,] when one has learned the perfection stage by a gradual process, one's own continuum {of mental C:44b
experience}‡ is purified immediately is indicated by the Lord himself in the *Journey to Laṅka Scripture*:[259]

> 'For instance, Mahāmati,† in a mirror the images of all objects A:6b
> appear without conceptualization, immediately. Likewise, Mahāmati, the Transcendent Lord purifies immediately the continua of all beings' own mental experience, which are nonconceptual ranges free of perception.
>
> 'For instance, Mahāmati, the orbs of the sun and moon immediately

---

satyadvayādvaidhīkāreṇa ātmānam abhisaṃbudhyati). TIB has slightly different grammar. It reads, "When, in order to arise through the process of gnosis, one becomes enlightened oneself in the nondual form of the two realities" (*gang gi tshe ye shes kyi rim gyis ldang ba'i phyir rang bzhin gyis 'od gsal ba'i bden pa gnyis la gnyis su med pa'i rnam pas bdag nyid mngon par rdzogs par sangs rgyas pa*).

258. *yuganaddha-vāhi-krama*; Tibetan reads merely "communion stage/process" (*zung du 'jug pa'i rim pa*).

259. See chapter 1, note 239, above.

> reveal the images of all objects by [their] light rays. (Likewise, Mahāmati, the Transcendent Lord instantaneously reveals an object that is the range of the Victors—the inconceivable gnosis—to beings who are free from the vestiges of negative conditioning of their own mind.)'[260]

Thus, it is said:

> So that beginner beings
> Might enter the ultimate reality,
> The perfect buddhas created
> This liberative art (in stages) like a staircase.[261]

(One should understand [this to mean that]) without the sequence of the five stages, one cannot realize the perfection stage samādhi."

260. This citation (in parentheses as it is only found in TIB) follows immediately after the passage cited above. In Nanjio's edition, it runs from p. 55, line 17, to p. 56, line 4. It is missing from SKT, yet its inclusion is warranted, I believe—otherwise one finds an argument for gradualism buttressed by a wholly-suddenist citation. It also presents the unpacking of the last simile, which would otherwise be left hanging. It could, however, be argued that the previous citation of the LAS has already established a gradualist interpretation, which this citation merely attenuates.

261. Harunaga Isaacson has identified this stanza as verse 176 of Kambala's *Ālokamālā*: see Lindtner, *A Garland of Light*, 72. It is also cited (similarly without attribution) in *Advayavajrasaṃgraha*: see Shāstri, *Advayavajrasaṃgraha*, 21.

This verse bears a strong similarity to PK I.2, which reads:

> To those established on the creation stage
> Who desire the perfection stage.
> The perfect buddhas created
> This art like a staircase.

(*utpattikrama-saṃsthānāṃ niṣpannakrama-kāṅkṣiṇāṃ | upāyaś caîṣa sambuddhaiḥ sopānam iva nirmitaḥ* ||).

2. Resolution of Doubts about the Integration of Body Isolation

The Vajra Student asked, "How at first, Lord, is isolation of one's own body to be learned?"

The Vajra Mentor replied, "Excellent, Great One, excellent! I will instruct you in detail about body isolation. Regarding that, the four elements produce the body [and] maintain all the heaps (*rāśi*) of the body [so] produced. The assemblage of the masses of flesh, veins, tendons, head, brain, A:7a
meninges,[262] †bone, marrow, small intestine, large intestine, kidneys, heart, stomach, lungs, liver,[263] urine, feces, (bladder,) upper digestive tract, lower digestive tract, fat, lymph, pus, blood, bile, phlegm, snot, hair, facial hair, nails, bodily hair, skin, hands,[264] feet, eyes, limbs, and so forth, is [referred to as] a 'heap.'[265]

"Further, in that regard, the five aggregates, the four elements, the six

262. Following Tib (*sha'i kham tshad | rtsa dang | rgyus pa dang | mgo bo dang | klad pa dang | klad rgyas*), Skt reads "mass of flesh, tendons, arteries, channels, meninges" (*māṃsapeśī-snāyu-śirā-dhamanī-mastaluṅga*).

263. The Tibetan word *mcher pa* seems to be ambiguous, meaning either "liver" or "spleen"; the Sanskrit reading *yakṛt* is unambiguously "liver." As seen below in the discussion of the earth element, there is another word for "spleen" (*plīha, mchin pa*). Chandra Das (434 and 436) and NTED (379 and 380), however, both maintain the opposite (i.e., *mchin pa*=liver, *mcher pa*=spleen).

264. Following ms C and Tib; ms A reads *śiraś*, "head." Either reading makes some sense. "Head and feet" make good sense given that ms A does not read "head" (*śiras*) as the fourth item, but "artery" (*śirā*), and so is not redundant. Given that Tib reads this former item as "head," "hands and feet" make a better reading.

265. This list might profitably be compared to that found in *Satipaṭṭhāna Sutta*, which reads: *kesā lomā nakhā dantā taco maṃsaṃ nahārū aṭṭhī aṭṭhi-miñja vakkaṃ hadayaṃ yakanaṃ kilomakaṃ pihakaṃ papphāsaṃ antaṃ anta-gunaṃ udariyaṃ karīsaṃ pittaṃ semhaṃ pubbo lohitaṃ sedo medo assu vasā kheḷo siṅghāṇikā lasikā muttan* (DN xxii.5). Twenty of the members of this list correspond exactly or very closely with those in the CMP list. Maurice

[sense] media, the five objects, and the five subjects[266] are called a 'heap.' Just as, for example, (many measures of) rice, barley, sesame seed, wheat, and peas[267] are called a 'heap,' likewise the assemblage that includes the body's limbs and digits is called a 'heap.' Among the assemblage of elements, the continua of critical wisdom, view, mentality, delusion, vestigial instincts, craving, and defilement are called an 'accumulation.' The accumulation—or heap—of consciousnesses, however, is not perceived, because it has no foundation (*ālaya*). Just as it says in the *Enquiry of Bhadrapāli*:[268]

> 'A consciousness resides nowhere in this body; [...][269] nor is a body obtained apart from consciousness. [...] Hence, O Bhadrapāli, one who does not see reality does not see this consciousness. One does not see it like [one sees] a myrobalan fruit (placed) in the palm of one's hand.'[270]

Walshe (*Thus Have I Heard*, 591n649) notes that "with the addition of 'brain' these 32 parts of the body are included as a meditation subject: cf. V[isuddhi]M[agga] 8.42ff."

266. *jñāna*: it does not seem here that the five "gnoses" are being indicated. TIB accordingly translates this as *shes pa*, not *ye shes*.

267. *mudga, mon sran; phaseolus mungo*, a near relative of the mung bean (*phaseolus aureus*).

268. *Bhadrapāli-paripṛcchā[-sūtra], bZang skyong gis zhus pa'i mdo*. This scripture does not seem to have survived in its original Sanskrit. A Tibetan translation (by Jinamitra and Surendrabodhi, with Bande Ye-shes-sde) may be found in DK, dKon-brtsegs, vol. cha, 71a¹–94b⁷ (Tōh. 83), under the title *'Phags pa tshong dpon bzang skyong gis zhus pa zhes bya ba theg pa chen po'i mdo* (*Ārya-bhadrapāla-śreṣṭhi-paripṛcchā-nāma-mahāyānasūtra*). This text is there considered the thirty-ninth chapter of the hundred-thousand-chapter *Ārya-mahā-ratnakūṭa-sūtra*.

269. There is an elision here, and further below. In full, DK reads: "Likewise, consciousness resides nowhere in this body. [It does not reside] in the eye, nor in the ear, nor in the nose sense organ. The production of a seed's sprout is a small being. Birth in a womb is small feeling. For example, if a sprout is produced and the time is right, it will produce flowers. If flowers are produced, fruit will be produced. Likewise, this consciousness element produces the body. If a body is produced, consciousness does not reside in any of the limbs or digits. Yet, if there is no consciousness, a body will not be produced" (*de bzhin du lus 'di la rnam par shes pa gang na yang mi gnas te | mig la yang ma yin | rna ba la yang ma yin | sna'i dbang po la yang ma yin no || sa bon gyi myu gu skye ba gang yin pa de ni sems pa chung ba yin no || mngal du skye ba de ni tshor ba chung ba yin te | dper na myu gu 'byung zhing dus tshigs dang ldan pa na me tog rnams 'grub ste | me tog grub na 'bras bu 'grub pa yod pa de bzhin de rnam par shes pa'i khams 'dis lus 'grub par 'gyur ro || lus grub pa na yan lag dang nying lag gang la yang rnam par shes pa mi gnas la | rnam par shes pa med na yang lus skye bar mi 'gyur ro ||*). This first sentence is found at f. 78b¹–78b³.

270. These latter two sentences are found at 83b⁵–83b⁶.

"Further, †this [body] of aggregates, elements, and media that is pred- A:7b
icated on beginningless ordinary pride[271] is now taught to have a nature composed of the fine atoms of all transcendent lords. {As} the Lord states in the Great Yoga Tantra, the {Glorious} *Esoteric Community*:[272]

> In short, the five aggregates are‡ C:45a
> Proclaimed to be the five buddhas.
> The vajra media themselves are
> The supreme maṇḍala of the bodhisattva[s].
>
> Earth is called Locanā.
> The water element is {traditionally known as} Māmakī.
> The fire (element) is {to be called} Pāṇḍara(vāsinī).
> Tārā is proclaimed to be air.
>
> The mantrin always meditates
> On forms, sounds, and so on, as divine.[273]

271. *prākṛtāhaṃkāra, tha mal pa'i nga rgyal.* This is a key concept in esoteric Buddhism. The basic notion is that beings' ordinary conception of themselves as limited, unenlightened beings is, fundamentally, due to delusion. This ordinary self-conception is to be eliminated in favor of a conception of themselves as divine: a "divine pride" (*devatāhaṃkāra, lha'i nga rgyal*).

272. This is, of course, the central, "root" scripture of Āryadeva's tradition. The work has been edited in Sanskrit by Bhattacharyya, Bagchi, Fremantle, and Matsunaga (see Bibliography under *Guhyasamāja Tantra*). A Tibetan translation may be found at: DK, rGyud, vol. ca, $90a^{1}$–$148a^{6}$ (Tōh. 442). Parts of the work have been translated into English by Fremantle (chapters I to XVII) and Alex Wayman (chapters V and VII in *Yoga of the Guhyasamāja Tantra*). It has also been translated into German by Peter Gäng (*Das Tantra der Verborgenen Vereinigung*).

273. This passage is excerpted from two places in the *Esoteric Community Tantra*. The first two verses are GST XVII.50–51. MS A has a variant reading for the last line, viz. *tejaḥ pāṇḍarākhyātā tārā vāyuprakīrtitā* ||, though Pandey's edition has another reading, viz. *pāṇḍarākhyā bhavet tejas tārā vāyuḥ prakīrtitā* ||.

The last (half-)verse is GST VII.14ab. It may be noted that both SKT and TIB support the reading *rūpa-śabdādi-* (which is also attested by some Tibetan versions, PU, and the Chinese translation), though most other extant MSS of the GST itself read *sparśa-śabdādi-*. Cf. Matsunaga, *Guhyasamājatantra*, 21.

"Further subdividing the aggregates, {elements,} and so on, each by five, they become hundredfold. As is stated in the {*Glorious*} *Secret Moon Drop*:[274]

> Clans are taught [to be] hundredfold;
> But through contraction, fivefold.
> They also become threefold
> By correlation with body, speech, and mind.[275]

At the very first we will teach [you] the division into one hundred clans.[276]

"Regarding that, the totality of the form aggregate is Vairocana. That being divided into five, it is constituted of the Five Transcendent Lords. Regarding that, forms having outer, inner, and both [outside and inside] shapes such as long and short are the constitution[277] of Vairocana. Forms
A:8a in the mode of self, †other, or both are that of Ratnasambhava. Exterior [and] interior forms of the five colors, [such as] blue, and so on, are that of Amitābha. Exterior [and] interior forms having the form of the luminance of the sun and moon are that of Amoghasiddhi. Forms that are made known[278] exclusively through personal experience are the constitution of Akṣobhya. [Thus] is explained the fivefold form aggregate.

274. *Guhyendutilaka*, *Zla gsang thig le*. This scripture was translated into Tibetan by Śraddhākaravarman and Rin-chen bZang-po as *dPal zla gsang thig le zhes bya ba rgyud kyi rgyal po chen po*, and may be found at: DK, rGyud, vol. ja, 247b[1]–303a[7] (Tōh. 477). As the title *Guhyendutilaka* is well attested in the extant literature, it is evident that the Sanskrit title given in the Tibetan versions is a false reconstruction; they read: *Śrī-candra-guhya-tilaka-nāma-mahātantra-rāja*.

275. DK, rGyud, vol. ja, 299a[5].

276. A chart detailing these hundred clans can be found in Appendix III.

277. *adhiṣṭhāna*; *byin gyis brlabs pa*; this term is difficult to translate consistently. It occurs most commonly in the technical term *svādhiṣṭhāna* (the topic of chapter 6 and one of the most important processes in this yogic system), which I render "self-consecration." "Consecration" does not seem to work in the present context, however, nor does the commonly used "blessing." Here—though the other usages are still valent—it seems closer to its general usage as "site, residence, abode." There may also be some suggestion of the more Dharmaśāstric meaning of "jurisdiction." In short, the doctrine of the hundred clans presents a pantheistic conception in which the entire world of ordinary experience is reenvisioned as the manifestation of enlightened beings. Hence, I have chosen to use the noun "constitution" (*adhiṣṭhāna*) and adjective "constituted of" (*adhiṣṭhita*) in this context. Note that (as indicated in the first line of each paragraph ["the totality . . . is . . ."]) this "constitution" is ultimately tantamount to a kind of identity relation: the universe *is* or is *made of* buddhas (it is *buddha-maya*).

278. *vijñapti-rūpa*; TIB suggests a reading of **a-vijñaptirūpa* (*rnam par rig byed ma yin pa*)—

"Speaking in reference to the samādhi of Ratnasambhava, the totality of the feeling aggregate is Ratnasambhava. That again is constituted of the Five Transcendent Lords. With regard to that, feelings arising from bile and conjunction [of all three humors][279] are [the constitution] of Akṣobhya. Feelings born from phlegm and wind are that of Ratnasambhava. Pleasurable feelings are that of Amitābha. Painful feelings are that of Amoghasiddhi. Ambivalent feelings are the constitution of Vairocana. [Thus] is explained the fivefold feeling aggregate.

"Speaking in reference to the samādhi of Amitābha, the totality of the discernment aggregate is Amitābha. With respect to the compositeness of things—[both] inanimate and animate—which occur here, on account of the[ir] division into the categories of legless, bipedal, and so on, there are distinctive terms for things. Those having been conceived by consciousness, one draws distinctions. That manner of knowing (*nimitta*) is properly designated 'the discernment aggregate.' That discernment again is constituted of the Five Transcendent Lords. {With regard to that,} †discernments of A:8b
bipeds are Akṣobhya's [constitution]. Discernments of quadrupeds are Ratnasambhava's. Discernments of those without legs are Amitābha's. Discernments of the many-legged are Amoghasiddhi's.[280] Discernments of stationary, inanimate beings ‡are the constitution of Vairocana. [Thus] is C:45b
explained the fivefold discernment aggregate.

"Speaking in reference to the samādhi of Amoghasiddhi: the totality of the propensity aggregate is Amoghasiddhi. It also is constituted of the Five Transcendent Lords. {With regard to that,} bodily propensities are Vairocana's [constitution]. Verbal propensities are Amitābha's. Mental propensities are Akṣobhya's. Propensities [toward] the three worlds[281] are

which may be preferable, if what is intended is the Abhidharmic category of that name that comprises the (outwardly) imperceptible "form" of vows taken, etc. This sentence would then be rendered "Unmanifest forms (*avijñaptirūpa*), which are only known through personal experience, are the constitution of Akṣobhya." Thanks to Robert Thurman for his suggestions in this regard.

279. That is, the three bodily "humors" of wind (*vāta, rlung*—associated with nervous, intellectual energy), bile (*pitta, mkhris pa*—associated with anger and heat), and phlegm (*kapha, bad kan*—associated with dullness and cold).

280. Tib reverses the order of Amitābha and Amoghasiddhi (such that Amoghasiddhi comes first), though the correspondence is the same. The textual pattern, however, is entirely consistent. Presumably, the Tibetan translators altered the pattern to accommodate the logical pattern of correspondences (i.e., two-legs, four, many, none, N/A).

281. Tib *khams gsum*; as Pandey points out in his edition, this is usually the equivalent for

Ratnasambhava's. Propensities [toward] liberation are the constitution of Amoghasiddhi. [Thus] is explained the fivefold propensity aggregate.

"Speaking in reference to the samādhi of Akṣobhya: that which grasps an object, delimits an object, [or] understands an object is consciousness. External objects are discerned according to the appearance of a consciousness in which they are situated; {and} consciousness is discerned according to an external object.[282] Thus, the establishment of a knower and a known is on the basis of their mutual relationship. That consciousness also, being divided into five, is constituted of the Five Transcendent Lords.[283] {With regard to that,} the totality of the consciousness aggregate is Akṣobhya.
A:9a Visual †consciousness is the constitution of Vairocana. Auditory consciousness is the constitution of Ratnasambhava; olfactory consciousness is Amitābha's; gustatory, Amoghasiddhi's; tactile consciousness is the constitution of Akṣobhya. [Thus] is explained the fivefold consciousness aggregate.

"This is the meaning of the [verse of] scripture:

> In short, the five aggregates are
> Proclaimed to be the five buddhas.

**tridhātu* (or, more common in this text, **tridhātuka*). In Buddhist discourse, this typically refers to the Realms of Desire, Form, and Formlessness (*kāma-*, *rūpa-*, and *arūp[y]a-dhātu*). Skt, however, reads the old Vedic *bhūrbhuvaḥ[svaḥ]*, "Earth, sky, and heaven"—called the "great utterances" (*mahā-vyāhṛti*), as they are uttered at the beginning of orthodox worship (forming as they do the beginning of the Gāyatrī Mantra). There are other instances in this work (in particular the use of *tryakṣara*) in which old orthodox terms are used with a distinctively Buddhist referent. As this is also a set of "three worlds," I have followed Tib with this stated cavil. The referent is, presumably, those propensities that are oriented to worldly affairs or conduce to perpetuating the life-cycle (*saṃsāra*), rather than liberation (*mokṣa*).

282. Following Skt, *vijñānārūḍhena cākāreṇa bāhyārthaḥ prajñāpyate | bāhyenārthena vijñānaṃ prajñāpyata iti ||*. Pandey emends *bāhyenārthena* to *bāhyārthena*—unnecessarily, in my opinion. Tib reads *rnam par shes pa la gnas pas kyang phyi'i don gyi rnam par rab tu brtags la | phyi'i don gyis kyang rnam par shes par brtags te ||*, suggesting that the translator read the beginning as **vijñānārūḍhena bāhyārthākāraḥ prajñāpyate*, "the appearance of external objects is designated according to the consciousness in which it resides."

283. ms C interpolates: "bodily volition should be known, as it is composed of fine atoms composed of transcendent lords, on account of the purity of the aggregates, and so on, in the body" (*kāya-saṃskāro veditavyaḥ tathāgata-maya-paramāṇu-parighaṭitatvena śuddhatvāt kāye skandhādīnām*).

Tibetan interpolates "*one should know that* the fivefold division of that consciousness is also constituted of the Five Transcendent Lords" (*rnam par shes pa de yang rnam pa lngar phye ba la de bzhin gshegs pa lngas byin gyis brlabs pa yin par shes par bya'o |*).

"Speaking in reference to the four elements: {with regard to that,} (one might ask) 'which is the earth element?' It is heaviness and solidity; its function is stability. {With regard to that,} (one might ask) 'which is the water element?' It is fluidity and wetness; its function is conglomeration. {With regard to that,} (one might ask) 'which is the fire element?' It is heat and maturation; its function is desiccation. {With regard to that,} (one might ask) 'which is the air element?' It is compression and diffusion, inhalation (of breath) and exhalation (of breath; its function is) lightness and agitation.[284]

"Having thus presented the characteristics of each of the four elements according to the manner[285] of the Universal Way, now in order to eliminate ordinary pride, they are described as constituted of the five buddhas according to the manner of the Adamantine Way.

"With regard to that, the totality of the earth element is (Buddha) Locanā. That (element) also being divided into five forms, it is constituted of the Five Transcendent Lords. That is to say, hair, bone, feces, spleen, and
heart are Vairocana's. Bodily hair, nails, †pus, and heart are Ratnasambha- A:9b
va's. Teeth, skin, flesh, and heart are Amitābha{'s}. Tendons, flesh, ribs, †and C:46a
heart are Amoghasiddhi{'s}. Bodily secretions, small intestine, bile, and heart are Akṣobhya's. As it says in the *Vajra Rosary*:[286]

> In dependence on the five hearts,
> Brought forth from the five continua,[287]
> Conjoined with five airs,[288]

284. MS C adds: "[its] function is breathing" (*vyūha-karmā*).

285. Skt *krama*; Tib translates this term quite formulaically as *rim pa*, usually "stage." The context clearly indicates that we should interpret it according to the wider semantic range of the Sanskrit *krama*, which includes the idea of a "way" or "manner."

286. *Vajramālā, rDo rje phreng ba*. One of the major explanatory tantras of the Esoteric Community Noble Tradition literature. A Sanskrit text of this work has not been found to date. A Tibetan translation (by Sujanaśrī and Zhi-ba'i 'od) may be found at: DK, rGyud, vol. ca, ff. 208a[1]–277b[3] (Tōh. 445), as *rNal 'byor chen po'i rgyud dpal rdo rje phreng ba mngon par brjod pa rgyud thams cad kyi snying po gsang ba rnam par phye ba zhes bya ba* (Sanskrit title given as *Śrī-vajramālābhidhāna-mahāyoga-tantra-sarvatantra-hṛdaya-rahasya-vibhaṅga-nāma*).

287. Reading *pañcatantu* (the reading of the mss, confirmed by Tib's *rgyud lnga*), rather than Pandey's *pañcatanu*. The interpretation of *tantu* is not entirely clear, however. I suspect it refers to five (subtle) veins in the body. I have settled on the rendering "continuum," as it captures the sense adequately while leaving room for interpretation.

288. Following Tib *rlung lnga* (**pañca-vāyu*); both mss read *svapna-vāyu*, "dream air[s]."

> [It is] the creator of the enjoyment of the five [objects of] desire.[289]

"Thus again, the element of earth in the exterior [world] is divided into five forms: the four continents and [Mount] Sumeru. (The King of Mountains,) Sumeru, is {Mahā-}Vairocana's (constitution). {Pūrva-}Videha is Akṣobhya's (constitution). Jambūdvīpa is Ratnasambhava's (constitution). {Apara-}Godānīya is Amitābha's (constitution). Uttarakuru is the constitution of Amoghasiddhi. [Thus] is explained the fivefold earth element.

"Speaking in reference to the samādhi of Māmakī: with regard to that, the totality of the element of water is Māmakī. It again is constituted of the Five Transcendent Lords. Phlegm and tears are the constitution of Vairocana. Urine is Akṣobhya's constitution. Sweat is the constitution of Ratnasambhava. Blood is the constitution of Amitābha. Saliva is the constitution of Amoghasiddhi.

"Externally, also five forms are seen: {With regard to} that, ocean water is
A:10a Akṣobhya{'s}. River water is Ratnasambhava's. Spring water[290] is Amitābha's. Pond water †is Amoghasiddhi's. The waters of a waterfall are the constitution of Vairocana. [Thus] is explained the fivefold water element.

"Speaking in reference to the samādhi of Pāṇḍaravāsinī: The totality of the element of fire is Pāṇḍaravāsinī. That again is constituted of the Five Transcendent Lords. The heat of the head is Vairocana's constitution. The heat of the heart is Akṣobhya's. The heat of the navel is Ratnasambhava's. The heat of all the limbs is Amitābha's. The heat of the belly is Amoghasiddhi's constitution.

"Externally, also, five forms are seen. With regard to that, the perpetual fire[291] is Akṣobhya's. Fire arisen from stones[292] is Vairocana's. Fire arisen

289. DK, rGyud, vol. ca, 263a².

290. *udbhidodaka* (following MS C and TIB [*bkod ma'i chu*]); MS A reads *svabhrodaka*; in a footnote to his edition, Pandey cites the *Amarakośa* and interprets this latter term as *su-* (i.e., *śobhana*) *abhrodaka* (cloud-water) (*su- śobhanam abhrodakaṃ meghavāri | 'abhraṃ megho vārivāhaḥ'*), so this could be rendered "pure rain water."

291. *āhavanīyāgni, rgyun bzhag gi me*; fire taken from the fire kept perpetually burning by brahminical householders. Traditionally, this is the eastern of the three fires of a brahminical sacrifice. See PSED, 377, and M-W, 162, col. 3.

292. *pāṣānodbhavāgni, rdo las byung ba'i me*; perhaps this refers to fire struck by flint?

from sun-crystals[293] is Ratnasambhava's. Fire arisen from {pieces of} wood is Amitābha's. Forest fires are the constitution of Amoghasiddhi. [Thus] is explained the fivefold fire element.

"Speaking in reference to the samādhi of Tārā: {with regard to} that, the totality of the element of air is Tārā. It also is constituted of the Five Transcendent Lords. With regard to that, {the air} called 'vitality,' which is situated in the heart, is Akṣobhya's [constitution]. (That called) the 'evacuative'[-air], which is situated in the anus,[294] is Ratnasambhava's. That which is called the 'ascending'[-air], which is situated in the throat, is Amitābha's. The 'metabolic'[-air], which is situated at the navel, is Amoghasiddhi's. That called the 'pervasive' [-air], which is situated in all the joints, ‡is the constitution of Vairocana. C:46b

"And, †explaining the function of these one-by-one: A:10b

> [It] always issues
> By the continua of the sense-doors
> From issuance and vitality control—
> [Hence, it is] called the 'vitality'[-air].
>
> Since it evacuates gas, urine, feces, and
> Like them, semen, and so on,
> The yogins always designate this
> The 'evacuative'[-air].

293. *sūryakāntodbhavāgni, me shel las byung ba'i me*; a type of crystal believed to produce fire when exposed to the sun's rays.

294. *guda*; this reading of Skt is very clear. The specificity of this referent is somewhat surprising however, as the evacuative air (*apāna*) is usually understood to function to excrete urine and semen also from their channels, not merely feces from the anus. Tib reads *'doms* (following the Peking, all other recensions read the erroneous *mdoms*), which has a broader referent: "abdomen" or "pelvic region" (compare the Sanskrit *vasti*), and this is (I believe) the way in which Tibetan medicine understands it. Though this latter would thus seem to make better sense, as Prof. Kenneth Zysk has indicated (personal communication, 15 December 2004), the *guda* (anus) is specified in *Caraka Saṃhita* 29.3 as one of the ten seats of the vital airs (which is its referent in our text). According to *Suśruta Saṃhita* 6.6, it is a site of a vital point (*marman*); and the term is further unambiguously analyzed by the eleventh-century commentator Cakrapāṇidatta into upper and lower segments corresponding to the rectum and anus. Thus, in this context at least, the referent must be the latter.

That which always brings together[295]
Eaten, chewed, lickable,
Potable, and suckable [foods] in all ways,
Is called the 'metabolic'[-air].[296]

Since it moves upward and draws together,
Since it consumes food and delicacies,
This comprehends the function of the 'ascending'[-air],
As it is connected with gnosis.

Pervading and holding,
Going and (likewise)[297] coming,
Since it pervades all of the joints,
It is called the 'pervasive'[-air].[298]

"Externally, also, five forms are seen. The eastern wind is Akṣobhya's. The southern wind is Ratnasambhava's. The western wind is Amitābha's. The northern wind is Amoghasiddhi's. The zenith wind is the constitution of Vairocana. [Thus] is explained the fivefold air element.

"Wherever there is one of these four great elements, there (all) four are. Therefore, they are not self-established, [and do not] have [an] intrinsic reality [that is] without mutual interdependence. Space, since it is beyond the senses and is uncompounded, is not a great element; {however,} as [it is said 'it is called] "space" because it makes room for all things,[299] that is to
A:11a say, †it performs the function of non-obstructing.'

295. SKT reads *samānayati* (from *sam+ā+√nī*), which generally means "uniting." TIB reads *mnyam gnas*, which usually means "residing together" or "being in a state of equality." It seems that TIB was seeking more to capture the play on words (*samāna* and *samānayati* with *mnyam du gnas* and *mnyam gnas par*) than the sense of the verse. See next note for my own approach to this problem (and its attendant problems).

296. For the sake of consistency, I have preserved my standard rendering of the technical term *samāna-vāyu* as "metabolic air." This does not allow me, however, to capture the play on words found in the derivation of the name. "Uniting air" might be a possible solution, but this rendering does not indicate its function in the process of digestion.

297. *de bzhin, tathā*; This is found in *both* TIB and both Sanskrit MSS, though Pandey omits it from his edition—presumably because it is unmetrical.

298. *Vajramālā Tantra*, DK, rGyud, vol. ca, f. 276b[2–5].

299. The intent here is to trace an ("hermeneutical") etymology (*nirukti*) between *avakāśa*-

"[This] is the meaning of this [verse of] scripture:

> Earth is called Locanā.
> The water element is {traditionally known as} Māmakī.
> The fire is {to be called} Pāṇḍara(vāsinī).
> Air is proclaimed to be Tārā.[300]

"Now, speaking in reference to the samādhi[s] of the {great} bodhisattvas, (the great ones,) Kṣitigarbha and so on:

"With regard to that, the totality of the visual media is Kṣitigarbha. That also, being divided into five forms, is constituted of the Five Transcendent Lords. [Located] in the interior of the eyeball, the visual sense organ that is the size of a grape—that is Akṣobhya's. The nature of the pupil[301] of the eye is Ratnasambhava's. Forms seen with the peripheral vision[302] are Amitābha's. The movement of the eye is Amoghasiddhi's. The perception[303] of the three forms is the constitution of Vairocana. [Thus] is explained the fivefold visual medium.

"Similarly, the totality of the aural media is Vajrapāṇi. Here, the aural sense organ [located] in the interior of the ear, which has a form [composed] of a collection of fine atoms [and which has][304] a greatly convoluted appearance[305]—that is Akṣobhya's. The nature of the ear is Vairocana's. The

---

dāna (giving or making room) and *ākāśa* (space). Tib reads "since it makes room, space performs the function of not obstructing all things" (*go 'byed par byed pas na nam mkha' ni dngos po thams cad la mi sgrib pa'i bya ba byed do*).

300. We here have a slightly different version of the verse than the one originally cited near the beginning of this chapter (see p. 135). This is true of both Skt and Tib.

301. *tārakā*; Tib reads (quite unambiguously) *mig 'bras dkar po* (lit. "white eyeball"), which seems to refer to the "white of the eye."

302. *tiryag-rūpa, zur gyis lta ba'i gzugs*: "forms (seen) 'obliquely' or 'out of the corner [of the eye].'"

303. *grahaṇa, 'dzin pa.*

304. It is not clear whether the shape described applies to the organ as a whole or to the fine atoms (*paramāṇu*) which make it up. The structure of the compound implies that the shape is that of the particles, but the text later (see below under "gustatory media") breaks this compound up so that the shape clearly applies to the organ. Given the nature of the shapes (ear=twisted, tongue=half-moon), I follow the latter interpretation.

305. Reading *bhūry-āgranthy-ākṛti-*. Pandey's edition reads *tūrya-granthy-ākṛti* "appearance of a *tūrya* (a type of musical instrument) [and/or] a knot." Depending on what a *tūrya* looks like (not specified in any of the works at my disposal, some of which suggest that it is merely

orifice of the ear is Amitābha's. The root of the ear is Amoghasiddhi's. The perception of the three sounds is Ratnasambhava's constitution. [Thus] is
A:11b explained the fivefold aural medium.†

C:47a "The totality of the olfactory media is Ākāśagarbha. †The olfactory sense organ [located] in the interior of the nose, which has a form [composed] of a collection of fine atoms [that have] the appearance of a (fine) instrument for applying eye medicine is Akṣobhya's. The nature of the nose is Vairocana's. The septum[306] is Ratnasambhava's. The nostrils are Amoghasiddhi's. The perception of the three scents is Amitābha's constitution. [Thus] is explained the fivefold olfactory medium.

"The totality of the gustatory media is Lokeśvara. With regard to that, the gustatory sense organ, which has a form [composed] of a collection of fine atoms and has the appearance of a half-moon—that is Akṣobhya's. The nature of the tongue is Vairocana's. The root of the tongue is Ratnasambhava's. The tip of the tongue is Amitābha's. The perception of the three flavors is Amoghasiddhi's constitution. [Thus] is explained the fivefold gustatory medium.

"The totality of the tactile media is Sarvanīvaraṇaviṣkambhin. With regard to that, the tactile sense organ, [composed] of a collection of fine atoms [and comprising] the entire body—that is Vairocana's. The nature of the bones is Ratnasambhava's. The nature of the flesh is Amitābha's. The nature of the skin is Amoghasiddhi's. The perception of the three [types of] contact is the constitution of Akṣobhya. [Thus] is explained the fivefold tactile medium.

---

a general term and not a specific instrument itself), this could be a satisfactory reading. However, the MSS seem clearly to read *bhūrya-*. As (to my knowledge) *bhūrya* does not mean anything, this must be read as *bhūri+agranthi*, which should be emended (I believe) to *bhūry-āgranthi* ("much twisted"). TIB is not of much help here. It reads *gro ga gcus te bcad pa lta bu*: like birch[-bark?] that is *bcus* ("winding" or "screwy") and *bcad pa* ("cut"). It, thus, seems to be based on a reading of **bhūrja-*. Harunaga Isaacson (personal communication 27 June 2005) has suggested that this could be read *bhūrjagranthy-ākṛti*, "shaped like a *bhūrjagranthi* (a kind of plant)."

306. *madhyāntaraṃ, nang gi dbus*. According to Prof. Kenneth Zysk (personal communication, 15 December 2004), this term does not occur in the early medical classics in connection with the nose. However, according to Prof. Zysk, the septum (which is the "inner middle" of the nose) is the site of a vital point (*marman*), and so seems a likely candidate as a referent for this term. MS C reads "inside the nose" (*ghrāṇābhyantaraṃ*).

"Speaking in reference to the samādhi of Samantabhadra,[307] the consciousness of the three radiances[308] in the interior of the body †is the mental A:12a
sense. Since it is the overlord of all the senses, it is introspectively known. Having taken as its object the Realm of Reality, due to the unreality of external objects, [and] having perfected itself through the enlightenment process of the phantasmic web (*māyājālābhisambodhikrama*), 'endowed with every one of the buddha qualities, it progresses from buddha-field to buddha-field.'[309] Thus is explained the samādhi of Samantabhadra.[310]

"[This] is the meaning of this [verse of] scripture:

> The vajra media themselves are
> The supreme maṇḍala of the bodhisattvas.[311]

"Speaking in reference to the samādhi of the object divinities,[312] the Great Yoga Tantra *Vajra Door {Goddess}*[313] proclaims ten airs, to wit: 'vitality,' 'evacuative,' 'ascending,' 'metabolic,' 'pervading,' 'upward-moving,' 're-moving,' 'co-moving,' 'out-moving,' and 'well-moving.'[314] With regard to

307. Following MS A; MS C and TIB read "Mañjuśrī" (*'jam dpal*). This variation would seem to reflect divergent streams within the tradition, rather than textual corruption.

308. Following SKT: *ābhāsa-traya-vijñānaṃ* (**snang ba gsum po'i rnam par shes pa*—note that TIB generally translates *ābhāsa*, by *snang ba* rather than *mched pa*, when it occurs alone). TIB reads "the three consciousnesses of luminance" (*snang ba'i rnam par shes pa gsum po*).

309. The quotation marks around "endowed with . . . buddhaverse(s)" represents an *iti* found in SKT after this phrase. I have placed the opening quotation mark (not found, obviously, in the Sanskrit) where I thought it belonged. This *iti*-construction is not found in TIB.

310. Again, MS C and TIB read "Mañjuśrī." See note 307, above.

311. GST XVII.50; see above, p. 135.

312. *viṣaya-devatā*; TIB specifies the gender: *yul rnams lha mo* (technically, "goddess [of the] objects," but given the context, it is clear that more than one goddess is meant).

313. *Vajramukhī-mahāyoga-tantra*, *rDo rje sgo zhes bya ba'i rnal 'byor chen po'i rgyud*. This scripture has not come down to us in either Sanskrit or Tibetan. Harunaga Isaacson (personal communication 27 June 2005) has noted another citation of this scripture in Abhayākaragupta's *Āmnāya-mañjarī* (Tōh. 1198: sDe-dge bsTan-'gyur, rGyud-'grel, vol. cha, ff. $1b^1$–$316a^7$), f. $196a^7$–$196b^1$, but as this seems to be drawn from the CMP it cannot be considered an independent witness.

314. *prāṇa-apāna-udāna-samāna-vyāna-udvāha-vivāha-saṃvāha-nirvāha-pravāha*; *srog dang | dur du sel ba dang | gyen du rgyu ba dang | mnyam du gnas pa dang | khyab byed dang | ldang zhing rgyu ba dang | rnam par rgyu ba dang | yang dag par rgyu ba dang | rab tu rgyu ba dang | nges par rgyu ba'o*. Note that TIB reverses the last two.

that, the five [main] airs—'vitality' and so on—in collaboration with[315] the (five) aggregates, perform the function[s] of the five aggregates. The five [auxiliary] airs—'upward-moving' and so on—in collaboration with the [five] sense organs, perform the function[s] of the senses.

"With regard to that, the air called 'upward-moving,' in collaboration
with the visual media, completes the fivefold activities of [perceiving visual]
form. That again—[i.e., the visual] form-object that is seen on account of
the assemblage of light, space,[316] mental functioning, and the visual sense
organ—that is Vairocana's [constitution]. [Visual] forms of play, flirtation,
and eroticism are Akṣobhya's. [Visual] forms to which one is attached are
A:12b Ratnasambhava's.[†‡] [Visual] forms that are discerned as pleasant, unpleas-
C:47b ant, and ambivalent are Amitābha's. [Visual] forms that perform all activities are the constitution of Amoghasiddhi. [Thus] is explained the fivefold
[visual] form-object.

"(The air called) 're-moving,' in collaboration with the aural media, performs the fivefold activities of [perceiving] sound. With regard to that, sounds inside the ear, and head (and) hair sounds, are Vairocana's [constitution]. Sounds of singing and stringed instruments are Ratnasambhava's. Palatal, labial, and vocal sounds are Amitābha's. Sounds of great trees, rivers, finger-snapping, clapping, drums, and other musical instruments are Amoghasiddhi's. The pacific and violent sounds of the syllable *hūṃ* are Akṣobhya's constitution. [Thus] is explained the fivefold sound-object.

"(The air called) 'co-moving,' in collaboration with the olfactory media,[317] performs the fivefold activities of [perceiving] scent. With regard to that, [all] scents without exception are Vairocana's. The scent of the entire body is Ratnasambhava's. The (perception of the distinction of the) three scents is Amitābha's. The scent of [vital] fluid[318] is Amoghasiddhi's. Unpleasant

315. Or "depending on," "residing in," "in connection with," "in relation to," or the like. Tib is odd here. This sentence and the one that follows are clearly parallel. The Sanskrit word rendered above as "[in] collaboration [with]" is (the gerund) *āśritya*. In the first sentence, Tib reads *brten te* ("depending on (the five aggregates)"), yet in the second it reads *gnas nas* ("residing in (the five sense organs)"). Both are suitable equivalents for *āśritya* (though perhaps the former should read **brten[d] nas*). Nonetheless, it is odd that the Tibetan translators did not choose one sense, but instead translated the same word in two adjacent, and *parallel* sentences with different equivalents.

316. Skt *ākāśa*; Tibetan reads *sgrib g.yogs med pa*, "non-obscuration."

317. Skt abbreviates, reading merely "nose" (*ghrāṇa*) rather than "olfactory media" (**ghrāṇāyatana*) as Tib.

318. *rasa-gandha*, the "smell of *rasa*"; this could mean the smell of water, taste, essence, semen,

scent[319] is the constitution of Akṣobhya. [Thus] is explained the fivefold scent-object.[320]

"(The air called) 'well-moving,' in collaboration with the gustatory media,[321] governs the fivefold gustatory object. With regard to that, sweet flavors are Vairocana's. Astringent flavors are Ratnasambhava's. Salty flavors are Amitābha's. Bitter flavors †are Akṣobhya's. The distinction of the A:13a
six flavors such as sharp, sour, {saline,} and so on, are the constitution of Amoghasiddhi. [Thus] is explained the fivefold gustatory object.

"{The air} called 'out-moving,' in collaboration with the tactile media, governs the fivefold tactile activities of strength, fortitude, [and] boldness such as personal combat and the like. With regard to that, the tactile sensation of staying on a single seat[322] is Vairocana's. The tactile sensation of embracing is Ratnasambhava's. The tactile sensation of kissing is Amitābha's. The tactile sensation of sucking[323] is Amoghasiddhi's. The perception of the nature of passion, dispassion, and moderate passion[324] from the tactile sensation of uniting the *liṅga* and[325] the *bhaga*[326] is the constitution of Akṣobhya. [Thus] is explained the fivefold tactile object.

---

mercury, poison, melted butter, gold, scallions, myrrh, or bodily fluid (among others). Noting the earlier mention of the "smell of the entire body" (*sarvāṅga-gandha*) and seeking to avoid using Sanskrit terms in the English translation, I have chosen the last, but this is rather arbitrary. Tib reads *ro'i dri*, which might be rendered "the smell of flavor" (though this does not seem a likely meaning), or perhaps "the smell of a corpse."

319. Following ms C, which reads *viṣama-gandha*. Tib (*dri mi zad pa*, "sharp/obdurate smell") supports this reading. ms A reads "the scent of objects" (*viṣaya-gandha*).

320. Tib reads *dri'i skye mched* (**gandhāyatana*) here, rather than **dri'i yul* (*gandha-viṣaya*). As Skt reads *gandha-viṣaya* and the pattern (set in the contexts of form, sound, and, below, tactile objects) is consistent, I have followed that reading. This same slip is repeated immediately below in the context of the gustatory objects.

321. Skt abbreviates, reading merely "tongue" (*jihvā*) rather than "olfactory media" (**jihvāyatana*) as Tib.

322. *ekāsanasthaḥ sparśaḥ, stan cig la gnas pa'i reg bya*. In general, this would refer to the tactile sensations of one who is an ascetic, who "sits [down to eat] only once per day." This practice is one of the standard ascetic practices (*dhūta-guṇa*).

323. *cūṣaṇa*; Tib reads *rngub pa*, "inhaling."

324. These three here serve as metonyms for the three sets of "prototypes" (*prakṛti*) of the subtle mind, which are described in greater detail in chapter 4, below. See also Appendix IV.

325. Sanskrit reads "in."

326. This refers, of course, to the uniting of the penis and vagina in sexual union. However, I have followed the Tibetan translators here in not rendering them in English, but retaining the Sanskrit terms.

"[This] is the meaning of this [verse of] scripture:

> The mantrin always meditates
> On forms, sounds, and so on, as divine.[327]

"Speaking in reference to the five gnoses: the mirror-like gnosis—[which
is] the immediate knowledge of a complete thing similar to the perception
of a reflection in a mirror—that is Vairocana's. The equality gnosis—[which
is] the understanding that all beings, [whether] legless, bipedal, quadrupe-
dal, or multi-pedal, have one form in being 'merely mind'—that is Ratna-
A:13b sambhava's. †The gnosis of individuating discernment—[which is] dwelling
without doubt in the discernment that, having analyzed and examined
one by one outer and inner things, such as aggregates and elements, [and,]
knowing them all to consist of buddha[s, discerns that] (the constituents
C:48a of) all things are (these) [buddhas], {numerous} like the petals of a lotus‡—
that is Amitābha's.[328] The function-accomplishing gnosis—which has the
nature of effecting the functioning of body, speech, and mind [which take]
action for the aims of self and other—that is Amoghasiddhi's. The completely pure gnosis of the Realm of Reality—which completely purifies the
vestigial instincts of conceptualizing good and evil (*śubhāśubha*), and so on,
is free of action and rebirth,[329] and completely purifies the obscurations of
body, speech, and mind—that is the constitution of Akṣobhya.

327. Here we get yet another slightly different version of the verse cited above, GST VII.14ab. (See chapter 2, note 273, above).

328. This translation reflects an eclectic attempt to reconcile the slightly divergent readings of Skt and Tib. Skt seems to define this gnosis as "dwelling without doubt in the discernment that all things are numerous like the petals of a lotus, having analyzed and examined one by one outer and inner things such as aggregates and elements [and] knowing them all to consist of buddha[s]" (*skandha-dhātvādi-bāhyādhyātmika-padārthān pṛthak pṛthag vibhajya pravivecya sarvaṃ buddha-mayam iti jñātvā sarva-dharmān bahava iti padma-dala-vat pratyavekṣya nirāśaṅkena viharaṇaṃ pratyavekṣaṇā-jñānaṃ*).

Tib seems to read: "dwelling without conceptuality in the discernment which, having analyzed and examined one by one outer and inner things such as aggregates and elements [and] knowing them all to be of the nature of buddha[s, discerns that] the constituents of all things are these [buddhas], like the petals of a lotus" (*phung po dang khams la sogs pa'i phyi dang nang gi dngos po rnams so sor rnam par phye ste rnam par brtags na thams cad kyang sangs rgyas kyi rang bzhin no zhes shes nas chos thams cad kyi cha shas ni 'di dag go zhes padma'i 'dab ma ltar so sor rtog cing rtog pa med pas gnas pa*).

329. *janman*; Tib reads "the defilements" (*nyon mongs pa*).

"Hence, [one] said:

> Aggregates, elements, and likewise, {sense} (media)
> Divided five by five—
> Are each constituted of the Five Transcendent Lords:
> How [could] life-cycle-action (*saṃsāra-karma*) occur?[330]
>
> In that way, the five (senses) together with external objects
> Are each properly [and] eternally constituted
> Of the Five Transcendent Lords.
> The three gnoses are the residence of [the] five also.[331]

"[This] is the meaning of this [previously cited verse of] scripture [from the *Secret Moon Drop*]:

> Clans are taught [to be] hundredfold."[332]

The Vajra Student asked, †"[My] doubts concerning (the establishment of) a body composed of the fine atoms of all Transcendent Lords by the sequence of the hundred clans have been dispelled. How, then, do they become 'fivefold through contraction?'" A:14a

330. Munidatta's commentary on the *Caryāgīti* (CGKV) cites this verse as from the *Sūtaka*, i.e., as from the CMP itself. See Kværne, *Anthology of Buddhist Tantric Songs*, 129.

331. Tib and Skt concur quite well in these two verses, except for the last line. Tib reads "[they] abide in the three and five gnoses also" (*ye shes lnga dang gsum du'ang yang dag gnas*). Skt reads *jñāna-trayaṃ pañca-samāśritaṃ ca*. This reading might be explained by the absence of the anusvāra after *-trayaṃ* in the text the Tibetan translators worked from, thus giving them the reading *jñāna-traya-pañca-samāśritaṃ ca*. I have followed Skt in the above translation, which makes more sense to me. For one, Skt is very clear. Further, it appears that we already have one hundred clans. With five aggregates, four elements, six sense media and five external objects (twenty categories in all), subdivided by five, one obtains one hundred clans. The three gnoses (again divided by five) are an additional set.

It is interesting to note that this verse mentions only three gnoses. This may be on account of the fact that this is mentioned in a yogic context—thus the three mentioned are those that are otherwise known as the three consciousnesses (*vijñāna*) or three radiances (*ābhāsa*). This may also adumbrate the discussion immediately following of the reduction of the hundred clans to five and three (and, eventually, one).

332. See above, p. 136.

The Vajra Mentor said, "The four elements produce the mass[333] of the body. From the gathering of the elements, the elemental derivatives (*bhautika*) occur. Hence, those elemental derivatives such as the form aggregate, which belong to the Transcendent Lord Clan, become a collection within[334] the earth element. Likewise, those of the Jewel Clan [become collected] in the water element; those of the Lotus Clan, in the fire element; those of the Action Clan, in the air element; [and] those of the Adamant Clan are collected in the consciousness element. For this reason, according to the division of elements and elemental derivatives in one's own body maṇḍala, the hundredfold heaps further become the nature of the five secret great realities (*tattva*).[335]

"Hence, it is said in the {Glorious} *Esoteric Community*:

> One should conceive in the middle of space
> A maṇḍala born from all vajras.

333. *piṇḍam*; this term can itself mean "body" or "flesh." Tib renders this *phung po*, which refers to a "heap" (another acceptable rendering of *piṇḍam*), but I think in this context it is best rendered "mass" or "matter."

334. This occurs in the locative (*pṛthivī-dhātau*), but we may be justified in reading this in a genitive sense as "a collection of the earth element" (cf. W.D. Whitney, *Sanskrit Grammar*, 5th edition, §303a). Tib reads the literalistic (though grammatically divergent) "since they gather the earth element, they go [near]" (*de ni sa yi khams sdud par byed pas nye bar 'gro'o*).

335. Or, perhaps, "five secret great elements." Here Skt and Tib diverge somewhat more significantly than usual. I have followed Skt, which seems to make good sense. Tib reads "by dividing one's own body maṇḍala according to elements and elemental derivatives, the five aggregates, which have become hundredfold, also become the nature of the five secrets [and] the nature of the five great elements." (*rang kyi lus kyi dkyil 'khor 'byung ba dang 'byung ba las gyur pa'i dbye bas phung po lnga rnams brgya gyur pa yang gsang ba lnga'i de kho na nyid 'byung ba chen po lnga'i de kho na nyid du 'gyur*).

There are two issues here. The first, concerning the reading "five aggregates," is reasonably clear. One suspects that somewhere in the transmission of Tib, someone added a knee-jerk "five" after the term *phung po* ("aggregate"), which of course come in a set of five. Interestingly, however, this reading is found in all the canonical versions I consulted (D, Co, N, and P). If this is so, then this interpolation must have occurred in the prototype(s) of these canonical versions. The Sanskrit term, however, is *rāśi* (not *skandha*) and there are, in this context at least, a hundred of them (analyzed above), which *include* the five aggregates.

The other problem is more difficult. The phrase I have rendered above as "of the nature of the five secret great realities" is *pañca-guhya-mahātattvātmikāḥ*. Āryadeva has just described how the five clans correspond to the five elements. It is possible (as noted above) that the correct reading is **pañca-guhya-mahābhūtātmikāḥ*; though again, Tib restores to something like **pañca-guhya-tattva-pañca-mahābhūta-tattvātmikāḥ*.

Should one desire the peaceful Vajradhṛk,
One should effect the assembling (*saṃhāra*).[336]

(And,) clarifying that very idea, the *Universal Secret Tantra*[337] says:

The human body is always viewed
As having five natures (*ātman*) on account of the five elements.
Those who always cultivate their own minds
By contemplation of its condition, become buddhas.[338]

(And) also the *Space-Like Tantra*[339] says:† A:14b

This entire world is of the nature of the five buddhas.
Let it be seen [like] a divine dance [or] picture,
In which [the] one called 'Great Bliss'
Dances, alone [but] with several æsthetic moods.[340]

336. This verse does not occur in this form in the *Guhyasamāja Tantra* as it has come down to us. The first two pādas seem to be a variant of GST XI.3ab. The third and fourth pādas are GST VIII.11cd.

337. *Sarva-rahasya-tantra, Thams cad gsang ba'i rgyud.* A Sanskrit text of this scripture does not seem to have come down to us. A Tibetan translation (by Padmākaravarman and Rin-chen bZang-po) is found at: DK, rGyud, vol. ta, 1b^1–10a^1 (Tōh. 481), as *Thams cad gsang ba zhes bya ba rgyud kyi rgyal po/Sarvarahasya-nāma-tantrarāja.* For more on this text (Tibetan text [from Peking edition], translation, and index), see A. Wayman, "The Sarvarahasyatantra," 521–69. See also Urga Kanjur (Rgyud, vol. ta, f. 1b^2 ff.). The cited verse is the first verse of the scripture, though it appears in rather different wording in the canonical text.

338. Tib reads: "In the five natures of the five elements, the human body should be designated. By meditating certainly that thing, one will become buddha by the power of their own mind" (*'byung ba nga yi bdag nyid lngar | mi yi lus ni brtag bya ste | dngos de nges par bsgoms pa yis | rang sems mthu yis sangs rgyas 'gyur* ||). The Tibetan canonical translation (P) corresponds more closely to Skt (see apparatus to Tibetan edition).

339. *Khasama-tantrarāja-nāma, Nam mkha' dang mnyam pa'i rgyud* (*kyi rgyal po zhes bya ba*). On this scripture, see note 340, below.

340. This verse is not found in the version of the *Khasama-tantra* preserved in DK (*dPal nam mkha' dang mnyam pa'i rgyud kyi rgyal po*, DK, rGyud, vol. ga, 199a^7–202a^1 [Tōh. 386]). This may be due to its not, in fact, being a citation from that Tantra. It is cited in Vanaratna's commentary on the *Vasantatilaka*, where it is attributed to the *Guhyendutilaka* (on which, see chapter 2, note 274, above) rather than the *Khasama-tantra*, though I have been unable to locate it in the Tibetan translation of that scripture. See RD, 15. A variant form of the verse also occurs in the *Yoginīsaṃcāra Tantra* (YST, p. 115), where the *Nibandha*

[This] is the meaning of this [previously cited verse of] scripture [from the *Secret Moon Drop*]:

> Through contraction (*saṃkṣepa*), fivefold."

The Vajra Student asked, "How do the five forms further become threefold?"

The Vajra Mentor replied, "Ratnasambhava becomes nondual with the body vajra. Amoghasiddhi becomes nondual with the speech vajra. Akṣobhya becomes nondual with the sixth transcendent lord. In that way, having started with one hundred clans, the buddhas and bodhisattvas,
C:48b which have the nature of the five clans, ‡become collected into one's own body, speech, and mind. Just as the Lord said in the Great Yoga Tantra, the {Glorious} *Esoteric Community*:

> Then, all those Transcendent Lords caused their own body, speech, and mind to enter the syllables of the three vajrasattvas.[341]

(And,)

> By focusing on body, speech, and mind,
> One will not grasp the [real] nature.
> By uniting with a mantra body
> There is neither enlightenment nor [meditative] cultivation.
>
> Having investigated, this—in brief—
> Is the characteristic of body, speech, and mind.

---

of Tathāgatarakṣita comments: "'the nature of the five buddhas' [means] 'the proper form of the Five Transcendent Lords, Vairocana, and so on.' 'This entire world' [means] 'this whole world, the form [aggregate], feeling [aggregate], and so on.' . . . 'The Sixth' [refers to] the sixth [transcendent lord] called 'Vajrasattva,' [of whom] 'Great Bliss' is another name. 'Dances, alone [but] with several æsthetic moods' [means] he alone is known under several forms." (YST, 301–2) Thanks to Harunaga Isaacson for directing me to these texts.

341. Following Skt, which corresponds to a passage at the end of GST XVII (Matsunaga, 111). Tib reads "then, all those transcendent lords entered their own body, speech, and mind, by the three inexhaustible vajras" (*de nas de bzhin gshegs pa thams cad mi zad pa'i rdo rje gsum gyis nyid kyi sku dang gsung dang thugs la rab tu zhugs par 'gyur ro*)—presumably reading **try-akṣaya-vajreṇa* instead of *tri-vajra-sattvākṣareṣu*. However, the Tibetan canonical translation of this passage (DK, rGyud, vol. ca, 148a[1]) corresponds to Skt.

One should cultivate the enlightenment-conjunction,[342]
The samādhi created by mantra.[343]

"The Great Yoga Tantra, the {Glorious} *Union of All Buddhas: †Magical* A:15a
Supreme Bliss of the Ḍākiṇīs[344] also illuminating this point, says:

Yoga is not born
In cast images, or the like.
Yogins who [practice] the great yoga of the spirit of
enlightenment
(Will become) divinities by that.

I (myself) am {verily} universal buddha{hood}!
And universal hero{ism}, too!
Through union with one's own divinity
So should one accomplish the self![345]

[This] is the meaning of this [previously-cited verse of] scripture [from the *Secret Moon Drop*]:

By correlation with body, speech, and mind,
They also become threefold."[346]

342. *bodhi-saṃyoga*; Tib reads "the rite of conjunction" (*sbyor ba'i cho ga*), reflecting a reading of **vidhi-saṃyoga*, which is the reading found in Matsunaga's edition. The reading *bodhi-saṃyoga* (found in both mss) is attested in several places, however, including PU, RD, and the Chinese translation of the GST (Taisho 885).

343. This pair of verses is GST VI.5–6.

344. *Sarva-buddha-samāyoga-ḍākinī-jāla-saṃvara-mahāyoga-tantra*; *Sangs rgyas thams cad dang mnyam par sbyor ba mkha' 'gro ma sgyu ma bde ba'i mchog*. This text does not seem to have come down to us in the Sanskrit. A Tibetan translation (by Lha Rinpoche) may be found at: DK, rGyud, vol. ka, 151b^{1}–193a^{6} (Tōh. 366). An alternative rendering (translator not specified, though the subsequent text is attributed to Smṛtijñānakīrti, revised by gZhon-nu grags-pa) may be found at: sTog Palace Kanjur, vol. 95 (rGyud nga), ff. 241a^{1}–295b^{2}.

345. These verses are SBS I.22 and I.24, which may be found in DK at f. 152a^{6} and 152a^{7}. The first verse is cited in the *Jñānasiddhi* (see Bhattacharyya, 85) as from the *Saṃvara Tantra* (which is how the SBS is typically cited in Sanskrit sources; see also CMP [B:64a]). The first line of the second verse is commonly cited/found: see, e.g., PK III.28ab.

346. See above, p. 136.

The Vajra Student asked, "[My] doubts about the ingathering—in one's own body, speech, and mind—of the buddhas and bodhisattvas that have the nature of all clans[347] have been dispelled. How again do the three clans become the body vajra with the nature of the indivisible three vajras? Speak, O Lord! Speak, O Teacher, Vajra Mentor!"

The Vajra Mentor replied, "Excellent! Excellent, Great One! For the sake of the practitioners of the [Esoteric] Community,[348] you inquire about the consummation of body isolation. Therefore, listen! Having explained to you the mutual causal relationship of body, speech, and mind, I will establish [you] in the body-vajra samādhi.

"The Lord says in the {Glorious} *Esoteric Community*:[349]

> By a body mantra-focused [and]
> By speech [is it[350]] impelled in the mind.
> A:15b One may accomplish the foremost accomplishment—†
> The beloved that satisfies the mind.[351]

The intention of this [statement] is this. With regard to that, being the body vajra{dhara}, having completed the assemblage of the tongue in the space [between] the palate [and] lips, one transforms into the speech vajra. There, the mind vajra is set in motion. Thus, from the conjunction of the three {vajras}, one may bring forth the accomplishment that satisfies the mind. That is the meaning.

"Having thus investigated the characteristic[s] of body, speech, mind

347. Tib reads *rtogs pa* (read *rtog pa*, **kalpa*) for Skt *kula* ("clan").

348. Following Skt, which reads merely *sāmājikānāṃ hitārthāya*; Tib reads "for the sake of those who enter the meaning of the Community" (*'dus pa'i don la zhugs pa rnams la phan par bya ba'i phyir*).

349. On this scripture, see chapter 2, note 272, above.

350. PU supplies the object that is impelled: "the Vajrasattva that abides in the heart" (*hṛdistho vajrasattvaḥ*).

351. GST VI.3 (Matsunaga, 17). Tib and Skt diverge significantly here in the first two pādas. Tib may be rendered: "The body focused on the meaning and speech also should be impelled by the mind." Again, the Tibetan canonical translation of this passage (DK, rGyud, vol. ca, 98b[6–7]) corresponds to Skt.

separately, now the characteristic of the indivisible three vajras is to be presented. (Since) it says in the {glorious} *Esoteric Community*:[352]

> You! Create [your] mind in the form of body, [your] body in the form of mind, (and) [your] mind, like vocal expression.[353]

The yoga of constitution (*adhiṣṭhānayoga*) is said [to be this]: having firmly created [oneself as a deity] with the thought "I am naturally pure (*prakṛti-śuddha*),"[354] one should devote oneself completely to [attaining the state of] Mahāvajradhara, †which has the nature of the indivisible three vajras." C:49a

352. On this scripture, see chapter 2, note 272, above.

353. This passage is found near the beginning of GST II (Matsunaga, 9, l. 13–14).

354. Tib (*sic*) reads "I am the natural lord" (*rang bzhin gyi bdag po'o*, **prakṛti-siddha*). I have emended Tib to read *rang bzhin gyis dag pa'o*, based on Skt. This seems like a clear case of textual corruption.

3. Resolution of Doubts about the Integration of Speech Isolation

The Vajra Student asked, "(As) [my] doubts regarding the instruction concerning body isolation have been dispelled, how, O Lord, should speech isolation be learned? How should it be accomplished? Speak, O Lord [and] Teacher, Vajra Mentor!"

The Vajra Mentor said, "Excellent, excellent, O Great One![†] The body A:16a
isolation [that I have] just described—the aggregates, elements, and media—and the array of deities therein is common to all, as it is a coarse yoga. But speech isolation is the extremely subtle gnosis of the yogins [that is] not the province of practitioners of the Universal Way. Even [among] practitioners of the Adamantine Way, it is not the range of those who practice the creation stage, as it is a subtle yoga.[355] Therefore, listen carefully! I will instruct you in detail about the speech-vajra samādhi according to the explanatory tantra[s].

"With regard to that, the previously cited (versified) scriptural statement that 'clans are taught to be hundredfold,' [refers] in common to body, speech, and mind isolations. With respect to that, the so-called 'speech isolation' is mantra reality; and that will not be known unless it is preceded

355. While Skt texts read "because it is a subtle yoga" (*sūkṣma-yoga-tvāt*), Tib reads "because it is extremely subtle" (*shin tu phra ba'i phyir*, **atyanta-sūkṣma-tvāt*).

Note that in this passage Āryadeva seems to be indicating that the line of demarcation between the creation and perfection stages lies between the practices of body isolation and speech isolation—a subject of some debate among later Tibetan scholastics. With regard to this claim, it is important to note that the stage of speech isolation either begins with or commences immediately after the crucial practices of vitality control (*prāṇāyāma*), here called "air reality," which serve to force the airs into the central channel (*avadhūti, rtsa dbu ma*). This technique is the *sine qua non* of the advanced yogic techniques of the Buddhist tantras. Hence, it marks a logical division in the stages of Tantric practice.

by air reality.[356] The so-called 'air reality' is vitality control (*prāṇāyāma*). Hence, a statement illustrating air reality is introduced in the *Glorious Esoteric Community*:

A five-colored {great} jewel
(Roughly) the size of a mustard [seed]
Should always be meditated by yoga
With perseverance on the tip of the nose.[357]

"Analyzing these vajra words according to definitive and interpretable meaning, it applies to the two types of deity yoga. (The teaching that) "the one meditating on the creation stage should meditate on the symbol of their own deity (merely) the size of a mustard seed[358] on the tip of [their]
A:16b nose for the purpose of stabilizing their own mind" †is a reference to the subtle yoga [of the creation stage].

This very [same verse] expresses the subtle yoga of those who have encountered the perfection stage samādhi: having created the three-syllabled[359] in the manner of [the three genders]—feminine, masculine, and neuter—by means of the vowels and consonants, [and] having harnessed the three-syllabled to [the three processes of] entering, abiding, and emerging, one should perform the vajra recitation—[which has the] nature of vitality control—according to the sequence of the four maṇḍalas.

356. *vāyu-tattva, rlung gi de kho na nyid*. For "unless it is preceded by air reality," Tib reads "without the process of air reality" (*rlung gi de kho na nyid kyi rim pa dang bral bas*). Note that this refers to the list of four "realities" (*tattva*) found in chapter 1 (see above, p. 123). Āryadeva here asserts that speech isolation is also called "mantra reality" (*mantra-tattva*). He here adds a fifth "reality" not mentioned before—air reality, which is ostensibly a propædeutic process of mastering the subtle yogas of vitality control (*prāṇāyāma*).

357. GST III.12: *pañca-varṇaṃ mahāratnaṃ sarṣapa-sthūla-mātrakam | nāsikāgre prayatnena bhāvayed yogataḥ sadā ||* Tib seems to suggest **sarṣapa-phala-mātrakam* (*yungs kar gyi ni 'bru tshad tsam*), which reading is attested in PU, though it is unmetrical. This verse is also cited in the "Vajrajāpa" chapter of the *Pañcakrama* (PK I.11). In fact, Āryadeva even introduces it with practically the same words, viz. CMP: *vāyu-tattvasyoddeśa-padaṃ śrī-guhyasamājād avatāryate*; PK: *vāyu-tattvoddeśa-padaṃ mūla-sūtrād evâvatāryate*.

358. *sarṣapa-phala*: as noted above, this reading is suggested by Tib, demonstrating that—according to Āryadeva at least—one is to understand *sarṣapa-sthūla-mātrakaṃ* to mean *sarṣapa-phala-pramāṇaṃ*.

359. *tryakṣara, yi ge gsum*; typically in Indic religious writings, this refers to the sacred syllable *oṃ* (analyzed into three syllables as *a-u-m*). In this esoteric Buddhist context, it refers to the three syllables *oṃ āḥ hūṃ*.

"Clarifying this point, the (*Esoteric*) *Community Appendix* (*Tantra*)[360] states:

> The breath made of the five gnoses,
> With the nature of the five elements—
> Emitting [it] at the lotus nose tip,
> [One] should imagine [it] in the form of a lump (*piṇḍa*).
>
> The five-colored great jewel
> Is traditionally known as "vitality control."[361]

"The explanation of this illustrative statement[362] is expressed in the explanatory tantra[363] of the Esoteric Community, the *Explanation of the Intention*:[364]

360. *samājottara*; *gsang ba 'dus pa'i rgyud phyi ma*; This refers to the *Guhyasamājottaratantra* (GSUT). Often included as the eighteenth chapter of the GST itself, this work is commentarial with regard to the rest of the Tantra. The Sanskrit text may be found in Bhattacharyya and Bagchi. A Tibetan translation (by Śraddhākaravarman and Rin-chen bZang-po) is found (as a separate text) in: DK, rGyud, vol. ca, ff. $148a^6$–$157b^7$ (Tōh. 443).

361. The Sanskrit text as found in the CMP differs somewhat from that found in the edited GSUT (vv. 147–48, Matsunaga, 124). However, this passage is also cited in the corresponding section of PK (i.e., the "Vajrajāpa-krama": PK I.14–15), which has essentially the same readings as the CMP. The citation as found in Tib corresponds exactly to the sTog Palace Kanjur version, vol. ca, f. $90b^{6-7}$ (also translated by Śraddhākaravarman and Rin-chen bZang-po). I have discussed this variant in detail in my "Tantalising Traces" (165–67). In short, all the extant texts of the Noble Tradition works (PK, CMP, PU) read "lotus nose tip," while all texts of the GSUT read "nose tip." Tsongkhapa (RṄSG, 313) prefers the latter reading, claiming (erroneously, I feel) that it is found in some Indian manuscripts and Tibetan translations of the Noble literature.

362. Skt reads *uddeśa-pada*, previously rendered in the Tibetan translation of this chapter as *bstan pa'i tshig*. Here, however, Tib reads *mdor bstan pa*, "brief illustration."

363. It is notable that—although he introduced the term at the beginning of this chapter and has mentioned the *Vajra Rosary* (*Vajramālā*) in chapter 2 above—this is the first time in this work that Āryadeva has specifically identified a work he cites as an "explanatory tantra" (*vyākhyā-tantra*). Such citations become crucial pieces of evidence for later Tibetan writers seeking to identify the precise denotation of the term "explanatory tantra of the Esoteric Community," a concept that is crucial to the hermeneutical practice of the Noble Tradition.

364. *Saṃdhyāvyākaraṇa-mahāyoga-tantra*; *dGongs pa lung ston pa zhes bya ba'i rnal 'byor chen po'i rgyud.* This is one of the central explanatory tantras on which the Noble Tradition relies in advancing its interpretation of the Esoteric Community. It is a hermeneutical and exegetical scripture. I am not aware of an extant Sanskrit text of this scripture, though parts

Then, the Lord Mahāvajrin proclaimed
The statement of the meaning of the vajra recitation.[365]
C:49b Having paid proper homage‡
To the sole mentor of beings, [he said]:

'(If) even this worldly tradition
Sets forth the spirit of enlightenment,
How will those in the future possibly
Understand the transcendent?

'The Dharma was taught by you
For abandonment of all views.
How so, then, the spirit of enlightenment?
A:17a That view has been made firm!†

'The expressed meaning is not understood
By those who are deluded about intentional speech,
They cling to the literal meaning
And say "[the meaning is] not otherwise."'

Then, the Lord Viśva
Said to Vajrapāṇi thereafter,
'Excellent, excellent, Secret Lord!
You have predicted those in the future.[366]

'The spirit of enlightenment should become air
And [become] situated in space.
[That air] is the very vitality of (all) beings,
With five natures [and] ten names.[367]

---

of it are cited in several extant Sanskrit śāstras. A Tibetan translation (by Dharmaśrībhadra and Rin-chen bZang-po) may be found in DK, rGyud, vol. ca, ff. 158a^{1}– 207b^{7}.

365. *vajrajāpārtha*; Tib reads "the meaning of the essence of vajra" (*rdo rje snying po'i don*, **vajrasārārtha*).

366. Skt is problematic here. Tib reads: "Then the Lord Viśva said to Vajrapāṇi, 'it is excellent, excellent that you inquire about the secret intention that is not understood'" (*khyod gsang dgong pa ma rtogs pa | 'dri bar byed pa legs so legs ||*).

367. These last two pādas are echoed in PK I.3a and I.3d, respectively. The whole verse reads:

'Known as the "twelve links of dependent origination,"
From the natures [it] may become three.
This chief principle of the senses
[Is] the spirit of enlightenment called "air."

'[As it is] thus unmanifest and subtle,
It is always called "manifest."
But on the basis of that, a being
May perform [ritual] actions, to [various] ends.

'Pacification and prosperity,
Domination and, likewise, destruction—
All that [comes] from the spirit of enlightenment
In dependence on the dwelling of the three Realities.

'All worldly significations
[And,] likewise, various fabrications
Evolve from the spirit of enlightenment;
Concepts always [evolve] from air.[368]

'Thing[s] such as pleasure and pain
Are produced from their seed[s].[369]
Those[370] [things have] the spirit of enlightenment as [their] nature,
[Being] nondual [with] the aggregates, and so on, like space.

'By the unification of critical wisdom and liberative art,
The spirit of enlightenment may become a being.

---

prāṇabhūtaś ca sattvānāṃ vāyvākhyaḥ sarva-karma-kṛt | vijñāna-vāhanaś caiṣa *pañcātmā daśadhā punaḥ* || (shared pādas in italics).

368. SKT differs from TIB here. TIB seems to read: "Just as worldly conventions and, likewise, various fabrications, concepts always emerge from the air called 'the spirit of enlightenment'" (*ji srid 'jig rten brtag pa dang | de bzhin brtag pa sna tshogs rnams | rnam rtog byang chub sems zhes pa'i | rlung las rtag tu 'byung ba yin |*).

369. TIB reads, "Pleasure, pain, and so on, are explained to be like the seeds of things" (*bde sdug la sogs chos rnams kyi | sa bon lta bur bshad pa yin |*).

370. Literally, "that" (*asau*); TIB reads "this" (*'di*).

The master who has abandoned
A:17b Study [and] meditation should himself recite.[†]

'By the distinction of day and night
In consequence of the moon and sun,
Breath[371] is that which pervades beings—
The one air of the spirit of enlightenment.

'Having abandoned good and evil results,
It becomes like unto the sky.'"[372]

The Vajra Student asked, "It has been said that 'air [has] five natures and ten names.' Out of [your] kindness, tell [me], Lord, the different names of each of the airs."

The Vajra Mentor said, "It is taught by the explanatory tantra just mentioned [the *Explanation of the Intention*]; we shall indicate it.[373]

> Then the Lord, having entered all the transcendent lords and likewise all the bodhisattvas, spoke of the ten airs in order to please the overlord of transcendent lords:[374]

'Vitality,' 'evacuative,' 'metabolic,'
'Ascending,' and 'pervasive,'
'Nāga,' 'kūrma,' 'kṛkara,'[375]
'Devadatta,' and 'dhanañjaya.'

371. Skt reads *niḥśvāsaḥ* ("breath"), but Tib reads *dngos po med pa*, i.e., "lack of reality." Presumably the translators read **niḥsvabhāvo* rather than *niḥśvāso hi*.

372. This passage may be found at DK, rGyud, vol. ca, ff. $168b^2$–$169a^2$.

373. Tib reads "extricate" (*dgrol*, *√muc*) for Skt "indicate" (*darśayāmaḥ*, **bstan par byed*).

374. All the texts have divergent readings of this introductory line. Here I follow my own conjectural reading. The reading of ms A is incoherent. Even after Pandey's emendation of *tathāgatādhipaśyate* to *tathāgatādhipateḥ* (based on Tib), one still lacks a main verb to resolve the action of the gerund. Such a verb is supplied in C (*āha*), which reading I have followed in the main, merely adding that element of (emended) A that is shared by Tib (i.e., "the overlord of transcendent lords," **tathāgatādhipateḥ/de bzhin gshegs pa bdag po*). Tib versifies this passage and reads: "Then all the transcendent lords | and likewise all the bodhisattvas | entered in order to please | that lord of transcendent lords. ||"

375. All these terms have meanings, of course: *nāga* means "snake" (or "elephant"), *kurma*

Having produced those, one again
Creates their form as female.[376]

"The (jargon) expressions by which these ten airs are referred to according to the tradition of the *Union of All Buddhas: Magical Supreme Bliss of the Ḍākiṇīs*[377] ‡ are: C:50a

koṭākhyaḥ,[378] koṭavaḥ, koṭaḥ, koṭābhaḥ, and kaṭīrakaḥ,
kolākhyaḥ, kolavaḥ, kolaḥ, kolābhaḥ, and, likewise, kaliḥ.[379]

These ten names were also declared with a literal intent in the Great Yoga Tantra the *Vajra Door {Goddess}*,[380] †as ten airs: vitality (*prāṇa*), evacuative (*apāna*), ascending (*udāna*), metabolic (*samāna*), pervasive (*vyāna*), up-moving (*udvāha*), re-moving (*vivāha*), co-moving (*saṃvāha*), well-moving (*pravāha*), and out-moving (*nirvāha*)." A:18a

The Vajra Student asked, "The ten airs—'vitality' and so forth—where do they reside in this body [and] what do they do? Speak, O Lord and Teacher, Vajra Mentor!"

"turtle," and so on. SKT reads *kṛkara/kṛkala*, "partridge," which is well-attested, but TIB *rtsangs pa* usually renders **kṛkalāsa*, "chameleon."

376. DK, rGyud, vol. ca, 158b[7]–159a[1].

377. On this scripture, see chapter 2, note 344, above.

378. I follow the reading of MS C and TIB here (rather than MS A's reading of *koṭākṣaḥ*), based on the verse in PU, which uses these terms as an example of non-literal (*naruta*) explanation: "Sounds such as '*koṭākhya*' and so on | Which do not exist in worldly treatises | Are the signs of the Transcendent Lords | That is known as the 'non-literal' ||" (*koṭākhyakādayaḥ śabdā loka-śāstra-bahiṣkṛtāḥ | tathāgatānāṃ saṃketā narutaṃ tat prakīrtitam* || See PU, 3).

379. Overall, my strategy in editing these terms, with the exception of the reading mentioned above (i.e., *koṭākhyaḥ*), has been to follow the apparent pattern in the phonemes. While all the variant readings of the Sanskrit texts may be found in the apparatus to my edition, it may be convenient to have the diplomatic readings of the MSS here for reference: MS A reads *koṭākṣaḥ, koṭacaḥ, koṭaḥ, koṭābhaḥ, kaṭīrakaḥ, kolākṣaḥ, kolavaḥ, kolaḥ, kolābhaḥ, kaliḥ;* MS C reads *koṭākhyaḥ, koṭavaḥ, koṭaḥ, koṭābhaḥ, kaṭīrakaḥ, kolākhyaḥ, kolavaḥ, kolaḥ, kolābhaḥ, kalaḥ;* TIB reads *koṭakhya, koṭava, koṭa, koṭavaścaśa, koṭīragaḥ, kolahya, kolavā, kola, kolavaśca, kola(tathā)*. The Tibetan canonical translation of this passage may be found at DK, rGyud, vol. ka, 186b[5].

380. On this scripture, see chapter 2, note 313, above.

The Vajra Mentor said, "The five [main] airs, residing in the parts of the body, perform the function[s] of the body. The five [auxiliary] airs, residing in the media such as the eye, and so forth, perform the function[s] of the senses.

"In regard to that, the (so-called) 'vitality (air),' which resides in the heart, is the Transcendent Lord Akṣobhya. The 'evacuative,' which resides in the anus, is the Transcendent Lord Ratnasambhava. The 'ascending,' which resides in the throat, is the Transcendent Lord Amitābha. The 'metabolic,' which resides at the navel, is the Transcendent Lord Amoghasiddhi. The 'pervasive,' which resides in all the joints, is the Transcendent Lord Vairocana. The 'upward-moving (air)' is [visual-]form. The 're-moving (air)' is sound. The 'co-moving (air)' is scent. The 'well-moving (air)' is flavor. The 'out-moving (air)' is tactile objects.

"These ten airs, moreover, become exhalation and inhalation. They also become of the nature of the four maṇḍalas, such as the air [maṇḍala] and so forth.[381] They also become of the nature of the four goddesses. They also
A:18b become {of the nature of} the five elements.[†] They also become {of the nature of} the five gnoses, such as the mirror(-like) [gnosis] and so forth. They also become of the nature of five [colored] light rays, such as white, and so forth. They also become of the nature of the Five Transcendent Lords. They also, having become the foundation of the three-syllabled, cause the performance of the vajra recitation by the process of entering, abiding, and emerging. These airs also, having become the support (*ādhāra*) of the syllable *a,* cause the enunciation of all speech. They also, having reached the unstruck [sound/nerve-center in the heart],[382] become insubstantial."

The Vajra Student asked, "How, Lord, do these ten airs, with [their] nature of being one [and] many, perform day and night the emitting [and] collecting in one's own body? Speak, O Lord and Teacher, Vajra Mentor!"

381. See the eight verses cited from the *Vajra Rosary* (*Vajramālā*) in response to the next question.

382. Following the reading of MS A, *anāhataṃ vyāpya.* MS C and Tib read *prāpya/thob pa* rather than *vyāpya,* which would not change the meaning. Tib translates *anāhataṃ* (the "unstruck [sound]") by *mi shigs pa* ("indestructible"), usually understood in the Tibetan tantric tradition as the *mi shigs pa'i thig le,* or "indestructible drop" located in the yogic heart center. For the meaning of this term in orthodox ("Hindu") esoterism, see s.v. *anāhata* in Brunner, *et al., Tāntrikābhidhānakośa* I, 117–18.

The Vajra Mentor replied, "Excellent, excellent, Great One! The air reality is not stated clearly in the root tantras, such as the *Glorious Compendium of Realities*,[383] and the appendix tantras. ‡[This is] because it is spoken of C:50b
intentionally. But in the explanatory tantra [the *Vajra Rosary*[384]] it is spoken of literally; that [shall be] introduced:

> Born from the nostril orifice,
> Fixed [in] the five buddha clans,
> The upward motion of the five airs
> Always courses in the body.
>
> Moving [in] the superficial nose,
> [It is] issued forth from that door.
> They are fourfold: Left and right and
> Both and languid.† A:19a
>
> [385]The element that flows from the right
> Is indeed the fire-maṇḍala.

383. *Śrī-tattvasaṃgraha, dPal de kho na nyid bsdus pa.* One of the most important Buddhist tantras, the STTS has been edited and published several times. Kanjin Horiuchi's is probably the best. It has also been published as: Isshi Yamada, *Sarva-tathāgata-tattva-saṅgraha nāma mahāyāna-sūtra*, and Lokesh Chandra, *Sarva-tathāgata-tattva-saṅgraha*. A Tibetan translation (by Śraddhākaravarman and Rin-chen bZang-po), *De bzhin gshegs pa thams cad kyi de kho na nyid bsdus pa zhes bya ba theg pa chen po'i mdo*, may be found at DK, rGyud, vol. nyi, 1b[1]–142a[7] (Tōh. 479). It has not been translated into English, except for selected passages, such as the Maheśvara subjugation myth, which has garnered a fair bit of scholarly attention of late.

Āryadeva's comment seems to suggest that ("historically") the practice of vital air yoga is not found in the teachings of the "Yoga Tantras," nor even their supplementary scriptures (presumably including the "root" Mahāyoga Tantras), but is a development only set forth in the explanatory tantras.

384. On this scripture, see chapter 2, note 286, above.

385. From this point until the line "should issue [the maṇḍala] of the Vajra Savior," this passage is found in the sDe-dge redaction of the *Vajramālā* in the twelfth chapter, "Explanation of Air Reality," from 222b[7] to 223a[2]. This is also the section (plus one following verse, "That which, upholding all the elements," etc.) that corresponds to the verses cited in the same context in the *Pañcakrama*; see PK I.17–23 (Mimaki and Tomabechi, 4–5).

[One] should issue this red-colored manifestation[386]
Of the Lotus Savior [Amitābha].

The element that flows from the left
[Is the] issuance of the air-maṇḍala.
Looking [darkish] yellow-green,[387]
[One] should issue [the maṇḍala] of the Action Savior
[Amoghasiddhi].

The element that flows from both
Resembles a golden color.
[One] should indeed also issue the maṇḍala of earth
Of the Jewel Savior [Ratnasambhava].

The languid, non-streaming element
Is immediately the water maṇḍala.
One should issue [the maṇḍala] of the Adamant Savior
[Akṣobhya],
[Which] looks like pure crystal.

That which, upholding all the elements,[388]
Comprises habitat and inhabitant [maṇḍalas]

386. Following MS C (also SUT), which reads *vyaktaṃ*; MS A reads *vaktraṃ* ("mouth, face, garment, beginning"); TIB reads *mchog* ("supreme").

387. *harita-śyāma-saṃkāśa*; or "looking like a greenish-yellow cuckoo"; TIB reads only "appearing greenish-yellow" (*ljang ser dag tu snang ba*).

388. TIB seems to read **samudgamya* (*yang dag 'byung*, "rising up/coming forth"), for *samuddhṛtya* ("upholding"), which latter reading is clearly attested in both MSS. There are also significant variants in the Tibetan texts. The reading of D (*khams kun yang dag 'byung ba ni*) is closer to SKT; P reads *khams gsum yang dag 'byung ba yi*.

[Is] the great body of Vairocana.[389]
[One] should issue [it in all directions][390] at the conclusion of
[the process of] death.[391]

One should always recite the[se] four maṇḍala[s]
Through meditative stabilization.
[They are] to be recited day and night always
By the count of the recitation of the mantra-practitioners.[392]

The Lord stated thus in the Great Yoga Tantra, the *Vajra Rosary*. Its meaning is this: one should issue forth light rays [in all directions] from nostrils of the vajra and lotus. That which goes upward issues from the tip[393] of the superficial nose by the processes of the left, right, both, and fixed.

"With regard to that, this [is the] process:[394] the air that exits from the left nose is the Transcendent Lord Amoghasiddhi; [He has] the nature of air [and appears as an] air maṇḍala †that has the very form of [darkish] yellow-green light rays.[395] The air that issues from the right nose is the A:19b

389. *vairocana-mahākāyo*; Tib seems to suggest "the body of Great Vairocana" (*rnam snang mdzad chen sku*, **mahāvairocana-kāya*).

390. The term *viniścaret* ("should issue [it in all directions]") is used in this verse, rather than the term *saṃcaret* ("flows"), which was used in all the foregoing verses.

Note that, although both Sanskrit mss read *na viniścaret*, I have opted for the reading *viniścaret*. This reading is to be preferred, as a) it better fits the meter, and b) it matches both Tib and the pattern of the verses preceding it. The error in our texts can, I believe, be attributed to a tendency for scribes to write *na* after *te* (as commonly found in the instrumental singular of the very common masculine and neuter a-stems). The presence of this error in these two rather independent witnesses is, then, due either to a) independent corruption (rather unlikely, perhaps), or b) an error in a remote ancestor of the two manuscript traditions.

391. SUT gives a more lucid version of this pāda, which reads "the great air of Vairocana should be issued from the dead body" (*vairocanasya mahāvāyur mṛtakāyād viniścaret*).

392. The Tibetan canonical translation of this passage may be found at DK, rGyud, vol. ca, $237b^5$–$238a^2$.

393. Skt *agra*; Tib reads "door" (*mgo*).

394. Note that in the discussion below, the order of Amitābha and Amoghasiddhi is reversed relative to the earlier textual citation.

395. Tib for this first sentence varies from the rest. It reads: "the air that exits from the left nose is the nature of the air of the Transcendent Lord Amoghasiddhi; it is the essence of the air maṇḍala, greenish-yellow in color with black light rays" (*sna g.yon pa nas nges par 'byung*

Transcendent Lord Amitābha; [He has] the nature of fire [and appears as a] fire-maṇḍala with the nature of red light rays. The air that exits from both noses is Ratnasambhava; [He appears as an] earth-maṇḍala with the nature of yellow light rays. The languid, slowly moving air is Akṣobhya; [He has] the nature of water[396] [and appears as a] water-maṇḍala with the nature of white light rays. The pervasive air, which pervades (all) four elemental maṇḍalas, does not exit. [Its] light rays are the Transcendent Lord Vairocana, [who has a] nature like space.[397]

"Nevertheless, (if) one should emit the light rays one by one, the light rays [will] depart five by five. For (all) four elements are pervaded by each single elemental maṇḍala. In each individual maṇḍala, the three-syllabled
C:51a mantra-overlord‡ should continually recite itself by the process(es) of entering, and so forth. [That is] the abbreviated (explanation) of air reality."

The Vajra Student asked, "By the grace of the Mentor,[398] I am well-educated in air reality by means of [both] scripture and realization. Now I wish to know the characteristics of mantra reality. Out of your kindness, [please] explain, O Lord and Teacher, Vajra Mentor."

A:20a The Vajra Mentor replied, †"Excellent, excellent, Great One! Of the so-called 'mantra reality,' only the mantras themselves are enunciated in the root tantras, such as the *Compendium of Realities*,[399] and the appendix tantras—the extraction of the mantra[s] (*mantroddhāra*) is not indi-

---

ba'i rlung ni de bzhin gshegs pa don yod par grub pa'i rlung gi ngo bo nyid ste| rlung gi dkyil 'khor mdog ljang ser 'od zer nag po'i ngo bo nyid do|). The remainder of the passage conforms to the Sanskrit phrasing.

396. MS C reads *svacchābdhatu*, which could be parsed as either *svaccha-abdhātu* ("clear water") or *svacchā-abdhātu* (water-water); this term is missing in MS A. Tib reads *gsal ba* ("clarity"), suggesting a reading of **svaccha*. I suspect that the original reading was *svacchā*, and that the scribe or editor of MS C added *abdhātu* as a gloss.

397. Tib and MS C diverge here from MS A (which I have followed). They read "The pervasive [air] is the air that pervades (all) four elemental maṇḍalas. Its light rays are not emitted and are pervasive. [It] is the Transcendent Lord Vairocana, with a space-like [infinite] nature."

398. Literally, "by the grace of the guru's feet" (*guru-pāda-prasāda*). Tib reads "by the kindness from the guru's mouth" (*bla ma'i zhal snga nas kyi bka' drin*).

399. *Śrī-tattva-saṃgraha-tantra*; *De kho na nyid bsdus pa'i rgyud*. See chapter 3, note 383, above.

cated. Rather, the extraction of mantra[s], the signification[s] of mantra[s] (*mantra-saṃketa*), the meaning[s] of mantra[s], [and] mantra reality are truly revealed by the Lord in the explanatory tantra[s]. Hence, those who do not understand the explanatory tantras, those who devote themselves to outer mantras, do not understand. Therefore, listen with diligence! I will instruct you in mantra reality[400] in accordance with the explanatory tantra[s]!

"With regard to that, mantras such as the serpent [mantra], and so on, are born from the vowels and consonants (*āli kāli*). Their Reality is the three-syllabled [mantra] arisen [from] the unstruck [sound].[401] Because all mantras—which have the nature[s] of feminine, masculine, and neuter[402]—enter the three-syllabled according to the personal instructions as received, the three-syllabled is the overlord of all mantras. Further, they individually, together with the unstruck, are produced by the syllables, three by three.

"Now, the function of the three-syllabled is to be taught. With regard to that, first, from the union of the three [syllables, one] produces a divinity-body. That [three-syllabled] itself causes embodiment[403] day and night by the process[es] of entering, abiding, and emerging. That itself, together with the vowels and consonants, having become face downward at the time of uniting the two organs, †[and] having been emitted in the form of A:20b semen from the secret-nostril orifice, produces the mass[es] of beings. That itself, having again gone upward by means of vitality control, [and] having opened the door[s] of the [sense] organs, [and] having emerged from the door of the superficial nose by the process[es] of left, right, and so on, [and] having effortlessly performed the vajra recitation, purifies the obscurations of previous action (*karma*). That itself, having observed the count of the recitation by the process[es] of day and night, performs all the rites such as pacification, and so forth, in dependence on the colors such as white, and so on, in the creation of a water-maṇḍala, and so forth.[404] ‡That itself, C:51b

400. Tib adds "only" (*'ba' zhig*).

401. *anāhata*; again, Tib reads "indestructible" (*mi shigs pa*).

402. Tib reads this as an attribute of the personal instructions, rather than "all mantras."

403. *deham dhārayati, lus 'dzin par byed pa*; literally, "causes a body to be held/borne."

404. This is typically expressed in ritual forms wherein one finds the correspondences: pacification/white/water/round; prosperity/yellow/earth/square; domination/red/fire/triangular; destructive/blue/air/half-circle, though these occasionally vary slightly. In addition to these correspondences, one also finds directional and deity correlations (though

visualized in the form of a syllable, having performed the recitation with the characteristics of vocal recitation, such as 'an utterly unmoving tongue tip,'[405] and so forth, performs all the rites such as pacification, and so forth, based on the [ritual] procedure[s] such as [use of representative] outer color[s], and so forth.[406] That itself, having purified food by the process[es] of the purification, arousing, and blazing of the three-syllabled, makes it faultless. Having done all in such a bodily condition, [and] having finally entered the unstruck [sound-center],[407] depending again on an ordinary body, in that very way it does all.

"Now, {the Lord} described the creation of the three-syllabled in the Great Yoga Tantra the *Explanation of the Intention*:[408]

> Beginning with one, but in the middle of nine,
> That which is not bound by [the] ten
> A:21a One should know that [to be] unbound—†
> He [who] knows [it knows] the supreme state.
>
> The phonemes—the vowels and consonants—
> Follow a count of nine.
> Bound by [the primary vowel] *a,* since [they are] united with one another—[409]

these often are reflexes of the colors involved). See, e.g., *Mahāvairocana-uttaratantra* and *Sarvadurgatipariśodhana-tantra.*

405. This is a reference to a passage from the *Sarvatathāgatatattvasaṃgraha*, see STTS (Chandra ed.), 208.

406. *bāhya-varṇādi-kriyām āśritya śāntikādi-sarva-karmāṇi karoti*; I believe this refers to the use of colors to indicate the specific ritual aims desired. On this, see note 404, above.

407. Again, Tib reads *mi shigs pa* for Skt *anāhata.*

408. On this scripture, see chapter 3, note 364, above. I have done my best to translate the words of the cited verses as literally as possible. The passage is elliptical and cryptic (intentionally so) in the original. Several commentaries on the PK—wherein most of the verses are cited in the same context—unpack their meaning, most concurring that they represent the extraction of the mantra (*mantroddhāra*), that is of the "three-syllabled" mantra *oṃ āḥ hūṃ*. The commentaries are, however, by no means uniformly in accord in their interpretations (see, e.g., note 411 below). Published Sanskrit commentaries (by Parahitarakṣita and Muniśrībhadra) may be found in PKṬ (23–25) and PKṬYM (44–51).

409. *abaddhā anyonyasaṃyogā*; I here follow the Tibetan interpretation of this term (as *bcings*), which is supported in part by the reading of ms C (as above). ms A reads *abaddhānyonyasaṃyogā*, which could be translated "mutually united with the unbound."

He who knows [that] is the mentor of the world
[of beings].[410]

That one who, knowing, should desire accomplishment
(*siddhi*),
The good fortune of the fruit of liberation,
That one [will] accomplish that very thing
Which, because formless, is free of form.

Linked with the reality limit (*bhūtānta*)[411]
[It is] fixed in the sixteen parts,[412] and so on,
Linked with the fifth [of the] fifth,
Joined with three [by] four,

Nasalized, with a long vowel,
With loss of vowel strengthening and conjunct,
Short, [it] may be all words,
Neither many nor one.

The one who desires whatever accomplishment
Is to be done by the meaning of the syllable 'ya,'
By the three—'ra' and so forth—
[One] accomplishes the aims of the world [of beings].

Those phonemes that are articulated from the back[413]
Those also that are [enunciated in] the forepart,

410. These first two verses are cited in RD, which comments, "since all these [Brahminical sciences] are derived from the syllable *a*, without that lord of all mantras, they cannot be uttered" (*etāni sarvaṇy akārād uddhriyanta iti sarvamantreśvaraṃ taṃ vinā teṣāṃ uccāro na vidyate* |); see RD, 72. This fits with Āryadeva's subsequent discussion of the syllable *a*.

411. PKṬYM comments that this refers to the syllable *u*; PKṬ says either *ū* or *u*; Lakṣmī's PK commentary (Tōh. 1842) glosses this as the syllable *ha*. As mentioned above (note 408), there is significant divergence in the commentarial sources.

412. *kalā*; following Tib (*cha*) in interpreting this term. While the general meaning of the term is "a small part" (cf. PSED, 545), in this context it is presumably referring to the sixteen vowels (including *anusvāra* and *visarga*).

413. *pṛṣṭhataḥ*; Tib reads "before" (*sngar*).

Those also—feminine, masculine, and neuter—
Are imagined as the elements, and so on.

Linked above [and] below,
Knowing that, they are joined with intelligence (*buddhi*).
Uttered by six; four and three and one;
Born from the one reality of the natureless.

Those, linked with the meaning 'ya' and so on,
A:21b The gnosis of the three times is born.†
The wise one considers the beings of the triple world
As like a dream or Indra's [phantasmic] web.[414]

This mantra is enunciation (*pravyāhāraṃ*),
Born from the nature of the natureless.
The form transformed from that
Is the divine perception.

Conventional, residing in the three realities,
The characteristic of the natural recitation,
Inexpressible,[415] unutterable—
This spirit of enlightenment is supreme.

That very triad should be one—
Not going, not coming,
Without cessation, utterly peaceful,
Free of permanence and destruction.

The [false] conception[s] not made by those who know the
three times
Have the indivisible character of space.
This is the ultimate, indeed—
[It has] a character that is introspectively known.

414. *indrajāla.* Tib reads *sgyu ma* (magic/phantasm, usually *māyā*), for Skt *svapna*, and *mig 'phrul* ("mirage") for *indrajāla*. For "the triple world" (*tridhātuke*, **khams gsum la*), Tib reads *rgyu mthar*.

415. *anākhyeyaṃ*; Tib reads "nameless" (*ming med*).

In all things to be done—
In falling asleep, and so forth—the one who knows yoga
Should always repeat [that which is] beyond the three times,
Inexpressible, [and] unutterable.

The recitation of Pāṇḍara, and so forth, are vocalized
Two hundred [and] twenty-five [times].

Duly multiplied by four,
The four yogas [become] nine hundred.

That nine hundred, which is seen
By the sequence of the twenty-four,
That also should become, from multiplication,
Twenty-one thousand six hundred.‡ C:52a

In this manner, according to the secret intention,
The subtle yoga [is] set forth.
Though [one be] devoid of study[416] and meditation,
In that way should the recitation be vocalized.[417]

That should be called the '{inner} mantra reality.'"[418]† A:22a

416. *adhyayana*; Tib specifies "reading" (*klog*), but this provides too limited a sense of this term.

417. As has been the case with most of the texts cited in this chapter, this passage also appears in the Vajrajāpa chapter of the *Pañcakrama*. PK I.27–45 are devoted to a long citation from this explanatory tantra. The verses cited here, with the exception of the last, are PK I. 35–45, with verses not found in PK appearing between 36 and 37, and 38 and 39, three lines between 40ab and 40cd, and seven in place of 42 and 43. The last verse in this citation, it seems, is PK I.55. All but the last four verses may be found at DK, rGyud, vol. ca, ff. 167a[3]–167b[2]; the final four verses may be found at f. 171a[6]–171b[1].

418. This passage from the *Saṃdhyāvyākaraṇa* is cited in PK in the context of explaining "mantra reality" (*mantratattva*); it is not specified there as "inner mantra reality." See the passages of PK just after I.24 and I.26: *idānīṃ mantra-tattvasyoddeśa-padaṃ mūla-sūtrād avatāryate* | . . . *ity uddeśa-padaṃ tasya nirdeśa-pratinirdeśam āha saṃdhyā-vyākaraṇa-vyākhyātantre tad avatāryate* | . . .) Tib does not include the qualification "inner," reading only "mantra reality."

The Vajra Student asked, "[My] doubts concerning the cause of the manifestation of inner vocal syllables have been dispelled. Yet, the Lord said 'short, [it] may be all words.' How does the short syllable *a* become the cause of the manifestation of all speech?[419]

The Vajra Mentor replied, "Excellent, excellent, Great One! In regard to this, the hidebound (*prāvacanikāḥ*), privileging grammar [above all else], consider only the verbal meaning. What's more, they do not understand the Reality of syllables as they really are, [such as] where, why, and how syllables and expressions manifest—because [this is exclusively] the range of the buddhas. Listen! I will instruct you following the teaching."[420]

"First of all, sound consists[421] of vowels and consonants. The 'vowels' (*āli*) are the sixteen vowels (*svara*), such as the syllable *a*, and so forth. The 'consonants' (*kāli*) are the thirty-three syllables (*varṇa*) such as the syllable *ka*, and so forth. The forty-nine letters,[422] which are combined with the sixteen vowels—all [are] known by the rules [and] conventions known as 'grammar,' up to and including grammatical commentary (*bhāṣya*), [under the rubrics] unanalyzable words (*asta*), simple words (*vyasta*), complex words (*samasta*), vowels, consonants, nasalization, surd breathing, euphonic combination, verbal roots, declension, nominal composition, analysis of compounds, and [suffixes such as] the feminine gender,[423] verbal inflections,
A:22b primary [and] secondary [nominal] suffixes, and so on.[424] †Hence, the

419. *vāc*; MS C and TIB read "words" (*vākya, tshig*).

420. *deśanā*; TIB reads "sequence/process of the teaching" (*bstan pa'i rim*).

421. *āli-kāli-mayaḥ*; TIB reads "is of the nature of vowels and consonants" (*ā li kā li rnams kyi rang bzhin*), though this is a stereotypical rendering of *-maya* at the end of a compound.

422. *lipika*; an interesting term to use in discussion of Sanskrit grammar, as such distinctively graphic notions are not traditionally part of this science.

423. *strī-liṅga*; TIB reads "the three genders" (*rtags gsum*, **tri-liṅga*). I believe this should be construed as referring to a mode of suffixation, taken in a list of four such suffixes: *strīliṅga, tiṅanta, kṛt*, and *taddhita*. Thanks to Gary Tubb and Ashok Aklujkar for guidance on this passage.

424. There are numerous minor differences between TIB and SKT here. Most important is that TIB construes *asta-vyasta-samasta-* with *lipikam* (*yi ge*), and renders it as "all, without exception" (*ma lus shing lus pa med pa*—typically the Tibetan rendering of *aśeṣa*). Although this expression (or *asta-vyasta* alone) is used elsewhere in the CMP with this sense (see A:33a and A:33b), here the expression seems to be used not in this idiomatic sense, but to refer to three specific grammatical categories.

worldly and transcendent sciences (*śāstra*) such as the eighty-four thousand Dharma teachings, scriptures (*sūtrānta*), tantras, ritual manuals, the Three Baskets, court poems, dramas, and so on, arise from words, sentences, [and] meters (*cchando*)—the *vṛtta* [meter], the *śloka* [meter], the *gāthā* [meter], the *daṇḍaka* [meter], and so forth. Relying on the teaching[s], all accomplishments (*siddhi*) will be obtained. As was said by the Lord in the *Journey to Laṅka Scripture*:[425]

> 'For instance, Mahāmati, some man holding a lamp, (may) search[426] for [his] wealth (and say, 'this is my wealth of such and such a kind in this place). Likewise, Mahāmati, by the lamp of the words of verbal conceptuality, the bodhisattvas, the great ones, enter into their own individual way[s] that are free of verbal conceptuality.[427]

"However, the very consciousness[428] of those varieties of phonemes that become words and sentences is this syllable *a*. Insofar as they are unconnected with the vowel *a*, the phonemes *ka*, and so on, cannot exist. Because they are merely consonant articulations, [they] cannot be pronounced.

"As the Lord said in the *Song of the Names* [*of Mañjuśrī*]:[429]

425. On this scripture, see chapter 1, note 239, above.

426. Tib (and Nanjio's edition of the LAS) read, "holding (aloft) a lamp, may look at his wealth [and say] 'this is my wealth of such and such a kind in this place" (*pradīpaṃ gṛhītvā dhanam avalokayed idaṃ me dhanam evaṃvidham asmin pradeśa iti, mar me thogs nas phyogs 'di na nga'i nor 'di lta bu 'di yod do zhes nor lta ba*). ms C has a lot of elision in this line and, in fact, includes the phrase *asmin pradeśa*, suggesting a text closer to LAS.

427. This passage may be found at LAS (Nanjio ed.), p. 155^{9-12}. There are a few difficulties with this passage. For one, Nanjio's edition reads "free of verbal conceptuality" in the nominative masculine plural (*-āḥ*), rather than the accusative feminine singular (*-āṃ*)—thus making it an adjective modifying the bodhisattvas, rather than the "way" they enter. In his translation, however, Suzuki reads it as modifying the "way" (which he translates as a "state," p. 134). The Tibetan can be found at DK, mDo, vol. ca, $117b^6$–$118a^1$.

Tib reads it as modifying "way," except that it does not read "way." In Tib, the bodhisattvas enter "the sphere of the individually known import" (*so sor rang gis rig pa'i don gyi yul, *pratisvasaṃvedyārthaviṣaya*?). LAS reads *ārya*, where Tib reads **artha*.

428. *vijñāna-bhūta*; presumably, to be taken here in the sense of an informing, vital principle.

429. *[Mañjuśrī]nāmasaṃgīti*; *mTshan yang dag par brjod pa*. Another major scripture of esoteric Buddhism. It has been edited in the original Sanskrit; see, e.g., Ronald M. Davidson, "The Litany of Names of Mañjuśrī." This also includes an English translation. A

'A' is the chief phoneme—
Most significant, the supreme syllable,

C:52b The great vitality,[430] unborn,†
Free of vocal utterance,
Supreme cause of all expression[s],
A:23a [It] illuminates all speech.† [431]

Hence, the Lord said, '[it is the] seed-word [that is] the door of all meditation. The syllable *a* is the door of all things (*dharma*), as it is primordially unarisen.' [It] is also called the 'connate syllable' (*sahajākṣara*). In the *Vajra Maṇḍala Ornament Tantra*,[432] too, [the Lord], clarifying the syllable *a,* said:

Blazing, like a lamp,
The center in the heart, the unstruck [sound]
The supreme syllable, subtle,
The syllable *a*—the supreme sovereign.[433]

"In that way, all the transcendent lords, knowing just as it is the character of vocal conceptuality, which by nature disappears upon being pronounced[434]—born from *a,* having *a* as its cause, derived [from] *a*—teach

---

Tibetan translation (by Kamalagupta and Rin-chen bZang-po, redacted by Shong bLo-gros brtan-pa), *'Jam dpal ye shes sems dpa'i don dam pa'i mtshan yang dag par brjod pa,* may be found at: DK, rGyud, vol. ka, ff. 1b¹–13b⁷ (Tōh. 360).

430. *mahāprāṇaḥ*; there seems to be a pun here, as this also means "aspirated" or "an aspirated consonant." Vowels, of course, cannot be aspirated. Thanks to Gary Tubb for this observation. Tib reads "emerging from within" (*khong nas 'byung ba*).

431. This passage may be found at MNS, vv. 28cd–29; DK, rGyud, vol. ka, 3a³.

432. *Vajra-maṇḍalālaṃkara-nāma-tantra, rDo rje dkyil 'khor rgyan zhes bya ba'i rgyud.* To my knowledge, this scripture has not come down to us in the original Sanskrit. A Tibetan translation (by Sugataśrī, Sa-skya Paṇḍita, bLo-gros brtan-pa), *dPal rdo rje snying po rgyan zhes bya ba'i rgyud kyi rgyal po,* may be found at: DK, rGyud, vol. tha, ff. 1b¹–82a⁷ (Tōh. 490).

433. This verse appears in the *Vajramaṇḍalālaṃkāra Tantra,* DK, rGyud, vol. tha, f. 42a⁷. It is similarly cited without attribution in AKṬ, 20, also in the context of commenting on MNS verse 28, and is unpacked in AKUN, 138.

434. This is an assertion of the Buddhist view of the nature of speech, *contra* the opposing

the Dharma to disciple-beings according to the inclinations and proclivities of beings[435] without regard for the niceties of grammar.[436]

"Hence, the Lord said in the *Journey to Laṅka Scripture*:[437]

> 'Mahāmati, the bodhisattva, the great one, should rely on the meaning, not on the "letter." Mahāmati, the noble man or woman who follows the "letter" will destroy themselves[438] and not cause others to understand the ultimate reality.
>
> 'For instance, Mahāmati, one may indicate something to another with (the tip of) the finger [and] that very one may turn [their] attention to looking at the fingertip itself. Likewise, Mahāmati, †those of the class of naïve ordinary beings, like children, persevere in obsession with the fingertip of the literal [meaning; and] thus [their] time will come [to die]. Having become fixated on the reality [that is] the fingertip of the literal [meaning], they will not seek the ultimate reality. A:23b

---

view of, e.g., the Mīmāṃsakas who, by way of defending the authority of the Veda, assert the permanence of the same.

435. The three texts have variant readings here. I believe there are good reasons for following the reading I have. MS A reads *sarvāśayānubhedena* (actually, it looks like *sarttvāśayānubhedena*), which is not objectionable, except that Āryadeva does not elsewhere use the term *anubheda*, except when referring to the "dissolving" meditation (see below, chapter 7, note 698). This leads me to believe that this is an error for the reading of MS C: *sattvāśayānuśayabhedena*—the compound *āśayānuśaya*, after all, is a commonplace of Buddhist literature and this makes perfect sense in context. TIB supports this, only it does not render both *āśaya* and *anuśaya*, reading merely *bsam pa* (usually *āśaya*) for both members of this common compound.

436. *śabdāpaśabda-nirapekṣaṃ*; literally, "without regard for [what is] grammatical speech [and what is] ungrammatical speech."

437. On this scripture, see chapter 1, note 239, above. The following citation consists of three passages from a connected discussion in LAS. I have marked the different passages by paragraph divisions in my translation. The first section is found at Nanjio, 194^{20}–195^{3}; the second at 196^{7-11}; the third at 197^{7-8}. The Tibetan can be found at DK, mDo, vol. ca, $133a^{3-4}$; $133b^{4-6}$; $134a^{3}$.

438. Following SKT; TIB reads "will fall away from ultimate reality (*bdag kyang don dam pa las nyams par byed*). According to Suzuki, a similar reading is to be found in the Sung and Wei (Chinese) translations of this scripture—a reading that he also favors.

> 'Hence, they [who are much learned in the meaning (*artha*), not merely the verbal conventions (*ruta*)] are to be attended by the one who desires reality. Therefore, the wrongheaded, who are obsessed with the literal meaning, are to be avoided by the one who seeks reality.'[439]

"'The manifestations of speech are fourfold,' as the Lord said in this very [same] scripture:

> 'Mahāmati, the form[s] of spoken conceptuality are fourfold; to wit, significant speech (*lakṣaṇa-vāc*), dream-speech (*svapna-vāc*), wicked-[concept]-obsession-speech (*dauṣṭhulya*[*vikalp*]-*ābhiniveśa-vāc*), [and] beginningless-conceptuality speech (*anādikāla-vikalpa-vāc*). Concerning that, Mahāmati, significant speech is produced from obsession with the sign of the form [of] its own concept. Furthermore, Mahāmati, dream-speech is produced from the recollection [of] objects previously experienced and from the absence of [its] conceived object.[440] Further, Mahāmati, wicked-concept-obsession-speech is produced from recollection [of] the action previously performed [by] beings.[441] Further, Mahāmati, beginningless-conceptuality speech is pro-
> A:24a duced from the vestiges [that are] the own seeds† [of] wickedness [that is] obsession with the [conceptual] elaborations [that have occurred since] primordial time. That, Mahāmati, is the fourfold characteristic of verbal conceptuality.[442]

439. For "by the one who seeks reality" (*arthānveṣiṇā*), Tib reads "reality is to be sought" (*don btsal bar bya'o, *artho 'nveṣanīyaḥ*).

440. The term here that I translate "conceived object" reads *pratinibaddha-viṣaya* in the mss. The LAS edition of Nanjio reads *prativibuddha-viṣaya*. As both expressions are obscure to me, I have preserved the former in the edition and followed the Tibetan interpretation (*rtog pa'i yul*) in my translation.

441. "Beings" (*sattva*) seems to be the proper reading. It is found in both mss of the CMP. Nanjio's edition reads "enemies" (*śatru*). Tib reads *sgras*, which would suggest **śabda-*, though this is almost certainly a corruption of *dgra*(*s*), i.e., *śatru-*.

442. This is one integral passage from the *Laṅkāvatāra-sūtra*, which can be found at Nanjio, p. 86^{3-12}. The Tibetan can be found at DK, mDo, vol. ca, $89a^{6}$–$89b^{2}$.

"By this reasoning, since sound emerges from *a,* it is undestroyed (*akṣara*).[443] Destroyed [means] annihilated. Undestroyed [means] unannihilated. That which has the space-like nature is reached through the door of sound; ⁺that is the perfection stage—the uncontrived, whose nature has [neither] beginning nor end.[444] C:53a

"As it is said in the *Teaching of One Method Scripture*:[445]

> These things (*dharma*) are taught by words and languages.
> Here one finds neither things nor words.
> Having entered the unity of method, facticity (*dharmatā*),
> [One] will reach the unexcelled, the supreme tolerance.[446]

(And,) as [it is] said in the Practice Tantra, *The Enlightenment of Vairocana*:[447]

443. The term used here, *akṣara*, also means, by extension, a "syllable" (because it is an "irreducible" element of speech). Tib renders this term here by *mi 'gyur ba*, "the unchanging," though it would normally use *mi shigs pa*. While this is an acceptable translation of *akṣara*, which can mean "undecaying, unalterable," given the gloss suggested by Āryadeva (*avināśa*, "un-annihilated"), I think "undestroyed" is a preferable English rendering.

444. Tib differs greatly from Skt. It reads "that which is taught through sounds of unreal nature is the uncontrived nature that has neither beginning nor end" (*mi bden pa'i ngo bo nyid kyi sgra'i sgo nas rab tu bstan pa de yang ma bcos pa'i thog ma dang tha ma med pa'i ngo bo nyid do*: perhaps **asadbhāva-śabda-dvāreṇa pradiṣṭaṃ tad apy akṛtānādi-nidhana-svabhāvam*).

445. *Eka-naya-nirdeśa-sūtra, Tshul gcig par bstan pa'i mdo.* I have not been able to identify this scripture. This verse is also cited by the *Subhāṣita-saṃgraha* as from this scripture though, given its overwhelming dependence on the CMP, it is likely that this latter was the source of the citation.

446. While corresponding closely for the first half of the verse, Tib diverges in the last two lines. It reads, "the one who engages the actual one method of reality will touch the unexcelled supreme tolerance" (*chos nyid tshul gcig dngos la'ang 'jug byed pa | bzod mchog bla na med la reg par 'gyur |*).

447. *Vairocanābhisaṃbodhi-caryā-tantra, rNam-par snang-mdzad mngon par byang chub pa zhes bya ba spyod pa'i rgyud.* A Sanskrit text of this scripture has not come to light. A Tibetan translation (by Śīlendrabodhi and dPal-brtsegs) may be found at: DK, rGyud, vol. tha, ff. $151b^2$–$260a^7$ (Tōh. 494). It has been translated into English from the Tibetan—see Stephen Hodge, trans., *Mahā-vairocana-abhisambodhi Tantra*, which work includes translations of its appendix tantra (*uttara-tantra*) and two commentaries by Buddhaguhya—and from the Chinese (see Chikyo Yamamoto, *Mahāvairocana Sūtra*). One might also consult A. Wayman and R. Tajima, *The Enlightenment of Vairocana*.

'However, Overlord of Secret Ones, the character of (secret) mantras is neither created, nor caused to be created, nor applauded by all the buddhas.[448]

'Why so? [Because of] the facticity of these things. That is to say, the facticity of these things is given[449] whether transcendent lords arise or do not arise; that is to say, [it is] the (secret-) mantra-facticity of all (secret-)mantras.[450]

'With regard to that, Overlord of Secret Ones, the Lord of the Desire Realm has a spell (*vidyā*) called "The Intoxicating." By means of that, he intoxicates[451] all the gods of the realms of desire†
A:24b [and] he causes various, {manifold,} delightful regions (endowed with many various flowers) to be seen. Having manifested various, manifold delights (and pleasures), he offers [them] to the gods of [the highest of all] the realm[s] of desire.[452] He also enjoys [them] himself.

'Thus, for instance, the god Maheśvara has a spell called "Swift [as] Thought." By means of that, he does all things[453] in the world-realms of the trichilio-great-chiliocosm. Having manifested all

448. Tib reads "all transcendent lords" (*de bzhin gshegs pa thams cad, *sarvatathāgata*).

449. *sthitā*; Tib reads "aboriginally present" (*ye nas gnas pa*).

450. This passage may be found at DK, rGyud, vol. tha, f. $170a^7$–$170b^2$. A translation may be found at Hodge, *Mahāvairocana Tantra*, 131.

451. *mūrcchayati*, lit. "he causes [them] to be senseless." Tib translates *brgyal bar byed,* which generally means "to make unconscious," but I think this cannot be meant in this context.

452. *paranirmita-vaśavartin, gzhan 'phrul dbang byed*. The account related here in the *Vairocanābhisambodhi Tantra* interprets the meaning of this name, which literally means "controlling (enjoyments) magically created by others" (cf. BHSD, 319). In Buddhist cosmology, this realm is considered to be the highest level of the 'Desire Realm' (*kāma-dhātu, 'dod pa'i khams*). The gods to whom these "delights" are offered, then, would seem to be a subset of those who are "intoxicated" earlier. The latter are "all the gods of the desire realms" (*sarvān kāmāvacarān devaputrān*), while the former (*paranirmita-vaśavartibhyo devebhyaḥ*) are the highest order of these.

453. *sarva-kāryaṃ*, lit. "all things that are to be done." Tib reads *sems can gyi dgos pa* ("the needs of sentient beings")—presumably the translators read **sattva-kāryaṃ*.

delights and pleasures, he offers [them] to the gods belonging to the realm[s] of purity.[454] He also enjoys [them] himself.

'Thus, for instance, by means of (secret) mantras an illusionist causes various, manifold things such as people, (waterfalls, lakes, pleasure gardens,) and so on, to be seen. Thus, for instance, by means of (secret) mantras [one][455] may cause illusions to be seen. Thus, for example, by means of (secret) mantras [one] may expel poison[s] as well as fever[s], and so on. Thus, for example, by means of mantras a deity propitiated [by] mantra offers beings happiness (*śreyas*).[456] Thus, for example, by means of (secret) mantras the heat of fire is destroyed and coolness arises.

'(Noble Ones,) on the basis of these illustrations, the potency of (secret) mantra should be firmly believed in. That potency of (secret) mantra does not issue from (secret) mantra(s)

454. *śuddhāvāsakāyikebhyo dev[aputr]ebhyaḥ, gnas gtsang ma'i ris kyi lha'i bu rnams la.* As in the last example (dealing with the gods of the Desire Realm), we here deal with the highest class of gods of the Form Realm (the next higher in the set of three realms).

455. TIB reads "demi-gods" (*lha ma yin rnams*) as the subject here. SKT does not mention a new subject.

456. My edition and translation follows MS A here, except that I have emended the (grammatically problematic) *śrayaḥ* ("protection") to *śreyaḥ* ("happiness"). MS C and TIB diverge in significant ways:

a) MS C gives two readings for this sentence. This is very interesting, as it indicates that MS C reflects fairly aggressive editorial intervention. It reads "Thus, for instance, by means of mantra Māra offers beings a deity propitiated [by] mantra; [or, there is] a second reading: by means of mantras a deity fashioned [of] mantra offers beings happiness" (*tadyathâpi nāma mantra-kalpikāṃ devatāṃ mantrair māras sattvebhyaḥ prayacchati* | *mantra-kalpitā devatā mantraiḥ śreyas sattvebhyaḥ prayacchati* | *iti dvitīyaḥ pāṭhaḥ* |).

b) TIB reads: "by means of secret mantra the goddesses called 'mātṛkā' send infectious diseases" (*ma mo zhes bya ba'i lha mo rnams ni gsang sngags kyis nad 'go ba gtong ngo* |). Interestingly, in the alternate reading found in MS C (mentioned above), the beginning of the line *mantrakalpikāṃ* looks very much like *mātṛkalpikāṃ*. Though it does not seem that this translation was based on (or based exclusively on) MS C, this is a curious coincidence.

> [themselves]. [It] does not enter into beings.[457] [It] is not obtained[458] from [its] reciter. And yet, Noble One(s), the facticity of mantra consecration does not exclude [its] production,
A:25a
> †as [it is] beyond the three times and comes into being in all ways [through] the inconceivable (profound) dependent co-origination.
>
> 'Hence, therefore, Noble One(s), the way of (secret) mantra should always constantly be practiced by [means of] understanding the nature of the inconceivable facticity.'[459]

"Having thus demonstrated the inconceivable potency of outer and
C:53b
inner gems, mantras, and medicines †by means of [scriptural] tradition and realization,[460] now [the Lord], describing just as it is the speech purification of the masses of perfected and unperfected beings, said in the *Enquiry of the Kinnara King Scripture*:[461]

457. *sattveṣu*, according to Hodge (*Mahā-vairocana Tantra*, 171), this reading is shared by the Chinese translation; Tib reads "substances, matter" (*rdzas*), in the ablative, not locative, resulting in something like "[it] does not even enter from matter/substance" (*rdzas las 'jug pa yang ma yin*).

458. *upalabhyate*; Tib interprets this term as "perceived" (*dmigs pa*).

459. *acintya-dharmatā*; Tib reads "inconceivable dharma" (*chos bsam gyis mi khyab pa, *acintya-dharma*). This passage may be found at DK, rGyud, vol. tha, f. 182a²–182b³.

460. *āgamādhigamābhyāṃ*; DCo read *rtogs pa dag*, thus preserving the dual number, but lacking the instrumental particle and the preceding *lung dang*. This makes the Tibetan read strangely—as, there being no particle between the direct object *mthu* (*prabhāvaṃ*) and (the instrument) *rtogs pa* (*adhigama*)—one would naturally construe these two as a dual object of the gerund *bstan nas* (*pratipādya*), thus "having shown the inconceivable power and understanding." I have accordingly emended Tib.

461. *Kinnararāja-paripṛcchā-sūtra, Mi'am ci'i rgyal pos zhus pa'i mdo.* I am not aware of an extant Sanskrit text for this scripture. A Tibetan translation (by Dpal gyi Lhun-po and dPal-brtsegs) may be found at: DK, mDo, vol. pha, ff. 254a¹–319a⁷ (Tōh. 157) as *'Phags pa mi'am ci'i rgyal po sdong pos zhus pa zhes bya ba theg pa chen po'i mdo/Ārya-druma-Kiṃnararājaparipṛcchā-nāma-mahāyāna-sūtra.* The term *kinnara* (or *kiṃnara*—lit. "a man, or what?!") refers to a mythical creature that is half man and half beast. A critical edition of this Tibetan translation (along with important discussion of the work and its recensions) has been published by Paul M. Harrison, *Druma-kinnara-rāja-paripṛcchā-sūtra.*

[462]'From whence, moreover, O Overlord of the Kinnara, do the vocal sounds (*rutaghoṣa*) of all beings issue forth?'

'From space, O Noble One, do the vocal sounds of all beings issue forth.'

'Do not, O Overlord of the Kinnara, the vocal sounds of all beings issue forth from the inner {cavity} (*adhyātma-koṣṭha*)?'

'What do you think, O Noble One? Do the vocal sounds of all beings come forth from a cavity within the body or from the mind?'

'O Overlord of the Kinnara, neither from the body nor the mind. Why so? The body is inanimate, motionless—like grass, a wall, a log, [or] a(n illusory) appearance. †The mind for its part is undemonstrable, like a phantasm, unobstructed,[463] imperceptible.' A:25b

'Nonetheless, O Noble One, in the absence of body and speech, from what other [could] vocalization (*ruta*) issue forth?'

'O Overlord of the Kinnara, the vocal proclamation of all beings is born from the space {[that is] non-mental-functioning (*amanaskāra*)}.'[464]

'{What do you think, O Noble One?} If space were not to exist, from whence would vocalizations issue forth?'

'In the absence of space, O Overlord of the Kinnara, [there could be] no issuing forth [of] vocalization whatsoever.'

462. MS C inserts a clause not found in MS A or TIB which reads, "one [of many], Noble One, ask[ed] the Overlord of the Kinnaras" (*anyatamaḥ kulaputra kinnarādhipatiṃ paripṛcchati*).

463. *apratighaṃ*; SS reads "incomparable" (*apratimaṃ*).

464. TIB is obscure (if not corrupt); it reads: "O Overlord of the Kinnara, the vocalization of all sentient beings [should be] understood to emerge from space" (*mi'am ci'i bdag po sems can rnams kyi sgra ni nam mkha' las 'byung bar rtogs so*). It does not mention the idea of *amanaskāra*.

'You should know it thus by this aphorism: "whichever vocal acts[465] issue forth, all of those issue forth from space." Vocalizations, {which} have space as their nature, are destroyed immediately upon being issued.[466] Destroyed, they become the very nature of space.[467]

'All things [are] the nature of space. They [are] either expressed or unexpressed. [They][468] do not lose their equality with the limit[s] of space [i.e., their limitlessness]. All things, O Noble One, [are] mere vocalization—without [either] signifier or signified—they are denoted by conventions. That usage also is non-
A:26a usage. That indeed that is usage according to vocal conventions †is not devoted to any thing whatsoever.[469]

465. *ruta-vyāpāra*; Tib reads "vocal designations" (*sgra'i tha snyad, *ruta-vyāhāra*).

466. *niryāta*; this is the reading of ms A, which seems to make the most sense. ms C and Tib (and SS, which tends to follow C) read "perceived" (*vijñāta, rnam par rig*) instead.

467. Interpreting this as if it read *ākāśa-svabhāvatāṃ*; read as is (locative, rather than accusative), it runs: "those that are destroyed are established in space-nature-ness."

468. There is no expressed subject here; both mss read (3rd person singular) *vijahāti*, though I think that the 3rd person plural *vijahati* is preferable given the plural referent throughout.

469. Tib differs markedly in this entire paragraph. It reads: "Hence, all things are called 'equal to space [i.e., infinite].' That lack of awareness, although [it] is not [something] to be conscious of, is expressed by vocalization and vocal signs. That expression is, furthermore, convention. Whoever understands in this way that which is expressed by vocalization is not devoted to any thing whatsoever" (*de'i phyir chos thams cad ni nam mkha' dang mnyam zhes bya ste | rnam par rig pa med pa de rnam par shes par bya ba ma yin mod kyi sgra dang sgra'i brdas brjod do | brjod pa de yang tha snyad do | gang sgras brjod pa 'di 'dra bar rab tu shes pa de ni chos gang la yang mngon par mi chags so |*).

Immediately after this citation, Tib inserts a large passage (consisting of the better part of one folio side, sDe 74a) that is not found in Skt. It reads:

> 'Who is not attached, does not proceed. Who does not proceed, does not wander. Who does not wander is unchanging. That which is unchanging is unborn. That which is unborn is indestructible. That which is indestructible is immaculate. That which is immaculate is pure. That which is pure is stainless. That which is stainless is brilliance. That which is brilliance is the nature of mind. That which is the nature of mind is engaging. That which is engaging is the subduer of all signs. That which is the subduer of all signs is called "entering into faultlessness." Whoever enters into the faultlessness of the bodhisattva attains tolerance of unborn things. Hence, the bodhisattva who enters into faultlessness is called "one who has attained the tolerance of unborn things."
>
> 'Whoever has attained tolerance, tolerates all. That one tolerates both the void and persons. Why? The void is not other than persons. Persons themselves are

"In that way, the great yogin who abides in the speech-vajra samādhi, hearing the words of perfected and unperfected beings—[words] whose nature is to express faults and qualities—is not attached, is not attracted,[470] is not afraid, is not terrified, does not waver. Having heard the distinctive arrangement of [meaningful] sounds [including such metres as the] *daṇḍaka* and *troṭaka*[471] [that appear in] the worldly and transcendent treatises, ‡he is not attached, is not corrupted, is not bewildered —for [that one] has understood all [meaningful] sounds.[472] As the Lord said in the *Scripture Teaching the Non-manifestation of All Things*:[473] C:54a

> 'O Divine One, were a bodhisattva, a great one, who is established in the employment of audible vocalizations (*śabda-ruta*) to be abused, [or] disparaged, by false and untrue[474] words for

---

> void. That one also tolerates both signs and signlessness. Why? The nature of signs is signlessness. That one tolerates both wishes and wishlessness. Why? The distinguishing characteristic of the nature of wishes is wishlessness. That one tolerates the natural nirvāṇa of all sentient beings. That one also tolerates the death, transmigration, and birth of sentient beings. Why? Death, transmigration, and birth have the nature of phantasm. Noble One, in that way the bodhisattva who has attained the tolerance of the birthlessness of things is not contradictory, for [that one] is not in contradiction with all things.'

Given that, when the main part of the CMP begins again after this citation, it takes up from the end of the quotation as found in those MSS (with the slight difference that it uses the word *anulīyate* instead of *abhiniviśate*), I believe that this passage is a Tibetan interpolation. This passage is found in KRP, Ch. 3; see Harrison, ed., 344–48.

470. *saṃhriyate*; following MS A (which reading seems the best counterpoint to the preceding *anulīyate*); MS C reads "is not defiled" (*saṃkliśyate*); TIB reads "is not overjoyed" (*yang dag par dga' bar mi bya*).

471. Following MS A; MS C reads *daṇḍaka-ch[ū]rṇaka* [*sic* for *cūrṇaka*], which could be rendered "verse and prose," as per the rendering in TIB *rgyun chags dang rkyang pa*.

472. TIB reads this somewhat differently: "because [that one] will understand the migration of all beings and" (*sems can thams cad kyi 'gro ba rtogs par 'gyur ba'i phyir dang* |)—and it adds the phrase, "because [it] is the reality of [meaningful] sound" (*sgra'i de kho na nyid yin pa'i phyir* |).

473. *Sarva-dharmāpravṛtti-nirdeśa-sūtra*; *Chos thams cad rab tu 'jug pa bstan par bya ba'i mdo*. I read this as *sarva-dharma-apravṛtti-*, which is also how the canonical Tibetan title interprets it; TIB seems to read **sarva-dharma-pravṛtti-*. A Tibetan translation (by Rin-chen 'Tsho) is contained in the bKa'-'gyur: *'Phags pa chos thams cad 'byung ba med par bstan pa zhes bya ba theg pa chen po'i mdo*, DK, mDo, vol. ma, ff. 267a[1]–296a[6] (Tōh. 180).

474. *asadbhūta*; TIB reads "disrespectful" (*bsnyen bkur ma yin pa*), suggesting the translators read **asatkṛta*.

> as many æons as there are grains of sand in the river Ganges, he would not give rise to an angry mind with regard to that [abuser]. Were he to be respected, treated as a mentor, esteemed, [and] offered the fundaments of all happiness [such as the four] requisites [of a monastic]—robes, alms, housing,[475] [and] medicine to cure the sick—for as many æons as there are grains of sand in the river Ganges, he would not give rise to loving mind with regard to that [respectful one].[476]

"In that way, the mantrin who stands in the speech-vajra samādhi [and
A:26b is] master of the eighth {stage}[477] †is not repelled,[478] is not attracted, by gain, loss, fame, infamy, blame, praise,[479] pleasure, [or] pain. Hence, having overcome all worldly motivations, [and] having passed beyond the creation stage,[480] the one who desires to seek mind isolation [should] attend to a spiritual guide (*kalyāṇa-mitra*)."

475. *śayanāsana, mal stan*; literally, "bedding and seats," M-W (1056) suggests a Buddhist meaning of "a dwelling, cell." For more information on this aspect of the monk's discipline (according to one influential Vinaya), see Gregory Schopen, "Hierarchy and Housing in a Buddhist Monastic Code."

476. This passage would seem to correspond to that found at: DK, mDo, vol. ma, f. 287b[6–7], though the wording is somewhat different.

477. This is only found in MS C.

478. *bādhyate*; TIB reads "bound" (*'ching ba*), suggesting **badhyate*.

479. TIB reads the more consistent order of "praise, blame" (*bstod pa dang | smad pa*), but both Sanskrit MSS read "blame, praise" (*-nindā-praśaṃsā-*).

480. This statement is hard to reconcile with other formulations found in this work. It would seem to suggest that Āryadeva seeks to draw the dividing line between the creation and perfection stages here—between speech isolation and mind isolation. However, at the beginning of the chapter, he described speech isolation as a subtle yoga, beyond the range of the creation stage, suggesting that the line should be drawn between body and speech isolations. I suggest that the topic of chapter 2 ("Speech Isolation") be understood as bridging creation and perfection stages. The first topic of the chapter, air reality (with which the chapter begins), is propædeutic—pre-perfection stage; the latter topic, mantra reality, is (as he says) speech isolation *per se*. Thus, he here notes that attainment of the speech-vajra samādhi (the mark of mastering speech isolation) signifies the definitive move beyond creation stage and into the thick of the perfection stage practices. That is, until a practitioner has mastered the speech-vajra samādhi, though s/he may be practicing "perfection stage" practices, s/he has not yet "passed beyond the creation stage."

4. Resolution of Doubts about the Integration of Mind Isolation

The Vajra Student asked, "Due to the grace of the Mentor, in due order after air reality, [my] doubts regarding mantra reality and speech isolation have also been dispelled. Now, how should one learn who desires to learn mind isolation? For the sake of those who aspire to the profound, explain [this] O Lord and Teacher, Vajra Mentor."

The Vajra Mentor replied, "Excellent, excellent, Great One! You inquire about [that which is] not the province of those who turn away from the [sacred] tradition of all the transcendent lords, exceedingly profound, supremely difficult to fathom—the range of the buddhas. As the Lord said in all the scriptural discourses,[481] 'the nature of mind is rootless, unlocated, without foundation, signless, colorless, shapeless, beyond the senses, not the province of the logicians.' Hence, the one who desires buddhahood, relying on the Adamantine Way [and] propitiating a spiritual guide, should seek the nature of his own mind.† A:27a

"For the Lord has said in the {*Glorious*} *Compendium of Realities Tantra*,[482] 'Know [Reality], O Noble One, by means of the meditative focus that attends to your own mind.'[483] The Glorious *Enlightenment of Vairocana*

481. *deśanā-pāṭha*; Tib reads "the words taught in all the tantras" (*rgyud thams cad las bstan pa'i tshig*—perhaps **sarva-tantra-deśanā-pāda*?). Note that this term was earlier (chapter 1) translated by the more appropriate *bshad pa'i gsung rab*.

482. On this scripture, see chapter 3, note 383 above.

483. Tib reads "Analyze your own mind, O Noble One, by means of meditative absorption" (*rigs kyi bu mnyam par gzhag pas rang gi sems so sor rtogs shig*). This is a well-known line from the opening chapter of STTS, see STTS (Horiuchi, ed.), 41.

Tantra[484] also says, '"Enlightenment" is thorough knowledge of one's own mind just as it is.' The *Method of the Three Baskets*[485] also says:

Far reaching, solitary,
Bodiless, dwelling in caves—
Those who contemplate [such a] mind
Are liberated from the bonds of Māra.[486]

"For this reason, the one who desires to manifest the phantasmic
C:54b samādhi, †having cast off all distraction [and] obscuration, [and] having propitiated the vajra mentors who have obtained the [sacred] tradition of all transcendent lords, should understand the prototypes [and] radiances —the three consciousnesses[487]—according to the explanatory tantras such as the *Glorious Gnosis Vajra Compendium*[488] and so on.

484. On this scripture, see chapter 3, note 447, above.

485. *Piṭaka-traya-naya, sDe snod gsum gyi tshul.* Given the verse that follows, this would seem to be some version of the *Dhammapada/Udānavarga. Dhammapada* 37 reads *dūraṅgamaṃ ekacaraṃ asarīraṃ guhāsayaṃ | ye cittaṃ saññamessanti mokkhanti mārabandhanā* |, which conforms closely to our cited verse. *Udānavarga* XXXI.8A reads: *dūraṃgamam ekacaram aśarīraṃ guhyāśayaṃ | ye cittaṃ damayiṣyanti vimokṣante mahābhayāt* ||. See Franz Bernhard, ed., *Udānavarga*, 410; Cf. Oskar von Hinüber and K. R. Norman, eds., *Dhammapada*, 11.

486. Tib has a five-pāda (rather than four-pāda) stanza here, which seems to correspond to *Udānavarga* XXXIII.55, a variation on the verse cited here. It reads:

The mind difficult to tame—
Solitary, far reaching,
Bodiless, dwelling in the cave of the sense[s]—
The one who tames [it],
I call a "brahmin,"
Liberated from the bonds of Māra.

Tib: *gcig pu 'gro zhing ring du rgyu | lus med dbang po'i phug na gnas | gdul bar dka' ba'i sems 'dul byed | de ni bram zer ngas bshad do | bdud kyi bcing ba las grol 'gyur* |. Bernhard (*Udānavarga*, 489) notes this is missing in the Tibetan ("Fehlt im Tibetischen [Tib. Uv. XXXIII. 67]")—reconstructed, it would seem to read something like this (based on Uv. XXXIII.55 [with apologies for the metrical flaws]): **ekacaram dūraṃgamam aśarīraṃ indriyāśayam | durdamaṃ cittam ye damiṣyanti brāhmaṇaṃ taṃ bravīmy aham || mucyante mārabandhanāt* |.

487. While Skt has the "three consciousnesses" and the "prototypes [and] radiances" in apposition, Tib reads this as a genitive relationship, i.e., "the prototypes [and] luminances of the three consciousnesses" (*rnam par shes pa gsum gyi rang bzhin snang ba*).

488. *Śrī-jñāna-vajra-samuccaya, dPal ye shes rdo rje kun las btus pa.* I am not aware that a Sanskrit text of this scripture has come down to us. Two variant texts by this name exist

"As the Lord said in the *Journey to Laṅka Scripture*:[489]

> 'And yet further, Mahāmati, the bodhisattva(, the great one,) who wishes to thoroughly understand the range of the concept[s] of subject and object [in] his own mental experience should do away with obstacles [such as] society, socializing, [and] torpor.[490]

Concerning that, all things have the three consciousnesses as their cause. That is to say, heaven and emancipation,[491] inanimate and animate [beings], subject and object, the twelve-limbed †wheel of dependent co-origination, A:27b concepts of good and evil,[492] light and darkness, female, male and neuter forms,[493] the creation, maintenance, and apocalypse [of the universe]—in brief, [everything] of the three worlds [that is] the range {of investigation} of the senses[494] may be[495] the three consciousnesses. As the Lord said in the *Enquiry of Bhadrapāli Scripture*:[496]

---

in Tibetan translation: one by Jñānakara and Khu dNgos-grub, revised by Tshul-khrims rGyal-ba, may be found at: DK, rGyud, vol. ca, 282a[1]–286a[6] (Tōh. 447); another, longer text, by Ākarasiddhi and Tshul-khrims rGyal-ba, may be found at DK, rGyud, vol. cha, 1b[1]–35b[7] (Tōh. 450).

489. On this scripture, see chapter 1, note 239, above.

490. This passage is found in Nanjio 49[7–9] (or Vaidya ed., 22, 1.25–26; or DK, mDo, vol. ca, 74a[3–4]). This is the end of the quotation from the LAS, though neither MS marks it with the expected *iti*. TIB includes the entire next paragraph (up to the citation from the *Bhadrapāliparipṛcchā*) in the LAS citation, marking it with *zhes gsung pa*. It seems clear, however, that the next paragraph is explanatory, not a quotation.

491. *apavarga*; TIB reads "hell" (*ngan 'gro*: literally, "bad rebirth/migration"), suggesting *apāya*. A good case can be made to emend here after TIB, but the Skt. MSS both read *apavarga*.

492. *śubhāśubha-vikalpaṃ*; TIB reads this as three things: "good and evil and concepts" (*dge ba dang | mi dge ba dang | rnam par rtog pa*).

493. *strī-pun-napuṃsakādy-ākāraṃ*; MS C and TIB read "[things with] the nature of male, female, and neuter, etc." (*strī-pun-napuṃsakādy-ātmakaṃ, skyes bu dang | bud med dang | ma ning la sogs pa'i bdag nyid can*).

494. *traidhātukaṃ indriya-pravicaya-gocaraṃ*; Again TIB renders apposition as genitive "the ranges of the senses of the three worlds" (*khams gsum po'i dbang po'i spyod yul rnams*).

495. *syāt*; TIB reads "is" (*yin*).

496. On this scripture, see chapter 2, note 268, above. Note that this citation consists of six separate passages (as found in the extant Tibetan version of the scripture) run together. For the convenient reference of the reader, I have set off the passages with asterisked paragraph breaks.

The Lord said, 'Bhadrapāli, the machine (*yantra*) that comes to be due to the predominance[497] of activity—that is produced from consciousness in accordance with activity.[498] Just so, the[499] machine of the body comes to be due to the predominance of consciousness. The product of various marvels[500] is this consciousness-element (*vijñāna-dhātu*). A creator, also, is this consciousness-element, for [it] creates the production of the body. Imperishable, also, is this consciousness-element, for it inhabits the realm of reality (*dharma-dhātu*). Of perfect intelligence is this consciousness-element, for [it] remembers [its] earlier bodily abodes.

'Like sunbeams, also, should this consciousness-element be regarded. For example, a sunbeam falls on the malodorous [such as] ritually impure offal [as well as] the redolent [such as] lotus flowers, and so on.[501] It does not develop a bond with the redolent, nor, separating from the malodorous, does [impurity] pass to the sun.[502] Just so, the consciousness-element takes birth in the wombs of swine, and so forth—even in eaters[503] of feces [and]
A:28a ordure—[yet] †the consciousness-element is not tainted by those faults.'[504]

* * * * *

497. *ādhikya*; Tib reads "by the power of" (*dbang gis*).

498. Tib reads "that device comes to be by the power of activity. That activity, further, is formless [and] produced from consciousness" (*'khrul 'khor de ni las kyi dbang gis 'jug ste | las de yang gzugs can ma yin zhing rnam par shes pa las mngon par grub pa'o*). The Tibetan translators may thus have read **tac ca karma arūpi*. Given the larger context of this citation, the device (*yantra*) in question would seem to be some sort of puppet.

499. Tib reads "this" (*'di*).

500. *āścarya*; ms C reads "product of many sources" (*āśraya*), which may be a better reading. Tib reads "enters into various bodies" (*lus sna tshogs la 'jug pa*).

501. Tib reads "the malodorous, the unclean, and corpses" (*dri nga ba dag dang mi gtsang ba dag dang | ro dag*).

502. Tib reads "yet they are not besmirched by that filth—the sun dispels bad odors, they do not recur" (*'on kyang dri des gos par yang mi 'gyur la | nyi ma yang dri nga ba bor te yang mi 'gro'o |*).

503. Tib reads "dog[s] who eat" (*za ba'i khyi*).

504. *doṣa*; Tib reads "by those bad activities" (*spyod pa ngan pa*). The above passage can be found in Tibetan translation in DK, dKon-brtsegs, vol. cha, ff. $76a^4$–$76b^1$. Note that there

Then Mahauṣadhi, bowing to the feet of the Lord, said this to the Lord, '[In] what form, O Lord, does consciousness issue forth from the body?'[505]

The Lord said, 'Excellent, excellent, O Mahauṣadhi! Just as you have now enjoined [me, so] {shall I instruct you.}[506] Supremely profound is this question. This[507] [is] a teaching [that is] the [proper] domain of the transcendent lords. Apart from a transcendent lord, none whatsoever [can be] found [who can] teach about[508] this consciousness.'

Then, Bhadrapāli said this to the Lord: 'Skilled in asking profound questions,[509] O Lord, is this crown prince Mahauṣadhi—and of subtle, ⁺acute[510] intellect.' C:55a

The Lord said, 'That, O Bhadrapāli, is because this crown prince Mahauṣadhi set down roots of virtue under the Lord Vipaśyin. Bhadrapāli, for five hundreds of lives this crown prince Mahauṣadhi became a non-Buddhist ascetic (*para-tīrthika*). He asked this: "What is this consciousness-element? Who[511] is this consciousness-element? What is this consciousness element like?[512] (Yet,) O Bhadrapāli, neither the going nor the coming

---

are some significant variants between the translation found in TIB and that found in the bKa'-'gyur.

505. TIB reads "of what kind of nature is the emission of consciousness from the body?" (*rnam par shes pa lus las 'pho ba de'i rang bzhin ji lta bu zhig lags*).

506. TIB reads "O Mahauṣadhi, just as you have requested of me just now, so it is. Excellent, excellent!" (*sman chen da ltar khyod kyis nga la ji skad du bskul ba de ni de bzhin te | legs so legs so |*).

507. MS C and TIB read "this question" (*'yaṃ praśnaḥ, dri ba 'di*).

508. Literally, "point out, indicate" (*nir+√diś*). Note that I have taken some liberties with this sentence's literal grammar, which reads "other than a Transcendent Lord, no teacher whatsoever [of] this consciousness is found."

509. TIB reads "in inquiring about the profound meaning" (*zab mo'i don zhu ba la*).

510. *sūkṣma-nipuṇa*; MS C adds "sharp" (*niśita*).

511. Both SKT and TIB are unanimous on this reading (*ko, gang*); however, the bKa'-'gyur version of this text reads "whose" (*su'i, *kasya*).

512. Literally, "how is this consciousness-element?"

of consciousness was encountered[513] by him. I will dispel his doubt.[514]

* * * * *

A:28b 'Moreover, †(if you wonder,) what is the meaning of "consciousness?" The seed produces the sprout of the body. From perception of consciousness, memory is obtained. Hence, the seed (*bīja*) is called "consciousness" (*vijñāna*).'[515]

* * * * *

'Thus, for example, the fruits of the jujube, date,[516] the [wild] mango,[517] (pear,)[518] pomegranate, bael,[519] and wood-apple[520] [trees]

513. *āsādita*; Tib reads "understood" (*khong du chud*).

514. These four paragraphs are found at DK, f. 82a[7]–82b[5].

515. Tib reads (or seems to read) "the seed (**bīja*) and the knowing (**jñāna*) are called 'consciousness' (*vijñāna*)" (*sa bon dang shes pa la rnam par shes pa zhes bya'o*). MS A seems to read something like Tib, though it seems flawed: *bījaṃ vijñānavijñānam ity ucyate*. Perhaps we should read **bījaṃ ca jñānaṃ ca vijñānam ity ucyate*?

This passage can be found at f. 75a[7]–75b[1] of DK. It occurs in the context of the Buddha answering important questions of Bhadrapāli concerning the activity of karma and consciousness across lives.

516. *kharjūra*; Tib reads *'bra go*, which seems ill-defined. The *Tshig mdzod chen mo* (p. 1987) has two definitions. The first is "the fruit called 'āmra fruit'" (*shing thog a mra zhes pa'i 'bras bu*) which, given that this is next in our list, seems unlikely. The second is the "*chi bi kha* fruit" (*shing thog chi bi kha*). Monier Williams has "Pterospermum ruberifolium" for *cibuka* (which might alternate for *cibika*). If the Tibetan transliteration is correct, this ought to be something like *chivikha*, but I could find no such entry in the dictionaries at my disposal. Chandra Das does not appear to have an entry for *'bra go*; Jäschke (399) merely says that it is "a medicine." NTED (769), on the other hand, gives "persimmon" as its referent in modern Tibetan (769).

517. *āmrātaka*; both M-W and PSED define this as a "hog-plum," but since hog-plums (*spondias lutea*) are not native to India, this would seem highly unlikely. However, a quick glance at the entry "hog-plum" in HJ (421) reveals that it is *spondias mangifera*, a "wild mango" of the same genus as the hog-plum, rather than the ordinary mango, *mangifera indica*.

518. *nyo ti* (or *nyo ting*); the Tibetan translators may have read **āmrāmṛta*, instead of *āmrātaka*, yielding two fruits instead of one.

519. *vilva* [also *bilva*], Tib *bil ba*; M-W defines this fruit as the "wood-apple," though that term is best applied to the next item (*kapittha*). The name bael (also bhel or bel) is directly derived from *vilva* and refers to the fruit *aegle marmelos*, also called the Bengal quince.

520. *kapittha*, Tib *ka pitta*; the fruit of *feronia elephantum*, properly called the "wood-apple." Chandra Das (6) merely notes that is "a very delicious fruit."

ripen into a variety of flavors. There is a ripening [of their] flavor potency with individual qualities [such as] bitter, sharp, sweet, sour, salty, and astringent, and so on. Some have a bitter flavor—some sweet.[521] Wherever the seeds of those vanished fruits [are], just there are [their] qualities transferred. Just so, wherever this consciousness-element is transferred [from the vanished body], just there is feeling transferred. Merit and demerit and memory also are transferred. Likewise, this consciousness-element, having abandoned the body, knows "this, my body, has been abandoned." Hence, this is called "the consciousness-element." It knows good action (*karma*); it knows bad action. It thus knows "these {my} actions are (my) constant companion;[522] I am their constant companion." Hence, it is called "consciousness."[523] †Furthermore, it makes known all the activities of this body—hence [it is] called "consciousness."[524] A:29a

* * * * *

'Consciousness resides nowhere in this body. Nor is a body obtained apart from consciousness.[525]

* * * * *

521. Tib reads "Some become sharp. Some become sour. Some become sweet." (*la la ni tsha bar 'gyur | la la ni skyur | la la ni mngar ro |*).

522. *samanubaddha* (*sic* for *samanubandha*), lit. "follow-ing/er"; Tib *phyi bzhin 'brang*.

523. A and Tib read "consciousness"; C reads "element of consciousness" (*vijñānasya dhātuḥ*).

524. Again, A and Tib read "consciousness," while C reads "consciousness-element" (*vijñān-adhātuḥ*). This passage may be found at DK, f. 80a[6]–80b[3].

525. This sentence may be found at DK, f. 78b[1]–78b[3]. There is an elision here. The bKa'-'gyur version reads: "Likewise, consciousness is not located anywhere in this body. *It is not in the eye. Nor is it in the ear. Nor is it in the nose sense organ. That which is the production of the sprout of the seed is small mind. Birth in a womb is small feeling. For example, if a sprout is produced and some time has passed, it will produce a flower. If a flower is produced, a fruit will be produced. Just so, the body is produced by this consciousness-element. If the body is produced, the consciousness is not located in any of the limbs or digits.* If there is no consciousness, a body will not be produced." (*de bzhin du lus 'di la rnam par shes pa gang na yang mi gnas te | mig la yang ma yin | rna ba la yang ma yin | sna'i dbang po la yang ma yin no || sa bon gyi myu gu skye ba gang yin pa de ni sems pa chung ba yin no || mngal du skye ba de ni tshor ba chung ba yin te | dper na myu gu 'byung zhing dus tshigs dang ldan pa na me tog rnams 'grub ste | me tog grub na 'bras bu 'grub pa yod pa de bzhin de rnam par shes pa'i khams 'dis lus 'grub par 'gyur ro || lus*

> 'Hence, Bhadrapāli, listen! One who does not see reality does not see this consciousness.[526]

Thus [it is] indicated in the scriptures of the Universal Way [that] consciousness [is] colorless, signless, shapeless, selfless,[527] mere self-awareness.[528]

"Nevertheless, without having entered the Great Adamantine Way [via] the Great Yoga Tantra, the {Glorious} (*Esoteric*) *Community*, one is not able to enact the thorough knowledge of one's own mind just as it is, even [were one to practice] for æons equal to the [number of] grains [of sand] in the river Ganges.[529] Hence, one should enact the thorough knowledge of the three consciousnesses just as they are through the grace of the Mentor in accordance with the [explanatory tantra, the] Great Yoga Tantra, the
C:55b *Glorious* †*Gnosis Vajra Compendium*.[530] Some vajra-words from that Tantra (shall be) introduced:

> Then the great bodhisattvas,[531] having paid homage [and] bowed to the feet of the Lord, once again asked, 'O Teacher! The so-called three consciousnesses are difficult to understand, supremely difficult to fathom. Tell [us], Lord! Tell [us], O Bliss-
> A:29b ful One, [of] the distinctions of the three consciousnesses.'†

> The Lord said, 'The consciousness that arises from brilliance —that very thing is called "mind" (*citta*) [and] "mentation"

---

grub pa na yan lag dang nyid lag gang la yang rnam par shes pa mi gnas la | rnam par shes pa med na yang lus skye bar mi 'gyur ro ||)

526. This last sentence may be found at DK, f. $83b^5$–$83b^6$. Tib reads "The one who does not see reality, does not know this consciousness" (*bden pa ma mthong bas ni rnam par shes pa 'di mi shes so*), though the earlier citation of this sentence (chapter 2, A:7a) and the canonical version read "see."

527. Following C: *asaṃsthānam anātmakaṃ*; A and Tib read "shapeless in nature" (*asaṃsthānātmakaṃ, dbyibs med pa'i bdag nyid can*).

528. *sva-saṃvitti-mātrakaṃ*; Tib reads "mere self-aware gnosis" (*rang rig pa'i ye shes tsam*).

529. Tib adds "and one will not see superficial reality" (*kun rdzob bden pa mthong bar mi 'gyur zhes so*).

530. On this scripture, see chapter 4, note 488, above.

531. *mahābodhisattvāḥ*; Tib reads "bodhisattva, great one" (*byang chub sems dpa' sems dpa' chen po*), though DK, rGyud, vol. cha, $2b^5$ reads *byang chub sems dpa' chen po*.

(*manas*). All things have that as [their] root, [having] the nature of defilement [or] purification. From that, [evolves] the imaginary duality, self and other.

'That consciousness is mounted on air. From air, fire. From fire, water. From water, earth. From those, [evolve] the five aggregates, six media, [and] five objects.[532] All those [are] mingled with air and consciousness. From that, [one] experiences very clearly the three consciousnesses, the manifestation of the prototypes and the radiances.[533] The prototypes are born from the radiance[s] as cause.'"[534]

[Then, the Vajra Mentor] declared at length an integrated full instruction [unpacking] those words of summary teaching:

"Concerning that, at first, the synonyms of the three consciousnesses [should be] taught for a while. The Lord called [them] 'critical wisdom [and] liberative art.' This explicit designation [demonstrates] the convention [of employing] neuter words [as done according to] intentional speech.[535] The imminence gnosis is not explicit[ly named in this twofold term]. Thence: 'mind, mentation,' and 'consciousness'; 'other-dependent, imagined, accomplished';[536] 'passion, hatred, ignorance'; 'the three natures,' and so on—these synonyms are [held] in common with those [who follow] the Universal Way and the like. But in the Adamantine Way, [the Lord] declared [these] synonyms: †"luminance, luminance-radiance, luminance- A:30a

532. Tib reads "five senses" (*dbang po lnga*), but DK (Tōh. 450) and the sTog Palace bKa'-'gyur version reads *yul lnga*, which accords with Skt.

533. Again, Tib reads apposition as genitive, i.e., "the manifestation/conduct (*rab tu spyod pa, pracāra*) of the prototypes [and] luminances of the three consciousnesses" (*rnam par shes pa gsum gyi rang bzhin snang ba la rab tu spyod pa*).

534. This passage may be found at DK, rGyud, vol. ca, $282a^{1-5}$, and DK, rGyud, vol. cha, $2b^{4}$–$3a^{2}$ (see also sTog Palace Kanjur, rGyud, vol. ca, $260a^{7}$–$260b^{5}$). The rendition in Tib is much clearer than those preserved in the bKa'-'gyur(s).

535. Āryadeva seems to suggest that all (or most) terms used in the intentional speech (*sandhyā-vacana*) of his school of esoteric Buddhism are in the neuter gender. While this is true of many of the terms he goes on to cite, it is not true of all.

536. i.e., the "three natures" of the Yogācāra school of Buddhist philosophy.

imminence'; 'void, extremely void, great void'; 'mind, mental factors, delusion'; 'passion, dispassion, moderate passion.'[537]

"Having thus indicated the synonyms of mind, now [its] own characteristic [nature], the nature that is to be introspectively known [shall be] taught through verbal means. The Lord said, 'mind has the character of space—free of color, shape, and so forth.' The Lord also explained that '[it] should be understood through [its] characteristics of radiance and perceptiveness (*anubhava*).' Hence, the personal instruction of that (shall be) introduced: that is to say, first the radiance[s],[538] then the prototype[s].

"With regard to that, 'luminance, luminance-radiance, and luminance-imminence' are the three radiances. The characteristic of luminance, first of all, [is that] its own form is incorporeal (*nirākāra*), without body [or]
C:56a speech. Just like †the shining of stainless moonbeams fills the sky in autumn, luminance [has] a clear-natured form—because [it is] the foundation (*ālambana*) of all things. This is the ultimate-reality spirit of enlightenment, whose nature is critical wisdom, the first void. *Aṃ* [is] the seed[-syllable] that relies on vocal means in order to stabilize [this kind of mind]. Beings
A:30b with little zeal (*adhimukti*)† do not understand the intentional speech of the transcendent lords. They have recourse to [visualizing the luminance mind] in the form of a moon disk. The superficial forms of the mind[539] manifest [as] a lotus, a female form, the symbol of the left, the symbol of night, [or] softness.[540]

"What, {secondly,} [is] the characteristic of luminance-radiance? [It] is free of subject-object [duality]; [and] its own form is incorporeal, without body or speech. Just like the shining of sunbeams fills [the sky] in the autumn, [radiance is] extremely clear [and] has an extremely stainless nature. [It is] the foundation of all things, completely wholesome, the spirit of enlightenment, the second stage, [whose] character is the extremely void. *Aḥ* [is the] seed[-syllable] that relies on vocal means in order to stabilize

537. i.e., these are all equivalent terms (*paryāya*) for the three levels of the subtle mind.

538. *ābhāsa*; Tib reads *kun tu snang ba* (**saṃbhāsa*?).

539. Here a technical term for the luminance (*āloka*) mind.

540. Compare PK II.12–13: *saṃvṛti-sphuṭa-rūpeṇa niśā-saṃjñā pradarśitā* || *strī-saṃjñā ca tathā proktā mandākāras tathaiva ca* | *vāma-saṃjñā punaś caiva candra-maṇḍala-paṅkajam* ||. In Tibetan: *kun rdzob gsal ba'i gzugs kyis ni* | *mtshan mo'i ming de nges par bshad* || *de bzhin bud med ming du brjod* | *'jam po lta bu'ang de bzhin no* | *gyon pa'i ming yang de nyid de* | *zla ba'i dkyil 'khor padma can* ||.

[this kind of mind]. Beings of little zeal do not understand the intentional speech of the transcendent lords. They have recourse to [visualizing the radiance mind] in the form of a sun disk. The superficial forms of mental factors[541] [manifest as] a five-pronged vajra, a jewel, a male form,[542] the symbol of the right, [or] a rough appearance.[543]

"What, {finally,} [is] luminance-imminence? Similarly, it has the character of space, its own form is incorporeal, without body or speech. It fills [the sky] just like the nature of the darkness of twilight. [It is] subtle, without support,[544] {Reality,} vitality control, [it] does not †travel, [it is] A:31a unconscious,[545] unwavering,[546] without[547] means of depending on a vocal seed[-syllable; it is] named 'perfection.'[548] This luminance-imminence has the characteristic mark of delusion, the great void. [These are] called the threefold consciousness.

"Having thus taught the personal instructions of all the buddhas, the characteristics of the three voids, now the flowing-forth (*spharaṇa*) of the prototypes at the appearance of each respective gnosis (shall be) presented.

"With regard to that, the prototypes of the gnosis of critical wisdom (*prajñā-jñāna*),[549] first of all, [are] the thirty-three moments, [to wit]:[550]

541. Here a technical term for the luminance-radiance (*ālokābhāsa*) mind.

542. MS C adds "the symbol of the male, the symbol of the day" (*puruṣa-saṃjñā vā divā-saṃjñā*). These are not found in A or TIB.

543. Compare PK II.21: *divā-puruṣa-saṃjñā ca kharākāraś ca dakṣiṇaḥ | sūrya-maṇḍala-saṃjñā ca vajrasaṃjñā tathaiva ca ||*. In Tibetan: *nyin mo skyes pa'i ming dang ni | rtsub mo g.yas par bstan pa yin | nyi ma'i dkyil 'khor ming dang ni | de bzhin du ni rdo rje'i ming ||*.

544. *nirālambakaṃ*; C and TIB read "selfless" (*anātmakaṃ, bdag med pa*).

545. *niścetanaṃ*; C reads *niśceṣṭatayā* ("because it is motionless"). TIB suggests that its translators read **niśceṣṭatayā niścetanaṃ*, construing the former with the preceding *na saṃkrāmati* (*mi rgyu bas rgyu ba med pa ste | sems med pa*).

546. MS C reads "the unwavering samādhi" (*asphalaka-samādhiḥ*).

547. TIB does not read a negative here.

548. *pariniṣpanna, yongs su grub pa*; i.e., the third of the three natures of the Yogācāra school.

549. Here referring to the first radiance, or level of the subtle mind, called "luminance" (*āloka*).

550. There is disagreement in the traditional sources about how to enumerate these thirty-three. The list I have given reflects my best attempt to make sense of the textual record, given that MSS A and C both treat nos. 18/19 and 23/24 as two (albeit differently). Yet, a cogent case can be made for considering 18 and 19 one prototype and dividing 24 into two. Only three (of ten) Indian commentators enumerate the prototypes and

1. Dispassion
2. Moderate dispassion
3. Extreme dispassion
4. Mental coming and going
5. Pain
6. Moderate pain
7. Extreme pain
8. Peace
9. Conceptualization
10. Fear
11. Moderate Fear
12. Extreme Fear
13. Craving
14. Moderate craving
15. Extreme craving
16. Clinging/Appropriation
17. Non-virtue
18. Hunger
19. Thirst
20. Feeling
21. Moderate feeling
22. Extreme feeling
23. Knower
24. Object grasped (by) knowing
25. Individuating analysis
26. Shame

C:56b 27. Compassion‡

28. Affection
29. Moderate affection
30. Extreme affection

---

these disagree. Vīryabhadra (Tōh. 1830) consolidates 18 and 19, and analyzes 24 thus: *viddhāraṇā* and *pada*. "Nāgabodhi's" *Arthabhāskaraṇa* (Tōh. 1833) considers 18 and 19 as two, omits 24 altogether, treats 28–30 as one, and omits 32, yielding only twenty-nine prototypes. "Nāgabodhi's" *Maṇimālā* (Tōh. 1840) lists thirty-one, omitting 5–7, treating 8 and 9 as one, 18 and 19 as two, analyzing 24 into two as *vit* and *dhāraṇāpada*, and omitting 32. Among Tibetans, Tsongkhapa has yet another accounting, considering 18 and 19 as two and arriving at thirty-three by claiming (on the authority of the 'Gos tradition: RṄSG, f. 210b[3]) that no. 4 should be "applied generally." Tib dodges the issue altogether by listing thirty-four prototypes!

31. Anxiety
32. Collecting
33. Envy† A:31b

"The prototypes of the gnosis of liberative art (*upāya-jñāna*)[551] [are] the forty moments, [to wit]:

34. Passion
35. Impassioned
36. Pleasure
37. Moderate pleasure
38. Extreme pleasure
39. Delight
40. Rapture
41. Amazement
42. Laughter
43. Satisfaction
44. Embracing
45. Kissing
46. Sucking
47. Stability
48. Heroism
49. Arrogance
50. Activity
51. Robbery
52. Force
53. Fortitude
54. Boldness
55. Moderate boldness
56. Supreme boldness
57. Aggression
58. Flirtation
59. Spite
60. Virtue
61. Clear Words

551. Here functioning as a synonym of the second radiance, or level of the subtle mind, "luminance-radiance" (*alokābhāsa*).

62. Truth/Reality
63. Untruth/Unreality
64. Certainty
65. Non-clinging
66. Donor
67. Impelling
68. Heroism
69. Shamelessness
70. Cunning
71. Wickedness
72. Violence
73. Scheming

"The prototypes of the gnosis of luminance-imminence (*ālokopalabdha-jñāna*) [are] the seven moments,[552] [to wit]:

74. Moderate Passion
75. Forgetfulness
76. Confusion
77. Muteness
78. Depression
79. Sloth
80. Dull[-minded]-ness[553]

These prototypes are the eightyfold moments. Distinguished directly,
A:32a [they] are one hundred and sixty; [they] function day and night[554] †within the egg-born [beings], and so on; [they] should not be divided according to male and female."[555]

552. C adds, "[or] prototypes" (*prakṛtayaḥ*); Tib adds "[or] characteristics of prototypes" (*rang bzhin gyi mtshan nyid*).

553. Tib reads "doubt" (*the tshom*).

554. *niśamaniśaṃ*; Tib interprets this as "day and night" (*nyin dang mtshan du*), usually *aharniśaṃ* (to which Pn emends). The term *niśāniśaṃ* is attested with the meaning "every night, always" (PSED, 924), but I have not found *niśamaniśam*. Perhaps it might also mean "latent [and] active." This, and the instance immediately below, are the only occurrences of this expression in the CMP. This reading is confirmed by the relevant verse in PK (II.26), on which see the next note.

555. This final passage is problematic. In terms of the meaning of the passage, one should

The Vajra Student asked, "[I have] no doubts [regarding] the eightyfold mind [which] functions day and night [and] is to be introspectively known by self and other. Nevertheless, demonstrate [its] proof (*pratyaya*) by means of [scriptural] tradition, O Lord and Teacher, Vajra Mentor!"

The Vajra Mentor said: "[It] was indicated by the Lord in the (*Esoteric*) *Community Appendix (Tantra)*[556] by means of an etymological explanation of the word 'mantra,' [to wit:]

> Whatever is born from conditions,
> By means of sense-organs and objects, is mentation.
> That mentation [is] called 'eighty.'
> The syllable 'tra' is derived from 'protection.'[557]

---

consult PK II.26, which reads: "those subtle prototypes, one hundred and sixty | manifest day and night, through the cause of their air-mount[s]" (*etāḥ prakṛtayaḥ sūkṣmāḥ śataṃ ṣaṣṭy-uttaraṃ divā | rātrau câpi pravartante vāyu-vāhana-hetunā ||*). Thus, on Nāgārjuna's authority, the multiplication from eighty to one hundred and sixty is based on the division of day and night. Āryadeva seems to be refuting an interpretation by which the multiplication would be on the basis of male and female.

Textually, all three witnesses diverge on this passage. Regarding the initial qualification (modifying the "moments"), I follow the reading of A and Tib (*bhidyamānāḥ*), rather than C (*vidyamānāḥ*). The problem in the final clause is more intractable. ms C reads *strī-puruṣayoḥ* (genitive dual) and has an alpha-privative before the following word, i.e., *a-bheda-bhinnaṃ*. ms A, however, reads *strī-puruṣa-yonibheda-bhinnaṃ*. Tib apparently followed a similar text, interpreting this as the word *yoni* ("womb") occurring before the word *-bheda*. It is not clear, however, where the Tibetan translators may have found a negative in this sentence. Perhaps a better reading of ms A would be to continue to read *strī-puruṣayoḥ*, but to read *nirbhedabhinnaṃ* thereafter. This would bring the readings of A and C into some kind of agreement.

Tib is very obscure. It reads something like this: "If the distinctive characteristics of the eighty prototypes are divided before one's very eyes, there are one hundred sixty; day and night those born from eggs, and so on, function day and night; it is not due to [their] being divided according to the categories of male and female womb" (*rang bzhin rnam pa brgyad cu po de dag gi mtshan nyid ni mngon sum du phye bar gyur na brgya drug cu ste | nyin dang mtshan du sgo nga las skyes pa la sogs pa rnams kyang nyin dang mtshan du spyod de pho dang mo'i skye gnas kyi dbye bas phye ba'i phyir ni ma yin no |*). The commentary attributed to Śākyamitra (which I believe to be a Tibetan apocryphon) is not helpful with respect to this passage.

556. *Samājottara*; *gSang ba 'dus pa'i rgyud phyi ma*; see chapter 3, note 360, above.

557. As noted in my edition, this verse seems to be a creative variant on a verse that is found in the extant text(s) of the *Guhyasamāja Uttaratantra* (GSUT, v. 70). The first two pādas are identical; however, in the extant version of the GSUT, the latter two lines give

These eightyfold prototypes become the ninety-eight defilements. Further, [they] become {the prototypes of} the sixty-two [wrong-] views, (and so on)."[558]

The Vajra Student asked, "It has been said that 'the gnosis of critical wisdom[559] [is] like the luminance of the moon—just exactly the void;[560] the gnosis of liberative art [is] like the radiance[561] of the sun—just exactly the extremely void; likewise, the gnosis of imminence [is] like the darkness of twilight—the characteristic of the great void; those are the three consciousnesses [that have] the character of space, [whose] own form [is] incorporeal, pervasive, [and] free of coming and going.' How [are they] emitted

---

the etymology (or "hermeneutical etymology," *nirukti*) of the term *mantra*: *man-* meaning "mind" (*manas*) and *-tra* meaning "protection" (*trāṇana*). The latter half of the etymology is preserved in our text, yet the former is transformed into a declaration that "that mind" should be called "eighty"—thus making the GSUT a scriptural authority for the doctrine of the eighty prototypes (*prakṛti*).

I must admit to some difficulty in imagining how Āryadeva thought this would go over with his readers. One assumes that most, if not all, would have known this famous verse already in its canonical form; and furthermore—though Āryadeva specifically identifies it as an etymology—the replacement line does not seem etymological at all (*man* ≢ *aśīti*). Prof. Ashok Aklujkar assures me that such a *nirukti* verse need only analyze one element of the term; so, technically, it is a suitable verse. However, I still wonder how much acceptance it could have garnered, given that the GSUT version must have been well-known by his audience and this is the only authoritative verse given in response to the doubt the Vajra Student expresses about the scriptural justification for this doctrine.

Interestingly, Tib does not correspond to Skt, but to the received version (more or less). This is noteworthy, as it makes the Vajra Mentor's "proof" something of a non-sequitur. It seems likely that we here see another example of Tibetan translators, rather than translating the citations as is, inserting previously completed, standard translations into newly translated works. On this, see my "Tantalising Traces," where I refer to Anne MacDonald's work on this (see her "Interpreting Prasannapadā 19.3–7," 163–64).

558. The texts diverge here. I follow ms A, which reads *dvāṣaṣṭi-dṛṣṭi-prakṛtayaḥ*; C reads merely *dvāṣaṣṭi-prakṛtayaḥ*; Tib seems to read **dvāṣaṣṭi-dṛṣṭy-ādayo* (*lta ba drug cu rtsa gnyis la sogs pa*). I am somewhat inclined to favor the reading of Tib here, as it seems strange for *prakṛti* to become *prakṛti*—rather, they should become *vikṛti* (effects of *prakṛti*). But even so, the readings of the Skt. mss are consistent enough and the sense is clear.

559. Tib reads "gnosis of critical wisdom and the void" (*shes rab dang stong pa'i ye shes*).

560. Both Tib and ms C read "voidness" (*śūnyatā, stong pa nyid*) but, given the context, this is an unacceptable reading.

561. Literally, "luminance" (*āloka*), but to keep the association going—i.e., luminance (*āloka*) is to [luminance-]radiance ([*ālok*]*ābhāsa*) as moon is to sun—I have taken a small liberty here with the translation.

and †[re-]collected in one's body day and night? Who is aware [of it]? Who is unaware? The one hundred and sixty prototypes, such as passion, dispassion, moderate passion, and so on—from the presence of what [can they be] perceived? Teach the [distinctive] indications (*kāraṇa*) regarding this, O Lord and Teacher, Vajra Mentor!" A:32b

The Vajra Mentor replied, "{In truth,} the three consciousnesses [are] rootless, unlocated, foundationless, signless, colorless, shapeless, beyond the senses. Nonetheless, [they are] radiant; thus, one is aware [of them when they are] conjoined with the air element. For the same reason that ‡the formless air-element may be perceived by inference by observing the actions of moving and shaking, and so on, [caused by the air], just so the formless radiance of consciousness may be perceived by inference, as it is inferrable from the [perceptible] prototypes such as passion, dispassion, moderate passion, and so forth. As is said in the *Transmigration of Consciousness Scripture*:[562] C:57a

> 'Thus, for instance, O Bhadrapāli, the formless, indemonstrable air-element appears concrete[563] on the basis of the material things it interacts with.[564] With regard to that, the indication[s are] the rumbling [and] clattering sound[s] of trees shaking and swaying [and] the feelings born from physical sensations of heat and cold. It is not perceived [by means of] its hands, feet, eyes, [or] face. Nor is it observed by means of its predominant color—dark or pale. Just so, Bhadrapāli, this consciousness-element †is not observed by means of [its own] form. It does not come in the A:33a

562. *Vijñāna-saṃkrānti-sūtra, rNam par shes pa 'pho ba'i mdo*. This is an alternative name for the *Bhadrapāli-paripṛcchā-sūtra* (on which see chapter 2, note 268, above). The attribution of this name to the scripture may be found at the end of the sūtra itself, wherein (as is not uncommon in Mahāyāna sūtras) it gives a list of names for the teaching it promulgates. There, Ānanda asks the Buddha the name under which the teaching should be known. The Buddha replies that it should be known as either the "Transmigration of Consciousness" or the "Enquiry of Bhadrapāli"; cf. DK, dKon-brtsegs, vol. cha, f. 94b[3].

563. *rūpī*, literally "with a form."

564. TIB reads this slightly differently: "Bhadrapāli, for example, although the consciousness-element is formless, it is demonstrable—perceived concretely from the ungraspable" (*bzang skyong dper na rlung gi khams gzugs can ma yin yang bstan du yod cing gzung du med pa las gzugs su snang ngo* |).

> appearance of form. Nevertheless, this consciousness-element should be understood by its distinctive indications.[565]

"By this reasoning, because of the formlessness of [both] the subtle element [air] and the radiance[s] of consciousness—having become intermixed like ghee poured into ghee—[they] accomplish all {worldly and} transcendent aims (*kṛtya*). As it is said in the *Unexcelled Intention*:[566]

> The gnosis that is just exactly self-awareness
> Is characteristicless, like space.
> However, it has divisions:
> Having the nature of twilight, night, and day.
>
> Luminance, luminance-radiance, and
> Likewise, luminance-imminence—
> Are called the 'threefold mind.'
> The support (*ādhāra*) of that is (to be) explained.
>
> Gnosis is intermixed
> With air, the subtle form.
> Having come forth from the paths of the sense[s],
> [It] engages objects.
>
> When, connected with radiance,
> Air becomes a conveyance;
> Then, [one] may produce all
> The prototypes of that without exception.
>
> Wherever air is located,
> The corresponding prototypes may be drawn out.[567]

565. This passage may be found at DK, dKon-brtsegs, vol. cha, f. 74b[1–3].

566. *Anuttarasaṃdhi, dGongs pa bla na med pa.* This text is none other than the (second chapter of the) *Pañcakrama*, the work whose thought Āryadeva is elucidating. The *Unexcelled Intention* is the special name for this chapter as found in the colophon: "*Anuttarasaṃdhir ity aparanāma Sarvaśuddhiviśuddhikramaḥ.*" This work seems to have circulated as an independent piece before being incorporated into PK. See Introduction above, pp. 57–58.

567. The verses cited here constitute PK II.28–32b.

Clarifying this (very) point, †[the Lord] spoke [this] intentional speech: 'Born instantaneously from gnosis, in the form of the space-illuminator,[568] pervader of the ten directions, blazing.' How [is it] 'born instantaneously from gnosis?' This means that the arising of radiance [takes] merely a moment, an instant, a mere trice, or the blink of an eye.[569] [Regarding] the meaning of 'in the form of the space-illuminator': a 'space-illuminator' illuminates space—one who is in the form of that [is a 'space-illuminator']. 'Pervader of the ten directions, blazing' [refers to] the radiance of the three luminances. 'Space-illuminator' does not [refer to] a firefly.[570] A:33b

"Hence, from entering the subtle element [air], there is[571] a radiance [for] merely a moment, an instant, a mere trice, or the blink of an eye.[572] Thence, the prototypes are experienced [for] merely a moment, an instant, a mere trice, or the blink of an eye.[573] What is unaware? Delusion. From just that everything is born. Then, from the air-element as cause, the prototypes, mutually following one another, are experienced by self and other day and night due to the discernment[574] of all objects without exception. †The great yogin who has thus understood the distinctions of the prototypes, the radiances, [and their] air-conveyance knows the pulsating thought-deeds of all beings—past, future,† and present. C:57b A:34a

"As the Lord said in the *Enquiry of the Kinnara King Scripture*:[575]

> 'Indeed, a perfectly-enlightened one is endowed with unobstructed gnosis. Why so? O Noble One, the past mental continua of all beings are exhausted, veiled, departed, [and] transformed—all of those the Transcendent Lord discerns. [He knows] by which causes those continua originated [and] by the

568. *khadyotaka, nam mkha' snang byed*, i.e., the sun.

569. Tib adds, "or a hand-clap" (*thal mo brdabs pa*).

570. This remark seems rather cryptic in English (as do most such traditional commentarial glosses in translation). Āryadeva is here clarifying that in this context the word *kha-dyotaka* (which I here translated rather literally as "space-illuminator") refers to the sun, not a firefly. The term is ambiguous in Sanskrit.

571. ms C and Tib read "the radiance[s] waver (*calati, g.yo ba*) for merely a moment . . ."

572. Tib adds "or a hand-clap."

573. Tib adds "or a hand-clap."

574. *vibhāga*; Tib reads "enjoyment" (*longs spyod, *avabhoga*?).

575. On this scripture, see chapter 3, note 461, above.

absence of which causes [they became] exhausted[576]—virtuous, unvirtuous, specified or unspecified—with [their] form[s], explanation[s, and] indication[s].[577]

'Now also at the present time the mental continua of all beings are produced—those also the Transcendent Lord discerns. [He knows] which mind arises after which [other] mind—virtuous, unvirtuous, specified, or unspecified—with [their] form[s], explanation[s, and] indication[s].

A:34b 'The future mental continua of all beings† (and their) mental factors—all of those also the Transcendent Lord discerns. [He knows] which mind arises after which [other] mind—virtuous, unvirtuous, specified, or unspecified—with [their] form[s], explanation[s, and] indication[s].

'Thus, O Noble One, a transcendent lord, saint, perfectly-enlightened one is indeed endowed with unobstructed gnosis.'[578]

"By this reasoning, the wise one (*jñānin*) who abides in the mind-vajra samādhi, putting aside obsession with various external things such as a wisher, that wished for, [or] a wish (*praṇidhāna*), confronts the self-consecration stage. From the words of the *Root Tantra*:[579] 'Know [Reality],

576. Tib adds "[and] departed" (*bral, *vigata*).

577. *sākāra, soddeśa, sanidarśana*; Tib has two renderings for this formula in this quotation. Here, in the first instance, it is translated "with [their] form[s], base[s], [and] reasons" (*rnam pa dang bcas pa | gzhi dang bcas | gtan tshigs dang bcas*). In the latter two instances, it is translated "with [their] form[s], regions, and the base[s] from which they come" (*rnam pa dang bcas | yul phyogs dang bcas | gzhi ci las gyur pa dang bcas*).

578. This passage may be found in KRP, chapter II; see Harrison, ed., 348–50.

579. *mūla-tantra, rtsa ba'i rgyud*. The tantra cited here as a "Root Tantra" is the *Sarva-tathāgata-tattva-saṃgraha* (STTS), on which see chapter 3, note 383, above. Though one might assume that the "Root Tantra" in this context would be the GST, the STTS is frequently so cited in writings on the "higher" esoteric systems (as, for instance, PU p. 208).

Tsongkhapa, in a discussion of the root and explanatory tantras of the Esoteric Community systems in RṄSG, comments that "it appears that it is also the intention of the *Caryā-melāpaka-pradīpa* [to take] the *Tattva-saṃgraha* as a root tantra from the perspective of the *Guhyasamāja*" (*'dus pa la bltos nas de nyid bsdus pa rtsa rgyud yin pa 'di spyod bsdus kyi'ang*

O Noble One, by means of the meditative focus that attends to your own mind.'[580]

"Thus relying on the explanatory tantra, [it may be said that], not[581]
having attained the thorough knowledge of their own mind just as it is in
accordance with the prototypes [and] radiances, beings who assert [phi-
losophical views about] action (*karma*) [are trapped] in the beginningless
life-cycle due to the bond[s] of action and defilement born from their own
conceptuality—like a cocoon-weaving [silk] worm. Having assembled a
great mass of suffering [and] having experienced the resultant ripening
of the good and evil action heaped up through an uninterrupted series of
births, †[and] having further abandoned [their] body[582] by the process of A:35a
(entering) the ultimate reality maṇḍala,[583] [one is] taken up [by] the air-
element, bound [to] feeling, trailing along [behind] craving,[584] fallen from
the Realm of Reality,[585] seized by recollection, bound [to] attend to virtue
and non-virtue,[586] like a child of five {or six} years seeing all, nourished by
scents, undaunted[587] by vajras and so on, ‡endowed with all the marks, [and C:58a
moving] with the speed of action and miracle (*ṛddhi*). After seven days,
standing in the interval [between] rebirths (*gati*), when impelled by the

---

dgongs par snang ngo |); see RṄSG, 31. Tsongkhapa is apparently basing himself in this very passage.

580. Again, this line comes from the first chapter of STTS (Horiuchi, ed., 41).

581. Tib reads a negative here, which seems to be missing in both Skt. mss. I have emended Skt, as it does not seem to make any sense that one who has thoroughly understood their own mind would be stuck in *saṃsāra*.

582. *kalevara*; Tib reads "aggregates" (*phung po*).

583. i.e., of dying and dissolving into the brilliance/*dharmakāya*.

584. "Feeling" and "craving" (*vedanā* and *tṛṣṇā*): factors 7 and 8 in the twelve limbs of dependent co-origination.

585. Following ms A (*dharmadhātu-niṣpattitaḥ*); ms C reads "the necessary consequence [of] the realm of reality" (*dharmadhātu-nisyanditaḥ*). Tib reads this as conjoined with the next phrase, yielding: "seized by recollection that is born from the sufficient cause of the realm of reality" (*chos kyi dbyings kyi rgyu mthun pa las byung ba'i dran pa, dharmadhātu-nisyanda-*[or, perhaps, *-nisyanditodbhūta-*]*-smṛti*).

586. *kuśalākuśalārambaṇa-saṃprayuktaḥ*; Tib reads "endowed with a mentality of virtuous and unvirtuous forms" (*dge ba dang mi dge ba'i rnam pa'i yid dang ldan pa*).

587. *anivārya*; following ms C and Tib (*mi bzlogs pa*); ms A reads *abhedyaḥ*, "not split (by vajras)." While this is a reasonable reading, it doesn't seem to make perfect sense, given the context.

good and evil actions born from their own conceptuality [and] having met with the [proper] causes and conditions, [that one] takes rebirth in the five realms[588] again and again in the manner of an irrigation machine[589] and experiences the suffering of the life-cycle.

588. *pañca-gati, 'gro ba lnga rnams*; i.e., gods, humans, animals, hungry ghosts, and hell-beings.

589. *ghaṭīyantra*; *zo chun gyi 'khrul 'khor*; a machine used for bringing up water; perhaps on the lines of the "Persian [water] wheel."

5. Resolution of Doubts about the Integration of the Discernment of the Consequences of Action (karma)

The Vajra Student said, "Lord, I [would like to] ask about another curious feature of consciousness. If, Lord, the three consciousnesses [and] the prototypes [and] radiances [are] formless, the air element is formless, and
action is formless, [and] likewise †it was stated by the Lord in the scriptural A:35b
discourses that [they] are void on account of their being mutual imagination,[590] how is the mind-made body bound[591] to the beginningless wheel of existence by good and evil action? Similarly, (if) having created virtue and non-virtue heaped up moment to moment here [in this world] due to these one hundred and sixty prototypes, [it] perishes,[592] how is that acquired again[593] in the afterlife?[594] Does that virtue and non-virtue come from elsewhere? Or rather, is it born from the vestigial instincts [of one's]

590. *anyonya-manyanā-bhāvāt*; the reading here is (or was) difficult. The final consonant is half-obliterated in MS A; and in MS C it does not match any other character (looking something like a *pa* in modern Devanāgarī). I believe this to be the correct reading. It fits the context nicely and is plausible based on the existing half-syllable in MS A. Tib, however, reads "because there is no mutual knowledge" (*phan tshun shes pa med pas*). It is possible that the translators followed the same reading as I do, but interpreted the long *a* on *manyanā* as coalesced with an alpha-privative before *bhāva* (i.e., *manyanā-abhāvāt*). Pandey's reconstruction (based evidently on Tib), *anyonyam aparijñānena*, is unacceptable—not least because it has too many syllables, but also since they do not match the undamaged section of MS A.

591. Tib reads "not bound" (*bcings par ma gyur*)—likely an old scribal error for *bcings par 'gyur*.

592. Tib reads the past passive participle "heaped up" (*upacitaṃ*) as a gerund, yielding "similarly, having heaped up virtue and non-virtue due to these hundred and sixty prototypes, that here (reading *'di nyid la* for *'di nyid*) is born and perishes in a moment, an instant" (*de bzhin du rang bzhin brgya drug cu po 'di rnams kyis dge ba dang mi dge ba rnams nye bar bsags nas de 'di nyid [la] skad cig thang cig tu skye zhing rab tu 'jig par 'gyur*).

593. Following A, which reads *punaḥ*; C (and Tib) read "again and again" (*punaḥ punaḥ, yang nas yang du*).

594. Literally, "another world" (*paraloka*).

own mind? Clear up these anxieties of mine,[595] O Lord and Teacher, Vajra Mentor!"

The Vajra Mentor replied, "Excellent, excellent, O Great One! The so-called thorough knowledge [of] the purification of action is exceedingly profound, the province [of the] buddha[s]. It is not, O Noble One, the territory of beginners or those who assert [philosophical views about] action. Hence, listen carefully! I [will] instruct you [concerning] the purification of action by [means of both] reasoning and [scriptural] tradition.

"With regard to that, first of all, the proper characteristic[s] of good and evil action are (to be) presented. With regard to that, [there are] the ten paths of virtuous action [and] their inverse—the (ten) paths of unvirtuous
A:36a action.† In the *Vajra Crown-Protrusion Tantra*,[596] the Lord stated [that] those paths arise from body, speech, and mind. That [shall be] introduced:

> The Lord said, 'Listen, O Overlord of Secret Ones! Threefold [are] the misdeeds of the body. Fourfold [are] the misdeeds of speech. [There are] three misdeeds of mind. From them, (beings) descend [into] hell.'
>
> Vajrapāṇī said, 'Speak, O Lord, speak, O Blissful One! Of what kind are the misdeeds of the sort [that relate to] the body, the misdeeds of the sort [that relate to] speech, [and] the misdeeds of the sort [that relate to] the mind?'
>
> The Lord said, 'Those misdeeds, O Overlord of Secret Ones, are [either] grave [or] common.[597] Beating [or] slaying of one's parents, respectable persons, and the like [is] a grave misdeed [of

595. or "for me" (*me*).

596. On this scripture, see chapter 1, note 236, above.

597. MS C adds an explanation here, which seems to have been added by an overzealous editor, based on an apparent misreading of the text. The passage begins *tad eva*, but MS C reads *deva-*, so it seems to add a third category of misdeed, that related to the gods (*deva*). (Presumably, the "heavy" [*guru*] misdeeds were interpreted as related to the mentor [*guru*]). As there was no further explanation of this category, the editor felt one should be added, so MS C then reads "with regard to that, damaging (*bhedana*) [representations of] the Holy Teaching such as a reliquary tower (*stūpa*) or a statue (*rūpa*) [is] a god-misdeed."

body]. The paths of unvirtuous action such as taking life, and so on, [are] common misdeed[s of body].

[598]'Misdeeds of speech—that is †to say, harsh speech [that comes] from rejecting the Holy Teaching—are misdeeds of speech. Harsh speech [regarding] one's mother, father, respectable persons, and the like, [are] grave misdeeds of speech. Some create obstacles to virtuous action [such as] telling lies [about] the beyond in conversation with persons of upright faith and conduct with brash words [like] "there is no afterlife." [This and] idle chatter, speaking behind the back, and likewise words of unvirtuous action (*akuśala-karma-vākya*) †are the common misdeeds of speech. C:58b A:36b

'The misdeeds of mind—that is to say, first of all, sloth—those [are] according to their prototype (*prakṛti*) [either] misdeeds [with] mind [as] prototype, misdeeds [with] mental factors [as] prototype, [or] misdeeds [with] delusion [as] prototype.'

Vajrapāṇi said, 'Speak, O Lord! Speak, O Blissful One, [about] the misdeeds [with] mind, mental factors, and delusion [as prototypes].'

The Lord said, 'Listen, Overlord of Secret Ones! The mind [influenced] by destructiveness [and] the mind [influenced] by aversion—that [mind] that is averse to the ten paths of virtuous action—[are] themselves the misdeed[s related to] mind. Arrogance, haughtiness, selfishness, wrath, forsaking[599] beings, passionate mind, stealing others' women [or] others' goods, a mind to deceive respectable persons [are] the mind-misdeed[s related to] mental factors. Rejecting [and/or] forgetting the ten paths of virtuous action [and/or] the six transcendent virtues, a face

598. Tib adds "what are the misdeeds of speech?" (*ngag gi nyes par spyod pa gang she na*).

599. Literally, "destroying" (*nāśana*), but this can also mean "forgetting," which seems more appropriate in this context.

troubled[600] by doubt on account of the darkness of mentation
[are] the common misdeeds of delusion.'

"Thus, the ignorant one (*ajñānin*), not knowing either the good deeds or the misdeeds of body, speech, and mind [as having] the nature of their respective prototypes, radiances, [and] air-mounts, having performed good and evil actions due to the I-habit and mine-habit [thinking,] 'my body, my
A:37a speech, my mind,' becomes wholly devoted to good and bad rebirths.† The wise one (*jñānin*) who has realized mind isolation by the process of the prototypes and radiances neither thinks nor conceptualizes either good deeds or misdeeds of body, speech, and mind—because the good and evil prototypes, born from the three voids, arising moment by moment due to their air-mounts [and] experiencing objects, repeatedly enter into the brilliance. As is said in the *Unexcelled Intention*:[601]

Just like clouds, [which are] not identical
[And have] manifold shapes and colors,
Are born from the expanse of the sky
[And] dissolve in that very place,

Just so, all the prototypes,
[Which have] the three radiances as cause,
Having gone forth into all [sense] fields,
Enter [again] into brilliance.

From not knowing the natures of those[602]
Those who are covered by the veil of unknowing,
Having performed good and evil actions,
C:59a Wander in the five realms [of rebirth].‡

600. Reading *dvandva-pāṅkita-vadano*. *Pāṅkita* would seem to be a causative past passive participle, "muddied, besmirched, troubled" (cf. *paṅka/paṅkaya*; MW, 574). Tib loses the metaphorical usage, rendering *pāṅkita* by "marked [by]" (*mtshan ma'i*); Pn consequently hyper-emends to *dvandvāṅkita-vadano*. Thanks to Yigal Bronner for assistance with this phrase.

601. On this work, see chapter 4, note 566, above.

602. I have settled on the reading of *eṣāṃ* (C and PK). A better reading would be *āsāṃ* (since *prakṛti* is feminine). Both A and Tib read *evaṃ* ("thus"), which seems to make little sense in the context (which has not described a way in which they are known).

> Having performed the "immediates,"[603] and so on,
> [One] is roasted in the hells.
> Having performed good [deeds] such as generosity, and so on,
> [One] is honored[604] in the heavens.† A:37b
>
> Having obtained limitless thousands of births
> In this way again and again,
> Because of this ripening of previous action,
> [One] suffers on account of ignorance.
>
> The combination[605] of prototypes and radiances
> By which beings are tormented—
> Knowing that very thing,
> The wise are liberated from the prison of existence.[606]

Clarifying this very point, the {Lord said} in the *Enquiry of the Kinnara King Scripture*:[607]

> The activity of the mind [is] uncompounded, formless, of that sort. Air [is] independent.[608] Knowing the prototypes of mind in all folk (*loka*), since those [natures] are [thereby] purified, there will be no production of the darkness of defilement at all.[609]

603. That is, the inexpiable sins, or "sins of immediate retribution" (*ānantarya*) that result in rebirth in hell immediately after one's death. PU (46) enumerates them as follows: killing one's mother, father, or a monk/saint (the Sanskrit text reads *bhikṣu*; its Tibetan translation reads *dgra bcom pa*, i.e., *arhat*), damaging a buddha's body, and abandoning the Holy Dharma: *ānantaryetyādi | mātṛ-pitṛ-bhikṣuvadha-buddha-pratimābheda-saddharma-pratikṣepakākhyāni pañca-karmāni maraṇānantaraṃ naraka-yātanād* [read: *naraka-pātanād*] *ānantaryāni* |; also, Peking bsTan-'gyur, vol. 60 (rGyud 'grel, vol. sa): *sems can mtshams med ces bya ba la sogs pa la | pha dang ma dang dgra bcom pa gsod pa dang | sangs rgyas kyi sku 'jig pa dang | dam pa'i chos spong ba zhes bya ba'i las lngas ni | 'chi ba'i dus byas ma thag tu dmyal bar ltung bar 'gyur bas na mtshams med pa ste* |.

604. Or "delighted" (√*mah*).

605. *-yogena*; Tib follows another meaning of *yoga*, and reads *tshul gyis* "the manner of . . . by which . . . ."

606. The cited verses are PK II.39–44.

607. On this scripture, see chapter 3, note 461, above.

608. *aśakta*; Tib reads "unobstructed" (*thogs pa med pa, *asaṅga*).

609. This passage is knotty. I have done my best to edit and render Skt (with reference to

Also, according to this reasoning, the great yogin who realizes mind isolation confronts liberation indifferent to the results of virtuous and unvirtuous action. Just as the Lord said in the *Diamond Cutter* [*Scripture*]:[610]

> If even good things (*dharmāḥ*) [are] to be abandoned, what need to mention bad things (*adharmāḥ*)?[611]

[The Lord] also said, in the Great Yoga Tantra the *Esoteric Community*:

> Those who have abandoned gnosis
> B:38a Perform the ten paths of virtuous action.[612†]

Thus, beings, not realizing the thorough knowledge of their own mind just as it is due to separation from spiritual guides, conceiving of [ideas such as] empty, vain, void,[613] good and evil, and so on, due to the I-habit and the mine-habit, experience suffering in the beginningless life-cycle.[614] Just as the

---

Tib). If one reads instrumental *kleśa-tamasā* (a possible, and more grammatical, reading of ms A's *kleśa-tamasya*) instead of genitive *kleśa-tamasaḥ* (ms C), one would read "there will be no production due to the darkness of defilement." Tib would seem to suggest: "the activities of mind [are] uncompounded [and] formless; due to the distinction according to function (*las*), air also is unobstructed. Since the one who knows the prototypes of the minds of all beings (*'jig rten*) is pure, it is not possible for defilements to arise." This citation does not correspond to any known passage in KRP (see Harrison, ed., 351).

610. *Vajracchedikā, rDo rje gcod pa*—the famous "Diamond Sūtra." Edited Sanskrit texts may be found at: F. Max Müller, ed., *Buddhist Texts from Japan*, and P. L. Vaidya, ed., *Mahāyāna-sūtra-saṃgraha*, vol. I, 75–89. A Tibetan translation (by Śilendrabodhi and Ye-shes-sde) may be found at: DK, Shes-phyin, vol. ka, 121a[1]–132b[7] (Tōh. 16).

611. This citation may be found in the Sanskrit at: Müller, 23; and Vaidya, 88. Tibetan may be found at: DK, Shes-phyin, vol. ka, f. 123a[3].

612. GST XVII.15ab. On this scripture, see chapter 2, note 272, above. See also chapter 9, p. 260 below, for an alternative citation of this passage.

613. *riktaṃ tucchaṃ śūnyaṃ*: a variation on the Buddhist Sanskrit cliché *riktakaṃ tucchakaṃ asārakaṃ*, "empty, vain, insubstantial." Cf. BHSD, 84.

614. Tib parses this differently, reading, "Thus, not realizing the thorough knowledge of their own mind just as it is due to separation from spiritual guides, having conceived the I-habit, the mine-habit, vain and insubstantial, due to conceiving of good and evil, and so on, beings experience suffering from the beginningless life-cycle." Note the duplication of "conceiving" (*kalpayitvā* becomes *brtags nas . . . brtags pas*) and the shift from gerund to instrumental in the latter emphasizing as it does the causal relationship. Also noteworthy is the reduction of *riktaṃ tucchaṃ śūnyaṃ* to *gsob dang gsog* (implying either **tuccham asāraṃ*, or perhaps **tucchaṃ riktaṃ*).

Lord said in the "Spiritual Guide Chapter" of the *Noble Eight-Thousand-Line Transcendent Virtue of Wisdom* [*Scripture*]:[615]

> Subhūti said: 'Lord, if all things [are] isolated [and] {all things} [are] void—how, Lord, is the defilement of all beings [to be] understood? How, Lord, is the purification of all beings [to be] understood?[616] The isolated,[617] Lord, is not defiled; nor, {Lord,} is {the isolated} purified. The void, Lord, is not defiled; nor, {Lord,} is {the void} purified. Lord, neither the isolated nor the void[618] is enlightened to the unexcelled, perfect enlightenment. The Holy Teaching,[619] Lord, is not found elsewhere than voidness.† Is, will, B:38b
> or has [anything] been enlightened to the unexcelled, perfect enlightenment? How are we to understand, Lord, the meaning of this statement?[620] Explain, Lord, explain, O Blissful One!'
>
> Thus addressed, the Lord said this to the Venerable Subhūti: 'What do you think, Subhūti? Have beings been engaged in the I-habit and the mine-habit for a long time?'
>
> Subhūti replied, 'It is so, Lord. It is so, O Blissful One. Beings have been engaged in the I-habit and the mine-habit {for a long time}.'‡ C:59b

615. *Āryāṣṭasāhasrikāyāṃ prajñāpāramitāyāṃ kalyāṇamitra-parivarte*, *Shes rab kyi pha rol tu phyin pa brgyad stong pa'i dge ba'i bshes gnyen gyi le'u*: chapter 22 of this extremely influential Mahāyāna Buddhist scripture. Sanskrit text may be found at: P. L. Vaidya, ed., *Aṣṭasāhasrikā Prajñāpāramitā*; and R. Mitra, *Aṣṭasāhasrikā Prajñāpāramitā*. A Tibetan translation (by Śākyasena, Jñānasiddhi, and Dharmatāśīla, with many revisors) may be found at: DK, Sher-phyin, Tōh. 12, $1b^1$–$286a^6$.

616. Tib reads "How, Lord, can there be defilement of sentient beings? How are [they] purified?" The version of this text in the Kanjur is closer to the Sanskrit of the CMP.

617. ms B adds "of beings."

618. Tib reads "voidness."

619. *saddharma*; ASPP reads "all things" (*sarvadharma*). Pn emends to ASPP.

620. Tib reads, "Lord, if other than isolation and voidness, whatever thing [such as] a past actual, perfect enlightenment of unexcelled, authentic, perfect enlightenment, or a present authentic, perfect enlightenment, or a future authentic, perfect enlightenment is not found, Lord, how does [one] seek the meaning of that statement?"

The Lord said, 'What do you think, Subhūti? Are [not] the I-habit and the mine-habit void?'

Subhūti replied, '[They are] void, Lord. [They are] void, O Blissful One.'

The Lord said, 'What do you think, Subhūti? [Do] beings circle in the life-cycle on account of the I-habit and the mine-habit?'

Subhūti replied, 'It is so, Lord. It is so, O Blissful One. Beings circle in the life-cycle on account of the I-habit and the mine-habit.'

The Lord said, 'Thus indeed, Subhūti, is the defilement of beings understood. Thus is [their] purification understood.'[621]

B:39a Just as †it is also said in the *Purification of All Karmic Obscurations Scripture*:[622]

'What do you think, monk? Is the unproduced produced, destroyed, defiled, or purified?'

'It is not so, Lord.'

The Lord asked, 'What do you think, monk? Do unproduced things go to hell? Do [they] go to the animal realm or the realm of Yama [the Lord of Death]?'

'[It is] unproduced; hence, Lord, [it] does not exist. How then [could there be] the taking of a bad rebirth?'

621. This passage may be found in ASPP, 198–99. An alternative English translation may be found in Conze, 237. The Tibetan canonical translation of this passage may be found at DK, brGyad sTong, vol. ka, 218a[5]–218b[5].

622. *Sarva-karmāvarana-viśuddhi-sūtra, Las kyi sgrib pa thams cad rnam par dag pa'i mdo.* I am not aware of an extant Sanskrit text of this scripture. A Tibetan translation of this scripture (by Jinamitra, Prajñāvarman, and Bande Ye-shes-sde, "etc.") may be found at DK, mDo, vol. tsha, ff. 284a[3]–297b[5].

'Thus, monk, all things are brilliance. (Yet,) naïve ordinary beings, conceiving the unreal, conceiving falsehood, conceiving "empty, vain, [and] void," go to (hell,) the animal realm or the realm of Yama [the Lord of Death].[623] {Do I not teach the Dharma,} monks, [that] from defilement of mind, beings are defiled, [and that they] are purified by purity of mind?'[624]

And, in the {*Secret*} *Treasury of the Transcendent Lord[s] Scripture*:[625]

[That one] is earnestly devoted to those [things] in which one should have faith, [such as the teaching that] 'all things are primordially pure.' I do not speak of a going to a lower rebirth of that being. For what reason? †The defilements do not have the existence of a heap.[626] Vanished [are] all defilements; [they] are produced from the complete assemblage [and] conjunction of causes and conditions. They are destroyed as soon as they are produced. That which is the flux of production of mind is the flux of the defilements.[627] B:39b

"{The Venerable Master} (Nāgārjuna)[628] also said, clarifying this point:

If all this is void
[And] intrinsically unproduced,

623. This passage may be found at DK, mDo, vol. tsha, f. 286a⁴–286b¹.

624. This final sentence may be found at DK, mDo, vol. tsha, f. 285b⁴⁻⁵.

625. *Tathāgata-guhya-koṣa-sūtra*; *de bzhin gshegs pa'i mdzod kyi mdo*. This scripture is cited in several works, e.g., SS (69–70) and the *Āmnāyamañjarī* of Abhayākaragupta. I have not otherwise been able to identify an extant Sanskrit text or a corresponding Tibetan translation of this scripture.

626. *rāśī-bhāva*; see discussion of the "heaps" of the body/mind" in chapter 2, above.

627. TIB reads "I do not say that if one who does not have faith in all dharmas has great faith and earnest devotion, that sentient being therefore goes to a bad rebirth. Why? Because the defilements have no aggregates. As all defilements are isolated, they are produced from the assemblage and conjunction of causes and conditions. Due merely to production, they will be destroyed. That which is creation and destruction is the destruction of the defilements."

628. TIB renders *bhaṭṭārakapāda* as "Nāgārjuna" (*klu sgrub*). This seems acceptable, given both that the last of the cited verses is from a work attributed to Nāgārjuna, and that Candrakīrti uses this term as a title for Nāgārjuna. See PU, 229.

How does action produce pleasure and suffering
Here in the life-cycle?

The naïve are defiled by suffering
On account of the imagined [and] other-dependent [natures],
Due to the I-habit and the mine-habit,
[And] likewise by the impurities [such as] passion, and so on.

All this is merely mind—
Arisen in the form of phantasm.
From that, [there comes] good and evil action;
From that, [there come] good and evil births.[629]

By this argument—according to [both] scripture and reasoning—all the transcendent lords, whose nature is great caring,[630] having seen all beings who have fallen into the torrent[631] of suffering [and are] without a refuge or last resort, having recognized the purity of the defilements[632] by means of the thorough knowledge of the nature of the defilements in accordance
C:60a with superficial reality,‡ [and] having purified superficial reality itself by means of ultimate reality, [those transcendent lords] cause [those beings]
B:40a to be established in the samādhi whose nature conduces to the real.†

629. The last verse in this citation occurs as verse 18 of the *Mahāyāna-viṃśikā* sometimes (though by no means certainly) attributed to Nāgārjuna. It has been edited by Giuseppe Tucci in *Minor Buddhist Texts,* Part I, p. 203. I have not been able to identify the first two verses.

630. great caring (*mahākṛpa*); Tib reads "great compassion" (*snying rje chen po*)—usually *mahākaruṇā*, though it is occasionally used to render *mahākṛpa* (typically, *brtse ba chen po*).

631. *arṇava*: in this context, "ocean" seems a bit tame and "torrent" seems to fit closest to the sense of *arṇava* as "agitated, foaming, restless" (cf. PSED, 228). Tib reads *dba'/rba klong*, "whirlpool" (cf. *Bod rgya tshig mdzod chen mo*, p. 193[7]: *rba rlabs kyi klong ngam dkyil*).

632. *kleśaviśuddhiṃ prabodhya*; Tib reads "having purified the defilements" (*nyon mongs pa rnam par dag par mdzad*).

6. Resolution of Doubts about the Integration of Superficial Reality

The Vajra Student said, "Out of your grace, analyzing the distinctive characteristics of body, speech, and mind [isolations] in accordance with the [scriptural] statements articulated just previously, the Venerable Master[633] has instructed [me about] the immediately previous samādhi, which has been ascertained; I [now] inquire about the particulars of the successively higher samādhis.[634]

"Having undertaken the creation stage, [its] consummation in body isolation [is] a mere confidence[635] characterized by the absence of the [actual] three vajras [of body, speech, and mind]. Hence, there is no divine form (at) [the stage of] body isolation; because the body [in that context] is merely an assemblage of fine atoms. Even the consummation of speech isolation is the thorough knowledge of merely the vajra recitation by the processes of entering, and so on. There, too, there is no divine form; because the nature of sound is like an echo. Even the consummation of mind isolation is merely the thorough knowledge of the prototypes and radiances. Even there the proper form of a deity endowed with the marks, such as possessing the best of all forms, is not found; because the mind is merely radiance.

"According to this reasoning, without a foundation in [the yogic practice

633. *bhaṭṭārakapāda*; given that the two other instances in which this term is used in the CMP both refer to Nāgārjuna (B:39b and B:51b; see also chapter 5, note 628, above), this would seem to be an indication that the Vajra Mentor in the CMP is meant to be Nāgārjuna himself.

634. Tib reads "Out of your kindness, I have found certainty through analysis of the distinguishing characteristics of the body, speech, and mind [isolations] in accordance with the scriptural statements spoken just previously. Begging from the Venerable Master's mouth also the distinctive characteristics of other samādhis, I ask for the distinctive characteristics of successively higher samādhis."

635. Or "zeal" (*adhimukti*).

of] superficial reality, one does not obtain establishment [as a deity].[636]
B:40b †Therefore, I desire, by the grace of the Mentor, to understand the production of a deity [body] by means of mere gnosis."

The Vajra Mentor replied, "Excellent, excellent, Great One! I will explain to you the inconceivable divinity reality (*devatā-tattva*), which is the personal instruction of all the buddhas descended through the successive generations of mentors,[637] which is not even the range of the lords of the ten stages.[638] Given the unreality of the aggregates, elements, and media,[639] the so-called 'thorough knowledge of one's own mind just as it is' is the assuming of a divine form, endowed with all the marks [of a great being], by merely the prototypes and radiances of the three gnoses. That also is described by the twelve similes, such as dream, phantasm, and so on. This is the mind-made body of the buddhas."

The Vajra Student asked, "It is said in the scriptural discourses that 'without the receptacle of the body, there is no manifestation of mind; without the mind, a body is not found.' How then, is a divine body endowed with all the marks such as hands and feet, and so on, created by merely the mind alone? Those who hold objectifying views will not accept [this teaching] without [proofs based on] scripture and realization. Therefore, for them, O Lord and Teacher, Vajra Mentor, teach the technique for easily making manifest the non-objectified divinity reality."

B:41a †The Vajra Mentor ‡replied, "Excellent, excellent, O Great One! Those
C:60b who are engaged in methods such as those of the [exoteric] scriptures, and so on, and even those who cultivate the creation stage, pronounce [and]

636. *pratiṣṭhā*; this is a technical term used for the consecration of images or statues. Tib reads only *gnas pa*, not *rab tu gnas pa*, which is a more readily-identifiable word for such consecration; though it is this sense that is clearly operative in this context. For more information on such consecration practices, see Yael Bentor, *Consecration of Images and Stūpas.*

637. *guru-parva-krama*; Tib reads "through the sequence of the lineage of gurus" (*bla ma brgyud pa'i rim pa*).

638. i.e., of full, or "tenth stage" bodhisattvas.

639. Tib reads "that called the 'thorough knowledge of one's own mind just as it is' is not among the aggregates, elements, and media" (*rang gi sems ji lta ba bzhin du yongs su shes pa zhes bya ba phung po dang khams dang skye mched rnams la yang med pa*).

have confidence in similes such as '(all things are)[640] like a phantasm, like a dream, like a reflection,' and so on. [However,] they do not understand the analogy[641] [to] the production of a divine [form], made of mind, by mere gnosis [according to] the personal instruction of the self-consecration. Hence, I will instruct you in the causes and conditions for the production of Vajrasattva according to the Yoga Tantra[s].

"The truth (*tathyaṃ*) [is that] mind [is] free of color and shape, mere radiance, whose nature is like space, difficult to contact like ultimate reality. However, the three luminances are radiant; and air is elemental, common, [and] light.[642] Consciousness is bound together with that air. From that is produced a phantasmic divine form, endowed with all qualities, beautiful, united with five[-colored] light rays, the two luminances—critical wisdom and liberative art [conjoined]. What is the conveyance (of) that? [It is] the air element. The mover (*yaḥ*), mind vajra, mounted [on it] like a horse, proceeds wherever it desires.[643]

Clarifying [this point, the Lord] said, in the *Transmigration of Consciousness Scripture*:[644]

> The Lord said, 'Mahauṣadhi, for the sake of [learning] this very pair of verses,[645] I hurled myself from a cliff at the peak of a mountain †and experienced many hundreds of thousands of tribulations. Mahauṣadhi, ask whatever you desire [and] I will tell [you].' B:41b

640. This is also found in MS C, but as it occurs three times in that text (and only once in TIB), I do not feel that it is integral to the original work.

641. SKT *aupamya*; TIB reads "through similes" (*dpes*).

642. *laghu*, *yang ba*; or "quick," or perhaps "subtle."

TIB reads this passage quite differently. It says, "However, the three luminances of mere luminance have air as their support; since they are common, they are light" (*de lta mod kyi snang ba tsam gyi snang ba gsum po rlung la brten par gyur pa dang | thun mong du gyur pas yang ba ste |*).

643. This is a difficult passage. In translating the initial *yaḥ* as a noun, rather than a more-typical relative pronoun, I am perhaps taking some liberties—and certainly deviating from the reading of the Tibetan translation team. However, as there is no correlative pronoun in this case, it does not seem to make sense to me any other way. The TIB reads, "That which is the mind vajra, mounted on that kind of air, proceeds wherever [it] wishes."

644. On this scripture, see chapter 4, note 562, above.

645. TIB reads "half a verse" (*tshigs su bcad pa phyed*).

Thus addressed, {the bodhisattva} Mahauṣadhi said this to the Lord: 'Lord, what [physical] form [does] this consciousness [take]?'[646]

The Lord said, '(It is like) the [physical] form of an illusionist's fire;[647] the [physical] form of the reflection of a person on the surface of water, whose form is [both] visible and invisible. Moreover, that of which you speak, Mahauṣadhi, [is] "how is one to see the shape of the unoriginated, of that which has already died?"[648]

'Thus, for example, a reflection on the surface of water resembles the form of a person. Yet, [it is] not to be regarded as the appearance of that in [that water].

'In fact, furthermore, Mahauṣadhi, that person [appearing] in the water, with [its] accompanying head, hands, and feet, is neither warm nor cold, nor [does it experience] bodily exhaustion. Nor is that body comparable [in terms of its] masses of flesh.[649] Nor is that reflection composed of elemental substances.[650] Nor

646. Tib reads "Lord, what is the nature of this consciousness" (*bcom ldan 'das rnam par shes pa 'di'i rang bzhin ci lags* |).

647. Skt and sTog read "fire" (*agni/me*); DCoP read "human" (*mi*), as does DK.

648. According to the Tibetan translation of the sūtra, there is a break here in the continuity of the quote. The paragraph above is DK, dKon-brtsegs, vol. cha. f. $83a^{2}$–$83a^{5}$.

Tib reads "It is like the nature of an illusionist's fire, the nature of the shadow of a person in water, not clear and unclear, (sDe and Co add: the nature of eye and space,) and the nature of existence. I must explain to you, Mahauṣadhi, since it has not been born yet, how one should initially regard a form that has just died" (*sman chen sgyu ma mkhan gyi me'i rang bzhin gang yin pa dang* | *mi'i grib ma chu'i nang du 'byung ba gsal ba ma yin zhing mi gsal ba'i rang bzhin gang yin pa dang* | *mig dang nam mkha'i rang bzhin gang yin pa dang* | *srid pa'i rang bzhin gang yin pa de bzhin no* | *gang yang sman chen khyod kyis skye ba med pa nyid kyis ji ltar thog mar 'chi bas byas pa'i gzugs blta bar bya zhes bya ba bshad par bya'o* |).

649. Tib reads "because it does not have flesh, fish flesh, and so on" (*de la sha dang nya sha la sogs pa mi srid pa'i phyir*).

650. Literally, "filled with the elements" (*dhātubhir vyākulā*); that is, it is not, like a normal body, made up of elemental substances. Tib reads "because it cannot be destroyed by the elements" (*khams kyis rnam par gzhig mi nus pa'i phyir*). *Vyākula* can indeed mean "disturbed or agitated by," but in this context—in which a contrast between a real body and a

> does that image of a person in the water make a sound—neither an unhappy sound nor a happy sound.† In that way, this consciousness, having cast off the bodily form that has already died, takes on the shape of its own form.'[651]‡ B:42a (C:61a)

That [consciousness] of naïve ordinary beings, destined for [future rebirths in] the life-cycle, [is] called 'a between-being.' That very [consciousness,] of those who have obtained the personal instruction of all buddhas[652] [passed down] through the successive generations of mentors, is this [that is] called 'the self-consecration stage,' perceived like a scroll-painting[653] [reflected] in the center of a mirror. In the same way, the selflessness [that is] the nature of the vajra body emanates,[654] endowed with the best of all forms, a {lovely} body (one never tires of looking at), an embodiment adorned with the thirty-two marks of a great person—in short, adorned with the qualities of all the buddhas. As the Lord said in the *Enlightenment of Vairocana Tantra*:[655]

> From [meditative] cultivation of Reality,
> One obtains a body like Indra's [rain]bow.[656]

This [is] its meaning: 'Indra' is Śakra. Just as the [rain]bow of Indra, adorned with the colors of five light rays, is distinctly visible in the vault of the sky, so too is the body to be perceived. †'One obtains from [meditative] cultivation of Reality' [means] one obtains from the personal instructions [learned at] the guru's feet; from [meditative] cultivation of Reality, [i.e.] aiming to perceive ultimate reality." B:42b

---

reflection is being drawn with regard to its sensations and compositions, I think the former reading is better.

651. Tib reads, "Likewise, this consciousness also, having cast off the nature of the body that has already died, takes on a form made of that." This last passage appears at: DK, dKon brtsegs, vol. cha, f. 91a[6]–91b[2].

652. Tib reads "all Transcendent Lords" (*de bzhin gshegs pa thams cad, *sarvatathāgata*).

653. *citra-paṭa*, this could also be a "multicolored cloth"; Tib reads "a cloth painting on a wall" (*rtsig pa'i ras ris*).

654. Tib reads "in the same way, itself is emanated by the nature of the Vajra(sattva) Body."

655. On this scripture, see chapter 3, note 447, above. These lines are not found therein.

656. This citation is also found in PKṬYM (61–62), and a variant is found at GS III.79.

The Vajra Student asked, "Lord, I [still] have some doubts. Why does one sleep for a long time? Why, having cast aside just the body [and] gone in a dream to the Realm of the Thirty(-Three)[657] or another foreign land, [and] having enjoyed [there] the five objects of [sense] desire, does one pass again into this body? Why, too, does one suffer the ripening of [karmic] effects from good and bad dream-visions? That is, is there a difference between the states of sleep and waking or not?"

The Vajra Mentor replied, "Excellent, excellent, Great One! In order to heal those suffering from the disease of clinging to physicality due to beginningless ordinary pride, and further, to make clear the personal instructions of the self-consecration stage, you inquire of the characteristics of dream.[658] Hence, listen with one-pointed mind! In accordance with the scriptures, I
B:43a will explain to you [the attainment] by means of dreaming †[of] a divine form like a reflection, which is the introspectively-known continuity of all [beings].[659]

> In the aggregates, elements, sense media, and sense organs, and
> so on,
> In those two gnoses [it is] well-assembled (*susaṃskṛta*) here.[660]
> Being the void, greatness, the one who sleeps
> May behold a dream by the force of [vital] wind.

657. *tridaśālaya*; Tib reads "the Abode of the Thirty-three" (*sum cu rtsa gsum pa'i gnas*). Cf. *Amarakośa*, v. 6.

658. Tib reads, "[Your] inquiry concerns the characteristics of dreaming so as to remove the doubts of those who conceive of the body as having the nature of a beginningless thing, and in order to clarify the explanation of the self-consecration."

659. Following text as emended; it could alternatively be emended to read, "in accordance with the sūtras and tantras, I will explain to you [the attainment] by means of dreaming [of] a reflection-like divine form of all, which is introspectively known." Tib reads, "Therefore, since you should understand well the divine body according to the sūtras and tantras—which [body] is the introspective self-awareness of everything and has been explained to be like a reflection through [the simile of] dreaming—listen with one-pointed mind!"

660. Tib reads "those two knowledges (*shes pa*) are well assembled here in the aggregates, elements and media, sense organs, and so on."

The one who longs for the results of dreams may not conceive
Any difference between dreaming and waking.
Night and day, being[s] experience dream[s];
For a very long time, they remain like a mere [lump of] earth.[661]

As long as the result of the action[s] performed has not ripened,
The air again proceeds to birth here.
[If] the result should ripen, the air verily goes
Elsewhere, quickly passing away in the world.

Just as ‡the victorious lords residing in the ten directions C:61b
Having no marrow, bone, [or] flesh in their bodies,
May, for the sake of beings, enter into an element[al form],
[And] perform deeds by means of an emanated body,

In the [same] way, the sleeping mind gradually wakens;
[It] may desire the result and a mass of [illusory] conceptuality.
Like dreams, verily, [are] all things;
The true and the false—both [are] unreal.

Illuminating this very point [the Lord] said in the *Purification of All Karmic Obscurations Scripture*:[662†] B:43b

'Monk, what do you think? Should the mind experience a dream during sleep, are you aware of the commission of passion?'[663]

'Lord, I am aware.'

661. Literally, "[there is] success in mere-earth-ness for a long time." Tib is unclear, but seems to concur: "having become unconscious (lit. touched the earth), they sleep for a long time."

662. On this scripture, see chapter 5, note 622, above.

663. or the "occurrence of passion" (*rāgam adhyāpannam*); Tib reads "when aware (*kun tu rtog pa'i tshe*) during a dream during sleep, do you experience the activity of passion?"

> The Lord said, 'What do you think, monk? Are you aware[664] of the commission of passion by means of the mind?'
>
> 'Just so, Lord.'
>
> 'Do you see, monk, any distinction or difference between the dreaming mind and other minds?'
>
> 'Lord, I do not observe any difference between a dreaming mind and other minds.'
>
> 'What do you think, monk? Have I taught [that] (all) thing[s are] like a dream?'[665]
>
> 'Just so, Lord.'[666]

Clarifying this very point, the Lord said in the Great Yoga Tantra, the *Glorious Esoteric Community*:[667]

> Thus, for instance, O Lords, All Transcendent Lords, the spirit of enlightenment causes the adamantine state that gives rise to the gnosis of all transcendent lords. That spirit of enlightenment does not reside in the body; it does not reside in speech; it does not reside in the mind. There is no arising of a thing that is not located in the triple world. This is the adamantine state that gives rise to the gnosis {of all transcendent lords}.
>
> O Lords, All Transcendent Lords, it is just so [with regard to]
> dreams. I should not teach [that there is] a dream state in the
> B:44a triple world. †Nor is it so [with regard to] persons; I should see
> [them as like a] dream. The functions of the triple world are like
> dreams, resemble dreams, are arisen from dreams. Just so, O

664. Tib reads "aren't you aware?"

665. Tib renders explicit this (presumed) meaning. Skt uses the singular: "dharma is like a dream" (*svapnopamo dharmaḥ*).

666. This passage may be found at DK, mDo, vol. tsha, ff. $285b^5$–$286a^1$.

667. On this scripture, see chapter 2, note 272, above.

> Lords, All Transcendent Lords, all buddhas and bodhisattvas of the world-realms in [all] ten directions, and all beings, all those should be understood as selfless [and like a] dream.[668]

Clarifying this very phantasmic samādhi, [the Lord] said in the Great Yoga Tantra, the *Gnosis Vajra Compendium*:[669]

> The great yoga[670] of mind and mental factors is the great bliss samādhi. That is indicated by the similes of phantasm, and so on. Hence, all transcendent lords [whose number is] like the sands of the streams of the Ganges river[s in all] the buddha-fields are like phantasm, like a moon in water, like a phantom [double], like a mirage, a dream, an echo, a city of gandharvas, Indra's net [i.e., an optical illusion], Śakra's bow [i.e., a rainbow], lightning, (water) bubbles, a mirror image. The great bliss samādhi is indicated by [these] twelve similes of phantasm.[671]

Thus, too, ⁺the transcendent lords of the ten directions reside[672] for as long (C:62a)
as the life-cycle lasts by means of the phantasmic samādhi. They frolic in, they delight with, they surround [themselves] with the five objects of [sensory] desire. ⁺According to their wishes, endowed with {all} qualities (of an B:44b
omniscient one), they pass from buddha-field to buddha-field. Thus, the one desiring liberation, recollecting the past, present, and future sufferings of the life-cycle, propitiating the vajra mentor diligently, [and] obtaining the personal instruction on the self-consecration stage, should seek the art of purifying that.

668. GST, chapter 15 (Matsunaga, 83–84).

669. On this scripture, see chapter 4, note 488, above.

670. *mahāyoga*; This reading is found in B and Tib; C and PKṬYM read *samāyoga*, which would be rendered "union."

671. This passage may be found at DK, rGyud, vol. ca, 283a$^{5-7}$ (Tōh. 447), and vol. cha, 5b$^{1-3}$ (Tōh. 450). See also sTog Palace Kanjur, rGyud, vol. ca, f. 261b$^{1-3}$.

672. *viharanti*; a word found at the beginning of nearly every Buddhist scripture, describing where the Buddha was then residing, and I have translated it accordingly. However, in later literature, it comes to mean strolling for pleasure and, given the verbs that follow in this context (*krīḍanti, ramanti, paricārayanti*) it seems that some degree of this latter connotation is meant in this context.

7. Resolution of Doubts about the Integration of Ultimate Reality[673]

The Vajra Student asked: "[My] doubts [regarding] the superficial reality have been dispelled; now, by your grace, I wish to know the discernment [of] the ultimate reality, the state of the purification of the radiances."

The Vajra Mentor said: "The so-called 'superficial reality'—a Vajrasattva form[-body] perfected by the process of self-consecration—can be known by means of the twelve similes of phantasm. However, the ultimate reality [is] bodiless (*amūrtika*), incomparable, devoid of all undertaking, introspectively known. One [only] comes to know it from the mouth of the Mentor.[674] As it is said in a scriptural discourse:

> Just as a lamp inside a[n earthen] pot
> Does not shine outside,
> [Yet,] when that pot is broken,
> The flame of the lamp then shines forth.
>
> (Likewise,) the pot is one's own body;† B:45a
> The lamp is Reality;

673. MS C and TIB construe—wrongly, I believe—the (incomplete) last clause of the chapter as standing in apposition to "ultimate reality" in the title (which, following standard Indic practice, occurs at the end of the text of the chapter). Thus, they read "Chapter 7: Resolution of Doubts Concerning Ultimate Reality, the Enlightenment Process that is the Universal Secret of the Purity of Yoga and Bliss" (MS C), and "Chapter 7: Resolution of Doubts Concerning Ultimate Reality, the Enlightenment Process of Joy Concerning the Purity of the Two Yogas" (TIB).

674. Literally, "hence, it is not known without the mouth of the guru"; TIB reads "hence, it is not known unless taught from the mouth of the guru."

When broken by the Mentor's word,[675]
The buddha-gnosis bursts into view.[676]

Sky is born from sky
Space perceives space—
In that very manner,[677] from the guru's mouth,
This method (*prayoga*) is taught.

"By this reasoning, because it occurs in the form of sound, [that whose] nature is radiance without beginning or end,[678] free of subject-object [duality], whose character is the superficial reality, [may be] known by that [same] sound. The ultimate reality, though, is uncontrived, space-like, [and] stainless in nature.[679] Clarifying this very point, [the Lord] said in the *Teaching of One Method Scripture*:[680]

These things (*dharma*) are taught by words and languages.
Here one finds neither things and words.
Having entered the unity of method, facticity,
[One] will reach the unexcelled, the supreme tolerance.[681]

675. Literally, "by the guru's mouth" (*vaktra*).

676. These two verses are also found in the *Abhibodhi-kramopadeśa* (Tōh. 1806: sDe-dge bsTan-'gyur, rGyud, vol. ngi, ff. 114b²–117a¹; these verses f. 115a⁷–115b¹) attributed to Āryadeva (see the Introduction for my reservations in attributing this text to the author of the CMP).

Noteworthy is the evident similarity of this sentiment to the idea in the Āraṇyakas and the Upaniṣads that "*ātman* is *brahman* in a pot" [i.e., a body], and that breaking the pot allows one to "realize the primordial unity of the individual soul with the plenitude of Being that was the Absolute" (see D. G. White, *The Alchemical Body*, 18).

677. *tathaiva*; TIB reads *de nyid* (**tad eva*).

678. *anādinidhanābhāsa-svabhāva;* TIB reads "without beginning or end, the unreal (or insubstantial) nature" (*dngos po med pa'i ngo bo nyid, *abhāva-svabhāva*).

679. TIB reads "equal to uncontrived space, stainless in nature" (*ma bcos pa'i nam mkha' dang mnyam pa dri ma med pa'i ngo bo nyid*); presumably the translators were reading *akṛtaka-kha-samaṃ,* rather than *akṛtakaṃ khasamaṃ*. Though *anusvara* are often missing or unclear in MS B, it is quite clearly marked here.

680. The very same verse from the *Ekanayanirdeśa-sūtra,* is cited in chapter 3. See chapter 3, note 445, above.

681. Following SKT; TIB reads rather differently: "the one who enters facticity, the one true

"Thus, the student who understands making cause and effect nondual, having received the permission of the delighted mentor,[682] having made the host maṇḍala (*gaṇa-maṇḍala*) according to the rite taught in the Tantra according to [his] means, at midnight, having presented to the mentor a consort (*mudrā*), who is well-educated, {well-bathed,} †with fragrant limbs B:45b
[and] adorned with all ornaments, [and] having worshipped with the secret and higher offerings (*pūjā*),[683] placing [his] right knee{cap} on the ground in front of the mentor, folding [his] hands,[684] ‡with a mind terrified by the C:62b
life-cycle, envisioning the teacher as a transcendent lord [appearing] right before [his] very eyes, [he] prays for enlightenment with this offering of praise:

Homage to you, O Best Vajra, Bestower of the Supreme!
Homage be unto you, Reality limit (incarnate)!
Homage to you, whose kernel is voidness![685]
Homage be unto you, Buddha-enlightenment![686]

Give me, Great Mentor,
The vision of enlightenment,
The great gnosis of all the buddhas,
The unexcelled universal void!

Give me, Great One,
That which is identical with your own personal experience![687]

---

method, will touch the unexcelled, supreme tolerance" (*chos nyid tshul gcig dngos la'ang 'jug byed pa | bzod mchog bla na med la reg par 'gyur |*).

682. Skt reads *guru-tuṣṭājñā*, properly "the delighted command of the guru," though I construe it as an "inverted word" compound. Tib reads *bla mas bstan pa'i lung*, which in normal Tibetan would signify "the oral transmission (*āgama*) taught by the guru." However, it might also reflect a reading of **guru-dṛṣṭājñā*, "the tried and true [i.e., time-honored] permission of the guru."

683. Tib reads "secret and other offerings" (*gsang ba dang de las gzhan pa'i mchod pa*).

684. *kṛta-kara-puṭa*; i.e., placing the palms together in supplication.

685. *śūnyatāgarbha*, "filled with voidness"; Tib reads slightly differently: "born from voidness" (*stong nyid las byung*).

686. This verse is identical to MNS v. 158 (see Davidson, 61).

687. *anubhava* (ms C); ms B reads *anubhāva*, "saving power"—an important concept in

Free of action and [re]birth,
I may attain enlightenment right here!

Apart from your lotus-feet,
There is no refuge elsewhere, O Lord!
Hence, be gracious, O Best of Buddhas,
B:46a Hero of Beings, Great Sage!'†[688]

Having thus heard the amazing divine
Supreme rite of supplication,
Generating compassion for the Student,
The glorious Mentor, the ocean of qualities,[689]

Assuming a kindly demeanor,
Sympathetic, ecstatic,
Should teach[690] the divine pledge—
The supreme, whose source is the Yoga Tantras.[691]

Then, the teacher, absorbed in samādhi,
{Should produce the spirit of enlightenment,}[692]
Placing the spirit of enlightenment
In a vase or a conch shell.

Then, beckoning to that Student,
Consecrated by all the buddhas,
[He] should offer his pledge (*samaya*)

Mahāyāna Buddhism, but one that does not fit well in this context. Tib reads *rang myong* (**svānubhava*).

688. This verse is identical to PK III.8 and GS V.25.

689. This verse is identical to PK III.9 and GS V.26.

690. Literally, "cause to be heard/learned" (*śrāvayet*).

691. This verse is similar to GS V.27.

692. This line is not found in Tib. I have followed ms B (*niṣpādayet*); ms C reads "should let fall the bodhicitta" (*nipātayet*). Either reading makes sense in the context; the latter seems rather more explicit. In this context, "bodhicitta" presumably refers to the seminal drop(s) produced in ritual union.

Together with that of his consort.[693]

The initiation is to be given
By [one] like a second vajradhara (*Vajrin*),
With words proclaiming the auspicious,
[And] sounds of various musical instruments.[694]

By the initiations of the three realms,
The Student, bowing with folded hands,
Should then be given the permission of that
As enjoined in the tantras.[695]

Garland, water, buddha,
Vajra, bell, and mirror,
Name, teacher, the permission—
This is the sequence of initiations.

Then, he should offer that one
The characteristic of enlightenment,† B:46b
Obtained from the abode of the sacred tradition
That comes from the successive generations of mentors.

"Concerning that, the enlightenment process is twofold; that is to say, inner and outer. First of all, the outer is taught: At the break of dawn, there is the radiance of delusion-darkness.[696] Until the sun rises, there is brilliance,

693. *nija-mudrā*; Tib reads "the seal of the victors" (*rgyal ba'i phyag rgya,* presumably reading *jina-mudrā*). This verse is identical to GS V.33cd–34ab.

694. This verse is similar to GS V.37cd–38ab.

695. This verse is identical to GS V.39cd–40ab.

696. Reading *avidyā-tamasābhāsaṃ* (ms C). ms B (corrected) reads "the radiance of the coppery delusion" (*avidyā-tāmrasya[sā?]bhāsaṃ*); however, the main text reads *adhiṣṭhātāmrasya*[*sā*?]*bhāsaṃ*, and while there seem to be marks above the syllables *adhiṣṭhā* to indicate that they should be replaced by the *avidyā* written above, the reading is interesting. As the moment of dawn is sometimes said to be the moment of consecration, it is not implausible, though it could just as well be a mistaken interpolation by an educated scribe. As this passage focuses on the four voids and not consecrations, I feel it is better omitted. Tib reads, "having passed beyond the luminance of delusion" (*ma rig pa'i snang ba 'das nas,* **avidyābhāsam atikramya*?)

the stainless form, clear, devoid of body, speech, and mind, the character of the universal void. At sunrise is the luminance-radiance. At the moment of sunset is delusion. At moonrise is luminance.

"Having thus explained the outer teaching of the four voids,[697] now the inner enlightenment, whose character is to be introspectively known, is taught by this process: Concerning that, the process is this: first, one may
B:47a see the form of a mirage, a mass of five-colored light rays. Second, †luminance, like the rays of the moon. Third, luminance-radiance, like the rays of the sun. Fourth, the form of darkness, the luminance-imminence. Then,
(C:63a) ‡at the moment the darkness lifts, brilliance, extremely bright, the nature of perpetual luminance, the ultimate reality, the particular, may be seen with the eye of gnosis. Having thus made the universal void directly manifest, the twofold meditation[698] should be taken up by this process:

"Concerning that, the process is this: in stainless water or a flowing stream[699] a globule melts; like that, gradually, the yogin always remembers [this] formulation of the 'dissolving' [process]. The waning of breath on a mirror is gradual, thus it becomes imperceptible; the 'holistic' process is regarded in that way {by those who know the rites}.

"Now, in order to eliminate the confusion of those obsessed with verbal expressions, the synonyms of the ultimate reality [shall] be introduced: first, 'brilliance,' 'universal void,' 'buddha-gnosis,' 'adamantine-gnosis,' 'unexcelled gnosis,' 'stainless,' 'natureless,' 'radianceless,' 'selfless,' 'nirvāṇa,'
B:47b 'beingless,' 'lifeless,' 'personless,' 'impurity-less,'[700] †'unarisen,' 'unceasing,' 'syllable-less,' 'wordless,' 'unperceived,' 'unexcelled,' 'inexpressible,' 'inconceivable,' 'limitless,' 'countless,' 'beyond the senses,' 'foundationless,' 'characterless,' 'uncompounded,'[701] 'signless,' 'unwavering,' 'not a [sense] object,' 'not an object of [ordinary] consciousness,' 'undeducible,' 'imperishable,' ('unincreasing,') 'wordless,'[702] 'obscurationless,' 'the one method,' 'auspicious' (*śivaṃ*), 'peaceful' (*śāntaṃ*), 'space-like,' 'naturally pure,' 'beginning-

697. TIB reads "fourfold voidness" (*stong pa nyid rnam pa bzhi*).

698. *dvividhaṃ dhyānaṃ*; this refers to the two modes of dissolving into the brilliance/void: the holistic (*piṇḍagrāha*) and dissolving (*anubheda*).

699. *toye nirmalake nadīsarasi vā*; TIB reads "ponds or streams" (*chu bo'am lteng ka'i chu*).

700. SKT inserts *nirmalaṃ* again—though this appeared above, perhaps meant to be construed specifically with "essenceless."

701. Or, "unimagined" (*anabhisaṃskṛta*).

702. This occurs twice in both the Sanskrit and Tibetan.

less,' 'middle-less,' 'endless,' 'not going, nor coming,' 'not far,' 'not near,' 'not one, nor many,' 'hard to reach,' 'difficult to discern,' 'meditation incarnate,' 'reality body' (*dharma-kāya*), 'reality limit,' 'limit of nonattachment,'[703] 'realm of reality,' 'bodiless,'[704] 'dustless,' 'limitless accomplishment,'[705] 'secret accomplishment,' 'purity of perfection,' 'purity of view,' 'purity of cause,' 'purity of effect,' 'purity of the three worlds,' 'purity of merit,' 'purity of sin,' 'purity of defilement,' 'purity of action,' [and] 'purity of [re]birth.'

'Transcendent virtue of wisdom,' 'mother of all buddhas,' ('knower of all,') 'knower of all forms,' 'knower of all paths,' 'suchness' (*tathatā*), 'not un-suchness' (*avitathatā*),[706] 'equality,' '{composed of} undecaying stores of merit {and gnosis},' 'bearer of gnosis,'[707] 'mother of all bodhisattvas,'
†'mother of all śrāvakas,' 'mother of all pratyekabuddhas,'[708] 'mother of all B:48a
folk,'[709] 'purifier of the divine eye,' 'bestower of the divine ear,' 'knower of others' minds and recollector of previous incarnations,'[710] 'performer of measureless marvels,' [and] 'destroyer of all defilements.'[711]

Likewise, the Great Yoga Tantra, the *Esoteric Community*,[712] ‡expres- C:63b
ses the characteristics of enlightenment by the six stanzas on the spirit of

703. *asaṅga-koṭi*; following the Tibetan translators' interpretation of the meaning of this term.

704. Or, perhaps, "imageless" or "aniconic" (*amūrtiḥ*).

705. *ananta-siddhiḥ*; Tib reads this as two entries: "limitless" and "accomplishment."

706. Tib reads "unmistaken suchness" (*mi nor ba de bzhin nyid, *avitatha-tathatā*).

707. *jñāna-vāhinī*; Tib reads "just-gnosis-ness" or "only gnosis itself" (*ye shes 'ba' zhig pa nyid*).

708. Due to the limitations of the English language (or, at least, my command of it), I have translated the final term of the last three Sanskrit compounds by "mother." They are, respectively, *-jananī*, *-dhātrī*, and *-janayitrī*. The Tibetan translators decided to try to mark this difference. They used *bskyed pa*, *yum*, and *skrun pa* ("producer," "mother," "begetter"). I considered using "progenitrix" or something similar (I imagine *skrun pa* has about the same, rather cold, resonance to a Tibetan-speaking audience), but all the Sanskrit terms refer to a "mother," and English has no other word that quite captures that image.

709. Or "mother of all worlds," *sarva-loka-dhātrī*; Tib reads "benefactor of all folk/worlds" (*'jig rten thams cad 'byin pa*), perhaps reflecting a reading *sarvaloka-dātrī*?

710. *para-citta-jñāna-pūrva-nivāsānusmaraṇa-karī*; Tib reads this as two different entries "knower of others' minds" (*gzhan gyi sems shes par byed pa*) and "recollector of previous incarnations" (*sngon gyi gnas rjes su dran par byed pa*).

711. All the epithets in this paragraph are feminine in Skt, though masculine in Tib.

712. On this scripture, see chapter 1, note 272, above.

enlightenment, [which begin] "unreal..." and so on.[713] Elsewhere, in a Yoga Tantra,[714] [the Lord] said:

> Beyond [meditative] cultivation [of] the whole body
> (*sarvāṅga*),
> Free of conceptuality and [conceptual] construction,[715]
> Beyond the head [and] the drop[716]—
> That[717] is the supreme maṇḍala.[718]
>
> It is to be entered by all [living] things.
> [It is] stainless in the form and the formless.
> Known [and] brought forth—mind [is]
> A maṇḍala in the form of a circle (*maṇḍala*).
>
> Being and nonbeing—both are extremes.
> Purity and impurity—these two are extremes.
> Rejecting both extremes,
> The learned one (*paṇḍita*) does not take a stand in the middle.[719]

713. These are the "famous" six verses found at GST II.3–8.

714. *anyatrāpi yogatantre*; Tib reads "in another Great Yoga Tantra."

715. *kalpanākalpa*; Tib suggests *kalpa* and *vikalpa* (*rtog dang rnam rtog*).

716. *mātrā-bindu*; this is difficult to interpret. I believe it is referring to the visualized dissolution process, in which the practitioner, having dissolved their body into a graphic syllable (often *hūṃ*), then dissolves this from the bottom up, into the brilliance/void. Thus, the last two visible elements of the syllable-body are the upper line of the *ha* and the *anusvāra*-drop above. Thus, this verse suggests that the ultimate reality/brilliance (the subject of this chapter) is the supreme maṇḍala, which one experiences after the dissolution of the head (*mātrā*) and the drop (*bindu*).

Tib roughly supports this interpretation, reading *gug skyed thig le*. According to the *Tshig-mdzod Chen-mo*, *gug kyed* refers to the vowels of the Tibetan syllabary, *gug* being *i* and *u*, *kyed* being *e* and *o* (*gug kyed: gug ni gi gu dang zhabs kyu gnyis dang | kyed ni 'breg bu dang na no gnyis |*); cf. *Tshig mdzod chen mo*, vol. I, 357. While this does not exactly correspond to my interpretation of the Sanskrit—the usual Tibetan term for *mātrā*, in this sense, being *mgo* ("head"), it indicates that the Tibetans understood *mātrā-bindu* to refer to lexical signs; and from there, my interpretation follows.

717. *etat*; Tib reads "this" (*'di*).

718. *Guhyendutilaka*, DK, rGyud, vol. ja, f. 251b[5]. This verse is cited in *Jñānasiddhi* (141, as *Guhyendutilaka*) and PU (45, as 'explanatory tantra'). The next verse is, f. 251b[6–7].

719. This verse is *Samādhirāja Sūtra* IX.27 (SRS, 48).

And,

> The eternal, limitless verity of space,
> The great foundation of all existence,[720]
> Magnificence (*vibhūti*), glory (*śrī*), splendor (*vibha*), royalty
> (*rājā*)—
> [It is] the fulfiller of all wishes.[721]

"What [is the use of] more [such] allusive expressions (*saṃdhyā[ya]-vacana*), of introducing [further] synonyms, insofar as the foundation of the ultimate reality is well-known from the eighty-four thousand dharma teachings [of the Lord], †by difficult expressions, by words of indeterminate B:48b
gender?"

Then, the Vajra Student, having understood the twofold enlightenment process, and the twofold meditation, and, having heard the introduction of the succession of names of the ultimate reality, casting off obsession with conceptual thought, with a delighted expression and folded hands, spoke this benediction:

> "O Buddha! O Buddha!
> O Teaching of the Dharma![722]
> O Pure Reality! O Pure Thing!
> Homage be unto you, O Spirit of Enlightenment!"[723]

Then, the Vajra Teacher, looking upon him as if he were another teacher, uttered [this] verse:

> "Free of all things
> Without aggregates, elements, media, subject or object,

720. *sarvabhūta*; Tib interprets this to mean "all living things" (*sems can kun*)—which it certainly can mean. However, in this context, I think the broader meaning is appropriate.

721. This verse is from *Paramādyamantrakalpakhaṇḍa*, DK, rGyud, vol. ta, f. 206a$^{2-3}$.

722. Tib reads "the teaching of the Dharma is a great wonder" (*chos kyi bshad pa ni ngo tshar che*).

723. This verse is GST II.8.

On account of the equality of objective selflessness,
One's own mind [is] primordially unarisen, the very essence of
voidness."[724]

[And,] focusing on nonduality, he bestowed the wisdom-gnosis initiation.

By this process, the Lord, the Glorious Lion of the Śākyas,[725] was roused by all the transcendent lords with the sound of finger snapping. Emerging from the unshakeable samādhi, seating [himself] at the root of [the tree of] enlightenment, at midnight he made manifest the brilliance. Rising by
B:49a the phantasmic samādhi, he turned the wheel of Dharma for beings. †Since then, as long as the Holy Dharma has existed, [it] has passed from mentor's mouth to mentor's mouth; the enlightenment process, the secret [of] the universal purity [of] the union of the pair, has [likewise so] passed.[726]

724. The verse is the second of the six "bodhicitta" verses (found in GST II, between those numbered 3 and 4 by Matsunaga, 10). It is the one spoken by the Lord Vairocana. The translation found in Tib corresponds (with two small exceptions) to the text found in the sTog Palace Kanjur (rGyud ca, f. 9b$^{1-2}$), wherein the (four line) Sanskrit verse is rendered in six (conventional, seven-syllable) Tibetan lines; it differs from the text found in DK (rGyud ca, f. 94b$^{2-3}$), wherein it is rendered in four, nine-syllable Tibetan lines.

725. The system of the Mahāyoga Tantras has its own account of the events that transpired under the Bodhi Tree on the night of the Buddha's enlightenment. Compare the ostensible quotation from *Lalitavistara Sūtra* in PK II, v. 53f. See also Ratnākaraśānti's commentary on Nāgārjuna's *Piṇḍīkṛtasādhana* (sDe-dge bsTan-'gyur, rGyud-'grel, vol. ci, ff. 1b^{4}–2b^{4}), which gives this account in some detail, as well as the later derivation by mKhas-grub-rje (Lessing and Wayman, 34–39), for a perspective from the later Tibetan tradition.

726. Tib takes this last clause ("the secret . . . passed") to be part of the chapter title. See chapter 7, note 673, above.

8. Resolution of Doubts about the Integration of the Realm of Unlocated Nirvāṇa

The Vajra Student asked: "[My] doubts [regarding] the realization of superficial reality have been dispelled. How, then, Lord, does one, having entered ultimate reality and ǂbecome insubstantial, [subsequently] arise? Who is (C:64a)
it that here experiences true bliss?[727] What is the irreversible? What is the point of 'liberation' (*mokṣa*)? From what [is one] liberated?"[728]

The Vajra Mentor said: "Excellent, excellent, Great One! The process of arising from brilliance is not the province of those who turn away from the [sacred] tradition[729] of the transcendent lords. I will instruct you according to the Great Yoga Tantra, the *Esoteric Community*.[730] Listen with one-pointed attention!

727. Following emended text, *sat-sukham*; Tib reads *mngon du phyogs pa* (**abhimukham*); ms B reads *svasukham*. Tsongkhapa, in his RṄSG (585–86), cites an alternative translation by Chag Lotsāwa, which reads *bde ba dam pa*—upon which I base my emendation of **sat-sukhaṃ*. The proper reading of this question is difficult to determine from context, as (as far as I can tell) this question, unlike the others, is not explicitly answered. See B:64a for an alleged citation from the GST that reads *satsukham*. Also note that the perfected state (*padavaraṃ*) is referred to as *sat-sukham* by Candrakīrti, PU, 230

728. Tib interprets this last question as "on account of what is one liberated?" (*ci'i phyir na grol bar 'gyur*—which RṄSG (f. 293b[2–3]) glosses as *de ltar thar pa'am grol bar 'gyur ba'i rgyu mtshan ci'i phyir zhes rgyu mtshan 'di 'dri ba'o:* inquiring about the cause, to wit 'on account of what cause is one liberated or freed in that way?'). Tib also adds a sixth question, to wit, "Who is liberated?" (*grol ba ni su zhig lags*—which RṄSG glosses as *grol ba po ni su zhig lags zhes gang zag gi ngo bo 'dri ba'o*: inquiring about the nature of the person, to wit 'who is the liberated one?'). Given that the last section of the chapter is devoted to describing the enlightened body and enumerating the names of the enlightened one, a good case could be made for including this question, though a) I hesitate to "reconstruct" one, and b) (though inconclusive as an argument) Chag and the surviving text do not include it.

729. Skt *saṃpradāya*; Tib reads "personal precepts" (*man ngag*).

730. On this scripture, see chapter 2, note 272, above.

"Here, in the Adamantine Way, having attained the eighth [bodhisattva] stage by means of repeated cultivation of the creation stage,[731] born again and again in fortunate rebirths, one propitiates a spiritual guide until one has attained the perfection stage. [Later,] the one who has realized {the iso-
B:49b lation of} body, speech,† and mind, having attained the tenth stage, gains the phantasmic samādhi. Having realized the phantasmic samādhi, one gains the purification of the radiances [of the subtle mind]. Arising from non-radiance, having manifested the body of a buddha[732] by means of the process that leads to communion, [that practitioner] resides, adorned with all the qualities [of a buddha] by means of the adamantine samādhi. As it was said by the Lord in the *Journey to Laṅka Scripture*:[733]

> [734]Reflecting in detail by following the experiences (*viṣaya*) of the samādhis of the sequence of stages according to the regular procedure [and] through confidence [that] the triple world [is] a phantasm of their own mind, [one] gains the phantasmic samādhi. (Therefore, Mahāmati,)[735] by merely entering into the non-appearance of his own mind, the one[736] who has reached the

731. Tib reads "having learned the creation stage" (*bskyed pa'i rim pa la bslabs nas*).

732. *buddha-kāya*; Tib reads "the deeds of a buddha" (*sangs rgyas kyi bya ba, buddha-kārya*). Tsongkhapa (RṄSG, 587) notes that, although Lo-chen's translation reads *bya ba* (**kārya*), Chag's translation reads *sku* (**kāya*), which he believes "clarifies the earlier translation" (*'gyur snga ma gsal du btang ngo*).

733. On this scripture, see chapter 1, note 239, above.

734. Tib includes an introductory passage from LAS not found in Skt, which gives the subject of the sentence with which the citation begins. It reads: "Mahāmati, by the process [in which] great compassion and skill in liberative art become effortless, by [considering] the similarity of all beings to phantasms and reflections, [their] beginningless conditionality, [their] isolation {LAS reads: freedom} from inner and outer objects, [and] the non-perception of [anything] outside the mind, the ones who have settled in signless[ness] . . . ."

Note that Tib and LAS read a plural subject, though Skt reads a singular. This last specification "those who have settled in signlessness" could also be read "those who have the consecration of signlessness" (*animittādhiṣṭhānānugatāḥ, mtshan ma med pa'i byin gyis brlabs pa rnams*), depending if one wants to emphasize the original exoteric context or the esoteric context in which the passage is re-presented.

735. This phrase is not found in either LAS or ms B—again suggesting that the passage may have been interpolated into the CMP translation from another translation, rather than translated anew in this context.

736. Tib reads "the bodhisattvas who . . ." This does not concur with either ms B or LAS.

> residence (*vihāra*) of the transcendent virtue of wisdom, without birth, [ritual] action, {[or] yoga,} obtains the adamantine-body samādhi, which conforms to the body of a transcendent lord. In that way, Mahāmati, the bodhisattva acquires the body of a transcendent lord, accompanied by emanations, adorned with the [ten] powers, the [five] superknowledges, the [ten] masteries, compassion,[737] [and] liberative art, appearing in all buddhafields and the sacred precincts of the orthodox ascetics, free of that mind, mentation, and mental consciousness, engendered [by] the consequence of a [spiritual] transformation. Hence, thus, Mahāmati, the bodhisattvas, the great ones,[738] who have acquired conformity with the body of a transcendent lord, †should be free of aggregates, elements, media, mind, cause, B:50a
> condition, [ritual] action, yoga, arising, abiding, destruction, conceptions, and [mental] elaborations.[739]

(Thus,) until the one[740] who is equipoised in the phantasmic samādhi attains realization of ultimate reality, [that one is] 'reversible.' Why? [Because] the three radiances [are] not purified.[741] As long as there exist conscious intentions (*vijñāna-saṃkalpa*), there is a linked continuity (*prabandha*) of the vestiges of defilement. From the linked continuity of defilement, [there is] rebirth. The state of purity is free of all intellection.[742] As is said in the {Great} Yoga Tantra, the (*Glorious*) *Supreme Prime*:[743]‡ C:64b

737. LAS and Tib read "caring and compassion" (*kṛpā-karuṇa, snying brtse ba dang snying rje*).

738. LAS adds "who follow the Mind Only" (*cittamātrānusāribhiḥ*). Tib includes this, but renders it in the optative, implying "should follow the Mind Only" (*sems tsam gyi rjes su 'brang bar bya'o*).

739. This passage may be found in LAS (Nanjio, ed.), 42–43; or LAS (Vaidya, ed.), 19–20.

740. Tib reads "those who are."

741. Tib reads "Why?' As long as the three luminances are not purified, there are conscious intentions," (*de ci'i phyir zhe na | ji srid du snang ba gsum rnam par dag par ma gyur pa de srid du ni rnam par shes pa'i kun du rtog pa'o |*).

742. Tib reads "that which is free of other minds is the state of purity" (*gang sems gzhan dag dang bral ba de ni rnam par dag pa'i gnas te |*).

743. *Śrī-paramādya-mahāyoga-tantra, dpal mchog dang po zhes bya ba'i rnal 'byor gyi rgyud* [*sic*]. A Sanskrit text of this work is not available, to my knowledge. A Tibetan translation

The state of purified passion—that is the state of the bodhisattva.
The state of purified hatred—that is the state of the bodhisattva.
The state of purified ignorance—that is the state of the bodhisattva.[744]

It was also stated by Kambalācāryapāda[745] in [his work, the] *Inner Sādhana*:[746]

[According to tradition,][747] that made of sound is coarse;
That made of intellection is subtle.
That which is free of intellection
Is the supreme state of the yogins.

"By this reasoning, whoever has obtained {the personal instruction on} [reaching] the brilliance by the enlightenment process, because their body, speech, and mind [are] stainless in nature [and] the universal void, [that one has] purified the three consciousnesses [and has] the nature of the transcendent virtue of wisdom—without intellection, {not}[748] silently, [being]
B:50b this realm of nirvāṇa, bodiless, †difficult to contact, free of action (*karma*) and [re]birth, brighter even than the light of the sun, moon, [and] wishing gems.[749]

(by Śraddhākaravarman and Rin-chen bZang-po) may be found at: DK, rGyud, vol. ta, 150b[1]–173a[1] (Tōh. 487).

744. Nothing precisely corresponding to this passage occurs in the current redactions of this tantra, though similar passages can be found at DK, rGyud, vol. ta, 151a[3] and 161a[5–6]. This verse does occur in the *Vajramaṇḍalālaṃkāra*, DK, rGyud, vol. tha, 4a[3–4].

745. Tib reads "the vajra teacher [vajrācārya] Kambala" (*rdo rje slob dpon kamba la*).

746. *Adhyātmasādhana, Nang gi bdag nyid sgrub thabs.* This verse is also cited in SS, p. 65. It is also cited (in a slightly different form) by Munidatta in his commentary on the *Caryāgīti* (CGKV), wherein it is attributed to "scripture" (*āgama*)—see Kværne, *Anthology of Buddhist Tantric Songs*, 148. Though this verse is thus cited in several places in the surviving literature, the work of which it allegedly derives has not come down to us.

747. Literally, "they [traditionally] state" (*prāhuḥ*).

748. I include this reluctantly: both mss read *na tūṣṇīṃ*; though Tib reads "silently" (*smra ba med pa*).

749. Literally, "the light-nature of sun, moon, and wishing gems is not brighter [than

"From that [brightness],[750] there is the arising of the darkness-radiance, the luminance-imminence.[751] From the luminance-imminence, there is the arising of the luminance-radiance, [whose] nature is the warmth[752] of the radiance of the bright sun's rays. From that, there is the arising of the pervasive wisdom-gnosis, [whose] nature is the cool of the radiance of the bright moon's rays.[753] [The Lord] said in the (*Glorious*) *Supreme Prime*[754] also:

> From space, [comes] that born [from] space—
> The whole of space[755] [is] the great sky.[756]

Hence, luminance is the unification of the four voids, like a multitude (*puñja*); [it has] the form of the space-illuminating [sun], shining in all world-realms; borne by the subtle element [air], [it has] the form of a shadow; [it has] the unsplittable, indivisible nature of the adamantine body—imperishable, free of impurity (*anāsrava*), free of the vestiges of all defilements, [with] mastery [of others] at will.[757] Like a fish [leaping] out

---

s/he]." Tib reads "bright like the nature of the light of sun, moon, fire, and wishing gems" (*nyi ma dang | zla ba dang | me dang | nor bu'i 'od kyis ngo bo nyid bzhin du gsal ba'o |*). Though I think this is a scribal error for *nyi ma dang | zla ba dang | yid bzhin nor bu'i 'od kyi ngo bo nyid shin tu gsal ba'o |*.

750. "Brightness" is specified in ms C, but is not found in ms A or Tib. Thus, I assume it is an interpolated clarification.

751. Tib reads "from that, there is the luminance of darkness, [i.e.] the luminance-imminence, and so on" (*de las mun pa'i snang ba ste snang ba nye bar thob pa la sogs par 'gyur ro*—presumably reading **tasmāt tāmasābhāsālokopalabdhādayo bhavati*).

752. *ātapaḥ*; a warmth which is especially associated with the sun.

753. Tib reads "there is the arising of the wisdom-gnosis, pervaded by the radiance of the nature of the cool rays of the bright moon" (*gsal ba zla ba'i 'od zer bsil ba'i ngo bo nyid kyi snang bas khyab pa shes rab kyi ye shes 'byung bar 'gyur ro*)—suggesting a reading of **svaccha-candra-raśmi-śītala-svabhāvābhāsa-vyāpta-prajñā-jñānodaya bhavati.*

754. See chapter 8, note 743, above.

755. *sarvākāśa*; Tib reads "universal void" (*thams cad stong pa, *sarvaśūnya*).

756. This verse does not appear in the *Paramādya Tantra* as we have it. It does, however, appear in STTS (Horiuchi, ed., vol. 2, p. 114). Thanks to Harunaga Isaacson for this information.

757. *icchā-vaśitā-prāpta*; or "having obtained mastery over desire?" This is not one of the usual ten "masteries" of a bodhisattva.

Tib renders this passage rather differently. It has: "Therefore, the host of luminances whose one foundation is voidness illuminates all world-realms like the sun. Together with

of water [or one] awakened [from] sleep,[758] the proper form of the body of supreme joy is created. Because it is the nature of mind and body (*nāma-rūpa*) [it is called] 'Mahāvajradhara.'[759] Because it is liberated from the bonds of the life-cycle, [it is] called 'liberation.'

"Clarifying this very point, [Padmavajra] said in the *Secret Accomplishment*:[760]

> Reality is to be known through personal experience.
> B:51a It cannot be communicated by another.†
> It is perceptible by means of the cultivation of devotion.[761]
> It is not perceptible by any other means.[762]

---

the subtle element, like a shadow, it has the nature of an unsplittable, indestructible vajra body; since it is free of transmigration and free of impurity—it is free of all the vestiges of the defilements; [it has] attained mastery by mere wish." (*de bas na stong pa nyid gzhi* [*sic* for *bzhi*] *gcig tu gyur pa'i snang ba'i tshogs nam mkha' snang byed lta bus 'jig rten gyi khams thams cad snang bar byas te | khams phra ba dang lhan cig tu grib ma dang 'dra bar gcad du med pa dang gzhig tu med pa'i rdo rje'i sku'i ngo bo nyid 'pho ba med cing zag pa med pas nyon mongs pa'i bag chags thams cad las rnam par grol ba 'dod pa tsam gyis dbang du gyur pa thob pa*).

758. Tib reads "[one] quickly wakened or roused [from] sleep" (*myur bar gnyid log cing sad pa*).

759. *yannāmarūpātmako mahāvajradhara iti*; Tib reads "the name of that which has the nature of form is 'Mahāvajradhara'" (*gzugs kyi bdag nyid can gyi ming ni rdo rje 'chang chen po zhes bya'o*). Tsongkhapa notes a variant translation by Chag Lotsāwa: "that which has the nature of mind and matter is 'Mahāvajradhara' (*gang ming dang gzugs kyi bdag nyid can rdo rje 'chang chen po*). As I have noted elsewhere (Wedemeyer, "Tantalising Traces"), neither Tibetan translation adequately conveys the Sanskrit idiom.

760. *Śrī-guhya-siddhi* (*dpal gsang ba grub pa*) by Padmavajra (slob dpon padma badzra). The full title of this work is *Sakala-tantra-sadbhāva-sañcodanī-śrīguhyasiddhi-nāma,* in Tibetan translation *rGyud ma lus pa'i don nges par skul bar byed pa dpal gsang ba grub pa zhes bya ba*, or *The Invoker of the Definitive Meaning of All Tantras called "The Glorious Secret Accomplishment."* An edition of this work in Sanskrit (and in a Tibetan translation by Kṛṣṇapaṇḍita and Tshul-khrims rGyal-ba) may be found in: S. Rinpoche and V. Dwivedi, eds., *Guhyādi-aṣṭasiddhi-saṃgraha*. An English translation and study of this important work is in progress by Ronald M. Davidson.

761. *bhakti-bhāvanayā*; Given the feminine, singular instrumental ending, I have construed this compound as a *tatpuruṣa* (though I suppose it could also be rendered as a *karmadhāraya*, i.e., "the cultivation which is devotion"). Both Tibetan translator teams (of CMP and GS: Śraddhākaravarman/Rin-bzang and Kṛṣṇapaṇḍita/Tshul-rgyal, respectively) construed it as a *dvandva*, i.e., "devotion and [meditative] cultivation" (reading *mos dang bsgoms pas* and *gus dang bsgom pas*, respectively).

762. Following Skt and the Kṛṣṇapaṇḍita/Tshul-rgyal translation; Śraddhākaravarman/Rin-bzang read "that pledge is not otherwise" (*dam tshig de ni gzhan du min*).

Understanding reality, thereafter[763]
Having undertaken the cultivation of devotion day and night,
There [is] the state of supreme nirvāṇa,
The unexcelled peace.

Then, through the force of that devotion,
The power of [meditative] cultivation is produced.[764]
There, the body is created
A supreme born from indescribable joy.

Come forth in the space of an instant,[765]
[It] radiates and contracts;
Illuminating this entire three[fold] world,[766]
Both animate and inanimate [things].

†Through the force of the power of [meditative] cultivation,[767] (C:65a)
[It is] auspicious (*śiva*),[768] constituted of critical wisdom and
liberative art,
Free of all defilements,

763. Following Skt and the Kṛṣṇapaṇḍita/Tshul-rgyal translation; Śraddhākaravarman/Rin-bzang read "abandoning reality [and] non-reality" (*de nyid de nyid min spangs te*).

764. Tib reads "That which is produced by the power of meditative cultivation | by the force of devotion [to] that and that" (*de dang de mos pa yi mthus | bsgoms pa'i stobs kyis gang sprul pa |*). Kṛṣṇapaṇḍita/Tshul-rgyal read "there, that which is produced by the very power of devotion and | by the power of meditative" (*der ni gus pa'i stobs nyid dang | bsgoms pa'i stobs kyis gang sprul pa |*).

765. *dhagity-ākāra-saṃbhūtaṃ*; ms C has an interesting reading for this line—evidently a later interpolation. It reads "come forth [from] the instantaneous gnosis" (*jhaṭiti-jñāna-saṃbhūtaṃ*). One wonders if this is an attempt by later "subitists" to read their doctrines back into earlier, gradualist sources. One may compare in this regard the subitist variant reading in the *Jñānasiddhi* (see Bhattacharyya, *Two Vajrayāna Works*, 81). Incidentally, David Snellgrove refers to this passage, basing his argument on the subitist reading; in so doing he (in my opinion) too easily prefers the Tibetan version, which supports the subitist reading (see *Indo-Tibetan Buddhism*, vol. I, 152–53, n. 67).

766. Skt *bhūrbhuvaḥsvaḥ*; Tib *khams gsum*. See chapter 2, note 281, above.

767. Both Tibetan texts have similar, though slightly variant, readings here. Tib reads "through the force of the reality of meditation" (*bsgom pa'i de nyid mthu yis ni*), suggesting *bhāvanā-tattva-samārthyāt*; Kṛṣṇapaṇḍita/Tshul-rgyal read "through the power of meditation on reality" (*de nyid bsgoms pa'i stobs kyis ni*), suggesting *tattva-bhāvanā-sāmarthyāt*.

768. The Tibetan translations render this as "peace" (*zhi ba*).

Adorned with all the marks [of a buddha],
Come forth from the gnosis of voidness,
Peerless, the supremely auspicious,[769]
Endowed with the best of all forms,
Without subject or object,
Gnosis, phantasmic, pure,
Clear, stainless in nature,
Transcending sound, smell, taste,
[And] likewise beyond touch.

The supreme is seen by the one
In samādhi, with the eye of gnosis—
Like phantasm [or] a shadow, divine
With the shape of a divinity.[770]

By successive pulsations of {the fire of} gnosis,
[Are created] bodies, various [and] multiple.
A body, appearing like Indra's [rain]bow,
Is obtained by the one who cultivates Reality.

By the force of the yoga of [meditative] cultivation,
And from preserving the pledges,
Such a form will be attained—
Inexpressible even by the victors.

Where there is no body, nor speech and mind, [is]
The state, omnipresent and supreme.[771]

769. GS here reads "the supreme state" (*paramaṃ padam*), though this may be the result of dittography.

770. Following SKT and Rin-bzang's CMP translation; GS reads "endowed with all saṃskāra" (*sarvasaṃskāra-saṃyutam*), while the Kṛṣṇapaṇḍita/Tshul-rgyal translation reads "endowed with good/divine saṃskāra (*'du byed bzang po dang ldan pa*, **divya-saṃskāra-saṃyutam*).

771. TIB reads "Where the supreme that is free of body, speech, and mind, which form the basis of avarice" (*gang du ser sna'i gnas gyur pa'i | lus ngag yid dang bral ba'i mchog |*). Presumably, the translator had a text more similar to the *textus receptus* (which reads the [metrically better] *yatra kāyo na vākcittaṃ sthānaṃ yat sarvagaṃ param |*), and read *mātsarya* for *yatsarva*.

There, by the power of the [sacred] tradition,[772]
The form of it becomes manifest.

Aho! Utter marvel!
Aho! Great peace beyond the senses!
Aho! Supreme profundity—† B:51b
The highest state of buddhahood![773]

"{All} the Transcendent Lords describe this very process of emergence in the Great Yoga Tantra, the *Glorious Esoteric Community*:[774]

Aho! Vajra! Aho! Vajra!
Aho! Vajra teaching!
Where there is no body, speech, and mind
There the [divine] form manifests.[775]

[It is] also described by the Venerable Master [Nāgārjuna thus]:

There is no hollow in your body;
Nor yet flesh, bone, or blood.
Like Indra's [rain]bow in space,
You display your body.

There is no illness in [your] body, nor impurity,
Nor yet the occurrence of hunger and thirst.
In order to conform with the world, you
Display [such] worldly activities.[776]

772. Tib reads "by the power of the authentic teaching" (*yang dag bstan dbang gis*), presumably reading **sampradeśa* or **samprakāśa* in place of *sampradāya*.

773. GS reads "the miracle of the spirit of enlightenment" (*bodhicitta-vikurvaṇam, byang chub sems kyi rnam 'phrul*).

Cited here are GS III.71–82, from the chapter entitled "The Teaching about Enlightenment" (*abhisambodhi-nirdeśa*).

774. On this scripture, see chapter 2, note 272, above.

775. This is GST XVII.38 (see Matsunaga, 102; Bhattacharyya, 135).

776. This is PK III.2–3. It is also identical to *Niraupamyastava*, vv. 18–19 (see CS[Tucci] 318, and CS[Patel] 319).

[The Lord] also says in the *Compendium of {All} Rituals*:[777]

> Having seized the pure heart,[778]
> [Perform] the manifestation of the adamantine body.
> Firm, {solid,} without hollow,
> One obtains the adamantine body.

The body of a transcendent lord is also described by Candraprabhakumāra in the *King of Samādhi Scripture*:[779]

> O Space-like, immaculate (*viraja*), possessing the best of forms,
> Bodiless,[780] characteristic-less, child of the wise,
> Profound ocean of virtues, compassionate,
> Lay your hand on my head, O incomparable one![781]

[Subhūti] also said in the *Noble Eight-Thousand (-Line Transcendent Virtue of Wisdom) [Scripture]*:[782]

> (Subhūti said, 'O Divine Ones!) I declare nirvāṇa to be like a
> B:52a phantasm, like a dream. †Even were there another thing greater than nirvāṇa, it too I would declare to be like a phantasm, like a dream.'[783]

777. *Sarva-kalpa-samuccaya, rTog pa kun las btus pa*; this refers to a section of the *Vajraśekhara Tantra*, wherein it may be found at DK, rGyud, vol. nya, f. 147b$^{4-5}$. This scripture was translated into Tibetan by Karmavajra and gZhon-nu tshul-khrims as *gSang ba rnal 'byor chen po'i rgyud rdo rje rtse mo*: DK, rGyud, vol. nya, ff. 142b^{1}–274a^{5} (Tōh. 480).

778. *hṛdaya*; TIB reads "mind" (*sems*).

779. *Samādhi-rāja-sūtra, Ting nge 'dzin rgyal po'i mdo*. An edited Sanskrit text of this sūtra can be found at: P. L. Vaidya, ed., *Samādhirājasūtra*. A Tibetan translation of this scripture (by Śilendrabodhi and Dharmatāśīla) can be found at: DK, mDo, vol. da, ff. 1b^{1}–170b^{7} (Tōh. 127).

780. *aśarīra*—this term connotes divinity (in Mīmāṃsa thought), as well as ascetic renunciation.

781. This verse occurs in only some extant versions of this scripture, in chapter 10, "Entering the City" (see Vaidya, ed., 313). The verse as it appears has an unmetrical final line, reading: *khasamā virajā vararūpadharā aśarīra alakṣaṇa prajñasūtā | sugambhīraguṇodadhi kāruṇikā dada mūrdhni pāṇi apratimā ||*. See also DK, mDo, vol. da, 29a$^{5-6}$.

782. On this scripture, see chapter 5, note 615, above.

783. This passage is a paraphrase of that found at ASPP, 20, which reads "Subhūti said,

Now, its distinctive qualities [are these]: It is neither material nor immaterial, neither true nor false. Thus, [it is] neither real nor even unreal, neither destructible nor permanent. [It] neither has an appearance nor does not; it is neither right (*dharma*) ‡nor wrong. It is neither defiled nor pure. C:65b
It is neither saṃsāra nor nirvāṇa. Neither permanent nor impermanent. Neither self nor not-self, nor [is it] other than the self.[784] It is neither inside nor outside. It is neither worldly nor transcendent. It is neither dual nor nondual.

Some of the synonyms of this completely perfected {adamantine} body of communion {itself}, [shall be] introduced: body of the great knowledge person (*mahāvidyā-puruṣa*), established in the procedure of two realities, constituted of prototypical brilliance, constituted of critical wisdom and liberative art, constituted of the three worlds, constituted of the three times,[785] constituted of the three ways, constituted of the three maṇḍalas, constituted of all clans; likewise, true person, pinnacle people,[786] great person, †preeminent person,[787] brave person, heroic person,[788] person to be B:52b
tamed,[789] taming person, supreme person, charioteer of people, person-lion, space-person, universal (person),[790] pure person.

Thus, it is called: one who has crossed the ocean of the life-cycle

---

'even nirvāṇa, O Divine Ones, I declare [to be] like phantasm, like a dream. What need to mention other things?' Those divine ones said, 'Even nirvāṇa, Noble Subhūti, you declare to be like phantasm, like a dream?' The Venerable Subhūti said, 'If there were, O Divine Ones, another thing greater than nirvāṇa, that too I would declare to be like a phantasm, like a dream.'" See also DK, brGyad sTong, vol. ka, $23a^{5-6}$.

784. Tib omits "nor not-self"; ms C omits "nor [is it] other than the self."

785. ms B and Tib; ms C reads "constituted of the three bodies" (*trikāyātmakaḥ, *sku gsum gyi bdag nyid can*).

786. *agrapuruṣa*; Tib renders this as *skyes bu mchog*—making it indistinguishable from *puruṣottama*, below.

787. *puruṣa-nāga;* Tib suggests "well born person" (*skyes bu cang shes, *ājāneya-puruṣa*).

788. "brave person, heroic person" (*puruṣa-śūra* and *puruṣa-vīra*): these terms are similar, each ending in a term for a "hero." Tib has rendered them as "heroic person, steadfast person" (*skyes bu dpa' bo dang | skyes bu brtan po*).

789. Tib reads "tame person" (*skyes bu 'dul ba*), rather than the expected *skyes bu 'dul bya.*

790. *sarvātmaka*; literally, "constituted of all." Tib reads "person" here, though both Sanskrit versions omit it. Or, rather, each contains it once: ms C construes it with "universal," ms B with "pure."

(*saṃsāra*),[791] one who has reached the [further] shore, one who has obtained beatitude,[792] one who has obtained fearlessness, one who has thrown down [all] obstacles,[793] one who has removed the thorn, one without fabrications, monk, saint, one who has destroyed the impurities, owner of nothing,[794] wandering ascetic (*śramaṇa*), priest (*brāhmaṇa*), warrior (*kṣatriya*), child of the buddhas, without defilement, powerful, one with a well-liberated mind, one with well-liberated critical wisdom, well born,[795] great elephant, one who has done what ought to be done, one who has done what is to be done, one who has laid down the burden, one who has achieved the aim, one whose connection with existence has dissolved, one whose mind is liberated through perfect knowledge,[796] one who has power over all minds, one who has attained the supreme transcendent virtue, one who stands on the further shore of the life-cycle, gnosis-body, self-created.

Defining this very adamantine samādhi, the Lord said in the *Hero's March (Samādhi) Scripture*:[797]

> Those who follow the buddha-experience (*buddha-viṣaya*) [are] true people. [They] who have attained this hero's march samādhi [are] masters of their own gnosis.[798] I do not call that one "a
> B:53a bodhisattva," who has not attained †this samādhi.[799] I do not call that one "a bodhisattva who has attained superknowledge," who

791. MS C *tīrṇa-saṃsāra-sāgara*; MS B reads *tīrṇa-pāragaḥ*, "one who goes across, who has crossed," which seems a bit redundant. TIB reads "one who has forded saṃsāra."

792. *kṣema-prāpta*; Or, perhaps in this context, "one who has come home."

793. TIB reads "ablaze with transcendent virtues" (*pha rol tu 'gro bas 'bar ba*).

794. *niṣkiñcana*, i.e., one who has voluntarily given up all possessions.

795. *ājāneyaḥ*; TIB renders this (not atypically) as "omniscient one" (*kun shes pa*), cf. BHSD, 90.

796. *samyagājñā-suvimuktacitta*; TIB reads "one whose mind is liberated through the authentic word/command" (*yang dag pa'i bkas sems rnam par grol ba*).

797. On this scripture, see chapter 1, note 243, above.

798. *svajñāna-vaśavartinaḥ*; TIB reads "masters of independent gnosis" (*rang dbang gi ye shes la dbang bgyid pa, *svavaśa-jñāna-vaśavartinaḥ*).

799. Literally, "because [that one] has not attained this samādhi." TIB renders this slightly differently: "That bodhisattva who has not attained this hero's march samādhi, I do not call a 'bodhisattva.'" This pattern continues throughout this passage, i.e., it renders *bodhisattva* with the direct object, rather than the predicate: "That bodhisattva who has not attained this hero's march samādhi, I do not call 'one who has attained superknowledge,'" etc.

has not attained this samādhi.[800] I do not call that one "a bodhisattva who has perfected generosity, ethics, tolerance, heroism, meditation, and critical wisdom,"[801] who has not attained this samādhi. I do not call that one an "erudite bodhisattva blessed with eloquence,"[802] who has not attained this samādhi. Therefore, Noble One,[803] the bodhisattva, {the great one,} who wants to follow all paths of emancipation[804] should ‡learn this hero's (C:66a) march samādhi.[805]"

800. Tib inserts here "That bodhisattva who has not attained this hero's march samādhi, I do not call a 'purified one.'"

801. Tib adds the seventh transcendent virtue, "liberative art" (*thabs, upāya*), to this list of six.

802. Tib devotes a separate sentence to each "learned" and "eloquent."

803. Tib reads "Noble Ones" (*rigs kyi bu dag*).

804. Tib adds "because [they are] free of vanity" (*rlom sems thams cad med pa'i phyir*).

805. This passage may be found in DK, mDo, vol. da, ff. 279b[4]–280a[3]. The corresponding passage may be found in Boin-Webb's English translation of Lamotte's French translation, p. 163.

9. *Resolution of Doubts about the Integration of the Bodhisattva*[806] *Practice with Elaboration, the Enlightenment of the Reality-Source, According to the Method of the "Union of All Buddhas: Magical Supreme Bliss of the Ḍākiṇīs"*[807]

The Vajra Student asked, "How shall the yogin—who, from learning and reflection, has discriminating understanding of the realities of all the stages,[808] who has been given the permission by the mentor, who wants to bring forth the blessing of omniscience [and] is exerting himself[809] [to that end]—persevere in the causal condition? How shall he conduct [himself]?[810] How shall he [meditatively] cultivate [himself]? How shall he practice the practices of [spiritual] discipline (*vrata-caryā*)? †[Please] explain, O Lord and Teacher, Vajra Mentor!" B:53b

The Vajra Mentor replied, "Excellent, excellent, O Great One! You inquire in order to dispel the doubts of those who have obtained the distinctive cause, who are ablaze with heroism, who are indifferent towards [their own] body and life, who, having transformed their own body,[811] want

806. Tib adds "great spiritual hero" (*sems dpa' chen po, mahāsattva*).

807. That is, the *Sarvabuddhasamāyoga-ḍākinījālasaṃvara* (SBS: Tōh. 366); on this scripture, see chapter 2, note 344, above.

808. *sakala-krama*; Tib reads "the stages together with their fruits" (*'bras bu dang bcas pa'i rim pas, *saphala-krama*).

809. *ghaṭamāna*; throughout the following discussion (in which this term plays an important role, consistently in contrast to the *parinispanna*), Tib renders this term as *slob pa* (usually *śikṣamāṇa*), "learning" rather than "exerting."

810. This question is missing in Tib. In Skt (ms B), the previous query is crossed out.

811. Skt reads *svarūpa-parāvṛttyā*; Tib reads "having turned away from grasping at their form" (*rang gi gzugs su 'dzin pa las yongs su log nas, *svarūpa-dhāra-parāvṛttyā*).

to perfect the result—the eight superhuman powers[812]—here in this very life. ([This is] excellent, excellent.) Hence, having put aside clinging to [material] things, out of desire for liberation, listen! [I will] describe to you the purification of [meditative] cultivation and the purification of practice,[813] in order.

"Now, [as] the two realities [are] nondual, cause and effect [are] also nondual. [As] cause and effect are nondual, that to be attained and the attainer[814] are also nondual. [As] that to be attained and the attainer [are] nondual, that to be [meditatively] cultivated and the cultivator [are] also nondual. [As] those [are] nondual,[815] neither are a practitioner (*sādhaka*), a practice (*sādhana*), or its result (*sādhya*) evident. Since those are not [truly] evident, who here cultivates [meditation]? Who [is it] that practices the practices? Upon analysis, there is no difference between the one exerting [himself in practice] and the perfected one. As it has been said:

> Nirvāṇa in the present life[816] [and]
> Having done what ought to be done[817] [are] that very [thing].[818]

812. *aṣṭaguṇaiśvarya, yon tan gyi dbang phyug brgyad*; according to M-W (234, citing *Sarvadarśana-saṃgraha*), these are: the power of becoming small (*aṇiman*), the power of becoming lightweight (*laghiman*), the power of becoming large (*mahiman*), power of attaining things (*prāpti*), irresistible will (*prākāmya*), power of domination (*vaśitva*), power of supremacy (*īśitva*), and the power of suppressing desire (*kāmāvasāyitva*).

813. Tib reads "the pure meditation and the pure practices of those who desire liberation" (*thar pa 'dod pa rnams kyi sgom pa rnam par dag pa dang | spyod pa rnam par dag pa*).

814. *prāpya-prāpaka*; Tib reads "attainment and the to-be-attained" (*thob pa dang thob par bya ba).*

815. Here, Tib switches from rendering the locative absolute expressions in the instrumental (i.e., *gnyis su med pas*), and renders it instead in the locative (i.e., *gnyis su med pa la*), suggesting a translation of "in nonduality."

816. Skt *dṛṣṭe dharme,* Tib *mthong ba'i chos.* On this term, Cristina Anna Scherrer-Schaub notes "l'expression *dṛṣṭa-dharma* ou *dṛṣṭo dharmo* (pāli, diṭṭadhammo ou diṭṭo dhammo), au sens de «vie présente» (synonyme, au locatif, de *ihaiva janmani . . .*), s'oppose dès les textes anciens à l'expression *saṃparāya* (pāli, saṃparāya) désignant la «vie future»." See Scherrer-Schaub, *Yuktiṣaṣṭikāvṛtti*, p. 170, n. 216.

817. *kṛta-kṛtya; bya ba byas pa*; an old Buddhist epithet for a saint (*arhat*). It is found above in the list of synonyms of the ultimate reality (B:52b).

818. This verse is identical to *Yuktiṣaṣṭikā* 11ab. This important work of Nāgārjuna has not survived in its original Sanskrit. An edition and French translation of the Tibetan translation are contained in: Scherrer-Schaub, *Yuktiṣaṣṭikāvṛtti.* This half-verse may be found in

†Thus, distinguishing [them based upon their] context, cause and effect appear in the world. Otherwise, there would be the faulty [logical] consequence of [things being] causeless. Hence, in the context of exerting [oneself in practice], a cultivator, [meditative] cultivation, and that to be cultivated, a practitioner, a practice, and its result, [and] practices too, are evident. [Of this] there is no doubt.[819] Here, the practitioner [is] superficial reality; the practice [is] ultimate reality. [What they] effect [is] the nondual gnosis. Hence, the thorough knowledge [that] reconciles [the duality] of cause and effect is here (explained as) [meditative] cultivation. As it was said in the *Universal Secret Tantra*:[820] B:54a

One should consider
Cause sealed by effect,
[And] effect sealed by cause, otherwise,
Accomplishments (*siddhi*) will not arise in ten million æons.[821]

"{Clarifying also} the purification of practice, {[it is] said}: 'When the nondual gnosis has been realized,[822] the periods of meditative equipoise and non-equipoise also become nondual. Those being nondual, who performs

---

Scherrer-Schaub's edition and translation on p. 46 (Tibetan) and p. 170 (French). See also Loizzo, et al., *Nāgārjuna's Reason Sixty*, 120, 157, 221, 282. According to Candrakīrti's commentary on this verse, the "very thing" spoken of here is the attainment of non-objectifying gnosis (*chos thams cad mi dmigs pa'i ye shes*). This is consonant with the preceding discussion in the CMP which addresses the nonduality—or non-evidence/non-objectification—of things like doer, deed, and so on.

819. The gradualism implicit in this passage is noteworthy.

Tib reads "one should have no doubt whether or not the practices of a cultivator, [meditative] cultivation, and that to be cultivated, a practitioner, a practice, and its result exist," or alternatively, "one should have no doubt about whether or not a cultivator, [meditative] cultivation, and that to be cultivated, a practitioner, a practice, and practices of its result exist" (*sgom pa po dang | sgom pa dang | sgom par bya ba dang | grub pa po dang | sgrub pa dang | bsgrub par bya ba'i spyod pa rnams kyang yod do zhes pa'am | med do zhes som nyir mi bya*). N and P specify "distinctive practices" (*khyad par gyi spyod pa*).

820. On this scripture, see chapter 2, note 337, above.

821. This verse does not seem to occur in the extant Tibetan translation of the work to which it is here attributed. This verse is, however, identical to that found in GSUT (cf. Matsunaga, ed., XVIII.79; Bhattacharyya, ed., 157; Bagchi, ed., XVIII.78).

822. *advaya-jñāne gate*; Tib specifies (gerund, not locative absolute) "having realized" (*rtogs nas*; usually, *adhigamya*).

practices? There being no actor, there too is no action,' [this is] common knowledge.[823] However, [the fact that] 'without the practices of [spiritual] discipline (*vrata-caryā*), [one] cannot destroy the vestiges of beginning-
C:66b less defilement,' is well known both in the world and in the scriptural dis-
B:54b courses.† As it is said‡ in the {*Glorious*} (*Esoteric*) *Community* (*Tantra*):[824]

> Vajrasattva, the Great King,
> Should be roused again and again.[825]

So, too, is it said in the *Secret Accomplishment*:[826]

> Giving up stretching your legs
> And relinquishing the hordes of the life-cycle,
> The foremost Vajrasattva[827] should be cultivated (*sādhayet*)
> Always with a zealously active mind,[828]
>
> Forsaking with sincere effort
> Anxiety, sloth, torpor, and the like—
> Otherwise, there could never be success (*siddhi*),
> Even in a billion æons.[829]

"Hence, clearing up[830] the stains of the vestiges of beginningless defilement by means of equipoise in the signless samādhi, doing away with

823. Literally, this passage runs: "'Due to such unreality of the actor, there is also the unreality of the action,' this is certain in the world."

824. On this scripture, see chapter 2, note 272, above.

825. GST, Ch. 14 (Matsunaga, ed., XIV.40ab; Bhattacharyya, ed., p.87; Bagchi, ed., XIV.40ab), reading *vajrasattvo mahārājaś codanīyo muhurmuhuḥ* (Bhattacharyya reads *mahārājo*).

826. On this work, see chapter 8, note 760, above.

827. *vajrasattvāgraṃ, rdo rje sems dpa' mchog*; C reads "that called 'Vajrasattva'" (*vajrasattvākhyāṃ*); the text of the Sarnath edition of the *Guhyasiddhi* reads "the command of Vajrasattva" (*vajrasattvājñāṃ*).

828. *udyukta-mānasaḥ, brtson dang ldan yid kyis*; the text of the Sarnath edition of the *Guhyasiddhi* reads "with a liberated mind" (*nirmukta-mānasaḥ*).

829. Literally, "in a hundred ten-millions of æons" (*kalpa-koṭi-śata*). The verses here cited are GS VI.2–3.

830. Skt *apahāya*; Tib reads "abandoning" (*spangs nas*).

thoughts of 'I will or will not perform the practices,'[831] and conquering the eight worldly concerns,[832] the one who seeks to secure the effortless result should practice according to [what is] said in the practices of yoga.[833] Therefore, I will expound the practices of [spiritual] discipline[834] by the grace of the mentor, insofar as [I am] able.

"First of all, the Lord, in the condition of a bodhisattva in his last existence,[835] having surveyed the continent [on which he was to be born] and so on,[836] having descended from residence [in] Tuṣita [Heaven], and displayed the fourfold †procedure—'genealogy,'[837] and so on—having manifested B:55a

831. Tib reads "abandoning mental constructions (**manaskāra*) such as "when [I] practice the practices, I practice' or "I do not practice" (*spyod pa spyad na spyod do zhe'am mi spyod do zhes bya ba'i yid la byed pa spangs nas*).

832. Skt *aṣṭa-loka-dharma*, Tib *'jig rten chos brgyad*; these have been cited before (at the end of chapter 3), but not by this name. They are seeking and avoiding (respectively) gain/loss, fame/infamy, praise/blame, and pleasure/pain.

833. *yoga-caryā*; Both B and C read very clearly a locative singular here. The reference, if there is a specific one, is unclear to me.

834. *vrata-caryā*; Tib reads "the authentic practices" (*yang dag par gyur pa'i spyod pa*).

835. *carama-bhavika-bodhisattvāvasthāyāṃ*; Tib reads "in the condition of a bodhisattva performing practices (*spyod pa mdzad pa'i spyod pa byang chub sems dpa' gnas skabs su*; **caryā-cārika-bodhisattvāvasthāyāṃ*).

836. This would refer to the tradition that the future buddha considers from Tuṣita the conditions of his final birth; the continent (*Jambudvīpa*), etc. The Tibetan tradition refers to them as the "five visions" (*gzigs pa rnam pa lnga*): buddhas always check first, before taking their final birth, to ascertain that the place (*yul*), caste (*rigs*), lineage (*rus*), mother (*yum*), and time (*dus*) of their birth are proper. The *Lalitavistara Sūtra* refers to four things the future buddha considers: time, land, country, and family; it discusses the proper mother separately, but immediately after (see, e.g., the English translation of this scripture: Gwendolyn Bays, trans., *The Voice of the Buddha*, vol. I, 36–49).

837. These four procedures (Skt *catur-vidha-nyāya*, Tib *tshul rnam pa bzhi*) are explained in the *Pradīpoddyotana* of Candrakīrti (PU I.19–23), both in exoteric and esoteric terms. The four are genealogy (*santāna*), foundation (*nidānaka*), derivation (*nirukti*), and cause (*hetu*). He explains [my translation]:

> Birth in a human incarnation
> Is said to be "genealogy."
> Departure from the middle of
> The retinue of queens is the "foundation." 19.
>
> The teaching of the vows in the Discipline (*vinaya*)
> Is said to be the "derivation."
> Practice of the Teaching by those who desire the fruit [of buddhahood]
> That is called the "cause." 20.

(cont'd)

himself in a form free of passion, undertook[838] the realization of the Four Noble Truths and the passion-free practices for those who aspire to the Individual [Way]. Further, for those who adhere to the Universal Way,[839] [He] undertook the realization of objective selflessness [such as that] of the eight consciousnesses, {the bodies,} and so on, and [undertook] the practices of the stages and transcendent virtues, and so on. Further, emanating in the form of a universal monarch for those who aspire to the profound [Adamantine Way, He] undertook the realization of the nonduality of the two realities and the practices of the objects of passion.[840]

"Hence, for those [with] a body that comprehends the two realities,[841] for those who discriminate [properly among] all things, for those who seek[842] the fruit of supreme great bliss—the practices of the Śrāvakas and the

---

This manner of passion-free teaching
Is accepted as fourfold.
In order to understand the import clear[ly]
I will explain according to the vehicle of the passionate teaching. 21.

Creation of the buddhas of the five clans
Is said to be "genealogy."
Again becoming one clan
Is taught as the "foundation." 22.

Holding the vajra, and so forth,
Is explained as "derivation."
Practices such as eroticism, and so forth,
Are explained as the "cause." 23.

For the Sanskrit text, see PU, 2–3.

838. This is not yet a finite verb in the text—but another of many gerunds; I have broken it up for clarity a- (*ston pa*) [the various kinds of practices]. Skt reads only one verb "undertook, practiced" (*pratipad*), which takes two objects.

839. *mahāyānābhinivișța*; Tib reads "those adhering to the vast" (*rgya chen po la mngon par zhen pa*). The Tibetan translators seem to have altered this to correspond to a common division of the Mahāyāna into the vast and profound (*rgya chen dang zab mo*—often associated with the Yogācāra and Madhyamaka traditions, respectively). However, it seems clear that Āryadeva is here contrasting the exoteric Mahāyāna approach with a "profound" approach characteristic of the Vajrayāna.

840. Tib reads "[He] demonstrated the practices of the things of passion in order that those who aspire to the profound may realize the two realities through passion" (*zab mo la lhag par mos pa rnams la 'dod chags kyis bden pa gnyis rtogs par bya ba'i phyir 'dod chags kyi chos kyi spyod pa ston par mdzad pa yin no*).

841. Presumably, here, a body characterized by the communion of the two esoteric realities, the phantasm body (superficial reality) and brilliance (ultimate reality).

842. Following B (*anveșin*); C reads "desire" (*abhilāșin*).

Scripturalists are not suitable.[843] Just as the Śrāvakas, and so on, who aspire to the Individual [Way], who engage in argumentation, who lack the self-invocation (*ātma-sādhana*), who have set out on the path of deeds (*kriyā*) such as generosity and ethics, who do not possess faith in the Reality-gnosis, who believe liberation to be [a] distant [goal],[844] not understanding pleasure as liberative art, seek enlightenment for a long time by means of arduous practices such as the twelve ascetic practices;[845] †nevertheless, they do B:55b
not obtain [it], as [they] lack the realization of the perfection stage. Hence, verily, the Lord said:

> Those who remain in the state of a monk,
> Those men who delight in logical disputation,
> And those who are aged—
> One should not teach Reality to them.

Hence, [The Lord] said in the Practice Tantra, *The Enlightenment of Vairocana*:[846]

> Learning gnosis without liberative art
> Was taught for the Śrāvakas,
> By the Great Hero,
> In order to introduce [it] to them.[847]

843. SKT *na yuktā* (TIB **mi rigs*). TIB reads "the practices in the manner of the Śrāvakas and the [Mahāyāna] Scriptures are not told" (*nyan thos dang mdo sde'i tshul dang ldan pa'i spyod pa ma gsungs te|*).

844. Cf. Kambala's *Ālokamālā* v. 14ab: in Lindtner's translation "A yogin should in no way think that liberation is far away" (*dūrasaṃjñī bhaven mokṣe na kathaṃ cana yogavit*). See ĀM, 17.

845. *dvādaśa-dhūta-guṇa, sbyang pa'i yon tan bcu gnyis*; that is, (according to the *Dharmasaṃgraha*), subsisting on alms (*paiṇḍapātika, bsod snyoms pa*), wearing three robes (*traicīvarkika, chos gos gsum pa*), not accepting food after having risen from one's seat (*khalupaścādbhaktika, zas phyis mi len pa*), remaining in sitting posture (*naiṣadyika, tsog pu ba*), residing wherever one is (*yathāsaṃstarika, gzhi ji bzhin pa*), residing at the foot of a tree (*vṛkṣamūlika, shing drung pa*), eating in one session (*ekāsanika, stan gcig pa*), living in the open air (*ābhyavakāśika, bla gab med pa*), dwelling in the forest (*āraṇyaka, dgon pa ba*), dwelling in charnel grounds (*śmāśānika, dur khrod pa*), wearing rags (*pāṃśukūlika, phyag dar khrod pa*), and wearing unwoven robes (*nāmantika, phying ba pa*). For a detailed discussion of these practices, see Reginald A. Ray, *Buddhist Saints in India*, 293ff.

846. On this scripture, see chapter 3, note 447, above.

847. This verse is found at the end of chapter 20 of the *Mahāvairocanābhisaṃbodhi*

[He] said in the *Root Scripture*[848] also:

> Those who have abandoned gnosis
> Desire the ten paths of virtuous action.[849]

Hence, verily, the Lord said:

> Monk[s], do not learn the Way of the Śrāvakas!
> Do not now practice that practice![850]
> Perform the enlightenment practice for the buddha-qualities;
> From this principle the self-created will come to be.[851]

Tantra. In his recent translation (from Tibetan and Chinese) of the root text and commentary of Buddhaguhya, Stephen Hodge renders this verse as follows: "Though ways of training have been taught | with the awareness lacking expedient means | the Great Hero expounded them | In order to help the Śrāvakas to it." He renders Buddhaguhya's commentary thus: "To explain the training of the Śrāvakas in the Awareness which lacks expedient means, the Bhagavat says that although he has taught such a training to the Śrāvakas, which lacks expedient means and insight, it was not taught as the definitive (*nītārtha*) one, but in order to guide them in accordance with their capacity." Cf. S. Hodge, *Mahāvairocana Tantra*, 342–43.

TIB reads "Gnosis without liberative art | and the [three] trainings [were] taught | By the Great Hero to the Śrāvakas | In order to lead [them] to it," (*thabs dang mi ldan ye shes dang | bslab pa dag kyang bshad pa ni | dpa' bo chen pos nyan thos rnams | de la gzud ba'i phyir bshad do*) or, in what I believe to be a corrupted reading found in P and N, "in order to care for them" (*de la gsung ba'i phyir bshad do*).

848. SKT *mūla-sūtra*; here this term refers to the GST (on which see chapter 2, note 272, above).

849. This verse is from GST XVII.15ab, with a slight alteration (i.e., *icchanti*, replacing *kurvanti*). It was previously cited in its usual version (see chapter 5, note 612, above). Again, Lochen has inserted the standard Tibetan translation, rather than rendering the idiosyncratic verse as found in the text.

850. Following C, *nâtha carīyatha tatra carīye*; TIB reads "Learn that practice of enlightenment!" (*byang chub spyod pa de la bslab bya ste*); B reads something like "enlightenment-practice that practice!" (*bodhicarīyata tatra carīye*).

851. TIB reads "The practice of enlightenment—the buddha-qualities and the cause will be self-emergent from this," or perhaps "by the practices of enlightenment the buddha-qualities will self-emerge from this cause" (*byang chub spyod pa[s] sangs rgyas yon tan dang | gleng gzhi 'di las rang 'byung dag tu 'gyur |*).

The source of this citation is not clear to me. Compare, however, *Samādhirājasūtra*, 37:96 (see apparatus to Sanskrit edition for citation).

"Therefore, from the distinctive cause, †the distinctive effect results. Just so, one should be assured that those who have recourse to the experience (*bhāva*) of enjoyment of [sense] objects such as [visual] form[s], and so on, [will] bring about the distinctive effect.[852] Contrariwise, one-pointedness of mind will not come about by means of arduous practices, for they damage the five sense organs. Just as the Lord said in the {Great Yoga} Tantra, the *Glorious Supreme Prime*:[853] (C:67a)

†By severe penitential observances,[854] B:56a
The body withers painful[ly].
Pain disturbs the mind;
Disturbance is incompatible with success (*siddhi*).[855]

[He] also said in the *Root Scripture*:[856]

By severe penitential observances,
The devotee will not succeed.
Devoted to the enjoyment of all desires, however,
[S/he] will quickly succeed."[857]

The Vajra Student asked, "It is said that

Passion, hatred, [and] ignorance
Are the three poisons in the world.[858]

852. Tib reads, "Likewise, one should know that the distinctive effect will be attained by the nature of the distinctive enjoyment of the five objects of desire such as form, and so on" (*de bzhin du gzugs la sogs pa'i 'dod pa lnga'i yul rnams la khyad par gyi longs spyod kyi ngo bor gyur pas khyad par gyi 'bras bu thob par 'gyur ba yin par shes par bya'o* |).

853. On this scripture, see chapter 8, note 743, above. The verse cited here could not be located in this scripture.

854. Tib reads "by unbearable vows of asceticism" (*dka' thub sdom pa mi bzad pas*).

855. *vikṣepāt siddhir anyathā*; literally, "due to disturbance, success [is] otherwise." Tib reads "due to disturbance, success is elsewhere" (*g.yengs pas dngos grub gzhan du 'gyur*). This verse is *Paramādyamantrakalpakhaṇḍa*, DK, rGyud, vol. ta, f. 242b$^{4-5}$.

856. *mūlasūtra*; Tib reads "Root Tantra" (*rtsa ba'i rgyud*). Here this term refers to the GST. On this scripture, see chapter 2, note 272, above.

857. This verse is GST VIII.3 (see Matsunaga, 20; Bhattacharyya, 27; Bagchi, 21).

858. A citation of a half-verse, probably from the *Mahāmāyūrīvidyārājñī*. See Shūyo Takubo,

and the Lord [Buddha] likewise taught that, since the [sense] objects, such as [visual] form, give rise to the defilements, [they] are the causes of lower rebirth (*apāya*). How, then, is this not mutually contradictory with [the assertion that] the one who is devoted to those will quickly accomplish the unexcelled state?"

The Vajra Mentor replied, "Excellent, excellent, Vajra Student; (it is excellent that) you inquire [about this], in order to eliminate the uncertainty of those who perform the passionate dharma. Hence, listen, O Great One![859] The Lord [Buddha] himself taught in the scriptures that the defilements such as passion are the cause of lower rebirth[860] for those with objectifying views such as Śrāvakas, as [they] do not thoroughly understand the intrinsic nature of defilement; while, through thorough understanding of the intrinsic nature [of defilement], they become the cause for enlighten-
B:56b ment. As †it is said in the Great Yoga Tantra, the *Glorious Supreme Prime*:[861]

> Passion, hatred, and ignorance—
> These three are poisonous.[862]
> Those who associate with the wicked[863]
> Become poisonous.
> But, those who associate with the immortal,
> They become immortal.[864]

---

ed., *Ārya-Mahā-Māyūrī Vidyā-Rājñī*, 59.

859. Following Skt (B). Tib reads "Hence, listen, as I will teach the great import!" (*de bas na don chen po bstan par bya yis nyon cig*). Skt suggests **de bas na sems dpa' chen po nyon cig*.

860. Tib reads "defilements are the condition for defilement" (*nyon mongs pa rnams ni... nyon mongs pa rnams kyi rkyen du 'gyur*). Tsongkhapa, in RNSG (Pek. ed., 68, f. 261a$^{7-8}$), refers to two "new translations of the CMP" that, he says, read "bad rebirth" (*ngan 'gro*) here, instead of "defilement" (*nyon mongs*). This reading conforms to Skt.

861. On this scripture, see chapter 8, note 743, above. Once again, this citation is from the *Paramādyamantrakalpakhaṇḍa*, DK, rGyud, vol. ta, f. 220b$^{4-5}$.

862. Tib reads "by grasping, become poison" (*'dzin pas dug tu 'gyur ba yin*).

863. *viṣama*, clearly this is meant to play on "poison" (*viṣa*).

864. *amṛta*; this also means ambrosia, and there is clearly an intent here to play ambrosia (*amṛta*) against poison (*viṣa*), as well as the wicked (*viṣama*) against the immortal (*amṛta*).

Tib reads (presumably reading **upaśānti* for *upayānti*): If poison itself is pacified (*upaśam*) | Poison eliminates poison. | By gradually relying on ambrosia (or 'relying on the process of ambrosia') | It will even become ambrosia itself." (*dug nyid nye bar zhi gyur na | dug ni dug med byas pa yin | bdud rtsi rim gyis brten nas ni | bdud rtsi nyid du 'gyur ba'ang yin |*).

[He] also said in the *Jewel Heap Scripture*:[865]

> 'Thus, for instance, Kāśyapa, a heap of filth[866] is beneficial to sugarcane fields(, rice fields, and) vineyards. Just so, (Kāśyapa,) the ("feces" of the) bodhisattva's defilements are beneficial (to the state of omniscience).[867]
>
> 'Thus, for instance, Kāśyapa, poison that is restrained by mantra [or medicinal] herbs does not kill.[868] Just so, the bodhisattva endowed with[869] critical wisdom and liberative art is not "killed"[870] by the defilements.'[871]

Hence,[872] [He] said in the Great {Yoga} Tantra, *Unfailing Success in Discipline*:[873]

865. *Ratnakūṭa-sūtra, dKon mchog brtsegs pa'i mdo.* The scripture here cited is the *Kāśyapa-parivarta.* Although *Ratnakūṭa* is also used (in Tibetan and Chinese contexts) for a class of scriptures *including* the *Kāśyapa-parivarta*, in Indian sources it refers merely to this one scripture (KP). See A. von Staël-Holstein, ed., *Kāśyapaparivarta.* A Tibetan translation of this important, early Mahāyāna scripture (by Jinamitra, Śīlendrabodhi, and Ye-shes sDe) may be found in the above work (as may a Chinese translation); it may also be found at: DK, dKon-brtsegs, vol. cha, ff. $119b^1$–$151b^7$ (Tōh. 87).

866. *saṃkāra-kūṭa*, usually a "heap of rubbish"; Tib reads "the manure of a large city" (*grong khyer chen po'i lud gang yin pa de*).

867. The elements marked by parentheses as occurring only in Tib are found in KP itself. Again, it is likely that the translators excerpted this passage from a prior translation, rather than translate this passage afresh from the CMP as found.

868. *na vinipātayati*; Tib and KP read "is not able to kill" (*'chi bar byed mi nus so, na śaknoti vinipātayitum*).

869. Tib reads "restrained by" (*yongs su zin pa*), in parallel with the preceding passage, suggesting **prajñopāya-parigṛhītaḥ*, rather than *prajñopāya-samanvitaḥ*. KP reads *jñānopāya-kauśalya-parigṛhītaḥ*.

870. There is a play on the verb *vi-ni-pat* here. Tibetan renders it in two different ways, appropriate to the context: i.e., poison does not "kill," and the defilements do not "cast down" a bodhisattva (into a moral "downfall").

871. This citation consists of two adjacent passages from the *Kāśyapaparivarta*, in inverted order. I have indicated this by a paragraph break in the translation. The first paragraph is KP §49; the latter is §48. See von Staël-Holstein, *Kāśyapa-parivarta*, 78–80.

872. *ataḥ*; Tib reads "furthermore" (*gzhan yang, *api ca*).

873. *Vinayāmoghasiddhi-mahā[yoga]tantra; 'Dul ba don yod par grub pa zhes bya ba'i rnal*

That by which the stupid one is bound,
Liberates the wise one.
This all is inverted
By the manifestation of enlightenment.

That which binds the foolish,
[And] makes them suffer in the vicinity of Raurava [Hell]—[874]
By those very things, [the wise] are liberated
Easily, by the power of critical wisdom.[875]

By this reasoning, there is no other practice (*sādhana*) to reach the result of unexcelled, great bliss—which [itself] becomes the cause for perfecting the
C:67b distinctive result[876]—‡than the distinctive transference (*samāropa*)[877] and
B:57a the distinctive transformation (*pariṇāma*).† Therefore, the perfection of the omniscient [state], such as the eight superhuman powers,[878] is realized by means of pleasurable food, residence, and so on. Thus, it is taught in the *Glorious Supreme Bliss*:[879]

The buddhahood of all is easily[880]
Obtained by bliss itself.[881]

"Concerning that, the practices of enlightenment[882] born from passion are threefold—that is, with elaboration, without elaboration, and com-

---

'byor chen po'i rgyud. I have not been able to identify this work; it may be a chapter title of another scripture.

874. Tib reads "will definitely end in Raurava" (*ngu 'bod mthar ni nges 'gyur ba*).

875. Tib reads "will attain happiness by the power of critical wisdom" (*shes rab stobs kyis bde ba thob |*).

876. Tib reads "delightful, distinctive result" (*khyad par can gyi 'bras bu yid du 'ong ba*).

877. Tib reads "exhortation" (*bskul ba, *saṃcodana?*).

878. Tib reads "endowed with the eight superhuman powers" (*yon tan dbang phyug brgyad la sogs pa dang ldan pa, *aṣṭāguṇaiśvaryādi-samanvita-*).

879. *Śrī-saṃvara*; *bDe mchog*; this is a citation from the SBS (on which scripture see chapter 2, note 344, above).

880. Play on words here difficult to render in English: "easily . . . by bliss" (*sukhaṃ sukhena*).

881. Though it does not entirely correspond to the Tibetan translation, it would seem to be SBS II.3ab (see DK, rGyud, vol. ka, f. 152b[3]).

882. *bodhicaryā*; Tib reads "the practices of a bodhisattva" (*byang chub sems dpa'i spyod pa, bodhisattvacaryā*).

pletely without elaboration. What, then, is practice with elaboration? That with elaboration is the extensive play (*āralli*) of all transcendent lords, as taught in the Transcendent Lord chapter and the Vajradhara chapter.[883] What is [practice] without elaboration? Because of the constant necessity of extensive business, sometimes play (*āralli*) may be done without elaboration.[884] What is [practice] completely without elaboration? Leaving aside all socializing, the one who lives and consumes only meditation (*dhyāna*)[885] may train in equipoise [with] a gnosis-consort[886]—that is [practice] completely without elaboration. Just as burning wood yields ashes, burning palmyra leaves yields †ashes, burning cotton[887] yields ashes—all turns to ashes B:57b
[when burnt]. Just so, by means of the threefold practices, [practitioners] will effect the state of Mahāvajradhara.[888]

"Now some practitioners, who follow [Yoga] Tantras such as the *Compendium of Realities*,[889] by means of [artistic] techniques such as actors' gestures, and histrionic expressions [such as] hand-gestures, songs, exultations, and swaying [of the limbs],[890] always [with] zealous mind day and night

883. *tathāgatāśvāse vajradharāśvāse ca*; TIB renders this literally: *de bzhin gshegs pa'i dbugs dbyung ba dang | rdo rje 'chang gi dbugs dbyung ba* ("the breath [or 'consolation'] of the transcendent lords and the breath of Vajradhara"). I believe, however, in this context we are justified in rendering this as "chapter, book section" (cf. BHSD, 110). Āryadeva is referring to the *Sarvabuddhasamāyoga Tantra* (SBS: the primary source for the "practices" in this chapter), presumably the fifth chapter, which devotes several sections to the *āśvāsa/dbugs-byung-ba* of the transcendent lords Vajrasattva, Vairocana, Padmanarteśvara, Vajrasūrya, and Paramāśva (see SBS: DK, rGyud, vol. ka, ff. $155b^3$–$159b^4$).

884. Reading *satata-vyāpi-kārya-vaśāt kvacid āralliḥ syāt*; an alternate reading (which may be preferable) is *satataṃ vyāpi-kārya-vaśāt kvacid vâralliḥ syāt*: "play may be [either] constant (*satataṃ*) or, due to the necessity of extensive business, occasional (*kvacit*)—that [is practice] without elaboration." Thanks to Gary Tubb, Harunaga Isaacson, and Yigal Bronner for assistance with this passage.

885. *kevala-dhyānāhāra-vihārī*; TIB suggests "the food of meditation, [and] living alone" (*bsam gtan gyi zas dang | gnas pa 'ba' zhig dang |*).

886. *jñānamudrā, ye shes kyi phyag rgya.*

887. *karpāsa*; this could also be "cotton tree. B is corrected from *kārpāsa* ("cotton [cloth]"). TIB reads "leaves of [the] cotton [plant]" (*ras bal gyi lo ma*).

888. Following C, *mahāvajradharapada*; B reads "the great vajra state" (*mahāvajrapada*). TIB reads "likewise, by all the three practices, the sought-after rank of Vajradhara will be born" (*de bzhin du spyod pa gsum car gyis kyang rdo rje 'dzin pa'i go 'phang mngon par 'dod pa nyid skye bar 'gyur ro*).

889. On this scripture, see chapter 3, note 383, above.

890. *hastamudrā-gītopahārākṣepābhinaya-naṭa-nartanādi-prayogaiḥ*. This list seems to correspond in the main to the first three of the four histrionic expressions (*abhinaya*) of

cultivate the accomplishment (*siddhi*) of the Great Seal (Mahāmudrā) by means of the practice with elaborations.[891] Likewise, some, inclining toward Great Yoga Tantra[s] such as the *Glorious Supreme Prime*,[892] invoke the state of great bliss[893] by means of the practices with elaboration [that are] the erotic play of all transcendent lords, including adopting the *paryaṅka* position and the nine dramatic moods,[894] and so on. But in this {Glorious} *Esoteric Community*,[895] only the [practice] without elaboration and the practice completely without elaboration is taught.

"Now, the practices with elaboration are introduced in the Great Yoga Tantra, the Glorious *Union of All Buddhas: Magical Supreme Bliss of the Ḍākiṇīs*:[896]

> Now, therefore, I will make known
> B:58a The highest, which pervades all,[897†]
> The Union of All Buddhas,
> Magical Supreme Bliss of the Ḍākiṇīs.

Indian classical dance: to wit, gesture (*aṅgika*: such as hand gestures [*hasta*]), vocal performance (*vācika*—esp. songs), and costumes (*āhārya*). (The fourth being *sāttvika*, "the entire psychological resources of the dancer-actor"; cf. "arts, South Asian" in *Encyclopædia Britannica* [2006], Encyclopædia Britannica Online. 30 Dec 2006 <http://search.eb.com/eb/article65249>). Our list diverges slightly from this list. The first two conform exactly. The third item in our list reads *upahāra* (which I have rendered "exultations"), but could be a corruption or alternative for [*upa*]*hārya*. The last element, *ākṣepa* ("swaying [of the limbs]), seems divergent—perhaps one could emend to **hastamudrā-gītopahāryādy-abhinaya-naṭa-nartana-prayogair*?

891. Tib reads "Also, some practitioners, following tantras such as the *Compendium of Realities*, [by means of] methods such as hand gestures, song-offerings, [and] gaits, [and] techniques such as dance, with an eternally zealous mind, day and night practice the *siddhi* of Mahāmudrā by means of the practices with elaboration."

892. On this scripture, see chapter 8, note 743, above.

893. Tib reads "Great Seal" (*mahāmudrā*).

894. *nava-nāṭya-rasa, nyams rnam pa dgu*; that is: the erotic (*śṛṅgāra*), heroic (*vīra*), disgusting (*bībhatsa*), furious (*raudra*), comic (*hāsya*), frightening (*bhayānaka*), piteous (*karuṇa*), wondrous (*adbhūta*), and peaceful (*śānta*). The *paryaṅka* position is one of several yogic postures and involves a kind of squatting attitude.

895. On this scripture, see chapter 2, note 272, above.

896. On this scripture, see chapter 2, note 344, above.

897. *sarvato viśvam uttamam*; Tib reads "the variegated supreme" (*rnam pa sna tshogs mchog gyur pa*).

Being secret, supreme, [and] delightful,[898]
[It is] always situated in all souls (*ātman*)—
The glorious, composed of all the buddhas,[899]
Bliss, the ascension of Vajrasattva.[900]

Great[901] divinity of [the] transcendent lords,
Adorned with lacework of jewels,[902]

[903]Thence, they [should] practice
In a splendrous, outspread velarium,
Endowed with bell[s],[904]
In a building or, instead, in parks [or] the like,
The Union of All Buddhas,
†Magical Supreme Bliss of the Ḍākinīs.[905] (C:68a)

There, sit on a seat at first,
Comfortable, soft to the touch,
Wrapped in fine cloth of multicolored lotuses—
That is the seat of all the buddhas,[906]

898. Tib reads "as [it is the] delight of the supreme secret" (*gsang ba mchog gi dgyes pa na*).

899. Tib suggests "the substance of all the glorious Buddhas" (*dpal ldan sangs rgyas kun gyi dngos*).

900. Tib suggests "Emergence of the bliss of Vajrasattva" (*rdo rje sems dpa'i bde 'byung ba*).

901. Tib reads "supreme" (*mchog*).

902. Tib reads "decked with jewel ornaments, and so on" (*rin chen rgyan la sogs pas spras*).

903. Tib inserts an extra verse between the two lines of this Skt verse: "Vajra songs and the various offerings | Magically manifested songs and cymbals | Flowers, incense compounds | Lamps, perfumes, and so forth | " (*rdo rje glu dang mchod la sogs | glu dang sil snyan rnam par 'phrul | me tog bdug pa'i sbyor ba dang | mar me dri dang sogs ldan par |*).

904. Tib reads "endowed with a bell and supreme victory banner" (*dril bu rgyal mtshan mchog dang ldan pa'i*).

905. Tib reads "[They] practice the Union of All Buddhas | Magical Supreme Bliss of the Ḍākinīs | [They] practice in either the triple world (**tribhuvana*) | Or in their own residence (**svasthāna*) | Or in a pleasure grove (**udyāna*) |" (*sangs rgyas thams cad mnyam sbyor ba | mkha' 'gro sgyu ma bde mchog bsgrub | yang na srid pa gsum dag gam | yang na bdag gi gnas dag gam | skyed mos tshal la sogs par bsgrub |*). See Tibetan edition for further readings from alternative translations.

906. *sarvabuddhāsana*; Tib reads "that universally pure seat" (*thams cad dag pa'i gdan*, **sarva-śuddhāsana*).

[907]Where they display
The forms of Vajrasattva,[908]
Made of all the elements,
Formed, too, of the root of vitality.[909]

The employment [of] the symbols (*cihna*) and seals (*mudrā*)[910]
By those face-to-face with their own presiding deity, [is as follows:]

Cast or molded,[911]
Polished, or well-decorated[912]—
A lovely image, the symbol-seal (*cihna-mudrā*),
Should [be] installed.

[913]By those face-to-face with their own presiding deity,[914]
A woman, well-dressed,[915]

907. Before this verse, Tib inserts an extra half-verse: "by displaying the lord of yoga | by the Union of All the Buddhas" (*sangs rgyas thams cad mnyam sbyor bas | sbyor ba'i dbang phyug rnam 'phrul bas |*).

908. *śrī-vajrasattva-rūpa*; Tib reads "[they] manifest the divinity of glorious Vajrasattva" (*rdo rje sems dpa' dpal gyi lha, *śrī-vajrasattva-deva*).

909. Tib reads "born of all the elemental natures and likewise vitality control (*prāṇāyāma*)" (*khams kyi rang bzhin thams cad dang | de bzhin srog dang rtsol las byung |*). RṄSG (f. $328b^{5-6}$) reads this line as: "born from the nature of elements and vitality and root" (*khams kyi rang bzhin dang srog dang rtsa las byung ba*); or, from Chag's translation: "born from the root of living beings" (*srog chags rtsa ba las byung ba*).

910. Following emended reading *cihna-mudrā*; B reads *siddhi-mudrā*; Tib suggests **siddha-mudrā*.

911. Tib reads "A cast image or relief-work" (*lugs ma'am yang na 'bur*).

912. Tib reads "consecrated [and] well-drawn" (*mngon par 'dus byas legs bris pa*)—apparently reading **vâbhisaṃskṛta* for *vâpi saṃskṛta*.

913. Tib inserts one and a half verses here that are not found in Skt. They read "On all those seats | Arrayed as [they] reside | Four-cornered [and] four-doored | Beautified by four arches | Place the door guardians— | vajra, jewel, lotus, and so forth |" (*stan de dag ni thams cad la | ji ltar gnas pa bzhin du dgod | gru bzhi pa la sgo bzhi pa | rta babs bzhi yis mdzas par byas | rdo rje rin chen padma sogs | sgo srung dang ni ldan par bya |*).

914. Tib reads "endowed with [their] own deity" (*rang gi lha dang ldan pa yi*).

915. *suprasādhita*; Tib reads "well-educated" (*legs bslabs pa*); though RṄSG (f. $329b^{1-2}$) notes that Pa-tshab's translation reads *legs bsgrubs*, which conforms to Skt.

Beautiful with [one's] own symbols and seals,[916]
Should be prepared—the host maṇḍala.[917]

I will expound in detail the meaning of these scriptur[al vers]es.

"At first, in an isolated region—such as a pleasure grove or the like—[which is] pleasing to the mind [and] free of unfortunate ones such as śrāvakas †and the like,[918] one should construct a brick, three-storied divine house, suitable for various activities.[919] There, on the first story, one should build the kitchen. On the second story, place the requisites [needed for] instrumental and vocal worship.[920] On the third story, Glorious Viśva, supremely fortunate,[921] should reside together with the yoginīs. B:58b

"Or, in a [single-story] cottage,[922] imagining a celestial palace[923] [with] a vajra peak [of] Mount Meru made of crystal, beryl, sapphire, emerald, and ruby on an adamantine spot, variously adorned, endowed with a firm encircling wall [as follows]:

Four-cornered, four-doored,
Adorned[924] with four archways,
Endowed with four lines (*sūtra*),
Adorned with eight pillars,
Strung with [pearl] garlands and half-garlands,[925]

916. Tib reads "marked with the seal of fortunate nature" or "fortunate in nature, marked with a seal" (*skal bzang rang bzhin phyag rgyas mtshan*).

917. DK, rGyud, vol. ka, 159b⁴–160a² (with variations similar to those discussed above).

918. *śrāvakādi-durbhaga*; Tib reads "unfortunate ones such as the unsuperficial" or "not in accordance with the method" (*tshul dang mi mthun pa la sogs pa skal pa ngan pa rnams*).

919. *vicitra-karma-yuktaṃ*; Tib reads "endowed with variegated/beautiful ornaments" (*rgyan rnam pa sna tshogs dang ldan pa*, **vicitrālaṃkāra-saṃyukta*).

920. *tantrī-gītakādi-pūjopakaraṇa*; literally, "the requisites of worship such as lutes and songs." Tib reads "the requisites of vocal and instrumental music such as lutes" (*pi wang la sogs pa glu gar dang rol mo'i mchod pa'i yo byad rnams*).

921. Reading *śrī-viśvaṃ subhagottamo*, which conforms to the Tibetan rendering *dpal sna tshogs skal ba bzang po'i mchog*; B reads *śrīvisvaśubhagottamo*.

922. Skt *bhū-gṛha*, Tib *sa'i khang pa*; literally "earth-house," usually a "cellar."

923. *kūṭāgāra*, *gzhal yas khang*; usually, an "upper room."

924. Tib reads "beautified" (*mdzes par byas*).

925. *hārārddhahāra*; Tib reads "nets and half-nets" (*dra ba dra ba phyed pa*).

Ornamented by silk, (flower) {garlands,} [and] wreaths,
Adorned with bell[s and] flags,
Ornamented by yak-tails[926] and the like,
[With] a half-moon and vajra [in the] corner[s] and
At the joints of the door-alcoves,
Adorned with beautiful paintings
On the balustrades, the panels flanking the doors, and so on.[927]

[928]With regard to that, the practitioner, with the permission of the mentor{s}, having worshipped the {great} lords of yogins—[both those] perfected and [those] unperfected—together with the beloveds, who have done away with ordinary pride, such as the companions (*sahacarī*) and
B:59a attendants (*anucarī*), †with a fearless heart[929] like a lion, should engage in the practice of the Great Seal (Mahāmudrā) by this process:

"Regarding that, this [is] the process: preceded by focusing on ultimate reality, having created oneself in the form of Vajrasattva by the process of self-consecration, adopting the role of the overlord of the maṇḍala, [one] enjoys material objects. Then, in order to reveal the female phantasmic forms [of] all transcendent lords,[930] one stands before the Lord, in the form of Saṃvarī,[931] with the nature of the passion lineage. One stands in the southern[932] direction, in the form of Ahosukhā, with the nature of the
C:68b lovemaking lineage. ‡One stands in the western direction, in the form of Pradīpā, with the nature of the wrath lineage. One stands in the northern

926. *cāmara*: "reckoned as one of the insignia of royalty," see PSED, 704.

927. *pakṣiṇī-krama-śīrṣādi-*. Tib diverges here, reading "beautified by variegated lotuses on [its] stairs, arches, doors, and so on" (*skas dang rta babs sgo la sogs | sna tshogs padmas mdzas byas pa |*) Presumably the translators read *padma* (lotus) rather than *paṭa* (painting), though their use of nonstandard architectural terminology is misleading.

928. Tib inserts "so it is taught" (*zhes bya ba bstan te*).

929. Literally, "mind" (*cetas*); Tib reads "with a mind that shuns nothing" (*'dzem pa med par gyur pa'i sems kyis*).

930. This is ambiguous. B could read "in order to reveal the form constituted of all the women of the transcendent lords" (*sarva-tathāgata-strī-mayākāra-pradarśanāya*). Tib reads "in order to show that all transcendent lords are like the magic of women" (*de bzhin gshegs pa thams cad bud med kyi sgyu ma lta bur rab tu bstan par bya ba'i phyir*).

931. Tib suggests Saṃvarīmāyā (*bde mchog sgyu ma*).

932. Tibetan has "right" (*g.yas*)—a literal translation of the Sanskrit *dakṣina* ("right, south").

direction, in the form of Śiṣyā, with the nature of the life lineage. These [are] the companions.

"One is situated in the south-east, in the form of Buddhabodhi, in order to purify ignorance. One is situated in the south-west, in the form of Dharmacakrā, †in order to purify the arrogance of rejecting the [task B:59b of] transcending the triple world.[933] One is situated in the north-west, in the form of Trailokyavijayā, in order to eliminate hatred. One is situated in the north-east, in the form of Kāmalatā, in order to eliminate passion and benightedness (*tamas*).

"One is situated in the outer south-east corner in the form of Śuṣirā, [the Flute Goddess]. One is situated in the outer south-west corner in the form of Nṛtyā, [the Dance Goddess],[934] bringing the triple world under [her] control by erotically playing the lute (*vīṇā*). One is situated in the outer northwest corner in the form of Vitatā,[935] [the Stringed Instrument Goddess,] playing a *mukunda*-drum in order to eliminate poison and fever.[936] One is situated in the outer northeast corner in the form of Ghanā,[937] [the Percussion Goddess,] playing a *muraja*-drum.

One is situated in the southeastern corner, outside {the curtain (*paṭṭikā*)}, in the form of Vajrapuṣpā, [the Adamantine Flower Goddess,] holding a B:60a flower in her hand. †One is situated in the southwestern corner, in the form of Vajradhūpā, [the Adamantine Incense Goddess,] bearing an incense censer. One is situated in the northwestern corner, in the form of Vajrālokā, [the Adamantine Lamp Goddess,] bearing a great lamp. One is situated in the northeastern corner, outside the curtain, in the form of Vajragandhā,[938] [the Adamantine Scent Goddess,] holding in her hand a conch-shell completely brimming with scents.

933. Reading *trailokya-laṅghanākṣepa-mada-viśodhanāya*; Tib seems to have read *-*pada-* (*gnas*) for *-mada-*, resulting in something like "in order to purify the states of controversy and doubt [in] the three worlds" (*khams gsum rgal cing gnon pa'i gnas rnam par sbyong ba'i phyir*).

934. Tib reads "*Bahutantrī [the Many-Stringed Instrument Goddess]" (*rgyud mangs*).

935. Tib reads "*Ekatantrī [the One-Stringed Instrument Goddess]" (*rgyud gcig*). *Vitata* does refer to a stringed instrument, but not necessarily (to my knowledge) one-stringed.

936. Tib reads "playing a large drum [and] eliminating poison and plague" (*rnga bo che rdung zhing dug dang rims rnam par sel ba*).

937. Tib reads "*Ghanatantrī [the Percussion Goddess]" (*rgyud stug po*).

938. Tib suggests, "*Vajralepanā, [the Scented Ointment Goddess]" (*rdo-rje byug-pa-ma*).

One is situated, guarding the eastern door, in the form of Turagā [the Horse Goddess,][939] desiccating the triple realm (*tribhuvana*) with breath from the mouth of Paramāśva, [the Supreme Horse]. One is situated guarding the southern door, in the form of Vajramukhī, [the Adamantine Door Goddess,][940] annihilating[941] the triple world. One is situated guarding the western door, in the form of Vajrālokā, [the Adamantine Luminance Goddess,] surveying the triple world. One is situated guarding the northern door, in the form of an ashen, destructive zombiess,[942] revivifying the three
B:60b worlds,[943] giving life even to [those] reduced to ashes.†

"Concerning that [rite], the Lord Great Bliss (Mahāsukha), the Universal Monarch, preceded by recollection of the samādhi that conduces to the real,[944] generates[945] the distinctive pride that 'I will delight all the transcendent lords who reside in my own body maṇḍala.' Having first savored the threefold [sense] objects such as [visual] form, and so on, [and] subsequently consecrating[946] all foods by the twofold[947] technique such as puri-
C:69a fication, and so on, ‡[He] recalls the natural, inner fire-offering-pit, [and] generating the pride that 'I will offer the {two} oblation{s}[948] in the center of

939. Tib *rta gdong*, "Horse-face."

940. Tib reads *rdo-rje phag gdong*, "Vajra Pig-face."

941. √*saṃhṛ*; Tib translates this literally as "uniting" (*sdud*).

942. Skt *vetālī* (m. *vetāla*); often this term is translated as "vampire" in Western works. Though I am not a real expert in the macabre, this term seems a little off the mark for, though it does mean a type of animated corpse, it tends to be understood with a much richer meaning (à la *Dracula*, *Nosferatu*, and their spin-offs). As the Sanskrit term signifies an evil spirit that occupies and animates dead bodies, the closest English term would seem to be "zombie." This also very nicely translates the sense of its Tibetan equivalent, *ro langs* ("animated corpse").

943. *bhūrbhuvaḥsvaḥ*; on the use of this term see chapter 2, note 281, above.

944. *bhūta-nayātmaka-samādhi*. This, of course, is the samādhi mentioned in the initial dialogue between Vajra Student and Vajra Mentor in chapter 1, above (see also the end of chapter 5). Tib reads "the samādhi with the nature of the method that came before" (*sngon byung ba'i tshul gyi bdag nyid can gyi ting nge 'dzin*)—presumably the translators read **pūrva-nayātmaka-samādhi* for *bhūta-nayātmaka-samādhi*.

945. This passage is a long series of gerunds; I have altered the grammar somewhat for clarity.

946. Tib reads "purifying" (*mngon par sbyangs*).

947. Tib reads "threefold" (*rnam pa gsum*).

948. Reading (accus. dual) *āhutī*, as per B; this could also be emended to (accus. sing.) *āhutiṃ*; Pandey emends to *āhutīḥ*; Tib reads *sbyin sreg*, "burnt offering," usually *homa*.

the three-pronged fire, the [very] mouth of the samādhi-being,' [He] consumes [it].[949] Then, [He] transforms [it] by means of bliss; [and it] becomes the elixir of immortality (*rasāyana*).[950]

"The practitioner, having thus gratified the body vajra by means of all kinds of food, delicacies, and drinks,[951] at the end he savors the fifth, the object of touch. By this procedure, too, having observed the retinue of goddesses such as the companions, and so on, [who are] skillful in lovemaking, he chooses[952] a consort according to [his] desire. Having set her in [his] lap,[953] generating the firm aspiration that 'I will perfect the power (*siddhi*) of the Great Seal,' †he performs the embracing, kissing, sucking, striking B:61a
with the nails, [emitting] cries of pleasure, [making erotic noises such as the song of the] kokila [bird and] the humming of bees, stimulating the veins, and so on.[954] Adopting the [sexual] positions such as the transcendent lord posture, the adamantine posture, the jewel posture, the lotus posture, the action posture, he should become engaged in action (*karma-stha*). Then, setting wisdom and art in equipoise through the friction[955] of the vajra and lotus, starting from the crown of the head, [He] makes all transcendent lords who have the nature of the aggregates, and so on—introspectively known as the proper form of the Transcendent Virtue of Wisdom—descend[956] from the seventy-two thousand psychic veins, in appearance [like] the (stainless)

949. *abhyavaharati*, "He 'tossed it back.'" Tib reads "[He] should enjoy the food" (*zas la spyad par bya*).

950. Tib reads "After that, having melted into bliss, [it] becomes *rasāyana*" (*de'i 'og tu bde bar yongs su zhu nas ra sa ya nar 'gyur ro*).

951. *bhakṣya-bhojya-peyādi*; thanks to Patrick Olivelle for help in clarifying this distinction. See also T. Yagi, "A Note on *bhojya-* and *bhakṣya*," 377–97. Tib reads *bza' ba dang bca' ba dang btung ba*: an edible and two drinkables, rather than the reverse.

952. Again, a long list of gerunds that I have recast slightly.

953. Tib reads "having chosen a consort, [he] unites [with her]" (*phyag rgya blangs nas nye bar bzhag*).

954. Interestingly, Tib renders much of this list in Sanskrit, rather than translating it to Tibetan—a sign perhaps of a certain reserve on the part of the translators? It reads: "*āliṅgana*, and *cumbana*, and *cūṣaṇa*, and *nakha-praharaṇa*, and *sītkara*, and *kokila*, and humming of bees, [and] exciting [the] *nāli* [veins], and so on" (*ā liṅga ṇa dang | tsumba na dang | tsu sha na dang | na ga pra ha ra ṇa dang | sītkara dang | ko ki la dang | bung ba'i sgra dang | nā li yang dag par bskul ba la sogs pa*).

955. *saṃharṣaṇa/saṃgharṣaṇa*; Tib reads "union" (*yang dag par 'dus pa*).

956. Reading *patataḥ* (following Tib *'babs*). The manuscript reads *yattataḥ*.

stream of a waterfall, liquified in [the form of] vowels and consonants, [by] the stages of passion, dispassion, and moderate passion.[957]

Thus, the yogin who has achieved eminence[958] through [repeated] cultivation of the samādhi of Glorious Great Bliss (Mahāsukha) right there in the host maṇḍala matures beings through inducements and deterrents (*nigrahānugraha*). Whomsoever should have a view that is obsessed with voidness, [for] that very one the Lord (Śrīmahāsukha), in the form of Mahāvairocana, provides a deterrent to [such a reified] view of voidness,
B:61b perfecting by means of the samādhi of great pacification †the character of unlocated nirvāṇa that is neither void nor yet non-void. Similarly, [for] those hard to tame [who are] extremely fierce,[959] having dissuaded [them from their] base view by means of the wrathful samādhi of Glorious Vajra Heruka,[960] [He] offers inducements. [For] those with false views, having perfected the ultimate reality in the form of Padmanarteśvara, [He] masters [them].[961] [For] the extremely base, envious[962] [and] greedy, in the form of Glorious Vajra Sūrya, [He] provides a deterrent to [their] defiled view through the samādhi of great prosperity {[and] a rain of all wealth and jewels.} [For] those extremely lacking in heroism, in the form of Paramāśva, [He] provides a deterrent to weak heroism through the haṭhayoga samādhi [and] through courage.[963]

C:69b "Regarding that, the Lord Glorious Mahāsukha, †in order to demonstrate the nature of the erotic play of the great *āralli* of the reality-source, exerts undivided attention. And, for mutual arousal, [He] performs the buddha-dance.[964] By this process is performed the symbolic procedure (*saṃketena*

957. *rāga-virāga-madhyarāga*; i.e., of the three sets of prototypes (*prakṛti*)—see chapter 4, above.

958. Skt *utkarṣa*; Tib reads "the supreme" (*mchog*).

959. Tib reads "extremely wild/mischevious" (*shin tu gdug, *atyanta-duṣṭa*).

960. Tib reads "the samādhi of the King of Wrath, Glorious Vajra Heruka" (*dpal rdo rje he ru ka'i khro bo'i rgyal po'i ting nge 'dzin*).

961. Tib reads "teaches the ultimate reality and controls [them]" (*don dam pa'i bden pa bstan nas dbang du mdzad do*).

962. *mātsarya*; Tib *ser sna can* (an attested equivalent for *mātsarya*, but better for *kṛpaṇa* or *kṣudra*), suggests "miserly."

963. *parākrameṇa*; Tib reads "through subduing the enemy" (*pha rol gnon pas*).

964. Following B, *buddha-nāṭya*; C and Tib read "buddha play/performance" (*buddha-nāṭaka, sangs rgyas kyi rol mo*).

vyavahāraḥ)—seal, counter-seal, salutation, counter-salutation, worship, †counter-worship, performance, counter-performance, song, counter-song, the bodily tokens, [and] the verbal tokens. B:62a

"Regarding that, the verbal tokens[965] are taught [thus]: 'oṃ ati hoḥ,' this vulgate (*mlecchā*) may indicate 'I pay homage.'[966] 'Oṃ pratikā' [is] counter-homage in return. 'Cchem (cchem)' [is] the mentor-salutation. 'Bhakṣa' [means] 'enter.' 'Ccho(ṃ)' [means] 'welcome.'[967] 'Cchaṃ' is shutting [the doors and windows].[968] 'Khaṃ' [means] 'enjoy [the victuals]!'[969] 'Kha' [means] 'eat!' 'Draṃ draṃ' [means] 'meat.' 'Śraṃ śraṃ' [means] 'blood.' 'Dreṃ dreṃ' [means] 'eat meat.' 'Jaṃ phaṃ' [means] 'vajra-water.'[970] 'Somaṃ' [means] 'the five ambrosias."[971] 'Iyati' [means] 'liquor.' 'Saṃvarī' [means] drinking [liquor]. 'Saṃvaraṃ' [means] 'water.' 'Supriyaṃ' [means] 'flowers.' 'Sañcayaṃ' [means] 'fruit.' 'Jālakaṃ' [means] 'clothing.' 'Kṣaṃ' [means] 'house.' 'Kṣorṇṇaṃ' [means] 'one's own house.' 'Kāmadaṃ' [means] 'the deity's house.' 'Kṣepaṇaṃ' [means] 'maṇḍala.' 'Bhodanaḥ' [means] 'maṇḍala-teacher.' 'Upāya' [means] 'student.' 'Mitraṃ' [means] 'the brethren.' 'Rañjitā' [means] 'the goddess.' 'Gopitā' [means] 'Vajrayoginī.'† B:62b
'Tatpurī' [means] 'ḍākinī.' 'Viklavā' [means] 'mothers.' 'Svamūkha' [means] 'fathers.' 'Yogyaḥ' [means] 'son.' 'Prīṃ prīṃ' [means] 'daughter.' 'Bahulā' [means] 'beautiful woman.' 'Loṭana' [means] 'illicit sex.'[972] 'Prīti' [means] 'edibles.'[973] 'Dhanuḥ' [means] 'give substances.' 'Śe śe' [means] 'go!' 'Pre pre' [means] 'come!' 'Traṃ' means 'it isn't.' 'Vihramo' [means] 'angry.' 'Cchora'

965. *cchomā* (Tib. *brda*). This term is sometimes said to derive from (proper) Skt. *chadman*. It appears in Hindu Tantra in the form *chummā*, of which André Padoux writes: "the term *chummā* denotes also one of the secret signs of recognition of the members of the esoteric initiatic Kula lineages called *ovalli**" (see Brunner et al., eds., *Tāntrikābhidhānakośa* II, 258).

966. Tib reads "the symbolic homage" (*brda'i phyag 'tshal lo*).

967. *svāgataṃ*; Tib reads "am [I] welcome?" (*legs par 'ongs sam*).

968. Tib reads "sit!" (*'dug shig*), rendering another sense of *avarundhana*.

969. *bhuñja*; Tib reads "eat!" (*zo shig pa'o*).

970. *vajrodaka, rdo rje'i chu*; i.e., urine.

971. *pañcāmṛta*; Tib reads "ambrosia-water" (*bdud rtsi'i chu*).

972. *agamyāgamana*; Tib reads "going and coming" (*'gro ba dang 'ong ba*). van der Kuijp ("Earliest Indian Reference," 196) interprets this term as "incest," but this seems too narrow.

973. Tib reads "eat!" (*zo shig pa'o, *bhakṣa*).

[means] 'killing.' 'Jīva' [means] 'protection.' 'Nīra' [means] 'averse.'[974] 'Hri' [means] 'passion.' 'Drava' [means] 'substance.'

"Worshipping regularly (*kramāt*), [one] says *suratas tvaṃ*. Recollecting one's own deity, [one] says *surato 'haṃ*. Exclaiming *anurāgayāmi* [is] the practice (*sādhana*) of Vajrasattva. Exclaiming *anubodhayāmi* [is] the Śrī Vairocana practice. Exclaiming *anumodayāmi* [is] the practice of (Śrī) Herukavajra. Exclaiming *anurāgayāmi* [is] the Śrī Padmanarteśvara prac-
B:63a tice.† Exclaiming *anumodayāmi* [is] the Vajrasūrya practice. Exclaiming *anumardayāmi*[975] [is] the practice of Paramāśva. [When] the goddesses are to be worshipped, [one says] this: *samayas tvam*.[976] To recollect one's own deity, [one] says: *samayo 'ham*. [This is] the worship of the host of the blessed maṇḍala of Śrī Vajrasattva. [This is] the procedure of the chapter [on] verbal tokens.

"Now, the bodily tokens are taught [thus]: touching[977] the crown of the head is paying homage. Touching the forehead is the counter-homage.
End MS C Fluttering the right eyebrow [means] 'the work is done.'[978] ‡[Fluttering] the left [means] 'victory.' Blinking[979] the left eye [means] 'beautiful woman.'[980] [Blinking] the right [means] 'handsome man.'[981] Touching the left
B:63b ear [means] 'well-gone.'[982] [Touching] the right [means] 'well said.' †Touching the right nostril [means] '[s/he asks for] incense.' [Touching] the left [means] '[s/he] asks for perfumes.' Lolling the tongue to the right [means] '[s/he asks for] meat.' [Lolling the tongue] to the left [means] '[s/he] asks for liquor.' Touching the left [side of] the belly[983] [means] '[s/he asks for]

974. *viraktaṃ*; Tib reads this as "passion-free" (*chags pa dang bral ba*).

975. Following B; C and Tib read *anuvarṣayāmi*.

976. Tib reads "When offering to any of the goddesses, one should use the five syllables *samayas tvaṃ*" (*lha mo gang yin pa rnams kyi mchod pa'i lan yin te | sa ma ya stvaṃ zhes bya ba'i tshig lngas so |*). This reference to "five syllables" is not found in Skt; nor does it make much sense. I suspect this is a scribal error for *tshig zlas so*.

977. Tib reads "rubbing" (*nyug pa*).

978. *kārya-siddhi*; C and Tib read "bodily powers" (*kāya-siddhi, sku'i dngos grub*).

979. *spandana*; Tib reads "touching" (*reg pa*).

980. *rūpavatī narī*; Tib reads "good woman" (*bud med bzang mo*).

981. *rūpavān naraḥ*; Tib reads "good man" (*skyes pa bzang po*).

982. *suṣṭhugata*; Tib reads "welcome" (*legs par 'ong pa*).

983. Tib reads "armpit" (*mchan khung*).

food.' [Touching] the right [side means] '[s/he] asks for condiments.'[984] [This is] the procedure of the chapter [on] bodily tokens.

"Thus, doing away with worldly meditation [and] casting away mental fancies,[985] the one who is always joyous in mind, playing [erotically] with the yoginīs,[986] having transformed his body[987] just like King Indrabhūti [and] become a vajra body, disappearing together with his harem,[988] goes from buddha-field to buddha-field endowed with the eight superhuman powers. As it is said in the *Root Tantra*:[989]

> The pleasures of all goddesses[990]
> Being enjoyed as one pleases,
> One should worship oneself
> Through union (*yoga*) [with] one's own personal divinity.[991]
> One should worship by the *anuyoga*
> All the pleasures of yoga.
> The one who savors[992] [these]
> Succeeds by [means of] *atiyoga*.

984. *vyañjana*; the Tibetan word used here, *tshod mo*, generally means "vegetables," but it is attested as an equivalent for *vyañjana* in Rong-zom Chos-kyi Bzang-po's (a contemporary of Rin-bzang) *Theg chen tshul 'jug*, where he explains "*vyañjana* is both the name of the minor marks [of a buddha] and a word for condiments (*tshod ma*)" (*bya dzā na zhes bya ba | dpe byad bzang po'i ming yang yin | tshod ma'i ming yang yin |*); it is clear that he is here referring to condiments, in that he further uses *tshod ma* as an analogy, stating, "just as condiments particularize and draw out the flavor of cooked food . . ." (*ji ltar tshod mas zan gyi ro bye brag du 'byed cing khrid par byed pa ltar |*); see *Rong zom bka' 'bum*, vol. ā, p. 74b[4] and 75a[1].

985. *manorājya*; Tib reads "mental hopes" (*yid la re ba*).

986. *yoginībhiḥ saha*; Tib reads "along with the yogins" (*rnal 'byor pa rnams dang lhan cig*).

987. Reading *tadvat kalevaraṃ* after SS; B reads "pure body" (*śuddha-kṣalevaraṃ—sic* for *śuddha-kalevaraṃ*), likely a scribal corruption of *tadvat kalevaraṃ*; Tib reads "aggregate body" (*phung po'i khog pa*, **skandha-kalevaraṃ*).

988. *antaḥpura*; Tib reads "retinue of queens" (*btsun mo'i tshogs*), which is also a fair rendering.

989. *mūlatantra*; Tib reads "Root Sūtra" (*rtsa ba'i mdo*). *Subhāṣitasaṃgraha* (59) also cites the verse as *mūlasūtra*. Here, this refers to SBS; see: DK, rGyud, vol. ka, f. 154a[3–6].

990. SS reads "all gods" (*sarvadeva-*); GST reads "all pleasures" (*sarvakāma-*).

991. This verse corresponds (more or less) to GST, VII.2. Interestingly, though Āryadeva here cites this verse in the context of the practice with elaboration (*prapañcatā caryā*), PU considers VII.1 to describe the practice with elaboration, and this verse (VII.2) to describe the practice without elaboration (*niṣprapañcatā caryā*). Cf. PU, 62.

992. *samāsvādayamānaḥ*; Tib reads "always" (*rtag tu*, **sadâsvādayamānaḥ*?).

B:64a Hence, the one who is the self of all †buddhas
By the bliss of alchemy (*rasāyana*),
May achieve {true} bliss—
The vitality, youth, and health of Vajrasattva.

The great body of all buddhas;
The (sweet) speech of all buddhas,
The great mind of all buddhas,
The great offering of all buddhas,
The great king of all buddhas,
The overlord of all vajradharas,
Lord of all world-lords (*lokeśvara*),
Lord of all wealth gods (*ratnādhipa*)—

The one who consorts with these
Is resurrected[993] as desired.
[He] succeeds [who is] the universal monarch,
The great accomplished one (*mahāsiddha*) of all goddesses.

"Or, those of small means, who are unable to constantly engage in the extensive elaboration of erotic play (*krīḍā*) by the process just described—for them the [practices] without elaboration and completely without elaboration are taught here in the {*Glorious*} *Supreme Bliss*.[994] Teaching th[ose] practice[s], [the Lord] said:

Daily or monthly
Or, similarly, yearly,
Or as authorized,
One should perform the Buddha Saṃvara.[995]

(And,)

993. *yāty utpatiṃ*; literally "he goes to birth."

994. *Saṃvara; bDe mchog.* This refers to the *Sarvabuddhasamāyoga-ḍākinījālasaṃvara* (SBS), on which scripture see chapter 2, note 344, above.

995. This verse is SBS V.5 (DK, rGyud, vol. ka, f. 155b⁵⁻⁶). Note that "perform" (√*nāṭ*) should here be understood as "act, imitate, dance."

Standing or sitting,
Or walking, in whatever situation,
Aroused[996] or chatting
Wherever, however.[997]

(And,)

Whatever should come through the sensory pathways† B:64b
All that is natural.
By the non-equipoised yoga
One should experience [it as] composed of all buddhas.[998]

* * * * *

Space-like, of space-like [infinite] form,
Unbounded, like the sea—
The epitome of the passionate dharma-way,
[Is] flirtation, the extensive erotic play.

Gathered [here is] the mere pith
In order to instruct student[s].
[In] how many lives
Can the passionate teaching [be] told?"

996. *praharṣa*; Tib reads "laughing" (*dgod/rgod*, **prahāsa*?).

997. Tib reads "wherever, however [one] practices is ok" (*gang na ji ltar spyod kyang rung*). This verse is SBS II.6 (f. 152b⁴⁻⁵).

998. This verse is SBS V.33 (ff. 156b⁷–157a¹); it also is found in both PK (III.36) and the *Cittaviśuddhi-prakaraṇa* attributed to Āryadeva (v. 76). The extant Sanskrit texts of both of these works read "well-" (*su-*) rather than "non-" (*a-*) equipoised yoga" (perhaps reflecting some negotiations between subitist and gradualist interpreters?), but the Tibetan versions of all of these texts seem to uniformly follow the latter reading. The reading of PK and CVP (*sarvaṃ buddhamayaṃ*) may be better than CMP ms B's reading (*sarva-buddhamayaṃ*), i.e., "one should experience all [of it as] composed of buddhas."

10. Resolution of Doubts about the Integration of the Practice without Elaboration

The Vajra Student said, "The practice with elaboration is quite clear. Teach the practice without elaboration, O Lord and Teacher, Vajra Mentor!"

The Vajra Mentor said, "Excellent, excellent, Great One! I will explain the practice without elaboration according to the tradition[999] of the Great Yoga Tantra, the Glorious *Esoteric Community*.[1000] Listen with one-pointed attention!

"In a region that is agreeable to the mind as described in the tantras, [that is]:

> In regions of great wilderness† B:65a
> Provided with fruits, flowers, and the like
> On a lonely mountain should
> This assembly of meditation be practiced.[1001]

Having consecrated[1002] {either} a [single-story] cottage[1003] {or a raised platform (*prāsāda*)} according {to the rite} as [it has been] explained, [and] having [imaginatively] created there a celestial palace with a vajra and jewel peak, with features such as having four corners, and so on, thereafter, the

999. *āmnāya*; Tib reads "personal instruction" (*man ngag*, usually **upadeśa*).

1000. On this scripture, see chapter 2, note 272, above.

1001. This verse, as cited here, is an eccentric version of GST XII.2 (it is identical until pāda d, which conforms to GST XI.35d—note that this latter verse is cited in a similar context at the beginning of chapter 11, below). The standard version reads "the assembly of all siddhis" (*sarva-siddhi-samuccayaṃ*) for "this assembly of meditation" (*idaṃ dhyāna-samuccayaṃ*).

1002. *saṃskṛtya*; this can also mean "having constructed"; Tib reads *mngon par sbyangs* (**abhisaṃskṛtya*), which is stronger in its connotations of ritual consecration.

1003. *bhūmi-gṛha*; see above, chapter 9 (note 922) for a parallel passage with *bhū-gṛha*.

great yogin who is free of ordinary pride, having also consecrated[1004] an external woman,[1005] he—along with the host of disciples[1006] who are connected to the same tribe[1007]—should commence the practice of the Great Seal (*mahāmudrā*) according to the process to be explained.

"Regarding that, the process is this: focusing first of all on ultimate reality, having arisen by the self-consecration process, one is situated in the attitude of the overlord of the maṇḍala, in imitation of the coming forth of Akṣobhya. Then, having visualized the forms of the divinities of the maṇḍala such as Vairocana, and so on—who are the component members of one's own body maṇḍala itself, an indivisible retinue, completely free of ordinary pride—having delighted the entire multitude,[1008] one enters ulti-
B:65b mate reality together with one's †consort through the holistic [or] dissolving process[es].[1009] Then, roused by the [four] goddesses by the purification of the four pure abodes (*brahma-vihāra*) [and] with the [four] verses[1010] such as "you, vajra mind," and so on,[1011] coming forth instantaneously[1012] by the process of self-consecration, one frolics in the nine æsthetic moods in order to enjoy the savor of supreme joy.

"Thus repeatedly entering the reality limit (*bhūta-koṭi*) [and] repeatedly emerging, one should savor the five objects of [sense] desire, which have

1004. *api saṃskṛtya*; this could also be an error for *abhisaṃskṛta*—Tib, in fact, has this reading (*mngon par sbyangs*).

1005. *bāhyāṅganā*; Tib reads "outer consort" (*phyi rol gyi phyag rgya, *bāhyamudrā*).

1006. *śiṣyagaṇa*; Tib reads "one's own disciple" (*rang gi slob ma*).

1007. *jāti*; Tib reads "clan" (*rigs, *kula*).

1008. *cakra*, literally "circle"; Tib reads "the deities of the circle of the maṇḍala without exception" (*dkyil 'khor gyi 'khor lo'i lha ma lus pa, *sakala-maṇḍala-cakra-deva*).

1009. For a brief description of these processes, see chapter 7 (B:47a, and note 698), above.

1010. These songs of the four goddesses (Māmakī, Buddhalocanā, Lokeśvaradayitā and Sarvatathāgatakāyavākcittasamayavajradayitā) are called the "four songs of arousal" (*catuś-codanāgīta*) in, e.g., GSUT; cf. GST XVIII.167 (Matsunaga, 125; Bhattacharyya, p. 165). The verses themselves are GST XVII.72–75. See apparatus to Sanskrit edition for text of these verses.

1011. Tib reads "by the verses 'vajra mind, you,' and so on, [which have] the meaning of the four brahmavihāras" (*tshang pa'i gnas bzhi'i don gyi rdo rje sems khyod ces bya ba la sogs pa'i tshigs su bcad pa rnams kyis*). This refers to GST XVII.72a.

1012. *jhaṭiti*, typically **cig car*; Tib reads *skad cig gis*, typically **kṣaṇāt*. The fact that this term occurs here (after being the object of intense criticism in chapter 1) is significant. It is also interesting that Tib glosses over this fact.

the nature of the five transcendent lords.[1013] As long as the mind does not become weary, one is absorbed in the play (*āralli*) of (all) the transcendent lord(s). There one enjoys the threefold visual objects, form, and so on.[1014] One enjoys the threefold aural objects such as vocal, string, and instrumental music, and so on. One enjoys the threefold olfactory objects such as flower, incense, ointments, and so on. One enjoys the threefold gustatory objects such as bitter, sharp, astringent, sour, and salty [flavors].

"Then, a sixteen-year old girl, virginal, with curvaceous body, bearing swelling breasts,[1015] {who comprehends proper (*gṛhīta*) conduct,}[1016†]—an B:66a
outcaste,[1017] laundress, garland-maker, dancer,[1018] flute-maker,[1019] labouress, craftswoman, cripple,[1020] or kinswoman[1021]—taking[1022] any one of those women, thereafter the great yogin whose nature is nonconceptuality, in

1013. Tib reads "Because [they] have the nature of the Five Transcendent Lords, [one] savors the five objects of desire" (*de bzhin gshegs pa lnga'i ngo bo nyid du gyur pas 'dod pa'i yon tan lnga rnam myong bar mdzad de*).

1014. Tib reads "one's own form, and so on" (*rang gi gzugs la sogs pa*).

1015. *pīna-stana-bhara-namrāvayavā*; or "with curvaceous limbs bearing swelling breasts"; Tib reads "a virgin with firm and large breasts" (*nu ma mkhrang shing rgyas pa'i na chung*).

1016. *gṛhīta-caryānvitā*; lit., "who possesses held conduct." As *anvita* means "understands" as well as "possesses," I have chosen "comprehends" as a suitable English term that comprehends both meanings.

1017. *caṇḍālī*; Tib reads *sme sha can*, which implies a "butcher" (more commonly in Tibetan, *bshan pa*). There is a similar list of such occupations in the *Caṇḍamahāroṣanatantra*—see George's edition, esp. 32–33.

1018. Tib reads "dancer, garland-maker" (*gar mkhan ma dang | phreng brgyud ma*).

1019. *veṇukārī* (Tib **smyug mkhan ma*); Tib reads "arrow-maker" (*mda' mkhan ma*). *Caṇḍamahāroṣaṇa-tantra* gives *kāṇḍakārī* as the equivalent for this latter term; Candra Das gives the equivalent *iṣukāra* of which he says (672), "n. of a low caste in ancient India who used to live by hunting. 2. an archer, an arrow-maker."

1020. *aṅga-vikalā*; Tib reads "anyone suitable *without* faulty limbs" (*gzhan gang yang rung yan lag mi dman pa*).

1021. *bandhu-bhūtā*; Tib reads "a woman who is a friend" (*rtsa lag tu gyur pa'i bud med*), which is another meaning of *bandhu* (which had a wide range of meanings). This is not a bad interpretation, perhaps, as this is a list of (orthodox-dharmically) unsuitable partners and the *Kāma Sūtra* specifies that one should not lie with a woman who is a friend.

1022. *gṛhītvā*; Tib is more explicit, reading not the expected *bzung nas*, but the (optative) *bgrod par bya*—literally, "should go to," with a strong implication of "should make love to." Cf. Candra Das, 281, who cites Csoma de Kőrös's authority for the gloss: "*buḏ-meḏ-la-ḇgroḏ-pa* to lie with a woman."

order to prove to himself the nature of all things,[1023] having consecrated by the process[es] of purification, and so on, the pledge [substances] to be consumed, [which are] forbidden[1024] [to be eaten] in the world,[1025] [and] casting away perception of worldly objects, consumes [them] in a private place.

In that way, one does not form ritual gestures (*mudrā*); [one does] not weary[1026] oneself [with] maṇḍalas, or [ritual] hearths, or shrines (*caitya*), or reciting [scriptural] texts; [one] does not pay homage to images of cloth, wood, or stone; [one] does not contemplate refuge [in] śrāvakas or pratyekabuddhas; [one] is not distracted by [auspicious or inauspicious] periods of time [such as] lunar days, [elevenfold] sub-divisions of the days, moments, [or] divisions of the zodiac.[1027] All this is effected internally.[1028]

"Should one, lacking the requisites, not be able to procure the entire
B:66b maṇḍala, then the practice without †elaboration should be practiced by the practitioner, who has the nature of the five secret great realities (*pañca-guhya-mahātattva*),[1029] according to this process:

The process is this: one is situated for the delight of [Lord] Mahāsukha [Great Bliss] in the (south)eastern corner in the form of Rūpavajrā [Form Adamant], whose soft lotus-hand holds a mirror [and] gazes with gentle[1030] eyes, whose swelling breast is completely crowded and beautified by strings

1023. Tib interprets this as follows, which also works: "in order to show that [that one] has the nature of all things" (*bdag nyid dngos po thams cad kyi bdag nyid du bstan par bya ba'i phyir*).

1024. *garhita*; Tib reads "reviled" (*smad pa*), which is another suitable meaning of *garhita*.

1025. These "pledges" (*samaya*) are, typically, the five meats (beef, dog, elephant, horse, and human meat) and the five ambrosias (feces, urine, blood, semen, and marrow). On these substances, and the interpretation of their use in esoteric Buddhist ritual, see my "Beef, Dog, and Other Mythologies."

1026. *kāya-kleśa*, more accurately "he does not pain his body with . . ."; Tib reads "bodily fatigue" (*lus kyi ngal dub*).

1027. *tithi-karaṇa-muhūrta-nakṣatra-kāla*; Tib (emended) reads "periods of time such as numbers of days, half-days, instants, or divisions of the zodiac" (*tshes grangs dang byed pa dang thang cig dang | skar ma'i dus*).

1028. *adhyātmanaîva sampādayati*; Tib reads "all of these are perfected only by the inner nature" (*'di dag thams cad ni nang gi bdag nyid kho nas rdzogs par byed do*).

1029. Tib reads "that practitioner, by [means of] the five aspects of reality" (*sgrub pa po des de kho na nyid rnam pa lngas*).

1030. *saumya*; Tib reads "peaceful" (*zhi ba'i*).

of pearls,[1031] [and] whose slightly loose garment reveals half of her curvaceous hips.[1032] One is situated in the south(western) corner in the form of Śabdavajrā [Sound Adamant], gazing wide-eyed, playing the lute (*vīṇā*) in imitation of the [low, sweet] song of the *kākalī*, singing song-stories that skillfully illuminate the teaching of the dharma of impassioned activities, [whose] composition [evokes the] amorous play [of the] erotic mood. One is situated in the (north)western corner, in the form of Gandhavajrā [Scent Adamant], gazing with smiling eyes, whose reddish lotus-hands are covered in lace, splendid with the lustre of long, glistening nails, in the form of a dancer (bearing) a bejewelled vessel containing scents of the perfumes (*kuṭī*) of the ten directions, redolent with the fragrances of saffron, aloewood,† musk, premium sandalwood, [and] camphor. One is situated in the B:67a north(eastern) corner in the form of Rasavajrā [Flavor Adamant], gazing with honeyed[1033] eyes, bearing a vessel of silver, gold, and jewels, holding food [as] wholesome [as] ambrosia, the divine victuals, [of] superlative flavor, [and] blended with various condiments. In order to delight [the Lord Great Bliss] Mahāsukha, one is situated in one's lap in the form of Sparśavajrā [Touch Adamant], whose body is ornamented with all [auspicious] marks,[1034] with an extremely delicate waist, {beautiful, bent and swaying}, with three folds [to her belly], with a navel deep and right-turning, large [and with] a thin line of hair disappearing into it,[1035] gentle-looking,[1036] with a smiling face, [and] an erotic, {playful, [and] charming} gait, languid[1037] [due to her] heavy hips and loins.

1031. *aśeṣa-muktā-hāra-vikaṭa-saṃkaṭa-pīna-payodharā*; Tib reads "resounding with [the sounds of] all her strings of pearls [hitting against one another], swaying, with breasts large and slightly soft" (*mu tig gi chun 'phyang ma lus par 'khrol zhing rnam par phye ba dang | nu ma rgyas shing cung zad mnyen pa dang*).

1032. Tib reads "clothes hanging free and showing a little of her lower body" (*gos grol zhing ro smad cung zad ston pas*).

1033. Tib reads "caring" (*brtse ba dang bcas pa'i*).

1034. *sarva-lakṣaṇālaṃkṛta-gātrā*; Tib reads "ornamented with all bodily marks" (*lus mtshan thams cad kyis brgyan pa*).

1035. *romarājy-antarita;* the ms is unclear, but this seems to be the reading, esp. as it is confirmed in SS. Tib reads "like a victory banner" (*rgyal mtshan ltar*), presumably reading some form based on *dhvaja*. Thanks to Wendy Doniger for guidance on this passage.

1036. *saumya-dṛṣṭā*; Tib reads "with peaceful gaze" (*zhi bas lta ba*).

1037. *stabdha-śṛṅgāra-lalita-komala-gati*; Tib reads "with leisurely and extremely sensuous gait" (*'gros dal zhing shin tu sgeg pa*).

"Then, [the Lord Great Bliss] Mahāsukha, in order to demonstrate the impassioned activities of the glorious pleasure of lovemaking,[1038] gladdening [the goddesses] through erotic techniques (*karaṇa*) such as embracing, kissing, sucking, fondling the breasts, striking [so as to cause] goosebumps,[1039]
B:67b biting, applying the nails, †bruising,[1040] swaying, needling,[1041] elbowing, and so on, setting in equipoise knower and known and critical wisdom and liberative art through the union of vajra and lotus, [and] sense-organs and objects, [such as] the jingling of agitated strings of pearls, bangles,[1042] gold bracelets, and armbands, [then] by wiggling, driving, and exciting the three veins—*madanātapatra*, *kūrmakaṇṭha*, [and] *śaśāṅka* —with three fingers, all the transcendent lords who have the nature of the aggregates, and so on, [as] vowels and consonants, become fluid in the form of the torrent of a waterfall[1043] [and,] having obtained the level of gnosis, [He, the Lord Mahāsukha,] relishes the state of supreme great bliss.[1044]

"Illuminating this very point, [the Lord] said in the *Root Tantra*:[1045]

The one impassioned for gnosis always
Enjoys the five objects of [sense] desire.[1046]

1038. Tib reads "in order to teach the joyous practices of the glorious Mahāsukha" (*bde ba chen po'i dpal rab tu dga' ba'i spyod pa bstan par bya ba'i phyir*).

1039. *pulakatāḍana*; Wayman (*Yoga*, 351) translates this a "beating with bristling hair," but *pulaka* clearly means some kind of "goosebumps" (a thrill or *frisson* when the hair stands on end).

1040. *mardana*, or "rubbing?"

1041. *sūci*; both PSED and M-W cite this as "a kind of coitus."

1042. *valaya*; also a bracelet. I am not sure how this is distinguished from the "gold bracelet" (*kaṭaka*) that follows. Perhaps it could instead be a "girdle," i.e., jewelry of some kind worn around the hips?

1043. *nirjharadhārā*; Tib reads "a stainless stream" (*dri ma med pa'i rgyun*, **nirmala-dhārā*).

1044. A parallel passage may be found in PU (225, l. 22–29).

1045. *mūla-tantra*; here, again, this refers to GST, on which see chapter 2, note 272, above. Tib reads "in order to clarify this very point, in the Root Scripture" (*don 'di nyid gsal bar bya ba'i phyir | rtsa ba'i mdo las |*).

1046. Or, "the one impassioned for the five gnoses should always enjoy the objects of [sense] desire." Tib implies "the one who desires the passionate gnosis, always relies on the objects of [sense] desire" (*chags can ye shes 'dod pa yis | rtag tu 'dod pa'i yon tan bsten |*). This verse is GST VII.7.

If Rupavajrā [Form Adamant], and so on, are not available, then it should be practiced together with Sparśavajrā [Touch Adamant] alone by means of the *saṃpuṭa* yoga.[1047] Because all the transcendent lords are contained in the body maṇḍala of the practitioner [and] all the goddesses are contained in the body maṇḍala of Sparśavajrā, therefore †it should be repeatedly cultivated nonconceptually by one with uninterrupted pride. Explaining this, [it says] in the *Root Scripture*:[1048] B:68a

> Now, Vajrapāṇi, the overlord of all transcendent lords, should emit the practice of the resolution of the consort discipline (*vidyā-vrata*) of the body, speech, and mind vajras of all transcendent lords from his own body, speech, and mind vajras.
>
> The [meditative] cultivation of body, speech, and mind
> Of the body, speech, and mind vajras—[1049]
> That is to be done in one's own form;
> Quick success (*siddhi*) will be obtained.
>
> Regarding that, this [is] the consort discipline of body, speech, and mind:[1050]
>
> [An] image bearing a crown of dreadlocks,
> Great, with a white-colored appearance—
> All should be produced according to the rite,
> Through the execution of the vows of mantra.
>
> Taking a sixteen-year-old [girl]
> Decked with all ornaments,

1047. Tib reads **saṃyoga* (*kun du sbyor ba*).

1048. *mūlasūtra*; Tib reads **mūlatantra* (*rtsa ba'i rgyud*). Again, this is GST (see chapter 2, note 272, above). This passage is GST XVI.91–103 (with verses 98–100 elided), see Matsunaga, ed., 94–95.

1049. Tib distinguishes the "body, speech, and mind vajras" with the honorific (*sku gsung thugs*), from the "cultivation of body, speech, and mind" in the non-honorific register (*lus dang ngag sems*).

1050. Tib reads "body, speech, and mind vajras" (*sku dang gsung dang thugs rdo rje*). Note that this (and the verses following) is still part of the citation from the GST.

With a pretty face [and] large eyes—having obtained
[Such a one, one] should perform the consort discipline.

One should meditate with the vajra-symbols (*vajra-cihna*),
Enjoying the state of Locanā.

[A girl] who knows how to employ ritual gestures and mantras,
Learned in mantra and tantra—
One should make [her] wife of the transcendent lord,
Consecrated as Buddhabodhi.

The one of great discipline (*mahāvratin*) should perform
The secret offering at four times.
He should enjoy all food and drink,
B:68b Including tubers and roots.[1051†]

Thus, may one become buddha quickly—
A great ocean of gnosis, a lord (*prabhu*).
One may obtain all that in only six months—
There is no doubt [of that].

The practitioner of firm resolve,
Should always wander in the forest, begging.
They, trembling with fear, give to that one
Food, divinely adorned.[1052]

Should the one of adamantine self prevail,
[The ordinary body] will perish [and he will become]
adamantine-indestructible.[1053]

1051. *kanda-mūla-phalaiḥ*, lit. "the fruits of tubers and roots"; Tib reads "trunk/tree, root, fruit" (*sdong bu rtsa ba 'bras bu*).

1052. Tib reads "good food" (*kha zas bzang po*).

1053. Basing myself here on PU (202), which glosses this verse by saying "[the verse] 'should . . . prevail' and so on speaks of the result of the practices. The yogin whose self is the three vajras may prevail; i.e., [he] will surpass the human condition (*mānuṣyabhāva*). The perishable, i.e., the ordinary body, 'will perish.' Transforming it, [it] will become unsplittable like adamant, 'indestructible,' i.e., imperishable" (***atikramed-ityādinā caryā-phalam āha | tri-***

Goddesses, snake-nymphs, great dryads,
Demi-goddesses, even women—
Having obtained [one], the consort discipline should be
performed
[In order] to enjoy the gnosis of the three vajras.

"Thus, those who undertake the six [practices] of love—pairing, embracing, holding hands, laughing, gazing, and copulating—enjoy the bliss of supreme joy moment by moment. In the perfected condition, as long as the life-cycle continues, they will be the embodiment of eternal joy. Clarifying this very point, [it] says in the *Assembly of All Deities Tantra*:[1054]

Setting the two organs in equipoise,
On the occasion of the rite of exertion,
The sage's accomplishment of a happy mind
Is known as the 'great bliss.'[1055†] B:69a

---

vajrātmā yogī atikramet mānuṣya-bhāvam abhibhavati naśyatîti nāśaṃ prākṛtaṃ śarīraṃ tat parāvṛttya vajra-vad abhedyam akṣaram avinaśvaraṃ bhavet |).

1054. *Sarvadeva-samāgama Tantra, Lha thams cad yang dag par 'dus pa'i rgyud.* I have not been able to identify an extant Sanskrit text of this scripture, nor a Tibetan translation. This verse is, however, also cited in the *Subhāṣita-saṃgraha* (cf. Bendall, 59). It is cited again in the CMP, below (B:71b).

1055. Tib reads "The mind attained with a joyous mind is called 'Great Bliss'" (*dga' ba'i sems kyis thugs 'grub pa | bde ba chen po zhes bya'o*). This verse is cited in SS (59), which reads *dhyeyo sa vidhir antare* |. Bendall cites alternatives for *dhyeyo*, viz. *dhyā yā* or *jyāyān*. Based on Tib and Bendall's indications, I had previously (Wedemeyer 1999, p. 346) suggested the emendation *vyāyāma-vidhir*—a reading confirmed by ms B.

11. Resolution of Doubts about the Integration of the Practice Completely without Elaboration

[The Vajra Mentor continued,] "Now, the practice completely without elaboration will be introduced. In a place congenial to the mind as described in the tantras, that is—

> On lonely mountains[1056]
> And by pooling streams,[1057]
> In charnel grounds and the like as well should
> This assembly of meditation be performed.[1058]

—dryads (*yakṣinī*), servants (*kiṅkarā*), and the like should be propitiated for the purpose of procuring food.[1059] Or, just provided with food from a ritual assistant[1060] or at a great [ritual] sacrifice,[1061] one should undertake the practices completely without elaboration by this process.

1056. *parvateṣu vivikteṣu*; TIB reads "on an extremely lonely mountain" (*ri bo shin tu dben pa*, **ativivikta-parvate*).

1057. *nadī-prasravaṇa*; this could also be interpreted as "by the torrents of streams"; TIB reads "banks and rivers" (*chu ngogs 'babs chu*).

1058. This verse is GST XI.35 (note also its similarity to the idiosyncratic version of GST XII.2 cited at the beginning of chapter 10, above). PU (104) comments that this verse describes the site of practice (*sādhana-sthāna*).

1059. Following TIB *kha zas sbyor ba'i phyir*; SKT reads *bhakta-sarāva-nimittaṃ*, "with *bhakta-sarāva* as the aim." *Sarāva* means a plate or dish; *bhakta* has several meanings—serving, cooking, food, meals, a worshipper/devotee. Thus, one could render this "with the aim of [procuring] dishes of food" or "with prepared dishes as the aim" or "with dishes [prepared by] a devotee as the aim." TIB is straightforward, so I have followed it here.

1060. *uttara-sādhaka*; TIB *sgrub pa'i grogs mchog* "a supreme practitioner-friend."

1061. *mahāsattra*; TIB (P and N) reads *tshogs chen pos*, suggesting **mahāsattreṇa* (alt. D reads *tshogs chen po'i*, **mahāsattrasya*). The former is not at all bad, since it would keep the terms

"Regarding that, this [is] the process: First of all, recalling the experience of the beginningless sufferings of the life-cycle, due to the wish [for] the bliss of nirvāṇa, the practitioner should abandon all socializing [and] should recognize [that] ultimately [there is] suffering even in the might of kings.[1062] Second, one should forsake the mind [desiring to] take possession of objects even [those] merely the size of a sesame seed.[1063] Third, focusing on ultimate reality,[1064] one should have no regard for [either one's] body or life. †As it says in the *King of Samādhi Scripture*:[1065]

B:69b

> 'Hence therefore, O Prince, the bodhisattva, (the great one,) desirous of this samādhi, who wishes to quickly [become] enlightened to the unexcelled, perfect enlightenment should have no regard for body or life.'[1066]

of the either-or (*vā . . . vā*) construction in the same case; but I think locative is acceptable in this context.

1062. Tib reads "should meditate on the experience of suffering [of all beings] even up to masters of empires" (*tha na rgyal srid kyi dbang phyug la'ang sdug bsngal gyi 'du shes bsgom par bya'o*). This would seem to be a kind of "sword of Damocles" meditation. For a Buddhist version of this, see "The Legend of Vītaśoka" in John S. Strong, *Legend of King Aśoka*, 221–26.

1063. Tib reads "one should forsake the mind that grasps at the [substantial] reality of even a sesame seed" (*til 'bru tsam la'ang dngos por 'dzin pa'i blo spang bar bya'o*). Other translations, however, conform better to the received Sanskrit. As I have noted elsewhere (Wedemeyer, "Tantalising Traces of the Labours of the Lotsāwas"), Tsongkhapa (RṄSG, p. 673) makes the following comments regarding this passage: "Concerning the second [of the four distinctive intentions], since the translation found in the two new translations, to wit 'one should forsake the mind [desiring to] take possession of objects even the size of a sesame seed,' is better, one should take this to refer to not taking, i.e., not accumulating, goods even [the size of] a sesame seed. One should not take this to refer to 'object grasping' in the sense of conceptual insistence on reality" (*gnyis pa ni 'gyur gsar gnyis las | dngos po til 'bru tsam la yang yongs su 'dzin pa'i blo dor bar bya'o | zhes bsgyur ba legs pas yo byad til tsam yang bsags te mi 'dzin pa la bya'i | bden zhen gyi dngos 'dzin mi byed pa la mi bya'o*).

1064. *paramārtha-satyaṃ saṃdhāya*; Tib reads "having faith in ultimate reality" (*don dam pa'i bden pa la dad pas, *paramārtha-satyaṃ śraddhāya*).

1065. On this scripture, see chapter 8, note 779, above.

1066. This citation is found in SRS Ch. XXII; see Vaidya, ed., 143, 143n4.

Likewise, neither the worldly, minor powers (*siddhi*) nor the transcendent eight great powers are to be sought, for [they are] distracting and mutable.[1067] As it says in the Great Yoga Tantra, *The Uncommon Secret*:[1068]

> Then, in the attainment of the supreme power of omniscience,[1069] one desires no power whatsoever. One is not to seek the speech power of all Materialists, [nor] the servant power, [nor] the wholesome vase power, [nor] the subterranean power, [nor] the political power, [nor] the domination power, [nor] the prosperity power,[1070] [nor] the destructive power. Why? Because the one who aims for the great power (*mahāsiddhi*) does not desire minor power[s]. [That one] cares only for[1071] the nonconceptual power.† B:70a

Likewise, it is said in the *Secret Accomplishment*:[1072]

> [Ritual] procedures, and so on, in truth[1073]
> Should always be shunned by the one who knows reality.
>
> One should not act otherwise than
> With the pride of Vajrasattva.[1074]

1067. *vikṣepatvāt vaivartikatvāc ca*; Tib suggests, "because one will become distracted and will regress" (*rnam par g.yeng bar 'gyur ba dang | phyir ldog par 'gyur ba'i phyir*). This term *vaivartika* is the same used in the sense of a bodhisattva being "irreversible" (see the beginning of chapter 8, above, for this usage), but here I think the sense, while related, is more ordinary.

Pandey marks this passage as a continuation of the SRS citation, but this does not seem to be the case.

1068. *Asādhāraṇa-guhya-mahāyogatantra*; *Thun mong ma yin pa'i gsang ba zhes bya ba'i rnal 'byor chen po'i rgyud.* I have not been able to identify this scripture either in Sanskrit or Tibetan.

1069. Tib reads "then, furthermore in order to gain the power of omniscience" (*de nas gzhan yang thams cad mkhyen pa'i dngos grub thob pa'i phyir*).

1070. Tib inverts order of prosperity and dominance.

1071. Tib reads "should be single-minded toward" (*la sems rtse gcig par 'gyur bar bya'o*).

1072. On this work, see chapter 8, note 760, above.

1073. Tib reads "effort [in] procedures, and so on" (*sbyor ba la sogs 'bad pa ni*).

1074. These two pādas are especially problematic. I have followed the conjecture of Bendall

[Ritual] procedures are not to be observed,
Situated in the pure reality.[1075]

By the yoga of the selfless[1076] state, meanwhile,
[One] investigates.

By [the one who] stands in the essenceless state
And [the one] endowed with the divine art,
[That] will be accomplished without analysis,
Which is enjoined a bit in the ritual manuals.

Through the power of the yoga of [meditative] cultivation,
[One] serves just oneself—
All [that occurs] in a moment,
Which has some of the character of accomplishment (*siddhi*).[1077]

Hence, having enthusiastically set [as one's] objective that, 'doing without an external [physical] woman, I will more quickly perfect the level of Mahāvajradhara by meditative union with a gnosis consort located in the heart,' the solitary one should meditate according to the process described below.

"The process is this: As long as there is the container of the aggregate[s], there is the nature of the three consciousnesses. [Due to] the prototypes and radiances, one's own self and the self of others[1078] function visibly in the
B:70b world.[1079] How? First, the radiance[s]. Second, the prototype[s]. That, †con-

(see SS, 60, note 5), reading *vajrasattvasyâhaṃkāraṃ*. Bendall comments, "Ms. (unmetrically) tvaṃ tadrūpaṃkkrūraṃ, where drū must be corrupted from ha and ṃkkū for ṅkā." B reads *vajrasattva-dhruvaṃ krūraṃ*, which is very similar to the reading of the SS MS, though this should come as no surprise, as the latter is very likely derived from CMP. GS reads *vajrasattvād ahaṃkāraṃ*.

1075. Tib reads "those who abide in the pure reality do not perform the procedures" (*dag pa'i de nyid la gnas pas | sbyor ba rnams kyang mi bya ste*).

1076. Following Tib (P) and Skt (*bdag med, nairātma-*), D and Co read *bdag nyid*. The GS translation by Kṛṣṇapaṇḍita also reads *bdag med*.

1077. This citation is GS VI.45cd–49ab.

1078. Reading *parātmā*; B reads "the supreme self" (*paramātmā*).

1079. Tib reads "the movement of the prototypes [and] luminances appears as self and other" (*rang bzhin gyis snang ba 'gro ba dag* (read: *bdag*) *dang gzhan la snang bar 'gyur ro*).

joined with air, wanders thereby in the ten directions. How? By the prototypes [such as] passion, dispassion, moderate passion, and so on. Likewise, the one hundred and sixty prototypes [such as] aggression, peace, delight, pain, hunger, thirst, feeling, and so on, operating in the mind day and night, ceased in delusion[1080] and again emerging, they wander by the force of air. From that, [occurs] agitation (*vyākulatā*) of the body. As long as the sense organs such as the eye, and so on, do not perceive [their] object[s], it will be dependent on that very thing, due to habituation from beginningless time. Then, from [repeated] cultivation of the selfless dharma through a series of births, the one who understands the procedure of burning,[1081] having brought together the prototypes and radiances, should focus on the ultimate reality by this process.[1082]

"Regarding that, the process is this: the aggregates, and so forth, enter the subtle element [air]. The subtle element further enters mind. Then, mind further enters mental factors. Mental factors further [enter] delusion. Thus fixated, [one] sleeps. At that time, [there is] forgetfulness of the feature[s] of entering [through] mind, mental factors, and delusion.[1083] †Subsequently, forgetfulness itself disappears; [and there is] the nature of gnosis, the 'brilliance.' Further, the air[s are] released; the prototypes depart.[1084] B:71a

1080. That is, the luminance-imminence (*ālokopalabdhaka*) state.

1081. *vidagdha-prayoga* (**rnam par bsreg pa'i sbyor ba*); Tib (mis)reads "the procedure of mixing" (*rnam par bsres pa'i sbyor ba*).

1082. Tib reads "Then, by habituation from one birth to another, by learning the dharma of selflessness and understanding the yoga of mixing, one becomes mixed as one with the luminances of the prototypes. By this process, one should perceive the ultimate reality" (*de nas skye ba gcig nas gcig tu goms pas bdag med pa'i chos la bslabs pas rnam par bsreg pa'i sbyor ba khong du chud nas rang bzhin gyis snang ba dang gcig tu 'dre par bya ste | rim pa 'dis don dam pa'i bden pa la dmigs par bya'o*).

1083. *tasmin kāle citta-caitasikāvidyā-praveśa-lakṣaṇa-vismṛtiḥ*; Tib reads "at this time, at the moment of entering mind, mentality, and delusion, one loses mindfulness" (*de la dus 'dir ni sems dang sems pa ma rig pa la rab tu zhugs pa'i skad cig la dran pa brjed pa'o, *tasmin kāle citta-caitasikāvidyā-praveśana-kṣaṇa-vismṛtiḥ*).

1084. Tib reads "Also, if liberated, one will find the intrinsic nature of air" (*yang grol ba na rlung gi rang bzhin rnyed de*).

Otherwise,[1085] a sleep[1086] state occurs. As long as consciousness does not depart,[1087] one sleeps. One becomes aware of the brilliance. That very thing is called the 'inner enlightenment,' which is to be introspectively known, free of body, speech, and mind, the ultimate reality.

"By this sequence, 'one should slay the array of transcendent lords' who reside in the body maṇḍala, i.e., one should cause them to enter suchness; [then,] 'one may obtain the most excellent accomplishment' (*siddhi*).[1088] That is to say, without requiring the practice[s] with elaboration or those without, the transformation of one's body will occur here more quickly. This very idea is expressed in the Great Yoga Tantra, the *Explanation of the Intention*:[1089]

> Should [one] see inner things such as form, and so on,
> [This] is called 'insight [meditation]' (*vipaśyanā*).
> Should one visualize Akṣobhya, and so on, corresponding in
> number [to the above],
> [This] is called 'tranquility [meditation]' (*śamatha*).
> On account of the insubstantiality of these two,
> [It] has the name 'suchness-tranquility.'[1090]

B:71b

> The yogin should make all buddhas†
> Enter the maṇḍala of suchness.[1091]

1085. *no cet*; Tib reads "at which time" (*gang gi tshe*, **ced* or **yadā*).

1086. *svapnāntara*; Tib interprets this as "another dream" (*rmi lam gzhan dag*).

1087. Tib reads "fluctuate" (*g.yo ba*).

1088. *sutarāṃ siddhiṃ*; or, "one will obtain *siddhi* more easily." Tib reads "one will obtain the siddhi of good fortune" (*skal pa bzang po'i dngos grub thob par 'gyur*, **subhaga-siddhiṃ āpnuyāt*).

Āryadeva is here implicitly commenting on GST VII.33cd. The parts I have nested in single quotation marks are passages from this half-verse.

1089. On this scripture, see chapter 3, note 364, above. Pandey's reading here of *mahā*-sandhyāvyākaraṇa cannot be sustained. For one, it would be the only instance in the CMP where Āryadeva adds such an honorific prefix to the name of a text. Given the overall pattern of his citation of other works, a reading of *āha* seems all but certain.

1090. Tib reads "since these two are insubstantial, suchness is explained as 'peace'" (*'di dag dngos med gyur pa yi | de bzhin nyid ni zhi bar bshad*).

1091. This passage may be found at DK, rGyud, vol. ca, f. 171a$^{4-5}$.

Further, it is said in the *Assembly of all Deities Tantra*:[1092]

> In the terrific[1093] fire of nirvāṇa,
> Not even ashes will survive.
> Hence, there is evident there
> Neither sense-object[s] nor [sense-]elements.

By this sequence, having ascertained the Mother of All Buddhas, whose form is understood through scripture and reasoning, [and] forsaking all play (*āralli*) and attachment to [sense-]objects, [one] should perform the practice of a *bhusuku*,[1094] by this process.

"Regarding that, the process [is] this: 'bhu' [means while] eating [one] pursues[1095] that alone; [one] should not think [that] one refuses socializing by difficult ascetical practices. 'Su' [means while] sleeping, one should make the consciousness that is characterized by delusion directly manifest; that very delusion does (not)[1096] again cause [such] consciousness to return, marked with the form of hook.[1097] [It] makes directly manifest brilliancy alone, stainless in nature. 'Ku' [means] one should go to the outhouse,[1098] with the aim of excreting feces and urine, [and one] experiences that alone. One rejects all socializing, and should not reflect on the nature of body, feelings, †objects, and sense organs. B:72a

"The practice completely without elaboration should be performed by means of the mad [spiritual] discipline (*unmatta-vrata*) according to the

1092. On this scripture, see chapter 10, note 1054, above.

1093. Tib reads "unbearable" (*mi bzad*).

1094. *Bhu-su-ku*, "one who eats, sleeps, and defecates." This term is left untranslated in Tib, though it is sometimes rendered in Tibetan tradition by the term *'du shes gsum pa*, "the one with three volitions." The most famous *bhusuku* in Buddhist literature is perhaps Ācārya Śāntideva, who is depicted as such in some Tibetan hagiographies.

1095. Reading *anusarati*; Tib suggests "contemplates" (*rjes su dran pa*, **anusmarati*).

1096. Tib reads *'dre bar mi byed*, "does not mix [with]"; Skt does not read a negative here, but the context seems to demand it. Perhaps this should be emended to *na punar āvartayati*.

1097. The meaning here is obscure to me. Tib seems to be missing something; it reads "that very delusion, like a hook, does not mix with any consciousness" (*ma rig pa lcags kyu lta bu de nyid kyis rnam par shes pa gang la'ang 'dre bar mi byed de*).

1098. Literally, "shed" (*kuṭi*); Tib is more explicit, reading "the toilet" (*bshang sa*).

process described in the explanatory tantra[s].[1099] Regarding that, the process [is] this:

> When the hero is nonconceptual,
> And has broken through worldly rectitude,[1100]
> He should do all deeds.[1101]
> The buddhas see him then.
>
> The naïve may analyze with reasoning—
> Proving everything, free of doubt.[1102]
> When the yogin makes no effort,
> Then the blessings rain down.[1103]
>
> Those entrenched in the obscurations of ignorance
> Associated with all sins
> Will unerringly have success (*siddhi*)
> In six months by the mad [spiritual] discipline.

1099. The "standard" Tibetan translation, that of Lo-chen Rin-chen bZang-po (as found in our edition) reads, "I will also explain the practices thoroughly without elaboration by the process related in the *Scripture Explaining the Mad Spiritual Discipline*" (*shin tu sprod pa med pa'i spyod pa smyon pa'i brtul zhugs bshad pa'i mdo las gsungs pa'i rim pas kyang bshad par bya'o*), suggesting the existence of a work known under that title. However, as Tsongkhapa points out (RṄSG, 678), both "new" translations of the CMP (those of Pa-tshab and Chag) read "one should practice [the practices] completely without elaboration by the mad [spiritual] discipline according to the method and process expressed in the explanatory tantra(s)" (*bshad pa'i rgyud las gsungs pa'i tshul dang rim pas smyon pa'i brtul zhugs kyis kyang shin tu spros med la spyad par bya*), which corresponds exactly to the surviving Sanskrit texts.

The first verse is also cited in the SS (62), which does not specify the source. However, Tsongkhapa claims (RṄSG, 678) that the passage is drawn from the sixteenth chapter of the *Vajra-maṇḍalālaṃkāra Tantra* (*rDo rje snying po rgyan gyi rgyud kyi le'u bcu drug pa*—on which, see chapter 3, note 432, above). However, I have not been able to locate this passage in that source.

1100. Tib reads "when one stands firm in nonconceptuality [and] abandons the worldly" (*gang tshe brtan par mi rtog la | gnas shing 'jig rten pa spangs te*).

1101. Tib reads "if one integrates all deeds" (*spyod pa thams cad bsdus byas na*).

1102. Following B; Tib follows the "standard" reading found also in SS, i.e., "who have totally eliminated doubts" (*sarvataś chinna-saṃśayaḥ*). Tib reads, in full, "Totally removing doubts by reasoning, as a child does" (*kun du the tshom gcod pa yis | rigs pas byis pa ji bzhin spyad |*).

1103. Tib reads "when the yogi has no passion, the attainments increase" (*gang tshe chags med rnal 'byor pa | de tshe phun sum tshogs 'phel 'gyur |*).

One should see all buddhas [as] oneself,
Worshipped[1104] with all [objects of] desire.
With neither weakness nor defect,
A body will be born—vitality at one's own volition.

[One] will gain, without struggle,
Unexcelled, supreme enlightenment.
They will succeed without effort,
Who long for the gratification of all desires.

The supremely profound state
[Is] permanent; going, standing, [or] sitting—
The expertise of the gnosis of brilliance† B:72b
[Is] always the mark of the yogins.

By this meditation-yoga,
One should make firm the mind-jewel.
They perform the consecration, too—
The buddhas who are installed in enlightenment.

Having thus become appointed,
One should manifest [oneself], devoted to existence.[1105]
As long as the mind is not wearied,
The wise one [is] mentally equipoised.

If wearied, though, he should then roam,
Doing as he pleases.
He should manifest the vast enlightenment,
With eyes slightly opened.

Laughing, talking, standing a bit,
He should do something or other—

1104. Tib (following the "standard" reading) reads "satiated" (*rab tu 'gengs, *prapūryate*).

1105. *bhāvayed bhāvatatparaḥ*; Tib reads "one should meditate on that with effort" (*de la 'bad pas sgom par bya, *bhāvayet tatra yatnataḥ*).

But the mind devoted to [meditative] cultivation
Will not be born, insofar as it is wearied.[1106]

Thus endowed with samādhi,[1107]
The mantrins of nonconceptuality
Setting aside a fixed period of time,
The unexcelled state will be accomplished.

Thus, conforming to the categories of weak, middling, and outstanding, the threefold practice will give rise to the sign[s] of the accomplishment of the Great Seal (*mahāmudrā-siddhi*) in the one who repeatedly cultivates [it] for a fortnight, a month, or up to six months, [respectively]. In that regard, this [is] the sign:

B:73a Subtle in form, light to the touch,†
Having attained omnipresence,
Brightness and firmness,
[Self-]mastery, [and] having come to the end of desire.[1108]

Further, too, the dream-signs are told in the Great Yoga Tantra, the {Glorious} *Esoteric Community*:[1109]

The attainment of the pinnacle of enlightened gnosis will
be seen—
The buddha-splendor—[1110]

1106. Tib reads "insofar as it is not wearied, [one should] be devoted to the mind of [meditative] cultivation" (*ji srid skyo bar mi 'gyur bar | sgom pa'i sems la zhen par bya |*).

1107. Tib reads "endowed with pledges" (*dam tshig ldan, *samaya-yuktasya*).

1108. This verse is also cited in SS (indeed, this entire passage from "thus, conforming" to "fixed in the meditation vajra" is plagiarized by the author of SS). Since the citation and its context is lifted verbatim from CMP, however, there is no further information to be gleaned as to its source. It is also cited in AKUN (172) and Abhayākaragupta's *Āmnāyamañjarī* (f. $190b^{4-5}$). In neither of these places is the source of the verse given, so it remains a mystery. Thanks to Harunaga Isaacson for providing these references.

1109. On this scripture, see chapter 2, note 272, above.

1110. Tib reads "like a buddha body" (*sangs rgyas sku dang tshungs par mthong, *buddha-[kāya]-saṃnibham*). The canonical Tibetan versions (N, P, D) read "sees the excellent buddha-light (or, sees the buddha-light excellently)" (*sangs rgyas 'od ni bzang por mthong*), which accords more closely with Skt *jñānasuprabham*.

And the beatific body of the buddha[s]
Itself is easily seen.[1111]
One sees [It] worshipped
By the great ones of the three worlds.

[That] born from the great pinnacle of gnosis
Will be seen worshipped always
With the five objects of [sense] desire, constantly
By the buddhas and bodhisattvas[1112]—
The great body of Vajrasattva,
The great fame of Vajradharma.

One's own form will be seen in a dream;
Those of great secret adamantine fame
Will bow down—the great buddhas
And bodhisattvas, the adamantine (*vajrinaḥ*).

[One] will see such dreams,
Which bestow the accomplishments of body, speech, and mind.

Dripping with ornaments of all [kinds],
A divine maiden, charming—
Seeing a boy [or] girl,
One realizes power (*siddhi*).

She will be seen, constant, standing in the field[s]
Of all buddhas of the ten directions.
They, constitutively happy-minded, give[1113†] B:73b
The delightful treasury of dharma.[1114]

1111. Tib reads "selfless, is quickly seen" (*bdag med pa ni myur du mthong*).

1112. Tib follows the canonical versions, reading "one will see the form of this great gnosis, constantly worshipped by the buddhas and bodhisattvas with the five objects of [sense] desire" (*ye shes chen po 'di yi gzugs | sangs rgyas byang chub sems dpa' yis | 'dod pa'i yon tan lnga rnams kyis | rtag tu mchog pa byed pa mthong | buddhaiś ca bodhisattvaiś ca pañcakāmaguṇair api | pūjitaṃ paśyate bimbaṃ mahājñāna-samaprabham |*). Tib does not translate the *samaprabha* element.

1113. Or, according to the reading of SS, "she . . . gives."

1114. Tib reads "One sees all the buddhas of the ten directions | Abiding in the [Buddha-]

All those who have attained the dharma body,
Surrounded by all beings[1115]
Will be seen in the period of yoga
[By] the one fixed in the meditation vajra."[1116]

The Vajra Student asked: "If a practitioner, even one who has seen reality, does[1117] not perform the threefold practice due to the distraction of work such as farming, trade, [or] service[1118] on account of the force of habituation to prior vestiges, and[/or] is not able to complete the rituals as related in the tantras on account of lacking the requisites—having died, may [such a practitioner] expect in the future life an [ordinary] rebirth, or will [that one] reach {Mahā}vajradharahood?"

The Vajra Mentor replied:

"There is nothing to be eliminated from this.
There is nothing to be added.
The real is to be shown by the real.
The one who sees the real is liberated.[1119]

---

verses, | Their minds overjoyed, | Granting the delightful treasury of dharma |" (*phyogs bcu'i sangs rgyas thams cad rnams | zhing na gnas pa nges par mthong | thugs ni dgyes par gyur nas kyang | chos mdzod yid du 'ong ba stsol |*).

1115. I have emended SKT here to read: *dharma-kāya-gataṃ sarvaṃ sarva-sattva-parivṛtam*. MS B is clearly faulty, reading *dharmakāyagataṃ sarva-sattva-sattva-parīvṛtam*. An alternative emendation (to *dharma-cakra-gataṃ kāyaṃ sarva-sattva-parivṛtam*), which is more in line with GST and TIB, yields "An embodiment, turning the wheel of dharma, surrounded by beings." GST reads "surrounded by all buddhas."

1116. TIB reads "will be seen by the pledge-yoga of the [one] fixed in the meditation vajra" (*chos kyi 'khor los sgyur ba'i sku | sems can kun gyis yongs bskor ba | bsam gtan rdo rje la gnas pa'i | dam tshig sbyor bas mthong bar 'gyur*).

This passage is GST XV.123–30. It is the better part of a section that begins "regarding that, this [is] the state of the great dream pledge" (*tatrêdaṃ mahāsvapna-samaya-padaṃ*).

1117. Literally, "should not"—i.e., an optative to be taken in the hypothetical sense.

1118. TIB reads "farming and work and trade and service" (*zhing dang | las dang | tshong dang | bsnyen bkur*).

1119. This verse, writes Christian Lindtner, "is very well-known and has been treated often. It may be from a lost work of Nāgārjuna." See Chr. Lindtner, "Adversaria Buddhica," p. 168. He references (among others) Louis de la Vallée Poussin, *Mélanges Chinois et Bouddhiques* I (394) and J. Takasaki, *A Study on the Ratnagotravibhaga*, 300. The former notes no less

The name of the perfection stage is 'seeing the real.' Due to seeing the real, views such as permanence, destruction, and transmigration cease.

"Nevertheless, depending on conventions, one may ascertain the purification of transmigration.[1120] †This—the aggregates, and so on—is not transferred to another world, since that would result in the faulty consequence of [things being] permanent. After death in another world, one is not born from another either, for this would result in the faulty consequence of [being produced] without a cause. Thus, for instance, a butter-lamp flame from a butter-lamp flame, an impression from a seal, and an echo from a sound—one cannot say that they are either the same [as] or different [than their sources]. Therefore, it says in the *Golden Radiance Scripture*:[1121] End MS B

> The Buddha does not [enter final] nirvāṇa.
> The Dharma does not decline.
> In order to discipline beings
> Nirvāṇa is shown.[1122]

than nine occurrences of the verse in Sanskrit and Pāli literature, among which it figures as verse 7 of the Tibetan version of the *Pratītyasamutpādahṛdaya* attributed to Nāgārjuna; as well as *Nāmasaṃgītiṭīkā* VI.5, where it is attributed to Nāgārjuna, as well as being found as *Abhisamayālaṃkāra* V.21 and *Ratnagotravibhāga* I.154 (versification as given by Johnston; La Vallée Poussin and Obermiller cite it as 152). The latter has characterized this verse as "one of the most famous verses in Mahāyānistic literature." Harunaga Isaacson (personal communication 15 May 2005) has indicated the same.

Tib reads: "In this there is nothing to reject. | There is nothing to present. | The real is seen in the real. | If one sees reality, one is liberated |" (*'di la bsal bya gang yang med | gzhag par bya ba ci yang med | yang dag nyid la yang dag lta | yang dag mthong na rnal par grol |*).

1120. The extant Sanskrit text ends at this point, as the final folio is missing.

1121. *Suvarṇa-bhāsa-sūtra, gSer 'od dam pa'i mdo.* An edition of the Sanskrit text has been published by Johannes Nobel: *Suvarṇabhāsottamasūtra* (1937). A Tibetan edition by the same author has been published as *Suvarṇaprabhāsottamasūtra*, vol. I (1944).

1122. This verse appears near the end of chapter 2 of Nobel's edition, which reads: *na buddhaḥ parinirvāti na dharmaḥ parihīyate | sattvānāṃ paripākāya parinirvāṇa deśayet |*. See Nobel, *Suvarṇa-bhāṣottama-sūtra* (1937), 19. Tib seems to follow a variant attested in PU (12): *na buddhaḥ parinirvāti na ca dharmo 'ntardhīyate | sattvānāṃ vinayārthāya nirvāṇam upadarśitam |*. Some Tibetan versions of this scripture follow the latter (i.e., reading *gdul*, "discipline"), while others follow the version attested in the former (i.e., reading *smin*, "develop/ripen/mature"). Otherwise all versions seem to agree. In Pandey's reconstruction of this section, he unfortunately follows the "standard" version, rather than the more appropriate form given in PU.

Likewise, the *Journey to Laṅka Scripture* says:[1123]

> Here, nothing arises or ceases
> Due to conditions.
> Only imaginary conditions
> Arise or cease.[1124]

"By this reasoning, the Lord Śākyamuni having performed all his [twelve] deeds, made a show of [entering] nirvāṇa. Likewise, one who has realized the perfection stage, having done everything, [enters] nirvāṇa in the world—have no doubt about this.

"Therefore, the one who knows Reality, although [he] may not have performed the practices as explained on account of not having the complete requisites, having abandoned all views [and] realized that 'death is the ultimate reality, birth is the superficial reality,' having at some time entered the brilliance, generates the firm resolution that 'having cast off the ordinary aggregates [i.e., died], I will arise by the process of self-consecration.'[1125] If he remains mentally fixated [on] that, he will not lose that mental fixation in the next life. Therefore, [he] will become omniscient. Hence, it is said:

> The human mind,
> Like a variegated jewel,
> Takes on the nature[1126]
> Of whatever[1127] it encounters.[1128]

1123. On this scripture, see chapter 1, note 239, above.

1124. This verse is LAS II.138: *na hy atrôtpadyate kiṃcit pratyayair na nirudhyate | utpadyante nirudhyante pratyayā eva kalpitāḥ* ||. See also DK, mDo, vol. ca, f. 140b[3]–140b[4].

1125. That is, "at death, I will become enlightened and arise in the form body of a buddha by the self-consecration process."

1126. Literally, "becomes that-constituted-ness" (*tanmayatāṃ yāti*).

1127. *yena yena bhāvena*; lit. "by whatever existent things." This term (*bhāva*), has a wide range of meanings. One of them is "resolution"; and this seems to be the way in which the Tibetan translators have construed it. They read *bsam pa*, "motivation." However, as seen in the verses from the *Citta-viśuddhi-prakaraṇa* (see note 1128, below), which specify "conceptions" (*vikalpa, rnam rtog*), this principle need not be confined to motivation/volition.

1128. This oft-cited verse also occurs in the *Advaya-vivaraṇa-prajñopāya-viniścaya-siddhi*; see Rinpoche and Dwivedi, eds., *Guhyādi-aṣṭa-siddhi-saṅgraha*, 217. It reads: *yena yena hi bhāvena manaḥ saṃyujyate nṛṇam | tena tanmayatāṃ yāti viśvarūpo maṇir yathā* ||.

(cont'd)

"Therefore, by transforming all this into the distinctive, due to that transformation, the distinctive result will emerge. Here it is explained:

> Birth is called 'superficial reality.'
> The name for death is 'ultimate reality.'
> Who finds those two processes by the grace of the guru
> Is a future buddha.
>
> The communion of those two realities,
> Inexpressible, without distinction between the two,
> Two names ultimately only the same—
> The one who knows that is here liberated from bondage.[1129]
>
> If someone falls from the peak of the king of mountains,
> Even if they don't want to plummet, they will.
> If one gains the beneficial verbal transmission by the grace of
> the guru,
> Even if they don't want to be liberated, they will be.[1130]

In the world, beings do not have the power to realize the Reality of meaningful words.[1131] They are like a drop of sesame oil in the water of a great ocean constantly agitated by a fierce wind. Therefore what little I have taken up and collected is like a lamp for the minds of those fortunate beings, terrified by the ultimate and the superficial.

That is, just as a jewel reflects the colors around it, so the mind will reflect the "coloration" of the intentions that motivate it. A similar sentiment is found at *Citta-viśuddhi-prakaraṇa* 27–28, which reads: "For example, if a crystal is pure | It will be colored by other colors. | Likewise this precious jewel [of a] mind | Is colored by the hues of conceptions. || If the mind-jewel is isolated | From the color of ordinary conceptions, [it is] | Primordially pure, unarisen, | Lacking intrinsic reality, stainless || (*yathaiva sphaṭikaḥ svacchaḥ pararāgeṇa rajyate | tathaiva citta-ratnaṃ tu kalpanā-rāga-rañjitam || prākṛta-kalpanā-rāgair viviktaṃ citta-ratnakaṃ | ādi-śuddham anutpannaṃ niḥsvabhāvam anāvilam* ||). See P. Patel, ed., *Cittaviśuddhiprakaraṇa*, 3.

1129. I have not been able to trace a source for these two verses.

1130. This final verse is identical to PK I.67.

1131. This would seem to be an allusion to his discussion of "meaningful words" (*artha-vacana*) and the modes of exoteric composition at the opening of the work. See chapter 1, note 214, above.

* * * * *

(Here ends the *Lamp for Integrating the Practices*, composed by the great mentor Āryadeva. It was translated, edited, and finalized by the Indian abbot Śraddhākaravarman and the editor/translator-monk Rinchen Zangpo.[1132] Herein are thirteen hundred Indian verses (*śloka*), comprising two volumes.)[1133]

[|| Śubham astu sarvasattvānām ||]

1132. This is the common colophon for all four redactions—D, Co, P, and N.

1133. This last sentence is found only in P and N. H.P. Shāstrī (*Catalogue of Palm-leaf*, vol. 2, p. 40) estimates the number of ślokas in MS B to be 550, yielding an estimate of ca. 1100 for the whole.

Appendixes

Appendix I
English-Sanskrit-Tibetan Glossary

Note: Though I had intended to include comprehensive English-Sanskrit-Tibetan glossaries here as a contribution to the further development of esoteric Buddhist lexicography, limitations of space and time have rendered this impracticable.

A tilde (~) before Tibetan entries indicates an attested equivalent that I judge to be either erroneous or imperfect.

English	Sanskrit	Tibetan
abode	āśraya	gnas
accomplished [nature], perfection, completely perfected	pariniṣpanna	yongs su grub pa, yongs su rdzogs pa
accomplishment	siddhi	dngos grub, grub
action, function, rite	karman	las
activity	karaṇa	bya ba
activity	kriyā	bya ba
acute	nipuṇa	mdzangs
adamant, adamantine	vajra	rdo rje
adamantine body	vajradeha	rdo rje lus
adamantine body samādhi	vajra-bimbopamaṃ-samādhi	ting nge 'dzin rdo rje'i gzugs lta bu
adamantine gnosis	vajra-jñāna	rdo rje'i ye shes
adamantine samādhi	vajropama-samādhi	rdo rje lta bu'i ting nge 'dzin
Adamantine Way	vajrayāna	rdo rje theg pa
æon	kalpa	bskal pa

English	Sanskrit	Tibetan
æsthetic mood	rasa	ro
afterlife	paraloka	’jig rten pha rol
aggregate	skandha	phung po
aim	kṛtya, kārya	bya ba, don
aim	artha	don
air	vāyu, māruta	rlung
air element	vāyu-dhātu	rlung gi khams
air reality	vāyu-tattva	rlung gi de kho na nyid
Ākāśagarbha	ākāśagarbha	nam mkha’i snying po
Akṣobhya	akṣobhya	mi bskyod pa
alchemy	rasāyana	ra sa ya na
ambrosia	amṛta	bdud rtsi
Amitābha	amitābha	snang ba mtha’ yas, ’od dpag tu med pa
Amoghasiddhi	amoghasiddhi	don yod grub pa
analogy	aupamya	dpe
animal realm	tiryag-yoni	dud ’gro’i skye gnas
animate	jaṅgama	rgyu ba
anxiety	cakita	dogs pa dang bcas pa
anxiety	kaukṛtya	’gyod pa
aphorism	paryāya	rnam grangs
apocalypse	pralaya	’jig pa
appearance	ākṛti	rnam pa
appearance	ākāra	rnam pa
āralli	āralli	a ra li
arduous practices	duṣkara-caryā	spyod pa dka’ ba
array	vinyāsa	rnam par dgod pa
arrogance	māna	khengs pa (nga rgyal)
art	upāya	thabs
ascending [air]	udāna	gyen rgyu, steng du rgyu ba
ascetic practice	niyama	brtul zhugs
attainer	prāpaka	thob par bya ba
attendant	anucarī	rjes su spyod pa

English	Sanskrit	Tibetan
audible vocalization	śabda-ruta	sgra grag pa
auspicious	śiva	zhi ba
authentic	sadbhāva	yang dag pa
bad	aśubha	mi dge ba
bad rebirth	durgati	ngan 'gro
basis	āśraya	gnas
bearer of gnosis	jñāna-vāhinī	ye shes 'ba' zhig pa nyid
beatific body	sambhogakāya	rdzogs longs spyod pa'i sku
beginner	ādikarmika	las dang po pa
beginningless [time]	anādi	thog ma med pa
being	sattva, jana, jagat, jantu	sems can, 'gro ba, skye bo
bell	ghaṇṭā	dril bu
beloved	priyā	
between-being	antarābhava	srid pa bar ma pa
beyond the senses	atīndriya	dbang po las 'das pa
bhusuku	bhusuku	bhu su ku
bile	pitta	mkhris pa
birth	janman	skye ba
birthless	anutpāda	skye ba med pa
blame	nindā	smad pa
blink of an eye	nimiṣa	mig btsums
Blissful One	sugata	bde bar gshegs pa
bodhisattva	bodhisattva	byang chub sems dpa'
bodiless	amūrti[ka]	lus med pa
bodily token	kāya-cchomā	lus kyi brda
body	kāya, deha, bimba, mūrti, śarīra, vigraha, kalevara	lus, sku
body isolation	kāya-viveka	lus rnam par dben pa
body vajra	kāya-vajra	sku rdo rje
boldness	sāhasa	dka' ba la sbyor ba
bond	bandhana, prabandha	bcing ba, 'ching ba
bow of Indra	indra-dhanu	lha'i dbang po'i gzhu
breath	niḥśvāsa, śvāsa	dbugs

English	Sanskrit	Tibetan
brilliance	prabhāsvara	'od gsal ba
buddha	buddha	sangs rgyas
buddha-field	buddha-kṣetra	sangs rgyas kyi zhing
buddhahood	buddhatva	sangs rgyas nyid
cause	hetu, kāraṇa	rgyu
ceaseless, unceasing	anirodha	'gag pa med pa
celestial palace	kūṭāgāra	gzhal yas khang
characteristic	lakṣaṇa	mtshan nyid
characterless	alakṣaṇa	mtshan nyid med pa
charnel ground	śmaśāna	dur khrod
chief principle	pradhāna	gtso
city of gandharvas	gandharva-nagara	dri za'i grong khyer
clan	kula	rigs
clinging to [material] things	bhāva-graha	dngos por 'dzin pa
coarse	sthūla	rags pa
color, phoneme	varṇa	kha dog
commission	adhyāpanna	spyod pa
common	sāmānya	tha mal pa
common knowledge	loke niścaya	nges pa
communion	yuganaddha	zung du 'brel pa, zung du 'jug pa
co-moving [air]	saṃvāha	yang dag par rgyu ba
companion	sahacarī	lhan cig spyod pa
comparable	upameya	~mi srid pa
compassion	karuṇā, kāruṇya	snying rje
completely perfected	pariniṣpanna	yongs su grub pa, yongs su rdzogs pa
completely without elaboration	atyanta-niṣprapañcatā	shin tu spros pa med pa
completely pure gnosis of the Realm of Reality	suviśuddha-dharmadhātu-jñānaṃ	chos kyi dbyings rnam par dag pa'i ye shes
conceit	manana	rlom sems
concept, conceptuality, conceptualizing, conception	vikalpa	rnam par rtog pa, rnam rtog

ENGLISH	SANSKRIT	TIBETAN
conch shell	śaṃkha	dung chos
condiment	vyañjana	tshod mo
condition	pratyaya	rkyen
condition	avasthā	gnas skabs
confidence	adhimukti	lhag par mos pa
confusion	bhrānti	'khrul pa
conjunction	sannipāta	'dus pa
connate	sahaja	lhan cig skyes pa
conscious intention	vijñāna-saṃkalpa	rnam par shes pa'i kun du rtog pa
consciousness	vijñāna	rnam par shes pa
consecrated	adhiṣṭhita	byin gyis brlabs pa
consecration	adhiṣṭhāna	byin gyis brlabs pa
consequences of action	karmānta	las kyi mtha'
consonant, 'letter'	vyañjana	gsal byed
consort	mudrā	phyag rgya
consort discipline	vidyā-vrata	rig pa'i brtul zhugs
constituted of	adhiṣṭhita	byin gyis brlabs pa
constitution [of]	adhiṣṭhāna	byin gyis brlabs pa
consummation	paryanta	mthar thug pa
contact, tactile object	sparśa	reg pa
Contentious Era	kali-yuga	rtsod pa'i dus
context of exertion	ghaṭamānāvasthā	slob bzhin pa'i gnas skabs
continuum, linked continuity	tantu, prabandha	rgyun, rgyud
conveyance	vāhana	bzhon pa
corpse	kalevara (kaḍevara)	lus, phung po
court poems	kāvya	snyan dngags
crafty	śaṭha	g.yo
craving, thirst	tṛṣṇā	sred pa, skom pa
creation	utpatti	bskyed pa, skye ba
creation stage, creation process	utpattikrama	bskyed pa'i rim pa

English	Sanskrit	Tibetan
critical wisdom	prajñā	shes rab
critical wisdom and liberative technique	prajñopāya	nas shes rab dang thabs
crown prince	rāja-kumāra	rgyal po'i bu gzhon nu
crown-protrusion	uṣṇīṣa	gtsug gtor
crucial point	artha-vaśa	don gyi dbang
cryptic expressions	nigūḍha-śabda	sgra sbas pa
crystal	sphaṭika	shel
ḍākinī	ḍākinī	mkha' 'gro ma
darkness	tāmasā	mun pa
death, passing away	maraṇa	'chi ba
deceitful	kapaṭa	sgyu
deed	kriyā	bya ba
deep investigation	parāmarṣa	yongs su tshol ba
defilement	saṃkleśa, kleśa	kun nas nyon mongs pa, nyon mongs pa
definitive meaning	nītārtha	nges pa'i don
delicacies	bhojya	myang, bca' ba
deluded	mohita	rmongs pa
delusion	avidyā	ma rig pa
dependent co-origination	pratītya-samutpāda	rten cing 'brel bar 'byung ba
depression	kheda	skyo ba
desire	kāma	'dod pa
Desire Realm	kāmadhātu	'dod pa'i khams
destruction	abhicāruka	mngon spyod
devotion	bhakti, parāyaṇa	mos, mchog tu gzhol ba
Dharma	dharma	chos
digits	pratyaṅga	nying lag
disagreeable	viṣama	mi zad pa
discernment	saṃjñā	'du shes
dispassion	virāga	'dod chags dang bral ba
dissolving [process]	anubheda	rjes su gzhig pa, gzhig pa
distinctive term	pṛthak-saṃjñā	ming tha dad pa

English	Sanskrit	Tibetan
divine body	devatā-vigraha	lha'i sku
divine form	devatā-rūpa	lha'i sku
divine perception	devatopalabdhika	lha ru nye bar dmigs pa
divine, divinity, deity	devatā	lha
divinity reality	devatā-tattva	lha'i de kho na nyid
divinity-body	devatā-mūrti	lha'i sku
domain	viṣaya	yul
domination	vaśya	dbang
doubt	saṃśaya	som nyi
dream	svapna	rmi lam
dreamlike	svapnopama	rmi lam lta bu, rmi lam dang 'dra ba
dual	dvaya	gnyis pa
dwelling	nilaya	gnas
dwelling place	āśraya	gnas, brten pa
earth	māhendra	dbang chen
echo	pratiśrutka	brag ca
effect	kārya	'bras bu
effortless	anābhoga	lhun gyis grub pa
eight great powers	aṣṭa-mahāsiddhi	grub pa chen po brgyad
eight superhuman powers	aṣṭaguṇaiśvarya	yon tan gyi dbang phyug brgyad
eight worldly concerns	aṣṭa-loka-dharma	'jig rten gyi chos brgyad
elegant	śṛṅgāra	snyan
element	dhātu	khams
elemental derivative	bhautika	'byung ba las gyur pa
elixir of immortality	rasāyana	ra sa ya na
eloquence	pratibhāna	spobs pa
emanated body	nirmāṇa-kāya	sprul pa'i sku
emancipation	apavarga, niryāṇa	nges par 'byung ba
embracing	āliṅgana	'khyud pa
emerging, emergence	vyutthāna	ldang ba
emitting, flowing forth	spharaṇa	spro ba, 'byung ba

English	Sanskrit	Tibetan
empty	rikta	gso ba
enjoyment	paribhoga, upabhoga	longs spyod, spyod pa
enlightenment	abhisaṃbodhi, bodhi	mngon par rdzogs par byang chub pa, byang chub
enlightenment process	abhisambodhi-krama, sambodhikrama	mngon par byang chub pa'i rim pa
entering	praveśa	'jug pa
enunciation	pravyāhāra	smra ba, brjod pa
envy	mātsarya	phrag dog
equality gnosis	samatā-jñāna	mnyam pa nyid kyi ye shes
equipoised	samāpanna	snyoms par zhugs pa
era	yuga	dus
erotic play	krīḍā	rol mo
eroticism	śṛṅgāra	steg pa
erudite	bahu-śruta	mang du thos pa
essenceless, insubstantial, naturelessness, essencelessness	niḥsvabhāva	dngos med, dngos po med pa
essencelessness	niḥsvabhāva	dngos med
establishment	siddhi	dgnos grub, grub
ethics	śīla	tshul khrims
etymological explanation	nirukti	sgra'i nges pa'i tshig
evacuative [air]	apāna	thur du sel ba
evil	aśubha	mi dge ba
excellent	sādhu	legs, legs so
exhalation	ucchvāsa	dbugs 'byin pa, dbugs 'byung ba
exhaustion	klamatha	dub pa
existence	bhava	srid pa
exoteric sciences	bāhya-śāstra	~dang po'i bstan bcos
experience	bhāva	dngos po
explanatory tantra	vyākhyā-tantra	bshad pa'i rgyud
extraction of the mantra	mantroddhāra	sngags btu ba

English	Sanskrit	Tibetan
extremely void	atiśūnya	shin tu stong pa
eye	cakṣu	mig
eye of gnosis	jñāna-cakṣu	ye shes kyi mig
facticity	dharmatā	chos nyid
faith	śraddhā	dad pa
fame	yaśas	grags pa
fault	doṣa	nyes pa
fear	bhīta	'jigs pa
feeling	vedanā	tshor ba
financial means	vibhava	'byor ba
fine atoms	paramāṇu	rdul phra rab
finger snapping	acchaṭā	se gol
fire	tejas, hutabhug, agni	me
fire-offering-pit	kuṇḍa	thab khung
five ambrosias	pañcāmṛta	~bdud rtsi'i chu
five gnoses	pañca-jñāna	ye shes lnga
five objects of [sense] desire	pañcakāmaguṇa	'dod pa'i yon tan lnga
five realms [of rebirth]	gati-pañcaka, pañcagati	'gro ba lnga
five subjects	pañca-jñāna	shes pa lnga
fivefold process	pañca-krama	go rims rnam pa lnga
fixed	sthita	gnas pa
flavor	rasa	ro
flesh	māṃsa	sha
flirtation	vilāsa	rnam par rol pa, rnam par sgeg pa
folk, world	loka	'jig rten pa
food	āhāra, bhakṣya	kha zas, bza' ba, zas
foot	pāda	zhabs
force	sāmarthya	stobs
form	rūpa	gzugs
form, appearance	ākāra	rnam pa
formless	arūpin, nirākāra	gzugs med pa, rnam pa med pa

English	Sanskrit	Tibetan
fortitude	utsāha	spro ba
foundation	ālaya, āśraya	gnas, gzhi
foundationless	anālaya	gzhi med pa, gnas med pa
four continents	catur-dvīpa	gling bzhi
Four Noble Truths	caturāryasatya	'phags pa'i bden pa rnam pa bzhi
four pure abodes	catur-brahma-vihāra	tshangs pa'i gnas pa bzhi
four voids	śūnya-catuṣṭaya	stong pa nyid rnam pa bzhi
fourfold procedure	caturvidha-nyāya	tshul rnam pa bzhi
free of impurity	anāsrava	zag pa med
free of perception, radianceless	nirābhāsa	snang ba med pa
fruit, result	phala	'bras bu
function	karman	las
function	kriyā	bya ba
function	vyāpāra	las, bya ba
function-accomplishing gnosis	kṛtyānuṣṭhāna-jñānaṃ	bya ba sgrub pa'i ye shes
gain	lābha	rnyed pa
Ganges river	gaṅgā	gaṅgā
gas	vāta	rlung
generosity	dāna	sbyin pa
ghee	ghṛta	mar
glorious	śrī	dpal
gnosis	jñāna	shes pa
gnosis being	jñāna-sattva	ye shes sems dpa'
gnosis consort	jñāna-mudrā	ye shes kyi phyag rgya
gnosis of brilliance	prabhāsvara-jñāna	'od gsal ye shes
gnosis of critical wisdom	prajñā-jñāna	shes rab kyi ye shes
gnosis of imminence	ālokopalabdha-jñāna	snang ba nye bar thob pa'i ye shes
gnosis of individuating discernment	pratyavekṣaṇā-jñānaṃ	so sor rtog pa'i ye shes
gnosis of liberative art	upāya-jñāna	thabs kyi ye shes

English	Sanskrit	Tibetan
gnosis-body	jñāna-mūrti	ye shes kyi sku
goddess	devī	lha mo
good and evil	śubhāśubha	dge ba dang mi dge ba
good deed	sucarita	legs par spyod pa
good rebirth	sugati	bde 'gro
good thing	dharma	chos
good, virtuous	kuśala, śubha	dge ba
grace	prasāda	bka' drin
gradual process	krama-vṛtti	rim gyis 'jug pa
gradually	kramaśaḥ	rim gyis, rim gyis 'jug pas
grammar	vyākaraṇa	byā ka ra ṇa
grave	guru	lci bar gyur pa
great bliss	mahāsukha	bde ba chen po
great caring	mahākṛpā	snying rje chen po
great elephant	mahānāga	glang po chen po
Great Hero	mahāvīra	dpa' bo chen po
great one	mahāsattva	sems dpa' chen po
great person	mahāpuruṣa	skyes bu chen po
Great Sage	mahāmuni	thub pa chen po
Great Seal	mahāmudrā	phyag rgya chen po
great void	mahāśūnya	stong pa chen po
Great Yoga	mahāyoga	rnal 'byor chen po
Great Yoga Tantra	mahāyoga-tantra	rnal 'byor chen po'i rgyud
habitat	ādhāra	rten
harem	antaḥpura	btsun mo'i tshogs
hatred	dveṣa	zhe sdang
heap	rāśi	spungs pa
heart	cetas	sems
heaven	svarga	mtho ris
hell	naraka	dmyal ba, dmyal, sems can dmyal ba
hero	vīra	dpa' bo

English	Sanskrit	Tibetan
hero's march samādhi	sūraṃgama-samādhi	dpa' bar 'gro ba'i ting nge 'dzin
heroism	vīrya	brtson pa, brtson 'grus
hidebound	prāvacanika	gsung rab
holistic [process]	piṇḍagraha	ril por 'dzin pa
Holy Teaching	saddharma	dam pa'i chos
host-maṇḍala	gaṇa-maṇḍala	tshogs kyi dkyil 'khor
human	nara	mi
hundred clans	śata-kula	rigs brgya
hunger	kṣut	bkres pa
ignorance	moha	gti mug
I-habit	ahaṃkāra	ngar 'dzin pa, bdag tu rlom pa
illicit sex	agamyāgamana	~'gro ba dang 'ong ba
illusionist	māyākāra	sgyu ma mkhan
images, radiance	avabhāsa	gzugs su snang ba, snang bar byed pa
imaginative yoga	kalpita-yoga	rtog pa'i rnal 'byor
immaterial	arūpa	gzugs med pa
immediate	yugapat	cig car
imminence gnosis	upalabdha-jñāna	nye bar thob pa'i ye shes
impassioned, red	rakta	kun du chags pa, dmar ba
imperceptible	avijñaptika	rnam par rig pa med pa
imperishable	akṣaya	mi zad pa, zad pa med pa
impermanent, impermanence	anitya	chad pa, mi rtag pa
impurity	mala	dri ma
inanimate	jaḍa, sthāvara	bems po, mi rgyu ba
inclination	āśaya	bsam pa
inconceivable	acintya	bsam gyis mi khyab pa
incorporeal	nirākāra	rnam pa med pa
indivisible	abheda, abhedya	dbyer med, mi phyed pa
Indra's [rain]bow	indrāyudha	'ja' tshon

English	Sanskrit	Tibetan
inexpressible	anabhilāpya, anākhyeya, avācya	brjod du med pa, ming med, tshig med pa, brjod med pa
inference	anumāna	rjes su dpag pa
inhabitant	ādheya	brten pa
inhalation	praśvāsa	dbyugs rngub pa, rngub par 'gyur ba
initiation	abhiṣeka	dbang bskur ba
instant	lava	thang cig
instantaneously	jhaṭiti	skad cig tsam gyis
insubstantial	niḥsvabhāva	dngos med
intellection	cintā	sems dpa' (sems pa)
intelligence, intellect	buddhi	blo, blo gros
intention	abhiprāya	dgongs pa
intentional speech	sandhyāya-vacana	dgongs te gsungs pa
intentional speech, allusive expression	sandhyā-vacana	dgongs pas bshad pa
intentional speech, spoken of intentionally	saṃdhyāya-bhāṣita, saṃdhyāya-vākya	dgongs par bshad, dgongs pa'i tshig
interpretable meaning	neyārtha	drang ba'i don
intrinsic character	sva-lakṣaṇa	rang gi mtshan nyid
introspectively known	pratyātmavedya	so so rang rig pa, rang gis rig pa, so so rang rig par gyur pa, so so rang gis rig pa
irreversible	avaivartika	phyir mi ldog pa
irrigation machine	ghaṭī-yantra	zo chun gyi 'khrul 'khor
isolated	vivikta	dben pa
jargon expressions	ruta	sgra ji bzhin ma yin pa
jewel	ratna	rin po che, rin chen
joy	ānanda	kun dga'
just as it is	yathābhūta	ji lta ba bzhin du
kindness	anukampā	[thugs] brtse ba
kissing	cumbana	'o byed pa
Kṣitigarbha	kṣitigarbha	sa'i snying po
language	ruta	skad

English	Sanskrit	Tibetan
languid	stabdha	dal [ba]
learned one	paṇḍita	mkhas pa
learning, instruction	śikṣā, śruta	bslab pa thos pa
letter	vyañjana	yi ge
letter	lipika	yi ge
liberation	mokṣa	thar pa, grol ba
liberative art, technique, art	upāya	thabs
life	jīvita, jāti	srog, tshe rabs
life-cycle, saṃsāra	saṃsāra	'khor ba
light	prabhā	'od
light ray, beam	kiraṇa, raśmi	'od zer
limbs	aṅga	yan lag
limitless	ananta	mtha' yas pa
literal meaning	yathāruta	sgra ji bzhin pa
Locanā, (Buddha) Locanā	locanā	spyan, sangs rgyas spyan
logical consequence	prasaṅga	thal ba
logical disputation	tarka	rtog
logicians	tārkika	rtog ge pa
Lokeśvara	lokeśvara	'jig rten dbang phyug
Lord	bhagavant	bcom ldan 'das
lord of the ten stages	daśabhūmīśvara	sa bcu'i dbang phyug
loss	alābha	ma rnyed pa
lotus (vagina)	padma	padma
lovely	lalita	rgya che ba
lovemaking	surata	rab tu dga' ba
lower rebirth	apāya	ngan 'gro, ngan song
luminance, light	āloka	snang ba
luminance-imminence	ālokopalabdha[ka]	snang ba nye bar thob pa, snang ba thob pa
luminance-radiance	ālokābhāsa	snang ba mched pa
lump	piṇḍa	gong bu
machine	yantra	'khrul 'khor
mad discipline	unmatta-vrata	smyon pa'i brtul zhugs

English	Sanskrit	Tibetan
Mahāvairocana	mahāvairocana	~rnam par snang mdzad
Māmakī	māmakī	mā ma kī
maṇḍala, orb	maṇḍala	dkyil 'khor
manifest	vyakta	gsal ba
manifestation	pravṛtti	'jug pa
manner	rūpa, krama, yoga, nyāya	gzugs, rim pa, rim, tshul
mantra	mantra	sngags
mantra body	mantra-mūrti	sngags kyi lus
mantra reality	mantra-tattva	sngags kyi de kho na nyid
mantrin	mantrin	sngags pa
Māra, demons	māra	bdud
mass	skandha	phung po
mass	piṇḍa	phung po
master	svāmin	bdag po
master of the eighth [stage]	aṣṭamīśvāra	sa brgyad pa'i dbang phyug
material	rūpa	gzugs
meaning, aim, object, point, in order to	artha	don
meditation	dhyāna	bsam gtan
meditative cultivation	bhāvanā	bsgom pa, bsgoms pa, sgom pa
meditative cultivator	bhāvaka	bsgom par bya ba
mental elaboration	prapañca	spros pa
mental fancies	manorājya	yid la re ba
mental functioning	manaskāra	yid la byed pa
mental factors	caitasika, caitasika-dharma	sems las byung ba, sems pa
mentation	manas	yid
mentor	guru	bla ma, slob dpon
mentor of the world	jagad-guru	'gro ba'i bla ma
mere trice	muhūrta	yud tsam
merely mind	citta-mātra[tā]	sems tsam
merit	puṇya	bsod nams
metabolic [air]	samāna	mnyam gnas, me dang mnyam du gnas pa

English	Sanskrit	Tibetan
mind	citta	sems, yid
mind and body	nāmarūpa	[ming gzugs]
mind isolation	citta-viveka	sems rnam par dben pa
mind vajra	citta-vajra	sems rdo rje
mind-made body	manomayadeha	yid kyi rang bzhin gyi lus
mind-made body	manomaya-kāya	yid kyi rang bzhin gyi sku
mind-vajra samādhi	citta-vajra-samādhi	thugs kyi ting nge 'dzin
mine-habit	mamakāra	ngar sems pa, nga yir 'dzin pa
miracle	ṛddhi	rdzu 'phrul
mirage	marīci[ka]	smig rgyu
mirror	ādarśa, darpaṇa	me long
mirror-like gnosis	ādarśa-jñāna	me long lta bu'i ye shes
misdeed	duścarita	nyes par spyod pa
mode	prakāra	rnam pa
moment	kṣana	skad cig
monk	bhikṣu	dge slong
moon	candra, śaśin, soma	zla ba
moon in water	udaka-candra	chu zla
Mount Sumeru	sumeru	ri'i rgyal po ri rab
mount, conveyance, vehicle	vāhana	bzhon pa
natural recitation	prakṛti-jāpa	rang bzhin bzlas pa
nature, essence, intrinsic reality	svabhāva	ngo bo nyid, rang bzhin, ngo bo
naturelessness	niḥsvabhāva	dngos med
navel	nābhi	lte ba
nine æsthetic moods	nava-nāṭya-rasa	nyams rnam pa dgu
nirvāṇa	nirvāṇa	mya ngan las 'das pa
noble one, noble man	kulaputra	rigs kyi bu
noble woman	kula-duhitṛ	rigs kyi bu mo
non-Buddhist ascetic	paratīrthika	gzhan mu stegs can
non-conceptual	nirvikalpa	rnam par rtog pa med pa
non-deceptive	avisaṃvādaka	mi slu ba

English	Sanskrit	Tibetan
nondual	advaya	gnyis su med pa, gnyis med
non-equipoised yoga	asamāhita-yoga	mnyam par ma bzhag sbyor ba
non-mental-functioning	amanaskāra	
nose	ghrāṇa	sna
not un-suchness	avitathatā	ma nor ba de bzhin nyid
not-self	anātman	bdag med
object	artha	don
object	grāhya	gzung ba, gzung
object	bhāva	dngos po, dgos por yod pa, ngo bo, dngos
object, form, manner, material	rūpa	gzugs
object, sphere, domain, province	viṣaya	yul, spyod yul
objectifying view	upalambha-dṛṣṭi	dmigs par lta ba
objective selflessness	dharma-nairātmya	chos la bdag med
objects of [sensory] desire	kāma-guṇa	'dod pa'i yon tan
obscuration	āvaraṇa	sgrib pa
obsessed	abhiniviṣṭa	mngon par zhen pa
obsession	abhiniveśa	mngon par zhen pa
obstacle	nivaraṇa	sgrib pa
one method	eka-naya	tshul gcig pa
one pointedness	ekāgratā	rtse gcig pa
one who has not seen reality	adṛṣṭa-satya	bden pa ma mthong ba
one without fabrications	niṣprapañca	spros pa med pa
one's own divinity	svādhidevatā	bdag nyid lha
optical illusion, Indra's phantasmic web	indrajāla	mig 'phrul
ordinary being	pṛthagjana	so so'i skye bo
ordinary body	prākṛta-deha	tha mal pa'i lus
ordinary pride	prākṛtāhaṃkāra	tha mal pa'i nga rgyal
orifice	chidra	bu ga

English	Sanskrit	Tibetan
other-dependent [nature]	paratantra	gzhan gyi dbang
out-moving [air]	nirvāha	nges par rgyu ba
overlord	adhipati	bdag po
overlord of mantras	mantrādhipati	sngags kyi bdag po
Overlord of Secret Ones	guhyakādhipati	gsang ba'i bdag po
own presiding deity	svādhidaiva	rang gi lha
pain	duḥkha	sdug bsngal
Pāṇḍarā	pāṇḍarā	gos dkar mo, gos dkar
passion	rāga	'dod chags, chags pa
passion-free practices	virāga-caryā	chags dang bral ba'i spyod pa
peerless	nirdvandva	gnyis med
penitential observances	duṣkara-niyama	dka' thub sdom pa
perception, vision	darśana, upalabdhi	snang ba, nye bar dmigs pa
perceptiveness, experience	anubhava	rjes su myong ba, myong
Perfect [Era]	kṛta[-yuga]	rdzogs ldan [gyi dus]
perfect buddha	sambuddha	rdzogs pa'i sangs rgyas
perfect enlightenment	samyak-saṃbodhi	yang dag par rdzogs pa'i byang chub
perfection	pariniṣpanna	yongs su grub pa, yongs su rdzogs pa
perfection stage	niṣpanna-krama	rdzogs pa'i rim pa, rdzogs pa'i go rims, rdzogs pa'i rim pa'i go rims
Perfectly Enlightened One	samyaksaṃbuddha	yang dag par rdzogs pa'i sangs rgyas
performance, drama	nāṭaka	gar
period of meditative equipoise	samāhitāvasthā	mnyam par bzhag pa'i gnas skabs
permanent, permanence	śāśvata	rtag pa
permission	anujñā	rjes su gnang ba
person	puruṣa	mi
personal experience	svasaṃvedya	rang gis rig pa
personal instruction	upadeśa	man ngag
pervasive [air]	vyāna	khyab byed

English	Sanskrit	Tibetan
phantasm	māyā	sgyu ma
phantasmic	māyopama	sgyu ma lta bu, sgyu ma 'dra
phantasmic web	māyā-jāla	sgyu 'phrul dra ba
phantasmic samādhi	māyopama-samādhi	sgyu ma lta bu'i ting nge 'dzin
phantom [double]	pratibhāsa	mig yor
phlegm	śleṣma	bad kan
phoneme	varṇa	yi ge, yig 'bru
play	līlā	'gying bag
play, āralli	āralli	a ra li
pleasant	manojña	yid du 'ong ba
pleasure	sukha	bde ba
pledge [substances]	samaya	dam tshig
point	artha	don
poison	viṣa	dug
potency	prabhāva	mthu
power	siddhi	dngos grub
practice	caryā	spyod pa
practice completely without elaboration	atyanta niṣprapañcatā caryā	shin tu spros pa med pa'i [spyod pa]
practice of spiritual discipline	vrata-caryā	brtul zhugs kyi spyod pa
practice tantra	caryā-tantra	spyod pa'i rgyud
practice with elaboration	prapañcacaryā, prapañcatā caryā	spros pa dang bcas pa'i spyod pa
practice without elaboration	niṣprapañca-caryā	spros pa med pa'i spyod pa
practice, art of accomplishment	sādhana	sgrub pa'i thabs
practices of enlightenment	bodhi-caryā	byang chub sems dpa'i spyod pa
practitioner	sādhaka	sgrub pa po
practitioners of the Adamantine Way	vajrayānikāḥ	rdo rje theg pa rnams
practitioner of the Universal Way	mahāyānika	theg pa chen po pa

English	Sanskrit	Tibetan
practitioners of the [Esoteric] Community	sāmājika	'dus pa'i don la zhugs pa rnams
praise	praśaṃsā	bstod pa
precinct of orthodox ascetic	tīrthāyana	mu stegs can gyi gnas su
predominance	ādhikya	dbang
pride	ahaṃkāra	nga rgyal, ngar 'dzin pa, bdag tu rlom pa
priest	brāhmaṇa	bram ze
primordially unarisen	ādyanutpanna	gzod nas ma skyes pa
prior impetus	pūrvāvedha	sngon gyi 'phen shugs
process	krama	rim pa, rim
process leading to communion	yuganaddha-vāhi-krama	zung du 'brel par 'jug pa'i rim pa
proclivity	anuśaya	
production of a divine form, production of a deity [body]	devatā-niṣpatti	lha'i sku rdzogs par 'gyur ba, lha nyid du bskyed pa
profound	gambhīra, gambhīrya	zab, zab pa
proof	pratyaya	yid ches par bgyi ba
propensity	saṃskāra	'du byed
prosperity	pauṣṭika	rgyas pa
prototype	prakṛti	rang bzhin
prototypes and radiances	prakṛty-ābhāsa	rang bzhin snang ba, rang bzhin gyi snang ba; rang bzhin gyis snang ba
prototypical brilliance	prakṛti-prabhāsvara	rang bzhin gyis 'od gsal ba
province	viṣaya	yul
psychic channel	nāḍī	nā li
pulsating	saṃspandita	rnam par g.yo ba
pure	śuddha	rnam dag, dag pa
purification	viśuddhi, vyavadāna	rnam par dag pa, rnam par sbyang ba
purification of the radiances	ābhāsa-viśuddhi	snang ba rnam par dag pa
purity	śuciḥ	gtsang
quality	guṇa	yon tan

English	Sanskrit	Tibetan
radiance	ābhāsa	snang ba, kun du snang ba
radiate	sphurat	spro
range	gocara	spyod yul, yul
Ratnasambhava	ratnasambhava	rin chen 'byung ldan
real	bhāva	dngos po
real	bhūta	yang dag pa
reality	bhāva	dngos po
Reality	tattva	de kho na nyid, de nyid
reality body	dharma-kāya	chos kyi sku
reality limit	bhūta-koṭi, bhūtānta	yang dag pa'i mtha', 'byung ba'i mtha'
reality-source	dharmodaya	chos 'byung ba
realization	adhigama	rtogs pa
realm of reality	dharmadhātu	chos kyi dbyings
Realm of the Thirty(-Three)	tridaśālaya	sum cu rtsa gsum pa'i gnas
Realm of Yama [Lord of Death]	yama-loka	gshin rje'i 'jig rten
reasoning	nyāya, yukti	tshul, rigs pa
rebirth, future life	punarbhava	yang srid pa, srid pa gzhan
recitation	japa	bzlas pa
reflection, image	pratibimba	gzugs brnyan
refuge	śaraṇa	skyabs
re-moving [air]	vivāha	rnam par rgyu ba
repeated cultivation	abhyāsa	bslabs
requisites for worship	pūjopakaraṇa	mchod pa'i yo byad
residence	vihāra	gnas
respectable persons	gurujana	bla mar gyur pa
result	phala	'bras bu
result [of practice]	sādhya	bsgrub par bya ba
retinue	parivāra	'khor
reversible	vaivartiko	phyir ldog pa
right	dharma	chos
ripening	vipāka	rnam par smin pa

English	**Sanskrit**	**Tibetan**
rite	karman	las
rite	vidhi	cho ga
ritual action	kriyā	bya ba
ritual gesture	mudrā	phyag rgya
ritual manual	kalpa	rtog pa
ritually-prepared	saṃskṛta	'dus byas pa
root of [the tree of] enlightenment	bodhi-mūla	byang chub kyi shing drung
root tantra	mūla-tantra	rtsa ba'i rgyud
rootless	amūla	rtsa ba med pa
roots of virtue	kuśala-mūla	dge ba'i rtsa ba
rosary, garland	mālā	phreng ba
sacred tradition	saṃpradāya	man ngag yang dag par 'gro ba
saint	arhant	dgra bcom pa
Śakra's bow [a rainbow]	śakrāyudha	'ja' tshon
salutation	vandana	phyag
samādhi	samādhi	ting nge 'dzin
samādhi whose nature conduces to the real	bhūta-nayātmaka-samādhi	yang dag pa'i tshul gyi bdag nyid can gyi ting nge 'dzin
samādhi-being	samādhi-sattvas	ting nge 'dzin sems dpa'
Samantabhadra	samantabhadra	~'jam dpal
Sarvanīvaraṇaviṣkambhin	sarvanivaraṇaviṣkambhin	sgrib pa thams cad rnam par sel ba
scents	gandha	dri
science, teaching	śāstra	bstan bcos
scriptural discourse	deśanā-pāṭha	bshad pa'i gsung rab, bstan pa'i tshig, lung gi tshig, gsungs pa'i tshig, lung las bshad pa,
scriptural tradition, scriptural statements	pravacana	gsung rab
Scripturalist	sautrāntika	mdo sde
scripture	sūtra, sūtraka, sūtrānta	mdo, mdo de

English	Sanskrit	Tibetan
scripture, [scriptural] tradition	āgama	lung
scroll-painting	citra-paṭa, paṭa	rtsig pa'i ras ris, ras ris
seal	mudrā	phyag rgya
seal reality	mudrā-tattva	phyag rgya'i de kho na nyid
seed, seed [syllable]	bīja	sa bon
self, nature	ātman	bdag, bdag nyid
self-awareness	sva-saṃvitti	rang rig, rang gi ye shes
self-consecration	svādhiṣṭhāna	bdag la byin gyis brlab pa
self-consecration stage	svādhiṣṭhāna-krama	bdag la byin gyis brlab pa['i rim pa]
self-created	svayaṃbhū	rang byung
self-invocation	ātma-sādhana	bdag la bsgrub pa
selfless	anātmaka	bdag med pa
semen	śukra	sa bon
sense medium	āyatana	skye mched
senses, sense organ	indriya	dbang po
sequence	krama, anupūrva, anukrama, parikrama	rim pa, rim, go rims
shadow, reflection	chāyā	grib ma
shaking	spandana	bskyod pa
shame	lajjā	ngo tsha shes pa
shape	saṃsthāna	dbyibs
shapeless	asaṃsthāna	dbyibs med pa
sign, manner of knowing	nimitta	mtshan ma
signification	saṃketa	brtag pa
signless	aliṅga, animitta	mtshan ma med pa
simile	dṛṣṭānta, upamā	dpe
sin	pāpa	sdig pa
single-mindedness	eka-smṛti	dran pa gcig pa
six transcendent virtues	ṣaṭpāramitā	pha rol tu phyin pa drug
size	pramāṇa	tshod tsam
skilled	yoga	mkhas pa

English	Sanskrit	Tibetan
sky	gagana, nabha	nam mkha'
sleep	svapna	gnyid log pa
sloth	ālasya, styāna	le lo, gnyid
socializing	saṃsarga	'du 'dzi
society	saṃgaṇikā	'du ba
song	gīta	glu
sound, word	śabda	sgra
space	ākāśa, ambara, kha	nam mkha'
space-like [infinite]	khasama, khopama	nam mkha' dang mnyam pa
specified	vyākṛta	lung du bstan pa
speech	vāk	ngag
speech isolation	vag-viveka	ngag rnam par dben pa
speech vajra	vāg-vajra	gsung† rdo rje
spell	vidyā	rig sngags
sphere	viṣaya	yul
spirit of enlightenment	bodhicitta	byang chub [kyi] sems
spiritual guide	kalyāṇa-mitra	dge ba'i bshes gnyen
Śrāvaka	śrāvaka	nyan thos
stage	bhūmi, krama	sa, rim [pa]
stainless	nirmala	dri ma med pa
state	pada, avasthā, bhāva	gnas, go 'phang, gnas skabs, dngos po
stationary, unwavering	acala	mi g.yo [ba]
store	saṃbhāra	tshogs
straightforward expression	uttāna-śabda	bshad pa'i sgra
strength, force	bala	stobs pa, stobs
student	śiṣya	slob ma
study	adhyayana	klog
subject	grāhaka	'dzin pa
subject reality	ātma-tattva	bdag gi de kho na nyid
subtle	sūkṣma	phra ba, zhib
subtle element [air]	sūkṣma-dhātu	khams phra ba
subtle yoga	sūkṣma-yoga	phra mo'i rnal 'byor

English	Sanskrit	Tibetan
success	siddhi	dngos grub
successive generations of mentors	guru-parva-krama	bla ma brgyud rim
suchness	tathatā	de bzhin nyid
sucking	cūṣaṇa	rngub pa
suffering	duḥkha	sdug bsngal, sdug
sun	aditya, ravi, sūrya, virocana	nyi ma
superficial	saṃvṛti-	kun rdzob [kyi]
superficial reality	saṃvṛti-satya	kun rdzob kyi bden pa, kun rdzob
superknowledge	abhijñā	mngon par shes pa
support	ādhāra	gzhi, rten
supreme joy	paramānanda	mchog tu dga' ba
syllable, undestroyed	akṣara	yi ge, mi 'gyur ba
symbol	cihna	mtshan ma
symbol-seal	cihna-mudrā	mtshan ma'i phyag rgya
synonym	paryāya	rnam grangs
synonym, succession of names	nāma-paryāya	ming gi rnam grangs
tactile object	sparśa	reg bya
tantra, continuity	tantra	rgyud
tantric appendix	uttara-tantra	rgyud phyi ma, rgyud bla ma
Tārā	tārā	sgrol ma
teacher	ācārya, śāstṛ	slob dpon, ston pa
teaching	deśanā, śāstra	bstan pa, bstan bcos
technique	upāya, vidhi	thabs, cho ga
ten airs	daśa vāyu	rlung bcu
ten paths of virtuous action	daśa-kuśala-karma-patha	dge ba bcu'i las kyi lam
territory	bhūmi	sa
that wished for	praṇidheya	smon par bya ba
that to be [meditatively] cultivated	bhāvya	sgom pa
that to be attained	prāpya	thob pa

English	Sanskrit	Tibetan
the Earth, earth	pṛthivi	sa chen po, sa
the naïve	bāla, bāliśa	byis pa'i skye bo, byis pa
the practice completely without elaboration	atyanta-niṣprapañca-caryā	shin tu spros pa med pa'i spyod pa
thing	bhāva, padārtha, dharma	dngos po, chos
thing to be done	kriyā	bya ba
thorough knowledge	parijñāna	yongs su shes pa, rtogs pa
thorough knowledge just as it is	yathābhūta-parijñāna	yang dag pa ji lta ba nyid shes pa
those who assert [philosophical views about] action	karma-vādin	las su smra ba
thought-deed, activity of the mind	citta-carita	sems kyi spyod pa
Three Baskets	tripiṭaka	sde snod gsum
three consciousnesses	vijñāna-traya	rnam par shes pa gsum
three luminances	āloka-traya	snang ba gsum po
three mandalas	trimaṇḍala	dkyil 'khor gsum
three natures	trisvabhāvam	ngo bo nyid gsum
three radiances	ābhāsa-traya	snang ba gsum
three Realities, three natures	tri-tattva	de nyid gsum
three times	try-adhva, trikāla	dus gsum
three voids	śūnya-traya	stong pa gsum
three ways	triyāna	theg pa gsum
three worlds	triloka	'jig rten gsum
Threefold [Era]	tretā[-yuga]	gsum ldan [gyi dus]
threefold practice	trividhacaryā	spyod pa rnam pa gsum, spyod pa gsum
threefold world, three worlds	bhūrbhuvaḥsvaḥ	khams gsum, sa 'og dang sa steng dang mtho ris
three-syllabled	akṣara-traya, tryakṣara	yi ge gsum
tolerance	kṣānti	bzod pa
tongue	jihvā	lce
torpor	middha	gnyid, rmugs

English	Sanskrit	Tibetan
tradition	āmnāya	man ngag
tradition, method	naya	tshul
transcendent virtue of wisdom	prajñāpāramitā	shes rab kyi pha rol tu phyin pa
transcendent	lokottara	'jig rten las 'das pa
transcendent lord	tathāgata	de bzhin gshegs pa
transference	samāropa	bskul bar 'gyur ba
transformation	parāvṛtti, pariṇāmana	yongs su log, yongs su gyur pa
tribulation, difficult	duṣkara	dka' ba, dka' thub
trichilio-great-chiliocosm	trisāhasra-mahāsāhasra-loka-dhātu	stong gsum gyi stong chen po'i 'jig rten gyi khams
triple realm	tri-bhuvanaṃ	srid pa gsum
triple world	traidhātuka	khams gsum
true bliss	satsukha	bde ba dam pa
truth	tathya	bden pa
Truth/Reality	satya	bden pa
Tuṣita [Heaven]	tuṣita	dga' ldan gyi gnas
twelve ascetical practices	dvādaśa-dhūta-guṇa	sbyangs pa'i yon tan bcu gnyis
twelve links of dependent origination	pratītya-dvādaśāṅga	rten 'brel bcu gnyis
twelve similes of phantasm	dvādaśa-māyā-dṛṣṭānta	sgyu ma'i dpe bcu gnyis
two [sexual] organs	dvayendriya	dbang po gnyis
two realities	satyadvaya	bden pa gnyis
Twofold [Era]	dvāpara[-yuga]	gnyis ldan [gyi dus]
ultimate reality	paramārtha-satya	don dam pa'i bden pa, don dam pa
unarisen	anutpanna	skye ba med pa
uncompounded	anabhisaṃskṛta, asaṃskṛta	'dus ma byas pa
uncontrived	akṛtaka	ma bcos pa
undeducible	apratarkya	brtag tu med pa
undominated	anabhibhūta	zil gyis mi non pa
unerring	akṣūṇa	mi 'chor ba

English	Sanskrit	Tibetan
unexcelled	anuttara	bla na med pa
unfortunate	durbhaga	skal pa ngan pa
unification	eka-yoga	gcig sbyor ba
union	yoga	sbyor ba
uniting the liṅga and the bhaga	bhaga-liṅga-yoga	bha ga dang liṅga'i sbyor ba
universal monarch	cakravarti	'khor los sgyur ba
Universal Vehicle	mahāyāna	theg pa chen po
universal void	sarva-śūnya	thams cad stong pa
unlocated	apratiṣṭhita	gnas [pa] med pa
unlocated nirvāṇa	apratiṣṭhita-nirvāṇa	mi gnas pa'i mya ngan las 'das pa
unmanifest	avyakta	mi mngon
unobstructed	asaṅga	thogs pa med pa
unproduced	anutpāda	skye ba med pa
unreal, unreality	abhāva, abhūta	med, med pa, yod ma yin, dngos po med pa, yang dag pa ma yin pa
unshakeable samādhi	āsphānaka-samādhi	mi g.yo ba'i ting nge 'dzin
unspecified	avyākṛta	lung du ma bstan pa
unspoken, syllable-less	anakṣara	yi ge bral, yi ge med pa
unstruck [sound]	anāhata	mi shigs pa
Untruth/Unreality	asatya	mi bden pa
unutterable	anuccārya	brjod du med pa
unvirtuous, non-virtue, bad	akuśala	mi dge ba
upward-moving [air]	udvāha	ldang zhing rgyu ba
utterance	udāhāra	brjod pa
utterly peaceful	praśānta	rab tu zhi ba
vain	tuccha	gsog
Vairocana	vairocana	rnam par snang mdzad
vajra (penis)	vajra	rdo rje
Vajra Mentor	vajraguru	rdo rje slob dpon
vajra recitation	vajra-jāpa	rdo rje bzlas pa
vajra teacher	vajrācārya	rdo rje slob dpon

English	Sanskrit	Tibetan
vajra word	vajra-pada	rdo rje'i tshig
Vajrapāṇi	vajrapāṇi	phyag na rdo rje, lag na rdo rje
Vajrasattva	vajrasattva	rdo rje sems dpa'
vase	kalaśa	bum pa
vehicle	vāhana	bzhon pa
Venerable Master (Nāgārjuna)	bhaṭṭāraka-pāda	rje btsun, klu sgrub
verbal token	vāk-cchomā	ngag gi brda
verse	gāthā, śloka	tshigs su bcad pa
vestige, vestigial instinct	vāsanā	bag chags
victor	jina	rgyal ba
victorious lord	jinendra	rgyal dbang po
view	dṛṣṭi	lta ba
virtuous and non-virtuous	śubhāśubha	dge ba dang mi dge ba
visualized, imagined [nature]	parikalpita	brtags, kun brtags pa
Viśva	viśva	sna tshogs pa
vital fluid	rasa	ro
vitality control	prāṇāyāma	srog dang rtsol ba
vitality, vitality [air]	prāṇa	srog
vocal acts	ruta-vyāpāra	tha snyad
vocal expression	vāk-pravyāhāra	tshig tu brjod pa
vocal proclamation	ruta-vijñapti	sgra
vocalization	ruta	sgra
void	śūnya	stong pa
voidness	śūnyatā	stong pa nyid
vowels	svara	dbyangs
vowels and consonants	ālikāli	ā li kā li
vulgate	mlecchā	
waking	jāgrat	gnyid ma log pa
wandering ascetic	śramaṇa	dge sbyong
warrior	kṣatriya	rgyal rigs

English	Sanskrit	Tibetan
water	salila, vāruṇa	chu
water bubbles	budbuda	chu'i chu bur
water element	abdhātu	chu'i khams
way of mantra	mantranaya	gsang sngags kyi tshul
Way of the Śrāvakas	śrāvaka-yāna	nyan thos theg pa
well born	ājāneya	kun shes pa
well-known	prasiddha	grags
well-moving [air]	pravāha	rab tu rgyu ba
wheel of existence	bhava-cakra	'khor ba
wheel, retinue	cakra	'khor lo, tshogs
wicked	dauṣṭhulya	gnas ngan len
wind	vāta	rlung
wisdom-gnosis	prajñā-jñāna	shes rab kyi ye shes
wisdom-gnosis initiation	prajñā-jñānābhiṣeka	shes rab dang ye shes kyi dbang bskur ba
wise one, the wise	jñānin	ye shes can
wish	praṇidhāna	smon lam
wisher	praṇidhāyaka	smon pa po
wishing gem	cintāmaṇi	yid bzhin nor bu
woman	strī	bud med
womb	yoni	~skye ba
word	pada	tshig
world	jagat	'gro ba
world of beings	jagat	'gro ba
worldly	laukika	'jig rten pa
worldly motivation	loka-dharma	'jig rten pa'i chos
world-realm	lokadhātu	'jig rten gyi khams
worship, offering	pūjā	mchod pa
wrong, bad thing	adharma	chos ma yin pa
yoginī	yoginī	rnal 'byor ma
zombiess	vetālī	ro langs ma

Appendix II
Index of Scriptural Authorities Cited in the CMP

NOTE: Reference numbers in parentheses indicate that the work is either not cited by name, or is mis-cited.

English Title	Tibetan Title	Sanskrit Title	Ref.
(unspecified scripture)			10b, 13b
(unspecified scripture)		(Mahāmāyūrī-vidyā-rājñī)	56a
Eight-Thousand-Line Transcendent Virtue of Wisdom [Scripture]	Shes rab kyi pha rol tu phyin pa brg-yad stong pa	Aṣṭasāhasrikā-prajñāpāramitā Aṣṭasāhasrikā	38a, 51b/52a
Adamantine Crown-Protrusion Tantra	rDo rje gtsug tor gyi rgyud	Vajroṣṇīṣa-tantra	3a, 36a/b
Assembly of All Deities Tantra	Lha thams cad yang dag par 'dus pa'i rgyud	Sarva-deva-samāgama-tantra	68b, 71b
Compendium of All Rituals	rTog pa kun las btus pa	Sarva-kalpa-samuccaya (Vajraśekhara Tantra)	51b
Compendium of Realities	de kho na nyid bsdus pa de kho na nyid bsdus pa'i rgyud	Tattva-samgraha Tattva-samgraha-tantra	18b, 20a, 27a, (34b), 57b
Diamond Cutter [Scripture]	rDo rje gcod pa	Vajracchedikā	37b
Enlightenment of Vairocana Tantra	rNam par snang mdzad mngon par byang chub pa'i rgyud rNam par snang mdzad mngon par byang chub pa zhes bya ba spyod pa'i rgyud	Vairocanābhisambodhi-tantra Vairocanābhisambodhi-caryā-tantra	24a, 27a, 42a, 55b
Enquiry of Bhadrapāli Scripture	bZang skyong gis zhus pa'i mdo bZang skyong gis zhus pa	Bhadrapāli-paripṛcchā-sūtra Bhadrapāli-paripṛcchā	7a, 27b, (32b/33a and 41a)

Enquiry of the Four Goddesses	Lha mo bzhis zhus pa	Caturdevī-paripṛcchā	2b
Enquiry of the Kinnara King Scripture	Mi'am ci'i rgyal pos zhus pa'i mdo Mi'am ci'i rgyal po ljon pas zhus pa'i mdo	Kinnara-rāja-paripṛcchā-sūtra	25a/b, 34a/b, 37b
Esoteric Community Appendix Tantra	gSang ba 'dus pa'i rgyud phyi ma	Samājottara	16b, 32a
Esoteric Community Tantra	gSang ba 'dus pa zhes bya ba rnal 'byor chen po'i rgyud gSang ba 'dus pa'i rgyud gSang ba 'dus pa	Guhyasamāja-mahāyoga-tantra Śrī-guhya-samāja Śrī-samāja	7b, 14a, 14b, 15a, 15b, 16a, 29a, 37b, 43b, 48a, 49a, 51b, 54b, (55b), (56a), 57b, 64b, (67b), (68a), (68b), 73a
Explanation of the Intention	dGongs pa lung ston pa zhes bya ba'i rnal 'byor chen po'i rgyud gSang ba 'dus pa'i bshad pa'i rgyud dGongs pa lung ston pa	Saṃdhyā-vyākaraṇa-mahāyoga-tantra Saṃdhyā-vyākaraṇa-samāja-vyākhyā-tantra	16b/17a, (17b), 20b/21a, 71a
explanatory tantra	bshad pa'i rgyud	vyākhyā-tantra	17b, 18b, 20a, 34b, 72a
(Glorious) Supreme Prime Tantra	dPal mchog dang po zhes bya ba rnal 'byor chen po'i rgyud dPal mchog dang po'i rgyud dPal mchog dang po	Paramādya-mahāyoga-tantra Paramādya	(48a), 50a, 50b, 55b/56a, 56b, 57b
Gnosis Vajra Compendium	Ye shes rdo rje kun las btus pa Ye shes rdo rje kun las btus pa zhes bya ba rnal 'byor chen po'i rgyud	Jñāna-vajra-samucchaya Jñāna-vajra-samuccaya-mahāyoga-tantra	27a, 29a, 44a
Golden Radiance Scripture	gSer 'od dam pa'i mdo	(Suvarṇa-prabhāsa-sūtra)	(lost folio)

English Title	Tibetan Title	Sanskrit Title	Ref.
Hero's March (Samādhi) Scripture	dPa' bar 'gro ba'i ting nge 'dzin gyi mdo	Śūraṅgama-sūtra	4a, 52b/53a
Inner Sādhana	Nang gi bdag nyid sgrub thabs	Adhyātmasādhana	50a
Jewel Heap Scripture	dKon mchog brtsegs pa'i mdo	Ratnakūṭasūtra (Kāśyapa-parivarta)	56b
Journey to Laṅka Scripture	Lang kar gshegs pa'i mdo	Laṅkāvatāra-sūtra	(2a), 3b, 6a, 22b, 23a, (23b/24a), 27a, 49b, (lost folio)
King of Samādhi Scripture	Ting nge 'dzin rgyal po'i mdo	Samādhi-rāja-sūtra	51b, 69b
Method of the Three Baskets	sDe snod gsum gyi tshul	Pitaka-traya-naya (Udānavarga/ Dhammapada)	27a
Purification of All Karmic Obscurations Scripture	Las kyi sgrib pa thams cad rnam par dag pa'i mdo	Sarva-karmāvaraṇa-viśuddhi-sūtra	39a, 43a/b
Root Sutra	rtsa ba'i rgyud	mūla-sūtra (GST)	56a, 68a
Root Sutra	rtsa ba'i mdo	mūla-sūtra (GST)	55b
Root Tantra	rtsa ba'i mdo	mūla-tantra	63b/64a (SBS), 67b (GST)
Root Tantra	rtsa ba'i rgyud	mūla-tantra (Tattva-saṃgraha)	34b
Scripture Teaching the Non-manifestation of all Things	Chos thams cad rab tu 'jug pa bstan par bya ba'i mdo	Sarvadharmāpravṛtti-nirdeśa-sūtra	26a

Scriptures of the Universal Way	Theg pa chen po'i mdo sde	Mahāyāna-sūtra	29a
Secret Accomplishment	gSang ba grub pa	Guhya-siddhi	50b/51a, 54b, 70a
Secret Moon Drop	Zla gsang thig le	Guhyendu-tilaka	7b, (13b), (14a), (14b), (15a), (48a)
{Secret} Treasury of the Transcendent Lord[s] Scripture	De bzhin gshegs pa'i mdzod kyi mdo	Tathāgata-guhya-koṣa-sūtra	39a
Song of the Names [of Mañjuśrī]	mTshan yang dag par brjod pa	Nāma-samgītī	22b
Space-Like Tantra	Nam mkha' dang mnyam pa'i rgyud	Khasama-tantra	(14a)
Supreme Bliss	bDe mchog	Saṃvara (Sarvabuddha-samāyoga)	57a, 64a
Teaching of One Method Scripture	Tshul gcig par bstan pa'i mdo	Eka-naya-nirdeśa-sūtra	24a, 45a
Transmigration of Consciousness Scripture (see Enquiry of Bhadrapāli Scripture)	rNam par shes pa 'pho ba'i mdo	Vijñāna-saṃkrānti-sūtra (a.k.a. Bhadrapāli-paripṛcchā)	32b/33a, 41a
The Uncommon Secret	Thun mong ma yin pa'i gsang ba zhes bya ba'i rnal 'byor chen po'i rgyud	Asādhāraṇa-guhya-mahāyoga-tantra	69b
Unexcelled Intention (a.k.a. PK, Chap. II)	dGongs pa bla na med pa	Anuttara-sandhi	33a, 37a/b
Unfailing Success in Discipline Tantra	'Dul ba don yod par grub pa zhes bya ba'i rnal 'byor chen po'i rgyud	Vinayāmoghasiddhi- mahātantra	56b
Union of All Buddhas: Magical Supreme Bliss of the Ḍākiṇīs	Sangs rgyas thams cad dang mnyam par sbyor ba mkha' 'gro ma sgyu ma bde ba'i mchog	Sarva-buddha-samāyoga-ḍākinī-jāla-saṃvara-mahāyoga-tantra	14b/15a, 17b, (57a), 57b/58a, (63b/64a)

English Title	Tibetan Title	Sanskrit Title	Ref.
Universal Secret Tantra	Thams cad gsang ba'i rgyud	Sarva-rahasya-tantra	14a, 54a (GSUT)
Vajra Door {Goddess}	rDo rje['i] sgo zhes bya ba rnal 'byor chen po'i rgyud	Vajramukhī-mahāyoga-tantra	12a, 17b
Vajra Rosary	rDo rje phreng ba zhes bya ba'i rnal 'byor chen po'i rgyud	Vajramālā[-mahāyoga-tantra]	9b, (10b), 18b/19a
Vajra Maṇḍala Ornament Tantra	rDo rje dkyil 'khor rgyan zhes bya ba'i rgyud	Vajra-maṇḍalālaṃkara-tantra	23a
Venerable Master	rje btsun gyi zhal snga nas	Bhaṭṭāraka-pāda (Pañca-krama)	51b
Venerable Master [Nāgārjuna]	kLu sgrub kyi zhal snga nas rJe btsun gyi zhal snga nas	Bhaṭṭāraka-pāda	39b, 51b
Yoga Tantra	rnal 'byor chen po'i rgyud	yoga-tantra	48a

Appendix III
Charts of the One Hundred Buddha Families

I. The Five Aggregates (25 families)

	Akṣobhya	Vairocana	Ratnasambhava	Amitābha	Amoghasiddhi
Form (Vairocana)	Forms made known only through personal experience	Forms having outer, inner, and both shapes such as long and short	Forms in the mode of self, other, or both	Exterior [and] interior forms of the five colors	Exterior [and] interior forms of luminance of the sun and moon
Feeling (Ratnasambhava)	Feelings arising from bile and conjunction [of three humours]	Ambivalent feelings	Feelings born from phlegm and air	Pleasurable feelings	Painful feelings
Discernment (Amitābha)	Discernments of bipeds	Discernments of inanimate beings	Discernments of quadrupeds	Discernments of those without legs	Discernments of the many-legged
Propensity (Amoghasiddhi)	Mental propensities	Bodily propensities	Propensities [toward] the three worlds	Verbal propensities	Propensities [toward] liberation
Consciousness (Akṣobhya)	Tactile consciousness	Visual consciousness	Auditory consciousness	Olfactory consciousness	Gustatory consciousness

II. The Four elements (20 families)

	Akṣobhya	Vairocana	Ratnasambhava	Amitābha	Amoghasiddhi
Earth element (Locanā)	Bodily secretions, small intestine, bile, and heart	Hair, bone, feces, spleen, and heart	Bodily hair, nails, pus, and heart	Teeth, skin, flesh, and heart	Tendons, flesh, ribs, and heart
external earth element	Pūrvavideha	Mount Sumeru	Jambudvīpa	Godānīya	Uttarakuru
Water element (Māmakī)	Urine	Phlegm and tears	Sweat	Blood	Saliva
external water element	Ocean water	Waters of waterfall	River water	Spring water	Pond water
Fire element (Pāṇḍaravāsinī)	Heat of the heart	Heat of the head	Heat of the navel	Heat of all the limbs	Heat of the belly
external fire element	Perpetual fire	Fire arisen from stones	Fire arisen from sun-crystals	Fire arisen from pieces of wood	Forest fires
Air element (Tārā)	Vitality air	Pervasive air	Evacuative air	Ascending air	Metabolic air
external air element	Eastern wind	Zenith wind	Southern wind	Western wind	Northern wind

III. The Five Media (25 families)					
	Akṣobhya	**Vairocana**	**Ratnasambhava**	**Amitābha**	**Amoghasiddhi**
Visual media (Kṣitigarbha)	Grape-sized visual sense organ	Perception of the three forms	Nature of the pupil of the eye	Forms seen with the peripheral vision	Movement of the eye
Aural media (Vajrapāṇi)	Greatly convoluted aural sense	Nature of the ear	Perception of the three sounds	Ear orifice	Root of the ear
Olfactory media (Ākāśagarbha)	*Śalākā*-shaped olfactory sense-organ	Nature of the nose	Septum	Perception of the three scents	Nostrils
Gustatory media (Lokeśvara)	Half-moon shaped gustatory sense organ	Nature of the tongue	Root of the tongue	Tip of the tongue	Perception of the three tastes
Tactile media (Sarvanīvaraṇa-viṣkambhin)	Perception of the three [types of] contact	Tactile sense organ (whole body)	Nature of bones	Nature of flesh	Nature of skin
Mental sense media (Samantabhadra / Mañjuśrī)					

IV. The Five Auxiliary Winds (25 families)

	Akṣobhya	**Vairocana**	**Ratnasambhava**	**Amitābha**	**Amoghasiddhi**
Upward moving (visual)	Forms of play, flirtation, and eroticism	Visual forms	Forms to which one is attached	Forms discerned as pleasant, unpleasant, and ambivalent	Forms that perform all activities
Re-moving wind (aural)	Pacific and violent sounds of the syllable *hūṃ*	Sounds in ear, head, or hair	Singing and stringed instruments	Palatal, labial, and vocal sounds	Sounds of great trees, rivers, snapping, clapping, drums and other musical instruments
Authentically moving (olfactory)	Unpleasant scents	All scents	Scent of the entire body	(Perception of the distinction of the) three scents	Scent of vital fluid
Well-moving wind (gustatory)	Bitter flavors	Sweet flavors	Astringent flavors	Salty flavors	Distinction of the six flavors
Certainly moving (tactile)	Perception of the nature of subtle mind from the tactile sensation of uniting *liṅga* and *bhaga*	Tactile sensation of *ekāsana-stha*	Tactile sensation of embracing	Tactile sensation of kissing	Tactile sensation of sucking

V. The Five Gnoses (5 families)

	Akṣobhya	Vairocana	Ratnasambhava	Amitābha	Amoghasiddhi
Five gnoses	Realm of Reality (*dharmadhātu*)	Mirror-like	Equality	Individuating discernment	Function-accomplishing

Appendix IV
Charts of the Eighty Prototypes (prakṛti) of the Subtle Mind according to the CMP and Pañcakrama

The levels of the subtle mind

Luminance (*āloka*): thirty-three prototypes
Radiance ([*ālok*]*ābhāsa*): forty prototypes
Imminence ([*ālok*]*opalabdha*]: seven prototypes
Brilliance (*prabhāsvara*)

1. The Thirty-three Prototypes of Luminance[1134]

Sanskrit of CMP (and PK)	Tibetan of CMP (PK)	English
virāgaḥ	'dod chags dang bral ba	1. Dispassion
madhyamavirāgaḥ	'dod chags dang bral ba bar ma	2. Moderate dispassion
ativirāgaḥ	shin tu 'dod chags dang bral ba	3. Extreme dispassion
manogatāgatam	yid kyis 'gro ba dang 'ong ba dag	4. Mental coming and going
śokaḥ	mya ngan	5. Pain
madhyamaśokaḥ	mya ngan bar ma	6. Moderate pain
atiśokaḥ	shin tu mya ngan du gyur pa	7. Extreme pain
saumyam	zhi ba	8. Peace
vikalpam	rnam par rtog pa	9. Conceptualization
bhītam (bhītaḥ)	'jigs pa	10. Fear

Table continues

1134. See above, note 70, for a discussion of disagreements in the traditional sources about how to enumerate these thirty-three.

Sanskrit of CMP (and PK)	Tibetan of CMP (PK)	English
madhyamabhītam (madhyamabhītaḥ)	'jigs pa bar ma	11. Moderate Fear
atibhītam (atibhītaḥ)	shin tu 'jigs pa	12. Extreme Fear
tṛṣṇā	sred pa	13. Craving
madhyamatṛṣṇā (madhyatṛṣṇā)	sred pa bar ma	14. Moderate craving
atitṛṣṇā	shin tu sred pa	15. Extreme craving
upādānam (upādānakam)	nye bar len pa	16. Clinging/ Appropriation
niḥśubham	mi dge ba	17. Non-virtue
kṣut	bkres pa	18. Hunger
tṛṣṇā (tṛṣā)	skom pa	19. Thirst
vedanā	tshor ba	20. Feeling
samavedanā	tshor ba bar ma	21. Moderate feeling
ativedanā	shin tu tshor ba	22. Extreme feeling
vettṛ	rig pa po	23. Knower
vid-dhāraṇāpadam	rig pa 'dzin pa'i gzhi (rig 'dzin gzhi)	24. Object grasped (by) Knowing
pratyavekṣaṇam	so sor rtog pa	25. Individuating analysis
lajjā	ngo tsha shes pa	26. Shame
kāruṇyam	snying rje	27. Compassion
snehaḥ	brtse ba	28. Affection
madhyamasnehaḥ	brtse ba bar ma	29. Moderate affection
atisnehaḥ	shin tu brtse ba	30. Extreme affection
cakitaṃ (saṃśayaḥ)	dogs pa dang bcas pa	31. Anxiety
sañcayaḥ	sdud pa	32. Collecting
mātsaryam	phrag dog	33. Envy

2. The Forty Prototypes of Radiance

Sanskrit of CMP (and PK)	Tibetan of CMP (PK)	English
rāgaḥ	chags pa	34. Passion
raktam	kun du chags pa	35. Impassioned
tuṣṭam	dga' ba	36. Pleasure
madhyamatuṣṭam	dga' ba bar ma	37. Moderate pleasure
atituṣṭam	shin tu dga' ba	38. Extreme pleasure
harṣaṇam	rangs pa	39. Delight
pramodyam	rab tu mgu ba	40. Rapture
vismayaḥ	ngo mtshar ba	41. Amazement
hasitam	dgod pa	42. Laughter
hlādaḥ (hlādana)	tshim pa	43. Satisfaction
āliṅganam	'khyud pa	44. Embracing
cumbanam	'o byed pa	45. Kissing
cūṣaṇam	'jib pa	46. Sucking
dhairyam	brtan pa	47. Stability
vīryam	brtson pa	48. Heroism
mānaḥ	khengs pa (nga rgyal)	49. Arrogance
karaṇam (kartṛ)	bya ba	50. Activity
haraṇam (hartṛ)	dbrog pa ('phrog)	51. Robbery
balam	stobs pa	52. Force
utsāhaḥ	spro ba	53. Fortitude
sāhasam	dka' ba la sbyor ba	54. Boldness
madhyamasāhasam	dka' ba la sbyor ba bar ma	55. Moderate boldness
uttamasāhasam	shin tu dka' ba la sbyor ba	56. Supreme boldness
raudram	drag pa	57. Aggression
vilāsaḥ	rnam par sgeg pa	58. Flirtation
vairam	'gres pa	59. Spite
śubham	dge ba	60. Virtue

Table continues

Sanskrit of CMP (and PK)	Tibetan of CMP (PK)	English
vāksphuṭam	tshig gsal ba	61. Clear Words
satyam	bden pa	62. Truth/Reality
asatyam	mi bden pa	63. Untruth/Unreality
niścayaḥ	nges pa	64. Certainty
nirupādānam	nye bar mi len pa	65. Non-clinging
dātṛtvam	sbyin pa po	66. Donor
codanam	bskul ba	67. Impelling
śauryam (sauratā)	dpa' ba (dpa' bo)	68. Heroism
alajjā	ngo tshar med pa	69. Shamelessness
dhūrtatvam	sgyu zin pa	70. Cunning
duṣṭam (duṣṭaḥ)	gdug pa	71. Wickedness
haṭham (haṭhaḥ)	mi srun pa	72. Violence
kauṭilyam (kuṭilaḥ)	gya gyu che ba	73. Scheming

3. The Seven Prototypes of Imminence

Sanskrit of CMP (and PK)	Tibetan of CMP (PK)	English
madhyamarāgaḥ	chags pa bar ma	74. Moderate Passion
vismṛtiḥ	brjed ngas pa	75. Forgetfulness
bhrāntiḥ	'khrul pa	76. Confusion
tūṣṇīm (tūṣṇī-bhāvaḥ)	mi smra ba	77. Muteness
khedaḥ	skyo ba	78. Depression
ālasyam	le lo	79. Sloth
dhandhatvam	the tshom	80. Dull[-minded]-ness

Appendix V
Schema of Questions Posed in the CMP

I. Chapter 1 (2 questions)

1. What is "Reality?" (2b)
2. Is the perfection stage a sequential process or instantaneous illumination by the instructions of the guru? (3b)

II. Chapter 2 (4 questions)

1. How does one learn body isolation? (6b)
2. How do the hundred clans become fivefold? (13b/14a)
3. How do the five further become threefold? (14b)
4. How do the three clans become the [single] body vajra with the nature of the indivisible three vajras? (15a)

III. Chapter 3 (6 questions)

1. How does one learn speech isolation? (15b)
2. What are the ten vital airs? (17b)
3. Where do the ten airs reside in the body and what do they do? (18a)
4. How do these ten airs day and night emit from and collect in the body? (18b)
5. What are the characteristics of mantra reality? (19b)
6. How is the syllable *a* "short" and how does it "become the cause of the manifestation of all speech?" (22a)

IV. Chapter 4 (3 questions)

1. How does one learn mind isolation? (26b)

2. What is the scriptural source for the teaching of the eightyfold mind? (32a)
3. How are the three consciousnesses emitted and re-collected in one's body day and night? Who is aware [of it]? Who is unaware? How can one discern the presence of the one hundred and sixty prototypes analogically? (32a/b)

V. Chapter 5 (1 question)

1. How is the mind-made body bound to the beginningless wheel of existence by good and evil action? How is virtue and non-virtue acquired again in the afterlife? Does that virtue and non-virtue come from elsewhere? Or is it born from the instincts of one's own mind? (35a/b)

VI. Chapter 6 (3 questions)

1. How does one produce a deity body by means of mere gnosis? (40a/b)
2. How is a divine body created by merely the mind alone? (40b)
3. Why does one sleep? Why does the consciousness return to the same body? Why does one suffer the ripening of karmic effects from good and bad dreams? Is there a difference between sleep and waking, or not? (42b)

VII. Chapter 7 (1 question)

1. What is the ultimate reality, the state of the purification of the radiances? (44b)

VIII. Chapter 8 (1 question)

1. How does one, having entered ultimate reality and become insubstantial, subsequently arise? Who is it that here experiences true bliss? What is the irreversible? What is the meaning of "liberation?" From what is one liberated? (49a)

IX. Chapter 9 (2 questions)

1. How shall the yogin persevere in the causal condition? How shall he conduct himself? How shall he meditatively cultivate himself? How shall he practice the practices of spiritual discipline? (53a/b)
2. How is it not mutually contradictory to teach both that the passion, hatred, and ignorance lead to a lower rebirth and that the one devoted to those will quickly accomplish the unexcelled state? (56a)

X. Chapter 10 (1 question)

1. What is the practice without elaboration? (64b)

XI. Chapter 11 (1 question)

1. If a practitioner who has seen reality does not perform the threefold practice due to the distraction of work and[/or] is not able to complete the rituals on account of lacking the requisites, having died, may he expect an ordinary rebirth or Mahāvajradharahood? (73b)

Appendix VI
Notes on the Textual Editions of the CMP[1135]

Until quite recently, it was thought that the CMP had not survived in its original Sanskrit. In 1977, Alex Wayman published a brief extract of a passage cited in the *Subhāṣita-saṃgraha* as an appendix to *Yoga of the Guhyasamājatantra*, in the belief that this was all that had survived of Āryadeva's work other than its Tibetan translation.[1136] In the meantime, further research into the surviving collections of Sanskrit manuscripts have unearthed previously unidentified texts of the CMP. It is upon these materials that the edition published in the first edition of this book was based, and it is that edition that is translated herein.

At present, the CMP is known to us through two witnesses. The first consists of two halves of one nearly complete palm-leaf manuscript (which I designate MSS A and B). The latter is currently available only as a decent photograph of the better part of another, paper manuscript (which I designate MS C). MS B was the first to be identified as belonging to the CMP, followed some years later by the identification of MS A.[1137] These texts were used as the basis of the first published edition of the CMP, which appeared

1135. These notes refer to the Sanskrit and Tibetan critical editions published in the first edition of this book (Wedemeyer, *Āryadeva's Lamp that Integrates the Practices*, 2007), which critical editions are now also presented in the online reading room at wisdomexperience.org. A slightly corrected version of my Sanskrit critical edition is available at sarit.indology.info/caryamelapakapradipa.xml.

1136. Actually, Wayman failed to publish the entire SS extract, as he mistook Āryadeva's citation of the Root Sūtra for the beginning of a new citation by the author of the SS. As I have indicated elsewhere ("Vajrayāna and its Doubles," 218), the passage from the CMP found there is much more extensive. (In fact, a great portion of the SS is composed of unattributed passages drawn from the CMP.)

1137. Notices of these identifications, by the staff of the Rare Buddhist Texts project at the Central Institute of Higher Tibetan Studies (Sarnath, Varanasi) were published in their house journal *Dhīḥ*, volume 10 (1990), 6, and vol. 25 (1998), 9–11, respectively.

in 2000.[1138] In early 2000, while searching Rāhul Sāṅkṛtyāyan's list of the manuscripts he photographed in Tibet in the 1930s, I myself discovered what I imagined must be another copy of the CMP. This turned out to be MS C. I subsequently discovered that this had already been tentatively identified by Tsukamoto et al. (in 1989)[1139] and Frank Bandurski in his 1994 catalog of the copies of the Rāhul Sāṅkṛtyāyan photos kept in the library of the University of Göttingen, based upon the Tibetan title written in along the top margin of the first folio of the text (not reported by Sāṅkṛtyāyan).[1140]

The older of the two manuscripts would seem to be that composed of MSS A and B.[1141] It is written on palm leaves, in an old Newari script[1142] in a neat and clear hand. The folios are numbered on each page on the verso. It has been corrected in at least two hands, and it also bears markings that I suspect derive from modern readers, notably the underlining of the names of works cited in the book.[1143] The leaves have one central hole (slightly to the left of center) for a string binding, set off from the text by vertical, dotted lines (only ca. the first ten folios). These two texts are to be found in the collections of the Asiatic Society of Bengal and the National Archives of Nepal, respectively. The two halves fit together perfectly, only one (the final) leaf seems to be missing from the whole. Tōru Tomabechi has suggested the name "Calcutta-Kathmandu Codex" for the reunited text. For clarity, I continue to refer to the texts independently, though I agree that they are parts of a whole. How exactly this manuscript came to reside in these two separate collections is not clear. However, I might hazard a guess that the paṇḍita who cataloged the manuscript in its original home in Kathmandu (the name Haraprasad Shāstri comes to mind) may have absconded

1138. Pandey, ed., *Caryāmelāpakapradīpam*.

1139. See Tsukamoto et al., *Descriptive Bibliography*, 237.

1140. See Bandurski, "Übersicht über die Göttinger Sammlungen," 66–67.

1141. I base this judgment largely on the fact that the script seems to me to be more archaic.

1142. Or, perhaps this might better be called "proto-Bengali." See Dimitrov, "Tables of the Old Bengali Script," 36. H.P. Shāstrī describes the script of MS A as "Bengali of the 13th century" (*Descriptive Catalogue*, 170), though he describes that of MS B as "Newari" (*Catalogue of Palm-leaf*, vol. 2, p. 40).

1143. Paṇḍit Sukh Dev Gwali of the Nepal National Archives reports that all the corrections were made in the 20th century, when the manuscripts were transferred from the Bīr Library to the National Archives. He estimates the text to be ca. 600 years old (personal communication, 31 December 2006).

with the first half of this MS, either with the permission of the authorities, or perhaps without. Why he only took the first half, however, remains a mystery.[1144]

At present, for all practical purposes, MS C exists only as a film taken in Tibet in the early part of the last century and preserved in the Rāhul Sāṅkrtyāyan Collection in Patna.[1145] A complete copy of this set of films is also kept in the library of the University of Göttingen, from which I obtained a copy. Based on this film, and the notes kept by Sāṅkṛtyāyan, we can say that it is written in an Old Bengali script[1146] in a neat and regular hand. It, too, bears a page number on each leaf, on the verso. It does not have marginal corrections, but there are signs that it may nonetheless have been corrected, with passages scraped off and rewritten, though this is hard to determine from a photo. Though described as a "palm leaf ms. from Tibet" by Sāṅkṛtyāyan,[1147] the regularity of the leaves suggests instead a paper manuscript. The pages are cut after the pattern of palm leaves, and bear two perforations for a string binding, one third of the way from either end. For reasons unknown to me, the front sides of the last set of folios (ten in all) do not appear to have been photographed, so every other page is missing for these last ten folios of MS C. The original film was taken in 1934 at the famous Ngor Monastery of Butön and I suspect it may date from about his era (early fourteenth century). With the invasion of Tibet by the Chinese and the subsequent looting and destruction of cultural artefacts, it is not clear whether these manuscripts have all survived. Many of them, however,

1144. The first half of the manuscript was evidently taken before it was accessioned or catalogued at the Bīr/Durbar Library. The half held by the Asiatic Society does not bear stamps from this library (as does the "Nepalese half"). And Shāstrī (*Catalogue of Palm-leaf*, vol. 2, p. 40) notes that "the Librarian [of the Durbar Library] has named the work Saṃśaya pariçheda [*sic*]," indicating that the two halves had been separated before his 1907 trip to Nepal—perhaps during the 1898–99 tour with Cecil Bendell and Binod Bihari Bhaṭṭacārya.

1145. The films reside in a building in Patna that is shared by the Patna Museum, the Bihar Research Society, and the K.P. Jayaswal Research Institute. It is not entirely clear which of these organizations has authority over the MSS, though I believe it to be the Bihar Research Society. There have been recent reports of the original films being stolen and sold by unscrupulous, presumably underpaid, employees. I do not have information as to the current state of the film of MS C.

1146. Sāṅkṛtyāyan calls it "Newari."

1147. Bandurski also describes the text as palm leaf ("Palmbl."); see Bandurski, "Übersicht," 66.

have resurfaced in Beijing in the possession of the Chinese authorities.[1148] Limited access to these texts has been granted to selected research teams (who allegedly pay exorbitant fees for the privilege). The current whereabouts of this text are unknown to me.

It must be confessed that the actual text of MS A used in preparing my edition was a microfilm copy of the manuscript I have described. Unfortunately, limitations of time and money did not allow me to travel to check my readings against the original text. Sole reliance on such derivative texts is methodologically problematic, as a copy of a manuscript is a new and distinct artefact, and thus does not preserve exactly the information contained in the original. Any proper edition, I believe, should be based first and foremost on the original texts, not on modern copies (even photographic or photomechanical ones). Nonetheless, as it is the case that nearly all contemporary published editions of Sanskrit works are similarly based on microfilm copies, I hope that the reader may in this case grant me the indulgence of "innocence by association."

One of the first challenges in creating a critical edition (after securing and collating the texts) is to attempt to determine the relationships between the witnesses, such that a critical method may be based in part upon "objective," genealogical considerations rather than allegedly more "subjective" critical judgement. That is, an editor seeks to determine if, for example, one text is a copy or descendent of another. If so, the derivative text is thereby given less weight when choosing among variant readings, since the variants in later copies are presumably the result of either textual change/corruption or later editorial intervention—neither attributable to the original author whose work is being reconstructed. Such considerations have significant impact on the relative weight to be given to variant readings and, thus, the results of critical editorial work. In a case such as ours, in which only two sources survive, such determinations may lead an editor to designate one a "copy text," which then becomes in essence the "default" reading.

My study of these manuscripts has led me to conclude that the two witnesses, the "Calcutta-Kathmandu Codex" (MSS A and B) and the Sāṅkṛtyāyan Photo (MS C), constitute what are called "radiant texts"; that is

1148. For a useful summary of the current situation with regard to Sanskrit manuscripts in Tibet and China, including avenues of access for researchers, see Ernst Steinkellner, *A Tale of Leaves*.

"texts that do not form an ancestral linear series but instead represent independent lines of descent from a common source."[1149] The pattern of variation is such that neither text may be considered the prototype of the other. Thus, even though the Calcutta-Kathmandu Codex seems to be the older text, it cannot be taken as a "copy text," as it does not have "presumptive authority by virtue of its genealogical position."[1150] Hence, it has not been possible to merely privilege one set of readings as derived from a more authoritative document than the other. Each set of variants has had to be weighed against a variety of factors (grammar, meter, sense, style, patterns of usage, etc.) in seeking to determine the original text as composed by the author. While some (misguided) purists may decry that the resulting edition is what is called an "eclectic text," I would argue that nearly all serious critical editing results in some way or other in such a text.

Complicating the editorial task somewhat, and adding to its eclecticism, are two facts. First, the fact that MS C seems quite likely to be eclectic itself—or what is sometimes called "contaminated." That is, it bears the mark of a prior editorial hand. This can be seen from several features. For instance, in the citation of the *Vajroṣṇīṣa Tantra* in chapter 5 (CMP, f. 36a), MS C contains added text inserted (apparently) to make sense of an erroneous reading. The reading does not follow the pattern of the rest of the passage, so I conclude that it was added by an overzealous editor.[1151] Further, there are a couple of occasions in which MS C adds glosses not found in the other texts, suggesting editorial intervention.[1152] The hand of a prior editor is even more clear in a passage in chapter 3 (CMP, f. 24b), where two variant readings of a cited sentence are given, marked by the editorial note "there is a second reading" (*iti dvitīyaḥ pāṭhaḥ*). Although such editorial intervention makes the readings of C somewhat more suspect, there are nonetheless many instances in which its readings are undeniably preferable.

External sources have also been consulted in the editorial process: largely citations of the CMP in other Sanskrit works, editions of works cited by the CMP, and parallel citations of verses also cited in the CMP. Another

1149. G. Thomas Tanselle, "Editing Without a Copy-text," 14.

1150. Tanselle, "Editing Without a Copy-text," 15.

1151. See note 597 to chapter 5 in the translation.

1152. E.g., the interpolation of *vyūha-karmā* in the definition of the air element in chapter 2 (CMP, f. 9a) and the gloss of *svacchā* by *abdhātu*, in chapter 3 (CMP, f. 19b).

reference has been the edition produced by the Rare Buddhist Texts project referred to above (designated Pn, for its editor Janardan Pandey). Although this edition is only based on the Calcutta-Kathmandu Codex, and (in my opinion) frequently fails to render that source adequately,[1153] I opted to note all the instances in which this edition departs from my reading of that manuscript; where it is not so marked, the reader may assume that Pn concurs with the reading I provide for A/B. Furthermore, I have compared each reading to that suggested by the eleventh-century Tibetan translation of the CMP by Śraddhākaravarman and Rinchen Zangpo (Tib) as well as citations of variant translations of the CMP found in the RṄSG of Tsongkhapa. These have, by their very nature, been given less weight than the evidence of the surviving manuscripts, but have nonetheless been taken very seriously as evidence by which to reconstruct the text.

As sources for my Tibetan edition, I consulted four texts: examples of the sDe-dge, Co-ne, sNar-thang, and Peking xylographic redactions of the work (marked by the sigils D, Co, N, and P, respectively). The sDe-dge redaction was consulted on the basis of a modern reprint of the original blockprint procured by the Library of Congress P.L. 480 program and held by Columbia University Libraries. The version of the Cone I consulted was a microfiche version produced by IASWR and held in the library of the American Institute of Buddhist Studies, Columbia University. The Peking is that reproduced in the photomechanical reprint made by Otani University under the editorial guidance of D. T. Suzuki. Finally, the sNar-thang redaction was consulted in two versions: a low-quality copy held by Columbia University Libraries, and an excellent print held by The Royal Library of Denmark (Det Kongelige Bibliotek, København, Danmark).

Concerning this edition, it must be borne in mind that what I have attempted is the restoration (within the limits of the extant witnesses and my own abilities) of the original translation as prepared by its authors, Śraddhākaravarman and Lochen Rinchen Zangpo. Thus, any errors or shortcomings native to this translation itself have been preserved. Much as I might have liked to have emended the text to bring it more into line with Āryadeva's original, to make it more consistent, or to render it in clearer

1153. In addition to inconsistent readings, the editors have followed an unfortunate policy of replacing unclear or damaged text with rather mechanical reconstructions from the Tibetan translation.

Tibetan syntax, this would have been an entirely different editorial project. Where I have emended the text based on context and/or the Sanskrit reading, this has been limited to rectifying what I believe to be errors in the transmission of the text, restoring what I conclude to have been the original reading.

Based on the pattern of variation, Tib seems to be based on sources very similar to ms C, though it shares some readings with A/B. Since ms C was found in Tibet, there is a remote possibility that it itself was the source upon which Tib was prepared, though I do not think the evidence bears this out.[1154] Hence, either its prototype is yet another radiant text, or it may have been based on more than one manuscript. The stemma of these variant redactions may be constructed as follows:

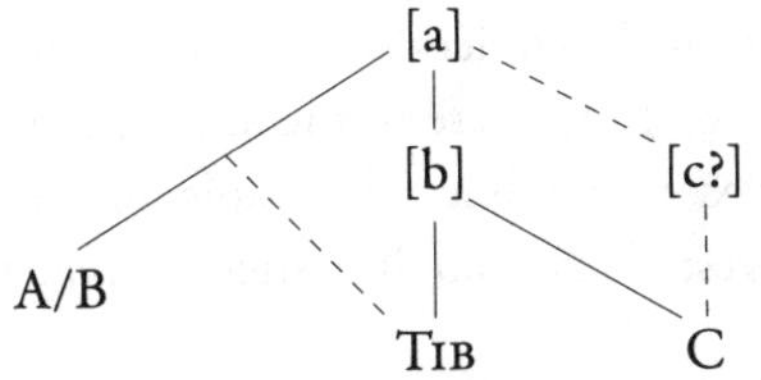

Although, in accordance with what I consider to be responsible and fully critical editorial practice,[1155] I have not arbitrarily restricted the range of readings that I would consider for inclusion in the reconstructed text, I am sympathetic to those who are uncomfortable with such a policy—due either to reservations about the very legitimacy of such an approach or (perhaps more appositely) to concerns about the soundness of my own editorial judgement. To such readers, I would offer two items of consolation. For one,

1154. For one, the script in which ms C is written suggests a later date than the eleventh century, when the translation was completed. Also, the contents do not match closely enough.

1155. In this, I largely follow the editorial school of G. Thomas Tanselle. He argues that most attempts to make editorial policy more "scientific" entail various strategies for limiting the scope of editorial freedom. Thus, the "copy text" policy seeks to ensure that the editor privileges the older witnesses (that are presumably closer to the original) over the (*ipso facto* derivative) later texts. As W. W. Greg has written, however, "the judgement of an editor, fallible as it must necessarily be, is likely to bring us closer to what the author wrote than the enforcement of an arbitrary rule" (Greg, "Rationale of the Copy-Text," cited in Tanselle, "Textual Study and Literary Judgment," 326). In the edition, I have therefore applied what I consider "scientific" principles of textual editing; but I have not arbitrarily sacrificed flexibility in editorial judgement.

unlike those editions properly censured as "eclectic," the decisions made are neither unsystematic nor based on pure whimsy. Each and every editorial choice has been based on consideration of the entire set of evidence available, and each has its specific rationale. Regrettably, due to the conventions of editorial publication (largely determined by the limitations of space and the similarly limited interest of readers), I have not included an argument for each editorial choice—for some I have stated my reasoning, for others the argument should be self-evident, yet others I have commented on in the apparatus to the translation, and the remaining may perhaps be reconstructed with but a little effort. Second, and more importantly, however—also in accordance with standard editorial practice—I have attempted to include in the published text all the information presented by the variant witnesses bearing on the CMP as a literary work.[1156] Hence—although inevitably I have had to make choices about which readings to include in the main text, and which to relegate to the apparatus—the reader is not forced to accept the text I offer, but will be able both to critically engage it as one possible, suggested text and, if desired, to reconstruct the "pure" readings of either MS.

To avoid burdening the text with too much apparatus, however, I have chosen not to list *all* variants in the text without exception. I have sought to err on the side of caution, however, as—aware of my own limitations—I am reluctant to make too quick a judgement about which readings are relevant and which are not. Nonetheless, I have not documented certain classes of predictable and/or (literarily, if not historically) meaningless variants. This includes the idiomatic usage of sibilants that varies between the texts and even within each text. MS A, for instance, tends to prefer the use of the dental sibilant (*s*) in contexts where "standard" Sanskrit employs the palatal (*ś*), resulting in *vajra-siṣya* instead of the standard *vajra-śiṣya*. MS C, on the other hand, frequently uses the palatal where standard usage employs the dental.[1157] I have, in such instances, preferred the standard usage and have not noted the idiosyncrasies of the texts unless I was already providing a variant reading for another reason. Furthermore, there are some idiosyn-

1156. That is, I have not included information that bears solely on the documentary sources of the CMP.

1157. Other examples include, e.g., *śarśapa* (C) for *sarśapa* (A), and *nisvāśo* (A) for *niśvāso* (C).

crasies of *sandhi* that I have not recorded, choosing instead to standardize the usage somewhat. For example, MS C tends to follow standard *sandhi* rules, while A/B tends to assimilate final *m* to the class (*varga*) of the following consonant: i.e., where MS C (and standard *sandhi*) reads *-ṃ n-* (e.g., *lakṣanaṃ nāma*), A tends to read *-n n-* (*lakṣanan nāma*). Likewise, one finds *-ñ c-* (e.g., *pustakañ ca*) instead of the more standard *-ṃ c-* (*pustakaṃ ca*), and so on. In general, sandhi has been regularized, though perhaps not as systematically as might be desired.[1158] Rather than clutter the apparatus more than necessary, such non-substantive variants have been excluded. Otherwise, wherever I have altered the text in any substantial way from that found in the manuscripts, I have marked the adopted reading as an "emendation." Some alterations that I felt were significant enough to mark, but not radical enough to merit being called "emendations," I have marked as "rectifications" (e.g., changing *prakṛtāhaṃkāra* to *prākṛtāhaṃkāra* at the beginning of chapter 10 [B:65a]). This distinction is somewhat tenuous, but I thought it important to flag for the reader which editorial changes were more or less intrusive.

Punctuation variants have also not been comprehensively noted. As with the morphological features, if a substantive variant also exists, variant punctuation has been noted in the apparatus, but in the absence of other grounds variant punctuation has not been included. On the whole, punctuation of the edition conforms to MSS A/B, though this has occasionally been emended for the sake of clarity. Scholars interested in such niceties of orthography will no doubt be able to consult the MSS themselves, whereas those interested in the literary work will, I presume, be happier without all the clutter.

In the apparatus to the Tibetan edition, I have similarly excluded variants when I did not consider them to be substantive. Thus, for example, occasional abbreviations (found frequently in N) such as *soḍ* for *sogs*, *yongsu* for *yongs su*, *sridu* for *srid du*, *'gyuro* for *'gyur ro*, *gsungso* for *gsungs so*, *gnyisu* for *gnyis su*, *namkha'* for *nam mkha'*, *yino* for *yin no*, etc., have not been noted in the apparatus. I have also excluded readings that are grammatically impossible. For example, D (f. 81b[1]) reads *sems can bmyal ba* for *sems can dmyal ba*.

1158. This is also true of internal morphological features. For instance, the MSS reading *napunsaka* (A and C) has been regularized to *napuṃsaka*. Variants such as *alaṅkāra*/*alaṃkāra*, etc., have likewise not been noted.

As *ba* cannot properly serve as a prefix for *ma*, the reading is thus untenable on morphological grounds and I have not reported it. Other minor, easily emended errors have also been passed over in silence. For example, in N (f. 65b^{6}), the text reads *longs* instead of *lobs*. This falls in the middle of a long, repetitive, stylized passage—all centering on the word *lobs*. To report such variants seems a waste of ink and paper. Similarly, the sNar-thang variant *spyon* for *spyan* in the famous verse about the four goddesses in chapter 2 is clearly not a helpful piece of information. I am certain there are instances in both editions in which, due to an excess of caution, I included more of these readings than necessary. For that I beg the reader's indulgence, as I have also (perhaps more stringently) endeavored to ensure that I do not omit potentially valuable information.[1159]

Concerning the conventions I have used, most obvious will be the decision to romanize both editions. In the case of the Sanskrit edition, this choice was simpler. Given that both source texts are written in characters for which no font is available, it seemed to me to do no greater violence by setting it in Roman script than recasting it in a modern Indian script such as Devanāgarī. Furthermore, romanization has the benefit of allowing word breaks to be indicated without the clutter of lots of unnatural *virāma*s. Likewise, it also allows for the marking of breaks between the individual semantic units of Sanskrit compounds (*samāsa*). Thus, I have chosen to indicate these breaks wherever possible with a hyphen. While in highly "literary" texts such marking of word breaks may obscure poetical polysemy, I do not find it to be a problem in this work. While a well written book, it does not have pretensions to *belles lettres*, so the compounds tend to analyze in one, straightforward manner. For professional Sanskritists, who may find such markings distracting or patronizing, I can only beg indulgence on behalf of those other (presumably more numerous) readers who may benefit from them. Finally, having struggled somewhat over the question of whether or not to mark breaks between lexemes when they occur by vowel coalescence, I decided that this was best done only between separate, inflected lexical units, and not to indicate them when internal to a compound. Thus, for

1159. I have, however—for the interest of scholars of Tibetan—included in the apparatus alternative renderings from the Tibetan translations by Chag Lotsāwa, as preserved in the writings of Tsongkhapa. In the RṄSG, Tsongkhapa makes frequent mention of alternative translations, among which figure four translations of the CMP: those by Lo-chen, 'Gos, Chag, and Pa-tshab.

example, one finds *kṛta-treta-dvāpara-yugeṣu* and *yathôktaṃ bhagavatā*, but *bhūta-nayātmakaḥ*.

In the Sanskrit edition, I have marked page breaks in the manuscripts by the superscript sigil † for those in MSS A and B, and ‡ for those in C. In the margins, one will find the page number beginning at that point—A/B in the left margin, C in the right. Insofar as possible to do so with accuracy, I have also marked the corresponding places in the Tibetan and English texts with the same sigla and corresponding marginal numbers. It is to be hoped that this will aid readers in cross-referencing the various texts. Page breaks in the Tibetan sources have been marked in that edition by superscript notations giving the sigil and page number. For example, $^{D:115a}$ marks the beginning of the recto of folio 115 of the sDe-dge redaction.

Bibliography

Microform Mss Utilized

A. Asiatic Society of Bengal Manuscript no. 4837. Palm leaf, 28.5 ′ 5 cm, 37 leaves, 6 lines per page, 50 syllables per line; Proto-Bengali script; incomplete. Title in catalog: *Vajrayāna-sādhanāṅgāni*.

B. Nepal-German Manuscript Preservation Project, National Archives Kathmandu. Ms. No. 3–363/ vi. bauddhatantra 82; Palm leaf, 28.5 ′ 5 cm, 36 leaves, 6 lines per page, 50 syllables per line; Proto-Bengali script; incomplete. Title in catalog: *Saṃśaya-pariccheda*.

C. Rahul Sāṅkrtyāyan Collection No. 100 (Göttingen catalog no. Xc 14/30, text no. 7). Paper, 12.33 ′ 2.16 inches, 9 lines per page, Old Bengali script, incomplete. Title in catalog: *Karmānta-vibhāga-melāvaṇa*, etc.

Sanskrit and Tibetan Sources

Sūtras and Tantras

Aṣṭasāhasrikā-prajñā-pāramitā-sūtra (*Ārya-aṣṭasāhasrikā-prajñāpāramitā, 'phags pa shes rab kyi pha rol tu phyin pa brgyad stong pa*). [Eight-Thousand-Line Transcendent Virtue of Wisdom Scripture].

- See Conze, below [English translation]
- See Mitra, below [Sanskrit text]
- See Vaidya, below [Sanskrit edition]
- sDe-dge bKa'-'gyur, Shes-phyin, vol. ka, ff. $1b^1$–$286a^6$ (Tōh. 12)

Bhadrapāli-paripṛcchā-sūtra (*Ārya-bhadrapāli-śreṣṭhi-paripṛcchā-nāma-mahāyāna-sūtra, 'Phags pa tshong dpon bzang skyong gis zhes pa zhes bya ba theg pa chen po'i mdo*) [Enquiry of Bhadrapāli Scripture; also cited as the Ejection of Consciousness Scripture]

- sDe-dge bKa'-'gyur, dKon-brtsegs, vol. cha, ff. 71a^{1}–94b^{7} (Tōh. 83)

Caṇḍamahāroṣaṇa Tantra

- See George, below [partial Sanskrit edition and English translation]

Caturdevī-paripṛcchā (*Lha mo bzhis yongs su zhus pa*) [The Enquiry of the Four Goddesses].

- sDe-dge bKa'-'gyur, vol ca, ff. 277b^{3}–281b^{7} (Tōh. 446).
- sTog Palace Kanjur, vol. 96 (rGyud, vol. ca), ff. 254a^{4}–259b^{4}.

Dhammapada

- See Hinüber, below [Pāli edition]

Guhyasamāja Tantra (*Sarvatathāgatakāyavākcittarahasya-guhyasamāja-nāma-mahākalparāja, De bzhin gshegs pa thams cad kyi sku gsung thugs kyi gsang chen gsang ba 'dus pa zhes bya ba brtag pa'i rgyal po chen po*) [The Esoteric Communion Tantra].

- See Bagchi, below [Sanskrit edition]
- See Bhattacharyya, below [Sanskrit edition]
- See Fremantle, below [Sanskrit and Tibetan editions and English translation]
- See Matsunaga, below [Sanskrit edition]
- sTog Palace Kanjur, vol. 96 (rGyud ca), ff. 1b^{1}–82b^{1}
- sDe-dge bKa'-'gyur, vol ca, ff. 90a^{1}–148a^{6} (Tōh. 442)

Guhyasamājottaratantra (*gSang ba 'dus pa'i rgyud phyi ma*). [Esoteric Communion Appendix Tantra].

- sDe-dge bKa'-'gyur, vol. ca, ff. 148a^{6}–157b^{7} (Tōh 443)
- sTog Palace Kanjur, vol. 96 (rGyud ca), ff. 82b^{1}–95b^{5}.
- See Bhattacharyya 1931, Bagchi 1965, below [Sanskrit ediitons]

Guhyendutilaka (*dPal zla gsang thig le zhes bya ba rgyud kyi rgyal po chen po*) [Secret Moon Drop Tantra].

- sDe-dge bKa'-'gyur, rGyud, vol. ja, ff. 247b^{1}–303a^{7} (Tōh. 477)
- sTog Palace Kanjur, vol. 97 (rGyud cha), ff. 226a^{3}–295b^{5}

Hevajra Tantra.

- See Snellgrove, below [Sanskrit and Tibetan texts and English translation]

Jñāna-vajra-samuccaya (*Ye shes rdo rje kun las btus pa*) [Gnosis Vajra Compendium].

- sDe-dge bKa'-'gyur, rGyud, vol. cha, ff. 1b^{1}–35b^{7} (Tōh. 450)
- sDe-dge bKa'-'gyur, rGyud, vol. ca, ff. 282a^{1}–286a^{6} (Tōh. 447)

Kāśyapaparivarta. [Kāśyapa Chapter].

- See von Staël-Holstein, below [Sanskrit and Tibetan texts]

Khasama-tantrarāja-nāma (*dPal nam-mkha' dang mnyam pa'i rgyud kyi rgyal po*). [The Space-Like Tantra].
- sDe-dge bKa'-'gyur, rGyud, vol. ga, ff. 199a^{7}–202a^{1} (Tōh. 386)

Kinnara-rāja-paripṛcchā-sūtra. (*'Phags pa mi'am ci'i rgyal po sdong pos zhus pa zhes bya ba theg pa chen po'i mdo*). [Enquiry of the Kinnara King].
- sDe-dge bKa'-'gyur, mDo, vol. pha, ff. 254a^{1}–319a^{7} (Tōh. 157)
- See Harrison, below [Tibetan edition]

Laṅkāvatāra Sūtra (*'Phags pa lang kar gshegs pa'i theg pa chen po'i mdo*) [Journey to Lanka Scripture].
- See Nanjio, below [Sanskrit edition]
- See Vaidya, below [Sanskrit edition]
- sDe-dge bKa'-'gyur, mDo, vol. ca, ff. 56a^{1}–191b^{7} (Tōh. 107)
- See Suzuki, below [English translation]

Mahāmāyūrī Vidyā-rājñī.
- See Takubo, below [Sanskrit edition]

Mañjuśrī-nāma-saṃgīti (*'Jam dpal mtshan yang dag par brjod pa*).
- See Davidson, below [Sanskrit edition and English translation]

Paramādya Tantra (*dPal mchog dang po'i rgyud*, or *dPal mchog dang po zhes bya ba theg pa chen po'i rtog pa'i rgyal po*). [Supreme Prime Tantra].
- sDe-dge bsTan-'gyur, rGyud, vol. ta, ff. 150b^{1}–173a^{4} (Tōh. 487)
- sTog Palace Kanjur, vol. 99 (rGyud nya), ff. 1b^{1}–35a^{3}
- Urga Kanjur, vol. 86 (rGyud ta), ff. 150b^{1}–173a^{4}

Paramādya-mantra-kalpa-khaṇḍa (*dPal mchog dang po'i sngags kyi rtog pa'i dum bu zhes bya ba*). [Supreme Prime Mantra Ritual Section].
- sDe-dge bKa'-'gyur, rGyud, vol. ta, f. 173a^{4}–265b^{7} (Tōh. 488)

Samādhi-rāja-sūtra. (*Ting nge 'dzin gyi rgyal po'i mdo*).
- See Vaidya, below [Sanskrit edition]

Saṃdhyā-vyākaraṇa-nāma-tantra (*dGongs pa lung ston pa zhes bya ba'i rgyud*). [Explanation of the Intention].
- sDe-dge bKa'-'gyur, rGyud, vol ca, ff. 158a^{1}–207b^{7} (Tōh. 444)
- sTog Palace Kanjur, vol. 96 (rGyud ca), ff. 95b^{5}–163b^{2}

Saṃvarodaya Tantra.
- See Tsuda, below [partial Sanskrit and Tibetan edition and English translation]

Sarva-buddha-samāyoga-ḍākini-jāla-saṃvara-nāma-uttaratantra (*dPal sangs rgyas thams cad dang mnyam par sbyor ba mkha' 'gro ma sgyu ma bde ba'i mchog ces bya ba'i rgyud phyi ma*). [Union of All Buddhas].

- sDe-dge bKa'-'gyur, rGyud, vol. ka, ff. 151b^{1}–193a^{6} (Tōh. 366)
- sTog Palace Kanjur, vol. 95 (rGyud nga), ff. 241a^{1}–295b^{2}
- Urga Kanjur, vol. 78 (rGyud ka), ff. 151a^{1}–193a^{6}

Sarva-kalpa-samuccaya-nāma-sarvabuddhasamāyogaḍākinījālasaṃvara-uttarottara-tantra (*rTog pa thams cad 'dus pa zhes bya ba sangs rgyas thams cad dang mnyam par sbyor ba mkha' 'gro sgyu ma bde ba'i mchog gi rgyud phyi ma'i phyi ma*). [Compendium of All Rituals].

- sDe-dge bKa'-'gyur, rGyud, vol. ka, ff. 193a^{6}–212a^{7} (Tōh. 367)
- sTog Palace Kanjur, vol. 95 (rGyud nga), ff. 295b^{2}–321a^{4}
- Urga Kanjur, vol. 78 (rGyud ka), ff. 193a^{6}–212a^{7}

Sarva-rahasya-nāma-tantrarāja (*Thams cad gsang ba zhes bya ba rgyud kyi rgyal po*). [The Universal Secret Tantra].

- sDe-dge bKa'-'gyur, rGyud, vol. ta, ff. 1b^{1}–10a^{1} (Tōh. 481)
- sTog Palace Kanjur, vol. 98 (rGyud ja), ff. 178a^{5}–189a^{2}
- Urga Kanjur, vol. 86 (rGyud ta), ff. 1b^{1}–10a^{1}
- See Wayman, below [Tibetan edition and English translation]

Sarva-tathāgata-tattva-saṅgraha [The Compendium of the Realities of all Transcendent Lords].

- See Horiuchi, below [Sanskrit edition]
- See Chandra, below [Sanskrit edition]
- See Yamada, below [Sanskrit edition]
- sDe-dge bKa'-'gyur, rGyud, vol. nya, ff. 1b^{1}–142a^{7} (Tōh. 479)
- sTog Palace Kanjur, vol. 97 (rGyud cha), ff. 295b^{6}–485a^{4}

Satipaṭṭhāna Sutta [Scripture of the Foundations of Mindfulness].

- See Davids and Carpenter, *Dīgha Nikāya*, below

Subhāṣita-saṃgraha.

- See Bendall, below [Sanskrit edition]

Śūraṅgama-samādhi Sūtra (*dPa' bar 'gro ba'i ting nge 'dzin gyi mdo*) [Hero's March Samādhi Scripture].

- sDe-dge bsTan-'gyur, mDo, vol. da, ff. 253b^{5}–316b^{6} (Tōh. 132)
- See Lamotte, below [French translation and English translation]

Suvarṇa-bhāsottama Sūtra. (*gSer 'od dam pa'i mdo*) [Holy Golden Light Scripture].

- See Nobel, *Suvarṇabhāsottamasūtra*, below [Sanskrit edition]
- See Nobel, *Suvarṇaprabhāsottamasūtra*, below [Tibetan edition]
- See Emmerick, below [English Translation]

Udānavarga.
- See Bernhard, below

Vajracchedika-sūtra (*Ārya-vajracchedika-nāma-prajñāpāramitā-mahāyāna-sūtra, 'Phags pa shes rab kyi pha rol tu phyin pa rdo rje gcod pa zhes bya ba theg pa chen po'i mdo*). [The Diamond Cutter Sutra].
- sDe-dge bKa'-'gyur, Shes-phyin, vol. ka, ff. 121a^1–132b^7 (Tōh. 16)
- See Müller, below [Sanskrit edition]

Vajra-mālā Tantra. (*rNal 'byor chen po'i rgyud dpal rdo rje phreng ba mngon par brjod pa rgyud thams cas kyi snying po gsang ba rnam par phye ba zhes bya ba*). [The Vajra Rosary Tantra].
- sDe-dge bKa'-'gyur, rGyud, vol. ca, ff. 208a^1–277b^3 (Tōh. 445)
- Urga Kanjur, vol. 82, ff. 208a^1–277b^1

Vajra-maṇḍalālaṃkāra Tantra (*dPal rdo rje snying po rgyan zhes bya ba'i rgyud kyi rgyal po chen po*). [The Vajra Maṇḍala Ornament Tantra].
- sDe-dge bKa'-'gyur, rGyud, vol. tha, 1b^1–82a^7 (Tōh. 490)

Vajraśekhara Tantra (gSang ba rnal 'byor chen po'i rgyud rDo rje rtse mo). [Vajra Pinnacle Tantra].
- sDe-dge bKa'-'gyur, rGyud, vol. nya, ff. 142b^1–274a^5 (Tōh. 480).

Vairocanābhisaṃbodhi Tantra [Enlightenment of Vairocana Tantra].
- sDe-dge bKa'-'gyur, rGyud, vol tha, ff. 151b^2–260a^7 (Tōh. 494)
- See Hodge, below [English translation]

Yoginī-sañcāra Tantra.
- See Pandey, below [Sanskrit and Tibetan editions]

Other Sanskrit and Tibetan Sources

Āryadeva. *Abhibodhi-kramopadeśa* (*mNgon par byang chub pa'i rim pa'i man ngag*) [Teaching on the Enlightenment Stage].
- Peking bsTan-'gyur vol. 62, #2671
- sDe-dge bsTan-'gyur, rGyud-'grel, vol. ngi, ff. 114b^2–117a^2 (Tōh. 1806)

———. *Caryā-melāpaka-pradīpa* (*Spyod pa bsdus pa'i sgron ma*) [Lamp for Integrating the Practices].
- Microfilm copy of MS from Asiatic Society of Bengal (A)
- Microfilm copy of MS from National Library of Nepal (B)
- Microfilm copy of MS from Bihar Research Society via Göttingen (C)
- See Pandey, below [Sanskrit and Tibetan editions]
- Co-ne bsTan-'gyur, vol. 163 (ngi), ff. 58a^2–107b^7

- sDe-dge bsTan-'gyur, rGyud-'grel, vol. ngi, ff. 57a²–106b⁷ (Tōh. 1803)
- sNar-thang bsTan-'gyur, vol. gi, ff. 62b²–118b⁵
- Peking bsTan-'gyur, vol. 61, (Pek. 2668)

———. *Catuḥśataka.*
- See Lang and Vaidya, below

———. *Cittaviśuddhi-prakaraṇa.*
- See Shāstrī 1898 and Patel 1949, below

———. *Cittāvaraṇa-viśodhana-nāma-prakaraṇa* (*Sems kyi sgrib pa rnam par sbyong ba zhes bya'i rab tu byed pa*) [Examination called, "Purification of the Obscurations of Mind"].
- Microfilm copy of MS from National Library of Nepal
- Peking bsTan-'gyur vol. 62, vol. gi, ff. 121b³–127a⁸ (#2669)
- sDe-dge bsTan-'gyur, rGyud-'grel, vol. ngi, ff. 106b⁷–112a³ (Tōh. 1804)
- sNar-thang bsTan-'gyur, vol. gi, ff. 118a⁵–124b²
- See also Patel, below [Sanskrit and two Tibetan translations]
- See also Shāstri, below [Sanskrit edition]

———. *Svādhiṣṭhāna-prabheda* (*bDag byin gyis brlab pa'i rim pa rnam par dbye ba*) [Discernment of the Self-Consecration Stage].
- Microfilm copy of MS from National Library of Nepal
- Peking bsTan-'gyur, vol. 62, #2670
- sDe-dge bsTan-'gyur, rGyud-'grel, vol. ngi, ff. 112a³–114b¹ (Tōh. 1805)
- See also Janārdan Pāṇḍey 1990, below [Sanskrit text]

Asaṅga/Maitreya. *Abhisamayālaṃkāra-prajñāpāramitopadeśa-śāstra.*
- See Stcherbatsky and Obermiller, below [Sanskrit and Tibetan texts]

———. *Mahāyānasūtrālaṃkāra.*
- See Bagchi, below [Sanskrit edition]

Bu-ston Rin-chen-grub. *Chos 'byung* [History of Buddhism].
- Bu-ston Chos-'byung. [Lhasa:] Krung-go Bod kyi shes rig dpe skrun khang, 1988
- See also Obermiller, below [English translation]

———. *The Collected Works of Bu-ston.* New Delhi: International Academy of Indian Culture, 1967.

Candrakīrti. *Guhyasamāja-tantra-pradīpodyotana-ṭīkā-ṣaṭkoṭi-vyākhyā* [The "Illumination of the Lamp" Commentary on the Esoteric Communion, Explanation of the Six Parameters].
- Microfilm MS from Bihar Research Society (via Göttingen).

- See Chakravarti, below [Sanskrit edition]
- sDe-dge bsTan-'gyur, rGyud, vol. ha, ff. 1b[1]–201b[2] (Tōh. 1785).

———. *Vajrasattvasādhana.*
- Microform MS from Bihar Research Society via Göttingens Universität.
- Peking bsTan-'gyur, rGyud-'grel, vol. gi, ff. 168b[3]–178a[2] (Pek. 2679).

———. *Yuktiṣaṣṭikā-vṛtti* [Commentary on the Reasoning Sixty].
- See Scherrer-Schaub, below [Tibetan edition and French translation]
- See Loizzo et al., below [Tibetan edition and English translation]

'Gos Lo-tsā-ba gZhon-nu-dpal. *The Blue Annals.* New Delhi: International Academy of Indian Culture, 1974.
- See Roerich, below [English translation]

'Gos Lo-tsā-ba Khug-pa Lhas-btsas. *gSang-'dus sTong-thun* [Survey of the Guhyasamāja]. New Delhi: Trayang, 1973.

Kambala. *Ālokamālā.*
- See Lindtner, below [Sanskrit and Tibetan editions and English translation]

mKhas-grub dGe-legs dPal-bzang. *rGyud-sde spyi'i rnam-gzhag.*
- See Lessing and Wayman, below [Tibetan edition and English translation]

———. *gSang-'dus bskyed-rim dngos-grub rgya-mtsho* (*rGyud thams cad kyi rgyal po dpal gsang ba 'dus pa'i bskyed rim dngos grub rgya mtsho*) [Esoteric Communion Creation Stage, "Ocean of Accomplishment"]. Varanasi: n.p., 1969.

Muniśrībhadra. *Pañcakramaṭippaṇī Yogimanoharā.*
- See Jiang and Tomabechi, below [Sanskrit diplomatic edition]

Naḍapāda (Nāropā). *Sekoddeśaṭīkā.*
- See Carelli, below [Sanskrit edition]

Nāgabodhi. *Pañcakramārthabhāskaraṇa-nāma* (*Rim pa lnga'i don gsal bar byed pa zhes bya ba*) [Illuminator of the Meaning of the Five Stages]
- Peking bsTan-'gyur, vol. 62, ff. 287b[6]–323b[7]
- sDe-dge bsTan-'gyur, rGyud-'grel, vol. ci, ff. 207b[3]–237a[7] (Tōh. 1833)

———. *Pañcakrama-ṭīkā-maṇimālā-nāma* (*Rim pa lnga pa'i bshad pa nor bu'i phreng ba zhes bya ba*) [Commentary on the *Five Stages*, called 'Jewel Rosary')
- Peking bsTan-'gyur, vol. 62, ff. 9a[2]–174a[6]
- sDe-dge bsTan-'gyur, rGyud-'grel, vol. chi, ff. 25a[1]–157a[7] (Tōh. 1840)

———. *Samāja-sādhana-vyavastholi-nāma* (*'Dus pa'i sgrub pa'i thabs rnam par gzhag pa'i rim pa zhes bya ba*). [Arranged Stages of the Community Sādhana].
- sDe-dge bsTan-'gyur, vol. ngi, ff. 121a[6]–131a[5] (Tōh. 1809)

———. *Śrī-guhyasamāja-maṇḍala-viṃśati-vidhi-nāma* (*dPal gsang ba 'dus pa'i dkyil 'khor gyi cho ga nyi shu pa zhes bya ba*). [The Maṇḍala Rite Twenty].
- sDe-dge bsTan-'gyur, vol. ngi, ff. 131a⁵–145b³ (Tōh. 1810)

Nāgārjuna. *Catuḥstava*. [Four Eulogies].
- See Patel and Tucci, below [Sanskrit and Tibetan editions]

———. *Pañcakrama* (*Rim pa lnga pa*) [The Five Stages].
- See Mimaki and Tomabechi, below [Sanskrit and Tibetan editions]
- See La Vallée-Poussin, below [Sanskrit edition]
- sDe-dge bsTan-'gyur, rGyud-'grel, vol. ngi, ff. 45a⁵–57a¹ (Tōh. 1802)

———. *Mahāyāna-viṃśikā*.
- See Tucci, *Minor Buddhist Texts*, below

———. *Śrī-guhysamāja-mahāyogatantra-utpattikrama-sādhana-sūtramelāpaka* (*rNal 'byor chen po'i rgyud dpal gsang ba 'dus pa'i bskyed pa'i rim pa bsgom pa'i thabs mdo dang bsras pa zhes bya ba*). [The Creation Stage Meditation of the Great Yoga Tantra the Glorious Esoteric Communion, "Integrating the Scriptures"].
- sDe-dge bsTan-'gyur, rGyud-'grel, vol. ngi, ff. 11a²–15b¹. (Tōh. 1797)

———. *Śrī-guhysamāja-maṇḍala-vidhi*. (*dPal gsang ba 'dus pa'i dkyil 'khor gyi cho ga zhes bya ba*). [Glorious Esoteric Communion Maṇḍala Rite].
- sDe-dge bsTan-'gyur, rGyud-'grel, vol. ngi, ff. 15b¹–35a⁷ (Tōh. 1798)

———. *Yuktiṣaṣṭikā*.
- See Scherrer-Schaub [Tibetan edition and French Translation]
- See Lindtner [Tibetan edition and English Translation]
- See Loizzo et al., below [Tibetan edition and English translation]

Ngag-dbang Kun-dga' bSod-nams, 'Jam-mgon A-myes Zhabs. *dPal gsang ba 'dus pa'i chos 'byung ba'i tshul legs par bshad pa gsang 'dus chos kun gsal ba'i nyin byed (gsang 'dus chos 'byung)* [History of the Guhyasamāja]. Dehradun: Sakya Center, 1985.

Ngag-dbang dPal-ldan, Chos-rje. *gSang-chen rgyud sde bzhi'i sa lam gyi rnam gzhag rgyud gzhung gsal byed ces bya ba*. [Presentation of the Stages and Paths of the Great Secret Four Classes of Tantras, called "Illuminator of the Tantric Treatises"]. Rgyud smad par khang, n.d.

Nyang-ral Nyi ma 'od zer. *Chos 'byung me tog snying po sbrang rtsi'i bcud*. [The History of Buddhism, Honey-essence of Flowers]. [Lhasa]: Bod ljongs mi dmangs dpe skrun khang, 1988.

Padmavajrapāda. *Guhyasiddhi* [The Secret Accomplishment].

- See Rinpoche, below [Sanskrit and Tibetan editions]

Parahitarakṣita. *Pañcakramaṭippaṇī.*

- See La Vallé Poussin 1894

Raviśrījñāna, Bhikṣu. *Amṛtakaṇikā-ṭippaṇī.*

- See Lal, below [Sanskrit and Tibetan texts]

Rong-zom Chos-kyi bZang-po. *Theg pa chen po'i mtshul la 'jug pa zhes bya ba bstan chos. Rong zom bka' 'bum.* 2 vols. Khreng Tu'u: Si khron mi rigs dpe skrun khang, 1999. TBRC W21617.

Śrīkṛṣṇācārya, Caryāvratī. *Vasantatilakā.*

- See Rinpoche, below [Sanskrit and Tibetan texts]

Tāranātha. *Dam pa'i chos rin po che 'phags pa'i yul du ji ltar dar ba'i tshul gsal bar ston pa dgos 'dod kun 'byung* [*rGya gar chos 'byung*, History of Buddhism].

- See Dorji, below [Tibetan facsimile edition]
- See Schiefner, below [German translation]
- See Chimpa and Chattopadhyaya, below [English translation]

———. *Rim lṅa 'grel chen rdo rje 'chang chen po'i dgongs pa: A Detailed Commentary on the Pañcakrama Instructions on the Practice of the Guhyasamāja Tantra.* [RṄGC: Great Commentary on the Five Stages]. Thimpu: Kunsang Topgey, 1976.

Tsong-kha-pa bLo-bzang Grags-pa. *The Collected Works (gSuṅ 'bum) of rJe Tsoṅ-kha-pa bLo-bzaṅ-grags-pa.* New Delhi: Ngawang Gelek Demo, 1975–.

———. *rGyud kyi rgyal po dpal gsang ba 'dus pa'i man ngag rim pa lnga rab tu gsal ba'i sgron me zhes bya ba* [RṄSG: The Personal Instruction in the King of Tantras the Glorious Esoteric Communion called the "Extremely Brilliant Lamp of the Five Stages"].

- *Collected Works*, vol. ja (vol. 11 of bound edition)

———. *rGyud thams cad kyi rgyal po dpal gsang ba 'dus pa'i rgya cher bshad pa sgron ma rab tu gsal ba'i tshig don ji bzhin 'byed pa'i mchan gyi yang 'grel* [Annotations on the extensive commentary of the Esoteric Communion].

- *Collected Works*, vol. nga (vols. 6 and 7 of bound edition)

Vanaratna. *Rahasyadīpikā* [Lamp of Secrets].

- See Rinpoche, below [Sanskrit and Tibetan texts]

Vibhūticandra. *Amṛtakaṇikodyota-nibandha.*

- See Lal, below [Sanskrit and Tibetan texts]

Vīryabhadra, *Pañcakrama-pañjikā-prabhāsārtha-nāma* (*Rim pa lnga pa'i dka' 'grel don gsal ba zhes bya ba*) [Commentary on the *Five Stages* called 'Shining Meaning'].

- Peking bsTan-'gyur, vol. 62, ff. 212a^{7}–255b^{1}
- sDe-dge bsTan-'gyur, rGyud-'grel, vol. ci, ff. 142b^{7}–180b^{2} (Tōh 1830)

dbYangs-can dGa'-ba'i bLo-gros. *dPal gsang ba 'dus-pa 'phags lugs dang mthun pa'i sngags kyi sa lam rnam gzhag legs bshad skal bzang 'jug ngogs zhes bya ba.* [The Presentation of the Stages and Paths of Mantra in accordance with the Ārya Tradition of the Esoteric Communion, called "Eloquent Entryway of the Fortunate"]. Dharamsala: Namgyal Monastery, 1979.

Modern Publications

Abé, Ryuichi. *The Weaving of Mantra: Kūkai and the Construction of Esoteric Buddhist Discourse.* New York: Columbia University Press, 1999.

Anonymous. "Arts, South Asian." In *Encyclopædia Britannica* [2006], Encyclopædia Britannica Online. 3 Dec 2006 <http://search.eb.com/ eb/article-65249>

Aris, Michael. *Hidden Treasures, Secret Lives: A Study of Pemalingpa (1450–1521) and the Sixth Dalai Lama (1683–1706).* London and New York: Kegan Paul International, 1989.

Bagchi, S., ed. *Guhyasamāja Tantra or Tathāgataguhyaka.* Buddhist Sanskrit Texts, no. 9. Darbhanga: Mithila Institute, 1965.

——, ed. *Mahāyānasūtrālankāraḥ.* Buddhist Sanskrit Texts, no. 13. Darbhanga: Mithilal Institute, 1970.

Bandurski, Frank. "Übersicht über die Göttinger Sammlungen der von Rāhula Sāṅkṛtyāyana in Tibet aufgefundenen buddhistischen Sanskrit-Texte." In Bandurski et al., eds., *Untersuchungen zur buddhistischen Literatur.* Sanskrit-Wörterbuch der buddhistischen Texte aus den Turfan-Funden, Beiheft 5. Göttingen: Vandenhoeck & Ruprecht, 1994.

Bays, Gwendolyn, trans. *The Voice of the Buddha: Beauty of Compassion.* Berkeley: Dharma Publishing, 1983.

Bechert, Heinz, ed. *Sanskrit-Wörterbuch der buddhistischen Texte aus den Turfan-Funden.* Göttingen: Vandenhoeck & Ruprecht, 1973–.

Bendall, Cecil, ed. *Subhāṣita-saṃgraha.* Louvain: J.-B. Istas, 1905.

Bentor, Yael. *Consecration of Images and Stūpas in Indo-Tibetan Tantric Buddhism.* Leiden/New York: Brill, 1996.

Bentor, Yael, and Dorjee, Penpa, ed. and trans. *The Essence of the Ocean of Attainments* (*dNgos grub rgya mtsho'i snying po*): *The Creation Stage of the Guhyasamāja Tantra according to Panchen Losang Chökyi Gyaltsen.* Studies in Indian and Tibetan Buddhism 21. Somerville MA: Wisdom Publications, 2019.

Bernhard, Franz, ed. *Udānavarga*. Band I. Göttingen: Vandenhoeck & Ruprecht, 1965.

Bhattacharyya, Benoytosh. *An Introduction to Buddhist Esoterism*. 1931. Delhi: Motilal Banarsidass, 1989.

———. *Two Vajrayāna Works*. Baroda: Oriental Institute, 1929.

Bhattacharyya, Benoytosh, ed. *Guhyasamāja Tantra or Tathāgataguhyaka*. Gaekwad's Oriental Series, no. 53. Baroda: Oriental Institute, 1931.

———, ed. *Sādhanamālā*, vol. 2. 1928. Baroda: Oriental Institute, 1968.

Brunner, H., G. Oberhammer, and A. Padoux, eds. *Tāntrikābhidhānakośa*. Vols. 1 and 2. Wein: Der Österreichischen Akademie der Wissenschaften, 2000 and 2004.

Bühler, Georg. *Indian Paleography*. 1904. New Delhi: Oriental Books Reprint Corporation, 1980.

Burnouf, Eugène. *Introduction à l'Histoire du Buddhism Indien*. Paris: Imprimerie Royale, 1844.

———. *Introduction à l'Histoire du Buddhisme Indien*. 2nd edition. Paris: Maisonneuve et Cie, 1876.

Campbell, John R., Robert A.F. Thurman, and the AIBS Translation Team, trans. and ed. *The Esoteric Community Tantra (Guhyasamāja Tantra)*, by Vajradhara Buddha; with *Its Illuminating Lamp Commentary (Pradīpoddyotana-nāma-ṭīkā)*, by Āchārya Chandrakīrti. Volume 1: Chapters 1–12. New York and Boston: American Institute of Buddhist Studies and Wisdom Publications, 2021.

Carelli, Mario E. *Sekoddeśaṭīkā of Naḍapāda (Nāropā): Being a Commentary of the Sekkodeśa Section of the Kālacakra Tantra*. Baroda: Oriental Institute, 1940.

Chakravarti, Chintaharan, ed. *Guhyasamājatantrapradīpodyotanaṭīkā-ṣaṭkoṭīvyākhyā*. Patna: Kashi Prasad Jayaswal Research Institute, 1984.

Chandra, Lokesh. *A Tibetan-Sanskrit Dictionary*. New Delhi: Mrs. Sharada Rani, 1985.

———. *Tibetan-Sanskrit Dictionary*. Seven ("supplementary") volumes. New Delhi: International Academy of Indian Culture and Aditya Prakashan, 1992–94.

———, ed. *Sarva-tathāgata-tattva-saṅgraha*. Delhi: Motilal Banarsidass, 1987.

Chimpa, Lama, and Alaka Chattopadhyaya, trans. *Tāranātha's History of Buddhism in India*. Ed. Debiprasad Chattopadhyaya. 1970. Calcutta: K. P. Bagchi & Co., 1980.

Cone, Margaret. *A Dictionary of Pali*. Pt. 1, a–kh. Oxford: Pali Text Society, 2001.

Conze, Edward, trans. *The Perfection of Wisdom in Eight Thousand Lines*. San Francisco: Four Seasons Foundation, 1973.

Das, Sarat Chandra. *A Tibetan-English Dictionary with Sanskrit Synonyms*. 1902. Kyoto: Rinsen Book Company, 1993.

Dasgupta, Shashi Bhusan. *An Introduction to Tantric Buddhism*. Calcutta: University of Calcutta, 1950.

Davids, T.W. Rhys, and J. Estlin Carpenter, eds. *The Dīgha Nikāya*. London: Pali Text Society, 1903.

Davids, T.W. Rhys, and William Stede, eds. *Pali-English Dictionary*. 1921–25. Oxford: Pali Text Society, 1999.

Davidson, Ronald M. "An Introduction to the Standards of Scriptural Authenticity in Indian Buddhism." In Robert E. Buswell, Jr., ed., *Chinese Buddhist Apocrypha*, 291–325. Honolulu: University of Hawaii Press, 1990.

———. "Imperial Agency in the Gsar-ma Treasure Texts during the Tibetan Renaissance: the *Rgyal po bla'i gter* and Related Literature." In Ronald M. Davidson and Christian K. Wedemeyer, eds., *Tibetan Buddhist Literature and Praxis: Studies in its Formative Period, 900–1400*, 125–47. Leiden: Brill, 2006.

———. *Indian Esoteric Buddhism: A Social History of the Tantric Movement*. New York: Columbia University Press, 2002.

———. "Reframing Sahaja: Genre, Representation, Ritual and Lineage," *Journal of Indian Philosophy* 30 (2002), 45–83.

———. "The Litany of Names of Mañjuśrī: Text and Translation of the *Mañjuśrīnāmasaṃgīti*." *Mélanges Chinois et Bouddhiques* 22: 1–69. Bruxelles: Institut Belge des Hautes Études Chinoises, 1981.

Davidson, Ronald, and Christian K. Wedemeyer, eds. *Tibetan Buddhist Literature and Praxis: Studies in its Formative Period, 900–1400*. Leiden: Brill, 2006.

De Bary, William Theodore. *The Buddhist Tradition in India, China and Japan*. 1969. New York: Vintage Books, 1972.

Dimitrov, Dragomir. "Tables of the Old Bengali Script (on the basis of a Nepalese manuscript of Daṇḍin's Kāvyādarśa)." In Dimitrov et al., eds., *Śikhisamuccayaḥ: Indian and Tibetan Studies (Collectanea Marpurgensia Indologica et Tibetica)*. Wiener Studies zur Tibetologie und Buddhismuskunde 53. Wien: Arbeitskreis für Tibetische und Buddhistische Studien, Universtät Wien, 2002.

Dorje, Gyurme, and Matthew Kapstein, trans. and ed. *The Nyingma School of Tibetan Buddhism: Its Fundamentals and History*. Boston: Wisdom Publications, 1991.

Dorji, Tseten, ed. *Five Historical Works of Tāranātha*. Tezu, Arunachal Pradesh: Tibetan Nyingmapa Monastery, 1974.

Edgerton, Franklin. *Buddhist Hybrid Sanskrit Grammar and Dictionary*. Two vols. 1953. Delhi: Motilal Banarsidass, 1985.

Emmerick, R.E., trans. *The Sūtra of Golden Light*. London: Luzac, 1970.

Fremantle, Francesca. "A Critical Study of the Guhyasamāja Tantra." Ph.D. dissertation, University of London, 1971.

Gäng, Peter. *Das Tantra der Verborgenen Vereinigung: Guhyasamāja-Tantra*. München: Eugen Diederichs Verlag, 1988.

George, Christopher. *The Caṇḍamahāroṣanatantra*. New Haven: American Oriental Society, 1974.

Goldstein, Melvyn, ed. *The New Tibetan-English Dictionary of Modern Tibetan*. Berkeley: University of California Press, 2001.

———. *Tibetan-English Dictionary of Modern Tibetan*. 4th edition. Kathmandu: Ranta Pustak Bhandar, 1994.

Gomez, Luis O. "Indian Materials on the Doctrine of Sudden Enlightenment." In Whalen Lai and Lewis R. Lancaster, eds., *Early Ch'an in China and Tibet*, 393–434. Berkeley: Asian Humanities Press, 1983.

Gupta, Sanjukta. *Lakṣmī Tantra: A Pāñcarātra Text*. Leiden: E. J. Brill, 1972.

Gyatso, Janet. *Apparitions of the Self: The Secret Autobiographies of a Tibetan Visionary*. Princeton, NJ: Princeton University Press, 1998.

———. "Drawn from the Tibetan Treasury: The *gTer ma* Literature." In Cabezón and Jackson, eds., *Tibetan Literature: Studies in Genre*, 147–69. Ithaca: Snow Lion, 1996.

Harrison, Paul, ed. *Druma-kinnara-rāja-paripṛcchā-sūtra: A Critical Edition of the Tibetan Text (Recension A) based on Eight Editions of the Kanjur and the Dunhuang Manuscript Fragment*. Tokyo: The International Institute for Buddhist Studies, 1992.

Harrison, Paul, trans. *The Samādhi of Direct Encounter with the Buddhas of the Present: An Annotated Translation of the Tibetan Version of the* Pratyutpanna-Buddha-Sammukhāvasthita-Samādhi-Sūtra. Studia Philologica Buddhica Monograph Series 5. Tokyo: The International Institute for Buddhist Studies, 1990.

Hercus, L.A., F.B.J. Kuiper, et. al. *Indological and Buddhist Studies: Volume in Honour of Professor J. W. de Jong on his Sixtieth Birthday*. Canberra: Faculty of Asian Studies [A.N.U.], 1982.

Hinüber, Oskar von, and K. R. Norman, eds. *Dhammapada*. Oxford: Pali Text Society, 1994

Hodge, Stephen, trans. *The Mahā-vairocana-abhisambodhi Tantra*. London: Routledge and Curzon, 2003.

Horiuchi, Kanjin, ed. *Sarva-tathāgata-tattva-samgrahaṃ Nāma Mahā-yāna-sūtram*. S.l.: s.n., 1968.

Isaacson, Harunaga. "Ratnākaraśānti's *Hevajrasahajasadyoga* (Studies in Ratnākaraśānti's Tantric Works 1)." In Raffaele Torella, ed., *Le Parole e i Marmi: Studi in Onore di Raniero Gnoli nel suo 70° Compleanno*, 457–87. Roma: Istituto Italiano per l'Africa e l'Oriente, 2001.

Jiang, Zhongxin, and Tōru Tomabechi. *The Pañcakramaṭippaṇī of Muniśrībhadra*. Berne: Peter Lang, 1996.

Jong, J. W. de. "A New History of Tantric Literature in India," (English précis of

Yukei Matsunaga, Mikkyō kyōten seiritsushi-ron, Kyōto, 1980), *Acta Indologica* 6 (1984): 91–113.

Kapstein, Matthew T. *The Tibetan Assimilation of Buddhism: Conversion, Contestation, and Memory*. Oxford & New York: Oxford University Press, 2000.

Katre, S.M. *Introduction to Indian Textual Criticism*. Poona: Deccan College Postgraduate and Research Institute, 1954.

Kharto, Dorje Wangchuk. *Thumi: dGongs gTer (The Complete Tibetan Verb Forms)*. Delhi: C. T. Kharto, n.d.

Kværne, Per. *An Anthology of Buddhist Tantric Songs*. 1977. Bangkok: White Orchid Press, 1986.

———. "On the Concept of Sahaja in Indian Buddhist Tantric Literature." In *Temenos: Studies in Comparative Religion*. Vol. 11–12. Helsinki: Suomen uskontotieteellinen seura, 1975–76.

Lal, Banarasi, ed. *Āryamañjuśrīnāmasaṁgīti with Amṛtakaṇikā-ṭippaṇī of Bhikṣu Raviśrījñāna and Amṛtakaṇikodyota-nibandha of Vibhūticandra*. Sarnath: Central Institute of Higher Tibetan Studies, 1994.

Lamotte, Étienne. *History of Indian Buddhism: From the Origins to the Śaka Era*. Trans. Sara Boin-Webb. Louvain-la-Neuve: Institut Orientaliste, 1988.

———. "La concentration de la marche héroïque," *Mélanges Chinois et Bouddhiques*, vol. 13. Bruxelles: Institut Belge des Hautes Études Chinoises, 1965.

———. *Śūraṃgamasamādhisūtra: The Concentration of Heroic Progress*. Trans. Sara Boin-Webb. Richmond: Curzon Press, 1998.

Lancaster, Lewis R. "The Oldest Mahāyāna Sūtra: Its Significance for the Study of Buddhist Development," *The Eastern Buddhist* 8.1 (May 1975), 30–41.

Lang, Karen. *Āryadeva's Catuḥśataka: on the bodhisattva's cultivation of merit and knowledge*. Copenhagen: Akademisk Forlag, 1986.

La Vallée-Poussin, Louis de. "À propos du Cittaviśuddhiprakaraṇa d'Āryadeva." *Bulletin of the School of Oriental and African Studies* 6.2: 411–15.

———. *Bouddhisme: Études et Materiaux: Ādikarmapradīpa: Bodhicaryāvatāraṭīkā*. London: Luzac, 1898.

———. *Bouddhisme: Opinions sur l'Histoire de la Dogmatique*. 5th edition. Paris: Gabriel Beauchesne, 1925.

———. *Études et Textes Tantriques: Pañcakrama*. Gand et Louvain: H. Engelcke [Gand] and J.-B. Istas [Louvain], 1896.

———. "Note sur le Pañcakrama." In *Proceedings of the 10th International Congress of Orientalists*, Part 1. Geneva: n.p., 1894. 137–46.

Lessing, F. D. and Alex Wayman. *Introduction to the Buddhist Tantric Systems*. 1968 (as *mKhas Grub rJe's Fundamentals of the Buddhist Tantras*). New York: Samuel Weiser, Inc., 1980.

Lindtner, Christian. "Adversaria Buddhica," *Wiener Zeitschrift für die Kunde Südasiens und Archiv für Indische Philosophie* 26 (1982): 167–94.

———. *Nagarjuniana: Studies in the Writings and Philosophy of Nāgārjuna*. Copenhagen: Akademisk Forlag, 1982.

Lindtner, Christian, ed. and trans. *A Garland of Light: Kambala's Ālokamālā*. Fremont, CA: Asian Humanities Press, 2003.

Loizzo, Joseph J. et al., trans. and ed. *Nāgārjuna's Reason Sixty with Chandrakīrti's Reason Sixty Commentary*. New York: American Institute of Buddhist Studies, 2007.

Lopez, Donald S., Jr. *Prisoners of Shangri-La: Tibetan Buddhism and the West*. Chicago & London: University of Chicago Press, 1998.

MacDonald, Anne. "Interpreting Prasannapadā 19.3–7 in Context: A Response to Claus Oetke," *Wiener Zeitschrift für die Kunde Südasiens* 47: 143–95.

Macdonell, Arthur Anthony. *A Practical Sanskrit-English Dictionary*. 1929. London: Oxford University Press, 1965.

Matsunaga, Yukei. "A Doubt to the Authority of the Guhyasamāja-ākhyāna-Tantras," *Journal of Indian and Buddhist Studies* 12.2 (1964): 16–25.

———. "Some Problems of the Guhyasamāja-Tantra." In Chandra, Lokesh, and Perala Ratnam, eds., *Studies in Indo-Asian Art and Culture*, Vol. 5. New Delhi: International Institute for Indian Culture, 1977.

———. *The Guhyasamājatantra: A New Critical Edition*. Osaka: Toho Shuppan, 1978.

Mayer, Robert. *A Scripture of the Ancient Tantra Collection: The Phur-pa bcu-gnyis*. Oxford: Kiscadale Publications, 1996.

Mayrhofer, Manfred. *Etymologisches Wörterbuch des Altindoarischen*. Indogermanische Bibliothek, II. Heidelberg: Carl Winter, 1986–2001.

Mimaki, Katsumi and Tōru Tomabechi, eds. *Pañcakrama: Sanskrit and Tibetan Texts Critically Edited with Verse Index and Facsimile Edition of the Sanskrit Manuscripts*. Tokyo: The Center for East Asian Cultural Studies for Unesco, 1994.

Mitra, Rajendralal. *Aṣṭasāhasrikā Prajñāpāramitā*. Calcutta: Asiatic Society, 1887.

Monier-Williams, Monier. *A Dictionary of English and Sanskrit*. 1851. Delhi: Motilal Banarsidass, 1999.

———. *A Sanskrit-English Dictionary*. 1899. Delhi: Motilal Banarsidass, 1990.

Müller, F. Max, ed. *Buddhist Texts from Japan: Vajracchedikā*. Oxford: Clarendon Press, 1881.

Nanjio, Bunyiu, ed. *The Laṅkāvatāra Sūtra*. Kyoto: Otani University Press, 1923.

Negi, J. S. *Bod skad dang legs sbyar gyi tshig mdzod chen mo* [Tibetan-Sanskrit Dictionary]. Volumes 1–13 (ka–ya). Sarnath: Central Institute of Higher Tibetan Studies, 1993–2003.

Nobel, Johannes. *Suvarṇabhāsottamasūtra*. Leipzig: Otto Harrassowitz, 1937.

———. *Suvarṇaprabhāsottamasūtra*, vol. 1, Leiden: E. J. Brill, 1944.

Obermiller, E., trans. *History of Buddhism (Chos-ḥbyung) by Bu-ston*. Part II: The

History of Buddhism in India and Tibet. Materialien zur Kunde des Buddhismus 19. Heidelberg: O. Harrasowitz, 1932.
Pāṇḍey, Janārdan. "Durlabh Granth Paricaya," *Dhīḥ: A Review of Rare Buddhist Texts* 10 (1990): 3–24.
———. "Durlabh Granth Paricaya," *Dhīḥ: A Review of Rare Buddhist Texts* 25 (1998): 9–18.
———, ed. *Yoginīsañcāra-tantram with Nibandha of Tathāgatarakṣita and Upadeśānusāriṇīvyākhyā of Alakakalaśa.* Sarnath: Central Institute for Higher Tibetan Studies, 1998.
Patel, Prabhubhai Bhikhabhai, ed. "Catuḥstava." *Indian Historical Quarterly* 8 (1932): 316–31; 689–705.
———. *Cittaviśuddhiprakaraṇa of Āryadeva.* [Santiniketan]: Visva-Bharati, 1949.
———. "Cittaviśuddhiprakaraṇa of Āryadeva." *Indian Historical Quarterly* 9 (1933): 705–21.
Ray, Reginald A. *Buddhist Saints in India.* New York and Oxford: Oxford University Press, 1994.
Rinpoche, Samdhong, and Vrajvallabh Dwivedi, eds., *Guhyādiaṣṭasiddhisaṃgraha.* Sarnath: Central Institute of Higher Tibetan Studies, 1987.
———. *Vasantatilakā of Caryāvratī Śrīkṛṣṇācārya with Commentary Rahasyadīpikā by Vanaratna.* Sarnath: Central Institute for Higher Tibetan Studies, 1990.
Roerich, George N., trans. *The Blue Annals.* 1949. Delhi: Motilal Banarsidass, 1988.
Ruegg, David S. *Buddha-nature, Mind and the Problem of Gradualism in a Comparative Perspective: On the Transmission and Reception of Buddhism in India and China.* 1990. Delhi: Heritage Publishers, 1992.
———. *The Literature of the Madhyamaka School of Philosophy in India.* Wiesbaden: Otto Harrassowitz, 1982.
———. "Towards a Chronology of the Madhyamaka School." In Hercus et al., *Indological and Buddhist Studies: Volume in Honour of Professor J. W. de Jong on his Sixtieth Birthday.* Canberra: Faculty of Asian Studies [A.N.U.], 1982. 505–30.
Sāṅkṛtyāyana, Rāhula. "Recherches Bouddhiques." *Journal Asiatique* 225 (Oct.–Dec. 1934): 195–230.
———. "Sanskrit Palm-leaf Mss. in Tibet," *Journal of the Bihar and Orissa Research Society* 21.1 (1935): 21–43.
———. "Search for Sanskrit Palm-leaf Mss. in Tibet," *Journal of the Bihar and Orissa Research Society* 24.4 (1938): 137–63.
———. "Second Search of Sanskrit Mss. in Tibet," *Journal of the Bihar and Orissa Research Society* 23.1 (1937): 1–57.
Scherrer-Schaub, Cristina Anna. *Yuktiṣaṣṭikāvṛtti: Commentaire à la soixantaine sur le raisonnement ou Du vrai enseignement de la causalité par le Maître indien*

Candrakīrti. Mélanges Chinois et Bouddhiques 25. Bruxelles: Institut Belge des Hautes Études Chinoises, 1991.

Schiefner, Anton. *Târanâtha's Geschichte des Buddhismus in Indien*. St. Petersburg: Commissionäre der Kaiserlichen Akademie der Wissenschaften, 1869.

Schopen, Gregory. "Hierarchy and Housing in a Buddhist Monastic Code: A Translation of the Sanskrit Text of the *Śayanāsanavastu* of the *Mūlasarvāstivada-vinaya*, Part One," *Buddhist Literature* 2 (2000): 92–196.

Shāstrī, Mahāmahopādhyāya Haraprasād, ed. *A Catalogue of Palm-leaf & Selected Paper Mss. belonging to the Durbar Library, Nepal*. 2 vols. Calcutta: Baptist Mission Press, 1905/1915.

———. *A Descriptive Catalogue of Sanskrit Manuscripts in the Government Collection under the Care of the Asiatic Society of Bengal*. Vol. 1, *Buddhist Manuscripts*. Calcutta: Baptist Mission Press, 1917.

———. *Advayavajrasaṃgraha*. Baroda: Oriental Institute, 1927.

———. "The discovery of a work by Āryadeva in Sanskrit," *Journal of the Asiatic Society of Bengal* 67.1 (1898): 175ff.

Skilling, Peter. "Trayastriṃśas Heaven and the Production of Scriptures." Paper presented at the Fourteenth Conference of the International Association of Buddhist Studies, London, England, 30 August 2005.

Snellgrove, David, ed. and trans. *Hevajra Tantra*. Two volumes. London: Oxford University Press, 1959.

———. *Indo-Tibetan Buddhism*. Two volumes. Boston: Shambhala, 1987.

von Staël-Holstein, A., ed. *The Kāśyapaparivarta: A Mahāyāna Sūtra of the Rantakūṭa Class*. 1926. Tokyo: Meicho Fukyū Kai, 1977.

Stcherbatsky, Th., and E. Obermiller. *Abhisamayālankāra-prajñāpāramitā-upadeśa-śāstra*. Bibliotheca Buddhica 23. 1929. Tokyo: Meicho-Fukyū-Kai, 1977.

Steinkellner, Ernst. *A Tale of Leaves: On Sanskrit Manuscripts in Tibet, their Past and their Future*. Amsterdam: Royal Netherlands Academy of Arts and Sciences, 2004.

———. "Remarks on Tantristic Hermeneutics." In L. Ligeti, ed., *Proceedings of the 1976 Csoma de Koros Symposium*. Budapest: Akadémiai Kiadó, 1978.

Strong, John S., trans. *The Legend of King Aśoka: A Study and Translation of the Aśokāvadāna*. Princeton: Princeton University Press, 1983.

Suzuki, Daisetz T., ed. *Chibetto Daijōkyō—The Tibetan Tripiṭaka*. Kyoto: Tripitaka Research Institute, 1955–61.

Suzuki, Daisetz T., trans. *The Laṅkāvatāra Sūtra: A Mahāyāna Text*. London: G. Routledge and Sons, Ltd., 1932.

Takasaki, Jikido. *A Study on the Ratnagotravibhāga (Uttaratantra)*. Serie Orientale Roma 33. Roma: Istituto Italiano per il Medio ed Estremo Oriente, 1966.

Takubo, Shūyo, ed. *Ārya-mahā-māyūrī Vidyā-rājñī*. Tokyo: Tokyo Sankibo, 1972.

Tanselle, G. Thomas. "Classical, Biblical, and Medieval Textual Criticism and Modern Editing." In Tanselle, *Textual Criticism and Scholarly Editing*, 274–321.

———. "Editing without a Copy Text." *Studies in Bibliography* 47 (1994): 1–42.

———. "Some Principles of Editorial Apparatus." In Tanselle, *Textual Criticism and Scholarly Editing*, 119–76.

———. "Texts of Documents and Texts of Works." In Tanselle, *Textual Criticism and Scholarly Editing*. 3–23.

———. *Textual Criticism and Scholarly Editing*. Charlottesville and London: The University Press of Virginia, 1990.

———. "Textual Study and Literary Judgement." In Tanselle, *Textual Criticism and Scholarly Editing*, 325–37.

Tatz, Mark, trans. *The Skill in Means (Upāyakauśalya) Sūtra*. Delhi: Motilal Banarsidass, 1994.

Thurman, Robert A.F. *The Holy Teaching of Vimalakīrti: A Mahāyāna Scripture*. 1976. University Park and London: The Pennsylvania State University Press, 1986.

———. *Tsong Khapa's Speech of Gold in the* Essence of True Eloquence: *Reason and Enlightenment in the Central Philosophy of Tibet*. Princeton, NJ: Princeton University Press, 1984.

———. "Vajra Hermeneutics." In Donald S. Lopez, Jr., ed., *Buddhist Hermeneutics*, 119–48. Honolulu: University of Hawaii Press, 1988.

Tomabechi, Tōru. "*Étude du Pañcakrama.*" PhD dissertation, Université de Lausanne, 2006.

Tsuda, Shiníchi. *The Saṁvarodaya-tantra: selected chapters*. Tokyo: The Hokuseido Press, 1974.

Tsukamoto, Keisho, Yukei Matsunaga, and Hirofumi Isoda. *A Descriptive Bibliography of the Sanskrit Buddhist Literature*. Vol. 4, *The Buddhist Tantra*. Kyoto: n.p., 1989.

Tucci, Giuseppe. "Animadversiones Indicae." *Journal of the Asiatic Society of Bengal* 26 (1930): 125–60.

———. *Minor Buddhist Texts*, Part I. 1956. Delhi: Motilal Banarsidass, 1982.

———. *Rin-chen-bzaṅ-po and the Renaissance of Buddhism in Tibet around the Millenium*. New Delhi: Aditya Prakashan, 1988.

———. "Some Glosses on the Guhyasamāja." In *Mélanges Chinois et Bouddhiques* 3: 339–53. Bruxelles: Institut Belge des Hautes Études Chinoises, 1935.

———. *Tibetan Painted Scrolls*. Three volumes. Roma: La Libreria della Stata, 1949.

———. "Two Hymns of the Catuḥstava of Nāgārjuna." *Journal of the Royal Asiatic Society* (1932): 309–25.

Vaidya, P. L. *Études sur Āryadeva et son Catuḥśataka: Chapitres 8–16*. Paris: Librarie Orientaliste Paul Geuthner, 1923.

Vaidya, P.L., ed. *Aṣṭasāhasrikā Prajñāpāramitā with Haribhadra's Commentary Called* Āloka. Darbhanga: Mithila Institute, 1960.

———. *Mahāyāna-sūtra-saṃgraha*, vol. 1. Darbhanga: Mithila Institute, 1961.
———. *Saddharmalaṅkāvatārasūtra*. Buddhist Sanskrit Texts, no. 3. Darbhanga: Mithila Institute, 1963.
———. *Samādhirājasūtra*. Darbhanga: Mithila Institute, 1961.
van der Kuijp, Leonard W.J. "The Earliest Indian Reference to Muslims in a Buddhist Philosophical Text of *Circa* 700." *Journal of Indian Philosophy* 34 (2006): 169–202.
Waddell, L. Austine. *The Buddhism of Tibet or Lamaism*. 1899. New Delhi: Asian Educational Services, 1991.
Walleser, Max. *The Life of Nāgārjuna from Tibetan and Chinese Sources*. Delhi: Nag Publishers, 1979.
Walshe, Maurice, trans. *Thus Have I Heard: The Long Discourses of the Buddha*. London: Wisdom Publications, 1989.
Wayman, Alex. "Observations on the History and Influence of the Buddhist Tantra in India and Tibet." In *Studies in the History of Buddhism*, ed. A. K. Narain. Delhi: B.R. Publications, 1980.
———. *The Buddhist Tantras: Light on Indo-Tibetan Esotericism*. 1973. Delhi: Motilal Banarsidass. 1993.
———. "The Sarvarahasyatantra." *Acta Indologica* 6 (1984): 521–69.
———. *Yoga of the Guhyasamājatantra*. 1977. Delhi: Motilal Banarsidass, 1991.
Wayman, Alex, and Ryujun Tajima. *The Enlightenment of Vairocana*. Delhi: Motilal Banarsidass, 1992.
Wedemeyer, Christian K. "Antinomianism and Gradualism: The Contextualization of the Practices of Sensual Enjoyment (*caryā*) in the Guhyasamāja Ārya Tradition," *Indian International Journal of Buddhist Studies*, New Series 3 (2002): 181–95.
———. "Beef, Dog, and Other Mythologies: Connotative Semiotics in Mahāyoga Tantra Ritual and Scripture." *Journal of the American Academy of Religion* 75.2 (June 2007): 383–417.
———. *Making Sense of Tantric Buddhism: History, Semiology, and Transgression in the Indian Traditions*. South Asia Across the Disciplines series. New York: Columbia University Press, 2013.
———. "On the Authenticity of the *Caryāmelāpakapradīpa Commentary* Attributed to Śākyamitra." Paper presented at the Fourteenth Conference of the International Association of Buddhist Studies, London, England, 2 September 2005.
———. "Sex and Death in Mainstream Eleventh-Century gSar-ma Esoterism: 'Gos Khug-pa Lhas-btsas, *caryā* (*spyod pa*), and *abhicāra* (*mngon par spyod pa*)." Paper presented at the Thirteenth Conference of the International Association of Buddhist Studies, Bangkok, Thailand, December 13, 2002.
———. "Tantalising Traces of the Labours of the Lotsāwas: Alternative Translations of Sanskrit Texts in the Writings of rJe Tsong-kha-pa." In Davidson and Wedemeyer, eds., *Tibetan Buddhist Literature and Praxis*, 149–82. Leiden: Brill, 2006.

———. "Tropes, Typologies, and Turnarounds: A Brief Genealogy of the Historiography of Tantric Buddhism." *History of Religions* 40.3 (Feb 2001): 223–59.

———. "Vajrayāna and its Doubles: A Critical Historiography, Exposition, and Translation of the Tantric works of Āryadeva." Ph.D. dissertation, Columbia University, 1999.

Wedemeyer, Christian K., trans. and ed. *Āryadeva's Lamp that Integrates the Practices (Caryāmelāpakapradīpa): The Gradual Path of Vajrayāna Buddhism According to the Esoteric Community Noble Tradition*. New York: American Institute of Buddhist Studies, 2007.

Weller, Friedrich. *Index to the Indian Text of the Kāśyapaparivarta*. Harvard Sino-Indian Series 2, pt. 1. Cambridge, MA: Harvard-Yenching Institute, 1935.

———. *Index to the Tibetan Translation of the Kāśyapaparivarta*. Harvard Sino-Indian Series 1. Cambridge, MA: Harvard-Yenching Institute, 1933.

West, M. L. *Textual Criticism and Editorial Technique Applicable to Greek and Latin Texts*. Stuttgart: B.G. Teubner, 1973.

White, David Gordon. *The Alchemical Body*. Chicago: The University of Chicago Press, 1996.

Whitney, William Dwight. *Sanskrit Grammar*. 5th edition. 1924. Delhi: Motilal Banarsidass, 1989.

———. *The Roots, Verb-forms, and Primary Derivatives of the Sanskrit Language*. Leipzig: Breitkopf and Härtel, 1885.

Williams, Raymond. *Marxism and Literature*. Oxford & New York: Oxford University Press, 1977.

Wylie, Turrell V. "Dating the Death of Nāropa." In L. A. Hercus et al., *Indological and Buddhist Studies: Volume in Honour of Professor J. W. de Jong on his Sixtieth Birthday*. Canberra: Faculty of Asian Studies [A.N.U.], 1982. 687–92.

Yagi, Toru. "A Note on *bhojya-* and *bhakṣya.*" In Yasuke Ikari, ed. *A Study of the Nīlamata—Aspects of Hinduism in Ancient Kashmir.* Kyoto: Institute for Research in Humanities, Kyoto University, 1994.

Yamada, Isshi. *Sarva-tathāgata-tattva-saṅgraha nāma mahāyāna-sūtra*. New Delhi: Mrs. Sharada Rani, 1981.

Yamamoto, Chikyo. *Mahāvairocana Sūtra*. New Delhi: International Academy of Indian Culture and Aditya Prakashan, 1990.

Yule, Col. Henry, and A. C. Burnell, eds. *Hobson-Jobson: A Glossary of Colloquial Anglo-Indian Words and Phrases, and of Kindred Terms, Etymological, Historical, Geographical and Discursive*. New edition edited by William Crooke. 1886. New Delhi: Rupa & Co., 1994.

Zhang, Yisun. *Bod rGya Tshig mDzod Chen Mo* [The Great Tibetan-Chinese Dictionary]. Three volumes. Lhasa: Mi Rigs dPe sKrun Khang, 1984.

Indexes

Index of Canonical Authors Cited

Indians

*Asvabhāva, 12
Āryadeva, xiii–xiv, xvi, xix–xxi, xxvii–xxix, xxxi–xxxii, xxxiv, 3, 5, 7, 9–11, 13–15, 20, 22–23, 34, 39, 40, 43–44, 46, 49–50, 52, 54–56, 58, 63, 65–66, 68, 70–81, 85–86, 88–89, 96–97, 100, 104–5, 107, 115, 124, 130, 135, 150, 157–59, 165, 171, 177, 179, 186, 195, 201–2, 205, 265, 277, 279, 296, 306, 359, 364
Bhartṛhari, 11
Bhāvaviveka, 12
Buddhaguhya, 12, 179, 260
Candrakīrti, xxviii-xxix, 7, 15, 18, 22–24, 41, 45, 49, 55–57, 89, 239, 255, 257
Jñānapāda, 7, 12, 24, 40, 42, 75
Kambala, 11–12, 80, 132, 242, 259
Maitreya, 32
Munidatta, 149, 242
Muniśrībhadra, 3, 13, 48, 170
Naḍapāda (Nāropā), 3, 13
Nāgabodhi, xiv, xxviii-xxix, 7, 19, 21–23, 32, 48, 55–57, 110, 198
Nāgārjuna, xiii–xiv, xvi, xviii–xix, 4, 7–8, 10–11, 15–24, 32–34, 38–40, 43–44, 46–49, 52, 55, 57–58, 66, 73–74, 76–77, 88, 98, 105, 123, 201, 217–19, 238, 247, 254–55, 302–3, 337, 344
Padmavajra, 12, 244
Ratnākaraśānti, 38, 105, 238
Śākyamitra, 48, 52–53, 55–60, 77, 123, 201
Tāranātha, 10, 14, 17–25, 31–33, 40, 77
Tathāgatarakṣita, 23, 152
Vīryabhadra, 198

Tibetans

Amey Zhab, Jamgön (A myes zhabs, 'Jam mgon), 15, 26, 28, 45, 57–59
Butön (Bu ston), 15, 27, 33, 51, 56, 58
Chag Lotsāwa (Chag lo tsā ba), 57–58, 106, 239, 244, 368
Gö Kugpa Lhaytsay ('Gos khug pa lhas btsas), 13, 130
Gö Lotsāwa Zhönu Pal ('Gos lo tsā ba gzhon nu dpal), 28
Guru Chöwang (Guru chos dbang), 32
Kaydrup Je Gelek Palzang (Mkhas grub rje dge legs dpal bzang), 4, 105
Nyang Ral Nyima Özer (Nyang nyi ma 'od zer), 28
Rongzom Chökyi Zangpo (Rong zom chos kyi bzang po), 277
Tsongkhapa (Tsong kha pa), xiv, xvi, 3–4, 15, 43, 45, 51, 54–55, 57–58, 86, 99, 106, 108, 115, 159, 198, 206–7, 239–40, 244, 262, 292, 298, 364, 368

Index of Canonical Texts Cited

Adamantine Crown-Protrusion Tantra (*Vajroṣṇīṣa-tantra*), 77, 96–97, 125, 210, 340, 363
Ālokamālā [ĀM], 11, 80, 132, 259
Arranged Stages of the Community Sādhana (*Samājasādhana-vyavastholi-krama*), 56
Assembly of All Deities Tantra (*Sarvadeva-samāgama Tantra*), 289, 297, 340
Caryāgītikoṣavṛtti [CGKV], 13, 124, 149, 242
Catuḥśataka, 11–12, 14
Cittaviśuddhiprakaraṇa [CVP], 49, 53–55, 279
Compendium of All Rituals (*Sarva-kalpasamuccaya*), 107, 248, 340
Compendium of Realities (*Tattva-saṃgraha* [STTS]), 85–86, 92, 110, 165, 168, 170, 187, 206–7, 243, 340
Diamond Cutter Scripture (*Vajracchedika Sūtra*), 97, 214, 340
Enlightenment of Vairocana Tantra (*Vairocanābhisambodhi*), 90, 100, 109, 152, 179–180, 187, 223, 238, 259–60, 340
Enquiry of Bhadrapāli Scripture (*Bhadra-pāli-paripṛcchā*), 68, 92, 95, 100, 134, 189, 203, 340, 343
Enquiry of the Four Goddesses (*Caturdevī-paripṛcchā*), 44–45, 124, 341
Enquiry of the Kinnara King Scripture (*Kinnara-rāja-paripṛcchā* [KRP]), 90, 95, 97, 182, 185, 205–6, 213–14, 341
Esoteric Community Appendix Tantra (*Guhyasamājottaratantra* [GSUT]), 38, 41–44, 94, 159, 201–2, 255, 282, 341, 344
Esoteric Community Tantra (*Guhya-samājatantra* [GST]), xiv, 3, 5–7, 12, 25–27, 28–29, 31, 38, 40–45, 47, 55–57, 64, 68, 73–74, 81, 83–85, 93, 97, 101, 107, 109–14, 124, 135, 145, 148, 151–55, 158–59, 194, 206, 214, 226–27, 235–39, 247, 256, 260–61, 266, 277, 281–82, 286–87, 291, 296, 300, 302, 341–42
Explanation of the Intention (*Saṃ-dhyāvyākaraṇa*), 44–46, 87–89, 159, 162, 170, 173, 296, 341
Extensive Explanation of the "Lamp for Integrating the Practices" (*Spyod pa bsdus pa'i sgron ma zhes bya ba'i rgya cher bshad pa*), 52, 58
Five Stages (*Pañcakrama* [PK], Nāgār-juna), xiii–xiv, xvi, 4, 7–8, 10, 21, 24, 32, 37, 40, 43–48, 50–53, 55–56, 58–61, 63, 73–75, 84, 95, 107, 132, 153, 158–60, 165, 170–71, 173, 196–97, 200–201, 204, 212–13, 232, 238, 247, 279, 305, 343, 351–54
Gnosis Vajra Compendium (*Jñānavajra-samuccaya*), 44–45, 57, 93, 101, 188, 194, 227, 341
Golden Radiance Scripture (*Suvarṇābhāsa-sūtra*), 115, 303, 341
Great Commentary on the Five Stages (*Rim lnga 'grel chen*, Tāranātha [RṄGC]), 17–19, 77, 123
Illumination of the Lamp (*Pradī-poddyotana* [PU]), 15, 18, 22–23, 45, 49–50, 57, 89, 121, 129, 135, 153–54,

158–59, 163, 206, 213, 217, 236, 239, 257–58, 277, 286, 288, 291, 303
Inner Sādhana (*Adhyātmasādhana*), 242, 342
Jewel Heap Scripture (*Ratnakūṭa-sūtra*), 109, 134, 263, 342
Journey to Laṅka Scripture (*Laṅkāvatāra-sūtra* [LAS]), 68, 78, 80, 88–89, 99, 106, 126, 131–32, 175, 177–78, 189, 240–41, 304, 342
Kāśyapa Chapter (*Kāśyapaparivarta* [KP]), 109, 263
King of Samādhi Scripture (*Samādhirājasūtra* [SRS]), 107, 236, 248, 260, 292–93, 342,
Method of the Three Baskets (*Piṭaka-traya-naya*), 92, 188, 342
Pañcakramaṭippaṇī Yogīmanoharā [PKṬYM], 13, 48, 124, 170–71, 223, 227
Purification of All Karmic Obscurations Scripture (*Sarvakarmāvaraṇaviśodhana-sūtra*), 98, 101, 216, 225
Rim lnga gsal sgron (Tsongkhapa [RṄSG]), 43, 45, 54, 57–58, 86, 108, 159, 198, 206–7, 239–40, 262, 268, 292, 298, 364, 368, 379
Samādhi of Direct Encounter with the Buddhas of the Present, 31
Secret Accomplishment (*Guhyasiddhi* [GS]), 11–12, 107, 223, 232–33, 244, 246–47, 256, 293–94, 343
Secret Moon Drop (*Guhyendutilaka*), 81, 136, 149, 151–53, 236, 343
Secret Treasury of the Transcendent Lords Scripture (*Tathāgataguhyakoṣa Sūtra*), 98, 239
Song of the Names of Mañjuśrī (*Mañjuśrī-nāma-saṃgīti* [MNS]), 88, 175–76, 231, 343
Space-Like Tantra (*Khasama-tantrarāja*), 151, 343
Subhāṣita-saṃgraha [SS], 13, 179, 183–84, 217, 242, 277, 285, 289, 294, 298, 300–301, 359
Supreme Prime (*Paramādya*) *Tantra*, 109–10, 241–43, 261–62, 266, 341
Survey of the Esoteric Community (*Gsang 'dus stong thun*, 'Gos Khug-pa Lhas-btsas), 3, 13, 58, 130
Teaching of One Method Scripture (*Ekanayanirdeśasūtra*), 90, 102, 179, 230, 343
Transmigration of Consciousness Scripture (*Vijñānasaṃkrānti-sūtra*), 100, 203, 221, 343
Uncommon Secret (*Asādhāraṇa-guhya*), 293, 343
Unexcelled Intention (*Anuttarasaṃdhi*), 48, 58, 95, 97, 204, 212, 343
Unfailing Success in Discipline Tantra (*Vinayāmoghasiddhi*), 109, 263, 343
Union of All Buddhas (*Sarvabuddha-samāyoga* [SBS]), 83, 110, 112, 153, 163, 253, 264–68, 277–79, 343
Universal Secret Tantra (*Sarva-rahasya*), 151, 255, 343–44
Vajra Crown-Protrusion Tantra. *See* Adamantine Crown-Protrusion Tantra
Vajra Door Goddess Tantra (*Vajramukhī*), 85, 145, 163, 344
Vajra Rosary Tantra (*Vajramālā*), 44–46, 85, 139, 142, 159, 164–67, 344
Vajra Maṇḍala Ornament Tantra (*Vajra-maṇḍalālaṃkāra-tantra*), 44, 87, 89, 176, 242, 344

General Index

A
Abhidharma, 30, 67, 80, 94
accomplishment (*siddhi*), 18, 22–23, 32, 64, 71–72, 79, 88, 95, 103, 107–8, 110, 114, 131, 154, 171, 175, 235, 255–56, 261, 266, 273, 276, 281, 287, 289, 293–94, 296, 298, 300–301, 309, 315–16, 327, 333. *See also* power (*siddhi*); success (*siddhi*); great power (*mahāsiddhi*)
accumulation
  as heap, 67, 81, 133–34, 150, 217, 319
  of gnosis and merit, 61
  of karma, 100
action(s) (*karma*), 50, 61, 63, 65, 69, 82–83, 87, 92, 95–98, 100, 122, 148–50, 166, 169, 178, 192–93, 203, 207–14, 218, 225, 232, 235, 242, 256, 260, 273, 309, 313, 333–34, 356
Adamantine Way (*Vajrayāna*), xvi, xix, 3–4, 28, 30, 39, 50, 53–54, 61, 66, 73, 78, 80, 84, 92–93, 108, 121–22, 124, 129, 139, 157, 187, 194–95, 240, 245, 258, 309, 327, 359
aggregate(s), 67, 81–82, 111, 115, 125, 129, 133, 135–38, 146, 148–50, 152, 157, 161, 207, 217, 220, 224, 237, 241, 273, 277, 294–95, 303–4, 310, 346
  consciousness, 138
  discernment, 137, 148
  five, 67, 81–82, 129, 133, 135–38, 146, 149–50, 157, 346
  form, 136
  propensity, 137–38
  unreality of, 220
air [element], 62, 82–83, 86, 95, 100, 135, 139, 141–43, 150, 203, 205, 207, 209, 221, 243, 295, 310, 332, 347, 363
  subtle element, 47, 62, 100, 204–5, 221, 243–44, 295, 332
air reality. *See* reality, air
airs [vital] (*vāyu*), 43–46, 64, 67–68, 82, 84–86, 90–91, 95–97, 99, 101, 115, 139, 141–42, 165, 310, 333
  five [main], 64, 68, 82, 84–85, 139, 146, 162–65
  five auxiliary [sensory], 64, 67–68, 82, 84–85, 129, 146, 162–65
  ten, 64, 82, 84–85, 145–46, 162–64, 333, 355
  vitality- (*prāṇa*), 67, 76, 79, 82, 84–86, 122, 129, 141, 145–46, 157–60, 162–64, 169, 176, 197, 268, 337, 347. *See also* vitality control; reality, air
Ākāśagarbha, 144, 310, 348
Akṣobhya, 42, 67, 83–84, 86, 136–44, 146–48, 152, 164, 166, 168, 282, 296, 310, 346–50
  samādhi of, 138
Amitābha, 42, 67, 83–84, 86, 136–44, 146–48, 164, 166–68, 310, 346–350
  samādhi of, 137
Amoghasiddhi, 67, 83–84, 86, 136–44, 146–48, 152, 164, 166–67, 310, 346–50
  samādhi of, 137
appendix tantra(s). *See* tantra(s), appendix
art of accomplishment (*sādhana*), 121
auctorative (-ization, etc.), 14, 17, 29, 32, 34, 37, 40

authorship, notion of, xiv–xv, 8–9, 11–12, 14, 29, 35–38, 57–58, 60, 77

B

beatific body (*sambhoga-kāya*). *See* body, beatific
between state (*antarābhava, bar do*), 56, 62–63, 68–69, 92, 95, 100–101, 115, 120
birth/rebirth, 9, 32, 36, 56, 61–64, 68–69, 82, 92, 95–98, 101, 107, 109, 111, 115, 134, 148, 185, 189–90, 193, 207–8, 212–13, 216–18, 223, 225, 232, 235, 240–42, 257, 262, 278, 295, 302, 304–5, 311, 317, 319, 322, 329, 357
bliss (great), 72, 110, 113, 227, 258, 264, 266, 272, 274, 284–86, 289, 319
bodhisattva, 25, 39, 42, 51, 69, 78, 81, 91, 97, 119, 121, 123, 126, 128–29, 135, 145, 152, 154, 162, 175, 177, 184–85, 189, 194, 220, 222, 227, 235, 240–43, 250–51, 253, 257, 263–65, 292–93, 301, 311
bodily humor(s), 137
body
  beatific (*sambhoga-kāya*), 63, 101 301, 311
  divine, 61, 63–65, 67, 69, 77–78, 81, 83, 87, 99–102, 104, 106, 135, 148, 220, 224, 246–47, 315, 328, 358
  emanation (*nirmāṇa-kāya*), 47, 56, 63, 87, 99, 101, 241, 315
  -maṇḍala. *See* maṇḍala, body
  ordinary, 61, 66–67, 70, 80–81, 102, 110, 114, 170, 288, 302, 325
  phantasm (*māyā-deha*), 53, 64–65, 70, 78, 92, 96, 98, 100–102, 105, 130, 258
  rainbow, 19, 32, 100–101
  reality (*dharma-kāya*), 61, 63, 130, 235, 302, 329
body isolation. *See* isolation, body
brilliance (*prabhāsvara*), 53, 61–65, 68–70, 77–78, 87, 91, 95, 97–98, 101–7, 111–13, 115, 130, 184, 194, 207, 212, 217, 233–34, 236, 238–39, 242, 249, 258, 295–96, 299, 304, 312, 318, 328, 351
Buddha(s), 16, 25, 27–32, 36–37, 44, 61, 63–65, 67, 70–71, 79–81, 89–90, 95, 98–105, 108–10, 115, 121, 129–30, 132, 135–36, 138–39, 148, 151–54, 163, 174, 180, 187, 192, 197, 203, 210, 213, 220, 223, 227, 231–33, 235, 237–38, 240, 246, 250, 253, 257–58, 262, 266–68, 277–79, 296–99, 301–5, 312, 326, 343, 345
  qualities of, 82, 101, 145, 223, 240, 260
  Śākyamuni, 25, 27, 32, 104–5, 108, 304
buddhahood, 39, 80, 91–92, 105–6, 109–10, 124, 187, 247, 257, 264, 312

C

Centrist (Madhyamaka) School, xvi, 7–12, 14–15, 17–18, 21, 24, 34, 38–41, 49, 98, 130, 258
clan(s), 154, 157, 249, 282, 312
  hundred, 53, 63, 67, 79–83, 129, 149–50, 152, 157, 320, 355
  five, 67, 81, 83, 129, 136, 149–50, 152, 165, 258, 355
  three, 63, 67, 83, 136, 154, 355
  one, 67, 83, 149, 258, 312
communion, xiii, 47–50, 61, 63, 65–66, 70, 77–80, 102, 105–7, 126, 131, 240, 249, 258, 305, 312, 328
conceptuality, 63, 95–96, 148, 175–76, 178, 207–8, 225, 236, 312. *See also* non-conceptuality
connate (*sahaja*), 89, 176, 313
consciousness(es), 62, 64, 68, 82, 88, 91–93, 95, 100, 134, 137–38, 145, 149, 175, 188–95, 197, 203–4, 209, 221–23, 234, 241–42, 258, 294, 296–97, 313, 334, 343, 346, 356
  eight, 258
  -element, 62, 83, 86, 92, 150, 190–91, 193, 203–4
  three, 64, 92, 93, 95, 145, 149, 188–89, 194–95, 203, 209, 242, 294, 334, 356. *See also* luminances/radiances, three
consecration, 46, 81, 99, 182, 220, 233, 281, 299, 313. *See also* self-consecration
consort (*mudrā*), 47, 65, 70, 72, 102, 111–15, 231, 233, 273, 282, 287–89, 313
  gnosis, 72, 114, 265, 294, 318
  -discipline (*vidyāvrata*). *See* practice(s), consort discipline
creation process (*utpattikrama*). *See* creation stage

creation stage, 16, 46–47, 56, 63–64, 67–69, 77, 79, 84, 99, 108, 121, 129, 132, 157–58, 186, 219–20, 240, 313
critical wisdom, 93, 122, 134, 161, 195–97, 202, 221, 245, 249–51, 263–64, 286, 314, 318

D

ḍākiṇī(s), 153, 163, 253, 266–67, 275, 314, 343
death, xvii, 9, 13, 28, 31, 56, 61–65, 68–69, 82, 86, 91–92, 96, 100–101, 104, 115, 167, 185, 213, 216–17, 303–5, 314, 329
defilement(s), 51, 68, 70–71, 79, 95, 97, 107–9, 130, 134, 148, 195, 202, 207, 214–18, 235, 241, 243–45, 250, 256, 262–63, 314
deity body, 64, 69, 99, 169, 220, 328, 356
delusion (*avidyā*), 71, 93, 96, 98, 103, 110, 134–35, 197, 205, 211–12, 233–34, 295, 297, 314. *See also* ignorance (*moha*)
dependent origination, 90, 161, 182, 189, 207, 314, 335
dharmadhātu. *See* Realm of Reality
dream(s)
  and sleep state, 69, 100–101, 224, 296, 356
  -body, 100–101, 224, 301
  reality as like, 77, 100, 114, 126, 172, 220–21, 227, 248–49, 315
  signs, 14, 114, 326–27

E

element(s), 38, 44, 47, 51, 62, 67, 81–83, 92, 94–95, 98, 100–101, 125, 109, 133–36, 139–43, 148–51, 157, 159, 161, 164–66, 168, 172, 179, 203, 205, 207, 209, 220–22, 224–25, 236–37, 241, 243–44, 268, 295, 297, 310, 315
  four, 62, 67, 81, 83, 86, 129, 133, 139, 142, 150, 168, 347
  consciousness-. *See* consciousness(es), -element
emanation body (*nirmāṇa-kāya*). *See* body, emanation
enlightenment, xvii, 5, 26, 30, 40, 49–50, 53, 55, 60–61, 63, 65–66, 69–73, 75, 78, 80, 82, 88, 90, 92–93, 98, 100, 102–10, 114–15, 121, 145, 152–53, 160–62, 170, 179, 187–88, 196, 215, 223, 226, 229, 231–38, 242, 247, 253, 259–60, 264, 292, 296, 299, 316, 326–27, 330, 332, 340
  inner and outer, 70, 103–4, 233–34
  -process of the phantasmic web, 82, 145
  See also spirit of enlightenment
erotic/sexual
  practices/techniques, 42, 72, 107, 113, 115, 147, 258, 286, 316
  play, 112, 115, 146, 266, 271, 274, 277–79, 285, 316, 349
  See also passion
explanatory tantra(s). *See* tantra(s), explanatory

F

facticity (*dharmatā*), 179–80, 182, 230, 317
fire-offering, 46, 72, 272, 317
five stages/fivefold process (*pañcakrama*), xiii, xiv, 46–50, 52–53, 56–59, 61, 64, 76–78, 80, 88, 90, 129, 132. *See also* isolation; self-consecration; communion
form body (*rūpa-kāya*), 61–63, 229, 304, 330
Four Goddesses, 41, 44–45, 81, 85, 105, 111, 124, 129, 164, 282, 341, 368. *See also* Locanā; Māmakī; Pāṇḍaravāsinī; Tārā; goddesses
Four Noble Truths, xxviii, 108, 258, 318
four procedures (*caturnyāya*), 45, 257

G

gnosis, 48, 61, 64, 68–69, 72, 77, 79, 84, 100, 102–6, 114, 119, 122, 129–32, 142, 148, 157, 164, 172, 195, 197, 199–200, 202, 204–6, 214, 220–21, 226, 230–31, 234–35, 238, 243, 245, 246, 250, 255, 259–60, 265, 286, 288–89, 294, 295, 299–301, 309, 311–12, 316–20, 324, 338, 356
  completely-pure, 148, 312
  equality, 148, 316
  five, 67, 134, 148–49, 158, 164, 286, 317, 350

function-accomplishing, 148, 318, 350
nondual, 48, 255
of critical-wisdom, 197, 202, 318
of imminence, 195, 202, 318
of individuating discernment, 148, 318, 350
of liberative art, 93, 199, 202, 318
of Reality, 122, 148, 259
goddess(es), 42, 72–73, 81, 85, 111, 113, 124, 129, 164, 181, 271–72, 275–78, 282, 286, 287, 289, 319, 341, 344, 368. *See also* Four Goddesses
gradual (process, path, etc.), xix, 5–6, 39, 50, 60–61, 65–66, 70–71, 73, 76, 78, 80, 108, 120, 127, 131–32, 245, 255, 279, 318. *See also* sudden; subitist; immediate; instantaneous
great power (*mahāsiddhi*), 26, 114, 293, 315. *See also* power (*siddhi*); success (*siddhi*); accomplishment (*siddhi*)
Great Seal (*Mahāmudrā*), 72, 111–12, 266, 270, 282, 300, 319. *See* seal, Great Seal
Great Yoga Tantra. *See* Tantra(s), Great Yoga

H

Heruka, 26, 274

I

I-habit, 212, 214–16, 218, 320. *See also* mine-habit
ignorance (*moha*), 93, 109, 195, 213, 241, 261–62, 271, 298, 320. *See also* delusion (*avidyā*)
immediate, 5, 126–27, 131, 148, 320. *See also* instantaneous; sudden; subitist; gradual
imminence. *See* luminances/radiances
Indrabhūti, 25–26, 28–29, 73, 112, 277
initiation(s), 26, 28, 46, 56, 70, 79, 102, 104–5, 230, 233, 238, 321, 338
buddha, 79, 102, 130, 233
sequence of, 102, 233
secret, 102
wisdom-gnosis, 104–105, 238, 338
instantaneous, 68, 78, 80, 132, 205, 245, 282, 321, 355. *See also* immediate; sudden; subitist; gradual
intentional/allusive speech (*saṃdhyā-vacana*), 43, 85, 112, 150, 165, 195–97, 205, 237, 321
interpretable meaning, 124, 158, 321
isolation(s)
body, xiii, 50, 63–67, 79–84, 99, 129, 131, 133, 157, 183, 186, 219, 240, 311, 355
mind, xiii, 50, 53–54, 63–65, 67–69, 79, 91–92, 99, 130–31, 157, 186–87, 212, 219, 324, 355
speech, xiii, 50, 63–65, 67–68, 79, 83–84, 86, 90–91, 99, 129–31, 157–58, 186–87, 219, 240, 332, 355
three, 39, 61, 63, 80, 99, 219

J

Jñānapāda Tradition, 7, 40, 42, 75

K

karma/karmic. *See* action(s) (*karma*)
Kṣitigarbha, 43, 321, 348

L

liberation (*mokṣa*), 54, 61, 64, 89, 104, 106–7, 122, 138, 171, 214, 227, 239, 244, 254, 259, 322, 346, 356
liberative art (*upāya*), 93, 132, 161, 195, 199, 202, 221, 240–41, 245, 249, 251, 259–60, 263, 318, 322
life-cycle (*saṃsāra*), 9, 61, 68–69, 82, 92, 95–96, 101, 114, 138, 149, 207–8, 214, 216, 218, 223, 227, 231, 244, 249–50, 256, 289, 292, 322
literal meaning, 160, 177–78, 322
Locanā, 42, 135, 139, 143, 288, 322
Lokeśvara, 42, 144, 278, 322
luminances/radiances (*ābhāsa*)
three (*ābhāsa-traya*), 64, 67–68, 82, 91–93, 95–96, 107, 145, 149, 195–96, 205, 212, 221, 241, 334. *See also* consciousness(es), three; prototypes; mind, subtle
luminance (*āloka*), 62, 64, 68, 91, 93–94, 103, 111, 145, 188, 195–97, 202, 204, 221, 233–34, 243, 322
-imminence (*upalabdhaka*), 62, 64, 68, 91, 93–94, 103, 111, 195–97, 200, 204, 234, 243, 295, 322

-radiance (*ābhāsa*), 62, 64, 68, 70, 91–97, 99–100, 103, 195–97, 199, 204, 234, 243, 322

M

mad spiritual discipline (*unmatta-vrata*). *See* practice(s), mad spiritual discipline
Mahāsukha (Lord), 272, 274, 284–86, 319
Mahāvajradhara, 48–49, 70, 108, 114, 155, 244, 265, 357
Mahāyāna. *See* Universal Way
Maheśvara, 165, 180
Māmakī, 42, 135, 140, 143, 282, 323, 347
maṇḍala, 4, 7, 16, 23, 26, 42, 44–47, 56, 62, 72–73, 84–87, 89, 95, 104, 106, 111–13, 135, 148, 150, 158, 164–69, 176, 207, 231, 236, 249, 269–70, 272, 275–76, 282, 284, 287, 296, 320, 323, 334, 344
  body, 47, 72, 112--13, 150, 272, 282, 287, 296
  elemental, 84–86, 168
  host, 231, 269, 274, 320
  supreme, 104, 135, 145, 236
  ultimate reality, 62, 104, 106, 207
Mañjuśrī, 88, 119, 145, 175, 343
mantra, xiii, 4, 18, 28, 67–68, 76–77, 84, 86–88, 90, 94, 121–23, 152–54, 157–58, 167–73, 180–82, 201–2, 287–88, 323, 338, 355
  body, 152, 154, 323
  extraction of, 168–70, 316
  overlord, 168–69, 326
  serpent, 169
  three-syllabled, 84, 86–88, 158, 168–70
  -reality. *See* reality, mantra
meditation, xvi, 30, 56, 71, 84, 103, 134, 162, 173, 176–77, 234–35, 237, 245, 251, 254, 265, 277, 281, 291–92, 296, 299–300, 302, 323
  holistic, 103, 130, 234, 282
  dissolving, 103, 130, 177, 234, 314
mental factors, 96, 196–97, 206, 211, 227, 295, 323
mind
  nature of, 54, 67, 68, 70, 91–93, 95, 184, 187, 196–97, 212, 221, 242, 244, 246
  subtle, 53, 62, 64, 67–68, 91–93, 95–97, 99–100, 103, 111, 147, 196–97, 199, 240, 349, 351, 353. *See also* luminances/radiances
mine-habit, 212, 214– 216, 218, 324. *See also* I-habit

N

Nāgārjuna, xiii, xxiii-xxiv, xvi, xxviii–xxix, 4, 7–8, 10–11, 15–24, 32–34, 38–40, 43–44, 46–49, 52, 55, 57–58, 66, 73–74, 76–77, 88, 98, 105, 123, 201, 217–19, 238, 247, 254–55, 302–3, 337, 344
nirvāṇa, 30, 64, 108, 110, 147, 203, 258, 267, 269, 273, 299, 318, 323, 329–330
Noble Tradition, xxviii, 3, 5–9, 11, 14–18, 20–25, 28–30, 33–34, 37, 39–47, 53, 55–57, 60–61, 63, 66, 70, 74–75, 78, 80, 90, 92, 105–6, 110, 121, 130, 139, 159
nonconceptuality, 148, 175, 236, 283, 298, 300. *See also* conceptuality
non-mental-functioning (*amanaskāra*), 183, 325
nonduality, 48, 62, 77, 87, 91, 125, 130–31, 152, 161, 231, 238, 249, 254–55, 258, 325

O

object(s)
  five, 107, 113, 134, 140, 144, 147, 149, 164, 195, 224, 227, 282–83, 286, 301
overlord
  of all mantras, 168–69, 326
  of all vajradharas, 278
  of the maṇḍala, 270, 282
  of Secret Ones, 125, 180, 210–11, 326
  of all the senses, 145
  of transcendent lords, 162, 180, 287
  of the Kinnara, 183

P

Padmanarteśvara, 265, 274, 276
Pāla Dynasty, 22–23
Pāṇḍaravāsinī, 42, 140, 347
passion/dispassion, 71, 93, 97,107, 109, 147, 195–96, 198–200, 203, 218, 225–26, 242, 258, 261–62, 264, 270–71, 274, 276, 279, 285–86, 295, 298, 314, 320, 326, 351, 353–54. *See also* erotic/sexual

perfection process (*niṣpannakrama*). *See* perfection stage
perfection stage, xiii, 46–47, 56, 63, 68, 74, 76, 78–80, 84, 89–91, 108, 115, 126, 129, 131–32, 157–58, 179, 186, 240, 259, 303–4, 326, 355. *See also* samādhi, perfection stage
phantasm body (*māyā-deha*). *See* body, phantasm
phantasm, twelve similes of, 79, 101–2, 130, 220, 227, 229, 335
phantasmical samādhi. *See* samādhi, phantasmical
play (*āralli*), 110, 114, 265, 274, 283, 297, 310, 327
pledge (*samaya*), 102, 113, 232, 244, 246, 284, 300, 302, 327
power(s) (*siddhi*), 22–23, 32, 79, 108, 131, 171, 175, 255–56, 261, 266, 273, 276, 281, 287, 293, 294, 296, 298, 300–301, 309, 316, 327, 333. *See also* accomplishment (*siddhi*); great power; success (*siddhi*)
  eight superhuman, 72, 108, 110, 254, 264, 277, 315
Practice Tantra. *See* Tantra(s), Practice
practice(s) (*caryā*)
  with elaboration, 28, 50, 65, 107, 110, 253, 264–66, 277, 281, 296, 327
  without elaboration, 50, 65, 72, 107, 110, 112–13, 264–66, 277–78, 281, 284, 296, 357
  completely without elaboration, 50, 65, 110, 112–15, 265–66, 278, 291, 297–98, 312, 327, 334
  bodhisattva, 42, 51, 78, 121, 253, 255, 257, 264
  mad spiritual discipline (*unmatta-vrata*), 114, 297, 298
  consort discipline (*vidyāvrata*), 65, 113, 287–89, 313
  of spiritual discipline (*vrata-caryā*), 65, 71, 108, 253, 256–57, 327
practice (*sādhana*), xxviii, 46–49, 52, 56–58, 72–74, 77, 105, 113, 121, 242, 254, 259, 264, 276, 327, 331, 342
pride
  divine, 64, 135
  ordinary, 67, 81–82, 100, 135, 139, 224, 270, 282, 325
prophecy (*vyākaraṇa*), 106
prototypes (*prakṛti*), 64, 67–68, 79, 91, 93–97, 99, 114, 130, 147, 188, 195, 197–205, 207, 209, 211–14, 219–20, 274, 294–95, 328, 351, 353–54
  eighty, 67–68, 91, 93–94, 200–202, 351–54
  one-hundred and sixty, 94, 200–201, 203, 209, 295
purity/purification, xxix, 21, 53, 66, 78–79, 87, 90, 96–98, 101, 108, 138, 170, 181–82, 195, 210, 215–18, 225, 229, 235–36, 238, 240–41, 254–55, 282, 284, 328, 342, 356

R

radiances, three. *See* luminances/radiances; consciousness(es), three; voids, three; mind, subtle
Ratnasambhava, 42, 67, 83–84, 86, 136–38, 140–44, 146–47, 152, 164, 166, 168, 329, 346–50
  samādhi of, 137
reality
  air, 43, 68, 84–86, 157–58, 165, 168, 186, 187, 310
  dharma, 77, 123
  divinity, 69, 76–77, 123, 220, 315
  limit, 48–49, 64, 69, 130, 171, 231, 234, 282, 329
  mantra, 68, 76–77, 84, 86, 88, 123, 157–58, 168–69, 173, 186–87, 323, 355,
  seal, 76–77, 123, 331
  self, 76–77, 123
  superficial, 50, 64, 69, 77, 79, 81, 98–99, 102, 125–26, 130–31, 194, 218–20, 229–30, 255, 258, 304–5, 333
  two, 38–39, 61, 63–66, 69, 77, 80, 125, 130–31, 249, 254, 258, 305, 335
  ultimate, 50, 62, 64, 69–70, 77–79, 101–6, 111, 114, 125–26, 130–32, 177, 196, 207, 218, 221, 223, 229–30, 234,

236–37, 239, 241, 254–55, 258, 270, 274, 282, 292, 295–96, 305, 335, 356. *See also* gnosis, of Reality
reality body (*dharma-kāya*). *See* body, reality
realm of reality (*dharmadhātu*), 62, 82, 130, 145, 148, 190, 207, 312, 329, 350
rebirth. *See* birth/rebirth
ritual, xxix, 18, 42, 46–47, 52, 56–57, 61, 69–70, 72–75, 87, 102, 104, 107, 112–114, 122–23, 161, 169, 170, 175, 190, 232, 241, 248, 281, 284, 288, 291, 293–94, 302, 330, 340, 357

S

sādhana. *See* practice (*sādhana*)
samādhi, 31, 48–49, 64, 68–71, 76–80, 91–92, 98. 101, 105, 123, 125–32, 137–38, 140–41, 143, 145, 153–54, 157–58, 180, 186, 188, 197, 206, 218–19, 227, 232, 238, 240–41, 246, 248, 250–51, 256, 272–74, 292, 300, 309, 320, 324, 327, 330, 336, 342. *See also* Akṣobhya; Amitābha; Amoghasiddhi; Ratnasambhava, samādhi of
  adamantine (*vajropama*), 240, 250, 309
  beginner's, 129
  body-vajra, 79, 83, 129, 154
  communion, 48, 79
  great bliss, 227
  hero's march, 78, 127–29, 250–51, 320, 342
  holistic and dissolving, 130
  mind-vajra, 79, 130, 147, 227, 324
  of single-mindedness, 79, 129
  of the perfection stage, 76, 78–80, 126, 129, 131–32, 157–58
  perfection (communion), 48, 79, 131
  phantasmical (*māyopama*), 48–49, 64, 69, 77–79, 92, 101, 126, 130, 188, 227, 238, 240–41, 327
  signless, 71, 256
  speech-vajra, 68, 79, 91, 130, 157, 185–86
  unshakeable, 105, 238, 336
  whose nature conduces to the real (*bhūta-nayātmaka-*), 77–78, 125, 272, 330, 369
Samantabhadra, 81, 145, 330, 348
  samādhi of, 145
saṃsāra. *See* life-cycle
Scripturalists, 108, 259
seal (*mudrā*), 76–77, 123, 233, 268–69, 275, 331
  accomplishment (*siddhi*), 268
  Great Seal (*Mahāmudrā*), 72, 111–12, 266, 270, 273, 282, 300, 319
self-consecration, 47, 49–50, 53, 64–65, 69, 99–100, 111–13, 115, 136, 221, 223–24, 227, 229, 270, 282, 304, 331. *See also* consecration
self-invocation, 259, 331
sense media, 67, 81–82, 85, 129, 134, 143–44, 146, 149, 164, 195, 220, 224, 348
sexual. *See* erotic/sexual
similes. *See* phantasm, twelve similes of
six parameters (*ṣaṭkoṭi*), 45, 57
spell (*vidyā*), 90, 180, 332
spirit of enlightenment, 102, 104, 153, 160–62, 172, 196, 226, 232, 235–37, 247, 332
  six stanzas on, 104, 235
spiritual friend/guide (*kalyāṇa-mitra*), 89, 91–92, 186–87, 214–15, 240, 332
Śrāvakas, 108–9, 112, 235, 258–60, 262, 269, 284, 338
subitist, 39, 73, 78, 80, 245, 279. *See also* sudden; immediate; instantaneous; gradual
subject and object, 62, 91, 189
subject(s), five, 134, 317
success (*siddhi*), 26, 88, 109, 256, 261, 263, 287, 298, 333, 343. *See also* accomplishment (*siddhi*); great power (*mahā-siddhi*); power (*siddhi*)
sudden, 5, 61, 65, 73, 80, 132. *See also* subitist; immediate; instantaneous; gradual
superficial reality. *See* reality, superficial
symbol (*cihna*), 84, 93, 158, 196–97, 268–69, 288, 333

T

tantra(s)
  appendix, 38, 41, 43–44, 85–86, 94, 159, 165, 179, 201, 333, 341

explanatory, xiv, 26, 40–45, 57, 60, 85–86, 90, 93, 114, 121, 139, 157, 159, 162, 165, 169, 173, 188, 194, 206–7, 236, 298, 316, 341
Great Yoga, 93, 100, 124, 135, 145, 152–53, 159, 163, 165, 167, 170, 194, 214, 226–27, 235–36, 239, 241, 247, 261–63, 266, 281, 293, 296, 300, 319, 341, 343
Practice, xxix, 18, 179, 259, 327, 340
root, 16, 26, 41–44, 47, 85–86, 135, 165, 168, 206, 261, 277, 286–87, 330, 342
Root, the (GST), 5, 25, 27, 29, 31, 41–42, 44–45, 47, 55, 57, 73, 83–85, 97, 101, 107, 109–13, 124, 135, 145, 148, 151–55, 158–59, 206, 214, 227, 236–39, 247, 256, 260–61, 277, 281–82, 286–87, 291, 296, 302, 342
Yoga, xiii, 49, 85, 98, 165, 221, 232, 236, 265, 344
Tārā, 42, 135, 141, 143, 333, 347
thirty-three moments, 197
three natures, 195, 197, 334
tokens (*cchomā*), 112, 275–77, 311, 337
Transcendent Lords. *See* Akṣobhya; Amitābha; Amoghasiddhi; Ratnasambhava; Vairocana
transcendent vitrue (*pāramitā*), 32, 39, 97, 103, 107, 211, 215, 235, 241, 248, 250–51, 258, 273, 331, 335, 340
transference (*samāropa*), 72, 110, 264, 335
transformation (*pariṇāma*), 72, 110, 114, 121–22, 264, 335
transmigration, 69, 100, 185, 203, 221, 244, 303, 343
Treasure Teachings (*gter ma*), 20–21, 31, 34
two realities. *See* reality, two

U

ultimate reality. *See* reality, ultimate
Universal Way (*Mahāyāna*), xiii, xvi, 7, 18, 30–31, 39–40, 61, 65, 71, 76, 84, 92–93, 98, 103, 108–9, 124, 126, 130, 134, 139, 157, 165, 182, 194–95, 203, 214–15, 218, 232, 258–59, 263, 327, 336, 343
unstruck [sound] (*anāhata*), 85, 87, 89, 164, 169, 170, 176, 336

V

Vairocana, 42, 67, 83, 86, 90, 92, 100, 109, 136–44, 146–48, 152, 167–68, 170, 179–80, 182, 187, 223, 238, 259–60, 265, 274, 276, 282, 323, 336, 340, 346–50
vajra recitation, 45, 47–50, 77, 79, 83–85, 87–89, 129, 158, 160, 164, 169, 219, 336
vajra(s)
body, 47, 67, 83, 87, 111–12, 114, 129, 152, 154, 219, 223, 244, 273, 277, 287, 311, 355. *See also* samādhi, body-vajra
speech, 47, 68, 83, 87, 91, 130, 152, 154, 157, 185–86, 219, 287, 332. *See also* samādhi, speech-vajra
mind, 47, 79, 83, 87, 130, 154, 206, 219, 221, 282, 287, 324. *See also* samādhi, mind-vajra
three, 47, 83, 152, 154–55, 219, 288–89, 355
Vajradhara, 28, 48–49, 70, 106–8, 114, 155, 233, 244, 265, 278, 294, 302, 357
Vajrapāṇi, 26, 45, 125, 143, 160, 210–11, 287, 337, 348
Vajrasattva, 23, 38, 83, 111, 119, 152, 154, 221, 229, 256, 265, 267–68, 270, 276, 278, 293, 294, 301, 337
Vajrayāna. *See* Adamantine Way
vestiges (*vasanā*), 51, 70–71, 108, 132, 178, 241, 243–44, 256, 302, 337
virtue, 62, 66, 191, 198–99, 207, 209, 248, 330, 336, 352–53, 356. *See also* transcendent virtue
Vision Teachings (*dag snang gi chos*), 14, 21–22, 31, 33, 36
vitality control (*prāṇāyāma*), 45, 67–68, 76, 79, 82, 84–86, 129, 141, 157–59, 169, 197, 268, 337
voidness(es), 39, 79, 101, 103–4, 111, 113, 202, 215, 231, 234, 238, 243, 246, 274, 337
eighteen great, 79, 130
void(s)
extremely, 93, 196, 202, 317
great, 93, 101, 130, 196–97, 202, 319
universal, 103, 119, 231, 234, 242–43, 336
three, 197, 212, 334

W

wind (*vāta*), 137, 142, 224, 338. *See also* airs [vital]
wisdom, critical. *See* critical wisdom

Y

yoga, xix, 4–6, 12, 41, 44–45, 47–48, 50, 53, 61, 63, 67–68, 79, 83–84, 91, 104, 106, 115, 121, 129, 153, 155, 157–58, 165, 173, 186, 213, 227, 229, 241, 246, 257, 268, 277–79, 287, 294–95, 299, 302, 320, 323, 325, 331–32, 336, 359
 imaginative, 63, 79, 129, 320
 non-equipoised, 279, 325
 of constitution, 155
 of meditative cultivation, 246, 294
Yoga Tantra. *See* Tantra(s), Yoga
Yogācāra, 39, 89, 195, 197, 258